Criminal Evidence

Robert M. Donley

330 Hudson Street, NY, NY 10013

Vice President, Portfolio Management: Andrew Gilfillan
Portfolio Manager: Gary Bauer
Editorial Assistant: Lynda Cramer
Senior Vice President, Marketing: David Gesell
Field Marketing Manager: Thomas Hayward
Product Marketing Manager: Kaylee Carlson
Senior Marketing Coordinator: Les Roberts
Director, Courseware and Content Producers: Brian Hyland
Managing Producer: Cynthia Zonneveld
Managing Producer: Jennifer Sargunar
Content Producer: Purnima Narayanan
Manager, Rights Management: Johanna Burke
Operations Specialist: Deidra Smith
Creative Digital Lead: Mary Siener
Managing Producer, Digital Studio: Autumn Benson
Content Producer, Digital Studio: Maura Barclay
Full-Service Management and Composition: iEnergizer Aptara®, Ltd.
Full Service Project Manager: Sadika Rehman
Cover Design: StudioMontage
Cover Photo: Brandon Bourdages/Shutterstock
Printer/Binder: Edwards Brothers
Cover Printer: Lehigh-Phoenix Color/Hagerstown
Text Font: 11/13 Goudy Old Style MT Pro

Library of Congress Cataloging-in-Publication Data available upon request.

7 2023

ISBN 10:   0-13-289906-X
ISBN 13: 978-0-13-289906-2

To my wife, Melissa, who believed in me
—*Robert Donley*

CONTENTS

APPENDICES

PREFACE

Without evidence, criminal law is nothing but theory, and no one has ever been convicted based on a mere theory. What is needed to put guilty people behind bars, and to ensure that innocent people remain free, is proof—solid, credible, and substantial proof. What happened, where and when it happened, who did it, how and why it happened—these are the questions that must be answered in order to turn statutes and rules into verdicts and sentences.

I wrote this book in order to provide students of criminal justice and legal studies with a comprehensive and clear understanding of the laws that determine what make evidence admissible in court, and the factors that make it credible to a jury. But in order to understand those laws, students also need to understand the context within which those laws and rules operate. We need to understand the principles that govern how evidence is collected and preserved. We need to understand the stages of the criminal process at which evidence is used, and how it is used. We need to understand the criminal law itself, which provides the legal framework within which evidence is analyzed and presented in court. We need to understand the types and forms that evidence can take, and how a jury will be influenced by those types and forms once the evidence has been placed before it. And, finally, we need to understand the larger constitutional protections that place limits on the gathering and use of evidence to prove a defendant's guilt.

The goal of this book is to explain the law of evidence and the context of that law in a manner that is accessible to students studying criminal justice as well as those studying law. For 14 years, I have taught hundreds of criminal justice and legal studies students how to understand evidence both online and in the classroom. This book captures the lessons and refinements of those years of experience, enhanced by research and analytical skills honed over a 12-year legal career. While rooted in long-standing and well-tested legal concepts, this book also provides a look at twenty-first-century challenges in the law of evidence, including the ways technology has affected the traditional rules and demanded a more flexible, creative approach to gathering and presenting evidence.

■ ORGANIZATION OF THE TEXT

Part One of this book provides the context within which the rules of evidence are applied. We begin in Chapter 1 with a look at the American court system, how it works, and the basic institutions that comprise it. Then, we turn to a discussion of the criminal law in Chapter 2, including how such laws are structured and defined in criminal statutes, the various elements that make up crimes, and the defenses that can be raised to defeat criminal liability. Next, in Chapter 3, we examine the criminal trial process itself, broken down into its component parts, and how evidence is used at each stage of that process to carry the case forward to a final verdict. We then introduce and contrast the types (direct, circumstantial, and demonstrative) and forms (testimonial and real) of evidence in Chapter 4, and look in Chapter 5 at the two key qualities of evidence: admissibility and weight. Finally, we examine in Chapter 6 the basic constitutional principles that govern the development and use of evidence in a criminal case.

Part One of this textbook serves two purposes. First, it provides you, the student, with the background understanding of the criminal justice system you need in order to place in proper context the statutes and rules of evidence you will learn in Part Two. Second, it teaches critical terminology and concepts that appear throughout our discussion of evidence law. There is much more that can be said about the criminal legal process, criminal law, and constitutional law than these six chapters contain, but they provide enough information that the law of evidence that follows will make sense.

Part Two of this textbook addresses the law of evidence itself. I have structured this part to follow a logical progression, moving from the most basic principles of admissibility to the more complex ones. Chapters 7 and 8 present the "threshold" concepts of the competence of witnesses and authenticity of real evidence, both of which must be satisfied before evidence can be presented to a jury. Chapter 9 discusses the third critical "threshold" requirement of relevance, and the various exceptions to that requirement are laid out in Chapter 10. Chapter 11 addresses the question of when hearsay evidence can be admitted, and Chapter 12 presents the limitation on admissibility provided by various privileges that protect confidential information from being offered in court. Finally, the textbook ends with a discussion in Chapter 13 of the unique concerns presented by witnesses, and how the credibility of witnesses is established and challenged before a jury.

■ PEDAGOGICAL FEATURES

The text includes a number of pedagogical features to facilitate students' learning of the material.

Court Opinions

Throughout this textbook, I discuss the law of evidence using the Federal Rules of Evidence, although I also interject considerations of state law where appropriate. My reason for focusing on the federal rules is that they form the basis for most state evidence rules, and therefore provide a more comprehensive and consistent understanding of evidence law than would be possible if I attempted to discuss that law from a multistate perspective. In order to take full advantage of this consistency, most of the court opinions contained in this textbook are from federal courts.

Each court opinion contained in this book is followed by two analytical questions that will help you understand what the opinion adds to the law of evidence.

Sample Trial Transcripts

To further illustrate the use of these rules, I include throughout the text, but primarily in Part Two, sample trial transcripts that demonstrate how rules would be applied in an actual trial. These transcripts, while fictitious, are realistic in order to provide you with a clear understanding of how the law of evidence works in the real world. To add to this realistic approach, I have also included a number of "practice tips" that provide guidance on how criminal justice and legal professionals can effectively work with the various rules and principles covered throughout the book.

Evidence and Technology

Recognizing the increasing role that technology plays in both the development and operation of evidence law, I have included in nearly every chapter a feature entitled "Evidence and Technology." These features discuss developing ways in which current technology is affecting the law of evidence, from how jurisdiction over Internet crimes is determined to the use of metadata in authenticating documents, and even whether a "like" on Facebook can be used against a defendant in court.

End-of-Chapter Summary, Web Excursions, and Practical Exercises

Each chapter is summarized in a series of discreet bullet points to make studying and retention easier, and accompanied by web excursions and practical exercises to further drive home the lessons of the chapter through hands-on experience.

Complete Trial Transcript with Annotations

This unique feature, included at the end of the text as an appendix, is a complete trial transcript, adapted from an actual criminal trial transcript. Through this appendix, I have included comments illustrating the application of the rules of evidence, as well as explanations of the tactical and strategic concerns that drive the prosecutor's and defense attorney's questions. This transcript provides an indepth, real-life illustration of the rules of evidence and the ways in which evidence is introduced and used before a jury in a typical criminal trial, and supplies instructors with a useful and comprehensive teaching tool.

The topics covered in this textbook, the features included in each chapter, and the comprehensive glossary of legal terms provided in the margins will provide you, the student, with a complete understanding of the law of evidence. It is my sincere hope that you will find this textbook accessible and interesting, and a valuable addition to the lexicon of works on this critical aspect of criminal justice.

■ INSTRUCTOR SUPPLEMENTS

Instructor's Manual with Test Bank Includes content outlines for classroom discussion, teaching suggestions, and answers to selected end-of-chapter questions from the text. This also contains a Word document version of the test bank.

TestGen This computerized test generation system gives you maximum flexibility in creating and administering tests on paper, electronically, or online. It provides state-of-the-art features for viewing and editing test bank questions, dragging a selected question into a test you are creating, and printing sleek, formatted tests in a variety of layouts. Select test items from test banks included with TestGen for quick test creation, or write your own questions from scratch. TestGen's random generator provides the option to display different text or calculated number values each time questions are used.

PowerPoint Presentations Our presentations are clear and straightforward. Photos, illustrations, charts, and tables from the book are included in the presentations when applicable.

To access supplementary materials online, instructors need to request an instructor access code. Go to www.pearsonhighered.com/irc, where you can register for an instructor access code. Within 48 hours after registering, you will receive a confirming email, including an instructor access code. Once you have received your code, go to the site and log on for full instructions on downloading the materials you wish to use.

■ ALTERNATE VERSIONS

eBooks This text is also available in multiple eBook formats. These are an exciting new choice for students looking to save money. As an alternative to purchasing the printed textbook, students can purchase an electronic version of the same content. With an eTextbook, students can search the text, make notes online, print out reading assignments that incorporate lecture notes, and bookmark important passages for later review. For more information, visit your favorite online eBook reseller or visit www.mypearsonstore.com.

■ ACKNOWLEDGMENTS

I thank the following people who assisted in the development of this textbook:

- My cherished colleagues and friends John DeLeo and Randi Teplitz, whose help, feedback, and legal knowledge have been an incalculable benefit to me as an author and a teacher.
- My colleague Jeffrey Goble, whose insights into criminal trial procedure were an invaluable resource in the writing of this textbook.
- My daughter Katelyn Donley, who assisted in the preparation of the trial transcript contained in the appendix, and who supported and encouraged me throughout the writing of this book.
- My wife Melissa Donley, whose support, patience, and understanding made the creation of this book possible.

Thanks also to the following reviewers, whose comments helped in the development of the book:

Erin Fay, Rowan University; Cumberland Country College; James Guffey, National University, LaJalla, CA; David De Haan, Keiser University; RaeLynn Oman, Salt Lake Community College; Wendy Vonnegut, Methodist University; Janet Foster Goodwill, Yakima Valley Community College; Kathleen Nicolaides, University of North Carolina, Charlotte; and Deborah Barrett, Rowan-Cabarrus Community. College.

 **ROBERT M. DONLEY** is a Professor of Legal Studies in the School of Professional Studies at Central Penn College, where he has taught in the legal studies and criminal justice programs since 2002. He also instructs graduate students in Central Penn's Master of Professional Studies program in Organizational Leadership.

Prior to his teaching career, Professor Donley practiced in a wide variety of legal fields, litigating cases throughout Pennsylvania. He graduated from Temple University School of Law in 1990, where he wrote for the Temple Law Review on the subject of juvenile justice. In addition to his legal and teaching experience, Professor Donley is also a certified mediator, and mediates disputes filed before the Pennsylvania Human Relations Commission.

Professor Donley lives in Lebanon, Pennsylvania, with his wife of 24 years, Melissa. His daughter, Katelyn, attends Central Penn College as a legal studies major, and plans to follow in her father's footsteps as an attorney.

Criminal Evidence

LEARNING OBJECTIVES

After reading this chapter, the student will be able to:

1. Explain the general structure of state and federal court systems.

2. Identify the four main levels of courts and describe the functions of each.

3. Explain the path of appeal in the federal and state court systems.

4. Distinguish between the criminal jurisdiction of federal and state court systems.

5. Describe the options open to an appellate court ruling on a trial judge's decisions.

6. Explain the interplay between federal and state court jurisdictions.

7. Contrast the scope and purpose of federal/state and local rules of court.

8. Identify the key subject areas of the Federal Rules of Evidence.

The American Court System | CHAPTER 1

■ INTRODUCTION

Most laws are substantive, telling us what we are and are not required or permitted to do as we live our lives and interact with our fellow human beings. The law of evidence is, by contrast, mainly procedural. It only has meaning in the context of proceedings before a court or other tribunal. Because of this, you must have firm grasp of how the court system works before you can understand evidence and its various legal principles.

This chapter introduces you to the basic structure and function of courts in the federal and state systems. As you read this chapter, keep in mind that every court system is unique, and must ultimately be dealt with on its own terms and according to its own rules.

The first part of this chapter addresses the overall structure of court systems, describing the four levels of courts and their functions. The chapter then looks at the jurisdiction and structure of the federal court system, followed by a similar look at state systems. The chapter ends with a discussion of rules of court and how they work, with a brief overview of the Federal Rules of Evidence that will figure prominently throughout this textbook.

■ GENERAL STRUCTURE OF COURT SYSTEMS

LEARNING OBJECTIVE 1
Explain the general structure of state and federal court systems.

Courts are part of governments, and in the United States there are two main levels of government: state and federal. While many believe that federal criminal courts are somehow "superior" to state criminal courts, this is not true. The vast majority of criminal cases are heard in state courts, and each of those state court systems operates according to its own laws and procedures. The federal courts have no say in how state courts operate, with one important exception: every state court must abide by the U.S. Constitution, and the federal courts have the final say about what the Constitution means.

Whether you are dealing with the federal courts or state courts, there are some common structures within these two systems. Most court systems consist of four levels: minor courts, trial courts, intermediate appellate courts, and courts of final appeal. Some states, like Montana and Wyoming, have only three levels—because of their small populations, they do not have intermediate courts of appeals.

LEARNING OBJECTIVE 2
Identify the four main levels of courts and describe the functions of each.

While courts within various state and federal systems have different names, they all serve essentially the same function. The following discussion outlines these functions and the various levels of courts where these functions are carried out. The principles set forth below are summarized in Figure 1-1, which depicts the path that cases take from minor courts to courts of final appeal.

Minor Courts

minor courts
Minor courts are courts of limited jurisdiction that hear small civil claims, issue arrest and search warrants, and conduct preliminary criminal proceedings.

Minor courts are courts that are very limited in their functions and powers. Judges at this level are often called "magistrates" or "justices of the peace." They hear civil cases involving relatively small amounts of money, in which capacity they are often referred to as "small claims courts." Magistrates are also involved in preliminary criminal proceedings such as the issuance of search and arrest warrants and preliminary arraignments.

Minor courts play an important role in the federal and state court systems. Magistrates provide access to justice to plaintiffs who might otherwise not be able to afford to take a case to court because the amount involved is relatively small. They also serve critical functions in criminal cases (such as issuing search and arrest warrants), making it possible to move cases forward promptly without waiting for the more "formal" courts to open. Magistrates may also conduct criminal trials, although these are usually limited to summary crimes like traffic citations and minor misdemeanors.[1]

Like all federal judges, federal magistrates are appointed by the President of the United States and confirmed by the Senate. In the state systems, most minor court judges are elected officials.

Trial Courts

trial court
Trial courts are courts that conduct criminal trials and sentencing proceedings, and rule upon legal issues that arise in the pretrial process, including the admissibility of evidence.

trial judge
A judge who presides over a trial court.

Criminal cases are usually prosecuted in the **trial court**. These courts are called "trial" courts because this is where trials and sentencing procedures take place, but these courts do much more than simply conduct trials and hand down punishments. From an evidence standpoint, **trial judges** play an active role in pretrial criminal process, often making rulings on admissibility and other legal issues that arise in the course of a criminal case. Trial courts have jurisdiction over every aspect of criminal cases from the moment they are first filed until a final decision on guilt is made and sentence is passed. More information about the involvement of trial court judges in the development of evidence will be discussed throughout this textbook.

EVIDENCE AND TECHNOLOGY

JURISDICTION OVER INTERNET CRIMES

"Proof of jurisdiction beyond a reasonable doubt is an integral component of the state's burden in a criminal prosecution. The state can meet its burden of showing that jurisdiction properly lies in a state court by presenting evidence that any or all of the essential elements of the alleged offense occurred in state" (21 Am.Jur.2d Criminal Law §422, citing *State* v. *Liggins*, 557 N.W.2d 263 (Iowa 1996); *State* v. *Squally*, 132 Wash.2d 333, 937 P.2d 1069 (1997); *State* v. *L.J.M.*, 129 Wash.2d 386, 918 P.2d 898 (1996)).

When the Internet is used to commit a crime, where exactly is the crime occurring? Is it in the state where the criminal is located and using his computer to carry out the crime? The state where the criminal harm occurs? Can a state have jurisdiction over a criminal case if it is simply the locus of the servers through which criminal electronic communications passed on their way from sender to receiver?

Many states have passed statutes that allow them to exercise jurisdiction over at least some types of Internet-based crimes. Some of these statutes are crime-specific and focus on the place where an electronic communication originated and the place where it was received. For instance, Alabama's jurisdiction over crimes relating to the electronic or online solicitation of children for sexual activity exists where the communications constituting such solicitation "either originate in or are received in this state" (Ala. Code 1975 §13A-6-126). This "send and receive" jurisdictional scheme is also employed in Arizona's statute prohibiting the use of electronic communication to "terrify, intimidate, threaten, or harass" (A.R.S. §13-2916), in North Carolina's statute defining a series of "computer-related crimes" (N.C.G.S.A. § 14-453.2). California uses the "send-receive" approach to establish jurisdiction over the criminal use of electronic communications to harass or annoy (West's Ann. Cal. Penal Code § 653m).

Other states take a different, much broader approach. Ohio's general criminal jurisdictional statute, for example, creates jurisdiction over any criminal who "causes or knowingly permits any writing, data, image, other telecommunication to be disseminated or transmitted into this state in violation of" Ohio law (R.C. § 2901.11). But the broadest jurisdictional provision of all is probably West Virginia's, whose computer crime statute provides jurisdiction in that state against any computer criminal who, in the process of committing his/her crime, "accesses, permits access to, causes access to or attempts to access a computer, computer network, computer data, computer resources, computer software, or computer program that is located, in whole or in part, within this state, or passes through this state in transit . . ." One commenter has doubted that this statute was actually meant to be used to prosecute every computer-related crime that passes through a server in West Virginia[2] (that would probably be more than the West Virginia criminal system could handle), but that is precisely what the statute's jurisdictional provision says.

Case law has followed a similar course as legislation when it comes to jurisdiction over computer-based crimes. In *People* v. *Jacobs*, 91 P.3d 438 (Colo. 2003), the defendant, who lived in Westminster, Colorado, engaged in a number of e-mail exchanges with a detective posing as the operator of a child prostitution ring in California. The defendant claimed that Colorado did not have subject matter jurisdiction over his crime because the prostitute was being supplied from California, not Colorado, but the court disagreed. Citing Colorado's state jurisdiction statute, which provides that Colorado courts have jurisdiction over offenses "if they are committed wholly or partly within the state," the court found that there was sufficient evidence to support jurisdiction,

(continued)

because the solicitations came from Colorado, the delivery of the prostitute and alleged sex acts were to occur in Colorado, and the defendant had inquired about the availability of prostitutes in the Colorado area (*Id*. at 442).

In *Hageseth* v. *Superior Court*, 150 Cal.App.4th 1399, 59 Cal.Rptr.3d 385 (Cal.Ct.App. 2007), the defendant, a Colorado physician, was accused of prescribing medication to a California resident, in violation of California law requiring such prescriptions to be written only by physicians licensed to practice medicine in that state (*Id*. at 1404, 59 Cal.Rptr.3d at 387). The physician prescribed the California resident Prozac by means of an Internet prescription website from which anyone anywhere in the country could request prescriptions and obtain medication (*Id*. at 1404, 59 Cal.Rptr.3d at 388). The defendant claimed that since he had not committed any part of his criminal act (i.e., the issuance of the unlawful prescription) in California, he could not be subject to California criminal jurisdiction (*Id*.). The court disagreed.

Acknowledging that the Internet presented unique opportunities for courts to modify existing theories of jurisdiction in criminal cases, the court nevertheless concluded that the defendant's actions in this case did not warrant a departure from the rule that California could exercise jurisdiction over crimes which had "deleterious effects" within the state, despite the fact that crime occurred via the Internet (*Id*. at 1420–1421, 59 Cal.Rptr.3d at 401–402). Responding to various concerns raised by the defendant, the court concluded that jurisdiction in California was proper because (a) the defendant must have known that California, like all states, did not permit physicians to practice medicine without a state license, (b) allowing jurisdiction to attach in California would deter others from committing crimes similar to the defendant's, and (c) such jurisdiction would not deter physicians licensed in other states from providing California residents lawful and beneficial forms of medical advice (*Id*. at 1422–1424, 59 Cal.Rptr.3d at 402–405).

In *Jaynes* v. *Commonwealth of Virginia*, 276 Va. 443, 666 S.E.2d 303 (2008), a defendant was charged in Virginia with sending unlawful "spam" to individuals using AOL e-mail addresses (*Id*. at 448–449, 666 S.E.2d at 305). Although the defendant's activities all took place at his home in North Carolina, the network servers through which AOL e-mails were routed were physically located in Virginia (*Id*.). The court held that the location of the AOL servers in Virginia alone could support a finding that the defendant's crime had been committed in Virginia, due in part to the fact that the location of AOL's servers was easily accessible to the defendant, who could therefore be charged with knowing that his illegal e-mails would be processed through those Virginia locations (*Id*. at 451, 666 S.E.2d at 307).

Admittedly, the case law on the issue of state jurisdiction over Internet-based crimes is hardly definitive. However, from the above-cited cases, some general rules can be distilled. First, a defendant can be charged with committing an Internet-based crime in the state where he himself is located, even if the effects of the crime are felt entire within another state. Second, he can be charged in the state where the crime's effects occur, even if he never personally enters that state or takes any actions within that state. Finally, where a computer network is involved in the crime, he can be charged in the state where the network servers are located, even if neither he nor the victim is located within that state.

These statutes and case law demonstrate the extensive breadth of jurisdiction states are exercising for crimes committed over the Internet. One can conclude, tentatively, that any state that is involved in a substantial manner in the commission of an Internet-based crime, either as the location of the criminal or the victim or as the means by which the criminal communications are electronically transferred, can find a basis for exercising jurisdiction.

Appellate Courts

Appellate courts exist primarily for one reason: to make sure that judges in trial courts have done their job properly. Appellate courts do this by reviewing the record before the trial court (which consists of the pleadings and other court filings, trial transcript, and other evidence admitted at trial), and deciding if there were any mistakes that require correction. Appellate courts do not, except in rare cases, hear testimony or consider any evidence that was not admitted at trial.

As noted above, most states and the federal court system have two levels of appellate court: an intermediate appellate court and a court of final appeal. Less populous states have only a single level of appellate court.

Intermediate appellate courts hear appeals directly from trial courts. In a criminal case, the defendant has an absolute right to appeal a conviction or sentence. The intermediate appellate court will review the **record** (a transcript of the testimony and the other evidence presented at trial) for errors identified by the parties, and will take appropriate action if any prejudicial errors are discovered. Defendants are able to appeal any issue that arises in the course of a criminal case, including a conviction and the sentence imposed by the judge. Prosecutors, on the other hand, cannot appeal an acquittal, although they can ask the appellate court to review other decisions of the trial court, such as the suppression of evidence.

> **PRACTICE TIP**
>
> Every decision a judge makes in a case relating to evidence is a potential basis for appeal by the side against whom that decision is made. Whenever a judge rules against you on an evidence issue, that decision should be noted as a possible issue to raise on appeal.

In the federal and most state systems, **courts of final appeal** hear appeals from the intermediate appellate courts. In less populous states where there is no intermediate appellate court, courts of final appeal hear appeals directly from trial courts. Otherwise, a party who is not satisfied with the decision of an intermediate appellate court must ask the court of final appeal for permission to take an appeal to that level. If permission is denied, then the decision of the intermediate appellate court stands. If permission is granted, then the court of final appeal will review the decision of the intermediate appellate court and decide if that court properly resolved the legal issues raised by the parties. Permission to appeal at this level will usually not be granted unless (1) the issue is of particular importance or (2) lower courts have made inconsistent decisions about the law involved in the case.

In both federal and state jurisdictions, sentences of death will be appealed directly to the court of final appeal. In the federal and some state systems, the appeal of a death sentence is mandatory; in others, the defendant has the option of a direct appeal.

Once the court of final appeal has made its decision, there is no additional level of appeal. The only exception is where a state court decision involves a question of federal constitutional law. In that case, an appeal can be taken to the U.S. Supreme Court on the federal constitutional issue only. Many of the most famous federal constitutional law cases, such as *Miranda v. Arizona* and *Roe v. Wade*, began as criminal cases in state courts.

The relationship between minor courts, trial courts, and appellate courts is illustrated in Figure 1-1.

appellate court
An appellate court reviews legal decisions made by the trial judge to determine whether any errors (legal mistakes) occurred that affected the outcome of the trial.

intermediate appellate court
An intermediate appellate court hears appeals directly from trial courts. Appealing to this level of court is a matter of right, but not all states have intermediate appellate courts.

record
The body of evidence admitted at trial, consisting of the transcript of oral testimony, exhibits, and other evidence, along with arguments, rulings, and other matters placed on the record by the court or the parties during trial.

court of final appeal
A court of final appeal hears appeals from intermediate appellate courts, or from trial courts where a state has no intermediate appellate court. Where an intermediate appellate court is available, appealing to a court of final appeal is a matter of permission, not of right.

LEARNING OBJECTIVE 3
Explain the path of appeal in the federal and state court systems.

Figure 1-1 The Path of Appeal

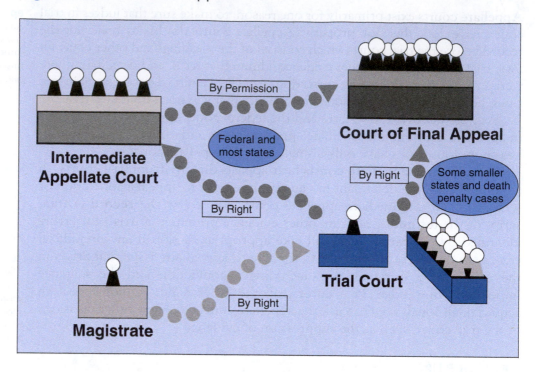

■ FEDERAL COURT SYSTEM

circuit
Circuits are the main divisions of the federal court system. There are eleven regional circuits comprised of various states and territories, along with the federal circuit and the D.C. circuit.

The federal court system stretches across the entire United States, which is divided into regions called "**circuits**." There are eleven regional circuits that are comprised of various states and the territories of Puerto Rico, the Virgin Islands, Guam, and the North Marina Islands. There is also a D.C. circuit (limited to the District of Columbia, which does not belong to any state) and a federal circuit, which hears cases where the federal government is a party.

district
Districts are subdivisions of circuits along state or territorial lines. Each state and territory has between one and four districts, depending on population.

Each regional circuit is divided into smaller areas called "**districts**." At the time of this writing, twenty-six states and all four territories have only one federal district (in other words, the district is the entire state). The remaining states have two, three, or four districts, depending on population. Figure 1-2 shows how the circuits and districts are organized.

Federal Jurisdiction

LEARNING OBJECTIVE 4
Distinguish between the criminal jurisdiction of federal and state court systems.

jurisdiction
The jurisdiction of a court is the power of that court to hear a particular case.

The **jurisdiction** of a court means the power of a court to hear a particular case. Federal courts can only hear criminal cases involving the violation of a federal criminal statute. The only exception to this rule is where a state criminal case is appealed to the U.S. Supreme Court on an issue of federal constitutional law, which is discussed in more detail below.

U.S. District Courts

Article III of the U.S. Constitution gave Congress the power to create "inferior" federal courts to supplement the U.S. Supreme Court. They did this by passing the Judiciary Act of 1789, Section 2 of which created the first thirteen federal judicial districts.

Figure 1-2 The Federal Court Circuits and Districts

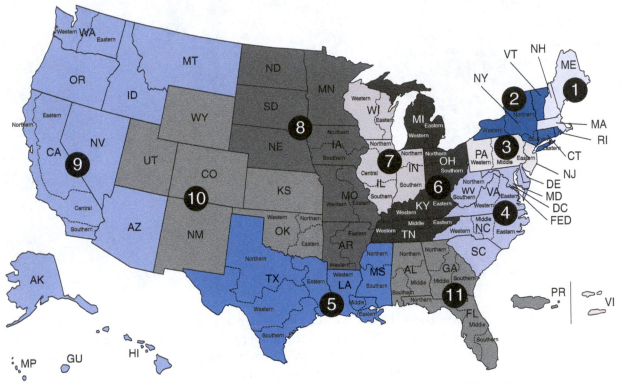

Source: Administrative Office of the U.S. Courts, 2013. http://www.uscourts.gov/uscourts/images/CircuitMap.pdf.

U.S. district courts sit in the various districts of the federal court system. This is where federal criminal cases are originally filed and where trials take place. Judges who sit on these courts are called **U.S. district judges**, and they are appointed by the President of the United States and approved by the Senate. These judges conduct criminal trials according to the Federal Rules of Criminal Procedure and Federal Rules of Evidence. Individual districts also have their own rules, called "local rules," which apply only in those districts. We will be discussing the Federal Rules of Evidence in more detail later in this chapter.

District judges are called upon to resolve legal issues in federal criminal cases. If a legal issue is sufficiently complex, a judge may write an **opinion** that expresses his/her reasoning and conclusions based on the facts of the case and the issues raised by the parties. Not every judge writes an opinion every time a legal issue is ruled on, but when an opinion is written it is often published in the **Federal Supplement**. Opinions relating specifically to federal rules, including the Federal Rules of Evidence, are also published in a separate reporter called "**Federal Rules Decisions**," or F.R.D. Opinions are important research tools, because they provide us with an understanding of how previous judges interpreted federal law and legal principles, allowing us to apply those interpretations to similar issues in other cases.

Circuit Courts of Appeals

U.S. circuit courts of appeals hear appeals from decisions made by district judges in that circuit (see Table 1-1). For instance, if a judge in the Eastern District of Washington makes a decision and the defendant wants to appeal

U.S. district court
U.S. district courts hear cases involving federal crimes that arise within a particular district. These are the trial courts of the federal court system.

U.S. district judge
A U.S. district judge presides over proceedings before a U.S. district court. These judges are appointed by the President of the United States with the approval of the Senate.

opinion
An opinion is written by a judge to explain the factual and legal reasoning behind a decision on an issue of law.

Federal Supplement
The reporter that contains opinions written by U.S. district judges, now in its second series.

Federal Rules Decisions
The reporter that compiles decisions handed down by U.S. district courts and circuit courts of appeals that relate directly to the interpretation and application of federal rules.

LEARNING OBJECTIVE 5
Describe the options open to an appellate court ruling on a trial judge's decisions.

The FBI, which is headquartered in Washington, DC, investigates crimes prosecuted in federal district courts.

Source: https://us.fotolia.com/id/54481054.

Orhan Çam/Fotolia

U.S. circuit court of appeals
A U.S. circuit court of appeals hears appeals from U.S. district courts within a particular circuit.

that decision, he/she would file his/her appeal in the U.S. Circuit Court of Appeals for the Ninth Circuit. Like appeals to other intermediate appellate courts, appealing a decision to a circuit court of appeals is a matter of right. No party can be denied an appeal to this court.

Circuit courts of appeals can also publish opinions that explain why they affirmed or reversed a district judge's decision. These decisions are found in the **Federal Reporter**, which is now in its third series. Like opinions of district judges, these opinions form the basis of research into issues of federal criminal law, but they carry greater weight because they come from a higher court within the federal system.

Federal Reporter
The reporter that contains opinions handed down by judges of the U.S. circuit courts of appeals, now in its third series.

The U.S. Supreme Court

U.S. Supreme Court
The court of final appeal in the federal system, consisting of nine justices appointed by the President of the United States and confirmed by the Senate. This court has the final authority to declare the meaning of federal law, including the U.S. Constitution.

At the pinnacle of the federal court system is the **U.S. Supreme Court**, which hears appeals in cases from all thirteen circuits. Those who sit on the U.S. Supreme Court are called "justices," and they are administered by the "Chief Justice." Like all federal judges, the justices of the Supreme Court are appointed by the President of the United States and approved by the Senate.

The Constitution says very little about the power of the Supreme Court. It is given original jurisdiction in certain cases, and appellate jurisdiction in all other cases. In 1803, the question arose as to whether Congress could give the Supreme Court the extra-Constitutional power to order the Secretary of State to deliver appointments made by a prior administration, by issuing a *writ of mandamus*. Original jurisdiction over such cases was given to the Supreme Court, not by the Constitution, but by the Judiciary Act of 1789. The Supreme Court, led by Chief Justice John Marshall, had to decide if Congress had the power to expand the Supreme Court's original jurisdiction in cases not specified in Article III of the Constitution.

The Court decided in *Marbury* v. *Madison* that Congress did not have such power. In his opinion in that case, Chief Justice Marshall eloquently established the federal courts as the final authority on whether acts of Congress were constitutionally valid, thereby providing a critical check on the power of Congress.

COURT OPINION 1-1

MARBURY V. MADISON, 5 U.S. 137 (1803)

The act to establish the judicial courts of the United States authorizes the supreme court "to issue writs of *mandamus*, in cases warranted by the principles and usages of law, to any courts appointed, or persons holding office, under the authority of the United States."

The secretary of state, being a person holding an office under the authority of the United States, is precisely within the letter of the description; and if this court is not authorized to issue a writ of mandamus to such an officer, it must be because the law is unconstitutional, and therefore absolutely incapable of conferring the authority, and assigning the duties which its words purport to confer and assign.

The constitution vests the whole judicial power of the United States in one supreme court, and such inferior courts as congress shall, from time to time, ordain and establish. . . .

In the distribution of this power it is declared that "the supreme court shall have original jurisdiction in all cases affecting ambassadors, other public ministers and consuls, and those in which a state shall be a party. In all other cases, the supreme court shall have appellate jurisdiction."

. . . . If congress remains at liberty to give this court appellate jurisdiction, where the constitution has declared their jurisdiction shall be original; and original jurisdiction where the constitution has declared it shall be appellate; the distribution of jurisdiction, made in the constitution, is form without substance.

. . .

It cannot be presumed that any clause in the constitution is intended to be without effect; and therefore such a construction is inadmissible, unless the words require it.

[The court determined that the issuance of a *writ of mandamus* is an exercise of original, not appellate, jurisdiction.] The authority, therefore, given to the supreme court, by the act establishing the judicial courts of the United States, to issue writs of mandamus to public officers, appears not to be warranted by the constitution; and it becomes necessary to enquire whether a jurisdiction, so conferred, can be exercised.

The question, whether an act, repugnant to the constitution, can become the law of the land, is a question deeply interesting to the United States; but, happily, not of an intricacy proportioned to its interest. It seems only necessary to recognize certain principles, supposed to have been long and well established, to decide it.

. . . . It is a proposition too plain to be contested, that the constitution controls any legislative act repugnant to it; or, that the legislature may alter the constitution by an ordinary act.

Between these alternatives there is no middle ground. The constitution is either a superior, paramount law, unchangeable by ordinary means, or it is on a level with ordinary legislative acts, and like other acts, is alterable when the legislature shall please to alter it.

If the former part of the alternative be true, then a legislative act contrary to the constitution is not law. . . .

If an act of the legislature, repugnant to the constitution, is void, does it, notwithstanding its invalidity, bind the courts, and oblige them to give it effect? Or, in other words, though it be not law, does it constitute a rule as operative as if it was a law? This would be to overthrow in fact what was established in theory; and would seem, at first view, an absurdity too gross to be insisted on. It shall, however, receive a more attentive consideration.

It is emphatically the province and duty of the judicial department to say what the law is. Those who apply the rule to particular cases, must of necessity expound and interpret that rule. If two laws conflict with each other, the courts must decide on the operation of each.

So if a law be in opposition to the constitution; if both the law and the constitution apply to a particular case, so that the court must either decide that case conformably to the law, disregarding the constitution; or conformably to the constitution, disregarding the law; the court must determine which of these conflicting rules governs the case. This is of the very essence of judicial duty.

If then the courts are to regard the constitution; and the constitution is superior to any ordinary act of the legislature; the constitution, and not such ordinary act, must govern the case to which they both apply.

Those then who controvert the principle that the constitution is to be considered, in court, as a paramount law, are reduced to the necessity of maintaining that courts must close their eyes on the constitution, and see only the law.

This doctrine would subvert the very foundation of all written constitutions. It would declare

(continued)

(continued)

that an act, which, according to the principles and theory of our government, is entirely void; is yet, in practice, completely obligatory. It would declare, that if the legislature shall do what is expressly forbidden, such act, notwithstanding the express prohibition, is in reality effectual. It would be giving to the legislature a practical and real omnipotence, with the same breath which professes to restrict their powers within narrow limits. It is prescribing limits, and declaring that those limits may be passed as pleasure.

That it thus reduces to nothing what we have deemed the greatest improvement on political institutions—a written constitution—would of itself be sufficient, in America, where written constitutions have been viewed with so much reverence, for rejecting the construction. . . .

Why . . . does [the Constitution] direct the judges to take an oath to support it? This oath certainly applies, in an especial manner, to their conduct in

their official character. How immoral to impose it on them, if they were to be used as the instruments, and the knowing instruments, for violating what they swear to support?

. . .

Thus, the particular phraseology of the constitution of the United States confirms and strengthens the principle, supposed to be essential to all written constitutions, that a law repugnant to the constitution is void. . . .

Questions

1. According to Chief Justice Marshall, what is the relationship between the U.S. Constitution and federal statutes?
2. On what ground did Chief Justice Marshall determine that courts have not only the power, but also the obligation to refuse to apply a law that violates the Constitution?

---

writ of certiorari
Permission given by the U.S. Supreme Court to file an appeal before that court.

Rule of Four
The rule that four U.S. Supreme Court justices must agree to hear an appeal before a *writ of certiorari* is granted.

Appealing a case to the U.S. Supreme Court is a matter of permission, not of right. Someone who wishes to appeal to this court must request a **writ of certiorari**. The petition for this writ must explain why an additional level of appeal is justified. Reasons might include that a case deals with issues that are of major importance in American law, or issues that have been dealt with inconsistently by the various circuits. Four justices must agree to hear an appeal before a *writ of certiorari* will be granted. This is known as the "**Rule of Four**." If the writ is not granted, then the decision of the circuit court of appeal will stand. How difficult it is to get an appeal heard by the U.S. Supreme Court is made evident by the fact that, of the almost 9,000 appeals on the Supreme Court's docket in 2011, only 66 were granted review![3]

As noted above, the U.S. Supreme Court can also hear appeals from the highest courts in the various states, where those cases involve issues of federal constitutional law. The U.S. Supreme Court will usually not hear such appeals unless they involve serious issues of constitutional law, or issues on which various circuits or states disagree. For this reason, relatively few state cases ever reach the U.S. Supreme Court, and those that do are usually quite noteworthy.

The United States Reports
The official reporter of opinions issued by the U.S. Supreme Court.

Opinions of the U.S. Supreme Court are absolutely binding on all federal courts, and state courts where they interpret federal law, and are therefore extremely important tools of research. These opinions are published in three separate reporters: **The United States Reports** (the official reporter), the Supreme Court Reporter published by West Publishing Company, and the Supreme Court Reporter, Lawyer's Edition.

There are only two ways a decision of the U.S. Supreme Court can be overturned. The first way is for the Supreme Court itself to overrule a previous decision. For instance, in the 1986 case of *Bowers* v. *Hardwick*, 478 U.S. 186 (1986), the Supreme Court upheld a Georgia state law that illegalized sodomy (oral and anal sex) among members of the same gender. The court ruled in that case that there was no constitutionally guaranteed right to privacy when it came to this particular form of sexual conduct. Seventeen years later, the Supreme Court overturned its own decision and ruled in the case of *Lawrence* v. *Texas*, 539 U.S. 558 (2003), that the Constitution does guarantee a right to privacy for all sexual acts between consenting adults. The effect of that decision was not simply to overrule *Bowers* v. *Hardwick*, but to invalidate all criminal sodomy laws in every state.

The second way a decision of the U.S. Supreme Court can be overturned is by constitutional amendment. Amendment of the Constitution requires a two-thirds majority of the House of Representatives and Senate, followed by ratification of the amendment by three-fourths of the states. Given this, the chances of overruling a Supreme Court decision by constitutional amendment are slim.

■ STATE COURT SYSTEMS

The vast majority of criminal cases in this country are decided by state courts. While more limited geographically than the federal court system (one state instead of the entire nation), state courts hear many more types of cases, because state laws deal with many more legal issues than federal laws. For instance, murder is not usually a federal crime, but it is a state crime. It only becomes a federal crime under certain circumstances, such as if the victim is a federal officer or agent.

Just as the federal courts are divided into regions based on state lines, state court systems are divided into regions, usually along county lines. The names given to the various levels of state courts vary from state to state, but each state has a trial court level, where cases are filed and trials take place, and at least one appellate court level, where appeals are taken from decisions of the trial court. In this sense, state court systems are similar to the federal court system, except that state appellate courts are not divided into distinct regions within the state like circuit courts are in the federal system.

Trial courts in state systems are usually organized along county lines, with a single trial court presiding over cases filed in one or two counties. Trial courts are often divided into sections or divisions, based on the particular kind of case involved, such as criminal cases, general civil cases (personal injury, breach of contract, real estate, etc.), probate cases (wills, estates, and trusts), and family cases (divorce, custody, and support), but these divisions are not separate courts. They are all part of the same trial court system.

Trial courts are known as "courts of record," because it is here that evidence is taken and the factual record of the case is created. The "record" consists of all of the court documents and evidence that forms the basis of the criminal case. Every word of testimony and every document and other evidence introduced at trial become part of this record. The trial court is the only place where such a record can be created. Appellate courts do not take testimony or consider any other evidence that is not part of the record at the time the appeal is filed. The practical effect of this rule is to make the trial court level, by far, the most important level of the entire trial process. In fact, every rule of evidence that will be discussed in this text has one purpose: to regulate what does and does not become part of the record in a given case.

The court structures of the 50 states are not uniform by any means. As Table 1-1 shows, nine states have a one-level appellate system, while the rest

Table 1-1   The Trial and Appellate Courts of All 50 States

State	Trial Court	Intermediate Appellate Court	Court of Final Appeal
Alabama	Circuit Court	Court of Civil Appeals Court of Criminal Appeals	Supreme Court
Alaska	Superior Court	Court of Appeals	Supreme Court
Arizona	Superior Court	Court of Appeals	Supreme Court
Arkansas	Circuit Court	Court of Appeals	Supreme Court
California	Superior Court	Court of Appeals	Supreme Court
Colorado	District Court	Court of Appeals	Supreme Court
Connecticut	Superior Court	Appellate Court	Supreme Court
Delaware	Superior Court	(None)	Supreme Court
Florida	Circuit Court	District Court of Appeals	Supreme Court
Georgia	Superior Court	Court of Appeals	Supreme Court
Hawaii	Circuit Court	Intermediate Court of Appeals	Supreme Court
Idaho	District Court	Court of Appeals	Supreme Court
Illinois	Circuit Court	Appellate Court	Supreme Court
Indiana	Superior Court Circuit Court	Court of Appeals	Supreme Court
Iowa	District Court	Court of Appeals	Supreme Court
Kansas	District Court	Court of Appeals	Supreme Court
Kentucky	Circuit Court	Court of Appeals	Supreme Court
Louisiana	District Court	Court of Appeals	Supreme Court
Maine	District Court Superior Court	(None)	Supreme Judicial Court
Maryland	Circuit Court	Court of Special Appeals	Court of Appeals
Massachusetts	District Court Superior Court	Appeals Court	Supreme Judicial Court
Michigan	Circuit Court	Court of Appeals	Supreme Court
Minnesota	District Court	Court of Appeals	Supreme Court
Mississippi	Circuit Court	Court of Appeals	Supreme Court
Missouri	Circuit Court	Court of Appeals	Supreme Court
Montana	District Court	(None)	Supreme Court
Nebraska	District Court	Court of Appeals	Supreme Court

Table 1-1 *(continued)*

State	Trial Court	Intermediate Appellate Court	Court of Final Appeal
Nevada	District Court	(None)	Supreme Court
New Hampshire	District Court	Superior Court	Supreme Court
New Jersey	Superior Court	Appellate Division of Superior Court	Supreme Court
New Mexico	District Court	Court of Appeals	Supreme Court
New York	Supreme Court County Court	Appellate Division of Supreme Court	Court of Appeals
North Carolina	Superior Court	Court of Appeals	Supreme Court
North Dakota	District Court	Temporary Court of Appeals	Supreme Court
Ohio	Court of Common Pleas	Court of Appeals	Supreme Court
Oklahoma	District Court	Court of Civil Appeals	Supreme Court (civil) Court of Criminal Appeals (criminal)
Oregon	Circuit Court	Court of Appeals	Supreme Court
Pennsylvania	Court of Common Pleas	Superior Court Commonwealth Court	Supreme Court
Rhode Island	Superior Court	(None)	Supreme Court
South Carolina	Circuit Court	Court of Appeals	Supreme Court
South Dakota	Circuit Court	(None)	Supreme Court
Tennessee	Circuit Court Chancery Court	Court of Appeals Court of Criminal Appeals	Supreme Court
Texas	District Courts County-Level Courts	Court of Appeals	Supreme Court (civil) Court of Criminal Appeals (criminal)
Utah	District Court	Court of Appeals	Supreme Court
Vermont	District Court	(None)	Supreme Court
Virginia	Circuit Court	Court of Appeals	Supreme Court
Washington	Superior Court	Court of Appeals	Supreme Court
West Virginia	Circuit Court	(None)	Supreme Court of Appeals
Wisconsin	Circuit Court	Court of Appeals	Supreme Court
Wyoming	District Court	(None)	Supreme Court

Source: Compiled by the author from information provided by the National Center for State Courts (State Court Structure Charts. (n.d.). Retrieved from http://www.courtstatistics.org/Other-Pages/State_Court_Structure_Charts.aspx).

LEARNING OBJECTIVE 6
Explain the interplay between federal and state court jurisdictions.

have at least one intermediate appellate court, and a few states (Alabama, Pennsylvania, and Tennessee) have more than one. Each state has a court of final appeal; two states (Oklahoma and Texas) have a separate court of final appeal for civil and criminal cases. Each state's court system has evolved to handle cases in the most appropriate and efficient manner, given the population and historical development of that state.

■ INTERPLAY BETWEEN FEDERAL AND STATE JURISDICTIONS

Violation of Both Federal and State Criminal Laws

In criminal cases, jurisdiction is usually an easy matter; if a defendant commits a state crime, then that state's court has jurisdiction, and if the defendant commits a federal crime, then the federal court has jurisdiction. What happens, though, if a defendant violates *both* federal *and* state criminal laws by committing a single criminal act? Where this happens, the defendant can be tried in federal court for violating federal criminal law, and in state court in a separate proceeding for violating the state's criminal law. While this might seem like double jeopardy (being tried twice for the same crime), it is not, because the defendant is not being tried twice for the *same* crime, but rather for two separate crimes committed through the same act.

Court opinion 1-2 illustrates how federal and state jurisdictions can apply to a single criminal action. The defendant, Johnson, received a violation notice for leaving her child unattended in a car, which was a crime under Maryland law. Because she committed the violation on federal property, she was also found guilty under the federal Assimilative Crimes Act, which makes it a federal crime to commit a state crime on federal property within the state. Johnson claimed that the federal court lacked jurisdiction over her case because the violation notice she received from federal officers cited only the Maryland statute as a basis of criminal liability, not the federal Assimilative Crimes Act. In other words, since a federal court only has jurisdiction over federal crimes, and she was not actually charged with a federal crime, the federal court could not hear her case. The U.S. District Court for the District of Maryland magistrate found that the notice, while defective, did not deprive the federal court of jurisdiction under the Assimilative Crimes Act, but had strong words to say about the sloppy way the federal officers completed the violation notice.

Criminal Acts Crossing State Lines

There are times when a criminal act will cross state lines. In that case, the federal government, under the Commerce Clause of the United States Constitution, has the power to prosecute the act as a federal crime. A notorious example of such a criminal statute is the 1910 Mann Act, which prohibited the trafficking of female across state lines for "immoral purposes." The idea was to prevent women from being transported for prostitution, but the vagueness of the term "immoral purposes" allowed prosecutions for much broader reasons. The Mann Act was amended in the 1970s and 1980s to resolve this problem. But even in its original form, it did not apply to any criminal activity that took place entirely within a single state. Such activity could only be criminalized under state law.

COURT OPINION 1-2

UNITED STATES V. JOHNSON, 131 F.SUPP.2D 721 (D.MD., 2001)

On the morning of October 23, 2000, at the Social Security Administration complex in Baltimore, Maryland, an officer with the General Services Administration issued a "United States District Court Violation Notice" to Defendant Valeria Johnson. Under the heading "Offense Charged," the officer wrote, "Article 5-801 (unattended child)." Under the heading "Offense Described," the officer wrote, "Did, being charged with the care of Darien Williams, a child under the age of 8 years old, allowed said child to be Locked/confined in a motor vehicle being out of his/her sight and while he/she was absent from."

Immediately before trial, counsel for the prosecution explained that "Article 5-801 (unattended child)" actually referred to Section 5-801 of the Family Law Article of the Maryland Code. Despite the ambiguity of the citation, defense counsel indicated that she was aware that the violation notice charged a violation under this section. Defendant did not contend that the violation notice gave her insufficient notice of the charge against her.

Instead, Defendant argued that the Court did not have jurisdiction. Defendant reasoned that because the violation notice did not mention the Assimilative Crimes Act in conjunction with the Maryland statute, it only charged a violation of state law. Because federal courts do not ordinarily have jurisdiction over state crimes, Defendant continued, this Court lacks jurisdiction over this case.

Analysis

Federal district courts have original jurisdiction over "all offenses against the laws of the United States" by virtue of Section 3231 of Title 18 of the United States Code. Under the Assimilative Crimes Act, Maryland crimes become federal crimes when they occur on federal lands within Maryland where federal jurisdiction exists. See *United States v. Raffield*, 82 F.3d 611, 611 (4th Cir. 1996) (citing 18 U.S.C. §§ 7(3), 13). Pursuant to the Assimilative Crimes Act, a violation of Section 5-801 of the Family Law Article of the Maryland Code is a federal crime when it occurs on federal property such as the Social Security Administration complex. Therefore, this Court has jurisdiction over such a case.

Defendant has cited no cases, and this Court has found none, that suggest that the Government's failure to refer to the Assimilative Crimes Act in the charging document renders that Act inapplicable to the crimes charged within. The Act applies of its own force to state law crimes committed on federal lands under federal jurisdiction, cf. *United States v. Robinson*, 495 F.2d 30, 33 (4th Cir. 1974) (noting that the Act "operates *ex proprio vigore*"), *overruled on other grounds by United States v. Young*, 916 F.2d 147, 151 (4th Cir. 1990), not merely when the Government invokes it. The Act, not the charging document, makes a violation of certain Maryland laws on federal land under federal jurisdiction a federal crime.

Although it did not deprive the Court of jurisdiction, Defendant could have argued that she did not receive adequate notice of the charge against her as a result of the officer's failure to refer to the Assimilative Crimes Act and correctly cite the Maryland statute in the violation notice. For petty offenses committed on federal enclaves, a "violation notice is the functional equivalent of an indictment or an information." *United States v. Moore*, 586 F.2d 1029, 1031 (4th Cir. 1978). Like indictments and informations, a violation notice should cite the statute that the defendant is charged with violating. See FED. R. CRIM. P. 7(c) (1) (providing that "[t]he indictment or information shall state for each count the official or customary citation of the statute, rule, regulation or other provision of law which the defendant is alleged therein to have violated"). Failure to do so does not justify dismissing the case, however, unless the Defendant was prejudiced by the omission. See *United States v. Brotzman*, 708 F. Supp. 713, 716 (D.Md.1989) (Smalkin, J.). In this case, the officer's failure to correctly cite the statutes did not require dismissal because she waived the issue and because—as demonstrated by her acquittal—she was not prejudiced by the omission.

Although the officer's failure to cite the statutes correctly did not require the Court to dismiss the charges, the Government should inform its law enforcement officers of the proper way to cite state crimes charged under the Assimilative Crimes Act. An officer should cite to both the Assimilative Crimes Act and the state statute. It can cite to the

(continued)

(continued)

former by writing "18 U.S.C. sec. 13" alongside the reference to the Maryland statute under the heading "Offense Charged."

Questions

1. Why did the federal magistrate decide that the defective violation notice did not deprive him of jurisdiction over Johnson's case?

2. Why did the magistrate feel so strongly that violation notices issued by federal officers should cite both the Maryland statute and the Assimilative Crimes Act?

Multiple State Jurisdiction

Federal criminal law may be violated by acts that cross state lines, but those same acts might also violate the criminal codes of the states where the acts take place. We have seen how the federal and state court systems can have jurisdiction over a single defendant for a single criminal act, but what about multiple states? Can a defendant be charged with a crime in more than one state, when only one criminal act was committed?

The answer is yes. A defendant can be charged with a crime in any state where an act in furtherance of that crime took place. To use a simple example, let's suppose that a defendant has committed bigamy by marrying a woman in California, and then later marrying another woman in Texas. Both states criminalize bigamy. The defendant could be charged with bigamy in both California and Texas, because even though the bigamous act (the second marriage) occurred solely in Texas, the first marriage that made the second marriage bigamous took place in California. Generally, states will interpret their own laws as broadly as possible to encompass criminal acts that took place in other states as well as their own.

Long-Arm Statutes

long-arm statute
A state statute that allows punishment of a defendant for acts committed outside the state, where those acts violate that state's criminal law.

Many states have passed "**long-arm statutes**" that criminalize conduct that violates that state's laws, but takes place outside the state. For instance, the state of Washington's long-arm statute provides that a person is liable for criminal punishment in the state of Washington if he "commits an act without the state which affects persons or property within the state, which, if committed within the state, would be a crime" (RCW 9A.04.030(5)). This "detrimental effects" approach to state criminal jurisdiction was first set forth by Justice Oliver Wendell Holmes in the 1911 case of *Strassheim* v. *Daily*, in which Justice Holmes wrote:

> "Acts done outside a jurisdiction, but intended to produce and producing detrimental effects within it, justify a state in punishing the cause of the harm as if he had been present at the effect, if the state should succeed in getting him within its power."

(*Strassheim* v. *Daily*, 221 U.S. 280, 285 (1911))

In the previous example, this ruling would give California the right to punish a defendant who committed bigamy in Texas, because the wife in California would certainly be detrimentally affected by the bigamous marriage.

Extradition

Article IV of the U.S. Constitution requires states to **extradite** fugitives from justice who are charged with crimes in another state. Under the federal Extradition Act (18 U.S.C. §3182), this requires that the fugitive be arrested in the state where he is located, and held for up to thirty days until an agent of the prosecuting state can arrive to take custody of the fugitive and transport him back to the prosecuting state. This means that a defendant charged with a crime in two states can be tried for that crime in one state, but will then have to be extradited to the second state to stand trial again. This, again, is not double jeopardy, because the defendant is not being charged for the same crime, but rather two different crimes arising from the same act.

extradition
The constitutionally mandated process by which a fugitive from justice is arrested and held in the state where he is located, for delivery into the custody of agents of the prosecuting state.

Conflict between Federal and State Laws in Criminal Cases

Clearly, an act that constitutes both a federal crime and a state crime can be prosecuted as such by both the federal and state judicial systems. But what happens when a federal criminal statute and a state criminal statute are inconsistent? In other words, what if an act committed within a state is legal under state law, but illegal under federal law?

The short answer to this question is that states do not have the power to undermine federal criminal law, and that a citizen can therefore be charged with a federal crime even if his/her actions are not criminal under state law. Such conflicts have occurred with respect to the manufacture and sale of medical marijuana in states that have legalized such activities. Growers and vendors of marijuana are safe from state prosecution, but are still subject to federal prosecution if their activities violate federal drug laws.

Conflicts can also occur when the federal court system levies punishments that are not permitted under state law. In the following case, a defendant was charged under federal law with a first-degree murder committed in Hawaii under circumstances that triggered the federal death penalty. The defendant argued that such a penalty infringed on the sovereignty of Hawaii, which did not impose the death penalty for any crime. The District Court of Hawaii addressed the question of whether a federal statute could impose a penalty that did not exist under state law.

COURT OPINION 1-3 _____

UNITED STATES V. TUCK CHONG, 123 F.SUPP.2D 563 (D.HAWAII, 1999)

Defendant . . . argues that the Government may not seek a sentence of death because Hawaii State law does not provide for the death penalty. Defendant argues that imposing a death sentence would violate Hawaii State sovereignty [and] the Tenth Amendment.

. . . . Defendant is charged with a federal capital crime, not a purely local offense outside federal jurisdiction. As such, the federal government has jurisdiction and may determine the appropriate sentence, independent of the State of Hawaii.

Defendant argues that the State of Hawaii did not delegate to the federal government the power to punish a criminal offender with the death penalty, and that the death penalty act contains no nexus with any power delegated to the federal government in the Constitution. Thus, Defendant contends that the implementation of the death penalty by the federal government violates the Tenth Amendment and Hawaii State sovereignty.

Defendant is incorrect, as his argument is based on the flawed premise that the federal government does not have the power under the United States Constitution to try and sentence crimes against the United States. This is simply untrue. Sentencing

(continued)

(continued)

Defendant according to federal law for a federal crime neither violates Hawaii State sovereignty nor the Tenth Amendment, under the doctrine of dual sovereignty.

In *United States v. Davis*, 906 F.2d 829 (2nd Cir. 1990), the Second Circuit explained the doctrine of dual sovereignty:

> One of the by-products of our nation's federal system is the doctrine of "dual sovereignty." . . . This doctrine rests upon the basic structure of our polity. The states and the national government are distinct political communities, drawing their separate sovereign power from different sources, each from the organic law that established it. Each has the power, inherent in any sovereign, independently to determine what shall be an offense against its authority and to punish such offenses.

> *Id.* at 832.

In this case, Defendant is charged, inter alia, with a violation of 18 U.S.C. § 924(j). Section 924(j) is a federal offense, and as previously discussed, this Court has found such a violation to be linked to interstate commerce.

It is well established that a federal district court has jurisdiction to prosecute federal crimes. The Tenth Circuit recently rejected the argument that such jurisdiction is absent because the States are sovereign. See *United States v. Lampley*, 127 F.3d 1231, 1245–46 (10th Cir. 1997), cert. denied, 522 U.S. 1137, 118 S.Ct. 1098, 140 L.Ed.2d 153 (1998). In finding that the federal court had original jurisdiction to prosecute crimes committed within the States, the court reasoned that "[t]he Supremacy Clause, the Civil War, the decisions of the Supreme Court, and acts of Congress make it clear that so long as there is a constitutionally authorized federal nexus, the federal government is free to act anywhere within the United States." *Id.* at 1246.

Thus, it is clear that in this case, the federal government has jurisdiction to prosecute Defendant, charged with a crime against the United States, in federal court. Moreover, the federal government has jurisdiction to determine the appropriate sentence under federal law. Congress determined that a sentence of death is available for a § 924(j) violation. According to the doctrine of dual sovereignty, the federal government has the power to provide for such a sentence, despite that the charged offense took place in a state that does not provide for a similar sentence. The federal government may, independent of the State of Hawaii, determine the appropriate punishment for a crime against the United States.

Thus, it is not necessary, as Defendant contends, that the State of Hawaii delegate such a power to the federal government, as the federal government rightly holds such power under the United States Constitution. According to the Tenth Amendment, any powers not delegated to the United States by the Constitution, nor prohibited by it to the States, are reserved to the States. Here, the Constitution has delegated the power to determine what shall be an offense against its authority and to punish such offenses. Such a power is not reserved to the States.

Moreover, under the Supremacy Clause of the United States Constitution, to any extent that State law conflicts with federal law, federal law preempts. . . . Under the pre-emption doctrine, which has its roots in the Supremacy Clause, state law is nullified to the extent that it actually conflicts with federal law. . . . Such a conflict arises when "compliance with both federal and state regulations is a physical impossibility." . . . or when state law "stands as an obstacle to the accomplishment and execution of the full purposes and objectives of Congress," . . . . Thus, to any extent that the sentence of death conflicts with Hawaii law, federal law governs.

. . .

In sum, the offense with which Defendant is charged is a federal crime. This Court has previously found that § 924(j) does not exceed Congress' power under the Commerce Clause, and that federal jurisdiction exists in the instant case. Under the foregoing authorities, it is evident that the federal government, independent of the State of Hawaii, is within its power to determine the appropriate sentence for the crime charged. Accordingly, the Court will not strike the death penalty notice, as neither Hawaii State sovereignty [nor] the Tenth Amendment . . . is threatened by the possibility of such a sentence.

Questions

1. Why did the Court feel that Hawaii's rejection of the death penalty did not affect the federal government's ability to impose it for a murder taking place in Hawaii?
2. What does this case tell us about how conflicts between federal and state laws are resolved?

■ RULES OF EVIDENCE

This brief overview of court structure is not intended to be exhaustive, but to provide some context for further discussions about court proceedings and issues involving the admissibility of evidence. Now, you will be introduced to the rules that courts use to resolve these issues: the **Rules of Evidence**.

Rules of Evidence can be found in the federal courts and most state courts, and cover nearly every type of evidence-related issue that can arise in the course of a criminal case. Throughout this text, we will be looking at the federal rules and various comparable state rules, but for now you should be aware of how the rules are organized, and what type of information they contain.

Court Rules

First, what do we mean by a "**rule of court**"? Statutes, as you may already know, are created by legislatures, and administrative agencies pass regulations. These types of laws are always subject to public scrutiny, because they apply to the public at large. It is not so with rules of court. These rules, which are generally procedural in nature, govern how courts operate. They only apply to those who are actually involved in court cases. For this reason, most courts may create, change, and eliminate rules with absolute impunity. There are exceptions to this rule (for instance, California's rules of court are found in the California Code of Civil Procedure, which is a statute passed by the legislature), but in most states, court rules are created by the courts themselves.

Federal and state rules are created by the highest court in the jurisdiction where they apply. There are four main types of rules: rules of civil procedure, which apply to all civil cases; rules of criminal procedure, which apply in criminal cases; rules of evidence, which apply to both civil and criminal

Rules of Evidence
Court rules that govern the admissibility and use of evidence before a trial court.

LEARNING OBJECTIVE 7
Contrast the scope and purpose of federal/state and local rules of court.

rule of court
A rule of court contains specific procedural instructions that apply to all courts within a certain jurisdiction. Rules of court are generally created, modified, and rescinded by the highest court within that jurisdiction.

What happens in a courtroom is governed by several layers of rules, from rules created by individual judges to state or federal rules that apply throughout the jurisdiction.
Source: https://us.fotolia.com/id/63138618?by=serie.

Aerogondo/Fotolia

cases; and rules of appellate procedure, which apply to appeals above the trial court level. Federal and state courts may also create additional sets of rules to govern courts of more limited jurisdiction (such as state probate courts or the federal tax court).

In addition to the state and federal rules, individual courts within each system may create rules that apply only in that court. These are called **local rules**. These rules are usually much more specific than the federal or state rules, because they address the everyday operation of the courts. Local rules are often used to fill in details left open by the more general rules, or to provide specific procedures for carrying out duties required under the state rules. They can also tell attorneys how to practice before that court. Nearly every level of court from the state trial court level to the U.S. Supreme Court has local rules that govern how that particular court operates.

For example, Pennsylvania Rule of Criminal Procedure 106 provides that "The court or issuing authority may, in the interests of justice, grant a continuance, on its own motion, or on the motion of either party." Pa.R.Crim. Pro 106(A). It does not, however, specify how to prepare or file a motion for a continuance (i.e., a delay in proceedings), because each Pennsylvania county will have different procedures for handling motions and scheduling court proceedings. The local rules will therefore inform lawyers what information to include in a motion for a continuance, where to file the motion, and how it will be processed by the court.

> **PRACTICE TIP**
>
> Anyone involved in criminal actions should have an up-to-date copy of the local rules of court for the county or district where the action is filed. These rules are often available for free on the county or district court's website, or from the county law library or clerk of courts for a nominal fee.

The Federal Rules of Evidence

Created in 1975, the **Federal Rules of Evidence** lay out rules that govern nearly every issue of evidence that might arise in the course of litigation. These rules are used as the model for many state rules of evidence, because they are so comprehensive and well organized.

The current version of the Federal Rules of Evidence are included in this textbook in their entirety as Appendix A. Throughout this textbook, you will be learning much more about these rules and how they operate.

---

local rules
Local rules govern proceedings in individual courts, as opposed to the entire court system as a whole.

Federal Rules of Evidence
Rules that govern the use and admissibility of evidence in federal trial courts. These rules have been used by many states as a model for their own rules of evidence.

LEARNING OBJECTIVE 8
Identify the key subject areas of the Federal Rules of Evidence.

KEY TERMS

CHAPTER SUMMARY

- The law of evidence is *procedural*, meaning that it only applies in the context of court proceedings.
- Far more criminal cases are heard in state courts than in federal courts.
- Federal courts do not control how state courts operate, except where the federal constitution is involved.
- The federal and nearly all state court systems have four levels: minor courts, trial courts, intermediate appellate courts, and courts of final appeal.
- Minor courts (often called *magistrates*) are limited in power, and are usually involved in issuing warrants and conducting preliminary criminal processes.
- Trial courts (or *trial judges*) hear criminal trials, and are active in resolving legal issues that arise prior to trial, including ruling on the admissibility of evidence.
- Appellate courts review legal decisions made by trial courts before and during trials, and determine whether those decisions were legally correct.
- Appeals to the intermediate appellate court are a matter of right, while appeals to the court of final appeal are a matter of permission, not of right, except in those few states that do not have an intermediate appellate court.
- The federal court system is divided into twelve circuits: ten regional circuits, the federal circuit, and the D.C. circuit.
- Each circuit is divided along state lines into districts. Each state has between one and four districts, depending on population.
- Federal courts have jurisdiction over federal crimes; state courts have jurisdiction over state crimes committed within that state's boundaries.
- U.S. district courts are the trial courts of the federal system.
- U.S. circuit courts of appeals are the intermediate appellate courts in the federal system.
- The U.S. Supreme Court is the highest court in the federal system, and hears appeals only where a *writ of certiorari* is granted.
- The U.S. Supreme Court can also hear appeals from state courts of final appeal where those cases involve issues of federal constitutional law.
- Court rules are rules created by courts to govern proceedings before those courts.
- State and federal rules are created by the highest court in each jurisdiction, and govern all court proceedings in that jurisdiction. There are four main kinds of state and federal rules: rules of civil procedure, rules of criminal procedure, rules of evidence, and rules of appellate procedure.
- Individual courts within the state and federal systems can also create *local rules*, which provide details in carrying out procedures required under the state or federal rules.
- The Federal Rules of Evidence provide a model for most states rules of evidence.

WEB EXCURSIONS

1. Visit the official United States Courts website at http://www.uscourts.gov. Using the resources of that website, answer the following questions:
   a. Which federal judicial district do you live in?
   b. Which circuit is your district located in?
   c. What are the names of the district judges serving in your district?
   d. What is the name, address, and phone number of the clerk of your district?
2. Using an Internet search engine such as Google, determine whether the county in which you live has its local rules available on the Web. If not, contact the county prothonotary and determine how you would go about getting a copy of the local rules.

PRACTICAL EXERCISE

1. You are the defense attorney in a case on appeal to the Supreme Court of any state. Your client, the defendant, is charged with raping his girlfriend three days after they allegedly broke up. Your client claims that he was still dating the victim when the sexual contact occurred, and that it was

consensual. The trial judge in the case refused to allow you to ask questions about the victim's previous sexual relationship with the defendant on the grounds that it might prejudice the jury unfairly. The state rules of evidence, however, clearly state that evidence of a victim's prior sexual relationship with the defendant is admissible where consent has been raised as a defense to rape. Based on this information, write an argument to the appeals court that supports your position that the judge's mistake in this case was prejudicial, not harmless. Base your argument on the likelihood that the jury would have accepted your client's consent defense if they had known that the victim had consented on many prior occasions.

ENDNOTES

1. The 1944 *United States* v. *Johnson* opinion cited later in this chapter was handed down by a federal magistrate.

2. Brenner, S.W. (2006). Cybercrime jurisdiction. *Crime, Law, and Social Change, 46,* 189–206.

3. Statistics provided by the United States Court website at http://www.uscourts.gov/uscourts/Statistics/JudicialBusiness/2012/appendices/A01Sep12.pdf.

lkiryo/123RF

LEARNING OBJECTIVES

After reading this chapter, the student will be able to:

1. Explain the concept of criminal guilt.

2. Understand what "elements" of crimes are and how they relate to the law of evidence.

3. Define the *actus reus* of a crime, including omission, status, and possession.

4. Identify and distinguish between the four types of *mens rea*.

5. Explain how conditions affect criminal liability.

6. Understand the element of harm and the concept of causation.

7. Define the basic defenses that are available to criminal defendants.

Criminal Law

■ INTRODUCTION

When we think of criminal cases, we usually think about the processes used to gather evidence and prove guilt: arrests, crime scene investigations, and trials. But how do we know if a defendant's actions constitute a crime? And how do we know what evidence we need in order to prove that crime? The answer to these two questions lies in **criminal law**, which defines the parameters of criminal liability. In this chapter, we will take a brief look at criminal law to understand the elements that comprise crimes, and how those elements function. We will also look at defenses that are available to criminal defendants to avoid liability for violating the criminal law.

■ THE ULTIMATE FACT QUESTION: GUILT

Guilt is the ultimate factual issue in every criminal case. If guilt is proven, then the defendant can be punished according to law. To understand how criminal law works, we need to understand what we mean when we say a defendant is guilty of a crime.

The concept of guilt is an old one. Every code of conduct ever created has embodied the notion that there are certain behaviors that cannot be

criminal law
The branch of law that defines the parameters of criminal liability.

LEARNING OBJECTIVE 1
Explain the concept of criminal guilt.

guilt
The ultimate fact that must be proven in a criminal case in order to punish the defendant.

tolerated by society, and anyone who exhibits those behaviors should be punished. In colonial times, before the U.S. Constitution was created, the concept of guilt extended beyond mere social harms deep into the realm of religion and morality. Societies founded by religion orders such as Quakers or Puritans passed laws that punished individuals for engaging in behavior that violated the religious teachings of those orders.

In modern times, American society does not generally base its criminal laws on purely religious or moral principles. We prohibit conduct that would injure society in some fashion, subject to the protections afforded by the Bill of Rights. For instance, we do not punish individuals simply for swearing, because such speech is protected by the First Amendment. We do, however, punish those whose communication consists of obscenity, because we have determined as a society that obscenity is not protected speech. Even where speech is not obscene, we prohibit certain *methods* of communication, such as spray-painting a message on the side of a public building. The point is that we no longer prohibit behavior simply because it is immoral or in violation of religious principles, but rather because it endangers the well-being and peaceful coexistence of our citizens, regardless of moral or religious beliefs.

One recent example of a morality-based crime is sodomy, usually defined as anal or oral sex. Many states outlawed sodomy in one form or another until 2003, when the U.S. Supreme Court ruled in *Lawrence* v. *Texas*, 539 U.S. 558 (2003), that such laws improperly infringed on the privacy of citizens and were therefore unconstitutional. Other so-called "victimless" crimes, such as prostitution or marijuana use, are the subjects of controversy over whether they should be criminal precisely because it is unclear whether they are criminalized on social or purely moral grounds.

Our concept of "guilt" is more restricted than it used to be. But one thing has not changed from colonial times: if behavior is prohibited, then those who engage in it are "guilty" and may be punished. This, then, is the ultimate issue that must be decided in any criminal case: is the defendant "guilty?" Now, we will look at how the criminal law answers this question.

LEARNING OBJECTIVE 2
Understand what "elements" of crimes are and how they relate to the law of evidence.

■ ELEMENTS OF CRIMES

To prove guilt, the government must prove specific facts that constitute the crime of which a defendant is accused. These facts go beyond the mere behavior of the defendant. For instance, a prosecutor cannot prove guilt in a murder case simply by proving that the defendant killed the victim. Causing the death of another human being is merely one fact among those that constitute the crime of murder.

elements of crimes
Facts that must be proven in order to find a defendant guilty of a crime.

The facts that make up crimes are called "**elements of crimes**." Most crimes consist of at least two elements: an action (called the *actus reus*, or "evil act") and a mental state (called the *mens rea*, or "evil mind"). In addition to these two basic elements, many crimes also include conditions, or facts that must exist apart from the defendant's actions and mental state. Some crimes also require that a certain kind of harm occur.

There are four basic elements of crimes:

- *Actus reus* (the defendant's behavior)
- *Mens rea* (the defendant's mental state)
- Conditions (sometimes)
- Harm (sometimes)

Each element of a crime represents a fact or set of facts that must be proven in order to determine the defendant's guilt. In every jurisdiction in the United States, the elements of crimes are set forth in **criminal codes**, which is a series of statutes defining each crime. Those elements must be sufficiently clear and specific so that a reasonably intelligent person can determine whether his behavior violates the statute.

If the elements of a crime are not sufficiently clear, then the statute is **void for vagueness** and cannot be enforced. This often happens when words used to define crimes are unclear or subject to more than one reasonable interpretation.

In *State v. Icon Entertainment Group, Inc.*, an adult nightclub was charged with violating Ohio law relating to the operation of a sexually oriented business after midnight. The defendant claimed that the activities that were prohibited after midnight were insufficiently defined in the statute, so that a reasonable person could not know whether he was breaking the law or not. The court carefully examined the statute and concluded that it was sufficiently clear that the defendant's activities violated the statute.

criminal code
A set of statutes that contains the criminal law in a particular jurisdiction.

void for vagueness
A statute is "void for vagueness" when it violates due process by failing to clearly identify the behavior that is being criminalized.

COURT OPINION 2-1

STATE V. ICON ENTERTAINMENT GROUP, INC., 160 OHIO MISC.2D 9, 937 N.E.2D 1112 (2010)

In these cases, the defendant is charged with two counts of illegally operating a sexually oriented business in violation of R.C. 2907.40(B). R.C. 2907.40(B) states:

> No sexually oriented business shall be or remain open for business between 12:00 midnight and 6:00 a.m. on any day, except that a sexually oriented business that holds a liquor permit pursuant to Chapter 4303 of the Revised Code may remain open until the hour specified in that permit if it does not conduct, offer, or allow sexually oriented entertainment activity in which the performers appear nude.

The defendant has moved to dismiss both complaints. . . . [T]he defendant argues that R.C. 2907.40(B) is unconstitutionally vague on its face. The state opposes these arguments by maintaining that the . . . statute is not unconstitutionally vague.

. . .

A vagueness challenge is rooted in due process, and due process prohibits a statute that "fails to give a person of ordinary intelligence fair notice that his contemplated conduct is forbidden." . . . "In order to survive a void-for-vagueness challenge, the statute at issue must be written so that a person of common intelligence is able to determine what conduct is prohibited, and the statute must provide sufficient standards to prevent arbitrary and discriminatory enforcement." . . . Due process, however, makes allowances for the limitations of language; it recognizes that "[m]any statutes will have some inherent vagueness." . . . Due process does not require that the legislature define every word or phrase that appears in a statute. . . . If words in the statute are undefined, they are to be "given the meaning commonly attributed to them."

. . .

In its assailment on the language of R.C. 2907.40(B), the defendant focuses on the phrase "sexually oriented entertainment activity." That phrase is not defined in R.C. 2907.40(A), nor is it defined elsewhere in the Revised Code. Defendant maintains that this lack of a statutory definition makes it impossible to guess what the statute prohibits. For example, it maintains that it is not possible to know if the statute applies in a case where a business permits performers to walk around in a state of nudity or presents a serious monologue in which the performer appears nude. The state argues that "sexually oriented" should clearly be understood in refers [sic]

(continued)

(continued)

to the statutorily defined term "sexually oriented business" and refers to an adult cabaret. It also refers to the dictionary definitions of the words "entertainment" and "activity." Under the state's construction, "sexually oriented entertainment activity" would refer to nude performances in an adult cabaret.

Although the entire phrase "sexually oriented entertainment activity" is not statutorily defined, that does not mean that a person of common intelligence cannot determine what conduct is forbidden. Nor does this, standing alone, somehow empower law enforcement to enforce the law in some random, arbitrary, or discriminatory way.

From the statute itself, two definitions are clear. "Nude" and "sexually oriented business" are both defined terms. "Nude" is defined by reference to R.C. 2907.39 and is "the showing of the human male or female genitals, pubic area, vulva, anus, anal cleft, or cleavage with less than a fully opaque covering; or the showing of the female breasts with less than a fully opaque covering of any part of the nipple." A "sexually oriented business" is "an adult bookstore, adult video store, adult cabaret, adult motion picture theater, sexual device shop, or sexual encounter center," each of which is defined in the statute. Therefore, persons of common intelligence are on notice that the prohibition in R.C. 2940.07(B) applies to certain businesses after midnight when someone appears who is displaying unclothed any of the specified anatomical parts.

The important phrases remaining are "sexually oriented," "entertainment activity," "conduct, offer, or allow," and "performer." These terms have commonly understood meanings. . . . Based on the common meaning of these terms, a person of reasonable intelligence would necessarily conclude that R.C. 2907.40(B) applies when one of the specified types of businesses acts as a venue for a person engaging in expressive activity as part of a course of conduct aimed at providing enjoyment or spectacle and when one or more of the people involved in the expressive activity shows any of the statutorily specified anatomical parts.

Placing these understandable terms in their statutory context provides even greater guidance. It is impossible but to conclude that since defendant *is* a "sexually oriented" business known as an adult cabaret *because* it features performances in which the performers display any of the statutorily specified anatomical parts discussed above, those performances *must themselves* be "sexually oriented" in nature, for without them, defendant would be neither an adult cabaret nor a "sexually oriented" business under Ohio law. . . . From there, the only reasonable reading of R.C. 2907.40(B) is that it would, at the very least, prohibit such an adult cabaret from featuring any such sexually oriented performances of which it is a purveyor after midnight. Since that conduct would fall well within what can reasonably be understood as the core meaning of R.C. 2907.40(B), then R.C. 2907.40(B) may validly be applied to prohibit that conduct. And since there is a valid application of the statute under those circumstances, it is impossible to conclude that R.C. 2907.40(B) is vague on its face.

Questions

1. Why did the defendant believe that the statute in this case was vague?
2. How did the court determine the meaning of the element "sexually oriented entertainment activity?"
3. Did the court find that the phrase "sexually oriented entertainment activity" could *never* be vague?

PRACTICE TIP

Since criminal statutes define the elements of a crime, and since the elements tell us what facts need to be proven in order to establish a defendant's guilt, anyone involved in gathering evidence to prove a crime should be very familiar with the criminal statute defining that crime, because the statute provides the "blueprint" to determine what evidence is needed to achieve a conviction.

While many crimes exist in all jurisdictions (e.g., murder, arson, and robbery), the elements that constitute those crimes can vary greatly from one jurisdiction to another. For example, Pennsylvania's criminal code defines "murder of the first degree" very simply as an "intentional killing" (18 Pa.C.S.

§2502(a)). The term "intentional killing" is defined as a killing that is "willful, deliberate, and premeditated" (18 Pa.C.S. §2502(d)). Under this statute, there are two elements, or facts, that need to be proven to find a defendant guilty of first-degree murder: (1) did the defendant kill the victim? (or put another way, was the victim's death caused by the defendant's actions?) and (2) was that killing willful, deliberate, and premeditated?

Virginia's capital murder statute (analogous to Pennsylvania's "murder of the first degree") also requires proof of a killing that was willful, deliberate, and premeditated. But that statute contains *fifteen* separate definitions of the term "capital murder," each with its own distinct set of additional elements (see Figure 2-1). In other words, while proving a willful, deliberate, and premeditated killing would be sufficient to obtain a conviction under

Figure 2-1 Virginia's Capital Murder Statute

The following offenses shall constitute capital murder, punishable as a Class 1 felony:

1. The willful, deliberate, and premeditated killing of any person in the commission of abduction, as defined in § 18.2-48, when such abduction was committed with the intent to extort money or a pecuniary benefit or with the intent to defile the victim of such abduction;

2. The willful, deliberate, and premeditated killing of any person by another for hire;

3. The willful, deliberate, and premeditated killing of any person by a prisoner confined in a state or local correctional facility as defined in § 53.1-1, or while in the custody of an employee thereof;

4. The willful, deliberate, and premeditated killing of any person in the commission of robbery or attempted robbery;

5. The willful, deliberate, and premeditated killing of any person in the commission of, or subsequent to, rape or attempted rape, forcible sodomy or attempted forcible sodomy or object sexual penetration;

6. The willful, deliberate, and premeditated killing of a law-enforcement officer as defined in § 9.1-101, a fire marshal appointed pursuant to § 27-30 or a deputy or an assistant fire marshal appointed pursuant to § 27-36, when such fire marshal or deputy or assistant fire marshal has police powers as set forth in §§ 27-34.2 and 27-34.2:1, an auxiliary police officer appointed or provided for pursuant to §§ 15.2-1731 and 15.2-1733, an auxiliary deputy sheriff appointed pursuant to § 15.2-1603, or any law-enforcement officer of another state or the United States having the power to arrest for a felony under the laws of such state or the United States, when such killing is for the purpose of interfering with the performance of his official duties;

7. The willful, deliberate, and premeditated killing of more than one person as a part of the same act or transaction;

8. The willful, deliberate, and premeditated killing of more than one person within a three-year period;

9. The willful, deliberate, and premeditated killing of any person in the commission of or attempted commission of a violation of § 18.2-248, involving a Schedule I or II controlled substance, when such killing is for the purpose of furthering the commission or attempted commission of such violation;

10. The willful, deliberate, and premeditated killing of any person by another pursuant to the direction or order of one who is engaged in a continuing criminal enterprise as defined in subsection I of § 18.2-248;

11. The willful, deliberate, and premeditated killing of a pregnant woman by one who knows that the woman is pregnant and has the intent to cause the involuntary termination of the woman's pregnancy without a live birth;

12. The willful, deliberate, and premeditated killing of a person under the age of fourteen by a person age twenty-one or older;

13. The willful, deliberate, and premeditated killing of any person by another in the commission of or attempted commission of an act of terrorism as defined in § 18.2-46.4;

14. The willful, deliberate, and premeditated killing of a justice of the Supreme Court, a judge of the Court of Appeals, a judge of a circuit court or district court, a retired judge sitting by designation or under temporary recall, or a substitute judge appointed under § 16.1-69.9:1 when the killing is for the purpose of interfering with his official duties as a judge; and

15. The willful, deliberate, and premeditated killing of any witness in a criminal case after a subpoena has been issued for such witness by the court, the clerk, or an attorney, when the killing is for the purpose of interfering with the person's duties in such case.

Source: Va.Code.Ann §18.3-31.

Prosecutors must prove to the jury that the defendant is guilty beyond a reasonable doubt.

Source: http://www.gettyimages.com/detail/photo/lawyer-showing-documents-to-jury-in-court-royalty-free-image/513067789.

Robert Daly/Getty Images

Pennsylvania's first-degree murder statute, it would be only part of the proof needed for a conviction under Virginia's capital murder statute.

When a defendant is charged with a crime in a particular jurisdiction, the prosecutor must prove, beyond a reasonable doubt, each element of the crime as stated in that jurisdiction's criminal statute. If a jury concluded that the prosecutor failed to prove even one of those elements, it would have to return a verdict of "not guilty."

Now, we will look at each of the four types of elements to understand how they affect the ultimate issue of a defendant's guilt.

Actus Reus

The ***actus reus*** of a crime is the physical action that the defendant must perform in order to commit the crime. Sometimes the action is not specifically defined, which is the case with Pennsylvania's first-degree murder statute described above. Such statutes define the action in terms of its result. It does not matter how the killing takes place, whether it is a shooting, a stabbing, a strangulation, or some other methods of ending someone's life. The act is simply a "killing," so any action that results in death is the *actus reus* of murder.

Other crimes define the act far more specifically. Rape, for instance, requires a very specific type of act: sexual intercourse. Different jurisdictions may define the term "sexual intercourse" differently, but however the term is defined, it is the action that constitutes the *actus reus* of rape.

Some criminal statutes do not prohibit action; they require it. For instance, in some jurisdictions certain citizens (e.g., doctors and child care providers) are required to report child abuse, and failing to do so can result in a criminal sanction. Every jurisdiction has laws making it a crime to fail to obey an order to court or to comply with the terms of a properly-served

LEARNING OBJECTIVE 3
Define the *actus reus* of a crime, including omission, status, and possession.

actus reus
The physical action that a criminal must take in order to commit a crime.

subpoena. Crimes in which the *actus reus* consists of *failing* to do something required by law are known as **crimes of omission**.

Possession of certain objects or substances (called **contraband**) can also be made illegal. In so-called **crimes of possession**, it is not the defendant's *actions* that are being prohibited, but rather the defendant's control over something that is illegal to possess. To be guilty of possession, the defendant must not only possess contraband, but also *know* about that possession. If someone slipped a package of cocaine into an unsuspecting traveler's suitcase, the traveler would not be guilty of possession.

For a relatively few crimes, the *actus reus* is a state of being. In other words, guilt is determined by the defendant's condition rather than his/her actions. The most common example is being intoxicated in public. It doesn't matter how the defendant became intoxicated. What matters is that he/she is in that condition while out in public. Such crimes are known as **status crimes**. Generally, it is not possible to illegalize a status unless it was assumed voluntarily, and even then these crimes are considered relatively minor.

In 2010, El Salvador passed a law making it illegal to belong to a criminal gang.[1] This is an example of a status crime that would clearly be unconstitutional in the United States, because of the First Amendment's guarantee of freedom of association. No matter how criminal the purposes of an organization, mere membership cannot be illegalized. Chicago tried to create such a law by making it illegal to loiter in the presence of suspected gang members, but the Supreme Court struck that law down as unconstitutional. Activities carried out by members of the gang can, however, result in convictions of nonparticipating members under a theory of conspiracy (*Chicago* v. *Morales*, 527 U.S. 41 (1999)).

Mens Rea

The *actus reus* element is the foundation of criminal behavior, telling us what a defendant must be *doing* in order to commit a crime. The **mens rea** element tells us what the defendant must have been *thinking or aware of* at the time the crime occurred. Under the Model Penal Code, which many jurisdictions follow as a template for their criminal codes, there are four basic types of *mens rea*: purpose, knowledge, recklessness, and negligence.

"**Purpose**" (or "intent" in some jurisdictions) is the most serious of the four types of *mens rea*. An action is "purposeful" if it is committed with a conscious purpose, either to commit the act or to cause the harm resulting from the act.

Some crimes require multiple levels of purpose or intent. For instance, some jurisdictions define "burglary" as entering a building with the intention of committing a crime inside that building. To prove guilt for such a crime, the prosecutor must prove two separate mental states, both existing at the time the defendant entered the building. The first mental state is the intention to enter the building, and the second is the intention to commit a crime inside the building. Because the first mental state triggers the actual *actus reus* of the crime (entering the building), it is called the **general intent**. The second mental state, which relates to *why* the defendant is entering the building, is called **specific intent**. In order to successfully prosecute the crime, both intents must be proven. These types of crime are known as **specific intent crimes**.

Intent can be proven by direct evidence, such as a confession, but it is usually proven by circumstantial evidence. This means that evidence is presented that proves that the defendant's actions were consistent with an intent to commit the crime, from which the jury can then infer that such an intent did exist. Proof, for instance, that a defendant pointed a loaded, functioning handgun at a victim's head at point-blank range and pulled the trigger, knowing that if the gun fired the victim would probably die from the resulting wound, is circumstantial evidence that the defendant intentionally killed the victim.

In the following case, the defendant was convicted of bank fraud by depositing a counterfeit check that he received unexpectedly. The defendant, Peters, claimed that the evidence was insufficient to allow a reasonable jury to infer that he *intentionally* committed the crime. He claimed that he believed the check he received was a settlement of a work-related injury he'd suffered the year before, despite the fact that he had filed no insurance claim, and his injury was not permanent or severe enough to warrant a $90,000 settlement. After making sure the check would clear, he deposited it and then moved most of the money to another account. His bank later notified him that the check was counterfeit. There was no evidence that Peters had the knowledge or the means to counterfeit the check himself.

COURT OPINION 2-2

UNITED STATES V. PETERS, 462 F.3D 953 (8TH CIR. 2006)

Peters argues that the district court should have entered a judgment of acquittal or granted a new trial on the bank fraud count because the government produced insufficient evidence that Peters knew the check was counterfeit and thus failed to prove the criminal intent element of the charge. To convict Peters of bank fraud, the government had to prove that Peters "knowingly" executed or attempted to execute "a scheme or artifice—(1) to defraud a financial institution; or (2) to obtain any of the moneys, funds, credits, assets, securities, or other property owned by, or under the custody or control of, a financial institution, by means of false or fraudulent pretenses, representations, or promises." 18 U.S.C. § 1344.

Peters contends that the evidence establishes only that he unexpectedly received a check and deposited it, innocently assuming the money was an especially generous insurance settlement for a work-related auto accident he had a year earlier. He argues that no reasonable jury could have found that this evidence proved the criminal intent element for bank fraud where the government failed to bring direct evidence that Peters knew that the check was counterfeit or had the ability to create or obtain a counterfeit check.

The government is permitted to and often does prove a defendant's criminal intent with circum-

stantial evidence. See *United States v. Idriss*, 436 F.3d 946, 950 (8th Cir. 2006). Direct evidence of a defendant's mental state frequently is unavailable, *United States v. Londondio*, 420 F.3d 777, 786 (8th Cir. 2005), and the jury "is entitled to scrutinize and make reasonable inferences from defendant's conduct and from all facts surrounding the incident in question." *United States v. Pitts*, 508 F.2d 1237, 1240 (8th Cir. 1974). Examples of circumstantial evidence from which a jury reasonably can infer criminal intent include the defendant's "furtive conduct," attempts to abandon the counterfeit material, and "false exculpatory statements." *Id.*

Viewed in the light most favorable to the verdict, the government's evidence showed that Peters deposited a check for $90,700 into his bank account and that this check, precisely addressed and payable to Peters and delivered to his home, was counterfeit. When Peters deposited the check into his existing savings account, the account balance was $6. In the months before Peters deposited the counterfeit check, Bremer Bank statements showed similarly low balances in his other accounts. Peters told a bank officer and, later, an FBI agent that he thought the check was an insurance settlement from an accident he was involved in a year earlier in a vehicle leased by his employer.

(continued)

(continued)

He admittedly had suffered no injury and filed no claim in the accident, however, and his employer's property damage claim was not filed with National States, a life and health insurance company. During the weeks after he deposited the counterfeit check, Peters spent approximately half of the $90,700 to pay creditors and make purchases. When the bank notified him that the check was counterfeit, he responded with an offer to repay the money.

Drawing all reasonable inferences favorable to the government, a reasonable jury could find that Peters knew the sizable check from an insurance company with which he had never filed a claim was counterfeit. When Peters presented that check to the bank for deposit into his account, he represented that he was entitled to the money. See *United States v. Ponec*, 163 F.3d 486, 489 (8th Cir. 1998). A reasonable jury could conclude beyond a reasonable doubt that, by presenting that large counterfeit check to a bank for deposit into his nearly empty account and spending nearly half the money in the next few weeks, Peters knowingly executed a scheme to obtain money from a financial institution by fraudulent representations in violation of the bank fraud statute, 18 U.S.C. § 1344.

Questions

1. What specific actions by Peters led the court to conclude that the evidence of his intent was sufficient to support his conviction?
2. How did the facts surrounding Peters' work-related injury lend weight to the conclusion that his belief in the check's authenticity was not reasonable?

"**Knowledge**" is a different mental state from "purpose," and is probably the hardest one to define. An act is performed knowingly if the actor knows, with substantial certainty, that a condition exists, or harm will result, which makes his actions criminal (Model Penal Code §2.202). Knowledge must exist at the time the criminal act is committed.

Suppose a man has decided to assassinate a high government official by setting off explosives in his car as he is being driven to a meeting across town. His purpose is to kill the official, but he knows with substantial certainty that the driver will also be killed. When the explosives go off, he has purposefully killed the official, and knowingly killed the driver.

"**Recklessness**" is a mental state that centers on the defendant's knowledge of the risk that his/her actions create. If someone drives drunk, no one, including the driver, knows whether harm might result. But the driver knows that there is a substantial risk that harm might result, and it is the knowledge of that risk that makes the driver's actions criminal.

The least severe mental state, negligence, rarely forms the basis of criminal liability. "**Negligence**," or what we normally think of as "carelessness," means that an actor is not aware of a substantial risk that his actions are criminal or harmful, but a reasonable person would be. To illustrate the difference between recklessness and negligence, suppose that someone drives through a red light, thereby creating a serious risk of causing an accident. If the driver knew that the light was red and simply does not want to stop, then he is recklessly creating the risk. If he was distracted and did not realize that the light was red, then he is negligently creating the risk.

There are some crimes that do not require the proof of any mental state at all. For instance, a person can be cited for speeding whether or not he/she intended or even realized he/she was doing so. These crimes, known as **strict liability crimes**, are usually minor, but not always. A notable example is statutory child rape, which in many jurisdictions does not require proof that the defendant knew the age of the victim at the time of the rape. Some states go even further,

knowledge
A crime is committed knowingly when the actor knows, with substantial certainty, that a condition exists, or harm will result, which makes his actions criminal.

recklessness
A mental state in which the defendant consciously disregards a substantial risk that a condition exists, or harm will result, which makes his/her actions criminal.

negligence
A mental state in which the defendant unreasonably fails to perceive a substantial risk that a condition exists, or harm will result, which makes his/her actions criminal.

strict liability crime
A crime that does not require proof of the defendant's mental state.

denying the defendant the right to prove, as a defense, that he/she was reasonably mistaken about the victim's age. The law generally disfavors strict liability crimes, though, because of the general idea that the wrongfulness of an act is difficult to determine without understanding the mind behind it.

Concurrence

concurrence
The connection between a defendant's mental state and his/her actions, by which the mental state triggers the actions.

In addition to proving the *actus reus* and the *mens rea*, it is also necessary to prove that the mental state triggered the act. This is known as **concurrence**. Suppose that a man decides he is going to kill his wife. He buys a gun and drives home from work intending to kill her the moment he gets home. He is so eager to commit the murder that he runs through a red light, striking and killing a pedestrian. The pedestrian, it so happens, is his wife. Did he murder his wife? No. He committed the required act (killing her) and had the requisite mental state (intent to kill her), but the killing was the result of his reckless driving, not his homicidal intention.

Although concurrence is an element that must be proven in order to find a defendant guilty, it is not difficult to prove in most cases, because the circumstances of the crime usually prove concurrence without any problem. In our example, the driver who killed his wife through negligence could not be charged with murder due to the lack of concurrence between his homicidal intent and the killing, but there clearly *was* concurrence between his recklessness and the killing, so he could be charged with involuntary manslaughter.

LEARNING OBJECTIVE 5
Explain how conditions affect criminal liability.

Conditions

condition
A fact that exists apart from the defendant's actions or mental state, which makes the defendant's actions criminal.

Often, an act, by itself, is not a crime even if it is committed with the required mental state, because the criminal law also imposes **conditions** that must exist to make the act criminal. Conditions are facts that exist apart from the defendant's actions and mental state. You can think of conditions as the *context* of the crime—the environment in which the act must occur in order for it to be a crime.

Take another look at Virginia's capital murder statute (Figure 2-1). Every one of the fifteen definitions of capital murder has the same *actus reus* and *mens rea*. The difference between the types lies entirely in the conditions that each definition requires. For instance, a conviction under subsection 4 of the statute would require the prosecutor to prove that the killing took place during a robbery or attempted robbery. By contrast, convicting a defendant under subsection 12 would require proof of the victim's age (under 14) and the defendant's age (21 or older) at the time of the killing. Proving conditions, if they exist in the applicable criminal statute, is absolutely vital to proof of guilt.

LEARNING OBJECTIVE 6
Understand the element of harm and the concept of causation.

Harm

harm crime
A crime that requires the proof of a particular harm in order to find the defendant guilty.

Some crimes require that a certain harm result from the act in order for the act to be criminal. These crimes are known as **harm crimes**, because harm is an element of the crime. It is not enough that the victim suffered *some* kind of harm. The harm must be that specified in the criminal statute.

The most obvious example of a *harm crime* is criminal homicide. Without a death, homicide cannot occur, so an inability to prove that the victim was killed would be fatal to the prosecutor's case. Similarly, getting a conviction on a charge of theft would require proof that the victim was actually deprived of property.

It is important not to confuse crimes that often *do* result in harm with those that have harm as an element. For example, the victim of a rape usually suffers some kind of physical, emotional, or psychological harm. But harm is not *required* to be proven in order to convict a defendant of rape. In other words, a defendant can be convicted of rape even if the victim suffered no physical or psychological harm whatsoever as a result of the rape. The same is true of some forms of assault that are based on a threat of harm rather than harm itself. There is no need to prove that a victim was actually frightened or suffered any mental stress as a result of the threat. All that matters is that the defendant threatened the victim with some form of physical harm, and that the victim reasonably believed that harm would occur.

This point raises the question of what exactly we mean by "harm." As we are considering the term here, the word "harm" is extremely broad. It does not have to be serious or debilitating harm. It can be merely offensive or unpleasant. But the point is that harm crimes require proof that some negative consequence, however the statute might define that consequence, was suffered by the victim as a result of the crime. Where this is the case, then the final element, causation, must also be proven.

Causation

Where harm is an element of a crime, it is not enough to prove that the harm occurred. The prosecutor must also prove that the defendant's criminal act caused the harm. This is known as the element of **causation**.

Causation is proven in two stages. First, there must be proof that the defendant's criminal act was a **cause-in-fact** of the harm. This means that, without the act, the harm would not have occurred. This does not mean that the harm would *never* have occurred, only that it would not have occurred *when* and *how* it did. For instance, shooting a person suffering from a terminal illness is a crime even though the person was going to die soon anyway, because without the shooting the person wouldn't have died in the manner he did and at the time he did.

The second stage of proving causation is to show that the harm was a foreseeable consequence of the defendant's act. "**Foreseeability**" means that the defendant could reasonably have expected the harm to result from the act *when the act occurred*. Foreseeability does not mean absolute certainty. It is *possible* that a person who is shot in the head by a defendant might survive, but if the victim does not survive, his death was still foreseeable. All that is required for this stage of causation is that a reasonable person in the defendant's position could have foreseen that the harm was likely to occur.

Figure 2-2 graphically illustrates the relationship between the four main elements of crimes.

causation
The connection between a defendant's actions and the harm that results from those actions. Causation must be proven in order to convict a defendant of a harm crime.

cause-in-fact
A defendant's action is a cause-in-fact of harm if the harm would not have occurred but for that action.

foreseeability
Harm is foreseeable if a defendant could reasonably expect the harm to result from his/her actions at the time those actions occurred.

Figure 2-2 Elements of Crimes

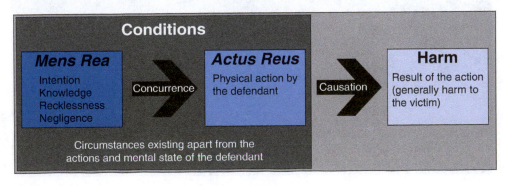

LEARNING OBJECTIVE 7
Define the basic defenses that are available to criminal defendants.

defense
A set of facts that allows a defendant to avoid criminal liability even though all of the elements of a crime can be proven.

justification
A defense that avoids criminal liability by claiming that a defendant's criminal actions were the right thing to do under the circumstances.

self-defense
A justification relieving a defendant of criminal liability where the crime was committed to avoid an imminent threat of bodily harm.

■ DEFENSES

Even if the elements of a crime are proven, a defendant can still avoid liability for that crime by successfully raising and proving a **defense**. Defenses, like crimes, consist of elements that are defined in the criminal code. Defenses are broken down into two categories: justifications and excuses.

Justifications

A **justification** for a crime challenges criminal liability by claiming that, although the defendant technically did violate a criminal statute, the violation was the right thing to do under the circumstances. There are a number of justifications that apply to crimes of varying severity.

> **PRACTICE TIP**
>
> Because defenses can relieve a defendant of criminal liability even if the elements of a crime are proven, evidence collection should from the start include any evidence that might refute potential defenses the defendant could foreseeably raise.

Self-Defense

Self-defense is a justification that is often used against charges of violent crimes such as murder and assault. In order to prove self-defense, a defendant must establish four facts:

1. The defendant believed that he/she was in danger of some kind of bodily harm.
2. The defendant's belief was reasonable under the circumstances.
3. The harm was imminent.
4. The force used by the defendant to avoid the harm was proportional to the threat.

Courts recognize a right to defend oneself and one's home from burglars, robbers, and other criminals who attempt to cause loss of life or property.

Source: https://us.fotolia.com/id/91837096.

Vchalup/Fotolia

Harm is "imminent" if it is threatened at the time the defendant acts, not at some future time. The proportionality requirement means that the steps the defendant takes to defend himself/herself must be appropriate for the level of threat the defendant is facing. A pro wrestler would not be justified in shooting an 80-year-old woman who is about to hit him with her fist, but he might be if she were attacking him with a knife.

In most jurisdictions, one can defend himself/herself against aggression even if he/she has an opportunity to retreat safely and avoid any harm. This rule is known as the **stand-your-ground rule**. Other jurisdictions limit the justification of self-defense through the "**retreat doctrine**," which holds that self-defense is available only where there is no reasonably safe method of retreating from the danger. Some jurisdictions that follow the retreat doctrine also apply the "**castle exception**," under which retreat is not required if the danger is encountered in one's own home.

In the following case, the defendant White Feather, a prison inmate, killed his cellmate, Running Bear, whom he alleged had made a credible threat against his life. White Feather raised the defense of self-defense, but the district court refused to instruct the jury that it could acquit him on that basis, because the evidence showed that he was not in imminent danger and that he had means of protecting himself other than killing his assailant. White Feather appealed on the grounds that the trial court erred in refusing to instruct the jury on self-defense.

stand-your-ground rule
A rule that permits a person to defend himself/herself against aggressive action even where he/she can safely retreat and avoid harm.

retreat doctrine
A doctrine limiting self-defense to situations where the defendant has no safe means of retreat from the danger.

castle exception
A limitation to the retreat doctrine that holds that a defendant is not required to retreat from his/her own home to avoid a threat of imminent harm.

COURT OPINION 2-3

UNITED STATES V. FEATHER, 768 F.3D 735 (7TH CIR. 2014)

This circuit recognizes three "lesser-evil" defenses that may justify otherwise unlawful action: duress, necessity, and self-defense. [*United States* v.] *Haynes*, 143 F.3d [1089,] 1091 [(7th Cir. 1998)]. Each of these defenses "rests on the belief that a person facing harm is justified in performing an act, otherwise illegal, less injurious than the impending loss." *Id*. Critically, to warrant a jury instruction on a lesser-evil justification defense, the defendant must present evidence that he faced actual, imminent harm and had no reasonable legal alternatives to avoid it. [*United States* v.] *Tokash*, 282 F.3d [962,] 969 [(7th Cir.2002)].

Imminence is an essential element for self-defense because the threatened harm may, in fact, be avoidable: "[I]f the threat is not imminent, a retreat or similar step avoids injury." *Haynes*, 143 F.3d at 1091. Importantly, a defendant's subjective belief that he had no available legal alternatives—even if objectively reasonable—is not enough to proceed with a justification defense if the evidence is insufficient to establish an actual, imminent threat of physical harm. *Tokash*, 282 F.3d at 969 (rejecting

an argument that the defendant's reasonable belief that he had no legal alternatives should suffice to permit a justification defense in the absence of a showing of imminence). For self-defense claims in particular, we have consistently held that the defendant must have evidence that he was under an imminent threat of death or serious bodily harm *and* that he had no reasonable legal alternatives to avoid that threat. *Id*.

The requirement of imminence is no less applicable in a prison than anywhere else. For example, in *Tokash* we rejected a necessity defense in a case involving inmates at USP–Marion who were caught in possession of concealed weapons. *Id*. at 965–68. The defendants pointed to an atmosphere of racial tension and frequent outbreaks of violence at the prison and argued that because the threat of violence was pervasive, they were entitled to assert a necessity defense. We resoundingly rejected this argument, explaining that evidence of frequent violence in a prison—an "inherently dangerous place [ ] . . . inhabited by violent people"—does not establish the kind of imminent threat required to support a

(continued)

(continued)

necessity defense. . . . *Haynes* involved a violent preemptive strike by a prisoner against a fellow inmate who frequently tormented him. 143 F.3d at 1089–90. We noted that "although prisons are nasty places, they are not jungles," and held that the imminence requirement was fully applicable. *Id.*

Here, the district court held that White Feather lacked evidence of an imminent threat. No other conclusion is remotely possible. Even if Running Bear was the initial aggressor, he was unconscious when White Feather dragged him out from under his bed and attacked him with the razor. An unconscious adversary does not pose an imminent threat of death or serious bodily harm.

White Feather insists that he waited to see if Running Bear "was alive and therefore an imminent threat again" before he acted. . . . As an initial matter, this argument contradicts White Feather's own testimony. He admitted on cross-examination that he had resolved to kill Running Bear earlier in the altercation, at the moment he was first assaulted, or at least at the point when he suffocated his unconscious victim. Perhaps more importantly, by White Feather's own account, Running Bear was still unconscious when he dragged him out from under the bed and cut his abdomen open:

Q. So you pull him—he's been laying there doing nothing. You pull him out, he's doing nothing, and then you slice him up; right?
A. Right.

That alone defeats the claim of self-defense, but for completeness we note that White Feather also failed to present evidence that he had no alternatives to the use of deadly force. A defendant seeking to justify his actions as a lesser evil must avail himself of reasonable legal alternatives to the use of unlawful force.

Again, this requirement applies equally in prison: "If prisoners could decide for themselves when to seek protection from the guards and when to settle matters by violence, prisons would be impossible to regulate." *Haynes*, 143 F.3d at 1091. . . .

White Feather had several legal alternatives to the use of deadly force. Most obviously, the cell was equipped with a duress button, and the government presented ample evidence about the operation of the duress signal and how it was designed to require prison guards to respond to the source of the alarm. In addition, the officer on duty in the L Unit on the night of December 1 testified that the unit was "very quiet," and that if an inmate yelled or banged on his cell door, a guard would hear and immediately respond.

In short, even accepting that Running Bear was the initial aggressor, there is no evidence that he posed an imminent threat when White Feather cut him open with the razor or that alternatives to this use of deadly force were unavailable. White Feather killed Running Bear slowly, deliberately, and savagely, while his victim was unconscious and posing no imminent threat, and in the presence of reasonable legal alternatives to the use of deadly force. Because no evidence supports White Feather's claim of self-defense, the district court properly refused to instruct the jury on the defense.

Questions

1. What would have been the outcome had White Feather instead been charged with assault for rendering his cellmate unconscious rather than killing him?
2. What does this case tell us about the notion that prisons are inherently violent and therefore the need for self-defense is *always* "imminent?"

Necessity

necessity
A justification in which a defendant commits a crime to avoid a harm greater than that that results from the crime itself.

Also known as the "choice of evils" defense, **necessity** justifies the commission of a crime where the only other alternative is worse than the crime itself. This defense only applies to lesser crimes such as trespass. For instance, trespassing on someone's lake-side property would be justified in order to harbor a boat that otherwise would be caught in a dangerous storm. For this defense to work, the evil avoided by the crime must outweigh the evil resulting from the crime.

Defense of Others

Defending someone else from imminent serious harm is also a justification, so long as the person being defended would have been entitled to defend himself/herself under the requirements for self-defense, but was unable to do so. This justification is not available if the defended individual would have been able to extricate himself/herself from the danger without the intervention of the defendant.

Defense of Property

Defending one's own property from harm can also justify certain types of crimes. This justification is not available for crimes that result in death or serious bodily injury, however, because property is not worth the life of the person threatening it. In other words, while the owner of property is permitted to physically restrain another person from taking or damaging his/her property, he/she is not permitted to shoot that person unless his/her or someone else's life is in danger.

Consent

Consent is a justification that centers on the victim's willingness to endure the crime. Consent is only available as a defense in four instances:

- Where the crime took place as part of a sporting event (e.g., football, hockey)
- Where the crime involved sexual conduct
- Where the crime did not cause bodily harm to the victim
- Where the victim benefitted from the crime (e.g., surgery)

Consent is not always available in these instances, however. For instance, where the criminality of a sexual act is based on the victim's age (such as statutory child rape), consent would not be a defense. Also, in order to take advantage of this defense, a defendant must prove that he did not exceed the scope of consent given by the victim. A football player who slugs another player in anger during a game can be charged with assault because consenting to potentially harmful contact during a football game does not include a deliberate punch.

Privilege

The justification of **privilege** exists where the defendant has a legal right to take actions that would otherwise constitute a crime. The classic example of a privilege is the right of a police officer to arrest a suspect. Normally, putting someone in handcuffs, forcing them into an automobile, and taking them away against their will would constitute the crimes of assault and kidnapping. But police officers who are acting within the scope of their duties are permitted to commit such acts without criminal liability. Privilege is contingent, however, on the legal correctness of the action. An officer who unduly beats a suspect, or who arrests someone without probable cause to believe that he/she committed a crime, would not be able to use this defense.

Excuses

Excuses are defenses that do not challenge the fact that a crime was committed or that it was the wrong thing to do, but instead claim that circumstances exist that should relieve the defendant from any punishment for the crime.

Insanity

The most notorious of excuses is **insanity**, although the use of this excuse is not as common as the average citizen might believe. The excuse of insanity

consent
A defense to criminal liability based on the willing acceptance of a crime by the victim.

privilege
A justification in which the defendant has the legal right to commit the crime.

excuse
A defense that claims that, under the circumstances, the defendant should not be punished for committing a crime despite its wrongness.

insanity
An excuse that relieves the defendant of criminal liability because of a mental disease or defect that prevents the defendant from recognizing the wrongness of his/her actions or from being able to conform his/her actions to the requirements of the law.

applies where a defendant has a mental disease or defect that prevents the defendant from recognizing the wrongness of his/her actions, or from being able to conform his/her actions to the requirements of the law.

Until the early 1980s, a defendant who raised insanity as a defense was not required to prove that he/she was insane. Rather, it was the duty of the prosecutor to prove that the defendant was *not* insane in order to obtain a conviction. Following the attempted assassination of President Ronald Reagan by John Hinckley, and Hinckley's subsequent acquittal based on his defense of insanity, the law was changed to place the burden on the defendant to produce evidence of insanity.

Intoxication

The excuse of intoxication challenges a defendant's criminal liability because the defendant's judgment and self-control were impaired by alcohol or drugs. This defense is usually not available unless the intoxication was involuntary. Where the defendant is charged with a specific intent crime, even voluntary intoxication can be used to show that the defendant was incapable of forming the requisite intent to commit the crime.

Age

Where a defendant is a minor, his/her age might be taken into account to determine whether he/she was sufficiently mature to be criminally liable for his/her actions. There was a time when children under the age of seven were automatically deemed incapable of criminal liability, but modern criminal law holds that a child's maturity will be determined on a case-by-case basis. If a child is not sufficiently mature to be held liable for a criminal violation, he/she might be released, or be subject to rehabilitation through the juvenile justice system.

Duress

duress
An excuse for criminal liability based on the fact that the defendant was forced or pressurized to commit the crime.

It is possible for a defendant to be forced or pressured into committing a crime. This force or pressure is called **duress**, and under some circumstances it can constitute an excuse for criminal activity. There are severe limitations on this defense, however. First, it cannot be used to excuse a serious crime such as homicide or rape. Second, the pressure on the defendant must be so powerful that a person of reasonable resolution would not be able to withstand it. Merely being teased or cajoled into committing a crime would not be sufficient. Some kind of serious harm to the physical, emotional, or financial well-being of the defendant or his/her loved one would probably be enough, so long as the crime is not violent.

Entrapment

This excuse is often misunderstood as being available whenever law enforcement provides the opportunity for someone to commit a crime. It is not entrapment for a police officer to masquerade as a drug user in order to get a dealer to sell so that an arrest can be made, or for a female officer to pose as a prostitute in order to arrest men who might solicit her services. Entrapment does not involve creating the *opportunity* for a crime; it involves creating the *motive* for the crime. In other words, law enforcement must persuade or entice someone to commit a crime that he/she would not have chosen to commit without that persuasion. If the officer posing as a prostitute targeted a man and aggressively pursued him until he finally agreed to use her services, she might have entrapped him. It depends on how far she went to break through his natural tendency to obey the law, and how long it took before that tendency was overridden. In one extreme case, *Jacobson* v. *United States*, 503 U.S. 540, 112 S.Ct. 1535, 118 L.Ed.2d 174 (1992), U.S. Postal Service employees spent two years in an elaborate scheme to convince the defendant to purchase child pornography. Such excessive and aggressive cajoling of an individual to get him/her to commit a crime is the kind of activity which is required to support a defense of entrapment.

PRACTICE TIP

In any sting operation, great or small, care must be taken not to entice an otherwise law-abiding citizen into committing a crime. The desire to commit a crime must originate with the target of the sting. Where the target steadfastly refuses to engage in criminal activity, the sting can turn into entrapment.

KEY TERMS

criminal law   27
guilt   27
elements of crimes   28
criminal code   29
void for vagueness   29
actus reus   32
crime of omission   33
contraband   33
crime of possession   33
status crime   33
mens rea   33
purpose   33
general intent   33

specific intent   33
specific intent
   crime   33
knowledge   35
recklessness   35
negligence   35
strict liability
   crime   35
concurrence   36
condition   36
harm crime   36
causation   37
cause-in-fact   37

foreseeability   37
defense   38
justification   38
self-defense   38
stand-your-ground rule   39
retreat doctrine   39
castle exception   39
necessity   40
consent   41
privilege   41
excuse   41
insanity   41
duress   42

CHAPTER SUMMARY

- Criminal law defines criminal liability, including the elements of crimes and defenses to crimes.
- The ultimate factual issue in any criminal case is guilt, as determined by the elements of the crime of which the defendant is accused.
- Each crime is comprised of elements defined in a criminal statute, including an act (*actus reus*) and a mental state (*mens rea*), often coupled with circumstances that must exist and harm that must result in order for the act to be criminal.
- A statute that fails to clearly define the elements of a crime may be void for vagueness.
- The elements of a crime can vary greatly from one jurisdiction to another.
- The *actus reus* of a crime is a physical act that the defendant must perform to commit the crime,

although some crimes are based on inaction (crimes of omission), possession, or status rather than an affirmative physical act.
- The *mens rea* of a crime is the mental state that must accompany the physical act, and can include purpose (or intent), knowledge, recklessness, or negligence.
- A crime may require proof of a general intent to commit the criminal act, but may also require a specific intent to commit an act or cause harm beyond the physical act of the crime itself.
- The only direct evidence of intent is a confession, but intent may be inferred from circumstantial evidence, such as the actions of the defendant.
- Knowledge involves a substantial certainty that one's actions constitute a crime or that a certain

harm will result, even if the criminal act or harm is not the defendant's conscious purpose.

- Recklessness occurs when a defendant knows there is a substantial risk of harm resulting from his/her actions, but chooses to ignore that risk.
- Negligence occurs when a defendant fails to perceive a substantial risk of harm that a reasonable person would have perceived.
- Some crimes, called strict liability crimes, do not require proof of any mental state.
- In addition to proving a criminal act and a required mental state, there must also be proof that the mental state triggered the criminal act.
- Many criminal statutes define conditions that must exist apart from the defendant's action and mental state, in order to make the defendant's actions criminal.
- Some crimes require that the defendant's actions result in specific harm in order to make those actions criminal.
- Where harm is required as an element of a crime, proof is required that the defendant's actions caused that harm, and that the harm was a foreseeable result of those actions.
- Where the elements of a crime are proven, defendant can avoid liability for the crime by establishing a defense, which can include a justification or an excuse.
- A justification is a defense that obviates the wrongness of a crime by arguing that, under the circumstances, the criminal act was the right thing for the defendant to do.
- Where a defendant has committed a crime of physical violence to protect himself/herself from an imminent danger, he/she will avoid criminal liability, although some states require that the defendant prove he/she could not reasonably and safely retreat from the danger, unless he/she was in his/her own home.
- Justifications include defending others and, in a limited sense, property, as well as necessity (choice of evils), the consent of the victim, and a privilege giving the defendant legal permission to commit the crime.
- Excuses are defenses in which circumstances relieve the defendant of punishment for his/her crime, despite the fact that his/her criminal actions were wrong.
- Insanity is an excuse that applies to defendants suffering from a mental disease or defect that makes them unable to distinguish right from wrong.
- Excuses include involuntary intoxication, the defendant's age where the defendant is too young to appreciate the wrongness of his/her conduct, duress sufficient to overcome a defendant's resistance to the commission of a crime, and entrapment by law enforcement, in which an otherwise law-abiding citizen is cajoled into committing a crime he/she would not otherwise have committed.

WEB EXCURSION

1. Using the Internet, find the text of your state's criminal statute for a specific crime such as rape, kidnapping, or theft. Then, find the text of another state's criminal statute for the same crime. Identify the *actus reus*, *mens rea*, conditions, and harm (if any) that must be proven for a conviction under both statutes. Then, answer the following questions:
   a. What significant differences exist in the elements of the two statutes?
   b. Under which state's statute do you believe it would be harder to prove the crime?

PRACTICAL EXERCISE

1. John stands outside of a bus terminal and watches the number 34 bus pull in. He has always had a terrible fear of the number 34, and believes that any bus bearing that number is evil and must be exorcised by use of magic arrows that John carries in a quiver at his side. The bus comes to a stop, and John places an arrow in his crossbow and takes aim. He

shoots one arrow, which strikes the left front tire of the bus. He then shoots another that passes through a window, striking Mike in the left shoulder. John fires another arrow that pierces the leg of the bus driver, and one final arrow that misses the bus completely but strikes a bystander waiting for another bus on the other side of the terminal.

a. Using your state's definitions of the crimes of assault and battery, evaluate John's criminal liability for his actions against Mike, the bus driver, and the bystander.

b. Using your state's definition of "insanity," would John's actions support that defense? If not, what additional facts would he need to prove to establish his legal insanity?

ENDNOTE

1. "El Salvador makes gang membership illegal in wake of attack on passenger bus that killed 17," *Fox News*, September 2, 2010, http://www.foxnews.com/world/2010/09/02/el-salvador-makes-gang-membership-illegal-wake-attack-passenger-bus-killed/ (accessed October 15, 2011).

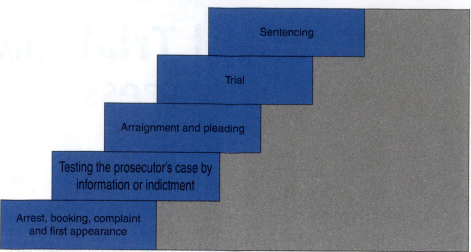

Figure 3-1 Stairway to Justice in the Federal Criminal System

■ THE FEDERAL CRIMINAL TRIAL PROCESS

Arrest, Booking, Complaint, and First Appearance

LEARNING OBJECTIVE 1
Explain the basic structure of the federal criminal trial process.

LEARNING OBJECTIVE 2
Identify the legal requirements for an arrest and explain preliminary post-arrest procedures.

When a defendant is arrested, he/she is taken into the custody of law enforcement and kept there until the court or the prosecutor allows his/her release. As you will learn in Chapter 6, an arrest cannot take place unless there is probable cause to believe that the person arrested actually committed a crime. A person cannot be arrested based on a mere suspicion of criminal activity, although the line between mere suspicion and probable cause is not always easy to identify.

> **PRACTICE TIP**
>
> Although not required unless an arrest is taking place in the suspect's home, an arrest warrant obtained from a judge or magistrate ensures that an arrest is properly based on probable cause, which avoids a number of constitutional pitfalls in the development of evidence after arrest.

booking
The administrative processes a criminal suspect is subjected to immediately following arrest.

Following an arrest, a suspect is "**booked,**" meaning that they are subjected to a number of routine administrative processes such as fingerprinting, having a mug shot taken, and recording identifying information such as the suspect's name, address, and Social Security number. So long as the arrest was lawful (i.e., supported by probable cause), any evidence obtained in a lawful manner during the booking process is admissible in court. The suspect is also brought before a magistrate (usually a federal magistrate or judge) for a **first appearance** to be informed of the charges against him/her and to find out if he/she wants counsel appointed. A preliminary hearing, if needed, is also scheduled at this time.

first appearance
A brief hearing in which a defendant appears before a magistrate and is informed of the charges against him/her and given the opportunity to request appointment of counsel.

complaint
A written statement of essential facts of the offenses with which a defendant is charged.

At some point during this process, a **complaint** will be filed that will basically start the criminal proceeding. Under Federal Rule of Criminal Procedure 3, the complaint is "a written statement of the essential facts constituting the offense charged." It is usually filed by federal investigators, and must generally be made under oath before a magistrate judge, but when permitted can also be made by telephone or electronically under Rule 4.1. The complaint's "essential facts" do not need to be supported by evidence in the complaint itself, although evidence supporting those facts will be required later in the proceedings.

Testing the Prosecutor's Case by Information or Indictment

LEARNING OBJECTIVE 3
Distinguish between the information and indictment processes.

Following these preliminary proceedings, the prosecutor's case must be tested to see if there is sufficient evidence to proceed to trial. In federal courts, this happens in one of two ways: an information and preliminary hearing or an indictment by a grand jury. Where the defendant is charged with a felony, an indictment is required unless waived by the defendant.

Information and Preliminary Hearing

Where no indictment is required, a government attorney will prepare and file an **information**, which is a written statement of the charges being brought against the defendant, and a summary of the evidence that supports those charges. Except where the defendant is charged with a misdemeanor or petty offense, or a felony in a case where the defendant has waived an indictment, the court must then hold a preliminary hearing, which must be held no later than 14 days following the first appearance where the defendant is in custody, or 21 days if the defendant is not in custody (F.R.Crim.P. 5.1).

information
A formal written accusation against the defendant filed by a government attorney.

A **preliminary hearing** takes place in front of a federal judge. The prosecutor presents the evidence he/she has in order to show that there is probable cause to justify further prosecution. The defendant and his/her counsel are present and may present evidence and challenge the prosecutor's evidence, but the defendant may not object to evidence on the grounds that it was illegally obtained. Once the evidence has been presented, the judge will either (a) find that there is probable cause to believe the defendant committed the offense, and hold the defendant for further proceedings, or (b) find that there is not probable cause to believe the defendant committed the offense, and release the defendant. Generally, a preliminary hearing does not constitute "jeopardy" for purposes of the prohibition against double jeopardy, so a release at this point can be followed by further charges and proceedings if additional evidence is obtained.

preliminary hearing
A hearing at which the prosecutor's case is tested by a magistrate to determine whether there is sufficient evidence to proceed to trial.

Indictment by a Grand Jury

An **indictment** is a decision made by a grand jury that there is sufficient evidence to justify charging a defendant with a crime. An indictment can be handed down before or after the defendant is arrested. Where a defendant has been charged under an indictment, there is no need for an information and preliminary hearing, because the grand jury has already weighed the evidence and found it sufficient to support bringing the defendant to trial. Indictments are only required when a defendant is charged with a felony.

indictment
A decision made by a grand jury to bring charges against a defendant, following presentation of evidence by a prosecutor sufficient to find probable cause that such charges are justified.

A **grand jury** is a panel of 16 to 23 citizens selected to hear evidence in federal criminal cases. A single grand jury can sit for up to 18 months, and pass judgment on any number of cases during that time. Government attorneys bring cases before a grand jury whenever an indictment is required under the federal rules.

grand jury
A panel of 16 to 23 citizens empowered to bring indictments against criminal defendants.

Grand jury proceedings are not open to the public, and the defendant has no right to present evidence or to even appear either in person or through counsel. The proceedings are secret, meaning that neither the grand jurors nor any attorneys appearing before the grand jury may disclose anything that happens in the grand jury room. The only exceptions are for the sharing of information between government attorneys, and even that is limited.

Witnesses, by contrast, are permitted to discuss their testimony freely unless the court orders otherwise.

Even the First Amendment right to a free press has to bow before the secrecy of grand jury proceedings. During the Watergate scandal involving President Richard Nixon's administration in the 1970s, two reporters for the *Washington Post*, Bob Woodward and Carl Bernstein, got in serious trouble for attempting to interview grand jurors who were hearing evidence against Nixon's top officials. The federal judge overseeing the case, John Sirica, seriously considered sending the reporters to jail for their attempt to violate the grand jury's secrecy. As it turned out, Judge Sirica merely admonished the reporters in his courtroom that they were not permitted to interview grand jurors, and he also restricted the interviewing of witnesses who were brought by prosecutors before the grand jury.

true bill
A decision of a grand jury that leads to an indictment.

Once a grand jury has heard the available evidence against a defendant, it returns a decision of "true bill" or "no true bill." If a decision of "**true bill**" is returned, then the defendant is indicted, and the case moves forward in the criminal system. A decision of "no true bill" is a determination that there is insufficient evidence to justify charges. This does not mean that the grand jury has found the defendant "not guilty," however. Further evidence can always be brought before the grand jury at a later time.

Where a defendant has already been arrested, an indictment must be handed down within 30 days after arrest, or the defendant must be released. Often, however, investigators and prosecutors will bring evidence before a grand jury and seek a true bill *before* an arrest is made. The grand jury's decision can then be used as a basis for an arrest warrant.

Proffer Session

proffer session
An informal meeting between the prosecutor and defense counsel where evidence of guilt is presented to open the door to plea negotiations.

During the investigative process leading up to an indictment or information, the investigators and prosecutor may feel that the evidence is solid enough to justify reaching out to the defendant and his/her counsel and schedule a **proffer session**. This is not a formal proceeding, but an informal meeting at which the prosecutor lays out the case against the defendant in order to open the door to a plea agreement. After having a chance to consult with his/her counsel, the defendant may decide to enter into a plea agreement and waive his/her right to a grand jury. The prosecutor would then proceed by information, thereby streamlining the process, and the details of the plea agreement would be negotiated by the parties prior to arraignment.

LEARNING OBJECTIVE 4
Explain the procedures and purposes of an arraignment.

PRACTICE TIP

When negotiating a plea, a key concern is whether there is sufficient evidence to convict a defendant of the crimes he/she is charged with. It is, therefore, important to develop evidence not only for trial, but also to convince a defendant that his/her chances of being proven guilty are good enough to justify pleading guilty rather than allowing a case to proceed to trial.

Arraignment and Pleading

arraignment
A proceeding at which a defendant is given the opportunity to enter a plea to criminal charges.

guilty plea
A plea by a criminal defendant that has the same effect as a conviction at trial.

An **arraignment** is a proceeding at which the defendant is notified of the charges in the indictment or information, and is given the opportunity to plead to the charges. Under Federal Rule of Criminal Procedure 11(a), the three options for pleas are guilty, not guilty, or (where the court permits) *nolo contendere* (or "no contest"). If a defendant pleads not guilty, then he/she is held over for trial. A **guilty plea**, by contrast, has the same effect as a

Much of the action in a criminal case occurs behind the scenes, in conversations between prosecutors, defense attorneys, and judges.
Source: https://us.fotolia.com/id/78630458.

conviction. The court is required under Rule 11 to make sure that a defendant who pleads guilty understands his/her right to plead not guilty and the consequences of a guilty plea before accepting it.

The plea of **nolo contendere** has the same effect as a guilty plea, with one important exception. A guilty plea can be used as an admission of wrongdoing in a subsequent civil or criminal trial; a plea of *nolo contendere* cannot. Suppose, for instance, a defendant pleads guilty to assaulting a man in a bar. When the man sues him in civil court for damages resulting from the attack, the guilty plea can be used as an admission that the defendant did, in fact, attack him, making it much easier to prove the victim's right to damages. If the defendant pleads *nolo contendere*, on the other hand, the victim will need to present evidence in the civil case proving that the defendant attacked him.

The vast majority of indicted criminal defendants plead guilty. But you should always remember that an indictment does not require the same level of proof as a conviction, and so it is entirely possible that an indicted defendant would be found not guilty at trial.

nolo contendere
A plea of "no contest" that has the same effect as a guilty plea, but that cannot be used as an admission of wrongdoing in subsequent civil or criminal actions filed against the same defendant.

Trial

The **criminal trial** is, of course, the centerpiece of the criminal trial process, although because of the commonality of guilty pleas, trials are the exception rather than the rule. The purpose of a trial can be simply stated: to determine the defendant's guilt. If the evidence presented by the prosecutor proves guilt beyond a reasonable doubt, then the defendant must be found guilty, or convicted. If not, then the defendant must be found not guilty, or acquitted.

As easily as the outcome of a trial can be stated, the reality of trials is far from simple. Trials can be extremely expensive and time consuming. One of the most expensive and longest trials in American history is the notorious McMartin preschool trial that took place in Los Angeles County, California, in the late 1980s, lasted for *three years*, and resulted in the acquittal or dismissal of all charges against the defendants.

LEARNING OBJECTIVE 5
Identify the key components and evidentiary concerns of each stage of a criminal trial.

criminal trial
A proceeding at which evidence is presented for the purpose of determining whether a defendant is guilty of the crimes charged.

Figure 3-2 The Six Stages of a Criminal Trial

Jury Selection	Opening Statements	Prosecutor's Case-in-Chief	Defendants' Case-in-Chief	Closing Arguments	Jury Instructions, Deliberation, and Verdict
		PRESENTATION OF EVIDENCE			

We will now look at the various parts of a criminal trial (see Figure 3-2), with a view toward understanding how evidence is used at each stage of the trial.

Stage 1: Jury Selection

jury selection
The process by which a jury is chosen for a particular criminal trial.

voir dire
The process of examining jurors to determine their fitness to sit on the jury of a particular criminal trial.

peremptory objections
Objections, limited in number, that either side can raise to the inclusion of a juror in the jury for a particular criminal trial, and that do not need to be based on any specific cause for excluding the juror.

Jury selection involves the examination of potential jurors (individuals called for jury duty, selected from various sources such as voting and driving license records) in a process known as **voir dire**. During *voir dire*, the judge, prosecutor, and defense attorney all ask questions of jurors to determine their fitness to hear the criminal case in question. The prosecutor and defense have the ability to object to specific jurors if there is good reason to believe the juror would not be able to hear the case impartially (e.g., a policeman's wife hearing a case involving a defendant accused of killing a police officer). In addition to objections for cause, the parties are also given a limited number of objections that they can use as they wish. These are called **peremptory objections**, and allow the parties to tailor the jury to some extent.

The court's concern about excluding prejudiced jurors was highlighted in the U.S. Supreme Court's decision in *Aldridge v. United States*. In that case, the defendant, a black man, was accused of first-degree murder in the killing of a white police officer in the District of Columbia. The trial judge refused to allow defense counsel to examine potential jurors about racial prejudice, which was a major concern in 1931. The defendant was convicted and sentenced to death.

COURT OPINION 3-1 _____

ALDRIDGE V. UNITED STATES, 283 U.S. 308, 51 S.CT. 470, 75 L.ED. 1054 (1931)

The petitioner was convicted, in the Supreme Court of the District of Columbia, of murder in the first degree, and was sentenced to death. The conviction was affirmed by the Court of Appeals, 47 F.(2d) 407. This Court granted a writ of certiorari, 282 U.S. 836, 51 S. Ct. 333, 75 L. Ed. _____, limited to the question raised by the exception to the ruling of the trial court on the examination on voir dire of prospective jurors.

The petitioner is a negro, and the deceased was a white man, a member of the police force of the District. The record shows the following proceedings on the examination of jurors on the voir dire:

[The court asked the jurors about typical matters that would affect their ability to render a fair verdict, such as any personal knowledge of the defendant or the deceased and their feelings on capital punishment.] 'Whereupon, with the consent of the court, counsel for the parties hereto approached the bench and in a whispered tone, out of the hearing of the prospective jurors, the following took place: [In the

(continued)

exchange, the defense counsel requested that the court permit questioning of jurors about possible racial prejudice, based on a previous case where such prejudice appeared to have influenced one juror's decision. The court denied the request.]

. . .

. . . We find no reason to doubt the nature of the inquiry which the counsel for the accused desired. It was admitted at the bar of this Court that the members of the jury were white. In asking that the question relative to 'racial prejudice' be put to the jurors, it is only reasonable to assume that counsel referred, not to immaterial matters, but to such a prejudice as would disqualify a juror because precluding an impartial verdict. [sic] The reference to what counsel had heard as to the attitude of a juror on the previous trial, where the jury had disagreed, indicated the purpose of the question, which was clear enough to invite appropriate action by the court. If the court had permitted the question, it doubtless would have been properly qualified. But the court, interrupting counsel, disposed of the inquiry summarily. The court failed to ask any question which could be deemed to cover the subject. . . .

The propriety of such an inquiry has been generally recognized. [The Court noted cases in Florida, Mississippi, North Carolina, Texas, and South Carolina which allows questions similar to the one requested by defense counsel in this case.]

. . .

The argument is advanced on behalf of the government that it would be detrimental to the administration of the law in the courts of the United States to allow questions to jurors as to racial or religious prejudices. We think that it would be far more injurious to permit it to be thought that persons entertaining a disqualifying prejudice were allowed to serve as jurors and that inquiries designed to elicit the fact of disqualification were barred. No surer way could be devised to bring the processes of justice into disrepute.

We are of the opinion that the ruling of the trial court on the voir dire was erroneous, and the judgment of conviction must for this reason be reversed.

Judgment reversed.

Questions

1. What reasonable basis did defense counsel rely on to justify his request for the examination of jurors for racial prejudice?
2. How did the Supreme Court distinguish between the proper and improper examination of jurors?

While allegations of facts relevant to the case may be disclosed during *voir dire*, no evidence is presented by either side. Once *voir dire* is concluded, the jury is empaneled and taken to the courtroom where the trial will be held.

Stage 2: Opening Statements

Opening statements are made by the prosecuting attorney and the defense counsel, in that order. These statements are intended to give the jury a roadmap for the evidence they are going to be hearing and seeing during the course of the trial. The attorneys summarize the evidence that they intend to present, with a view toward impressing on the jury members' minds the interpretation of the evidence they want the jury to adopt. Attorneys giving opening statements do not present the evidence objectively; rather, they describe the evidence in as favorable a light as possible for their side of the case.

While opening statements are a form of advocacy, they have limitations. First, no evidence that will not be admitted at trial can be referred to in an opening statement, especially evidence that has been excluded from evidence by the court prior to trial. Throughout this book, you will learn the various reasons why evidence may not be permitted at trial. The mere mention of such evidence in an opening statement could provide grounds for a mistrial if the judge feels that the jury has been prejudiced by that reference.

Figure 3-3 is an excerpt of the opening statement of Joseph Hartzler, the lead prosecutor in the trial of Timothy McVeigh, the man who on April 19, 1995,

opening statements
Statements to the jury by each side in a criminal case, providing the jury with a summary or "roadmap" of the evidence to be presented at trial.

Figure 3-3 Excerpt of Opening Statement of Joseph Hartzler in Trial of Timothy McVeigh

Opening Statement by Prosecutor Joseph Hartzler

April 24, 1997

Ladies and gentlemen of the jury, April 19th, 1995, was a beautiful day in Oklahoma City—at least it started out as a beautiful day. The sun was shining. Flowers were blooming. It was springtime in Oklahoma City. Sometime after six o'clock that morning, Tevin Garrett's mother woke him up to get him ready for the day. He was only 16 months old. He was a toddler; and as some of you know that have experience with toddlers, he had a keen eye for mischief. He would often pull on the cord of her curling iron in the morning, pull it off the counter top until it fell down, often till it fell down on him.

That morning, she picked him up and wrestled with him on her bed before she got him dressed. She remembers this morning because that was the last morning of his life.

. . .

At nine o'clock that morning, two things happened almost simultaneously. In the Water Resources Building—that's another building to the west of the Murrah Building across the street—an ordinary legal proceeding began in one of the hearing rooms; and at the same time, in front of the Murrah Building, a large Ryder truck pulled up into a vacant parking space in front of the building and parked right beneath those plate glass windows from the day-care center.

What these two separate but almost simultaneous events have in common is that they—they both involved grievances of some sort. The legal proceeding had to do with water rights. It wasn't a legal proceeding as we are having here, because there was no court reporter. It was a tape-recorded proceeding, and you will hear the tape recording of that proceeding. It was an ordinary, everyday-across-America, typical legal proceeding in which one party has a grievance and brings it into court or into a hearing to resolve it, to resolve it not by violence and terror but to resolve it in the same way we are resolving matters here, by constitutional due process.

And across the street, the Ryder truck was there also to resolve a grievance; but the truck wasn't here to resolve the grievance by means of due process or by any other democratic means. The truck was there to impose the will of Timothy McVeigh on the rest of America and to do so by premeditated violence and terror, by murdering innocent men, women, and children, in hopes of seeing blood flow in the streets of America.

At 9:02 that morning, two minutes after the water rights proceeding began, a catastrophic explosion ripped the air in downtown Oklahoma City. It instantaneously demolished the entire front of the Murrah Building, brought down tons and tons of concrete and metal, dismembered people inside, and it destroyed, forever, scores and scores and scores of lives, lives of innocent Americans: clerks, secretaries, law enforcement officers, credit union employees, citizens applying for Social Security, and little kids.

All the children I mentioned earlier, all of them died, and more; dozens and dozens of other men, women, children, cousins, loved ones, grandparents, grandchildren, ordinary Americans going about their business. And the only reason they died, the only reason that they are no longer with us, no longer with their loved ones, is that they were in a building owned by a government that Timothy McVeigh so hated that with premeditated intent and a well-designed plan that he had developed over months and months before the bombing, he chose to take their innocent lives to serve his twisted purpose.

In plain, simple language, it was an act of terror, violence, intend—intended to serve selfish political purpose.

The man who committed this act is sitting in this courtroom behind me, and he's the one that committed those murders.

After he did so, he fled the scene; and he avoided even damaging his eardrums, because he had earplugs with him.

. . .

As his Honor told you, my name is Joe Hartzler. My colleagues and I represent the United States of America. In this case, we'll work together as a team. I'm not going to reintroduce everyone. Over the course of the next few weeks, you'll get to know us, I believe.

As you see—as you'll see, there was a lot of evidence against McVeigh. We'll present a lot of evidence against McVeigh. We'll try to make your decision ultimately easy. That's our goal.

There are a number of us, but we won't stumble over each other. You'll see that each of us has a different role, presenting different segments and different types of evidence. We intend to do so fairly.

When we're finished, we will have proven—we will have proven to you beyond any reasonable doubt that Timothy McVeigh destroyed the Murrah Building and killed people inside by means of a huge fertilizer bomb built inside a Ryder truck. . . .

Source: Opening statement of prosecutor Joseph Hartzler in the Timothy McVeigh trial. (n.d.). Retrieved from http://law2.umkc.edu/faculty/projects/ftrials/mcveigh/prosecutionopen.html.

detonated a truck bomb outside the Alfred P. Murrah Federal Building in Oklahoma City, Oklahoma, killing 168 people in the worst instance of domestic terrorism until September 11, 2001.

This excerpt gives you a sense of how evidence is presented in an opening statement. As you can see, the opening statement does not need to be a dry recitation of facts. It can be couched in extremely emotional terms, designed to secure the jury's sympathies and arouse its anger. But a wise attorney will make absolutely sure to present evidence proving, or at least supporting, all of the facts included in the opening statement. The opposing side will be quick to exploit any discrepancies between an opening statement and the evidence to convince the jury that the errant party promised more than it could deliver.

Stage 3: Prosecutor's Case-in-Chief

The presentation of evidence is, of course, the primary purpose of a trial. In any criminal case, the prosecutor has the burden of proving, beyond a reasonable doubt, that the defendant is guilty of the crimes charged. The **prosecutor's case-in-chief** is the stage of the trial where that burden must be met.

You will recall in our discussion of criminal law in Chapter 2 how crimes are composed of elements, which are facts that must be true in order for a defendant's actions to violate the criminal law. The prosecutor's case-in-chief has one goal: to present enough evidence to meet the burden of proof for *every element* of the crime or crimes with which the defendant is charged. For the prosecutor to fail to prove just one element of a crime beyond a reasonable doubt means that it has failed in its attempt to prove the defendant guilty. The jury (or the judge in a bench trial) is the ultimate decision maker about whether the prosecutor has succeeded or failed in that attempt.

prosecutor's case-in-chief
The trial stage at which the prosecutor must present sufficient evidence to prove the defendant's guilt beyond a reasonable doubt.

PRACTICE TIP

In a jury trial, it is the jury, not the judge, who needs to understand the evidence. Evidence must be prepared and presented as directly and simply as possible, so that a jury of individuals without legal experience or training will be able to comprehend, digest, and analyze it.

The rest of this book will be devoted to explaining what evidence can and cannot be admitted at trial, and how that evidence affects the outcome of the trial. For now, you should be aware that it is not enough to present evidence that is *technically* sufficient to prove a defendant's guilt. Each juror must be *convinced* that the evidence is sufficient, and this requires that the presentation of evidence be clear and organized so as to lead the jurors to the conclusion the prosecutor wants them to reach. The best evidence in the world is not enough to secure a conviction unless the jury understands it and is able to derive the correct conclusions from it. This is why opening statements are so important—the roadmap they provide will help the jury navigate through possible days or weeks of testimony, and focus its attention on the evidence that will ultimately convince it to render a verdict of guilty.

During the prosecutor's case-in-chief, the defense counsel has the opportunity to challenge the admissibility of evidence and to cross-examine witnesses for the prosecution. Challenging admissibility is done through **objections** raised during the testimony, and those objections can be based on any number of legal restrictions on the admissibility of evidence. (We will

objections
Challenges to the admissibility of evidence raised during the course of a trial.

discuss those restrictions in detail in Part II of this text.) Generally, if the defense counsel fails to object to a piece of evidence as soon as it is presented, then the objection is waived and cannot be made later.

When an objection is made, the judge must either **sustain** it, meaning that the judge agrees with the objection, or **overrule** it, meaning that the judge does not agree. If necessary, the judge will allow the attorneys to argue for or against the admissibility of the evidence. Where evidence is potentially prejudicial to the jury's decision, the judge may invite the attorneys to the bench in a quiet discussion known as a **sidebar**, so that the jury will not hear the discussion taking place, or, if an extended discussion is required, the judge may order the jury to be removed from the courtroom.

If a judge sustains an objection, then presentation of the offered evidence will not be permitted. In many cases, however, an objection is made only after the jury has already heard the evidence, especially when it takes the form of testimony. When this happens, the judge will issue a **cautionary instruction** to the jurors, admonishing them to ignore the evidence they heard, and not to take it into account in their deliberations. This may be sufficient to overcome any damage the evidence did, but if not, the defense counsel may move for a **mistrial**. If a mistrial is granted, the trial is terminated, and the process must start all over against with the selection of a new jury. Obviously, mistrials are *not* favored, but if a jury has been tainted by improper evidence, a mistrial may be the only way to ensure that the defendant has a fair hearing.

Defense counsel also has the opportunity to cross-examine witnesses. The right of cross-examination is guaranteed in the Sixth Amendment to the U.S. Constitution, and is a critical part of the adversarial process. We will discuss this right in detail in Chapter 6, and the subject of cross-examination itself thoroughly in Chapter 13. The purpose of cross-examination is simply stated: to make the jury question the credibility of the witness by poking holes in his/her testimony or demonstrating that he/she does not possess the knowledge he/she claims to possess. The skillful cross-examination of a key witness is one of the defense attorney's most powerful means of preventing the prosecuting attorney from meeting his/her burden of proof.

The prosecutor's case-in-chief involves the deliberate, careful, and painstaking presentation of evidence, and can often last for days, weeks, or even months. Needless to say, jurors who are sitting in a trial where this stage lasts for a long time are challenged to remain focused and to retain the evidence in their minds until the end of the trial. Most courts do not allow jurors to take notes, on the somewhat questionable premise that the jurors' notes should not be used by other jury members as a substitute for the actual evidence. More and more courts are relaxing this rule, however. In any event, helping the jury retain critical information and focus on the evidence that will ultimately lead to a guilty verdict is one of the great tasks of a prosecuting attorney.

After the prosecutor's case-in-chief is concluded, the defendant has the right to file a **motion for a judgment of acquittal** under Rule 29. In state courts, this is sometimes referred to as a motion for a directed verdict. In essence, the defendant is asking the court to make a ruling that the evidence put forth by the prosecutor failed to meet its burden of proof for conviction. The motion can be made after all of the evidence has been presented, or at any time up to 14 days following a guilty verdict. Granting this motion has the same effect as if the jury had entered a verdict of "not guilty."

---

sustain
A ruling by a trial judge that an objection to the admissibility of evidence is correct, and that the evidence should not be admitted.

overrule
A ruling by a trial judge that an objection to the admissibility of evidence is not correct, and that the evidence should be admitted.

sidebar
A discussion between a judge and attorneys during trial on a question of admissibility, taking place out of the jury's hearing.

cautionary instruction
An instruction by the court to the jury to disregard evidence in its deliberations.

mistrial
The termination of a trial, usually because the jury has been exposed to evidence that is inadmissible, and cannot be adequately addressed through a cautionary instruction.

motion for a judgment of acquittal
A motion made by the defendant asking the court to rule as a matter of law that the prosecutor's evidence is insufficient to support a conviction. Granting this motion has the same effect as a verdict of not guilty.

EVIDENCE AND TECHNOLOGY

TECHNOLOGY IN THE COURTROOM

Courtroom technology has been a topic of some discussion and interest for years. At one time, the controversial subject was whether courtroom proceedings should be recorded or videotaped. The "traditionalists" who resisted such technological advances were concerned that such practices would diminish the gravity of the courtroom, turning it into a production where lawyers would play to the camera and jurors would be distracted by how they appeared on video. Following the televised O.J. Simpson trial, the idea of cameras in courtrooms became less controversial, although some would argue that the Simpson trial itself proved the traditionalist's point.

Now, the focus of technology in the courtroom is not the recording of proceedings for public consumption, but rather the use of technology as a way of presenting evidence. The ubiquity of computers, laptops, tablets, cell phones, and wireless technology, along with the incorporation of technology into the mainstream of communications and the widespread digitization of documents, has presented possibilities for changing the nature of courtroom presentation of evidence as never before. While we are a long way from seeing every courtroom adapt to these technological advances, it is not difficult to imagine, in the near future, a justice system where the presentation of evidence in high definition at every juror's seat and the testimony of witnesses whose faces appear on screen rather than at a witness stand may become the norm rather than the exception.

Acknowledging the "coolness" factor that high-tech courtrooms present, the value of technology can also be assessed in terms of economy. In the past, a lawyer who wished to present a photograph, chart, or document in a manner where the entire jury could see it and he/she could also point to it as he/she presented was forced to spend hundreds of dollars on large presentation boards held up by easels. Now, a lawyer in a properly equipped courtroom can simply put the evidence on his/her laptop and project it or transfer it digitally to a screen for all to see. Witnesses who might have to be brought to court over long distances at a cost of thousands of dollars can present testimony directly from their homes or offices by means of a webcam and wireless connection.

Those who resist these technological changes raise good points. For one thing, these processes depend on the viability of the technology, which, as anyone who uses a computer knows, can fail without warning at quite inopportune moments. A witness who is present at trial can testify even if the electricity goes out or the wireless connection is lost. Regarding economy, technology is expensive, and refitting a courtroom to accommodate anything but the most basic computer systems could tax the average county court's budget to the breaking point, not to mention the ongoing cost of maintenance and payroll for the technicians who will need to be on call in case the system breaks down.

It is probably fair to say that it will be some time before courts in general catch up to the whirlwind of technological advances that have occurred and continue to occur every day in the present age. Lawyers who become too dependent on technology for their practices might actually find themselves at a disadvantage when faced with a courtroom that still depends on old-fashioned methods to present evidence. But it is also likely that technology will find its way into most courtrooms eventually, at least to some extent, although a wise court will still maintain low-tech options, just in case the lights go out.

Stage 4: The Defendant's Case-in-Chief

The defendant's primary task at trial is the same as a defensive line in football: to counter the advancement of the prosecutor and prevent him/her from reaching the goal, which in this case is conviction. In addition to cross-examining witnesses and raising objection during the prosecutor's case-in-chief, the defendant has the right to present evidence of his/her own. This presentation of evidence, known as the **defendant's case-in-chief**, can serve one or more of three purposes:

defendant's case-in-chief
The presentation of evidence by the defendant for the purpose of rebutting evidence of guilt and establishing facts supporting the defendant's innocence or proving affirmative defenses.

- to rebut the prosecutor's evidence;
- to establish facts (such as an alibi) that support the defendant's innocence; and
- to prove affirmative defenses such as insanity or self-defense.

Rebutting the prosecutor's evidence is simply a matter of presenting evidence that either contradicts the prosecutor's evidence or provides additional information that makes that evidence less credible or less incriminating. If the prosecutor presents an eyewitness to the crime, the defense may counter with another eyewitness who was present at the scene of the crime but did not see the defendant commit it. The defense may also counter the prosecutor's eyewitness by presenting evidence that the conditions were such that the witness could not have seen or heard what he/she claimed to.

The defendant may also introduce evidence that affirmatively supports the defendant's innocence. Evidence establishing an alibi is one example, proving that the defendant was not at the scene of the crime when the crime took place. Remember, the defendant does not need to convince the jury of his/her innocence. He/she only needs to present evidence sufficient to raise a reasonable doubt about his/her guilt. Even if the jury is skeptical of the defendant's evidence, it may be enough to raise some doubt about whether the defendant was actually present when the crime took place, and that may be all that is needed to prevent a conviction.

affirmative defense
A set of facts that relieves a defendant of liability for a crime. A defendant must present evidence to support an affirmative defense by a preponderance of the evidence.

Finally, a defendant may present evidence of an **affirmative defense**, such as those discussed in Chapter 2. Generally, a defendant must prove an affirmative defense by at least a preponderance of the evidence, meaning that the evidence supporting the defense must outweigh, to some extent, evidence refuting the defense. In many cases, proving an affirmative defense requires that the defendant himself/herself testify.

A defendant taking the stand is problematic, because a prosecutor has the same right to cross-examine defense witnesses as the defense has to cross-examine prosecution witnesses. When a defendant chooses to testify, he/she is opening himself/herself up to cross-examination, and that cross-examination can cover any issue that is raised by the defendant's testimony. A defendant must therefore decide if his/her own testimony has a good enough chance of helping his/her case to justify waiving his/her Fifth Amendment right against self-incrimination.

Stage 5: Closing Arguments

closing arguments
Arguments by each side in a criminal case to persuade the jury that the presented evidence requires a verdict in that side's favor.

Once all of the evidence supporting and refuting guilt has been presented, the prosecutor and defense counsel present their **closing arguments**, in that order. This is a departure from many state procedures, which allow the prosecutor, as the party with the burden of proof, to go last in closing arguments. Under Rule 29.1, however, the federal prosecutor also has the opportunity to rebut the defense's closing argument.

Closing arguments are the point at which the respective sides do their best to convince the jury that the evidence, taken as a whole, requires a verdict in their favor. These arguments are more forceful than opening statements, because they are based on evidence the jury has actually seen and heard, and because the attorneys are now able to draw inference and conclusions from the evidence, which they could not do in their opening statements.

Because the evidence has already been presented, attorneys must be careful in their closing arguments not to refer to evidence that the court has ruled inadmissible or that was not actually presented during the trial, or to make any other statement that might improperly influence the jury or appeal to its passions or prejudices. Doing so can result in a cautionary instruction or a mistrial if the evidence is likely to prejudice the jury's decision.

In *United States* v. *Baptiste*, a case involving tax fraud, the prosecutor improperly referred to the money stolen by the defendant as "your money" (meaning the jurors' own tax money) in his closing argument to the jury. The defendant moved for a mistrial on the grounds that the prosecutor had essentially suggested that the jurors, as taxpayers, had a financial interest in the outcome of the case. The judge denied the motion for a mistrial, issuing a cautionary instruction instead, and the defendant appealed his conviction based in part on this issue.

COURT OPINION 3-2

UNITED STATES V. BAPTISTE, 618 FED. APPX. 593 (11TH CIR. 2015)

Defendant Marie Jean Baptiste appeals her conviction for three counts of theft of United States property, in violation of 18 U.S.C. § 641. On appeal, Defendant . . . argues that the district court erred in denying her motion for a mistrial, based on the prosecutor's improper statement during his rebuttal closing argument. . . . After careful review, we affirm.

In September 2012, refunds from three fraudulently-filed federal income tax returns (totaling $3,280) were deposited into Defendant's Higher One student bank account. That same day, Defendant walked into a Chase Bank branch and used her Higher One debit card and driver's license to withdraw $2,400 from that account. Through subsequent ATM withdrawals and debit card purchases, all of the fraudulent tax proceeds were withdrawn from Defendant's Higher One account. Defendant was indicted for three counts of theft of money or property of the United States. She pled not guilty, was tried by a jury trial, and found guilty.

. . .

During the Government's rebuttal closing argument, Defendant moved for a mistrial after the Government referred to taxpayers' money as "your money." The district court denied the motion, but did provide a curative instruction. The jury found Defendant guilty on all three counts.

B. Motion for Mistrial

At trial, Defendant moved for a mistrial after the Government stated, in its rebuttal argument, that:

> In opening, I stated that this is not the largest case, but you did learn during the course of this trial that . . . the defendant's conduct . . . is part of a larger scheme. . . . And you also learned how serious this case is, how it is a serious federal offense to steal government money. And the government, this is your money, the taxpayers.

The district court sustained Defendant's objection to this statement, but denied Defendant's mistrial motion and instead gave a curative instruction.

On appeal, Defendant argues that the Government's "your money" comment was improper, the district court's curative instruction did not undo the harm, and the court erred in denying Defendant's motion for a mistrial. We review the denial of a motion for a mistrial for an abuse of discretion. *United States v. Ettinger*, 344 F.3d 1149, 1161 (11th Cir. 2003). A defendant is entitled to a grant of a mistrial only upon a showing of substantial prejudice. *Id.* If the district court gives a curative instruction, reversal is appropriate only if the evidence "is so highly prejudicial as to be incurable" by the district court's instruction.

(continued)

(continued)

United States v. Garcia, 405 F.3d 1260, 1272 (11th Cir. 2005).

During closing arguments, a prosecutor is "forbidden to make improper suggestions, insinuations and assertions calculated to mislead the jury and may not appeal to the jury's passion or prejudice." *United States v. Rodriguez*, 765 F.2d 1546, 1560 (11th Cir. 1985) (quotation marks omitted). Specifically, the prosecutor may not invoke the individual pecuniary interests of the jury as taxpayers. *United States v. Smyth*, 556 F.2d 1179, 1185 (5th Cir. 1977).

Given the above case authority, the prosecutor should not have made a comment that appealed to the jurors' pecuniary interests as taxpayers. *See id.* Nevertheless, Defendant has not shown that the result of her trial would have been different, had the comment not been made. The district court promptly sustained Defendant's objection and instructed the jury to disregard the Government's comment. After denying Defendant's motion for a mistrial, the court subsequently gave a curative instruction [cautioning the jury not to consider any personal interest as taxpayers in the case], and it then confirmed with the jurors that they understood and would be able to follow the instruction. After the jury returned its verdict (and Defendant renewed her motion for a mistrial), the court found, based in part on its observations of the jurors' reactions to the curative instruction, that a reasonable probability did not exist that the Government's improper comment affected the outcome of the trial.

Moreover, the Government introduced significant evidence of Defendant's guilt. . . .

Additionally, contrary to Defendant's argument, the improper comment was an isolated part of the prosecutor's closing argument, having been made only once by him. Thus, in light of the curative instruction and substantial evidence of Defendant's guilt, we conclude that the improper comment was harmless and that the district court did not abuse its discretion in denying Defendant's motion for a mistrial.

Questions

1. Do you agree with the Eleventh Circuit that the prosecutor's reference to "your money" did not justify a mistrial?
2. What significance did the court place on the fact that the prosecutor presented plenty of evidence of the defendant's guilt?

Stage 6: Jury Instructions, Deliberation, and Verdict

Once the evidence has been presented and the parties have made their arguments for conviction or acquittal, the rest of the trial belongs to the jury. This stage of the trial has three parts: jury instructions, deliberation, and verdict.

jury instructions
Also known as the "charge to the jury," the instructions on the law relevant to a case given by a judge to a jury before it deliberates.

Jury instructions, sometimes called the "charge to the jury," consist of a miniature legal education given by the judge to the jurors, encompassing the legal principles involved in each crime the defendant is charged with, and each defense raised by the defendant. Jurors usually have no legal training, and must be told what elements constitute each crime and defense, and what level of proof is required for a conviction. They must also be instructed on their duty as jurors to weigh the evidence fairly and impartially, and their right as jurors to decide for themselves how much weight must be given to each piece of evidence.

The parties may request that specific instructions be provided to the jury on certain points of law. Under Rule 30, such requests must be made at the close of the evidence unless the court sets an earlier time. These requests provide the parties with an opportunity to influence how the jury will view the evidence in its deliberations, although in most cases the law surrounding a particular trial is fairly clear and not subject to a lot of interpretation or variation.

model jury instructions
Instructions prescribed by a court as a guide for lawyer and judges in formulating a charge to the jury.

Instructions can be quite lengthy depending on the complexity of the trial, and many courts use **model jury instructions** in order to facilitate this task. Model jury instructions are basic form instructions that are endorsed within

Figure 3-4 Third Circuit Court of Appeals Model Jury Instructions, Section 3.01

3.01 **Role of Jury**

Members of the jury, you have seen and heard all the evidence and the arguments of the lawyers. Now I will instruct you on the law.

You have two duties as a jury. Your first duty is to decide the facts from the evidence that you have heard and seen in court during this trial. That is your job and yours alone. I play no part in finding the facts. You should not take anything I may have said or done during the trial as indicating what I think of the evidence or what I think about what your verdict should be.

Your second duty is to apply the law that I give you to the facts. My role now is to explain to you the legal principles that must guide you in your decisions. You must apply my instructions carefully. Each of the instructions is important, and you must apply all of them. You must not substitute or follow your own notion or opinion about what the law is or ought to be. You must apply the law that I give to you, whether you agree with it or not.

Whatever your verdict, it will have to be unanimous. All of you will have to agree on it or there will be no verdict. In the jury room, you will discuss the case among yourselves, but ultimately each of you will have to make up his or her own mind. This is a responsibility that each of you has and that you cannot avoid.

During your deliberations, you must not communicate with or provide any information to anyone by any means about this case. You may not use any electronic device or media, such as the telephone, a cell phone, smartphone, iPhone, Blackberry or computer, the Internet, any Internet service, any text or instant messaging service, any Internet chat room, blog, or website such as Facebook, MySpace, LinkedIn, YouTube, or Twitter, to communicate to anyone any information about this case or to conduct any research about this case until I accept your verdict. In other words, you cannot talk to anyone on the phone, correspond with anyone, or electronically communicate with anyone about this case. You can only discuss the case in the jury room with your fellow jurors during deliberations.

You may not use these electronic means to investigate or communicate about the case because it is important that you decide this case based solely on the evidence presented in this courtroom. You are only permitted to discuss the case with your fellow jurors during deliberations because they have seen and heard the same evidence you have. In our judicial system, it is important that you are not influenced by anything or anyone outside of this courtroom.

Perform these duties fairly and impartially. Do not allow sympathy, prejudice, fear, or public opinion to influence you. You should also not be influenced by any person's race, color, religion, national ancestry, or gender *(sexual orientation, profession, occupation, celebrity, economic circumstances, or position in life or in the community).*

Source: Model Criminal Jury Table of Contents and Instructions, **Third Circuit**, United States Court of Appeals. (n.d.). Retrieved from http://www.ca3.uscourts.gov./model-criminal-jury-table-contents-and-instructions.

certain judicial jurisdictions in order to make sure that all juries are given consistent, correct instructions. Figure 3-4 shows the first section of the Third Circuit Court of Appeals Model Jury Instructions for criminal cases.

Obviously, juries may not be entirely clear on every point of law relevant to a case when they begin their deliberations, so juries are permitted to ask the judge for clarification or additional instructions as their deliberations proceed.

PRACTICE TIP

Judges decide whether and how to instruct juries on the law, but the parties recommend instructions that will support their interpretation of the law and theory of the case. Developing careful and clear jury instructions, supported by strong legal precedent, can therefore have a huge impact on both the legal issues that the jury is permitted to decide and the outcome of that decision.

Jury deliberations are the only part of the trial which the parties are not permitted to participate in, or even witness. During deliberations, the jury meets in secret and discusses the evidence until it either reaches a verdict or determines that it is unable to do so. Under Rule 31, a jury's **verdict** in favor

jury deliberations
The conference of jurors following the conclusion of the presentation of evidence in which the jury considers the evidence and attempts to form a verdict.

verdict
The decision of a jury regarding the defendant's guilt.

hung jury
A jury that, after deliberating, is unable to agree on a unanimous verdict of either guilty or not guilty.

of conviction or acquittal must be unanimous. If the jury is unable to reach a unanimous decision, then the court may declare a **hung jury**, which has the same effect as a mistrial. Because hung juries render the entire trial process moot, judges can refuse to accept a hung jury, and order the jury to keep deliberating until it reaches a unanimous decision one way or the other.

While the jury has broad discretion to consider and discuss the evidence however it chooses, there are some limitations on what a jury can do. First, the jury can only consider evidence properly admitted at trial, and may not create its own evidence via experimentation or by any other means. This restriction may surprise fans of the movie *Twelve Angry Men*, in which a jury considered quite a bit of evidence not admitted at trial, including a re-enactment of a witness' testimony and the presentation of a weapon identical to the murder weapon purchased by one of the jurors the night before. In a real trial, such extrajudicial evidence would never be permitted to influence a jury's deliberations, and the mere introduction of such evidence during deliberations could be grounds for a mistrial.

sequestration
The isolation of a jury during deliberations to prevent them from being exposed to any external information related to the case.

Second, a jury may not consider any information that may have been publicized about a trial in the press or news media. For this reason, juries will often be **sequestered** throughout a trial, meaning that they are housed in a controlled environment (usually a hotel) and forbidden from reading any newspaper, Internet, or other coverage of the trial or anything related to the trial until a verdict is reached. Since jury deliberations can sometimes go on for days, this can be quite an onerous condition, and provides an incentive for juries to work hard to reach a verdict so that their isolation can be as brief as possible.

Once a jury has reached a verdict, the foreman notifies the judge, and the jury and parties are called into the courtroom, where the verdict is read aloud by either the judge or the foreman. At this point, either party may request a **jury poll** under Rule 31(d), which means that each juror must announce his/her agreement with the verdict. If any juror fails to agree with the verdict, then the judge is required to send the jury back to deliberate further.

jury poll
The questioning of each individual juror as to his or her agreement with the verdict announced by the foreman.

The rendering of a verdict ends the trial, but not the case. The court must enter a judgment of conviction, which is a legal ruling that the defendant is guilty of the charges to which he/she pleaded guilty or was found guilty by a jury. Once this judgment is entered, the defendant can then be sentenced.

LEARNING OBJECTIVE 6
Explain the federal sentencing process for both capital and non-capital crimes.

Sentencing

The sentencing process is separate from the determination of the defendant's guilt or innocence. In this stage of the proceedings, the defendant's guilt has already been established, and therefore his/her constitutional rights under the Fourth, Fifth, and Sixth Amendments are severely reduced. He/she still has the right to be represented by counsel, but may no longer cross-examine witnesses or refuse to testify on behalf of the prosecutor.

Incarceration

Sentences of imprisonment in federal criminal courts are governed by sentencing guidelines formulated by the U.S. Sentencing Commission. Federal sentencing guidelines are based on two primary factors: the offense committed and the defendant's prior criminal record. Figure 3-5 is a basic federal sentencing table, which combines these two factors to determine the sentence to be imposed on the defendant. The numbers in the table refer to months of incarceration.

The federal sentencing guidelines prescribe a specific offense score for every federal crime. Figure 3-6 shows the offense scores prescribed for a

Figure 3-5 Federal Sentencing Table

SENTENCING TABLE
(in months of imprisonment)

| Offense Level | Criminal History Category (Criminal History Points) | | | | | |
	I (0 or 1)	II (2 or 3)	III (4, 5, 6)	IV (7, 8, 9)	V (10, 11, 12)	VI (13 or more)
1	0-6	0-6	0-6	0-6	0-6	0-6
2	0-6	0-6	0-6	0-6	0-6	1-7
3	0-6	0-6	0-6	0-6	2-8	3-9
4	0-6	0-6	0-6	2-8	4-10	6-12
5	0-6	0-6	1-7	4-10	6-12	9-15
6	0-6	1-7	2-8	6-12	9-15	12-18
7	0-6	2-8	4-10	8-14	12-18	15-21
8	0-6	4-10	6-12	10-16	15-21	18-24
9	4-10	6-12	8-14	12-18	18-24	21-27
10	6-12	8-14	10-16	15-21	21-27	24-30
11	8-14	10-16	12-18	18-24	24-30	27-33
12	10-16	12-18	15-21	21-27	27-33	30-37
13	12-18	15-21	18-24	24-30	30-37	33-41
14	15-21	18-24	21-27	27-33	33-41	37-46
15	18-24	21-27	24-30	30-37	37-46	41-51
16	21-27	24-30	27-33	33-41	41-51	46-57
17	24-30	27-33	30-37	37-46	46-57	51-63
18	27-33	30-37	33-41	41-51	51-63	57-71
19	30-37	33-41	37-46	46-57	57-71	63-78
20	33-41	37-46	41-51	51-63	63-78	70-87
21	37-46	41-51	46-57	57-71	70-87	77-96
22	41-51	46-57	51-63	63-78	77-96	84-105
23	46-57	51-63	57-71	70-87	84-105	92-115
24	51-63	57-71	63-78	77-96	92-115	100-125
25	57-71	63-78	70-87	84-105	100-125	110-137
26	63-78	70-87	78-97	92-115	110-137	120-150
27	70-87	78-97	87-108	100-125	120-150	130-162
28	78-97	87-108	97-121	110-137	130-162	140-175
29	87-108	97-121	108-135	121-151	140-175	151-188
30	97-121	108-135	121-151	135-168	151-188	168-210
31	108-135	121-151	135-168	151-188	168-210	188-235
32	121-151	135-168	151-188	168-210	188-235	210-262
33	135-168	151-188	168-210	188-235	210-262	235-293
34	151-188	168-210	188-235	210-262	235-293	262-327
35	168-210	188-235	210-262	235-293	262-327	292-365
36	188-235	210-262	235-293	262-327	292-365	324-405
37	210-262	235-293	262-327	292-365	324-405	360-life
38	235-293	262-327	292-365	324-405	360-life	360-life
39	262-327	292-365	324-405	360-life	360-life	360-life
40	292-365	324-405	360-life	360-life	360-life	360-life
41	324-405	360-life	360-life	360-life	360-life	360-life
42	360-life	360-life	360-life	360-life	360-life	360-life
43	life	life	life	life	life	life

Zones: Zone A, Zone B, Zone C, Zone D

Source: 2015 Guidelines Manual, United States Sentencing Commission. (n.d.). Retrieved from http://www.ussc.gov/guidelines/2015-guidelines-manual.

Figure 3-6 Sentencing Guidelines for Selected Federal Crimes

Crime	Base Offense Level
First-Degree Murder	43
Attempted First-Degree Murder	33
Assault With Intent To Commit First-Degree Murder	33
Conspiracy Or Solicitation To Commit Murder	33
Second-Degree Murder	38
Voluntary Manslaughter	29
Involuntary Manslaughter 1. Criminally negligent conduct 2. Reckless conduct 3. Reckless operation of a means of transportation	1. 12 2. 18 3. 22

Aggravated Assault	(a) Base Offense Level: 14
	
	(b) Specific Offense Characteristics
	
	  (1) If the assault involved more than minimal planning, increase by **2** levels.
	
	  (2) If (A) a firearm was discharged, increase by **5** levels; (B) a dangerous weapon (including a firearm) was otherwise used, increase by **4** levels; (C) a dangerous weapon (including a firearm) was brandished or its use was threatened, increase by **3** levels.
	
	  (3) If the victim sustained bodily injury, increase the offense level according to the seriousness of the injury:
	
	    Degree of Bodily Injury — **Increase in Level**
	    (A) Bodily Injury — add **3**
	    (B) Serious Bodily Injury — add **5**
	    (C) Permanent or Life-Threatening Bodily Injury — add **7**
	    (D) If the degree of injury is between that specified in subdivisions (A) and (B), — add **4** levels; or
	    (E) If the degree of injury is between that specified in subdivisions (B) and (C), — add **6** levels.
	
	    However, the cumulative adjustments from application of subdivisions (2) and (3) shall not exceed **10** levels.
	
	  (4) If the offense involved strangling, suffocating, or attempting to strangle or suffocate a spouse, intimate partner, or dating partner, increase by **3** levels.
	
	  However, the cumulative adjustments from application of subdivisions (2), (3), and (4) shall not exceed **12** levels.
	
	  (5) If the assault was motivated by a payment or offer of money or other thing of value, increase by **2** levels.
	
	  (6) If the offense involved the violation of a court protection order, increase by **2** levels.
	
	  (7) If the defendant was convicted under 18 U.S.C. § 111(b) or § 115, increase by **2** levels.

Source: 2015 Guidelines Manual, United States Sentencing Commission. (n.d.). Retrieved from http://www.ussc.gov/guidelines/2015-guidelines-manual.

selected group of crimes. As you can see, some crimes (like first- and second-degree murders) are given a single offense score, while others (like involuntary manslaughter and aggravated assault) are given varying scores depending on certain factors surrounding the crime.

The offense score can be adjusted based on certain aggravating and mitigating factors. **Aggravating factors** increase the offense score, while **mitigating factors** decrease it. Here is a partial list of the factors contained in the sentencing guidelines:

Aggravating factors:

- Crime was motivated by the victim or anyone else's race, color, religion, national origin, ethnicity, gender, gender identity, disability, or sexual orientation.
- Victim was unusually vulnerable to criminal activity due to age, physical or mental condition, or some other factor.
- Crime was motivated by the fact that the victim is a current or former government employee or family member thereof.
- The victim was physically restrained in the course of the crime.
- The crime involved or was intended to promote terrorism (this increases the criminal history score as well).
- The crime involved a federal law relating to genocide, torture, war crimes, or the use or recruitment of child soldiers.
- The defendant organized, led, managed, or supervised the criminal activity.
- The defendant used or attempted to use a minor to commit or conceal the crime.
- The defendant used body armor in the commission of a violent or drug-trafficking crime.
- The defendant recklessly endangered another person while fleeing law enforcement.

Mitigating factors:

- Defendant's participation in the crime was minimal or minor.
- The defendant clearly demonstrates acceptance of responsibility for his/her crime.

Figure 3-7 contains the basic calculation method for criminal history scores. When this score is calculated along with the offense score, the sentence for a

> **aggravating factors**
> Factors that may be considered by a judge in increasing a sentence above that prescribed by sentencing guidelines.
>
> **mitigating factors**
> Factors that may be considered by a judge in decreasing a sentence below that prescribed by sentencing guidelines.

Figure 3-7 Criminal History Category Guidelines

§ 4 A1.1. Criminal History Category

The total points from subsections (a) through (e) determine the criminal history category in the Sentencing Table in Chapter Five, Part A.

(a) Add **3** points for each prior sentence of imprisonment exceeding one year and one month.

(b) Add **2** points for each prior sentence of imprisonment of at least sixty days not counted in (a).

(c) Add **1** point for each prior sentence not counted in (a) or (b), up to a total of **4** points for this subsection.

(d) Add **2** points if the defendant committed the instant offense while under any criminal justice sentence, including probation, parole, supervised release, imprisonment, work release, or escape status.

(e) Add **1** point for each prior sentence resulting from a conviction of a crime of violence that did not receive any points under (a), (b), or (c) above because such sentence was counted as a single sentence, up to a total of **3** points for this subsection.

Source: 2015 Guidelines Manual, United States Sentencing Commission. (n.d.). Retrieved from http://www.ussc.gov/guidelines/2015-guidelines-manual.

given defendant can be achieved by finding the appropriate range on the federal sentencing table. For instance, if a defendant is charged with involuntary manslaughter caused by the reckless use of an automobile (offense score 22) and he previously served a five-year federal sentence (criminal record score 3), then his prescribed sentence under the table is 46–67 months.

Under 18 U.S.C. § 3553, federal judges must sentence defendants in accordance with the federal sentencing guidelines unless the judge determines that there are additional aggravating or mitigating circumstances that are not addressed sufficiently in the guidelines themselves. If the judge feels that the available evidence is not enough to allow him/her to make a decision about sentencing, he/she can request a **presentencing report** from the probation officer assigned to the convicted defendant. This presentencing report will inform the judge of a defendant's prior criminal history, the level of cooperation in the current criminal case, and any other facts that could be helpful to the judge in deciding whether to impose a sentence that varies from that prescribed under the Guidelines. The Guidelines themselves also provide some advisory assistance to judges by specifying grounds for departure from the guideline sentence (United States Sentencing Commission, Guidelines Manual, §5K2.0 (November 2014)).

The interplay between the presentencing report and the judge's analysis of aggravating or mitigating factors is an important one. A judge needs the information contained in the presentencing report in order to determine whether and how to apply to guidelines and, if necessary, to go outside the guideline's parameters in order to impose a fair and effective sentence. Since much of this information is not relevant to the specific crime with which the defendant was charged in the criminal case, the information the judge requires may not be part of the record at the time he/she is considering sentence.

presentencing report
A report prepared by a probation officer, providing a judge with facts that will affect the judge's decision regarding a defendant's sentence.

Death

The federal system and 31 states impose a sentence of death for the most serious crimes (see Table 3-1). The U.S. Supreme Court held in 2008 that the state and federal government could not impose the death penalty for any crimes not resulting in the death of the victim or constituting crimes against the state (*Kennedy v. Louisiana*, 554 U.S. 407, 413 (2008)). The federal death penalty statute is found at 18 U.S.C.A. §3591 et seq., and authorizes judges to impose the death penalty for treason, espionage, and certain crimes resulting in the death of the victim. Under Section 3591, however, no defendant who was a minor when the offense was committed may be put to death.

Section 3592 of the federal statute specifies certain mitigating and aggravating factors, which a judge must consider when imposing the death penalty. As with sentencing in general, an aggravating factor is one that worsens the crime and makes the defendant more deserving of death. There are several sets of these circumstances in Section 3592 relating to different types of crimes. In homicide cases, for example, a judge must consider whether:

- the death occurred in the course of the commission of certain other crimes (like terrorism, hijacking, or kidnapping);
- the defendant was previously convicted of certain other deadly crimes or other serious offenses, including serious drug offenses, sexual assault, or child molestation;
- the crime involved torture, serious physical abuse, or multiple killings or grave risk of death to more than one person;

Table 3-1 List of States with and without the Death Penalty

States with the Death Penalty			States without the Death Penalty		
Alabama	Arizona	Arkansas	Alaska	Connecticut	Hawaii
California	Colorado	Delaware	Illinois	Iowa	Maine
Florida	Georgia	Idaho	Maryland	Massachusetts	Michigan
Indiana	Kansas	Kentucky	Minnesota	Nebraska	New Jersey
Louisiana	Mississippi	Missouri	New Mexico	New York	North Dakota
Montana	Nevada	New Hampshire	Rhode Island	Vermont	West Virginia
North Carolina	Ohio	Oklahoma	Wisconsin		
Oregon	Pennsylvania	South Carolina			
South Dakota	Tennessee	Texas			
Utah	Virginia	Washington			
Wyoming					

Source: Information provided by the Death Penalty Information Center (http://www.deathpenaltyinfo.org/states-and-without-death-penalty).

- the defendant paid for, or was paid for, the commission of the crime;
- the victim was a high public official, or particularly vulnerable to the crime as a result of age, youth, or infirmity; and
- the crimes occurred while engaging a continuing criminal enterprise involving the sale of drugs to minors.

In addition to aggravating circumstances, there is also a list of mitigating circumstances that will weigh against imposition of the death penalty. There is only one set of these circumstances that applies to all crimes, including:

- The defendant had an impaired capacity of appreciating the wrongfulness of his/her conduct or to conform his/her conduct to the requirements of law.
- The defendant was under unusual and substantial duress.
- The defendant's participation in the crime was minor.
- The defendant had no prior criminal record.
- The defendant was mentally or emotionally disturbed at the time of the offense.
- Other participants in the crime who were equally culpable did not receive the death sentence.
- The victim consented to the crime.

In addition to these, the statute allows a judge to consider any other mitigating factors in the defendant's background, record, or character that would weigh against the death penalty.

■ DEVELOPING THE BODY OF EVIDENCE

As we have seen, the entire criminal trial process, from arrest to appeal, is driven by evidence. An arrest requires evidence supporting probable cause. A preliminary hearing or indictment requires evidence supporting the

LEARNING OBJECTIVE 7
Explain how the body of evidence is developed before, during, and after an arrest.

Investigation at a crime scene is the critical step in building the body of evidence needed to convict a criminal.

Source: http://www.123rf.com/ search.php?word=crime+scene+ investigation&imgtype=0&t_ word=&t_lang=en&oriSearch=law yer+evidence+jury&orderby= 0&sti=mu55q7pb28jjmqm9bo|& mediapopup=21892625.

Paul Fleet/123RF

defendant's guilt. The purpose of a trial is to determine whether there is enough evidence to prove the defendant's guilt beyond a reasonable doubt. The sentence is based on evidence relevant to the application of the sentencing guidelines.

In this section, we're going to look at how the body of evidence is developed, from the moment the crime is committed through the beginning of the criminal trial. Generally, most of the evidence will be developed in the early stages of the process.

Crime Scene Investigation

probable cause
Articulable facts that support a reasonable belief that a crime is being or has been committed.

crime scene investigation
The initial investigation of the scene where a crime took place, usually conducted by specially trained law enforcement officers.

physical evidence
Evidence that is not testimonial in nature.

When a suspect is arrested, the arresting officer must have **probable cause** to believe that the suspect committed a crime. Probable cause must be based on evidence known to or reasonably believed by the officer at the time of the arrest, not afterward. An arrest made without probable cause is not legitimized by later evidence showing that the defendant did, in fact, commit the crime.

Prior to arrest, law enforcement needs to gather evidence supporting probable cause. This evidence can be developed through crime scene investigation, the interviewing of witnesses or the suspect himself/herself, or any other method of developing proof that the suspect committed the crime. **Crime scene investigation** is exactly what it sounds like—the exploration of the scene of the crime to find evidence that can then be used to justify an arrest, and later to support a conviction. While first responders secure the scene to prevent any evidence from being destroyed (often using the famous yellow "Police Line—Do Not Cross" tape), crime scene investigators go over it in meticulous detail to make sure all physical evidence is discovered and preserved. **Physical evidence** is any evidence that is not testimonial in nature. Bodily fluid, weapons and ammunition, fingerprints, pry bars, drug residue, clothing, hairs, and anything else that provides insight into who committed a crime and how it was committed is the subject of a crime scene investigation. It is critical that any evidence is preserved in exactly the form it is in when it is found. Otherwise, its value as evidence will be lost. Where evidence cannot be seized and taken from the crime scene, photographs are taken to preserve at least the image of the evidence as it was when the crime took place.

In addition to finding and preserving physical evidence, investigators also interview witnesses and record their statements and contact information for future use. While a witness' crime scene statement is not admissible in court to prove guilt (that requires a sworn statement or courtroom testimony), it can be used to support probable cause for an arrest. Where a police officer has caught a defendant in the act of committing a crime, the observations of the police officer himself/herself can be used for the same purpose. As you will learn in Chapter 6, an arrest warrant is seldom required for a valid arrest, but evidence supporting probable cause is always required.

Evidence-Gathering during Arrest

During an arrest, the arresting officer is permitted to search for evidence. If the officer has a search warrant, then the search can cover the area specified in the warrant. Even without a warrant, the officer can conduct a limited search of the suspect's person and clothing, any object or container the suspect is carrying at the time, and any area within the suspect's reach. This is called a **search incident to an arrest**. The purpose of such a search is to make sure that the suspect is not armed, and to preserve any evidence that the suspect might otherwise be able to destroy. Any evidence obtained during this type of search can be used against the suspect so long as the arrest was proper and the search did not exceed its constitutional bounds.

search incident to an arrest
A search of a suspect's body, clothing, and immediate vicinity, conducted during the course of a valid arrest.

The scope of those "constitutional bounds" was explored by the Iowa Supreme Court in *State* v. *Gaskins*, in which a safe was seized from the suspect's car after the suspect had already been handcuffed and placed into a squad car. The court had to decide if a search of a vehicle in which the suspect was located immediately prior to arrest could be considered a "search incident to arrest" after the suspect had been removed from the vehicle and was no longer able to gain access to it.

Evidence-Gathering after Arrest

After the arrest, law enforcement officers can use all available search procedures to gather further evidence of the defendant's guilt. They can interrogate the suspect and witnesses, take blood and DNA samples, and conduct full searches of any area where they have probable cause to believe evidence might be found. These processes are discussed in more detail in Chapter 6 as well, but you should remember at this point that every search must be conducted according to the limits established under the Fourth Amendment of the Constitution and any corresponding provisions of the applicable state constitution. Otherwise, evidence found during the search will not be admissible to prove the suspect's guilt.

LEARNING OBJECTIVE 9
Outline the processes used to gather evidence after an arrest and the constitutional concerns raised by those processes.

Following the arrest, as noted earlier, the suspect is subject to the booking process. During this process, the suspect will be fingerprinted, photographed, and interviewed for information to be entered into a log kept by the law enforcement agency. Although this is all a very preliminary part of the

COURT OPINION 3-3

STATE V. GASKINS, 866 N.W.2D 1 (IOWA, 2015)

[Jesse Gaskins was arrested for possession of marijuana with intent to deliver and illegal possession of a handgun. Upon being stopped for driving with expired license plates, the arresting officer detected an odor of burnt marijuana and asked the suspect if there was any marijuana in the vehicle. After Gaskins first denied the presence of marijuana and then admitting to a small amount, the arresting officer searched further and discovered and opened a safe containing a handgun and more marijuana. The evidence was seized and used at trial to secure Gaskins' conviction. On appeal, Gaskins claimed that it was error to admit the contents of the safe, because no warrant had been obtained before the safe was opened. The trial court ruled that the search of the safe was a valid search incident to an arrest. This appeal followed.]

. . .

Police searched Gaskins's vehicle and opened the safe without a warrant. "A warrantless search is presumed unreasonable" unless an exception applies. . . . The only exception to the warrant requirement litigated in the district court—and thus the only one at issue in this appeal—is search incident to arrest (SITA). . . . "The [SITA] exception derives from interests in officer safety and evidence preservation that are typically implicated in arrest situations." *Gant*, 556 U.S. at 338, 129 S.Ct. at 1716, 173 L.Ed.2d at 493. Importantly, however, "[t]he [SITA] exception to the warrant requirement must be narrowly construed and limited to accommodating only those interests it was created to serve." *State v. McGrane*, 733 N.W.2d 671, 677 (Iowa 2007). . . .

The seminal decision exploring the SITA exception to the warrant requirement is *Chimel v. California*, 395 U.S. 752, 762–63, 89 S.Ct. 2034, 2040, 23 L.Ed.2d 685, 693–94 (1969)[, which limited searches at the time of the arrest to the search of "the arrestee's person and the area 'within his immediate control'—construing that phrase to mean the area from which he might gain possession of a weapon or destructible evidence."]

In *Belton* [v. *New York*], the Supreme Court confronted the question of the extent to which the *Chimel* principles should apply in adjudicating a Fourth Amendment challenge to the search of an automobile conducted incident to the arrest of an occupant. . . . The [*Belton*] Court held that "when a policeman has made a lawful custodial arrest of the occupant of an automobile, he may, as a contemporaneous incident of that arrest, search the passenger compartment of that automobile." *Id*. at 460, 101 S.Ct. at 2864, 69 L.Ed.2d at 775. The Court based its conclusion on the notion that the entire passenger compartment is "generally, even if not inevitably, within 'the area into which an arrestee might reach.' " *Id*. (quoting *Chimel*, 395 U.S. at 763, 89 S.Ct. at 2040, 23 L.Ed.2d at 694).

[The court noted that Iowa adopted the ruling in *Belton* in 1981, but that the *Belton* ruling came under substantial criticism after that, culminating in the Supreme Court opinion in *Arizona v. Gant*, which] authorizes officers to search a suspect's vehicle incident to the suspect's arrest "only if the arrestee is within reaching distance of the passenger compartment at the time of the search *or* it is reasonable to believe the vehicle contains evidence of the offense of arrest." *Id*. at 351, 129 S.Ct. at 1723, 173 L.Ed.2d at 501 (emphasis added). In effect, *Gant* added a third justification under the Fourth Amendment for searching an automobile incident to the arrest of a recent occupant: a "more general sort of evidence-gathering" pertaining to the crime of arrest. *Thornton*, 541 U.S. at 629, 124 S.Ct. at 2135, 158 L.Ed.2d at 918; *see Gant*, 556 U.S. at 343, 129 S.Ct. at 1719, 173 L.Ed.2d at 496 (noting the evidence-gathering rationale "does not follow from *Chimel*").

. . .

Applying the rule in *Belton*, we concluded the dual purposes of promoting officer safety and preventing evidence destruction justified a warrantless search even when it occurred "after the arrestee ha[d] been handcuffed and restrained outside the vehicle." *State v. Edgington*, 487 N.W.2d 675, 677 (Iowa 1992); *see Sanders*, 312 N.W.2d at 537, 539. . . . In contrast to the group of states that adopted and followed *Belton* in interpreting their state constitutions, several others have departed from *Belton*, focusing on the specific and narrow *Chimel* considerations underpinning the SITA exception to the warrant requirement. . . .

We now agree with the approach taken by the courts that have rejected the *Belton* rule that authorized warrantless searches of containers without regard to the *Chimel* considerations of officer safety and protecting evidence. "When lines need to be drawn in creating rules, they should be drawn thoughtfully along the logical contours of the rationales giving rise to the rules, and not as artificial lines drawn elsewhere that are unrelated to those

(continued)

rationales." *Rowell*, 188 P.3d at 101; *see also Valdez*, 224 P.3d at 758 (reminding readers of "the danger of wandering from the narrow principled justifications of the [SITA] exception, even if such wandering is done an inch at a time"). . . . [The court, however, rejected the "general evidence-gathering" rationale for a warrantless search in *Gant*, holding that the Iowa Constitution does not allow any search that is not required either to protect the safety of officers or to prevent the destruction of evidence by suspects, even where there is reason to believe that the vehicle holds evidence of a crime.]

Applying these principles to the facts of this case, we conclude the search of Gaskins's locked safe was not a valid SITA under article I, section 8. Two police officers were on the scene. Although the van had two occupants, both Gaskins and his passenger were secured in a squad car before the search of the vehicle and the safe were undertaken. The officer who performed the search testified there was no way Gaskins could have retrieved anything from the locked safe while in custody in the squad car. *See Pittman*, 127 P.3d at 1122 ("Handcuffed and secured in the patrol car, Defendant had no realistic opportunity to escape, wrestle the car keys from the officer, rush over to his locked car, unlock the door, and seize the weapon from under the seat."). . . .

[The court then considered, and rejected, several public policy concerns raised by the prosecutor, including the difficulty in obtaining a warrant quickly and the possibility that a child might gain access to the vehicle and its dangerous contents, both of which were obviated by the fact that the vehicle was impounded immediately after the arrest.]

[T]he SITA exception to the warrant requirement under article I, section 8 is tethered to its original underlying dual justifications. When we apply those justifications in this case, we conclude the search of Gaskins's van and safe was not a valid warrantless SITA under the Iowa Constitution because at the time the police officer conducted it there was no danger to the officer or likelihood that Gaskins could access the vehicle to obtain a weapon or destroy evidence. Of course, our holding that the warrantless search of the van was not justified under article I, section 8 as a SITA does not mean the van was immune from search; our holding "is instead that a warrant is generally required before such a search." *Riley v. California*, ——U.S. ——, ——, 134 S.Ct. 2473, 2493, 189 L.Ed.2d 430, 451 (2014).

Questions

1. What were the main reasons that the search of Gaskins' vehicle was not a valid search incident to an arrest?
2. What options did the arresting officers have to search Gaskins' vehicle for evidence, other than searching it at the time they arrested him?

criminal process, it still plays an important role in the development of evidence. Fingerprints found at the scene can be matched to a suspect's prints taken during booking, and "mug shots" can be used in photographic lineups to help witnesses identify the suspect as the perpetrator.

Probably the most important step in developing evidence during the post-arrest process is the **interrogation**, which includes any attempt by law enforcement to get information directly from a defendant's mind through written or oral communication. If law enforcement officers attempt to obtain evidence after arrest by questioning the suspect or doing anything designed to get the suspect to talk, they are conducting an "interrogation," and the suspect must be read his/her **Miranda rights** *before* such an investigation takes place. If the suspect indicates a desire not to answer questions, the interrogation must stop. If the suspect demands a lawyer, then the interrogation must stop until a lawyer is present. Within these limitations, any information that a suspect gives to law enforcement after being properly informed of his/her *Miranda* rights can be used as evidence against him/her to prove guilt.

interrogation
The questioning of a suspect, or any other deliberate attempt to obtain information from a suspect's mind.

Miranda rights
Three rights, prescribed by the U.S. Supreme Court in *Miranda* v. *Arizona*, that a suspect must be made aware of before he/she can be interrogated following arrest. These rights include: the right to remain silent, the right to counsel, the right to have counsel provided if the suspect is unable to afford his/her own. The suspect must also be notified that anything said by him/her can be used against him/her in court.

The Fifth Amendment does not apply, however, to all evidence obtained from a suspect during the post-arrest process. In *Schmerber* v. *California*, the U.S. Supreme Court held that blood tests performed on a suspect without his/her consent, and used as evidence supporting his/her guilt on charges of DUI, did not constitute a violation of his/her Fifth Amendment privilege against self-incrimination.

COURT OPINION 3-4 _____

SCHMERBER V. CALIFORNIA, 384 U.S. 757, 86 S.CT. 1826, 16 L.ED.2D 908 (1966)

Petitioner was convicted in Los Angeles Municipal Court of the criminal offense of driving an automobile while under the influence of intoxicating liquor [based in part on the results of a blood alcohol test performed at the direction of law enforcement and without the defendant's consent. The defendant appealed his conviction, claiming, among other things, that the compulsory blood alcohol test violated his Fifth Amendment privilege against self-incrimination].

. . .

II. The Privilege Against Self-Incrimination Claim

. . . We . . . must now decide whether the withdrawal of the blood and admission in evidence of the analysis involved in this case violated petitioner's privilege. We hold that the privilege protects an accused only from being compelled to testify against himself, or otherwise provide the State with evidence of a testimonial or communicative nature, and that the withdrawal of blood and use of the analysis in question in this case did not involve compulsion to these ends.

It could not be denied that in requiring petitioner to submit to the withdrawal and chemical analysis of his blood the State compelled him to submit to an attempt to discover evidence that might be used to prosecute him for a criminal offense. He submitted only after the police officer rejected his objection and directed the physician to proceed. The officer's direction to the physician to administer the test over petitioner's objection constituted compulsion for the purposes of the privilege. The critical question, then, is whether petitioner was thus compelled 'to be a witness against himself.'

. . . In Miranda v. Arizona, 384 U.S. 436, at 460, 86 S.Ct. 1602, at 1620, 16 L.Ed.2d 694, at 715, the Court said of the interests protected by the privilege: 'All these policies point to one overriding thought: the constitutional foundation underlying the privilege is the respect a government—state or federal—must accord to the dignity and integrity of its citizens, . . . The withdrawal of blood necessarily involves puncturing the skin for extraction, and the percent by weight of alcohol in that blood, as established by chemical analysis, is evidence of criminal guilt. Compelled submission fails on one view to respect the 'inviolability of the human personality.' Moreover, since it enables the State to rely on evidence forced from the accused, the compulsion violates at least one meaning of the requirement that the State procure the evidence against an accused 'by its own independent labors.'

As the passage in Miranda implicitly recognizes, however, the privilege has never been given the full scope which the values it helps to protect suggest. History and a long line of authorities in lower courts have consistently limited its protection to situations in which the State seeks to submerge those values by obtaining the evidence against an accused through 'the cruel, simple expedient of compelling it from his own mouth. *** In sum, the privilege is fulfilled only when the person is guaranteed the right 'to remain silent unless he chooses to speak in the unfettered exercise of his own will. " *Ibid*. . . .

It is clear that the protection of the privilege reaches an accused's communications, whatever form they might take, and the compulsion of responses which are also communications, for example, compliance with a subpoena to produce one's papers. Boyd v. United States, 116 U.S. 616, 6 S.Ct. 524, 29 L.Ed. 746. On the other hand, both federal and state courts have usually held that it offers no protection against compulsion to submit to fingerprinting, photographing, or measurements, to write or speak for identification, to appear in court, to stand, to assume a stance, to walk, or to make a particular gesture. The distinction which has emerged, often expressed in different ways, is that the privilege is a bar against compelling 'communications' or 'testimony,' but that compulsion which makes a suspect or accused the source of 'real or physical evidence' does not violate it.

Although we agree that this distinction is a helpful framework for analysis, we are not to be under-

(continued)

stood to agree with past applications in all instances. There will be many cases in which such a distinction is not readily drawn. Some tests seemingly directed to obtain 'physical evidence,' for example, lie detector tests measuring changes in body function during interrogation, may actually be directed to eliciting responses which are essentially testimonial. . . .

In the present case, however, no such problem of application is presented. Not even a shadow of testimonial compulsion upon or enforced communication by the accused was involved either in the extraction or in the chemical analysis. Petitioner's testimonial capacities were in no way implicated; indeed, his participation, except as a donor, was irrelevant to the results of the test, which depend on chemical analysis and on that alone. Since the blood test evidence, although an incriminating product of compulsion, was neither petitioner's testimony nor evidence relating to some communicative act or writing by the petitioner, it was not inadmissible on privilege grounds.

Questions

1. How does the court define a "communicative act" for purposes of applying the Fifth Amendment's protection against self-incrimination?
2. What other types of evidence could a suspect be forced to provide without requiring a "communicative act"?

The *Schmerber* decision has been applied many times in cases where non-testimonial evidence is obtained from a defendant without his/her consent. In *People* v. *Gutierrez*, an off-duty police officer attempted to exclude the results of a breathalyzer test from a hearing challenging the rescission of his driver's license. Relying on *Schmerber*, the court denied Gutierrez's motion and allowed the evidence.

COURT OPINION 3-5 _____

PEOPLE V. GUTIERREZ, 38 N.E.3D 521 (2015)

. . . Defendant was a police officer with the Aurora police department. On December 24, 2013, defendant was off duty, driving in his personal vehicle, when he rear-ended another vehicle at an intersection within the jurisdiction of the Aurora police department. The other driver called the police. After waiting approximately 30 minutes to one hour without police arriving, defendant and the other driver exchanged information, and defendant left the scene of the accident and drove home.

After arriving home, defendant received a phone call from Sergeant Weber of the Aurora police department, requesting that defendant return to the scene of the accident. Defendant drove back to the scene. Illinois State Trooper David DeGraff administered to defendant a PBT. The result of the PBT was a 0.249 BAC. Defendant was arrested for driving under the influence of alcohol (625 ILCS 5/11–501 (West 2012)).

Defendant refused further chemical testing, and his driver's license was suspended. Defendant filed a petition to rescind the suspension. The petition requested a hearing pursuant to section 2–118 of the Illinois Vehicle Code (Code) (625 ILCS 5/2–118 (West 2012)).

Defendant filed a motion *in limine* seeking to exclude the PBT results from being admitted at the hearing on the petition to rescind. The motion alleged that the PBT was administered "for the purposes of an Aurora Police Department administrative employee disciplinary investigation" and was therefore not consensual, as required by section 11–501.5(a) of the Code (PBT statute) (625 ILCS 5/11–501.5(a) (West 2012)). In addition, the motion claimed that the results of the PBT were compelled testimony in violation of the fifth amendment (U.S. Const., amend. V). Furthermore, the motion argued that the results of the PBT were not reliable.

(continued)

(continued)

At a hearing on the motion *in limine*, defendant argued that the PBT was an "administrative blow," and therefore admission of the PBT at trial would violate defendant's fifth amendment right against self-incrimination. Defendant testified that when he arrived on the scene, Sergeant Bodman told him that he was required to take the PBT test as an administrative blow. DeGraff administered the PBT using a device that belonged to the Aurora police department. According to defendant, DeGraff seemed unaware of how to properly operate the device. He twice administered the test unsuccessfully before obtaining a reading on the third try. Defendant testified that he did not consent to taking the PBT but that DeGraff never told him that he was required to take it.

DeGraff testified that he was a friend and neighbor of defendant's. He was called to the scene to help investigate because the Aurora police who responded were concerned that they had a conflict of interest in investigating a fellow Aurora police officer. When defendant arrived back on the scene, DeGraff detected an odor of alcohol on defendant's breath. DeGraff stated that he was "slightly unfamiliar" with the PBT device he used because it was a different model than the device he typically used. Bodman requested that DeGraff administer the PBT as an administrative blow. DeGraff could not remember whether he told defendant that the PBT test was mandatory.

The court denied the motion *in limine*. It found that the PBT was an administrative search, and therefore the results were admissible so long as the PBT was not merely a subterfuge for discovering criminal activity. The court found that the PBT was not a subterfuge.

The cause proceeded to a hearing on defendant's petition to rescind. The issue before the court was whether there were reasonable grounds for officers to believe that defendant was under the influence of alcohol. 625 ILCS 5/2–118.1(b)(2) (West 2012). The court said, "Frankly, without the portable breath test, the Court would not find that there was reasonable grounds for the defendant to be arrested, so really this whole motion hinges on the admissibility of the portable breath test." The court found that the combination of the PBT results, the odor of alcohol emitting from defendant, and the collision established reasonable grounds for officers to arrest defendant. The court denied the petition to rescind.

Analysis

On appeal, defendant argues that the court should have granted his motion *in limine* and excluded evidence of the PBT results from the hearing on his petition to rescind. He further argues that, without admission of the PBT results, the court would have granted his petition to rescind. He therefore asks us to reverse the court's decision denying the petition.

. . .

We agree with the trial court that in the present case the decision on the petition to rescind turned on the admissibility of the PBT results. Therefore, we restrict our analysis to the trial court's decision on defendant's motion *in limine* seeking to preclude the PBT results. A court's decision on a motion *in limine* is reviewed for an abuse of discretion. *People v. Robinson*, 368 Ill.App.3d 963, 974, 307 Ill.Dec. 232, 859 N.E.2d 232 (2006).

Defendant first argues that the PBT results were inadmissible under the fifth amendment's protection against self-incrimination. U.S. Const., amend. V. Defendant cites to *Garrity v. New Jersey*, 385 U.S. 493, 87 S.Ct. 616, 17 L.Ed.2d 562 (1967), and its progeny for the proposition that the potential employment disciplinary consequences for refusing the PBT compelled him to take the PBT, in violation of the fifth amendment. See, *e.g., People v. Smith*, 399 Ill. App. 3d 534, 541, 339 Ill. Dec. 220, 926 N.E.2d 452 (2010) (holding that statements made under threat of employment termination could not be used to incriminate defendant at a criminal proceeding).

Defendant's argument fails on two levels. First, the fifth amendment protects against the use of *testimonial* evidence, not physical evidence such as the PBT results. See *Schmerber v. California*, 384 U.S. 757, 764–65, 86 S.Ct. 1826, 16 L.Ed.2d 908 (1966) (fifth amendment did not bar blood-alcohol analysis results, as results were not testimonial). Second, the fifth amendment prevents the introduction of compelled testimony at criminal proceedings rather than civil proceedings, such as summary suspension proceedings. U.S. Const., amend. V ("nor shall be compelled in any criminal case to be a witness against himself"); *People v. Hall*, 378 Ill.App.3d 666, 670, 317 Ill.Dec. 511, 882 N.E.2d 85 (2007). The fifth amendment and the holding of *Garrity*, 385 U.S. 493, 87 S.Ct. 616, did not preclude the admission of the PBT results.

Questions

1. Why did Gutierrez believe his breathalyzer test violated his Fifth Amendment rights?
2. What does the court's holding tell us about the continued vitality of the *Schmerber* v. *California* decision?

Time Limitations on Evidence Gathering

A person can be arrested without evidence sufficient to prove guilt beyond a reasonable doubt, but if insufficient evidence is developed after an arrest to support a finding of guilt, then proceeding with a criminal prosecution may be unwise. An individual may not be subjected to **double jeopardy**, meaning that once a suspect has been brought to trial and found not guilty, he/she cannot be retried for the same crime no matter how much additional evidence of his/her guilt is found.

At the same time, prolonging the evidence-gathering process can also be problematic, for several reasons. First, the constitution guarantees a **speedy trial**, meaning that the defendant cannot be held too long after arrest without being brought to trial. The Speedy Trial Act of 1974 (18 U.S.C. §3161 et seq.) requires that an information or indictment be filed no later than 30 days after a suspect is arrested, and that trial begin no later than 70 days after that (18 U.S.C. §3161(b) and (c)). If these time limits (or any extension permitted under Section 3161(h)) are not met, then the charges against the defendant must be dropped, and the court has the power to dismiss the charges with prejudice, meaning that no further prosecution of the defendant will be permitted (18 U.S.C. §3162). The statute also provides, however, that compliance with the Speedy Trial Act's provisions do not necessarily prevent a general claim that a defendant's right to a speedy trial was violated under the Sixth Amendment of the U.S. Constitution.

In *United States* v. *Abdush-Shakur*, the defendant was indicted three times. The first indictment was voluntarily withdrawn by the prosecutor, and the second was dismissed without prejudice because of the delay in bringing his case to trial. The third indictment was not dismissed, and the defendant was tried and found guilty. The court's analysis of the defendant's motion to dismiss the third indictment provides interesting insight into how the Speedy Trial Act applies, and how it differs from a claim that the defendant's Sixth Amendment right to a speedy trial was violated.

LEARNING OBJECTIVE 10
Discuss legal obligations relating to evidence-gathering, including time limitations, disclosure requirements, and the duty to preserve evidence.

double jeopardy
The trying of a defendant twice for the same crime based on the same actions.

speedy trial
Trial without undue delay, the right to which is guaranteed under the Sixth Amendment of the U.S. Constitution.

COURT OPINION 3-6

UNITED STATES V. ABDUSH-SHAKUR, 465 F.3D 458, 71 FED. R. EVID. SERV. 470 (10TH CIR. 2006)

On December 2, 2004, Shakir Abdush-Shakur, an inmate at the United States Prison at Leavenworth, was convicted of attempted murder, and possession of a handmade knife by a prison inmate, arising out of the May 18, 2003 stabbing of prison Senior Officer Specialist, Timothy McDonald. On March 9, 2005, he was sentenced to a total of 240 months imprisonment. He appeals from his conviction alleging various trial errors. We affirm.

Background

On May 29, 2003, Abdush-Shakur was charged in a two-count indictment with attempted murder and possession of a prohibited object in violation of 18 U.S.C. §§ 1113 and 1791(a)(2), respectively. After several successful motions for continuance lodged by defense counsel, trial was set for December 9, 2003. On December 3, 2003, the government filed a motion for a continuance of the trial date, followed the next day by the government's motion to dismiss the indictment due to the illness of government counsel. On December 8, 2003, the indictment was dismissed without prejudice over the objection of Abdush-Shakur.

On April 1, 2004, a second indictment charging the same offenses was filed under the same case number. On May 17, 2004, Abdush-Shakur filed a

(continued)

(continued)

motion to dismiss the indictment for violation of his right to speedy trial. The court granted his motion on June 28, 2004, and dismissed the indictment without prejudice. On September 16, 2004, the government filed a third indictment. Although filed under a new case number the substance remained unchanged. Abdush-Shakur moved to dismiss the third indictment on October 18, 2004. On October 27, 2004, the district court denied the motion. On November 10, 2004, a superseding third indictment was filed adding Abdush-Shakur's former name of Leonard Cunningham, but making no other changes.

. . . . On December 2, 2004, the jury convicted Abdush-Shakur of attempted murder and possession of a prohibited object.

Discussion

Abdush-Shakur asserts the district court erred . . . by denying his motion to dismiss the indictment as a violation of the Speedy Trial Act and his Sixth Amendment and Due Process rights. . . .

I. MOTION TO DISMISS

Abdush-Shakur argued to the district court that the third indictment should be dismissed as a violation of the Speedy Trial Act and his Sixth Amendment and Due Process rights. The district court denied the motions to dismiss. Abdush-Shakur reasserts his arguments on appeal.

A. SPEEDY TRIAL ACT

. . .

Congress enacted the Speedy Trial Act in part because "the Supreme Court had been reluctant to define specific time periods under the speedy trial guarantee of the Sixth Amendment. . . ." *Vogl*, 374 F.3d at 982. While the Speedy Trial Act certainly adds protection to a defendant's already existing Fifth and Sixth Amendment rights, statutes of limitations remain "the primary guarantee against bringing overly stale criminal charges." *United States v. Marion*, 404 U.S. 307, 322, 92 S.Ct. 455, 30 L.Ed.2d 468 (1971) (discussing Sixth Amendment right to a speedy trial).

The Speedy Trial Act "requires that the trial of a criminal defendant commence within seventy days of the filing of the indictment, or from the date that the defendant first appears before a judicial officer, whichever is later." *United States v. Gomez*, 67 F.3d

1515, 1519 (10th Cir. 1995); 18 U.S.C. § 3161(c)(1). Subject to statutory exclusions, "[i]f a defendant is not brought to trial within the seventy-day deadline, dismissal of the indictment is mandatory." *United States v. Doran*, 882 F.2d 1511, 1517 (10th Cir. 1989).[2] The "indictment shall be dismissed on motion of the defendant." *United States v. Vaughn*, 370 F.3d 1049, 1055 (10th Cir. 2004).

Nevertheless, the district court retains broad discretion whether to dismiss the indictment with or without prejudice. *Doran*, 882 F.2d at 1518. 18 U.S.C. § 3162(a) provides:

> In determining whether to dismiss . . . with or without prejudice, the court shall consider, among others, each of the following factors: the seriousness of the offense; the facts and circumstances of the case which led to the dismissal; and the impact of a reprosecution on the administration of this chapter and on the administration of justice.

. . . "[T]he application of the more severe sanction of dismissal with prejudice . . . should be reserved for more egregious violations." *Cano-Silva*, 402 F.3d at 1035. A violation of the speedy trial requirement, by itself, is not a sufficient basis for dismissal with prejudice. *Id.*

Based on the record before us, the district court did not err by dismissing the second indictment without prejudice.[1] First, as Abdush-Shakur concedes, attempted murder is a serious offense. Second, contrary to Abdush-Shakur's assertion, the delay between his initial appearance and his trial was not "completely due to the Government" (Appellant's Br. at 36.). It is true that the illness of government counsel contributed to the delay. . . . However, the government's behavior in this case was not egregious. There is no indication the government was dilatory or neglectful in its prosecution of Abdush-Shakur, or that it otherwise acted in bad faith. See *Taylor*, 487 U.S. at 338-39, 108 S.Ct.

---

[1] Under § 3161(d) (1), if an indictment is dismissed upon motion of the defendant and he is subsequently re-indicted with the same offense, the new indictment begins a new seventy-day period . . . Thus, because the Second Indictment was dismissed on Abdush-Shakur's motion, the Third Indictment began a new seventy-day period. . . . However, where the government moves to dismiss the indictment, as it did with the First Indictment here, and then refiles a second indictment alleging the same charges, the government does not get a new seventy-day clock. . . . "The reason for this rule is obvious. If the clock began anew, the government could circumvent the limitations of the Speedy Trial Act by repeatedly dismissing and refiling charges against a defendant." [*United States v. Hoslett*, 998 F.2d 648, 658 n. 12 (9th Cir. 1993).] . . .

(continued)

2413. Indeed, at the hearing on Abdush-Shakur's motion to dismiss the Second Indictment, defense counsel agreed "all parties acted professionally." (R. Vol. IV at 51.) Moreover, as the district court pointed out, another important source of delay was three continuances requested by Abdush-Shakur and allowed by the court . . .

Reprosecution of this case did not negatively affect the administration of justice. Abdush-Shakur concedes his incarceration throughout the proceedings was based on his sentence for the commission of another crime. Nor, as the district court pointed out, would penalizing the government for the delay deter any similar behavior in the future. Where the delay caused by the government is unintentional and the district court takes it upon itself to share in the blame for the delay, the administration of justice is not served by dismissal with prejudice. . . .

Finally, there is no evidence of sufficient prejudice to Abdush-Shakur to require dismissal with prejudice. . . . Thus, the second indictment was appropriately dismissed without prejudice and any intervening time between indictments was not covered by the Speedy Trial Act.

B. SIXTH AMENDMENT RIGHT TO A SPEEDY TRIAL

Abdush-Shakur claims the delay between his first indictment on May 29, 2003, and his third indictment on September 16, 2004, violates his Sixth Amendment right to a speedy trial. We think not.

> The Sixth Amendment right to a speedy trial is . . . not primarily intended to prevent prejudice to the defense caused by passage of time; that interest is protected primarily by the Due Process Clause and by statutes of limitations. The speedy trial guarantee is designed to minimize the possibility of lengthy incarceration prior to trial, to reduce the lesser, but nevertheless substantial, impairment of liberty imposed on an accused while released on bail, and to shorten the disruption of life caused by arrest and the presence of unresolved criminal charges.

United States v. MacDonald, 456 U.S. 1, 8, 102 S. Ct. 1497, 71 L.Ed.2d 696 (1982).

In determining whether a defendant's Sixth Amendment right to a speedy trial has been violated, a court must balance four factors: (1) the length of delay; (2) the reason for delay; (3) the defendant's assertion of his right; and (4) any prejudice to the defendant. . . . "None of these factors, taken by itself, is either a necessary or sufficient condition to the finding of a deprivation of the right of speedy trial. Rather, they are related factors and must be considered together with such other circumstances as may be relevant." *United States v. Gomez*, 67 F.3d 1515, 1521 (10th Cir. 1995) (quotation omitted). It is unusual to find a Sixth Amendment violation when the Speedy Trial Act has been satisfied. *United States v. Sprouts*, 282 F.3d 1037, 1042 (8th Cir. 2002).

"We need only inquire into the other factors if the period of delay is 'presumptively prejudicial.' " *Lugo*, 170 F.3d at 1002 (quoting *United States v. Dirden*, 38 F.3d 1131, 1137 (10th Cir. 1994)). In this case, the parties disagree as to whether the relevant period of delay under consideration was eleven or fourteen months. The latter delay, but not the former, might qualify as presumptively prejudicial. See *Gomez*, 67 F.3d at 1523 (twelve and one-half month delay held not prejudicial).

Regardless of the length of delay, the second prong—the reason for the delay, clearly does not suggest a violation of the Abdush-Shakur's Sixth Amendment rights. As discussed above, prior to the government's request for a continuance due to the poor health of one of its counsel, Abdush-Shakur himself requested three continuances, the latest occurring in October of 2003. Delays attributable to the defendant do not weigh against the government. *Dirden*, 38 F.3d at 1138. We find little merit in defendant's assertion of his Sixth Amendment right to a speedy trial in the wake of the government's legitimate request for a continuance when the defendant has sat on his hands for seven months and requested several continuances of his own. Finally, as discussed above, there was little showing of actual prejudice to Abdush-Shakur. Thus, Abdush-Shakur failed to establish a violation of his Sixth Amendment right to a speedy trial based on the total delay in this case.

Questions

1. What are the similarities between the court's analysis of the fact for purposes of applying the Speedy Trial Act and its analysis for purposes of determining a violation of the Sixth Amendment's right to a speedy trial?
2. What kind of "prejudice" would the defendant have to show in order to justify dismissing his case with prejudice?

Note that the time periods under the Speedy Trial Act only begin to run when the defendant is arrested, so under the act the government could have more time to develop evidence simply by delaying the arrest. This is also problematic, however, since the Speedy Trial Act is not the only clock ticking in a criminal case. As we have seen, the Sixth Amendment's right to a speedy trial is a separate concern that could prevent prosecution even if the Speedy Trial Act itself is not violated.

limitations period
A period of time, prescribed by statute, within which the prosecution of a defendant must be started after the crime is committed.

In addition, as the *Abdush-Shakur* court noted, most federal and state crimes have a **limitations period** within which a prosecution must be started after the commission of an offense. The federal limitations period for most crimes is five years, although there is no limitations period for crimes punishable by death, acts of terrorism, or certain federal sex offenses (Doyle, *Statutes of Limitation in Federal Criminal Cases: An Overview*, p. 1 (Congressional Research Service, October 1, 2012)). If this time period expires without charges being filed, then the prosecutor would be forever barred from bringing those charges.

Once an arrest is made, the need to bring charges promptly and to bring the case to trial within a reasonable time limits the time the government has to develop evidence in favor of conviction. Despite the ability to make an arrest without sufficient evidence to prove guilt beyond a reasonable doubt, such evidence must be available soon after the arrest is made if the defendant's Sixth Amendment right to a speedy trial is to be preserved.

Disclosure of Evidence

One of the mainstays of Hollywood-style courtroom drama is the entrance of the "surprise witness," who shows up when all hope is lost to provide the key testimony needed to put the villainous defendant away for life. While such dramatic reversals of fortune make for good cinema, the fact is that the law seldom allows such surprises to occur in real-life trials.

discovery
The disclosure of evidence by one side in a criminal case to the other.

Federal Rule of Criminal Procedure 16 requires disclosure of any evidence that is obtained before, during, or after arrest to the defendant and his/her counsel upon request. The process of requesting evidence from the other party in a criminal case is called **discovery**. The prosecutor is also entitled to evidence developed by the defendant, but that right is limited compared to the disclosure rights of the defendant.

The Duty to Preserve Documents

Once a document is the subject of a discovery request, it would obviously be illegal for the custodian to destroy it. But is there an affirmative duty to preserve relevant evidence even if no one has yet asked for it? Destroying relevant evidence or otherwise making it unavailable to the other party for trial is called **spoliation**, and can result in severe sanctions against the party responsible for the unavailability of the evidence.

spoliation
The loss or destruction of real evidence.

There are statutes and regulations in every jurisdiction that require certain types of businesses to maintain records and preserve them for a prescribed period of time. The federal statute known as Sarbanes–Oxley, for example, was designed to increase accountability in the area of corporate finance, and contains stiff penalties for the destruction of documents relating to fraud investigations, as well as affirmative mandates to preserve corporate audit records. Section 802 of Sarbanes–Oxley specifies what kinds of duties and penalties are imposed with respect to such types of documents.

State statutes can also require the preservation of documents. For instance, the Pennsylvania Fair Educational Opportunities Act requires that "any records, documents and data dealing with, or pertaining to, the admission, rejections, expulsion or suspension of students" be preserved for three years (24 P.S. §5004(a)(5)).

Obviously, when the retention of documents is required by statute, there is no need to foresee whether the document might be the subject of a lawsuit to create a duty of retention and preservation.

KEY TERMS

booking 48
first appearance 48
complaint 48
information 49
preliminary hearing 49
indictment 49
grand jury 49
true bill 50
proffer session 50
arraignment 50
guilty plea 50
nolo contendere 51
criminal trial 51
jury selection 52
voir dire 52
peremptory objections 52
opening statements 53

prosecutor's case-in-chief 55
objections 55
sustain 56
overrule 56
sidebar 56
cautionary instruction 56
mistrial 56
motion for a judgment of
  acquittal 56
defendant's case-in-chief 58
affirmative defense 58
closing arguments 58
jury instructions 60
model jury instructions 60
jury deliberations 61
verdict 61
hung jury 62

sequestration 62
jury poll 62
aggravating factors 65
mitigating factors 65
presentencing report 66
probable cause 68
crime scene investigation 68
physical evidence 68
search incident to an
  arrest 69
interrogation 71
Miranda rights 71
double jeopardy 75
speedy trial 75
limitations period 78
discovery 78
spoliation 78

CHAPTER SUMMARY

- The federal criminal trial process consists of five stages: (1) arrest, booking, complaint, and first appearance; (2) testing the prosecutor's case by indictment or information; (3) arraignment and pleading; (4) trial; and (5) sentencing.

- When a suspect is arrested, the suspect is booked, which is an administrative process including fingerprinting and photographing, among others.

- Evidence obtained during the booking process is lawful so long as the arrest itself was lawful.

- After booking, the suspect is brought before a judge for a first appearance, at which he/she is informed of the charges and given the opportunity to have counsel appointed.

- At some point during the initial post-arrest process, a complaint will be filed detailing the facts constituting the offenses charged.

- The complaint is filed by a federal investigator, under oath, and officially begins the criminal case.

- After a complaint is filed, the prosecutor's case is tested by information or indictment to see if there is sufficient evidence to proceed with a trial.

- If no indictment is required, the government will file an information, which is a written statement of the charges and a summary of the evidence of those charges.

- Once an information is filed, the court may need to hold a preliminary hearing to hear evidence supporting the charges.

- If the judge determines that there is insufficient evidence in an information or at a preliminary hearing to justify taking the case to trial, the charges will be dismissed.

- Where an indictment is required or desired, a prosecutor presents evidence supporting the charges to a grand jury, which meets in secret without the presence of the defendant or his/her counsel.
- Upon hearing the evidence, a grand jury returns a decision of "true bill," upon which an indictment is issued, or "no true bill," in which case no indictment is issued.
- Once the prosecutor's case has been tested, the defendant is arraigned. An arraignment is a proceeding where the defendant is given an opportunity to plead to the charges contained in an information or indictment.
- If the defendant pleads guilty, and the court accepts the plea after making sure that the defendant understands its ramifications, the defendant is immediately sentenced.
- A plea of *nolo contendere* (no contest) has the same effect as a plea of guilty, but cannot be used as an admission of liability in any subsequent civil or criminal trial.
- If the defendant pleads not guilty, the case goes to trial, which is a proceeding at which evidence is presented to prove the defendant's guilt beyond a reasonable doubt.
- A trial consists of six stages: (1) jury selection; (2) opening statements; (3) the prosecutor's case-in-chief; (4) the defendant's case-in-chief; (5) closing statements; and (6) jury instructions, deliberations, and verdict.
- Jury selection involves the examination and exclusion of potential jurors for a variety of reasons, including prejudice and partiality toward the parties in the case.
- During *voir dire*, the parties question jurors to determine their fitness to sit on the jury for that particular trial. One jury pool may provide jurors for several different trials.
- Each side in the case may object to a juror for cause (such as prejudice), and may exercise a limited number of peremptory objections, which exclude a juror without cause.
- Following jury selection and empanelment, each side gives an opening statement, with the prosecutor presenting first.
- Opening statements summarize the evidence each side will present to the jury, providing a roadmap for the jury to follow during trial, but may not include evidence that will not be presented at trial.
- The prosecutor's case-in-chief is the stage where the prosecutor must present evidence meeting

- the burden of proving the defendant's guilt beyond a reasonable doubt.
- During the prosecutor's case-in-chief, the defense counsel can object to evidence presented by the prosecutor. If the judge overrules the objection, the evidence is admitted, but if the judge sustains the objection, the evidence is excluded from the jury's consideration.
- If a piece of evidence is not objected to at the time it is presented, the objection is waived and cannot be raised later as a basis for overturning the jury's decision.
- An objection may require discussion outside the hearing of the jury, in which case the judge will either dismiss the jury from the courtroom or conduct a sidebar with the attorneys at the bench, out of the jury's hearing.
- Where an objection is raised only after the jury has heard the evidence, then the judge may issue a cautionary instruction to the jury to disregard what they have heard in their deliberations.
- If the inadmissible evidence to which the jury is exposed is so prejudicial that a cautionary instruction will not suffice, the judge may declare a mistrial, terminating the trial.
- During the prosecutor's case-in-chief, the defendant may also cross-examine witnesses in an attempt to challenge the veracity of their testimony and damage their credibility in the eyes of the jury.
- Once a prosecutor has rested his/her case-in-chief, the defendant may make a motion for a judgment of acquittal, claiming that the prosecutor's evidence was insufficient to meet the burden of proving the defendant's guilt beyond a reasonable doubt.
- Granting a motion for judgment of acquittal has the same effect as a "not guilty" verdict by the jury.
- After the prosecutor has rested, the defendant may then present his/her case-in-chief for the purpose of rebutting the prosecutor's evidence, presenting additional evidence that the defendant is not guilty, and supporting affirmative defenses.
- Although the defendant is not required to do so, the defendant may present evidence proving that he/she did not commit the crime, or challenging the factual accuracy or credibility of the prosecutor's evidence.
- During the defendant's case-in-chief, the prosecutor has the right to object to evidence and cross-examine witnesses, including the defendant

if he/she chooses to take the stand in his/her own defense.

- After the defendant has rested, the parties present their closing argument, with the prosecutor going first with the right to rebut following the defendant's closing argument.
- Closing arguments are presentations that attempt to persuade the jury that the evidence either does or does not support a verdict of guilty.
- Closing arguments are limited to the evidence that was actually presented at trial, and may not improperly inflame the jury's passion or prejudice.
- After closing arguments, the judge issues jury instructions, or the charge to the jury, informing the jurors of the legal principles governing the case and their verdict.
- Once the jury has been instructed, it deliberates in secret until it reaches a verdict or is unable to do so.
- If a jury is unable to reach a unanimous verdict either for or against guilt, it is a hung jury and the trial ends without a verdict, although a judge may refuse to accept a hung jury and require the jury to continue deliberating.
- During deliberations, a jury may not consider any evidence that was not admitted during the trial. Juries may be sequestered to prevent exposure to public information about a trial.
- Once the jury has reached a verdict, the verdict is announced in open court, thus ending the trial. Either party may request jury poll, which means that the judge asks each jurors if he or she agrees with the verdict.
- A defendant found guilty at trial must be sentenced according to the federal sentencing guidelines, which prescribe ranges of months of incarceration based on the severity of the crime and the defendant's prior criminal record.
- Under the guidelines, each crime is given an offense score, and each defendant is assigned a number of points based on his/her criminal history, and these scores are used to determine the appropriate sentence.
- A judge may impose a sentence outside the guidelines based on prescribed mitigation or aggravating circumstances.
- To assist the judge in sentencing, a probation officer may be required to provide a presentencing report, containing facts relating to the defendant's prior criminal record and the existence of aggravating or mitigating factors.
- Where a sentence of death is prescribed for the defendant's crime, the judge must also consider aggravating or mitigating factors in choosing whether to sentence the defendant to death or life imprisonment.
- Evidence can be developed throughout the trial process, before, during, and after the arrest.
- In order to gather evidence sufficient to support an arrest, law enforcement officers may need to engage in crime scene investigation, which is the careful examination of the crime scene for physical evidence such bodily fluid, fingerprints, implements of the crime, and any other tangible evidence.
- All physical evidence obtained at a crime scene must be preserved in the condition it is found in at the scene, or its value as evidence will be lost.
- When a defendant is arrested, the arresting officer may conduct a search of the defendant's person, anything the defendant is carrying, and the defendant's immediate surroundings, for evidence supporting the defendant's guilt.
- Following an arrest, law enforcement may use all available methods to obtain further evidence supporting the defendant's guilt, including interrogating the suspect and witnesses, obtaining DNA and blood samples, and conducting searches of any area that they reasonably believe might hold evidence of the crime,
- All constitutional requirements for searching and seizing evidence must be complied with in order for that evidence to be used at trial.
- If a suspect is in custody and interrogated, the suspect must be read his/her *Miranda* rights before any evidence obtained from him/her can be used at trial.
- It is important that the criminal trial process not move forward before sufficient evidence is obtained to support a conviction, because once a defendant is found not guilty, he/she may not be charged again with the same crime under the constitutional prohibition against double jeopardy.
- Likewise, it is important not to proceed too slowly, because federal law requires that a defendant be brought to trial no later than 70 days after an information or indictment is filed, which must in turn occur no later than 30 days after the defendant is arrested.
- Many crimes have limitations periods, which are the time periods within which criminal charges must be filed following the commission of an offense.
- Evidence obtained by a prosecutor during the investigation of a crime must be provided to the defense upon request. The prosecutor also has a more limited right to receive evidence obtained by the defendant.

WEB EXCURSIONS

1. Using Web resources, find a detailed explanation of your state's criminal trial process. Can you see any notable differences between your state's processes and the federal process discussed in this chapter?

2. Find your state's sentencing rules or guidelines on the Web. Compare your state's punishments with punishments for comparable crimes under the federal guidelines. Is your state harsher in its punishment of crimes than the federal system?

PRACTICAL EXERCISES

1. Interview a law enforcement officer in your municipality to determine how that agency investigates crimes. If possible, ask for a copy of any materials used to train law enforcement in crime investigation, and review that material carefully to see how specific investigations were conducted.

2. Sit in on a criminal trial in your area. Take notes about what evidence is presented, and how the various stages of the trial unfold.

LEARNING OBJECTIVES

After reading this chapter, the student will be able to:

1. Distinguish between direct and circumstantial evidence.

2. Explain the meaning of demonstrative evidence and its use in a criminal case.

3. Illustrate the three methods of proving facts without evidence.

4. Compare and contrast conclusive and rebuttable presumptions.

5. Define testimony and explain its limitations.

6. Distinguish between the use of documents and things as real evidence.

Types and Forms of Evidence

CHAPTER 4

■ INTRODUCTION

Everything you have learned so far about the nature and function of evidence can be summarized by three critical points:

1. To prove that a defendant committed a crime, you must prove that he/she satisfied all of its elements.
2. To prove that the elements of a crime have been satisfied, you must prove evidentiary facts that relate to each of those elements.
3. To prove evidentiary facts, you must provide evidence of those facts.

This chapter will describe and analyze the various ways in which evidence is categorized. We will begin by explaining the three *types* of evidence: direct evidence, circumstantial evidence, and demonstrative evidence. We will also look at ways that proof can occur without evidence. Then, we will examine the *form* that evidence takes. There are two basic forms of evidence: testimonial and real. Real evidence can be broken down into two other forms: documents and things.

LEARNING OBJECTIVE 1
Distinguish between direct and circumstantial evidence.

direct evidence
Evidence that proves a fact without the need for an inference by the trier of fact.

■ TYPES OF EVIDENCE

Direct Evidence

Direct evidence is evidence that is so connected to the fact it seeks to prove that if you believe the evidence, you *must* accept the fact as true. For example, suppose a witness in a manslaughter case testifies that he actually saw the defendant's car run a red light before it collided with the victim, a pedestrian. If the jury believes that witness, then they *must* conclude that the defendant's car ran the red light. The only alternative is to conclude that the witness is either lying or mistaken.

Direct evidence is the most persuasive kind of evidence, because it usually comes from personal, firsthand experience with the factual issue being decided. Eyewitnesses are one example, but there are many others. For instance, a photograph of damage to the car that struck the pedestrian would be direct evidence of the damage that the photograph depicts. The results of a blood alcohol test would be direct evidence of a defendant's blood alcohol content. A surveillance video showing the defendant running the red light would be direct evidence that he did, in fact, run the red light. The evidence can be attacked on the ground that it is not trustworthy, but if the jury believes the evidence, then it has no choice but to believe the fact that the evidence is offered to prove.

Direct evidence has its limits, however. It cannot be used to directly prove any fact *other* than the one it specifically relates to. For instance, the eyewitness' testimony and surveillance video showing that the defendant ran a red light does not directly prove *why* the defendant did so. The photograph of damage to the defendant's car does not directly prove what part of the plaintiff's body was struck. The blood alcohol test does not directly prove that the defendant's ability to drive was actually impaired.

As useful as direct evidence is, it usually proves fairly narrow evidentiary issues, not larger factual issues that form the elements of a crime. This is particularly true where the element in question is a defendant's state of mind (i.e., whether he acted purposefully, recklessly, etc.), which is a factual issue in nearly all criminal cases. A person can directly experience his own state of mind, but no one else can. This means that *the only direct evidence of person's state of mind is a confession.* If the defendant will not confess, then his state of mind must be proven through indirect, or *circumstantial*, evidence.

> **PRACTICE TIP**
>
> Given the critical importance of a confession, it is just as critically important to make sure that any confession obtained from defendant is obtained in compliance with constitutional requirements such as *Miranda* warnings and that the confession is voluntary and not coerced.

Circumstantial Evidence

circumstantial evidence
Evidence that proves a fact by inference. A jury can accept circumstantial evidence as true without accepting the fact the evidence seeks to prove.

Circumstantial evidence is different from direct evidence, because a jury can believe circumstantial evidence and still conclude that the fact it is offered to prove is not true. This evidence requires the trier of fact to *infer* facts that are not proven in order to make the connection between the evidence and the fact the evidence is offered to prove (see Figure 4-1). For instance, suppose an eyewitness is called to testify that a defendant ran a red light. Unfortunately, the witness did not actually see the defendant run the red light. She can testify only that that she saw the traffic light turn yellow as the defendant's car approached the intersection. The jury can accept that evidence as true and still conclude that the light was yellow when the defendant entered the

Figure 4-1 Direct and Circumstantial Evidence

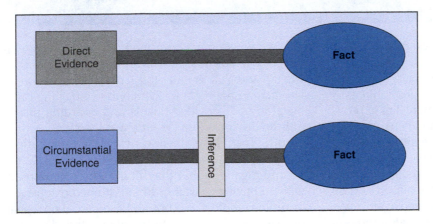

intersection. The witness' testimony may make it more *likely* that the defendant entered the intersection against a red light, but it doesn't prove it *directly*.

Where direct evidence of a fact is not available, circumstantial evidence is often introduced to support other circumstantial evidence in proving a factual issue. This is called *corroboration*, a concept discussed in more detail in Chapter 5. In our hypothetical manslaughter case, suppose a second witness testified that the traffic light was red when the defendant's car hit the victim. This doesn't prove exactly when the light turned red, and the jury could still conclude that the light was yellow when the defendant entered the intersection. But this evidence supports (or *corroborates*) the testimony of the first witness, and makes it even more likely that the defendant entered the intersection illegally.

The next two Court Opinions illustrate the use of circumstantial evidence to prove material elements of a crime. In *United States* v. *Yoshida*, the defendant was convicted of illegally bringing aliens from the People's Republic of China into the United States. Her conviction was based largely on inferences drawn from her actions during a flight with the aliens from China to the United States. She claimed that this evidence was insufficient to support a criminal conviction, in the absence of any direct evidence that she was involved with the aliens or leading them in their illegal flight. In *United States* v. *Thomas*, circumstantial evidence was presented to prove the identity of the perpetrator, Chapman, in a wire fraud case where no victim or witness ever actually saw the defendant while the crime was being committed. In both cases, the court held that the circumstantial evidence was sufficient to allow a jury to find that the material element was proven beyond a reasonable doubt.

COURT OPINION 4-1

UNITED STATES V. YOSHIDA, 303 F.3D 1145 (9TH CIR. 2002)

Section 1324(a)(1)(A)(iv) makes it a crime to (1) encourage or induce, (2) an alien to come to the United States, (3) while knowing or in reckless disregard of the fact that such coming to, entry or residence is or will be in violation of law. 8 U.S.C. § 1324(a)(1)(A)(iv). We have held that " 'to convict a person of violating section 1324(a)(1)(A), the government must show that the defendant acted with crim-

inal intent', i.e., the intent to violate United States immigration laws." *United States v. Barajas–Montiel*, 185 F.3d 947, 951 (9th Cir. 1999) (quoting *United States v. Nguyen*, 73 F.3d 887, 893 (9th Cir. 1995)).

Yoshida admits that Zhuan, Cheng, and Yue are aliens, but she claims that there is insufficient evidence that she (1) knew or recklessly disregarded the fact that the aliens were not lawfully in the United

(continued)

(continued)

States, and (2) knowingly encouraged or induced in some way their presence in the United States. Yoshida contends that in order for the jury to convict her for encouraging or inducing an alien to illegally enter the United States, the government had to prove that she gave support or help to the aliens. Yoshida argues that her mere presence at the airport and her simultaneous boarding of the plane were insufficient to establish that she committed the crimes.

Yoshida's "mere presence" at the airport and on the flight is not the only evidence offered against her. A number of events revealed at trial creates a series of inescapable inferences leading to the rational conclusion that Yoshida knowingly "encouraged and induced" Zhuan, Cheng, and Yue to enter the United States and that she did so with knowledge or in reckless disregard of the fact that their entry was in violation of law. For example, the government offered evidence that prior to boarding the flight that would take them to the United States none of the three aliens knew for which flight their tickets were valid, from which gate the plane departed, what time the plane was to depart, or how to find the departure gate. Yoshida clearly filled in these essential blanks. Thus, it was reasonable for the jury to infer that Yoshida helped the aliens enter the United States by leading them through the airport, to the correct departure gate, to the correct airplane, at the appointed time.

Furthermore, the government presented direct evidence that Yoshida concealed baggage claim checks in her underwear bearing the fake names of two of the aliens. A reasonable explanation for Yoshida's possession of the two baggage claim checks is that she obtained them by interacting with whoever in the smuggling organization obtained the boarding passes that were given to the three aliens. The fact that she hid the claim checks in her underwear is also evidence of guilty knowledge of her illegal acts.

We reject Yoshida's argument that her possession of the baggage claim checks was insufficient for a jury to conclude that she had assisted the aliens or had any link to them. While there might be some situations involving an unlucky airline passenger who innocently walks through an airport ahead of aliens, simultaneously shows up at a gate with a group of aliens, boards an aircraft at the same time as aliens, and is seated directly behind the aliens for the duration of the flight, this situation is clearly distinguishable. The fact that Yoshida concealed the baggage claims bearing the fake names of the aliens in the bulge in her underwear is strong evidence that she was not some unlucky bystander, but rather an escort for Zhuan, Cheng, and Yue.

The government also offered circumstantial evidence that Yoshida knowingly encouraged Zhuan, Cheng, and Yue to enter the United States. Yoshida led them to the flight for which the smuggling organization had provided tickets and boarding passes only an instant before Yoshida was identified as their escort. Yoshida walked quickly after the aliens caught up with her, and she timed their arrival at the boarding gate so that they could enter the aircraft without having to wait or be questioned extensively by airline employees. Though Yoshida did not speak or make eye contact with the aliens, the aliens followed her through the airport, boarded the same plane at the same time, and sat in the row ahead of her. Further, Yoshida's I–94 form indicated that her final destination was the Miyako Hotel in Las Vegas, but no business license was found for this hotel. The jury could reasonably conclude that no such hotel existed and thus, Yoshida's stated purpose for her trip was false.

From all of this evidence, a reasonable jury could easily conclude that Yoshida knowingly led the aliens to the flight and timed their arrival at the gate to assure that she and the aliens could promptly enter the aircraft without extensive questioning. It was also reasonable to conclude that Yoshida intentionally avoided overt communication with the aliens to preserve the appearance that she was not their escort. Finally, a jury could reasonably conclude that Yoshida's real purpose for the trip was to participate in the smuggling operation, rather than to stay at a nonexistent hotel. Although the government's case consisted of largely circumstantial evidence and required the jury to make reasonable inferences, circumstantial evidence can form a sufficient basis for conviction.

. . .Here, the jury had ample evidence before it to conclude, beyond a reasonable doubt, that Yoshida encouraged the aliens to enter the United States, with knowledge or in reckless disregard of the fact that the aliens' entry was in violation of law.

Questions

1. What circumstantial evidence did the prosecution offer to prove that the defendant was knowingly escorting aliens into the United States?
2. What does this case tell you about the ability to secure a criminal conviction based solely on circumstantial evidence? Do you believe after reading this case that direct evidence is more likely to result in a conviction than circumstantial evidence?

COURT OPINION 4-2 _____

UNITED STATES V. THOMAS, 763 F.3D 689 (7TH CIR. 2014)

[Chapman's] main argument is that no evidence was introduced at trial to link him, the person sitting at the defendant's table, with the "Lamar Chapman" who participated in the scheme. In this connection, he places great weight on the fact that no witness made an in-court identification of him at trial.

In essence, Chapman is arguing that identification is unique among facts required for conviction, in that (in his view) it can be established exclusively through direct, in-court testimony, and never through circumstantial evidence. That is an interesting theory, but it is not one for which we find any support in the law. Though in-court identification is preferred to prove identity, it is not required if the defendant's identity can be inferred from the circumstances. See *United States v. Prieto*, 549 F.3d 513, 525 (7th Cir. 2008). . . .

In the final analysis, the defendant's identity is nothing more or less than an element that must be established beyond a reasonable doubt in order to demonstrate guilt. That is, of course, a demanding standard, and if there were any reason to think that the "Chapman" in the courtroom was not the same "Chapman" involved in the scheme, the defense was free to make this argument, and the prosecution would have borne the risk of uncertainty. Identity, in short, is not a unique issue that can be proved only by someone pointing a finger at the defendant in the courtroom. Indeed, the Federal Rules of Evidence allow for a variety of means of proving identity: it is a permissible use of "other acts" evidence under Rule 404(b)(2), and Rule 901(b) lists several ways by which evidence can be linked to a defendant beyond direct witness testimony, including handwriting and voice comparisons, distinctive characteristics, and telephone records. If the evidence at trial was sufficient to permit jurors to find beyond a reasonable doubt that the man seated at the defense table was the same person referred to in the account of the offense, then there is no reason to overturn the jury's conviction based on the government's alleged failure to prove identity.

Judged against that standard, a reasonable jury could find that Chapman's identity as the "Chapman" identified by the evidence was established beyond a reasonable doubt. Chapman's son-in-law testified that Chapman ran one of the "businesses" identified with the scheme (the firm of Alexander, Cavanaugh, and Block), and he identified Chapman's signature on a letter to one of the targeted lenders. The son-in-law never suggested that the person on trial was not his father-in-law, nor that there was any sort of identity mix-up. If there were anything to this point, Chapman could have cross-examined his son-in-law about it. The fact that he did not is one reason for the jury to infer, reasonably, that the correct "Chapman" had been brought before the court. Further evidence supporting that inference included telephone records from AT&T that linked Chapman's phone to one used in the scheme and provided a link to his address.

. . .

Proof of identity can be especially difficult when crimes can be committed from a remote location and without direct contact with the victim—a possibility that is likely to become increasingly common as technology continues to evolve. Chapman played his role in the scheme entirely from the other end of a cell phone or via correspondence, and so it would be all but impossible for any of the victims or investigators to take the stand and say that Chapman was the person they "saw" committing the wire fraud. Someone may be able to identify the person in the courtroom as Lamar Christopher Chapman, but that would hardly solve the problem of proving that he was the Lamar Chapman involved in the scheme; it would prove only that 1) this man is named Lamar Chapman and 2) the Lamar Chapman name was used in the scheme. With such crimes, juries will often be forced to rely on circumstantial evidence to determine that the defendant has been correctly identified. That evidence may be substantial, but it does require in the end that an inference be drawn. . . .

In today's world, as this scheme illustrates, frauds can be committed without ever meeting the victims face-to-face. The evidence here was sufficient to show, for Chapman, that the government had the right person in the dock.

Questions

1. How did the court see Chapman's son-in-law's testimony as circumstantial evidence of his identity?
2. What does this opinion imply about the use of circumstantial evidence to prove all crimes committed over the Internet?

demonstrative evidence
Evidence that demonstrates a fact to a jury (e.g., a model, illustration, chart, photograph, etc.).

Demonstrative Evidence

While direct and circumstantial evidence are distinguished on the basis of how directly they prove a fact, **demonstrative evidence** is defined more by its function. The purpose of demonstrative evidence is to prove a fact by *demonstrating* the fact to the trier of fact. Models, illustrations, charts, graphs, and photographs can all be demonstrative.

The reason we distinguish demonstrative evidence from direct and circumstantial evidence is that demonstrative evidence is not meant to prove a fact in and of itself. Rather, it is offered to provide a frame of reference for the trier of fact to understand the information that is being conveyed by a witness. It is, therefore, neither direct nor circumstantial.

PRACTICE TIP

When considering the use of demonstrative evidence, care must be taken to ensure that the demonstration does not go beyond the facts proven by direct and circumstantial evidence or contain information that will unfairly prejudice the jury.

Demonstrative evidence allows a trier of fact to visualize what is being offered as evidence. An excellent example of demonstrative evidence is the *Zapruder film* that was used as evidence in the conspiracy trial of Clay Shaw. Mr. Shaw was accused of participating in a conspiracy that climaxed in the assassination of President John F. Kennedy in Dallas, Texas, in 1963. The general conclusion of those who investigated that assassination was that Lee Harvey Oswald acted alone in killing the President, but New Orleans District Attorney Jim Garrison believed that others had been involved. In order to prove this, he used the *Zapruder film*, which was shot by a Dallas citizen named Abraham Zapruder, and clearly captured the assassination, including the fatal gunshot that killed President Kennedy. Using this film, Garrison attempted to prove that more than one shooter was involved, and that therefore there had to have been a conspiracy in the assassination.

By showing the *Zapruder film* to the jury in Clay Shaw's trial, the jury was able to see firsthand what happened in the ten seconds during which the shots were fired. They were able to see President Kennedy clutching his throat, where the first bullet penetrated. They were able to see Texas governor John Connally, who was riding with the President and was also shot, react to the bullet striking him. And they were able to see the horrifying moment when the third bullet struck President Kennedy in the head. The *Zapruder film* did not, by itself, directly or even circumstantially proved that Clay Shaw was part of a conspiracy, but it provided an essential opportunity for the jury to directly visualize what was being argued by Garrison: that there were multiple shooters involved in the assassination.

Here is a brief excerpt from Jim Garrison's closing argument in the Clay Shaw trial where he discusses why the jury was shown the *Zapruder film*. His words clearly illustrate the purpose of demonstrative evidence.

> "We presented a number of eyewitnesses as well as an expert witness as well as the Zapruder film, to show that the fatal wound of the President came from the front . . .. You heard in this courtroom in recent weeks, eyewitness after eyewitness after eyewitness and, above all, you saw one eyewitness which was indifferent to power—the Zapruder film. The lens of the camera is totally indifferent to power and it tells what happened as it saw it happen . . .."[1]

Proof without Evidence

Most evidence can be classified into the types and forms described above. But there are three ways of proving a fact that eliminate the need for the presentation of evidence at all. We can think of these methods as "substitutes" for evidence, because they make it unnecessary to present evidence to prove a fact. There are three such substitutes: presumptions, stipulations, and judicial notice.

LEARNING OBJECTIVE 3
Illustrate the three methods of proving facts without evidence.

Presumptions

A **presumption** is a fact that is automatically taken as true if other facts are proven or disproven. This may sound a lot like direct evidence, but there are two important differences. First, the fact proven through a presumption might not directly relate to the evidence presented as proof. Second, presumptions are determined as a matter of law by the judge, not as a matter of fact by the jury. When a presumption exists, the court will instruct the jury that it *must* conclude the factual issue according to the presumption. It does not have any choice in the matter.

There are two types of presumptions: conclusive and rebuttable. A **conclusive presumption** means that a jury must find that one fact is true if other facts are proven, even in the face of evidence that the presumed fact is not true. An example of a conclusive presumption is the presumption of innocence. Where a jury concludes that a prosecutor has failed to meet its burden of proving guilt beyond a reasonable doubt, it *must* find the defendant not guilty.

There are very few conclusive presumptions in the American legal system. The reason for this is that facts are generally held to be proven better through evidence than they are through artificial mechanisms of law. But much more common are rebuttable presumptions.

A **rebuttable presumption** exists where a jury must accept a fact as true upon the proof of other facts, but the opposing party is permitted to present evidence to *rebut* the presumed fact, or, in other words, to prove it is not true. This means that a rebuttable presumption will favor the truth of the presumed fact, but will not deprive the other party the opportunity to prove that the presumed fact is not true.

An example of a rebuttable presumption is the **presumption of legitimacy**. Suppose a man is charged with failing to pay support for his estranged wife's child. He claims that he did not pay support because the child is not his. Paternity is now a factual issue in the case, a question that would normally be answered through blood tests or DNA analysis. But the prosecutor does not need to provide such advanced technical evidence to prove paternity if the child's mother became pregnant while she was married to the defendant. The fact of marriage creates a presumption that the defendant is the father of the child, because the law will presume that every child is legitimate. This presumption can be *only* rebutted by evidence proving that the defendant was either sterile or completely unavailable (such as being deployed overseas in the military) at the time of conception. In other words, to rebut the presumption, the defendant must prove that it was *impossible*, not just extremely unlikely, for him to be the father. Unless such evidence is presented, the jury *must* conclude that the defendant is the father of the child. While the presumption of legitimacy is rebuttable, it is only rebuttable in a very limited way. If the defendant was not sterile or unavailable at the time of conception, it would not matter if

presumption
A fact that is taken as true when another fact is proven or disproven.

LEARNING OBJECTIVE 4
Compare and contrast conclusive and rebuttable presumptions.

conclusive presumption
A presumption that requires a fact to be taken as true if other facts are proven or disproven, notwithstanding evidence that the presumed fact is not true.

rebuttable presumption
A presumption that can be overcome by presenting evidence that the presumed fact is not true.

presumption of legitimacy
A rebuttable presumption that the man who is married to a woman who gives birth to a child is the father of the child.

Table 4-1   Conclusive and Rebuttable Presumptions

Conclusive Presumptions

- *Presumption of knowledge of law*: Except where knowledge of a specific legal duty is an element of the crime with which the defendant is charged, every defendant is conclusively presumed to know what the law prohibits (*United States* v. *Spy Factory, Inc.*, 960 F.Supp. 684 (S.D.N.Y., 1997)).
- *Presumption of unfavorable testimony*: If a party who has exclusive access to a material witness fails to call him at trial, it is presumed that the witness' testimony would be unfavorable to that party (*United States* v. *Bran*, 950 F.Supp.2d 863, 875 (E.D.Va., 2013)).

Rebuttable Presumptions

- *Presumption of identity*: A person arrested pursuant to an indictment, whose name is identical to that listed in the indictment, is presumed to be the person indicted, and must produce evidence rebutting that presumption in order to be released from custody (*Smith* v. *United States*, 92 F.2d 460 (9th Cir. 1937)).
- *Presumption of sanity*: Every criminal defendant is presumed sane, and has the burden of proving otherwise by a preponderance of the evidence (*Clark* v. *Arizona*, 126 S.Ct. 2709 (2006)).
- *Presumption of continued membership in conspiracy*: Once one's membership in a conspiracy has been proven, that membership is presumed to have continued unless evidence to the contrary is produced (*United States* v. *Carvelli*, 340 F.Supp. 1295, 1304 (E.D.N.Y., 1972)).

he produced DNA tests proving that he was not the father. For the sake of the child, the presumption would still hold.

Table 4-1 illustrates a few more conclusive and rebuttable presumptions that have been applied in federal criminal cases. Always remember that just because a legal principle exists in one jurisdiction that does not mean it exists in all of them.

Stipulations

Whenever a criminal action is filed, there are usually a number of factual issues that the parties can agree upon. These usually relates to evidentiary facts that either are obvious or cannot be reasonably challenged. For example, suppose a man is shot dead by his wife, who is then charged with murder. The identity of the victim and the fact that the defendant was married to the victim are probably not facts that would seriously be challenged by the defendant, simply because they are so easy to prove. In such instances, the parties can enter into a **stipulation**, which is an agreement that certain facts are true and must be taken as true by the jury.

Stipulations usually involve facts that are relatively unimportant to the outcome of the trial. By stipulating to such facts, not only is a party saving time at trial, he/she is often generating good will with the court by making a trial move forward more quickly. It should be remembered, however, that in criminal cases the prosecutor has the burden of proving every element of the crime, and the defendant has the burden of proving every element of an affirmative defense. Stipulations allow facts to be established that will help the prosecutor or the defense meet that burden more easily.

stipulation
An agreement between a prosecutor and defense attorney that a fact is true without evidence.

PRACTICE TIP

Throughout the process of preparing a case for trial, it is useful to think about facts that neither party is really contesting, and to consider seeking a stipulation of those facts from the other side. Stipulations should always be considered in light of the benefit of having a witness present facts directly at trial as opposed to having a stipulation read to the jury.

Would a defendant ever agree to stipulate to a fact that is a key element in a case? Yes, if the defendant wished to avoid testimony that would engender sympathy or outrage in the jury. For instance, suppose a prosecutor in a rape case wishes to call the victim's child, who will testify that she saw her mother staggering home following the rape, and that she saw a wet stain on her mother's dress. Such testimony would have a powerful emotional impact on the jury, and it is very unlikely that the jury would fail to believe the child. In such a case, the defendant may stipulate that the child was present when her mother came home, that her mother was staggering as though she were in pain, and that the stain actually existed. Such a stipulation would make the child's testimony unnecessary and avoid the emotional effect the testimony would have on the jury. Of course, if the prosecution refused to accept the stipulation, then the child would have to testify, but offers to stipulate are often made in open court, and the prosecutor might anger the judge and the jury by placing the child through the trauma of testifying when it isn't necessary, despite the tactical loss.

It is often necessary to clearly limit stipulations so that they do not include facts that are actually in dispute. In the above example, the defendant would agree to stipulate that there was a stain on the mother's dress, but would not stipulate as to what that stain was, or how it got there. A stipulation that the mother was staggering and seemed to be in pain would not constitute a stipulation as to *why* the mother was in that condition. Since the child would have no firsthand knowledge about the origin or nature of the stain or the reason for her mother's behavior, the child's testimony could not include such facts anyway, so there is no reason to stipulate to them.

Stipulations can be made between the parties prior to trial or at trial. In rare instances, the parties are able to stipulate to all of the facts in a case, and submit the case to the court to be determined on those stipulated facts. In such cases, a trial is not necessary because there are literally no facts left for a jury to decide.

The following Court Opinion presents an unusual take on stipulations in criminal trials. The defendant, Leonard, stipulated at his criminal trial that there was probable cause for his arrest. After his criminal case was dismissed, Leonard filed a civil lawsuit against the Los Angeles police officer who arrested him for false imprisonment. The trial court found in favor of Leonard, holding that Leonard's stipulation in the criminal case that probable cause existed for his arrest did not apply to the civil case. On appeal, the California appellate court reversed the trial court's decision, holding that the stipulation was binding in the civil case, and providing a useful explanation of the purpose and nature of stipulations in criminal trials.

COURT OPINION 4-3

LEONARD V. CITY OF LOS ANGELES

Defendant City of Los Angeles appeals from a judgment entered against it on plaintiff's suit for false imprisonment. Following a nonjury trial the court found that defendant city had, without probable cause, wrongfully arrested and imprisoned plaintiff.

Facts

. . .We are here concerned with the effect of a stipulation that probable cause existed, made in the criminal case between the City Attorney and Leonard's defense counsel prior to the time the criminal complaint was dismissed in the municipal court. The superior court found that, when plaintiff appeared in the municipal criminal court on October 15, 1965, 'after consulting his attorney and being informed of all the consequences, plaintiff WILLIE B. LEONARD, in open Court, stipulated that his arrest was made with probable cause' and thereafter the criminal complaint was dismissed . . . .

[I]t generally is held that a stipulation between the parties may not bind a court on questions of law, and this includes legal conclusions to be drawn from admitted or stipulated facts. [citations omitted] A party to a criminal action can, however, and with binding effect, stipulate to evidentiary matters and to the existence or nonexistence of facts [citations omitted] and to any of the steps of an action or proceeding. [citations omitted] A binding stipulation admitting evidence may be made, even if such evidence is otherwise inadmissible. It also is held that, by stipulation, a criminal defendant may waive benefits granted to him by the Constitution. [citations omitted].

Whether reasonable or probable cause exists, generally presents a question of mixed fact and law. Here, however, the parties to the criminal proceedings stipulated to no facts but only that the arrest was made with probable cause . . ..

When a proposed stipulation is accepted by the other side, such stipulation becomes binding upon the court so long as it is not illegal or contrary to public policy. [citations omitted] In the criminal case pending against Leonard the only practical effect of the stipulation, had the case gone to trial, would have been to require that items seized in the search be admitted into evidence; the lawfulness or unlawfulness of Leonard's arrest would not have been relevant to proving him guilty of violating Pen. Code s 485.

We are not unaware that the stipulation undoubtedly was solicited and made in order to foreclose the very type of civil suit with which we are here involved. However, we are not now concerned with its purpose but with the right of the parties to make such a stipulation and its binding effect upon the trial court in the civil case.

. . .

Respondent at no time moved to be relieved from his stipulation and it has been ruled that "Relief from a stipulation may not be granted when requested for the first time upon appeal. The proper course is to make timely application to the court in which the stipulation was made, by a motion requesting relief, notice of which should be given to the opposing party. A hearing should then be had on affidavits and counter-affidavits." [citations omitted] Respondent never claimed the stipulation was entered into by mistake, inadvertence, fraud or misrepresentation, nor did he ask to be relieved of its effect. [citations omitted]

Our record does not disclose evidence of coercion. The mere fact that Leonard, as a criminal defendant, stipulated to probable cause no more establishes coercion than pleading guilty to a lesser included offense, pursuant to a plea bargain, establishes that such plea was coerced. [citations omitted] Furthermore, and in respect to any claimed coercion, the trial court specifically found that plaintiff authorized the stipulation 'after consulting his attorney and being informed of all the consequences.'

. . .

It is our opinion the trial court erred in holding that the stipulation was 'a conclusion of law and is not binding upon this Court in the within civil action.'

Questions

1. For what reasons might a defendant choose to stipulate to facts that the prosecutor would otherwise have to prove?
2. What factors does a court look at to determine whether a defendant's stipulation in a criminal case is valid?

Figure 4-2 Facts Judicially Noticed in Federal Courts

- Drug dealers are likely to be armed and dangerous (*United States* v. *Crespo*, 868 F.Supp. 79 (M.D.Pa. 1994)).

- A Porsche is especially vulnerable to theft in New York City (*United States* v. *Mundy*, 806 F.Supp. 373 (E.D.N.Y., 1992)).

- A particular Bronx neighborhood where shooting occurred was dangerous, particularly late at night (*Reynoso* v. *Leonardo*, 735 F.Supp. 134 (S.D.N.Y. 1990)).

- Gasoline, when ignited, not only burns but may explode (*United States* v. *Beldin*, 737 F.2d 450 (5th Cir. 1984)).

- Cocaine hydrochloride contains cocaine (*United States* v. *Gould*, 536 F.2d 216 (8th Cir. 1976)).

- The practice of sodomy is inherently inimical to the general integrity of the human person (*Dawson* v. *Vance*, 329 F. Supp. 1320 (S.D.Texas, 1971)).

- All members of the Jehovah's Witnesses religious sect are called "ministers" (*United States* v. *Brooks*, 298 F.Supp. 254 (W.D.La., 1969)).

- Innocent persons sometimes fly from the scene of a crime through fear of being apprehended as guilty parties or from an unwillingness to appear as witnesses (*Bailey* v. *United States*, 416 F.2d 1110 (D.C.D.C., 1969)).

- Cells used for solitary confinement are not designed for comfort (*Townsend* v. *Henderson*, 405 F.2d 324 (6th Cir. 1968)).

- Members of Congress rely heavily on staff in such matters as the revision of existing legislation (*United States* v. *Wallace & Tiernan, Inc.*, 349 F.2d 222 (D.C.Cir. 1965)).

Judicial Notice

There are some facts that are so well known, so beyond question, that it would be a waste of time to require a party to prove them in court. For example, no judge would require a party to prove that George Washington was the first President of the United States or that the first moon landing occurred in 1969. They can also include facts that, while not common knowledge universally, are commonly known within the area where the court sits. The authenticity of a local newspaper, or the identity of the current mayor or governor, would be examples of such facts.

Where such facts are part of the proof a party wishes to present in court, the judge can accept those facts as true without proof. This is known as **judicial notice**. If a judge takes judicial notice of a fact, the fact is established as true, and the jury must accept it as true. Judicial notice can be requested by a party before or during trial. A judge can also take judicial notice of a fact even if neither party requests it.

Figure 4-2 lists some facts of which federal courts have taken judicial notice.

It's instructive to note that not all of the facts listed in Figure 4-2 are facts that are cast in historical stone. Whether a particular neighborhood is dangerous or whether an expensive car is more likely to be stolen in one city as opposed to another are facts that can change over time. The "fact" relating to sodomy is clearly a function of the social mores and values of the mid-twentieth century, which may no longer be considered valid in today's more sexually tolerant environment. For this reason, it is important to remember that a decision by one judge to take judicial notice of a fact does not bind any other judge in another case to do the same.

judicial notice
A declaration by a court that a fact is true without supporting evidence, usually used for facts that are common knowledge.

■ FORMS OF EVIDENCE

Testimony

Testimonial evidence is evidence that comes from the mind of a witness. Testimonial evidence is usually oral and given under oath at trial, but this need not be the case. The testimony of a deceased witness can be provided

LEARNING OBJECTIVE 5
Define testimony and explain its limitations.

testimonial evidence
Evidence that comes from the mind of a witness, usually through an oral statement by the witness.

Eyewitnesses are a critical component of any criminal case, whether at the investigative or trial stage.

Source: http://www.alamy.com/ stock-photo-police-officer-takes-a-report-of-a-crime-from-a-senior-citizen-19165220.html.

Tom Carter/Alamy Stock Photo

through a transcript of the witness' deposition or a statement given under oath to an investigator. What defines testimonial evidence is that it derives solely from the perceptions and memory of a human being, which creates a number of problems we will explore in later chapters of this textbook.

> **PRACTICE TIP**
>
> When the absence of a witness from trial can be anticipated (where, for instance, a witness is suffering the final stages of a terminal illness or is critically injured), the witness' testimony can be preserved by taking his or her sworn deposition in the presence of counsel for the other party in the case, with the opportunity to cross-examine. So long as the witness is competent, the deposition can be used in lieu of live testimony at trial.

LEARNING OBJECTIVE 6
Distinguish between the use of documents and things as real evidence.

real evidence
Evidence that exists apart from the mind of a witness. Real evidence can be categorized as documentary evidence (or documents) and physical evidence (or things).

documentary evidence (document)
Evidence that proves a fact based upon information that the evidence contains or states.

physical evidence (thing)
Evidence that proves a fact based upon the physical properties of the evidence.

Real Evidence

Real evidence is evidence that exists apart from the mind of any one person. This generally breaks down into two categories: documentary evidence (or **documents**) and physical evidence (or **things**).

The difference between documents and things is not as obvious as it first appears. A document is usually thought of as a piece of paper with writing on it, but this is only one type of document. In order to understand the difference between documents and things, it is necessary to focus on where the value of the evidence lies. A document's value as evidence is based upon the information it contains, in either written or some other form. Physical evidence, on the other hand, is valuable as evidence based upon what it *is*, in other words, its physical nature.

To illustrate this difference, suppose a prosecutor wishes to introduce a videotape at trial. If the videotape is evidence because it contains a surveillance recording of the defendant committing a crime, then it is a document. If the same information were transferred to another videotape or a DVD, the value of the information as evidence would still be preserved so long as the accuracy of the copy could be established. But suppose the videotape were being introduced because the defendant used it as a weapon to strike the victim on the head. In that case, it would not matter what was on the tape. The tape could contain home movies, a feature film, or a documentary on the life cycle of Australian cicadas. It is the physical object itself, not what is on the tape, that constitutes the evidence. The videotape would therefore be considered a thing, not a document.

This illustration shows one of the major differences between documentary and physical evidence. Documentary evidence can be duplicated, but physical evidence cannot. Documentary evidence can be destroyed or damaged in some way, but if it was duplicated before it was destroyed, it can still be used as evidence. By contrast, if physical evidence is destroyed or damaged, the evidence is lost. We will address the issues surrounding the use of duplicates of documents as evidence and the preservation of physical evidence elsewhere in this textbook. For now, you should remember that documentary evidence is valuable based on what it contains, and physical evidence is valuable based on what it is.

PRACTICE TIP

Whenever you have a case that is dependent upon a piece of physical evidence, you need to take whatever steps are possible to preserve it in its original form, including accounting for every person who handled the evidence and how it was handled from the time it was first discovered until it is presented in court.

The difference between testimony and real evidence is important for a number of reasons. First, real evidence is more durable than testimonial, because it is not affected nearly as much by the passage of time. If properly preserved, a document or thing will remain as it is indefinitely, but testimony can be lost forever if a witness dies or suffers memory loss.

Another important difference between testimony and real evidence is that testimony is far more susceptible to interpretation than real evidence. A person's testimony can be affected by perception, bias, prejudice, and many other factors that have nothing to do with what really happened. Real evidence generally speaks for itself, and the jury can view the evidence firsthand (as with the *Zapruder film* mentioned earlier).

Later in this textbook, you will learn about the rules governing the introduction and use of testimony and real evidence at trial. For now, you should be aware of the basic differences that distinguish these types of evidence.

KEY TERMS

direct evidence 86	presumption of	real evidence 96
circumstantial evidence 86	legitimacy 91	documentary evidence
demonstrative evidence 90	stipulation 92	(document) 96
conclusive presumption 91	judicial notice 95	physical evidence
rebuttable presumption 91	testimonial evidence 95	(thing) 96

CHAPTER SUMMARY

- There are three types of evidence that can be offered to prove or disprove factual issues: direct evidence, circumstantial evidence, and demonstrative evidence.

- Direct evidence is evidence that directly proves a fact; if the evidence is believed, then the fact must be accepted as true.

- Circumstantial evidence requires an inference in order to prove a fact; the trier of fact can believe the evidence, and still conclude that the fact is not true.

- Demonstrative evidence illustrates a fact for the trier of fact to help clarify other evidence, such as testimony, and to give the trier of fact first-hand experience with the fact being proven.

- There are three ways in which facts can be proven without evidence: presumptions, stipulations, and judicial notice.

- Presumptions require a jury to accept a fact as true if other facts are proven or disproven; a judge decides whether a presumption applies in a given case.

- Stipulations are agreements between the parties that certain facts are true, without the need for proof.

- Judicial notice establishes facts based on common knowledge, as determined by the judge.

- There are two basic forms of evidence: testimonial and real.

- Testimonial evidence comes from the mind of a witness, and is presented in the form of oral testimony at trial.

- Real evidence consists of two types: documents (documentary evidence) and things (physical evidence).

- Documentary evidence is valuable as evidence based upon what it contains, and can be duplicated without losing its value.

- Physical evidence is valuable as evidence based upon what it is, and must be preserved in its original state in order to retain its value.

- Real evidence is more durable than testimonial evidence, and is less susceptible to interpretation, perception, bias, or prejudice.

WEB EXCURSION

1. Using Google or another search engine, find the transcript of a criminal trial. Read the testimony and determine how much of the testimony is direct evidence of the crime and how much is circumstantial. If you were on the jury, what evidence presented at the trial would you find most persuasive to support a guilty verdict?

PRACTICAL EXERCISES

1. Write down a fact about yourself. Now pretend that you need to prove that fact in court. Think about any testimony or documents you might offer to prove the fact. Write down three pieces of direct evidence, and three pieces of circumstantial evidence, that you could offer in court. Rank them according to which evidence you feel would best prove the fact about yourself.

2. For each of the following pieces of evidence, determine the type of the evidence (direct or circumstantial) and the form of the evidence (testimony, document, or thing).

   a. Defendant's mother says, "He was home that day!" (offered to establish that defendant was not at crime scene when murder occurred).

   b. Small bag of marijuana taken from defendant's front jacket pocket (offered to prove that defendant was in possession of marijuana).

   c. Photograph of the defendant dated two days prior to a rape showing defendant clean-shaven and with short hair (offered to prove that defendant was not the rapist, where the victim claimed that the rapist had long hair and a full beard).

d. Carburetor from plaintiff's pickup showing dents and score marks consistent with a small sledgehammer belonging to the defendant (offered to prove defendant guilty of smashing plaintiff's pickup with a sledgehammer).

e. Plaintiff's sister says, "I know he's lied to people all his life" (offered to prove defendant's guilt in a case of theft by deception).

f. Receipt showing that the defendant's credit card was used to purchase items at the victim's store ten minutes before robbery (offered to prove defendant was at the scene of the crime when the crime occurred).

g. Videotape from surveillance camera showing defendant taking items from the victim's store shelves and stuffing them in his trousers (offered to prove defendant's guilt on a charge of shoplifting).

h. A memo from the defendant to his boss that says, "I believe I am going to have to resign soon under a cloud of suspicion" (offered to prove defendant's guilt on a charge of embezzling money from his employer).

i. Eyewitness to an accident says, "Yeah, he must have been going at least 50" (offered to prove defendant was speeding in a 35-mile-per-hour zone).

j. Rape victim's rap sheet showing numerous previous convictions for prostitution (offered to prove defendant's claim that plaintiff consented to sexual intercourse).

ENDNOTE

1. http://www.prouty.org/closing.html (accessed May 6, 2011).

Robert Daly/Getty Images

LEARNING OBJECTIVES

After reading this chapter, the student will be able to:

1. Define what it means for evidence to be admissible.

2. Distinguish between an offer of evidence and the admission of evidence.

3. Explain a motion to suppress and how it works.

4. Illustrate the process of making, responding to, and ruling on an objection.

5. Explain how to preserve an issue for appeal, and when preservation is unnecessary.

6. Define the factors of admissibility of evidence.

7. Explain the weight formula and its elements, including probative value, credibility, and corroboration.

8. Illustrate the meaning of various burdens of proof in a criminal trial.

The Admissibility and Weight of Evidence | CHAPTER 5

■ INTRODUCTION

In Chapter 4, you learned what we mean by "evidence," and about the various types and forms that evidence can take. You also learned a basic principle of evidence: that the purpose of each piece of evidence is to influence the decision of the trier of fact regarding the factual issues raised in the case. In this chapter, you will begin to explore two concepts that determine whether, and how, evidence will affect the trier of fact's decision: the **admissibility** of evidence, and the **weight** of evidence. These concepts will be thoroughly explained throughout the remainder of this textbook, but first they must be introduced.

admissibility
The ability to present evidence to a jury by satisfying legal requirements.

weight
The degree to which evidence influences a jury's decision.

■ ADMISSIBILITY

When evidence of any type is presented to a jury, it is "admitted" into evidence. Not all evidence can be admitted; there are limitations on admissibility that will be discussed throughout this textbook. For now, you should concentrate on understanding the basic concept of admissibility.

LEARNING OBJECTIVE 1
Define what it means for evidence to be admissible.

inadmissible
Evidence that does not meet the legal requirements for admissibility and cannot be presented to a jury.

The law of evidence imposes limitations on the admissibility of evidence in order to make sure that a jury is not exposed to information that is not trustworthy or appropriate, or that would unfairly prejudice its decision on the facts of a case. Evidence that does not fall within these limitations is **inadmissible**, and cannot be presented to the jury in any form.

These limitations will often keep information away from the jury that would be helpful in determining what really happened in a case. Whenever you hear of a defendant being released or found not guilty on a "technicality," more often than not it means that the rules governing admissibility did not permit the jury to hear evidence that would have resulted in a conviction. While this may be a frustrating aspect of legal practice for prosecutors, it is essential that these rules are enforced so that juries' determinations are based on facts, not suppositions or prejudices.

Later, you will be introduced to the primary factors that determine whether evidence is admissible. Now, we will look at how admissibility is determined in a criminal trial. You should remember that the question of admissibility can be raised at any time during a criminal case, not only at trial.

LEARNING OBJECTIVE 2
Distinguish between an offer of evidence and the admission of evidence.

offer
To seek to bring evidence before a jury.

Challenging Admissibility

Offer versus Admission

First, let us be clear on the difference between what it means to **offer** evidence and what it means to *admit* evidence. Evidence is offered by a party when the party seeks to bring it before the trier of fact. Generally, the body of evidence created in a criminal trial is under the control of the prosecutor and defense counsel, since they alone decide what evidence they will offer into the record. It is not possible for either the court or the jury to consider evidence that the parties have not chosen to offer into evidence. To do so would be a violation of the proper function of the court and the jury.[1]

It is possible that a party may choose not to offer evidence that could conceivably help that party's case. For instance, a prosecutor may choose not to call one of several eyewitnesses to a crime, because he/she knows that the witness will present a poor image to the jury and could damage the overall credibility of the case. Defense counsel may choose not to introduce a document that, while supporting the defendant's case in general, would give the jury a bad opinion of the defendant's character. These decisions are *tactical* in nature, and are usually made based on the intuition and expertise of the attorneys involved in building the body of evidence.

In contrast to offering evidence, admitting evidence is a decision that lies solely within the discretion of the trial judge. That decision is not tactical at all: if a piece of evidence meets the legal requirements for admissibility laid out in subsequent chapters of this book, then the evidence must be admitted. A judge cannot refuse to admit evidence simply because he/she feels it would be a tactical mistake to offer it. Once a piece of evidence is offered, it must be admitted so long as the legal requirements of admission are met.

Having clarified the difference between offer and admission, we can turn to the procedures by which the admissibility of evidence is determined.

LEARNING OBJECTIVE 3
Explain a motion to suppress and how it works.

suppression of evidence
A determination by a judge prior to trial that evidence is not admissible.

motion to suppress
A motion filed by a defendant seeking a pretrial ruling that evidence is not admissible.

Suppression

If a piece of evidence is sure to be offered by a prosecutor at trial, the defense counsel can ask the court to **suppress** that evidence before the trial begins. A **motion to suppress** is a request by defense counsel for the court to rule on the admissibility of evidence before it is offered at trial. These motions are often based on constitutional challenges to the evidence, arising from how the evidence was obtained. These constitutional challenges are outlined in the discussion of the exclusionary rule in Chapter 6.

Once a motion to suppress is filed, the court must rule on that motion before the evidence can become part of the record. If the court grants the motion, then the evidence is deemed inadmissible. If the court denies the motion, then the evidence is not inadmissible based on the grounds set forth in the motion, although its admissibility is still open to challenge on other grounds, and the prosecutor does not have to offer evidence even if the court has decided that it is admissible.

Objections

Most questions about admissibility arise at trial, not before. If a party wishes to challenge the admissibility of a piece of evidence, he/she must do so the moment the evidence is offered by raising an *objection*. A judge will usually not, on his/her own, question the admissibility of evidence that is not objected to.

Think of an objection like hitting the "pause" button on your DVD player. It stops the presentation of evidence until the judge determines whether the evidence is admissible or not. When an objection is raised, the judge might rule on it immediately if the ruling is obvious, or he/she might ask the attorney offering the evidence to justify the offer by explaining its admissibility. If the judge or the attorneys do not wish such an argument to occur in front of the jury, any of them can call for a sidebar, which is an off-the-record discussion at the bench between the judge and counsel. If the argument may be protracted, the judge can excuse the jury from the courtroom before the argument takes place. This makes sense, because if a judge decides not to admit evidence, the jury is not permitted to hear the evidence, and so the jury shouldn't listen to discussions about admissibility when the substance of the evidence will be revealed. In any event, the judge will usually make a ruling on the objection before the trial continues.

Where an objection is based on relevance, it will be necessary for the offering attorney to explain how the evidence relates to a fact at issue in the case. This explanation is known as an "**offer of proof**," and often requires an attorney to "tip his/her hand" and reveal additional evidence he/she plans to offer. How this occurs is illustrated in Sample Trial Transcript 5-1.

> **LEARNING OBJECTIVE 4**
> Illustrate the process of making, responding to, and ruling on an objection.

offer of proof
A presentation of information about evidence that helps the judge determine its admissibility.

SAMPLE TRIAL TRANSCRIPT 5-1

Objection and Offer of Proof

Defense attorney (cross-examining a prosecution witness):	Mrs. Jones, isn't it true that you used to date the defendant, and in fact were lovers?
Prosecutor:	Objection, your Honor. That information is not relevant to this case and is therefore not admissible.
Defense attorney:	Your Honor, I am going to establish that Mrs. Jones' relationship with the defendant ended badly, to show that she is prejudiced against the defendant and would desire to see him go to jail.
Judge:	The objection is overruled.

In Sample Trial Transcript 5-1, the prosecutor raised an objection based on the fact that the proposed evidence, Mrs. Jones' previous relationship with the defendant, was not relevant to the case. Defense counsel then made an offer of proof by explaining why the evidence was relevant. Based on this dialogue, the judge overruled the objection, meaning that the judge concluded that the reason for relevance provided by the defense was sufficient to overcome the objection.

If a judge agrees with an objection and decides that evidence should not be admitted, the objection is *sustained*. If the judge disagrees with the objection and decides that the evidence *should* be admitted, the objection is *overruled*. Depending on the nature of the objection, the attorney may be able to overcome a sustained objection by presenting the evidence in a different form or by a different method, or the attorney may need to abandon the evidence completely. More information about these options will be provided later when we discuss the examination of witnesses.

Preserving Issues of Admissibility for Appeal

LEARNING OBJECTIVE 5
Explain how to preserve an issue for appeal, and when preservation is unnecessary.

error
A legal mistake committed by a trial judge.

harmless error
An error that does not meaningfully affect the outcome of the trial or a party's ability to fairly present his/her case.

prejudicial error
An error that affects a substantial right of a party by denying him/her the ability to present his/her case fully and fairly.

Defendants, and in some cases prosecutors, can file an appeal after a judgment has been entered on a verdict in a criminal case. Often, appeals are filed based on rulings of trial judges on issues of admissibility. This makes sense, since the decision to include or exclude evidence at trial can have a profound impact on the trial's outcome.

The decision whether or not to admit evidence is a question of law for the judge to determine. This means that an appeals court can substitute its own judgment for that of the judge. But for that to happen, a party who disagrees with a judge's decision must preserve the issue for appeal by giving the trial judge the opportunity to correct the mistake before it is taken up on appeal.

When a judge makes a legal mistake, or **error**, in deciding an issue of admissibility, the first question is whether the error is harmless or prejudicial. An error is **harmless** if it does not affect a substantial right of the party (F.R.Crim.P. 52(a)). In other words, if the error did not meaningfully affect the outcome of the trial or a party's ability to fairly present his/her case, then the error was harmless. A trial judge's decision, even if that decision was in error, will not be reversed on appeal if the error was harmless.

A **prejudicial error**, by contrast, is one that does affect a substantial right of the party by denying him/her the ability to present his/her case fully and fairly.[2] Prejudicial errors can be raised on appeal, and if the appellate court agrees an error was made, the erroneous decision can be reversed. But whether that happens depends on whether the issue of the trial judge's error was waived by the party by failing to properly preserve it for appeal.

Under Federal Rule of Evidence 103, prejudicial errors that admit evidence must be preserved by raising a timely objection or motion to strike the evidence from the record. Generally, this means that the party challenging the evidence must immediately object to it, or if it has already been placed on the record, ask the court to strike it. If the evidence is admitted and the presentation of evidence proceeds without any objection, then the error, if any, is waived and cannot be raised on appeal.

The objecting party must object to the admission on *specific* grounds, unless the grounds are obvious. If a party's objection, for instance, claims that offered evidence is irrelevant, and the court overrules that objection and allows the evidence, then the only question that can be raised on appeal is whether the court properly ruled on the issue of relevance. Grounds for objecting to evidence that are not raised at trial are waived (*United States* v. *Ruffin*, 575 F.2d 346, 355 (2nd Cir. 1978) (holding that defendant's objection to an IRS computer printout solely on the grounds of relevance did not allow him to raise on appeal the printout's inadmissibility on grounds of hearsay)).

PRACTICE TIP
When preparing a case for trial, identify any possible objections that might be raised to evidence that the other side may be offering, so those objections can be immediately raised should that evidence be presented.

When the ruling excludes evidence, then the party offering the evidence must preserve the issue for appeal by making an offer of proof (see above). In other words, whether evidence is being admitted or excluded, the parties must give the trial judge the opportunity to make a correct ruling based on the legal arguments presented in the objection or the evidentiary basis presented in the offer of proof.

Rule 103 provides an exception to the requirement of an objection or offer of proof where an error constitutes **"plain error."** This rule provides an appellate court with the ability to review an error on appeal even if it was not properly preserved at trial, if the appellate court concludes that the error is so substantial that it "seriously affects the fairness, integrity, or public reputation of judicial proceedings" (*United States* v. *Keigue*, 318 F.3d. 437, 445 (2nd Cir. 2003), *quoting United States* v. *Cotton*, 535 U.S. 625, 122 S.Ct. 1781, 1785, 152 L.Ed.2d 860 (2002)).

In *Keigue*, the trial judge during sentencing applied the 1998 federal sentencing guidelines rather than the 2001 guidelines applicable when the defendant was sentenced. The new guidelines were published only one month before sentencing, but were clearly applicable to the defendant's case (*Id.* at 439–440). Under both sets of guidelines, the defendant's offense and prior history scores were the same, but the applicable sentence under the 1998 guidelines was 12 to 18 months, whereas the sentence under the 2001 guidelines was 10 to 16 months (*Id.* at 440). The defendant did not object to the use of the 1998 guidelines at his sentencing, but raised the issue on appeal (*Id.*).

plain error
A prejudicial error that seriously affects the fairness, integrity, or public reputation of judicial proceedings, and that does not need to be preserved for appeal.

COURT OPINION 5-1

UNITED STATES V. KEIGUE, 318 F.3d. 437 (2nd Cir. 2003)

The government argues that Keigue's failure to bring the expired Guidelines issue to the attention of the district court requires that we undertake a traditional plain error analysis, which precludes us from correcting an error unless it affects a defendant's "substantial rights." . . . For the purpose of our inquiry, we assume without deciding that traditional plain error analysis applies.

To establish plain error, a court must find "1) an error, 2) that is plain, 3) that affects substantial rights." *United States v. Gordon*, 291 F.3d 181, 191 (2d Cir. 2002). Under this analysis, there must be an "'error,' or deviation from a legal rule which has not been

waived." . . . That error is considered "plain" if it is "'clear' or 'obvious' at the time of appellate consideration." *Gordon*, 291 F.3d at 193 (citation omitted). Such an error affects the "'substantial rights' [of a defendant] if [it] is 'prejudicial' and 'affect[s] the outcome of the district court proceedings.'" *Id.* (citation omitted). If an error meets these first three requirements, "the Court engages in a fourth consideration: whether or not to exercise its discretion to correct the error. The plain error should be corrected only if it 'seriously affects the fairness, integrity, or public reputation of judicial proceedings.'" *Id.* at 191 . . .

(continued)

(continued)

1. An Error Was Committed

The Sentencing Guidelines explicitly mandate that a court use the version of the Guidelines in effect on the date of the defendant's sentencing. . . . Consequently, it was error for the district court to calculate Keigue's offense level using the expired version of the Guidelines in effect on the date the offense was committed.

2. The Error Was Plain and Affected Substantial Rights

We have held that where there is "no *ex post facto* problem, it [is] plain error to fail to apply" the version of the Guidelines in effect at the time of the sentencing. *Keller*, 58 F.3d at 893. At the same time, under other circumstances, we have declined to find plain error in instances where a defendant could have received the same sentence in the absence of the alleged error, reasoning that such an error does not affect the "substantial rights" of a defendant. . . .

[W]e believe that, had the correct range been used, there is a strong likelihood that the district court's intention to sentence Keigue in the "middle" of the applicable range would have resulted in his receiving a sentence of 13 months rather than the 16 months actually imposed under what all parties agree was the incorrect Guidelines range. Because we believe Keigue received a longer sentence than the court intended to give, we conclude that his "substantial rights" were affected. *See Martinez-Rios*, 143 F.3d at 676.

3. Left Uncorrected, the Error Seriously Affects the Fairness, Integrity and Public Reputation of Judicial Proceedings

The effect on Keigue's substantial rights does not end our inquiry. "Rule 52(b) is permissive, not mandatory."

United States v. Olano, 507 U.S. 725, 735, 113 S.Ct. 1770, 123 L.Ed.2d 508 (1993). While we have authority to correct a forfeited error that is "plain" and affects the "substantial rights" of a defendant, we are not required to exercise that authority. *See id.* As the Supreme Court recently confirmed, "an appellate court may . . . exercise its discretion to notice a forfeited error, but only if [ ] the error seriously affects the fairness, integrity, or public reputation of judicial proceedings." *United States v. Cotton*, 535 U.S. 625, 122 S.Ct. 1781, 1785, 152 L.Ed.2d 860 (2002) (internal citations and quotation marks omitted). Here, we choose to exercise our discretion and correct the error. To allow an oversight like the one described above to remain uncorrected and increase the length of a defendant's sentence would seriously undermine the public's confidence in the judicial process. . . .

Accordingly, we hold that where, as here, the record permits the inference that a defendant *would* have received a different, shorter sentence absent the unobjected-to error, the defendant's substantial rights have been affected within the meaning of Rule 52(b). . . .

Here, because we have reason to believe that, absent the error, the district court's stated intention to sentence Keigue in the "middle" of the sentencing range would have led to a shorter sentence under the lower range, we conclude that he has established plain error.

Questions

1. What "substantial right" of the defendant was implicated in the trial court use of expired sentencing guidelines?
2. How did the court address the fact that Keigue's sentence fell within the appropriate sentencing range under both the 1998 and 2001 guidelines?

---

reverse
The overturning of the decision of a trial court where prejudicial error has occurred.

affirm
Permitting a trial court's decision to stand where no prejudicial error has occurred.

remand
The return of a case to a trial court for further proceedings in compliance with an appellate court's interpretation of the law.

Outcome of an Appeal on Issue of Admissibility

When an appellate court finds that a trial judge has committed prejudicial error relating to an issue of credibility, then the appellate court will **reverse**, or overturn, that decision. Otherwise, the appellate court will **affirm** the decision, and allow it to stand.

A reversal can lead to several different outcomes on appeal depending on the nature of the error and the impact it had on the trial. If an appellate court reverses a decision made at trial that related to the admissibility of the evidence and prejudiced the result of the trial, then the most common outcome is for the appellate court to **remand** the case to the trial court, and order that a new trial be held with an entirely new jury. If, however, the judge's error occurred in denying a motion to suppress evidence that was made prior to trial and immediately appealed, then the appellate court will remand the case and order the case to proceed to trial. If the judge's error occurred during sentencing (as occurred in *Keigue, supra*), then the appellate court will remand the case for a new sentencing hearing, but not a new trial.[3]

The Factors of Admissibility

There are eight **factors** that determine whether evidence is admissible. You should think of these factors as tests of admissibility. A piece of evidence is admissible if, and only if, it passes all eight tests (see Figure 5-1). Each of these factors will be discussed in much more detail later.

- *Competence*: This factor applies mainly to testimony. A witness is competent to testify if he or she is capable of communicating the truth and understands the duty all witnesses have to tell the truth.
- *Authenticity*: This factor applies to real evidence. A piece of evidence is authentic if it is what the party offering it claims it to be. The authenticity of a piece of evidence must be established before it can be admitted at trial.
- *Relevance*: To be admitted, evidence must be relevant to an issue in the case. Relevance means that the evidence tends to prove or disprove a fact that is an issue in the case. Relevant evidence can still be excluded based on three exceptions:
  - *Overly prejudicial*: Even if evidence is competent or authentic and relevant, there are times when the probative value of the evidence is outweighed by the prejudicial effect it would have on the jury. Such evidence is not admissible.
  - *Cumulative*: Evidence that merely duplicates other evidence without adding anything to the jury's understanding of the case is not admissible.
  - *Against public policy*: There are times when evidence is not admissible, not because there is anything wrong with the evidence itself, but because its disclosure would cause harm to society.
- *Hearsay*: This is evidence that contains statements by persons who are not on the witness stand. If the evidence is being offered to prove that those statements are true, then the statements are generally not admissible, but there are a number of exceptions to this rule.
- *Privilege*: The law protects certain relationships, such as the attorney–client relationship or the physician–patient relationship, from the disclosure of information that is obtained because of that relationship. This protection is known as privilege, and privileged information is not admissible in court.

LEARNING OBJECTIVE 6
Define the factors of admissibility of evidence.

factors of admissibility
The factors that determine whether evidence is admissible. They are competence, authenticity, relevance, hearsay, prejudice, privilege, cumulativeness, and public policy.

Figure 5-1 The Factors of Admissibility

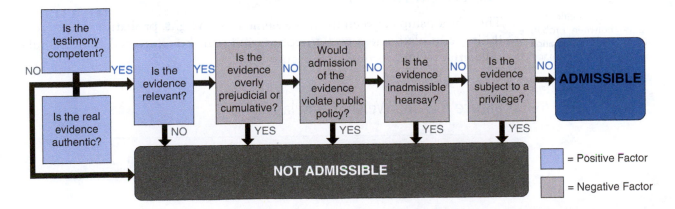

Juries are responsible to determine the credibility of witnesses and weight of other evidence based on their experience and common sense.

Source: https://us.fotolia.com/id/82348830.

Bikeriderlondon/Shutterstock

■ WEIGHT

Determining whether a plaintiff or prosecutor has met his/her burden of proof is not merely a matter of how many pieces of evidence are on either side. Think of a balance scale that has five one-ounce weights on the left side, and one ten-ounce weight on the right side. Will the scale tip toward the left because that side has a greater number of weights? Of course not. It will tip to the right because that side has the greatest total weight. In the same way, the testimony of one witness can outweigh the testimony of five witnesses, if that one witness' testimony is given more weight by the jury.

This principle was put to the test in the case of *United States* v. *Goodale*, where a defendant was convicted of federal sexual abuse charges, each conviction based on the uncorroborated testimony of a single witness, the victim. After a verdict of guilty was returned, the defendant sought to have his conviction overturned, claiming that the jury did not have sufficient evidence to convict.

What determines how much weight a piece of evidence has? The weight of evidence depends on three factors: its probative value, its credibility, and its corroboration.

The Weight Formula

The relationship between the three elements of weight, probative value, credibility, cumulativeness and corroboration, can be expressed in a formula called **the weight formula** (see Figure 5-2).

LEARNING OBJECTIVE 7
Explain the weight formula and its elements, including probative value, credibility, and corroboration.

the weight formula
A formula that loosely demonstrates the association between probative value, credibility, and corroboration in determining the weight of evidence.

Figure 5-2 The Weight Formula

Weight = (Probative value + Credibility) * Corroboration

COURT OPINION 5-2

UNITED STATES V. GOODALE, 738 F.3d 917 (8th Cir. 2013)

Goodale maintains M.R.'s testimony is insufficient to prove Counts 1 and 3—that Goodale transported him across state lines to engage in sexual activity before the age of 12. Goodale contends Z.G.'s testimony is insufficient to prove Count 4—that Goodale transported him in interstate commerce to engage in sexual activity before the age of 18. This court reviews the denial of a motion for judgment of acquittal de novo, "viewing the evidence in the light most favorable to the government, drawing all reasonable inferences in favor of the jury's verdict, and reversing only if no reasonable jury could have found the defendant guilty." *United States v. Gregoire*, 638 F.3d 962, 968 (8th Cir. 2011).
. . .

At trial, M.R. testified that he traveled from Iowa to Minnesota with Goodale and engaged in sexual conduct in Minnesota when he was younger than 12. [Transcript of testimony omitted.]

Similarly, Z.G. testified that he engaged in sexual acts with Goodale beginning when he was seven. He also testified that he engaged in sexual acts with Goodale in Minnesota. Z.G. did not remember the age or date on which he began engaging in sexual acts with Goodale in Minnesota.

Reviewing the sufficiency of the evidence, "[i]t is axiomatic that [this court does] not pass upon the credibility of witnesses or the weight to be given their testimony." *United States v. Clay*, 618 F.3d 946, 950 (8th Cir. 2010). "Credibility determinations are uniquely within the province of the trier of fact, and 'are entitled to special deference.'" *Sullivan v. Minnesota*, 818 F.2d 664, 666 (8th Cir. 1987), *quoting United States v. Manning*, 787 F.2d 431, 435 (8th Cir. 1986). "[A] victim's testimony alone is sufficient to persuade a reasonable jury of the defendant's guilt beyond a reasonable doubt." *United States v. Gabe*, 237 F.3d 954, 961 (8th Cir. 2001) (upholding a conviction for abusive sexual contact based on the testimony of the teenage victim), *citing United States v. Wright*, 119 F.3d 630, 633–34 (8th Cir. 1997). . . .

Here, the jury heard lengthy, detailed testimony from M.R. and Z.G., both of whom were 13 at the time of trial. M.R. testified that Goodale began engaging in sexual conduct with him when he was eight. He further testified that he engaged in sexual acts in Minnesota when he was nine or ten. On cross-examination, M.R. stated that he remembered this age "[b]ecause when I was eight was the first time that I met Mike and a year after we started going to Minnesota

and hanging out there." Z.G. similarly testified that Goodale first performed sex acts on him when he was seven. Although Z.G. did not remember when Goodale began taking him to Minnesota, he did remember that Goodale engaged in sexual activity with him in Rochester and Albert Lea. Z.G. also testified he saw sex acts between Goodale and M.R. in Minnesota. According to both boys, Goodale expected sexual touching when they traveled to hotels, and most of the time it occurred. This testimony establishes the elements of Counts 1, 3, and 4. *See Wright*, 119 F.3d at 634 (noting that had the child victim "been the government's sole witness against Wright, it would have been perfectly proper for the jury to credit [her] testimony and convict Wright"), *citing United States v. Martinez*, 958 F.2d 217, 218 (8th Cir. 1992).

The jury also heard substantial evidence corroborating M.R. and Z.G. Receipts and testimony from hotel employees showed that Goodale stayed with a child at hotels in Rochester, Albert Lea, Austin, and Bloomington (four cities M.R. said he traveled to with Goodale and engaged in sexual activity). Some of these trips occurred before M.R. turned 12. Two jailhouse cooperators testified that Goodale admitted to having sex with his nephew in Minnesota hotels. Both remembered Goodale stating he had taken his nephew to the Mall of America. One cooperator also said Goodale admitted to giving boys video games in exchange for sex. Goodale's father testified that Goodale stayed at hotels in Minnesota with M.R. and Z.G., and that the boys slept in the same bed with him when they stayed the night at his house. Finally, text messages sent and received from Goodale's cell phone showed him communicating with M.R. and Z.G. about trips to Minnesota.

In sum, this evidence was sufficient to support the jury's verdicts on Counts 1, 3, and 4. The district court properly denied the motion for judgment of acquittal and the motion for a new trial.

Questions

1. What does this case tell us about the jury's power to assign weight to the testimony of a single witness?
2. How does the corroborative testimony, none of which proved any of the elements of the crimes Goodale was charged with, support the court's decision that the evidence was sufficient to support the jury's verdict?

This is, of course, an inexact formula at best, since it includes factors that will vary from one juror to another. But on the whole this formula accurately depicts the relationship between these three factors in determining the weight that a jury will give to evidence.

Probative Value

probative value
The degree to which a piece of evidence proves the fact it is offered to prove.

Probative value means how well a piece of evidence proves a fact. Evidence in a murder case might include a signed confession by the defendant, the murder weapon, a piece of cloth found at the murder scene that matches the defendant's jacket, and a Pepsi can, also found at the murder scene. Which of these pieces of evidence has the greatest probative value? Obviously, the confession, because it is direct evidence that the defendant did, in fact, commit the murder. The murder weapon is also very probative, particularly if it yielded fingerprints that match the defendant's. The cloth from the defendant's jacket is not as probative, because it proves only that the defendant was at the murder scene, but not that he committed the murder. The Pepsi can is hardly probative at all, even if it were proven that the defendant liked Pepsi and drank it frequently, because a lot of people drink Pepsi and the can could have belonged to anyone.

Notice how the probative value of evidence can vary depending on other evidence. The murder weapon is more probative with fingerprints than without. Likewise, if the defendant's fingerprints are found on the Pepsi can, its probative value is much greater. How much probative value the jury assigns to a particular piece of evidence is usually determined in light of all of the evidence taken together, not each piece in isolation.

Credibility

credibility
The degree to which a witness or piece of evidence is believed by the jury.

The **credibility** of evidence has to do with whether it is believable. This is usually determined by a jury based on their experiences, upbringing, personalities, and even personal biases. Much of the work a lawyer does in preparing a case involves making sure that the evidence that is presented (particularly testimony) is believed by the jury. Later in this text, you will be learning about the factors that make evidence credible. For now, understand that evidence that is not believed is obviously not going to have much weight on a jury's decision.

As the *Goodale* case, above, demonstrates, credibility is a matter solely for the jury to decide, not the judge or any appellate court. Figure 5-3 contains the Model Jury Instructions recommended by the New York court system for informing the jury of its power to determine credibility and the factors it might take into account in weighing that credibility.

Corroboration

corroboration
The degree to which the credibility of a piece of evidence is supported by other credible evidence.

You previously learned what it means for evidence to be **corroborative**. Corroborative evidence supports other evidence without duplicating it. The more a piece of evidence is supported by corroborating evidence, the greater weight it is given by a jury.

While corroboration is usually a factor relating to credibility and weight, there are times when it can also affect the admissibility of evidence. There are some principles of law that require evidence to be corroborated before it can lead to a conclusion of guilt. Article III of the U.S. Constitution, for example, requires that an accusation of treason be corroborated by two witnesses.

Figure 5-3 New York Model Jury Instructions on Credibility

Credibility of Witnesses

As judges of the facts, you alone determine the truthfulness and accuracy of the testimony of each witness. You must decide whether a witness told the truth and was accurate, or instead, testified falsely or was mistaken. You must also decide what importance to give to the testimony you accept as truthful and accurate. It is the quality of the testimony that is controlling, not the number of witnesses who testify.

Accept in Whole or in Part (Falsus in Uno)

If you find that any witness has intentionally testified falsely as to any material fact, you may disregard that witness's entire testimony. Or, you may disregard so much of it as you find was untruthful, and accept so much of it as you find to have been truthful and accurate.

Credibility factors

There is no particular formula for evaluating the truthfulness and accuracy of another person's statements or testimony. You bring to this process all of your varied experiences. In life, you frequently decide the truthfulness and accuracy of statements made to you by other people. The same factors used to make those decisions, should be used in this case when evaluating the testimony.

In General

Some of the factors that you may wish to consider in evaluating the testimony of a witness are as follows:

Did the witness have an opportunity to see or hear the events about which he or she testified?

Did the witness have the ability to recall those events accurately?

Was the testimony of the witness plausible and likely to be true, or was it implausible and not likely to be true?

Was the testimony of the witness consistent or inconsistent with other testimony or evidence in the case?

Did the manner in which the witness testified reflect upon the truthfulness of that witness's testimony?

To what extent, if any, did the witness's background, training, education, or experience affect the believability of that witness's testimony?

Did the witness have a bias, hostility or some other attitude that affected the truthfulness of the witness's testimony?

Motive

You may consider whether a witness had, or did not have, a motive to lie.

If a witness had a motive to lie, you may consider whether and to what extent, if any, that motive affected the truthfulness of that witness's testimony.

If a witness did not have a motive to lie, you may consider that as well in evaluating the witness's truthfulness.

Interest/Lack of Interest

You may consider whether a witness has any interest in the outcome of the case, or instead, whether the witness has no such interest.

You are not required to reject the testimony of an interested witness, or to accept the testimony of a witness who has no interest in the outcome of the case.

You may, however, consider whether an interest in the outcome, or the lack of such interest, affected the truthfulness of the witness's testimony.

Previous Criminal Conduct

You may consider whether a witness has been convicted of a crime or has engaged in criminal conduct, and if so, whether and to what extent it affects the truthfulness of that witness's testimony.

You are not required to reject the testimony of a witness who has been convicted of a crime or has engaged in criminal conduct, or to accept the testimony of a witness who has not.

You may, however, consider whether a witness's criminal conviction or conduct has affected the truthfulness of the witness's testimony.

Inconsistent Statements

You may consider whether a witness made statements at this trial that are inconsistent with each other. You may also consider whether a witness made previous statements that are inconsistent with his or her testimony at trial.

(continued)

Figure 5-3 *(continued)*

If a witness has made such inconsistent statements, you may consider whether and to what extent they affect the truthfulness or accuracy of that witness's testimony here at this trial.

The contents of a prior inconsistent statement are not proof of what happened. You may use evidence of a prior inconsistent statement only to evaluate the truthfulness or accuracy of the witness's testimony here at trial.

Consistency

You may consider whether a witness's testimony is consistent with the testimony of other witnesses or with other evidence in the case.

If there were inconsistencies by or among witnesses, you may consider whether they were significant inconsistencies related to important facts, or instead were the kind of minor inconsistencies that one might expect from multiple witnesses to the same event?

Source: Criminal Jury Instructions. (n.d.). Retrieved from http://www.nycourts.gov/judges/cji/1-General/cjigc.shtml.

Corroboration is also required when guilt is based on a defendant's out-of-court confession. The so-called "corroboration rule" guarantees that convictions will not be based on confessions that may be the result of coercion or, even if voluntary, may not reflect the truth. In *United States v. Ramirez*, the Sixth Circuit applied the corroboration rule to determine the propriety of a guilty verdict based on the defendant's extrajudicial statements relating to her involvement in a conspiracy.

COURT OPINION 5-3

UNITED STATES V. RAMIREZ, 635 F.3d 249 (6th Cir. 2011)

A defendant cannot be convicted based solely on her uncorroborated statements or confessions. *Smith v. United States*, 348 U.S. 147, 153–54, 75 S.Ct. 194, 99 L.Ed. 192 (1954). The purpose of this rule is to avoid errors in convictions based upon untrue confessions and to promote sound law enforcement by requiring police investigations to extend their efforts beyond the words of the accused. *Wong Sun v. United States*, 371 U.S. 471, 489, 83 S.Ct. 407, 9 L.Ed.2d 441 (1963); *Smith*, 348 U.S. at 153, 75 S.Ct. 194. This rule also ensures that an appropriate investigation is done prior to prosecution. See *Smith*, 348 U.S. at 152, 75 S.Ct. 194.

The corroboration rule "prevents errors in convictions based upon untrue confessions alone." *United States v. Davis*, 459 F.2d 167, 170 (6th Cir. 1972). Though a statement may not be involuntary within the meaning of the exclusionary rule, its reliability may still be suspect if it is extracted from a person under the pressure of police investigation because his or her words may reflect the strain and confusion of the situation, rather than a clear reflec-

tion of the past. *Smith*, 348 U.S. at 153, 75 S.Ct. 194. The government may provide corroboration by introducing substantial evidence apart from the defendant's admissions. *Id.* at 157, 75 S.Ct. 194. "An out-of-court admission is adequately corroborated if the corroborating evidence 'supports the essential facts admitted sufficiently to justify a jury inference of their truth.'" *United States v. Pennell*, 737 F.2d 521, 527 (6th Cir. 1984) (*quoting Opper v. United States*, 348 U.S. 84, 92–93, 75 S.Ct. 158, 99 L.Ed. 101 (1954)). Corroborative evidence need not establish each element of the offense. *Opper*, 348 U.S. at 93, 75 S.Ct. 158. In other words, the "corroborative evidence does not have to prove the offense beyond a reasonable doubt, or even by a preponderance, as long as there is substantial independent evidence that the offense has been committed, and the evidence as a whole proves beyond a reasonable doubt that defendant is guilty." *Davis*, 459 F.2d at 171 (*quoting Smith*, 348 U.S. at 156, 75 S.Ct. 194).

The court serves as a gatekeeper with regard to whether an admission by the defendant has been

(continued)

(continued)

sufficiently corroborated to ensure its reliability. *United States v. Bryce*, 208 F.3d 346, 355 (2d Cir. 1999). "[O]ne available mode of corroboration is for the independent evidence to bolster the confession itself and thereby prove the offense 'through' the statements of the accused." *Smith*, 348 U.S. at 156, 75 S.Ct. 194. A confession is adequately corroborated where "[e]xtrinsic proof . . . fortifies the truth of the confession, without independently establishing the crime charged." *United States v. Ybarra*, 70 F.3d 362, 365 (5th Cir. 1995). So long as portions of the defendant's statement are corroborated by "substantial independent evidence" that "tend[s] to establish the trustworthiness of the statement," then the elements of the crime may be established by the defendant's statements. *Opper*, 348 U.S. at 93, 75 S.Ct. 158; *see also United States v. Brown*, 617 F.3d 857, 863 (6th Cir. 2010) (finding that "independent corroboration of one part of the statement may corroborate the entire statement").

When determining whether the defendant's statements were corroborated and whether the evidence as a whole was sufficient, a court must view the evidence in the light most favorable to the United States. See *Pennell*, 737 F.2d at 537. The court must refrain from "weigh[ing] the evidence, mak[ing] credibility determinations, or substitut[ing] [its] judgment for the jury's verdict." *United States v. Crossley*, 224 F.3d 847, 855 (6th Cir. 2000). A court will not lightly disturb a jury's verdict based on the corroboration rule because the "rule does not infringe on the province of the primary finder of facts." *Smith*, 348 U.S. at 153, 75 S.Ct. 194. Furthermore, an aggressive corroboration requirement could result in "the restrictions it imposes surpass[ing] the dangers which gave rise to them." *Id.*

Questions

1. Why are courts concerned about allowing juries to hear out-of-court confessions without evidence corroborating the truth of the confession?
2. What does the court mean by calling itself the "gatekeeper" with respect to the corroboration of confessions?

Even where corroboration is not *required* for a conviction to be based on evidence, corroboration adds greatly to the weight of evidence by making it more likely that the evidence is true. In this way, corroboration enhances both the credibility and probative value of the evidence being corroborated. This is why, in the weight formula described above, corroboration is shown as a multiplier for the combined factors of probative value and credibility.

PRACTICE TIP

Whenever testimony or real evidence is being considered as evidence in a case, its intrinsic credibility and probative value should be assessed to determine whether corroborative evidence will be needed to provide the evidence with sufficient weight.

■ BURDEN OF PROOF

To prove a fact in court, it is not enough to present *some* evidence that the fact is true. Rather, the party who is trying to prove the fact must present enough evidence to meet the **burden of proof** imposed by law. This means that the evidence that proves that the fact is true must *outweigh* evidence that the fact is not true. The law defines various burdens of proof for different purposes within criminal law.

LEARNING OBJECTIVE 8
Illustrate the meaning of various burdens of proof in a criminal trial.

burden of proof
The level of proof required in order to prove a fact under the law.

beyond a reasonable doubt
The burden of proof applicable in criminal cases, in which evidence of guilt so outweighs evidence against guilt that no reasonable person could doubt the defendant's guilt.

The highest burden of proof is required to prove that a defendant is guilty of a crime. Guilt must be proven **beyond a reasonable doubt**. In other words, evidence of guilt must outweigh evidence of innocence to such an extent that no reasonable person could doubt that the defendant is, in fact, guilty. The proof of each element of a crime must meet this standard. If just one element of the crime is not proven beyond a reasonable doubt, then the defendant must be found not guilty.

By contrast, defendants who claim a defense (such as self-defense or insanity) must present evidence supporting that defense that *slightly* outweighs evidence against the defense. This standard is called a **preponderance of the evidence**.

preponderance of the evidence
The burden of proof application to criminal defenses, in which evidence supporting the defendant must slightly outweigh evidence against the defense.

To help illustrate how admissibility and weight affect the outcome of a trial, think of a trial as a standard balance scale (not a very original metaphor, but a good one). With this type of scale, the more weight placed on one side, the more the scale tips to that side. If you put a feather on one side and a rock on the other, the scale will tip toward the rock. You could even put two or three or ten feathers on one side, and one rock will tip the balance the other way. It is the weight of the items, not their number, that determines how the scale will tip. If the combined weight on one side exceeds the combined weight on the other side, the scale will tip. How far it will tip depends on the difference in the combined weight on each side.

The same holds true with the scale of justice. Evidence that is introduced at trial is placed on one side of the scale or the other, depending on whether it tends to prove or disprove guilt (in criminal cases) or liability (in civil cases). In order to be placed on the scale, evidence must be *admissible*. This means that the evidence must satisfy the requirements to be presented to the trier of fact for consideration. Whether evidence is admissible is a question of law to be decided by the judge.

The scale of justice is evenly balanced.

Source: http://www.123rf.com/search.php?word=scales+of+justice&imgtype=&Submit=+&t_word=&t_lang=en&orderby=0&sti=lrvr03tndk73aop5oo|&mediapopup=10539380.

Figure 5-4 Burdens of Proof

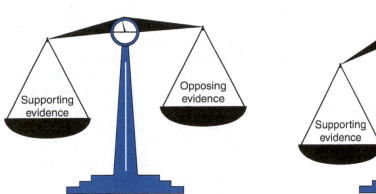
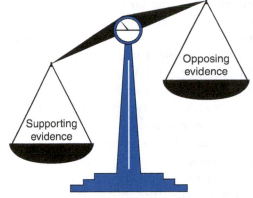

Preponderance of the evidence   **Beyond a reasonable doubt**

Once the evidence is admitted (placed on the scale), the degree to which that evidence tips the scale one way or the other is determined by its *weight* (just like on a real scale). Weight is determined by the trier of fact, based on the factors discussed above.

For now, remember these basic rules about the admissibility and weight: admissibility determines whether the evidence goes onto the scale, and weight determines how much the evidence will tip the scale one way or the other. Figure 5-4 graphically illustrates the difference between the "beyond a reasonable doubt" and "preponderance of the evidence" burdens of proof.

KEY TERMS

admissibility 101	harmless error 104	probative value 110
weight 101	prejudicial error 104	credibility 110
inadmissible 102	plain error 105	corroboration 110
offer 102	reverse 106	burden of proof 113
suppression of evidence 102	affirm 106	beyond a reasonable
motion to suppress 102	remand 106	doubt 114
offer of proof 103	factors of admissibility 107	preponderance of the
error 104	the weight formula 108	evidence 114

CHAPTER SUMMARY

- Evidence affects the outcome of a trial (civil or criminal) based on the admissibility of the evidence and the weight assigned to it by the jury.
- A judge determines whether evidence offered by the parties is admissible, meaning that it can be presented to the jury.
- The admissibility of evidence can be determined before trial through a motion to suppress.

- At trial, a party opposing the admission of evidence must object to that evidence.
- A party supporting the admission of evidence may be required to make an offer of proof explaining why the evidence is admissible.
- When a court rules on the admissibility of evidence, its decision can be raised on appeal if it was prejudicial, meaning that it affected the outcome of the case.

- Prejudicial error in the admission of evidence cannot be reversed by an appellate court unless the issue was preserved by raising an objection or making an offer of proof at trial, unless the error constitutes "plain error."
- Generally, evidence is admissible if it is competent, authentic, and relevant, and if it is not overly prejudicial or cumulative, its admission will not violate public policy, it is not inadmissible hearsay, and it is not privileged.
- Whether evidence is admissible is a question of law, determined by the judge.
- "Weight" refers to the *actual* effect that admissible evidence will have on the outcome of the trial, based on the probative value, corroboration, and credibility of the evidence.
- What weight will be given to a piece of evidence is determined by the trier of fact, which in criminal cases is usually a jury.
- Weight is determined by the probative value a jury assigns to a piece of evidence, as well as the credibility of the evidence as determined by the jury.
- Corroborative evidence increases the probative value and credibility of evidence, thereby adding additional weight to the evidence.
- The prosecutor in a criminal case has a burden of proving guilt beyond a reasonable doubt, meaning that the scale must tip substantially in favor of guilt.

WEB EXCURSION

1. Using Google or another search engine, find the transcript for a criminal trial, preferably in your own jurisdiction. Read the transcript and then answer the following questions:
   a. How often were objections made?
   b. How often were they sustained?
   c. Are you satisfied with the way the objections were ruled upon by the court?
   d. Did any of the objections seem unnecessary?
   e. If you were on the jury, how would you assess the credibility and probative value of the testimony?
   f. What witness would you give the greatest weight to when deciding on a verdict?

PRACTICAL EXERCISE

1. Carefully read the following factual scenario, and then answer the questions that follow:
   Raymond has been accused of murdering his girlfriend, Pauline. The prosecutor's theory is that Raymond shot Pauline in revenge for breaking up with him. Her body was found slumped over the desk in her office, with a single bullet wound in her temple. There were no eyewitnesses (or earwitnesses) to the shooting. The coroner estimates that Pauline died between 6:00 P.M. and 9:00 P.M. A .357 magnum handgun was found lying on the floor in front of the desk. Ballistics reports have proven that this was the weapon used to kill Pauline, and a standard check of the state's gun register indicates that Raymond is the gun's registered owner. A forensic lab examined fingerprints taken from the gun. The report concludes that the fingerprints probably did not (repeat: DID NOT) belong to Raymond. A search of Pauline's desk turned up a photograph of her and Raymond kissing in a pay photo booth on the boardwalk at Wildwood Beach. One witness, Pauline's secretary Harold, has given a sworn statement to the effect that he saw Raymond walking into Pauline's office building at 5:00 P.M., looking very upset. Another witness, Raymond's mother Helen, has given a sworn statement that Raymond showed up at her house, 30 miles from Pauline's office, at 5:30 P.M. on the day of the murder, and remained with her until 9:30 that night.
   a. Make a list of each piece of evidence mentioned in this scenario that indicates that Raymond is *guilty* of murdering Pauline.
   b. Make a list of each piece of evidence that indicates that Raymond is *not guilty* of murdering Pauline.

c. Is there any evidence mentioned in the scenario that does not appear on either list? If so, explain why you did not include that evidence on either list.

d. Pretend you are a juror who has heard this evidence at trial. How would you decide the issue of Raymond's guilt?

ENDNOTES

1. If you have ever seen the movie "*Twelve Angry Men*," you have seen an example of how this principle can be violated. In that movie, one of the jurors comes into the jury room with a piece of evidence (a switchblade) that neither the prosecutor nor the defense offered into the record. While the moment made for a dramatic twist to the story line in that movie, the use of evidence not offered by the parties would have resulted in a mistrial in any real court of law.

2. There are few federal cases defining what constitutes a "substantial right" for purposes of this rule, but those who have ruled on the issue focus on the impact the evidence had on outcome of the case and the ability of the defendant to fairly defend himself/herself at trial. In *Cutshall v. United States*, 252 F.2d 677 (6th Cir. 1958), for instance, the trial court refused to allow the defendant to present evidence of ownership of the premises where illegal liquor was found, thereby depriving the defendant of a substantial right to rebut a presumption that provided strong evidence of his guilt (*Id.* at 678). By contrast, the Seventh Circuit in *United States v. Micklus*, 581 F.2d 612 (1978), upheld a trial court's refusal to allow evidence of the source of a weapon used in the commission of a crime, where the source of the weapon was immaterial and the witness was given sufficient opportunity to develop the story without such evidence (*Id.* at 617). These and other federal cases indicate that Rule 103 does not allow an error to be raised on appeal when it did not meaningfully impact the development of relevant evidence in the case.

3. The most extreme form of appellate outcome is when the appellate court reverses a conviction and does not remand the case for a new trial, but orders that a judgment of acquittal be entered. Such an outcome usually occurs only where the law under which the defendant was convicted has been found unconstitutional or otherwise invalid, not where the issue on appeal is whether or not evidence should be admitted.

Mesut Dogan/123.RF

LEARNING OBJECTIVES

After reading this chapter, the student will be able to:

1. Explain the meaning and application of the exclusionary rule.

2. Illustrate the "fruit of the poisonous tree" doctrine and its exceptions.

3. Distinguish between searches and seizures under the Fourth Amendment.

4. Outline the process for obtaining a warrant.

5. Explain the concept of probable cause.

6. Distinguish between searches that require probable cause and those that do not.

7. Distinguish between searches that require a warrant and those that do not.

8. Explain the difference between voluntary encounter, stop, and arrest.

9. Identify the circumstances when a warrant is required to make an arrest.

10. Explain the origins of the *Miranda* warnings.

11. Illustrate the situations where *Miranda* warnings are required.

Constitutionality of Evidence and the Exclusionary Rule

CHAPTER 6

◼ INTRODUCTION

Before we begin to learn about the factors that form the core of the law of evidence, we must look at a source of law that transcends the entire spectrum of criminal law: the Constitution. Because this is a text on evidence and not constitutional law, this chapter will not attempt an exhaustive discussion of constitutional principles that apply to criminal proceedings. This is not a primer on how police officers should or should not conduct searches, seizures, or interrogations. Rather, this chapter will provide an overview of those constitutional provisions that most directly affect the admissibility of evidence in a criminal trial. Later, we will look at other constitutional provisions, specifically the Sixth Amendment, that govern the examination of witnesses and the rights of a defendant to counsel and to confront and cross-examine witnesses for the prosecution.

With respect to admissibility, we will be focusing our discussion on the two rights that most directly affect evidence in criminal cases: the right against unreasonable searches and seizures found in the Fourth Amendment, and the right against self-incrimination found in the Fifth Amendment. Specifically, we will discuss how these rights are enforced through the exclusionary rule, a principle of law that forbids the admission of evidence obtained in violation of these rights.

■ THE EXCLUSIONARY RULE

LEARNING OBJECTIVE 1
Explain the meaning and application of the exclusionary rule.

exclusionary rule
The rule that evidence obtained in violation of a defendant's constitutional rights cannot be used to prove his/her guilt at trial.

Fourteenth Amendment
Constitutional amendment that has been used to apply specific federal constitutional rights to states.

LEARNING OBJECTIVE 2
Illustrate the "fruit of the poisonous tree" doctrine and its exceptions.

the fruit of the poisonous tree doctrine
The application of the exclusionary rule to all evidence resulting from a constitutional violation.

independent source rule
Exception to the fruit of the poisonous tree doctrine that allows evidence that could have been obtained from a constitutionally valid source.

inevitable discovery rule
Exception to the fruit of the poisonous tree doctrine that allows evidence that would inevitably have been discovered even without the constitutionally improper evidence.

collateral use rule
Exception to the exclusionary rule that allows evidence obtained in violation of a defendant's rights to be used for purposes other than proving guilt at trial.

The **exclusionary rule** provides that evidence obtained in violation of a defendant's constitutional rights cannot be used against him/her to prove guilt in a criminal trial. This rule is not found in the Constitution, but was created over time through a number of Supreme Court decisions, culminating in the 1914 case of *Weeks* v. *United States*, 232 U.S. 383 (1914), which applied the rule on a federal level, and the 1961 decision of *Mapp* v. *Ohio*, 367 U.S. 643 (1961), which applied it to the states under the **Fourteenth Amendment**.[1] The rule was necessitated by the fact that the Bill of Rights is not self-enforcing, providing no incentive to law enforcement officers and prosecutors to respect defendants' constitutional rights. After all, if it is easier to obtain evidence of a crime by violating the defendant's rights and use that evidence to prove guilt, why bother respecting those rights? The exclusionary rule provided this missing incentive by prohibiting the admission of any evidence obtained in violation of the defendants' rights.

The reach of this rule extends further than the actual evidence that was unconstitutionally obtained. Through "**the fruit of the poisonous tree doctrine**," the exclusionary rule applies to any evidence that was obtained as a result of a constitutional violation, even if that evidence was not the *direct* result of the violation. For instance, suppose a police officer conducts an illegal search of a suspected drug dealer's apartment, and discovers an address book with the names and addresses of the suspect's customers. The address book would obviously not be admissible under the exclusionary rule, but what about the testimony of the addicts who are tracked down from the entries in the address book and subpoenaed to testify against the suspect? Their testimony would be considered "fruit of the poisonous tree," and would be inadmissible under the exclusionary rule.

There are a few circumstances where the fruit of the poisonous tree doctrine does not apply. For instance, the prosecution could still call any of the suspect's customers whom they knew about through other, legitimately obtained sources (the **"independent source" rule**), or if their investigation would inevitably have led them to that witness even if they hadn't obtained the address book (the **"inevitable discovery" rule**). But any evidence that was obtained solely as a result of the violation of the defendant's rights will be excluded, and it is up to the prosecutor to prove that the evidence falls outside the scope of the "fruit of the poisonous tree" doctrine.

It should be noted that the exclusionary rule and fruit of the poisonous tree doctrine prohibit evidence only when it is used to prove the defendant's guilt or innocence. It does not prevent that evidence from being used for other purposes (the **"collateral use" rule**). For instance, in our drug dealer example, if the defendant took the stand and testified that he didn't know a certain person listed in the address book, the address book could be used to prove he was lying (in other words, to impeach his testimony). So long as the evidence is not being used to directly prove the defendant guilty of the crime he stands accused of, the exclusionary rule is satisfied.

Now that we understand what the exclusionary rule is, let's take a look at the rights that must be honored to prevent it from being applied.

■ FOURTH AMENDMENT PROTECTION AGAINST UNREASONABLE SEARCHES AND SEIZURES

LEARNING OBJECTIVE 3
Distinguish between searches and seizures under the Fourth Amendment.

The Fourth Amendment of the U.S. Constitution reads as follows: "The right of the people to be secure in their persons, houses, papers, and effects, against unreasonable searches and seizures, shall not be violated, and no Warrants shall issue, but upon probable cause, supported by Oath or affirmation, and particularly describing the place to be searched, and the persons or things to be seized."

The meaning of this Amendment has undergone an extraordinary evolution since it was added to the Constitution, but the end product of that evolution is fairly easy to state. Searches (the examination of a person's belongings, including his/her own body, and taking of evidence therefrom) and seizures (the arrest or detention of a person against his/her will) cannot occur without a warrant, subject to a number of exceptions. These exceptions complicate the application of the Fourth Amendment.

Warrants and Probable Cause

LEARNING OBJECTIVE 4
Outline the process for obtaining a warrant.

Taking the Fourth Amendment on its face, it would seem that any search for evidence or seizure of a person accused of a crime would require a warrant issued upon probable cause. Let's begin by looking at those two concepts.

LEARNING OBJECTIVE 5
Explain the concept of probable cause.

A **warrant** is written permission from a court to conduct a search or make an arrest. There are two kinds of warrants: a **search warrant** and an **arrest warrant**. To obtain a warrant, a police officer completes a **probable cause affidavit** that lists all of the facts known to the officer establishing probable cause for the search or arrest. This affidavit is then presented to a magistrate (usually a minor court judge) who then examines the warrant to see if it meets the probable cause standard required under the Fourth Amendment. If it does, then the magistrate will issue the warrant.

warrant
Written permission issued by a magistrate to conduct a search or make an arrest.

search warrant
A warrant to conduct a search.

arrest warrant
A warrant to make an arrest.

probable cause affidavit
A sworn statement by a police officer containing facts to support the issuance of a search or arrest warrant.

Figure 6-1 contains the text of a probable cause affidavit that was filed by FBI Agent Henry Gibbons to search the car of Oklahoma City bomber Timothy McVeigh, who committed the worst act of terrorism on American soil before 9/11. Notice how carefully the agent laid out the facts he could prove in order to make a connection between the crime and the car he wished to search.

A warrant has to be specific. In other words, it must specify either the area to be searched or the person to be arrested. Specificity in a search area is determined by how much area is encompassed by the facts in the officer's affidavit. If the facts support a conclusion that an entire building may contain evidence of a crime, then an entire building might be searched. But an officer cannot obtain a warrant to search an entire apartment building because he believes that one of the apartments may contain evidence, but he doesn't know which one. Likewise, an arrest warrant must identify the person to be arrested. The person does not need to be identified by name, however, if the description is sufficient to pinpoint exactly who the suspect is. The sole resident of an apartment or the record owner of a particular automobile might be sufficient, but a warrant will not issue for all of the residents of an apartment building if only one is suspected of committing a crime.

Figure 6-1 Text of Probable Cause Affidavit to Search Car Belonging to Timothy McVeigh

United States District Court

WESTERN DISTRICT OF OKLAHOMA

APPLICATION AND AFFIDAVIT FOR SEARCH WARRANT

In the matter of the search of AUTOMOBILE LOCATED AT 1977 MERCURY MARQUIS AUTOMOBILE LOCATED AT 1009 N.W 4TH STREET OKLAHOMA CITY, OKLAHOMA

I, Henry C Gibbons, being duly sworn depose and say I am a Special Agent. Federal Bureau of Investigation, and have reason to believe that on the premises known as, AUTOMOBILE: Yellow 1977 Mercury Marquis, currently located at 1009 N W. 4th Street, Oklahoma City, Oklahoma, in the Western District of Oklahoma, there is now contained certain property, namely yellow 1977 Mercury Marquis, and for which a comprehensive forensic examination of its contents could reveal items. including but not limited to, hair, fibers, oil, fuel, soil, grass, chemicals and fingerprints which has been used as the means of committing a criminal offense and which is property that constitutes evidence of the commission of a criminal offense specifically a violation of Title 18, United States Code, Section 844(f).The facts to support a finding of Probable Cause are as follows: See attached Affidavit of Special Agent Henry C. Gibbons, Federal Bureau of Investigation, which is incorporated by reference herein. Continued on the attached sheet and made a part hereof

HENRY C. GBBONS

Special Agent

Federal Bureau of Investigation

Sworn to before me and subscribed in my presence on this 5th day of May, 1995, at Oklahoma City, Oklahoma.

DAVID L. RUSSEL UNITED STATES DISTRICT JUDGE

AFFIDAVIT

I, HENRY C. GIBBONS, being duly sworn, Hereby state that I am an agent with the Federal Bureau of Investigation, having been so employed for 26 years and as such am vested with the authority to investigate violations of federal laws, including Title 18, United States Code, Section 844(f) This affidavit is submitted in support of a search warrant for a 1977 yellow Mercury Marquis in the possession of the Federal Bureau of Investigation(FBI). Further, Affiant states:

1. The following information was received by the Federal Bureau of Investigation during the period April 19, 1995 to May 4, 1995.

2. On April 19, 1995, a powerful explosive device detonated in front of the Alfred P. Murrah Federal Building in Oklahoma City, Oklahoma, at approximately 9:00 a.m. Among the many people killed by the bombing are employees of the numerous federal agencies which had offices in the building.

3. Investigation by Federal agents at the scene of the explosion has determined that the explosive was contained in a 1993 Ford truck owned by Ryder Rental Company. a. A partial vehicle identification number (VIN) was found at the scene of the explosion and determined to be from a part of the truck that contained the explosive device. 57/5/45 B. The Vin which was completely reconstructed was traced back to a truck owned by Ryder Rentals of Miami, Florida. c. Ryder Rentals informed the FBI that the truck was assigned to a rental company known as Elliot's Body Shop in Junction City Kansas.

4. The rental agent at Elliot's Body Shop in Junction City_was interviewed by the FBI_on April 19, 1995, and advised that two persons had rented the truck on April 17, 1995. The individual who signed the rental agreement provided the following information: a. the person who signed the rental agreement identified himself as Bob Kling, SSAN 962-42-9694, South Dakota driver's license number YF942A6, and provided a home address of 428 Maple Drive, Omaha, Nebraska, telephone 913-238-2425. The person listed the destination as 428 Maple Drive, Redfield, South Dakota. b. Subsequent investigation conducted by the F3I determined all that information to be false.

5. An employee of Elliot's Body Shop in Junction City, Kansas, identified Timothy McVeigh from a photographic array as the person who rented a Ryder truck on April 17, 1995, and signed the rental agreement.

6. An employee of the Dreamland Motel in Junction City, Kansas, identified Timothy McVeigh as a guest at the motel from April 14, 1995, through April 18, 1995. This employee, when shown a photo lineup identified Timothy McVeigh's picture as the individual who registered at the motel under the name of Tim McVeigh, listed his automobile as a Mercury bearing an Arizona license plate, and provided a Michigan address, on NorthVan Dyke in Decker Michigan.

7. On April 17, 1995, Timothy James McVeigh was arrested in Noble County, Oklahoma, on traffic and weapons offenses and was thereafter incarcerated on those charges in Perry, Oklahoma. McVeigh's arrest occurred approximately

Figure 6-1 (continued)

60–70 miles north of Oklahoma City, Oklahoma, approximately 1 hour and 20 minutes after the April 19, 1995, explosion that damaged the Alfred P. Murrah Federal Building. At the time of his arrest, McVeigh was driving a 1977 yellow Mercury Marquis.

8. On April 21, 1995, a criminal complaint was filed charging Timothy James McVeigh with a violation of 18 U.S.C. 844 f) based on his involvement of the bombing of the Murrah Federal Building. Later that day, McVeigh was taken into federal custody.

9. On April 27, 1995, a preliminary hearing was held on this charge, evidence was presented and the federal magistrate judge found that there was probable cause to believe that an offense had been committed and that McVeigh committed it.

10. Based on interviews and other evidence developed by the FBI, there is reason to believe McVeigh did not act alone in committing this offense: a. The employee at Elliot's Body Shop in Junction City, Kansas, where the truck subsequently used as the bomb vehicle was rented, has advised that the vehicle was picked up by two persons; b. Two witnesses at the scene of the Alfred P Murrah building on April 19, 1955, observed a person believed to be Timothy James McVeigh with another person departing the area of the Murrah Building shortly before the bombing. One of these witnesses observed the person they believed to be Timothy James McVeigh leave the area in a yellow or cream-colored Mercury;

11. Supervisory Special Agent (SSA) James T. Thurman, Chief, Explosives Unit Washington, D.C., Bomb Data Center, FBI Laboratory, advised that: a the bomb which detonated in front of the Murrah Federal Building on April 19, 1995, contained a high explosive main charge initiated by as yet unknown methods; b. an explosive device of the magnitude which exploded in Oklahoma City on April 19, 1995, would have been constructed over a period of time utilizing a large quantity of both paraphernalia and materials, which may have included, but not been limited to, the following: fertilizer, fuel oil, chemicals, dynamite, military explosives, detonators (blasting caps), electrical or non-electrical fusing systems, wires, batteries, timing devices, burning type fuse, mixing and other containers. c. The construction of an explosive device similar to the one believed to have caused the damage to the Murrah Building would necessarily have involved the efforts of more than one person. '

12. On. April 21, 1995, United States District Judge David L. Russell authorized a search warrant for the 1977 Mercury Marquis based upon an application and affidavit of the United States. Among the items located during the course of the search of the 1977 yellow Mercury Marquis were human hairs of value for comparison purposes of more than one person.

13. On May 2, 1995, FBI Supervisory Special Agent (SSA) Richard S. Hahn advised affiant that during the course of the initial search, a test for latent fingerprints utilizing Cyano Acrylate was not conducted. SSA Hahn advised that the Cyano Acrylate search procedure can produce latent finger prints of value which other tests cannot produce.

14. A comprehensive forensic processing and examination of the vehicle and its contents could reveal hair, fibers, oil, fuel, soil, grass, chemicals and fingerprints which could be used to identify the presence of other persons present in the vehicle with Timothy James McVeigh and/or the presence of chemicals which could be used in the construction of the explosive device, and/or could be used to place the vehicle at locations where the explosive device may have been constructed, and/or could provide other evidence of the relationship of the vehicle and its owner to the explosion in Oklahoma City, Oklahoma. Moreover, during the course of this investigation, evidentiary items, including man-made and natural fibers, hairs, cloth, oil, fuel, other compounds, soil and grass have been seized from the Dreamland motel room, described paragraph 6 where McVeigh stayed, and from a location at Geary State Fishing Lake, approximately six miles south of Junction City, Kansas, where witnesses described seeing a Ryder truck parked next to a pickup truck in an unpaved area on April 18, 1995. The pickup truck was described as a 1980–1987 Chevrolet or GMC truck, dark blue or brown in color, with possibly a white camper shell back. Terry Nichols, who has admitted that he is an associate of McVeigh, and who has stated that he loaned his pickup truck to McVeigh on April 18, 1995, in Junction City, Kansas, owns a 1984 GMC blue pick-up truck with a white camper top. An additional, comprehensive processing and examination of the yellow 1977 Mercury Marquis is needed in order to obtain representative samples and quantities capable of analysis for purposes of comparison with the items described above.

15. Based upon the aforesaid, your affiant believes that probable cause exists to believe that the yellow 1977 Mercury Marquis, which is currently in FBI custody, is property which has been used as a means of committing a violation of Section 844(f) of Title 18, United States Code. Affiant also believes that probable cause exists to believe that the yellow 1977 Mercury Marquis currently in FBI custody consists of and contains items, both visible and latent, which are evidence of a criminal offense, namely Section 844(f) of Title 18, United States Code, or which can be compared to items seized and identified which are such evidence.

(continued)

Figure 6-1 (continued)

16. Based on the aforesaid and Rule 41(b), Federal Rules of Criminal Procedure, affiant wishes to seize said vehicle as evidence and to examine and process said vehicle and its contents Affiant believes there is a probable cause for law enforcement officials to conduct laboratory examinations on this vehicle and its contents for trace evidence materials to associate the vehicle with the bombing of the Alfred P. Murrah Federal Building, the mixing of explosives and to link said vehicle to any other coconspirators. Further your affiant sayeth not.

Henry C. GIBBONS

Special Agent

Federal Bureau of Investigation

ITEMS TO BE SEIZED 1977 MERCURY + MARQUIS

1. Explosive materials and residue including but not limited to the following: Military explosives, C4, ammonium nitrate, dynamite, water gels, emulsions, detonating cord, explosive boosters, free flowing powders, including but not limited to black powder, pyrodex and smokeless powder and explosive detonators including but not limited to electric and non-electric.

2. Fusing systems including but not limited to clocks, timers, radio transmitters, servo motors and components, wires, electrical and/or mechanical switches, time fuse, chemical delays, and/or any other source of power.

3. Non-explosive construction materials including but not limited to tape, wiring, adhesives, fasteners, containers, nails, staples, or any other material necessary to assemble IED devices.

4. Non-explosive fragmentation material including nails, screws, wire and other metal fragment which could be used to enhance the damage effect of the explosion.

5. IED construction tools which would include but are not limited to screwdrivers, clampers, wire strippers, knives, pliers, hammers, fingernail clippers, files, electrical tools such as saws, drills and presses.

6. Documentation which would include but not limited to schematics, blueprints, receipts for purchase of items, "how to" magazines, books and pamphlets which described construction, design and assembly techniques, directions, maps and blueprints of target sites and potential target sites, communications, memos and photographs which would include descriptive information such as telephone numbers, addresses, affiliations and contact points of individuals involved in a conspiracy to manufacture, transport and/or detonate the explosive device used at the Alfred P. Murrah building on April 19, 1995.

7. Any assembled explosives and/or detonation device.

8. Photographs, maps, hotel receipts, rental receipts, notes, ledgers, phone numbers, address books, commercial transportation receipts, and firearms, ammunition, digital pager(s), cellular phones, chemical formulas, and/or recipes for explosives. For which items there is probable cause stated in the Affidavit in support of the Application for the Search of the 1977 Mercury Marquis, and which items are evidence and instrumentalities of a violation of 18 U.S.C. + 371 and 844(f).

Source: Warrant for the search of Timothy McVeigh's 1977 Mercury Marquis. (n.d.). Retrieved from http://law2.umkc.edu/faculty/projects/ftrials/mcveigh/mcveighwarrant.html.

The Fourth Amendment's second requirement is *probable cause*. This is a slippery concept at best, because it is defined in terms of probabilities, not certainties. Probable cause exists if an officer can articulate specific facts that lead to a reasonable belief that a given area contains evidence of a crime (in the case of a search warrant) or that a particular person has committed a crime (in the case of an arrest warrant). There can be probable cause to search an area that has no evidence, or to arrest someone who has not committed a crime. Probable cause can be based on direct observation of a crime (for instance, a police officer sees a man grabbing a woman's purse) or on hearsay (a woman tells a police officer, "That man just stole my purse!"). But whatever the support, the facts must be sufficient and specific enough that a reasonable person can conclude a crime may have been committed. A hunch or "feeling" is not enough to support probable cause, no matter how certain the officer is that he/she is right.

Exceptions to the Probable Cause and Warrant Requirements for Searches

LEARNING OBJECTIVE 6
Distinguish between searches that require probable cause and those that do not.

When can a search be conducted without a warrant or probable cause? The answer to that question could fill an entire textbook, but what follows is a general overview of the exceptions to the warrant requirement for searches.

Non-Searches—No Probable Cause Needed

Under the right circumstances, evidence can be obtained without a warrant, or even without probable cause, because the process used to obtain it did not fall within the meaning of a "search" under the Fourth Amendment.

One type of "non-search" is a **"plain-view" search**. When a police officer is legitimately in the presence of evidence that is in plain view, that evidence may be seized and used to support a criminal conviction. For example, if a police officer stops a car for speeding, and the officer looks through the window and sees an illegal firearm lying on the backseat in plain view, that is not a search, and the firearm can be legitimately taken and used as evidence.

Another type of "non-search" is an **"open fields" search**. Where a landowner has a field that is not part of the land immediately around his house (known as "curtilage") and that field is not fenced in so that it cannot be accessed, then police are free to search that field without a warrant or probable cause. Any evidence of crime contained in that field can be taken and used as evidence.

A third type of "non-search" is the search of abandoned property. When property is abandoned by its owner, there is no longer any expectation of privacy in that property, and it can be searched without limitation. A common example is a bag of trash put out for the trash collector. Once the bag is placed on the sidewalk with the intention that it will be hauled away, it is fair game. Another example is where a suspect is fleeing from police and throws away evidence (such as drugs or a gun) during the chase. Once the evidence is thrown away, it can be taken and used at trial to prove the defendant's guilt.

plain-view search
A "non-search" in which a police officer comes upon evidence of a crime that is in plain view.

PRACTICE TIP
Because anything in plain view is not subject to the Fourth Amendment requirements for a reasonable search, police officers should always be as observant as possible when coming upon any suspicious scene or activity.

open fields search
The search of open land that is not fenced in or otherwise protected from public access.

Frisks—Reasonable Suspicion, Not Probable Cause

Frisks, also known as "pat-downs," take place in the course of a "*Terry* stop" (discussed further below), named after the case of *Terry* v. *Ohio* in which these types of "stops and frisks" were first given constitutional approval by the Supreme Court. When a suspect is stopped with a reasonable suspicion that he/she may be involved in criminal activity, the police officer conducting the stop may pat the suspect's outer clothing to make sure the suspect is not armed. This is not a search for evidence *per se*, but if evidence of a crime (such as an illegally possessed firearm) is uncovered, then it can be used as evidence to support a conviction for that crime. Because this search is so limited, it not only can be conducted without a warrant, but does not even require probable cause. All that is needed to justify a frisk is (a) a legitimate *Terry* stop, and (b) a reasonable suspicion that the suspect may be armed.

frisk
A pat-down of a suspect's clothing during a *Terry* stop for the purpose of determining whether the suspect is armed.

Consent—No Probable Cause Needed

A suspect is free to waive his/her Fourth Amendment rights and **consent** to a search, so long as his/her consent is voluntary. There is no need to tell a defendant that he/she has the right not to consent before it is given, so long as there is no undue pressure being placed on the defendant. Such pressure

consent
Permission given by a suspect to conduct a search.

could consist of threats ("Things will go harder for you if you make us get a warrant") or promises of reward ("If you let us search your car, we'll put in a good word with the judge"). Once consent is given, the search must remain within the scope of the consent. This means that if a defendant consents to the search of his/her house, the search cannot extend to his/her garage unless it is part of the house. A defendant who consents to the search of his/her "car" presumably give consent to search the entire car, including the trunk. But consent can be limited or withdrawn at any time, even after the search begins.

In the following case, the defendant claimed that his companion did not give proper consent to the search of the vehicle in which both were riding, and that even if such consent was proper, it was withdrawn. Based on the conversation between the police officer and the defendant's companion, the court concluded that consent was given and not withdrawn.

COURT OPINION 6-1

UNITED STATES V. LOPEZ-MENDOZA, 601 F.3d 861 (8th Cir. 2010)

According to Lopez–Mendoza, Vargas–Miranda did not voluntarily consent to the search of the car. . . . "The government bears the burden of proving voluntary consent by a preponderance of the evidence and must show that on the totality of the circumstances the officer reasonably believed that the search was consensual." *United States v. Almendares*, 397 F.3d 653, 660 (8th Cir. 2005).

> In evaluating the reasonableness of the officer's belief, we consider the characteristics of the person consenting, including the party's age, intelligence and education, whether he was under the influence of drugs or alcohol, whether he was informed of his right to withhold consent, and whether he was aware of rights afforded criminal suspects. We also consider the environment in which the alleged consent took place, specifically (1) the length of time he was detained; (2) whether the police threatened, physically intimidated, or punished him; (3) whether the police made promises or misrepresentations; (4) whether he was in custody or under arrest when the consent was given; (5) whether the consent occurred in a public or secluded place; and (6) whether he stood by silently . . . as the search occurred.

United States v. Esquivias, 416 F.3d 696, 700 (8th Cir. 2005) (internal quotations and citations omitted).

When Deputy Brown asked to look at the vehicle, Vargas–Miranda said "go ahead." Lopez–Mendoza emphasizes that, a moment later, Vargas–Miranda added: "You ain't got no right. I wasn't even driving." According to Lopez–Mendoza,

the follow-up statement shows that Vargas–Miranda was not voluntarily consenting, but merely acquiescing to Deputy Brown's authority.

As the district court correctly found, Vargas–Miranda—an adult, conversant in English—conversed with the (visibly) armed Deputy Brown in the convenience store. Vargas–Miranda gave consent to search the car in front of a gas station that was open for business. He was not under arrest when Deputy Brown asked to look in the car; he had his driver's license, the vehicle insurance card, and was free to leave. Vargas–Miranda and Lopez–Mendoza watched the search without objecting or indicating the search should be stopped. On these facts, Deputy Brown reasonably believed Vargas–Miranda consented. . . .

Lopez–Mendoza argues that "go ahead" is insufficient to evidence consent, citing *United States v. Morgan*, 270 F.3d 625 (8th Cir. 2001). *Morgan* is inapposite. There, the officer asked to search the defendant's van. The defendant asked what would happen if she refused. The officer answered he would walk his drug dog around the car. The defendant said, "go ahead." *Id*. at 628. This court held that "Morgan did not voluntarily consent to a search of the van when she said 'go ahead' " (but held that the officer had probable cause once the dog alerted). *Id*. at 631–32. Here, Vargas–Miranda said "go ahead" in direct response to Deputy Brown's initial request to search.

Lopez–Mendoza asserts that, if given, consent was withdrawn when Vargas–Miranda said: "You

(continued)

(continued)

ain't got no right. I wasn't even driving." "Conduct withdrawing consent must be an act clearly inconsistent with the apparent consent to search, an unambiguous statement challenging the officer's authority to conduct the search, or some combination of both." *United States v. Sanders*, 424 F.3d 768, 774 (8th Cir. 2005).

Critically, the exchange did not end with Vargas–Miranda asserting "you ain't got no right." Deputy Brown quickly clarified: "Well I'm asking you. I'm just asking you. I'm asking you. But like you said, it's all consensual. I'm just asking you." The deputy went on to say, "Well, I'll tell you what, since

you said I could look, I'm going to go ahead and look real quick, and then get you guys on your way." In response, Vargas–Miranda nodded, reasonably communicating his consent.

Questions

1. Who has the burden of proving whether consent was properly given for a search?
2. What statements by the police officer and Vargas–Miranda were critical to the court's determination that consent was properly given and not withdrawn?

Terry J Alcorn/Getty Images

When arresting a suspect, the police are permitted to search the suspect's person for evidence without a warrant.

Source: http://www.gettyimages.com/detail/photo/arrested-royalty-free-image/155132563.

Searches for Evidence on Probable Cause—No Warrant Needed

The exceptions to the warrant requirement are more limited where a search is being conducted specifically to find evidence of a crime in a place where the defendant has an expectation of privacy and has not consented. Such searches require probable cause, and can be conducted in only three circumstances: a search incident to an arrest, a vehicle search, and a container search.

A *search incident to an arrest*, as the name implies, occurs when a valid arrest is made. This means that the arrest must be supported by probable cause. If it is, then a search may be conducted of the suspect's body, clothing, any items the suspect is carrying (such as a purse or backpack), and the area within the suspect's reach at the time the arrest occurs. This search is

LEARNING OBJECTIVE 7
Distinguish between searches that require a warrant and those that do not.

permitted without a warrant because it is reasonable to allow an arresting officer to find evidence that the suspect can easily reach and possibly destroy during the course of the arrest. It also allows the officer to protect his/her own safety by searching and finding any weapons that may be within reach.

PRACTICE TIP

Whenever a suspect is likely to have evidence of a crime on his/her person, it is critically important to make sure that an arrest is constitutionally valid, or else all of the evidence seized during that arrest will be excluded from evidence.

vehicle search
A warrantless search of a vehicle on probable cause that the vehicle contains evidence of a crime.

A **vehicle search** is permitted without a warrant so long as there is probable cause to believe that the vehicle contains evidence of a crime. The reason for this is simple: vehicles are mobile, and could disappear in the few hours it might take a police officer to get a warrant. This type of search includes the entire vehicle, including the trunk and any container found within the vehicle.

container search
The warrantless seizure of a container upon probable cause that the container contains evidence of a crime.

A **container search** applies to any container that an officer has probable cause to believe might contain evidence. The warrantless part of this search includes only seizing and securing the container, however. Once the container is secured, then a warrant must be obtained to open it and search its contents. Note, though, that if the container is transparent, there is nothing stopping the police officer from examining the contents from the outside without opening it. If contraband is found, then the search becomes a "plain-view" search, and the contents can be seized without a warrant.

EVIDENCE AND TECHNOLOGY

SEIZURE AND ANALYSIS OF CELL PHONES WITHOUT A WARRANT

Most physical evidence that is uncovered during an arrest is relatively easy to preserve, because possession of the evidence provides the investigator with complete control over it. One notable exception is where electronic devices such as computers or laptops are discovered. These present a unique challenge, because it is possible to alter the content of those devices remotely.

Seizing a cell phone is no different than seizing any other kind of evidence. There must be probable cause that the cell phone contains evidence of a crime, and, in some instances, a warrant must be obtained. A cell phone found on a suspect's person or within grabbing distance at the time of the arrest would be subject to the search-incident-to-an-arrest exception to the warrant requirement. The presence of a cell phone at a crime scene may provide probable cause for a seizure, but if the cell phone does not belong to the suspect, that question may not be as clear, as shown in the following case of *King* v. *City of Indianapolis*.

Although the rules do not change for electronic evidence, electronic devices do present some unique challenges when it comes to preserving the evidence they contain. One such challenge is the need to prevent remote changes in or destruction of the contents of a cell phone after it is seized. Applications can be placed on cell phones that allow the phone to be wiped clean of data, destroying any evidence the phone might contain. To prevent this, one expert recommends that the phone be isolated from wireless signals immediately after seizure and protected from any electronic signals which might be used to destroy or alter data contained on the device.[2]

As with all forms of physical evidence, the value of evidence obtained from electronic devices depends entirely on the ability of investigators to maintain that evidence in the condition it was when the device was seized. For this reason, the forensic analysis of electronic devices should be left to the experts and never attempted by an officer who is not trained in conducting such analyses (*Ibid.*).

COURT OPINION 6-2 _____

KING V. CITY OF INDIANAPOLIS, 969 F.Supp.2d 1085 (S.D.Ind., 2013)

[Police officers were sued for violating the civil rights of a bystander who used his cell phone to video record the arrest of a suspect. Police forcibly seized the phone as potential evidence of resisting arrest by the suspect. The officers claimed qualified immunity from the lawsuit, because their seizure of the cell phone was supported by probable cause and was reasonable. The Defendant claimed that the seizure violated his fourth amendment rights, in that it was unreasonable to seize his phone without a warrant and without probable cause.]

As an initial matter, the Court finds that there is a clearly established right to be free from the warrantless seizure of a cell phone. This right is especially clear in the instant circumstances, where Mr. King was video recording police activity and crime, but was not himself engaged in unlawful activity at the time the iPhone was seized. Mr. King has not provided any analogous case law, likewise, the Court has not found any. However, the lack of analogous cases is not determinative because the right to be free from warrantless seizures is an obvious and clearly established right.

The remaining issue is whether the warrantless seizure of Mr. King's phone was justified by exigent circumstances, a doctrine usually applied to warrantless entries or searches. "The exigent circumstances doctrine recognizes that there may be situations in which law enforcement officials may be presented with 'a compelling need' to conduct a search, but have 'no time to secure a warrant.' " *Bogan v. City of Chi.*, 644 F.3d 563, 571 (7th Cir. 2011) (*quoting United States v. Dowell*, 724 F.2d 599, 602 (7th Cir. 1984)). When reviewing a warrantless search or seizure to determine if exigent circumstances existed, courts ask whether "a reasonable officer had a reasonable belief that there was a compelling need to act and no time to obtain a warrant." *Id.* (*quoting United States v. Andrews*, 442 F.3d 996, 1000 (7th Cir. 2006) (additional quotation omitted)). The determination is made on the totality of facts and circumstances from the position of the officer. *Id.* Relevant to this case, "the need 'to prevent the imminent destruction of evidence' has long been recognized as a sufficient justification for a warrantless search." *Kentucky v. King*, —— U.S. ——, 131 S.Ct. 1849, 1856, 179 L.Ed.2d 865 (2011) (*quoting Brigham City, Utah v. Stuart*, 547 U.S. 398, 403, 126 S.Ct. 1943, 164 L.Ed.2d 650 (2006)).

. . . Defendants claim that the potential imminent destruction of evidence—i.e., the video Mr. King was recording—created an exigent circumstance justifying the seizure of the iPhone. Taking the facts most favorable to Mr. King, it is not clear that the destruction of evidence was imminent, nor that the seizure was motivated by a need for the evidence. The Court is not convinced that a reasonable officer would feel, first, that the evidence was necessary and, second, that there was a compelling need to act and no time to obtain a warrant for the evidence. Therefore, qualified immunity is not granted on this claim.

Questions

1. Why did the court conclude that the seizure of Mr. King's phone may have been unreasonable?
2. Aside from taking the phone at the scene, what could the officers have done to obtain the phone without violating Mr. King's rights?

All Other Searches

If a search does not fall within one of the categories discussed above, then it cannot be conducted without a warrant. If it is, or if one of the above searches is conducted without fulfilling the requirements to justify the search, then the exclusionary rule would prohibit the admission of any evidence resulting from that search.

LEARNING OBJECTIVE 8
Explain the difference between voluntary encounter, stop, and arrest.

voluntary encounter
An encounter between a police officer and another person where the person is free to walk away.

Exceptions to the Warrant Requirement for Seizures

Voluntary Encounters—No Probable Cause Needed

When a person is stopped by a police officer on the street, is the person free to walk away? That's the key question in determining whether a person has been "seized" under the Fourth Amendment (see Figure 6-2 below). If the answer to that question is "yes," then there is no seizure, and the person is experiencing a "**voluntary encounter.**" Anything that is said during a voluntary encounter can be used against the person to support a criminal conviction.

Whether a person is engaged in a voluntary encounter or not depends on factors that are difficult to define. We assess the nature of the encounter from the viewpoint of the person being questioned by the police officers. Did the officers do anything (speak in a commanding voice, order the person not to move, surround the person, or take an aggressive or controlling posture) that would make a reasonable person believe he/she was not free to walk away? If so, then the encounter is probably not voluntary. Still, a person's own internal mental barriers, whether they are created out of fear or respect or wariness, will not turn a voluntary encounter into a seizure. We ask whether a reasonable person would feel that his/her freedom of movement was being curtailed.

Figure 6-2 Requirements for Types of Fourth Amendment Searches and Seizures

	NON-FOURTH AMENDMENT		FOURTH AMENDMENT		
	VOLUNTARY ENCOUNTER		STOP		ARREST
SEIZURES	NO INTERFERENCE WITH FREEDOM OF MOVEMENT	REASONABLE SUSPICION THAT CRIME MAY BE COMMITTED	LIMITED INTERFERENCE WITH FREEDOM OF MOVEMENT	PROBABLE CAUSE THAT CRIME IS BEING COMMITTED	WARRANT REQUIRED if arrest takes place in suspect's home
SEARCHES	1. Plain-view search 2. Open fields 3. Abandoned property 4. Public places 5. Consent search		FRISK (also requires reasonable suspicion that suspect is armed)		SEARCH FOR EVIDENCE WARRANT REQUIRED UNLESS: • Search incident to arrest • Vehicle search • Emergency search

The Terry Stop—Reasonable Suspicion, Not Probable Cause

Until 1968, the only standard court followed to determine the propriety of a seizure was probable cause. If a police officer had probable cause to believe someone committed a crime, then that person could be arrested. Otherwise, no restriction of the person's freedom was constitutionally possible. The officer could question a suspected criminal, but could not stop him/her from walking away if the evidence did not support an arrest.

In 1968, in the case of *Terry* v. *Ohio*, the U.S. Supreme Court added a second layer to the constitutional question of whether a seizure is reasonable. In that case, the police officer, Martin McFadden, who had over 30 years' experience as a detective, observed two men standing on a street corner in downtown Cleveland. One by one, they each repeatedly walked to a store that was not open for business, looked inside, and returned to the corner to talk to the other. They did this about a dozen times. Then, they were briefly joined by a third man. As they began leaving the scene, McFadden, suspecting that the men might be preparing a robbery of the store, followed them. Since he suspected they might be preparing for a robbery, he feared they might be armed. He approached them in front of a store where they had once again joined the third man, identified himself as a police officer, and asked for their names. When he received only a mumbled response, McFadden grabbed Terry, and holding him between himself and the other two, felt his pocket for a weapon. McFadden felt something that might have been a weapon, but, unable to retrieve it, he made the men enter the store and removed Terry's coat. He recovered a firearm, and charged Terry with illegal possession.

Terry sought to exclude the firearm as evidence because McFadden did not have probable cause to arrest him when he grabbed and searched him. Terry was convicted, and appealed his conviction, eventually to the U.S. Supreme Court. In its landmark ruling, the court held that McFadden's limited stop and search of Terry was not a violation of the Fourth Amendment.

COURT OPINION 6-3 _____

TERRY V. OHIO, 392 U.S. 1, 88 S.Ct. 1868 (1968)

The Fourth Amendment provides that 'the right of the people to be secure in their persons, houses, papers, and effects, against unreasonable searches and seizures, shall not be violated ***.' This inestimable right of personal security belongs as much to the citizen on the streets of our cities as to the homeowner closeted in his study to dispose of his secret affairs. . . .

We have recently held that 'the Fourth Amendment protects people, not places,' Katz v. United States, 389 U.S. 347, 351, 88 S.Ct. 507, 511, 19 L.Ed.2d 576 (1967), and wherever an individual may harbor a reasonable 'expectation of privacy,' *id.*, at 361, 88 S.Ct. at 507, (Mr. Justice

Harlan, concurring), he is entitled to be free from unreasonable governmental intrusion. Of course, the specific content and incidents of this right must be shaped by the context in which it is asserted. For 'what the Constitution forbids is not all searches and seizures, but unreasonable searches and seizures.' . . . The question is whether in all the circumstances of this on-the-street encounter, his right to personal security was violated by an unreasonable search and seizure.

. . .[I]t is frequently argued that in dealing with the rapidly unfolding and often dangerous situations on city streets the police are in need of an escalating set of flexible responses, graduated in

(continued)

(continued)

relation to the amount of information they possess. For this purpose it is urged that distinctions should be made between a 'stop' and an 'arrest' (or a 'seizure' of a person), and between a 'frisk' and a 'search.' Thus, it is argued, the police should be allowed to 'stop' a person and detain him briefly for questioning upon suspicion that he may be connected with criminal activity. Upon suspicion that the person may be armed, the police should have the power to 'frisk' him for weapons. If the 'stop' and the 'frisk' give rise to probable cause to believe that the suspect has committed a crime, then the police should be empowered to make a formal 'arrest,' and a full incident 'search' of the person. This scheme is justified in part upon the notion that a 'stop' and a 'frisk' amount to a mere 'minor inconvenience and petty indignity,' which can properly be imposed upon the citizen in the interest of effective law enforcement on the basis of a police officer's suspicion. . . .

[W]e turn our attention to the quite narrow question posed by the facts before us: whether it is always unreasonable for a policeman to seize a person and subject him to a limited search for weapons unless there is probable cause for an arrest. . . .

. . .

[I]n justifying the particular intrusion the police officer must be able to point to specific and articulable facts which, taken together with rational inferences from those facts, reasonably warrant that intrusion. The scheme of the Fourth Amendment becomes meaningful only when it is assured that at some point the conduct of those charged with enforcing the laws can be subjected to the more detached, neutral scrutiny of a judge who must evaluate the reasonableness of a particular search or seizure in light of the particular circumstances. And in making that assessment it is imperative that the facts be judged against an objective standard: would the facts available to the officer at the moment of the seizure or the search 'warrant a man of reasonable caution in the belief' that the action taken was appropriate? [citations omitted] . . .

Applying these principles to this case, we consider first the nature and extent of the governmental interests involved. One general interest is of course that of effective crime prevention and detection; it is this interest which underlies the recognition that a police officer may in appropriate circumstances and in an appropriate manner approach a person for purposes of investigating possibly criminal behavior even though there is no probable cause to make an arrest. [The court concluded that Officer McFadden was justified in approaching and stopping Terry and Chilton based on the suspiciousness of their behavior.] It would have been poor police work indeed for an officer of 30 years' experience in the detection of thievery from stores in this same neighborhood to have failed to investigate this behavior further.

[Regarding the legality of McFadden's frisk of Terry, w]e are now concerned with more than the governmental interest in investigating crime; in addition, there is the more immediate interest of the police officer in taking steps to assure himself that the person with whom he is dealing is not armed with a weapon that could unexpectedly and fatally be used against him. Certainly it would be unreasonable to require that police officers take unnecessary risks in the performance of their duties. American criminals have a long tradition of armed violence, and every year in this country many law enforcement officers are killed in the line of duty, and thousands more are wounded. Virtually all of these deaths and a substantial portion of the injuries are inflicted with guns and knives.

In view of these facts, we cannot blind ourselves to the need for law enforcement officers to protect themselves and other prospective victims of violence in situations where they may lack probable cause for an arrest. When an officer is justified in believing that the individual whose suspicious behavior he is investigating at close range is armed and presently dangerous to the officer or to others, it would appear to be clearly unreasonable to deny the officer the power to take necessary measures to determine whether the person is in fact carrying a weapon and to neutralize the threat of physical harm.

. . .

Our evaluation of the proper balance that has to be struck in this type of case leads us to conclude that there must be a narrowly drawn authority to permit a reasonable search for weapons for the protection of the police officer, where he has reason to believe that he is dealing with an armed and dangerous individual, regardless of whether he has probable cause to arrest the individual for a crime. The officer need not be absolutely certain that the individual is armed; the issue is whether a reasonably prudent man in the circumstances would be warranted in the belief that his safety or that of others was in danger. . . .

(continued)

(continued)

. . . The actions of Terry and Chilton were consistent with McFadden's hypothesis that these men were contemplating a daylight robbery—which, it is reasonable to assume, would be likely to involve the use of weapons—and nothing in their conduct from the time he first noticed them until the time he confronted them and identified himself as a police officer gave him sufficient reason to negate that hypothesis. Although the trio had departed the original scene, there was nothing to indicate abandonment of an intent to commit a robbery at some point. Thus, when Officer McFadden approached the three men gathered before the display window at Zucker's store he had observed enough to make it quite reasonable to fear that they were armed; and nothing in their response to his hailing them, identifying himself as a police officer, and asking their names served to dispel that reasonable belief. We cannot say his decision at that point to seize Terry and pat his clothing for weapons was the product of a volatile or inventive imagination, or

was undertaken simply as an act of harassment; the record evidences the tempered act of a policeman who in the course of an investigation had to make a quick decision as to how to protect himself and others from possible danger, and took limited steps to do so.

. . .

We conclude that the revolver seized from Terry was properly admitted in evidence against him. . . .

Questions

1. What facts were most important to the *Terry* court in deciding that Officer McFadden did NOT violate the Fourth Amendment when he stopped and frisked *Terry* and Chilton?
2. Re-read the Fourth Amendment. Does its language appear to allow for any search or seizure on less than probable cause? How did the *Terry* court justify this discrepancy?

Before *Terry* v. *Ohio*, police faced a dilemma when confronted by suspicious behavior that did not rise to the level of probable cause. The *Terry* case itself was a perfect example of this dilemma. Fortunately, the court recognized the difficult position the police officer was in, and carved out a limited exception to the requirement of probable cause where a police officer can articulate facts that support a reasonable suspicion that a crime may be occurring or about the occur.

The **Terry** **stop** is a very limited exception to the probable cause requirement, because it only allows a brief stop while a police officer questions the suspect and determines if there is any probable cause to arrest. If the stop does not yield any evidence to support probable cause within a reasonable time, then the suspect must be released. How much time is required depends on the circumstances, although one rule of thumb allows for 20 minutes before the stop becomes an illegal arrest.

Terry stop
A brief investigative stop of a suspect for the purpose of determining whether there is probable cause to arrest.

LEARNING OBJECTIVE 9
Identify the circumstances when a warrant is required to make an arrest.

Arrest—Probable Cause (Always) but Seldom a Warrant

An **arrest** is the greatest infringement on the right to move freely, because an arrested suspect can be detained indefinitely and taken away from the place where the arrest occurs. An arrest cannot occur without probable cause under *any* circumstances. However, it can very easily occur without a warrant. In fact, the *only* time a warrant is required in order to arrest someone is when that person is being arrested in his/her home. Otherwise, no warrant is needed, although a hearing, called a **probable cause hearing**, will be held soon after the arrest in order to ensure that probable cause for the arrest did, in fact, exist.

arrest
Indefinite detention of a suspect upon probable cause that the suspect has committed a crime.

probable cause hearing
A hearing that determines whether there was probable cause for a warrantless arrest.

An arrest cannot take place unless and until the police have probable cause to believe that the person being arrested committed a crime.

Source: http://www.123rf.com/search. php?word=arrest+suspect& imgtype=0&t_word=&t_lang=en &oriSearch=arrest+suspect+search& sti=lbegh28as98r027ff0|&mediapo pup=940472.

Ernest Prim/123RF

The question of when a person is in his/her "home" is a tricky one, considering the fact that "home" can be just about anywhere. Is a person in his/her "home" when he/she is living in a hotel, a motel, or a boarding house? The answer depends on how long he/she is staying there, and whether he/she has anywhere more permanent to live.

There are exceptions to the rule that an arrest in the home requires a warrant, where there is probable cause to believe that a warrantless arrest in the home is necessary to prevent the destruction of evidence or to prevent harm to the officers or anyone else. For instance, if a police officer is called to a home on a domestic violence call and arrives to find a wife about to shoot or stab her husband, they don't need a warrant to arrest her. These exceptions are very limited, however, because the sanctity of the home is paramount in the law, and can be violated only in the most extraordinary circumstances.

LEARNING OBJECTIVE 10
Explain the origins of the *Miranda* warnings.

■ FIFTH AMENDMENT PROTECTION AGAINST SELF-INCRIMINATION

"You have the right to remain silent."

These words are the mainstay of many a police drama, and for good reason. They represent one of the few clearly defined, bright-line rules granted to police officers by the Supreme Court. The circumstances under which they are needed, though, deserve some explanation.

In Chapter 4, you learned that a confession is the only direct evidence of a suspect's state of mind. A confession is worth a thousand witnesses, because no one has better firsthand knowledge of the commission of a crime than the criminal himself/herself. This makes the confession an extremely powerful evidentiary tool: the Holy Grail, as it were, of criminal evidence. Because it is such a powerful piece of evidence, a confession is also the source of great temptation by police and investigators to overreach the proper bounds of constitutional conduct.

The Fifth Amendment covers a lot of ground, but for our purposes the key provision is as follows: "No person . . . shall be compelled in any criminal case to be a witness against himself." The key word in this provision is "compelled." There is nothing wrong with using anything a defendant says against him/her as evidence in a criminal case, so long as he/she was not *compelled* to make that statement.

Forced confessions are prohibited not merely because they are wrong, but because they are unreliable. The goal of criminal justice is not only to convict the guilty, but to avoid convicting the innocent. If a man confesses to a crime under threat, is he confessing because he committed the crime, or simply to prevent the threat from becoming reality? There's no way to know. Forced confessions are bad evidence, and bad evidence has no place in front of a jury.

But even without threats, the experience of being arrested and interrogated on suspicion of a crime is an extremely stressful, even traumatic, experience, especially for those who are unfamiliar with the criminal justice system and how it works. Someone who sits in an interrogation room, surrounded by police officers who are trying to convince him to confess, may not even be aware he has any choice. This is especially true if he is not schooled in his constitutional rights, as many weren't in 1966 when the Supreme Court decided *Miranda* v. *Arizona.* 384 U.S. 436, 86 S.Ct. 1602, 16 L.Ed.2d 694 (1966).

In *Miranda,* the defendant gave an oral confession after several hours of interrogation without an attorney. He was then asked to sign a written confession. The form the confession was printed on advised him that he had the right to an attorney, and stated that his confession was made voluntarily. The problem was, he had already confessed orally, before he was advised of any of his constitutional rights. He had no reason to believe that his oral confession couldn't be used against him even if he didn't sign the written one. So he signed it, thinking at that point that he had nothing left to lose.

> **LEARNING OBJECTIVE 11**
> Illustrate the situations where *Miranda* warnings are required.

The Supreme Court overturned the conviction of *Miranda* that was based on his confession. It held, in a rule that clearly defined what police officers interrogating suspects must do, that no confession can be used as evidence unless it is *preceded* by a statement informing the defendant of four things:

- that he has the right to remain silent (an application of the Fifth Amendment);
- that anything he says can be used against him in court;
- that he has a right to have an attorney present during questioning (a right found in the Sixth Amendment); and
- that if he cannot afford an attorney, one will be appointed for him by the court (an application of the Supreme Court's holding in *Gideon* v. *Wainwright,* 372 U.S. 335 (1963)).

Miranda rights
The rights of which every suspect in custody must be notified before an interrogation is permitted.

Miranda established a "bright-line" test for constitutionally valid interrogations. If a suspect is in custody (meaning that he/she has been arrested), and if he/she is going to be interrogated (meaning that anything is going to be done to get him/her to make incriminating statements), then he/she *must* be advised of his/her **Miranda rights**. If he/she is, then anything he/she says can be used as evidence. If not, then nothing he/she says can be used as evidence.

The Fifth Amendment also requires that any interrogation stop immediately if a defendant indicates that he/she does not want to talk, or that he/she wants a lawyer present during questioning. This means that police cannot try and persuade the defendant to talk by any means once those rights have been invoked.

PRACTICE TIP

To avoid application of the exclusionary rule to any confession that might be obtained from a suspect, no attempt should be made to elicit any information orally from a suspect who had clearly indicated his/her desire not to speak during an interrogation.

In *Mincey* v. *Arizona*, the U.S. Supreme Court addressed the question of whether statements made by a defendant in the hospital during an interrogation that persisted after he indicated his desire not to answer questions without his lawyer present could be used to impeach his testimony at trial. Although the exclusionary rule does not usually apply to "collateral uses" such as impeachment (see above), the Supreme Court held that the violation of *Mincey*'s rights was so egregious in this case that his "sickbed statements" should not be permitted to be used for any purpose.

COURT OPINION 6-4

MINCEY V. ARIZONA, 437 U.S. 385, 98 S.Ct. 2408 (1978)

[The court held that evidence obtained from a warrantless search of the defendant petitioner's apartment was inadmissible as a violation of the defendant's Fourth Amendment rights.] Since there will presumably be a new trial in this case, it is appropriate to consider also the petitioner's contention that statements he made from a hospital bed were involuntary, and therefore could not constitutionally be used against him at his trial.

Mincey was brought to the hospital after the shooting and taken immediately to the emergency room where he was examined and treated. He had sustained a wound in his hip, resulting in damage to the sciatic nerve and partial paralysis of his right leg. Tubes were inserted into his throat to help him breathe, and through his nose into his stomach to keep him from vomiting; a catheter was inserted into his bladder. He received various drugs, and a device was attached to his arm so that he could be fed intravenously. He was then taken to the intensive care unit.

At about eight o'clock that evening, Detective Hust of the Tucson Police Department came to the intensive care unit to interrogate him. Mincey was unable to talk because of the tube in his mouth, and so he responded to Detective Hust's questions by writing answers on pieces of paper provided by the hospital. Hust told Mincey he was under arrest for the murder of a police officer, gave him the warnings required by *Miranda v. Arizona*, 384 U.S. 436, 86 S.Ct. 1602, 16 L.Ed.2d 694, and began to ask questions about the events that had taken place in Mincey's apartment a few hours earlier. Although Mincey asked repeatedly that the interrogation stop until he could get a lawyer, Hust continued to question him until almost midnight.

. . .

It is hard to imagine a situation less conducive to the exercise of "a rational intellect and a free will" than Mincey's. He had been seriously wounded just a few hours earlier, and had arrived at the hospital

(continued)

(continued)

"depressed almost to the point of coma," according to his attending physician. Although he had received some treatment, his condition at the time of Hust's interrogation was still sufficiently serious that he was in the intensive care unit. He complained to Hust that the pain in his leg was "unbearable." He was evidently confused and unable to think clearly about either the events of that afternoon or the circumstances of his interrogation, since some of his written answers were on their face not entirely coherent. Finally, while Mincey was being questioned he was lying on his back on a hospital bed, encumbered by tubes, needles, and breathing apparatus. He was, in short, "at the complete mercy" of Detective Hust, unable to escape or resist the thrust of Hust's interrogation. Cf. *Beecher v. Alabama*, 389 U.S. 35, 38, 88 S.Ct. 189, 191, 19 L.Ed.2d 35.

In this debilitated and helpless condition, Mincey clearly expressed his wish not to be interrogated. As soon as Hust's questions turned to the details of the afternoon's events, Mincey wrote: "This is all I can say without a lawyer." Hust nonetheless continued to question him, and a nurse who was present suggested it would be best if Mincey answered. Mincey gave unresponsive or uninformative answers to several more questions, and then said again that he did not want to talk without a lawyer. Hust ignored that request and another made immediately thereafter. Indeed, throughout the interrogation Mincey vainly asked Hust to desist. Moreover, he complained several times that he was confused or unable to think clearly, or that he could answer more accurately the

next day. But despite Mincey's entreaties to be let alone, Hust ceased the interrogation only during intervals when Mincey lost consciousness or received medical treatment, and after each such interruption returned relentlessly to his task. The statements at issue were thus the result of virtually continuous questioning of a seriously and painfully wounded man on the edge of consciousness.

. . .

It is apparent from the record in this case that Mincey's statements were not "the product of his free and rational choice." *Greenwald v. Wisconsin*, 390 U.S. 519, 521, 88 S.Ct. 1152, 1154, 20 L.Ed.2d 77. To the contrary, the undisputed evidence makes clear that Mincey wanted not to answer Detective Hust. But Mincey was weakened by pain and shock, isolated from family, friends, and legal counsel, and barely conscious, and his will was simply overborne. Due process of law requires that statements obtained as these were cannot be used in any way against a defendant at his trial.

Questions

1. *Mincey* was read his *Miranda* rights and understood those rights. Why, then, did the court conclude that his statements could not be admitted against him?
2. What should the investigators have done in order to ensure that *Mincey*'s interrogation did not violate the Fifth Amendment?

Recently the Court of Appeals of Wisconsin applied the standards set forth in *Mincey* in the case of *State* v. *Bullock*, holding that the defendant's questioning by police was not a violation of his Fifth Amendment rights, and distinguishing the defendant's circumstances from those of the defendant in *Mincey*.

COURT OPINION 6-5

STATE V. BULLOCK, 844 N.W.2d 429 (2014)

On appeal, Bullock argues that the trial court erred in denying his motion to suppress because neither his statement to Officer Phelps nor his statement to Detectives Young and Gulbrandson was voluntary. . . .

"A defendant's statements are voluntary if they are the product of a free and unconstrained will, reflecting deliberateness of choice, as opposed to the result of a conspicuously unequal confrontation in

(continued)

(continued)

which the pressures brought to bear on the defendant by representatives of the State exceeded the defendant's ability to resist." *State v. Hoppe*, 2003 WI 43, 36, 261 Wis.2d 294, 661 N.W.2d 407. To determine whether a defendant's statements are voluntary, we apply a "totality of the circumstances" test. *See id.*, 38. "The totality of the circumstances analysis involves a balancing of the personal characteristics of the defendant against the pressures imposed upon the defendant by law enforcement officers." *Id*. The personal characteristics of the defendant that we consider "include the defendant's age, education and intelligence, physical and emotional condition, and prior experience with law enforcement." *See id.*, 39.

. . . Bullock claims that his physical condition and Officer Phelps' decision to ask him questions, despite his injuries and disorientation, is analogous to circumstances surrounding police questioning of a hospitalized man that the United States Supreme Court found improper in *Mincey*.

Similarly, with regard to his statement to Detectives Gulbrandson and Young, Bullock sets forth several factors that he claims place the circumstances surrounding his statement in line with—or even more egregious than—*Mincey*: (1) he was questioned by two detectives, instead of one; (2) he was in the hospital's intensive care unit and taking medications for his pain, and he made moaning sounds due to his pain; and (3) he could not tell the detectives what day it was.

We disagree with Bullock regarding both statements. Bullock highlights only a few of the numerous factors we must consider in weighing the totality of the circumstances of his statements. . . . Evaluating all of the circumstances the law requires us to consider leads us to conclude that Bullock's statements to Officer Phelps and Detectives Gulbrandson and Young were voluntarily made. Moreover, as we will explain below, *Mincey* is inapposite.

Turning first to Bullock's personal characteristics, . . .while Bullock's injuries were described by Officer Phelps as "extensive," and while Bullock did make moaning sounds due to his pain at the beginning of the hospital interview, there is no indication that the pain interfered with his ability to speak with law enforcement in these particular circumstances . . .

. . .

Turning next to "the pressures imposed by police," . . . we conclude that the record is devoid of any information that would lead us to conclude that the police officers who questioned Bullock acted improperly. Bullock does not argue that the length of questioning was improper, not does he argue that there was any delay in arraignment. . . . As for the general conditions under which he gave his statements, Bullock takes issue with the fact that *two* detectives questioned him at the hospital, but that fact, without more, is not enough to evince coercion. . . . In addition, Bullock does not argue that he should have been read his *Miranda* rights before giving his statement to Officer Phelps, nor does he argue that he did not understand the *Miranda* warnings given by Detectives Gulbrandson and Young in his hospital room.

[A]s the trial court found, and as Bullock does not refute, "[t]here were no threats made," nor any raised voices, "[n]or any kind of indication of any kind of pressure put on him by the officers." This last point forms the lynchpin of our analysis, as our supreme court has clearly held "that in order to justify a finding of involuntariness, there must be some affirmative evidence of improper police practices deliberately used to procure" a statement. . . .

Furthermore, neither Bullock's personal characteristics nor the actions of police in this case mirror the facts of *Mincey*, the case on which Bullock primarily relies to support his contentions. First, the physical condition of the defendant in *Mincey* was far worse; indeed, the Supreme Court described him as "seriously and painfully wounded . . . on the edge of consciousness." *See [Mincey]*, 437 U.S. at 401, 98 S.Ct. 2408. The court also noted:

> [Mincey] had sustained a wound in his hip, resulting in damage to the sciatic nerve and partial paralysis of his right leg. Tubes were inserted into his throat to help him breathe, and through his nose into his stomach to keep him from vomiting; a catheter was inserted into his bladder. He received various drugs, and a device was attached to his arm so that he could be fed intravenously. He was then taken to the intensive care unit . . .. Mincey was unable to talk because of the tube in his mouth, and so he responded to Detective Hust's questions by writing answers on pieces of paper provided by the hospital.

See id. at 396, 98 S.Ct. 2408 (some formatting altered). Second, unlike Officer Phelps and Detectives Gulbrandson and Young, the police officer who questioned Mincey undoubtedly coerced Mincey into giving a statement. . . . No such misconduct occurred in Bullock's case.

. . .

(continued)

(continued)

In sum, the totality of the circumstances shows that Bullock's statements were "the product of a free and unconstrained will, reflecting deliberateness of choice." *See Hoppe*, 261 Wis.2d 294, 36, 661 N.W.2d 407. We therefore conclude that the trial court properly denied Bullock's motion to suppress.

Questions

1. What were the key factors leading the Bullock court to distinguish this case from *Mincey*?
2. Why did the court feel that, under the circumstances, Bullock's statements were made voluntarily?

It should be noted that reading a defendant the *Miranda* warning is necessary only when the suspect is being taken into custody and interrogated. The *Miranda* warnings are *not* an essential part of the arresting process, and they are not required during a voluntary encounter or a stop. But the moment an arrest occurs, they must be read to the defendant if any questions are going to be asked. And if the defendant has any trouble understanding them (for instance, if the defendant does not speak English), those issues must be addressed or the interrogation cannot proceed.

KEY TERMS

exclusionary rule   120
Fourteenth Amendment   120
the fruit of the poisonous tree
   doctrine   120
independent source rule   120
inevitable discovery rule   120
collateral use rule   120
warrant   121

search warrant   121
arrest warrant   121
probable cause affidavit   121
plain-view search   125
open field search   125
frisk   125
consent   125
search incident to an arrest   127

vehicle search   128
container search   128
voluntary encounter   130
Terry stop   133
arrest   133
probable cause
   hearing   133
Miranda rights   136

CHAPTER SUMMARY

- The exclusionary rule prohibits the admission of evidence that is obtained in violation of the defendant's constitutional rights.
- Under the "fruit of the poisonous tree" doctrine, the exclusionary rule applies to all evidence obtained as a result of a constitutional violation.
- Evidence that is obtained from sources independent of the constitutional violation, or that would have been inevitably discovered by valid means, is not prohibited under the exclusionary rule.

- Evidence not used to prove a defendant's guilt is not barred by the exclusionary rule.
- While the Fourth Amendment seems to require a warrant for every search and seizure, many occur without warrants.
- A warrant is permission to search or arrest, given by a magistrate based on facts contained in an affidavit of probable cause filed by a law enforcement officer.
- To be valid, a warrant must specify the area to be searched or the person to be arrested.

- Probable cause exists when the officer can articulate facts that support a reasonable belief that a crime is occurring or has occurred.
- Plain-view searches and searches of open fields and abandoned property are not "searches" within the meaning of the Fourth Amendment, and can occur without probable cause.
- Frisks are pat-downs of a suspect's outer clothing to determine if he/she is armed, and are valid as long as they occur during a valid *Terry* stop and are supported by a reasonable suspicion that the suspect may be armed.
- Consent searches can take place without probable cause or a warrant as long as the suspect's consent was given voluntarily and the search does not exceed the scope of the consent.
- Voluntary encounters, where a person reasonably believes he/she is free to walk away from a questioning officer, are not "seizures" within the meaning of the Fourth Amendment.
- A *Terry* stop is a brief investigative stop that may occur based on a reasonable suspicion that a crime may have been committed, for the purpose of determining if there is probable cause to arrest.
- An arrest cannot occur without probable cause, but a warrant is only required when the suspect is arrested in his/her home, unless emergency conditions allow a warrantless arrest.
- In order to satisfy the Fifth Amendment, a suspect who is being interrogated must be informed of his/her right to remain silent and his/her right to counsel.
- The *Miranda* rights are only required when a suspect is in custody and when police intend to interrogate him/her.

WEB EXCURSION

1. Using Google or another search engine, find court opinions or articles describing cases in your state where a conviction has been overturned based on an improper search and seizure or confession. Given what you now know about how evidence is affected by constitutional concerns, do you believe that justice was served in that case?

PRACTICAL EXERCISE

1. Determine in the following scenario what evidence, if any, would be inadmissible under the exclusionary rule.

   a. A police officer stops a car being driven erratically down a busy freeway. The driver is a woman in her late 70s, who is obviously shaken and nervous when the police officer approaches. She immediately begins apologizing profusely before the officer has a chance to say anything. The officer asks the woman to produce her driver's license and registration, at which point the woman leans over and, while retrieving the items from her glove box, slips a small package beneath the passenger seat of the car. The officer asks what the package was, and the woman replies, "Oh, nothing." The officer asks the woman to step out of the car, which she does, and then asks her if she will consent to a search of her car. She replies, "I guess I don't have much choice, do I?" and the police officer replies, "Well, ma'am, it's up to you if you want to consent, but I need to know what you put beneath the seat." She then says, "All right, go ahead and look." The police officer retrieves the package and opens it to find a small mace sprayer. "I thought you'd be mad if you saw that," the woman said. The police officer then searches the rest of the car and discovers a small amount of marijuana underneath the driver's side seat. He promptly arrests the woman for drug possession.

   b. Based on information obtained from a much-used informant, a police officer knocks on the door of a suspected drug dealer. Moments later, the door opens. The suspect sees the officer and quickly closes the door. The police officer then kicks the door in and grabs the suspect, who immediately surrenders to him. He conducts a pat-down search of the man's clothes and finds a vial of pills in the man's front left pocket. The officer recognizes the pills as amphetamines. The officer places the vial in his shirt pocket and proceeds to arrest the man for drug possession.

c. A police officer has a warrant, based on an affidavit of probable cause that relied primarily on information obtained from an often-used and reliable informant, which authorizes the search for "any controlled substances or paraphernalia for the use of controlled substances found at a house located at 50 W. Lucian Lane, Morrisdale, Pennsylvania." The officer proceeds to the correct house and knocks and announces his presence. There is no answer, so the police officer breaks down the door. Finding no one in the house, the officer begins his search. As he does so, he discovers a wide array of illicit drugs and drug paraphernalia. While searching a room that contains a computer, the police officer accidentally nudges the computer mouse, causing the computer monitor to activate. The monitor shows a standard Windows desktop. The police officer continues the search. After a few minutes, the computer monitor goes blank for a second, and then a series of pornographic pictures begin to appear as a type of screen saver. The police officer watches the screen and realizes after a few minutes that many of the pictures are of underage girls. The officer then sits down at the computer, does a search for picture files, and discovers a folder filled with hundreds of child pornography files. Just then, the suspected drug dealer returns home. The police officer arrests him for drug possession and for possession of child pornography.

ENDNOTES

1. The Fourteenth Amendment, that requires states to provide due process and equal protection of the laws to its citizens, is the main vehicle by which the Bill of Rights has been applied to criminal cases in state courts.

2. Dixon, E. (September 1, 2011). Best Practices in Mobile Phone Investigations. *Evidence Technology Magazine*, September–October, 2011, page 27.

Rich Legg/Getty Images

LEARNING OBJECTIVES

After reading this chapter, the student will be able to:

1. Explain what it means for a witness to be competent to testify.

2. Distinguish between testimony based on firsthand knowledge and testimony that is not.

3. Understand the purpose of the oath witnesses are required to take before testifying.

4. Explain the process of laying a foundation and conducting a *voir dire* to prove competence.

5. Explain how age, mental illness, and language affect competence in federal courts.

6. Explain the circumstances under which a lay witness can offer an opinion.

7. Illustrate the standards for admissibility of expert opinions.

8. Understand and apply the *Frye* and *Daubert* tests to the content of expert testimony.

Competence

CHAPTER 7

■ INTRODUCTION

Competence and authenticity, while dealing with two very different forms of evidence (testimony and real evidence, respectively), have this in common: they are both "threshold" requirements without which evidence will not even be considered for admission into the record of a criminal case. A witness' competence to testify, if challenged, must be established before one word of testimony can be received. The authenticity of a piece of real evidence must be established before the jury can even consider it as evidence. For this reason, we begin our discussion of admissibility with these two concepts: competence in this chapter and authenticity in Chapter 8.

■ THE MEANING OF "COMPETENCE"

LEARNING OBJECTIVE 1
Explain what it means for a witness to be competent to testify.

competence
The ability of a witness to testify truthfully.

"**Competence**" refers to the ability of a witness to testify truthfully about a matter involved in a case. Federal Rules of Evidence 601 through 606 lay out the basic foundation of competence in federal courts. Under Rule 601(a), every person is presumed to be competent unless a statute or other rule provides otherwise.

143

Competence has nothing to do with the *willingness* of a witness to testify truthfully. That issue relates to credibility, which is discussed in Chapter 13.

Minimum Standards of Competence

A competent witness is simply one who meets the minimum qualifications to testify before a jury, and as Rule 601 points out, the presumption of competence is a strong one.

Personal Knowledge

LEARNING OBJECTIVE 2
Distinguish between testimony based on firsthand knowledge and testimony that is not.

personal knowledge
Knowledge that originates in the mind of a witness through his/her own perception or mental processes.

The primary qualification for a competent witness is that his/her testimony must be based on personal knowledge. Rule 602 states that "A witness may testify to a matter only if evidence is introduced sufficient to support a finding that the witness has personal knowledge of the matter." By "**personal knowledge**," we mean knowledge that originated in the mind of the witness through his/her own perceptions or mental processes, not knowledge that was placed in his/her mind by someone else.

For example, if I'm standing in a convenience store when it is robbed, I am competent to testify about everything I saw and heard while the robbery was taking place. I can testify about the physical appearance of the robber, where he was standing, what he said, what he took, whether shots were fired, and so forth. If I told my friend, who was not there, everything I saw and heard, my friend would not be competent to testify about the robbery, because her knowledge is based on my perceptions rather than her own. She is, however, competent to testify about the words I spoke when I described the robbery to her, because she heard those words with her own ears. So my friend could be called to court to testify that the story I told her was, or was not, the same as the story I told to the police or when I testified in court. But she would not be permitted to say a single word in court about the actual robbery.

laying a foundation for competence
The production of evidence necessary to establish the competence of a witness.

Rule 602 also requires evidence to be presented proving that the witness' testimony is based on personal knowledge. This is known as **laying a foundation for competence**, and it is an essential part of the questioning of a witness. Usually, laying a foundation for competence is not difficult. When calling me as a witness to the robbery in the above example, the prosecuting attorney would lay a foundation for my competence by asking me where I was and what I was doing at the time of the robbery. Once I testified that I was at the convenience store when the robbery occurred, the requirement of Rule 602 would be satisfied, and I could proceed to describe what I saw and heard. The defense counsel can challenge the truthfulness or accuracy of my testimony, but he/she cannot challenge my competence to give it.

SAMPLE TRIAL TRANSCRIPT 7-1

Establishing Personal Knowledge

Prosecutor:	Mr. Jensen, were you present in the defendant's office when the check was signed?
Mr. Jensen:	Yes, I was.
Prosecutor:	And did you see the defendant place his signature on the check?
Mr. Jensen:	Yes, I did.

Prosecutor:	Now, Mr. Jensen, who was the check made out to?
Attorney 2:	Objection, your Honor. There is nothing on the record to indicate that Mr. Jensen is competent to answer questions about the contents of the check.
Judge:	Sustained.
Attorney 1:	Mr. Jensen, did you have the opportunity to see what was written on the check before it was signed?
Witness:	Yes, I did.
Attorney 1:	And who was the check made out to?
Witness:	It was made out to Barry Johnson.

Why did the judge sustain the objection about Mr. Jensen's competence? Because the attorney questioning him had not asked him the critical question: did you see the check itself? He only asked if Mr. Jensen had seen the check being signed. Until a foundation was laid showing that Mr. Jensen had actually seen the check, there was nothing to prove that Mr. Jensen's knowledge about the contents of the check was firsthand.

In the following case, *United States v. Diaz*, the defendant was arrested as part of a conspiracy to engage in drug trafficking and various firearms-related offenses. Several of his co-conspirators were arrested based on statements by a police officer that he had seen the co-conspirators engaged in a drug transaction. Diaz sought to introduce testimony of the mother of one of the co-conspirators to impeach the police officer's testimony by showing that he could not have seen a drug transaction taking place, because of the circumstances of the arrest of the two co-conspirators. Based on the offer of proof provided by Diaz to support the witness' testimony, the trial judge refused to allow the witness to testify based on her lack of competence. Diaz appealed his conviction, claiming in part that the trial judge erred in excluding the witness' testimony.

COURT OPINION 7-1 _____

UNITED STATES V. DIAZ, 670 F.3d 332 (1ST Cir. 2012)

Rodríguez–Romero's first argument is that the district court violated his constitutional right to present a complete defense by refusing to let him introduce extrinsic evidence that he claims "could have" impeached Police Officer Víctor M. Veguilla Figuero. On October 24, 2008, Veguilla arrested Rodríguez–Romero with 150 vials of crack outside a home in Guayama, Puerto Rico. Rodríguez–Romero had stopped in front of the house in a grey Ford Taurus. Veguilla testified that he received an instruction to arrest Rodríguez–Romero from a colleague, Officer Pérez, who claimed to have witnessed Rodríguez–Romero conducting a drug sale with a co-conspirator named David de León. On the same day, Pérez arrested David de León.

At trial, Rodríguez–Romero sought to introduce the testimony of Tomasa Colón–Pérez, David de León's mother and the owner of the house in front of which Rodríguez–Romero was arrested. The district court reviewed Colon–Pérez's testimony outside the presence of the jury. Colon–Pérez's offer of proof was that, on the evening of October 24, 2008, she was sitting outside her house when police officers ran into her house and arrested her son, David. She witnessed the officers handcuff her son, and then a female officer escorted her into a bedroom, where Colon–Pérez remained for a period of time. She was allowed to exit the bedroom and kiss her son before the officers escorted him out of the house through

(continued)

(continued)

the "door in the back of the room which leads to the yard." The officers then brought Colon–Pérez back into the bedroom. About two hours went by, according to Colon–Pérez, at which point the officers standing in the bedroom with her said something to the effect of, "It's about to arrive. It's about to arrive." A few minutes later, the officers said, "It arrived. The car arrived." Colon–Pérez then heard a voice in the house say, "David, David." From the bedroom, she could not see who was speaking, nor could she identify the voice. Colón–Pérez was inside her home, could not see outside, and did not witness Rodríguez–Romero's arrest.

Though the offer of proof at trial was less than lucid, Rodríguez–Romero's attorney apparently sought to introduce Colon–Pérez's testimony in order to impeach Veguilla by showing that: (1) Officer Pérez could not have witnessed David de León and Rodríguez–Romero conducting a drug sale, because de León was already under arrest at that point; and (2) more generally, the events that day could not have transpired as Veguilla claimed they had, since de León was arrested two hours before Rodríguez–Romero.

Rodríguez–Romero's argument fails. Colón–Pérez did not witness the arrest of Rodríguez–Romero, which is the arrest Veguilla conducted and about which he testified. Colón–Pérez contradicted none of the specific events that Veguilla described in his testimony. Veguilla did not testify that the drug sale between de León and Rodríguez–Romero occurred outside Colón–Pérez's house, that de León and Rodríguez–Romero were immediately arrested following the sale, or that de León was still present at the house when Veguilla arrested Rodríguez–Romero. Nor did Colón–Pérez see the car that was allegedly "arriving" such that she could establish

that the activity she heard two hours after her son's arrest was indeed the arrest of Rodríguez–Romero.

Rodríguez–Romero argues that the exclusion of Colón–Pérez's testimony denied him "a meaningful opportunity to present a complete defense," a right the Constitution guarantees, "[w]hether rooted directly in the Due Process Clause of the Fourteenth Amendment, or in the Compulsory Process or Confrontation clauses of the Sixth Amendment." *Crane v. Kentucky*, 476 U.S. 683, 690, 106 S.Ct. 2142, 90 L.Ed.2d 636 (1986) (internal citation and quotation marks omitted). Yet a defendant's right to present relevant evidence in his own defense "is not unlimited, but rather is subject to reasonable restrictions." *United States v. Scheffer*, 523 U.S. 303, 308, 118 S.Ct. 1261, 140 L.Ed.2d 413 (1998). *See also Taylor v. Illinois*, 484 U.S. 400, 410, 108 S.Ct. 646, 98 L.Ed.2d 798 (1988) ("The accused does not have an unfettered right to offer testimony that is incompetent, privileged, or otherwise inadmissible under standard rules of evidence."). A witness cannot testify to a matter unless there is evidence sufficient to support a finding that she has personal knowledge of the matter. Fed.R.Evid. 602. We fail to see how Colón–Pérez had sufficient personal knowledge to testify regarding Rodríguez–Romero's arrest, *see id.*, nor do we understand how her testimony would have been relevant to impeach Veguilla, *see* Fed.R.Evid. 401, 403. We thus affirm.

Questions

1. For what purpose did Diaz seek to introduce the testimony of Tomasa Colón–Pérez?
2. Why did the court decide that Tomasa Colón–Pérez's testimony was neither competent nor relevant to impeach Officer Veguilla's testimony?

LEARNING OBJECTIVE 3
Understand the purpose of the oath witnesses are required to take before testifying.

The Oath

Rule 603 requires the administration of an *oath* to testify truthfully. The purpose of the oath is simply to make sure the witness understands that he/she had a duty to tell the truth. The oath must be "in a form designed to impress that duty on the witness's conscience." Usually, this is accomplished with the familiar, "Do you solemnly swear or affirm that the testimony you are about to give in this matter shall be the truth, the whole truth, and nothing but the truth?"[1]

In one court in which the author once practiced, the oath was somewhat more elaborate: "Do you swear before God, the searcher of all hearts, that the testimony you shall give in this matter shall be the truth, the whole truth, and nothing but the truth, as you shall answer on that Last Great Day?" Such strong admonitions of divine accountability, or even a belief by the witness in a higher power, are not required in order to fulfill the requirement of Rule 603. But failing to take the oath disqualifies a witness from testifying.

Voir Dire to Establish General Competence

There are times when the competence of a witness may be called into question, not due to a lack of personal knowledge, but due to factors such as age or mental illness that may affect the witness' ability to tell the truth or understand the duty to do so. The federal rules say nothing about age or mental capacity as a barrier to competence, and the explanatory notes accompanying Rule 601 specifically deny any such requirement. Such factors generally affect the witness' credibility rather than his/her competence. But state rules may still require a threshold level of competence to be established based on age or mental capacity. Where these issues are raised by opposing counsel, a more extensive examination of the witness may be needed to ensure that he/she is competent. This examination, called a ***voir dire***, may take place in open court, or, if the witness is very young or susceptible to anxiety, in the judge's chambers with all counsel present.

A *voir dire* to establish general competence is not meant to elicit evidentiary testimony from the witness. Its sole purpose is to ensure that the witness is capable of telling the truth and understands the duty to tell the truth. If those foundational elements of competence cannot be laid to the judge's satisfaction, then the witness will not be permitted to testify.

> **LEARNING OBJECTIVE 4**
> Explain the process of laying a foundation and conducting a *voir dire* to prove competence.

> **voir dire**
> A proceeding at which the competence of a witness is established.

> **LEARNING OBJECTIVE 5**
> Explain how age, mental illness, and language affect competence in federal courts.

> **PRACTICE TIP**
> Whenever you are depending on a witness whose competence might be called into question, it is critically important to examine that witness before trial to ensure that competence can be established, and to prepare the witness for the likelihood that a *voir dire* will take place.

SAMPLE TRIAL TRANSCRIPT 7-2

Voir Dire of a Child Witness

Prosecutor:	The state calls Tommy McPaulson to the stand.
Defense:	Your Honor, we would ask for an offer of proof on the competence of this witness.
Judge:	Very well. Let's do this in chambers. [The judge, attorneys, and witness go to the judge's chambers.]
Judge:	Tommy, how old are you?
Tommy:	Seven.
Judge:	Tommy, do you understand why you are here today?
Tommy:	Yeah, I gotta tell you what happened.
Judge:	That's right. And when you tell what happened, do you understand that it is important that you tell the truth?

Tommy:	Yeah.
Judge:	Do you know what happens to people who don't tell the truth?
Tommy:	Yeah. They get in a lot of trouble, and maybe even get a time out or have to sit in the corner.
Judge:	And those are bad things, aren't they?
Tommy:	Yeah. Really bad.
Judge:	So when you tell the people out in the courtroom what happened, are you going to tell them the truth?
Tommy:	Yes.
Judge:	And you know that it is very important to tell the truth when you talk to those people, right?
Tommy:	Yeah. I wouldn't ever lie, because lying is really bad.
Judge:	Now when you talk to those people, do you remember the things you are going to say to them?
Tommy:	Yeah.
Judge:	Do you remember them for yourself, or were you told what to say?
Tommy:	No, I remember it myself. I remember everything that happened real good.
Judge:	And you understand, don't you, that when you tell the people out there what you remember, you have to tell it just like it happened?
Tommy:	Yeah, because it would be a lie if I didn't.
Judge:	Thank you, Tommy. (To the attorneys) Do either of you have any questions for Tommy?
Attorneys:	No, Your Honor.
Judge:	Let's go back out to the courtroom. (In the courtroom) Back on the record, I have examined the witness and find that he is competent to testify. Please proceed.

Interpretation

A witness is competent if he/she can accurately express the truth, but what if he/she can only do so in a language other than English? In situations where a witness does not speak English, or does not speak it well enough to testifying meaningfully, an **interpreter** must be used. An interpreter is not simply someone who is bilingual. Knowing how to say something in two languages does not mean that the person can translate between the languages, because of the idiosyncrasies of dialect and expressions that do not translate literally. A qualified interpreter would understand the different syntax and grammar used in each language, and interprets not only the words, but also the meaning.

The most qualified interpreters are highly trained expert in language translation who is familiar with the dialect as well as the language spoken by the witness, and able to translate both to and from that language and dialect. Under Rule 604, "an interpreter must be qualified and must give an oath or affirmation to make a true translation." This requires an expert *voir dire*, which will be discussed in more detail below.

interpreter
One skilled in the ability to translate from one language and dialect into another.

An unusual application of Rule 604 occurred in the following case, in which the prosecutor's main witness was deaf and unable to communicate orally. The court allowed the witness' wife to interpret for him. The defendant challenged this decision based on the alleged bias of the interpreter as well as her lack of interpreting skill, both of which would normally present serious issues of due process. Here, however, the appellate court found that the interpreter, despite being the wife of the key prosecution witness, was a proper choice under the circumstances.

COURT OPINION 7-2

UNITED STATES V. BALL, 988 F.2d 7 (5th Cir. 1993)

The Government's principal evidence was the testimony of Dudley Wriley. Neither party disputes that Dudley Wriley was deaf, his spoken words unintelligible, or that his wife was appointed and sworn as an interpreter of his speech. Ball, however, asserts that it was improper to appoint an interpreter where, as here, the witness could have responded to counsel's questions through written statements or other unspecified means.

. . . . The trial court held a hearing outside the presence of the jury to determine the proper procedure to elicit Dudley Wriley's testimony. The Government proposed to have Wriley's wife, Ophelia Wriley, act as an interpreter to which Ball objected, but failed to offer an alternative. Thereafter, the trial court gave the parties an opportunity to question Wriley's wife with respect to her ability and qualifications and the opportunity to test the adequacy of her interpretive skills by allowing counsel from both sides to ask questions of Wriley through his wife. The trial court found that the long-standing relationship between the witness and his wife allowed the two to communicate with one another freely and then qualified her as an expert pursuant to Federal Rules of Evidence Rules 604 and 702. The defendant renewed his objection to the use of an interpreter, but he continued to offer no alternative to the Government's proposed method of eliciting the testimony and his objection was overruled. Under these circumstances, we find the trial court's initial decision to appoint an interpreter to have been within its sound discretion.

Ball next argues that the trial court erred in failing to terminate the questioning of Wriley when it became necessary for his wife to repeat and rephrase questions posed by counsel. Ball further contends that the trial court erred in allowing Wriley's wife to interject statements outside the scope of her husband's

responses to the questions posed. At the trial level, Ball's objection was limited to receiving the testimony through an interpreter and Ball's qualitative objections are raised for the first time on appeal. In the absence of an objection below, we may only reverse the conviction if the trial court's error, if any, rises to the level of plain error. *See United States v. King*, 505 F.2d 602, 605 (5th Cir. 1974).

It is well established that an interpreter must have no interest in the outcome of a criminal proceeding if he or she is to act in his or her professional capacity during the course of those proceedings. There is, however, no absolute bar against appointing a witness' relative to act as an interpreter when circumstances warrant such an appointment. *See United States v. Addonizio*, 451 F.2d 49, 68 (3d Cir. 1971), *cert. denied*, 405 U.S. 936, 92 S.Ct. 949, 30 L.Ed.2d 812 (1972). Rather, the trial court must take into consideration the unique circumstances of each case including the interpreter's interest and involvement in the case, the necessity of having a family member act as an interpreter, and available alternative modes of testimony. Here, the interpreter's only connection to the defendant was that she was married to a witness at the defendant's trial. Moreover, the nature of the witness's handicap made it necessary for the trial court to appoint someone familiar with the witness and "prevented the court from obtaining a wholly disinterested person." *See Prince v. Beto*, 426 F.2d 875, 876 (5th Cir. 1970). In the absence of the slightest showing that the interpreter harbored any feelings of malice or prejudice toward the defendant, we find no reason to believe that Mrs. Wriley's interest in the trial's outcome was so prodigious as to pose a threat to the fairness of the proceedings. *Id.* at 876-77.

Defendant's argument that the interpretation provided by Wriley's wife was of such poor quality

(continued)

(continued)

as to deprive the defendant of a fair trial and his rights to due process is also without merit. Our review of the record of the proceedings below revealed that the interpreter posed the questions asked to her husband as they were stated to her by counsel and re-phrased those questions only when it was necessary to assist her husband in understanding a particular question. Mrs. Wriley's translation of the defendant's statements were likewise to the point and without superfluous explanation. On the one occasion when Mrs. Wriley interjected a statement that fell outside the scope of her husband's response to a question, she relayed a fact within her personal knowledge that had little, if any, bearing on the defendant's participation in the alleged criminal conduct. . . . Finally, the trial court went to great lengths to instruct the jury regarding Mrs. Wriley's limited role within the proceedings thereby ensuring that her particular participation as an interpreter was well understood by the jury. We therefore hold that the district court did not commit error, let alone, plain error.

Questions

1. On what basis did the defendant claim that the wife of a witness is not qualified under Rule 604 to act as an interpreter?
2. What does this case tell us about the ability of a witness to be qualified as an expert based on her personal experience as opposed to formal training?

Judges and Jurors

Under Rule 605, a judge may never testify in a trial over which he/she is presiding. Rule 606 provides that a juror may not testify as a witness before the other jurors. The only subject matter a juror can testify to relates to the integrity of the jury's deliberations and verdict. Under Rule 606(b), a juror can testify to

- extraneous prejudicial information that was improperly brought to the jury's attention;
- an outside influence that was improperly brought to bear on any juror; or
- a mistake made in entering the verdict on the verdict form.

Except for these limited concerns, no juror can sit in the witness chair and remain a juror.

Opinion Testimony

A special issue of competence is raised when a witness is asked to give an **opinion** as part of his/her testimony. Opinions generally consist of the witness' conclusions about the facts, rather than simply a recitation of the facts themselves. Opinions are problematic because it is the jury, not the witness, that is empowered to make conclusions about the facts of a case. In many circumstances, though, the conclusions of a witness are helpful, even necessary, for a complete picture of the facts to be laid before the jury. Such opinions are divided into two categories: lay and expert.

Opinions by Lay Witnesses

Rule 701 states that a **lay witness** (i.e., "nonexpert") is competent to give an opinion where it is (a) "rationally based on the perception of the witness," (b) "helpful to a clear understanding of the witness' testimony or the

opinion
A statement of a witness' conclusion about a fact.

LEARNING OBJECTIVE 6
Explain the circumstances under which a lay witness can offer an opinion.

lay witness
An opinion witness who is not offering an opinion as an expert.

determination of a fact in issue," and (c) "not based on scientific, technical, or other specialized knowledge" that falls within the scope of expert testimony. This means that a witness can give an opinion so long as it is based on what the witness himself/herself saw or heard, it is going to make it easier for the jury to do its job of deciding the facts of the case, and it isn't something the witness would need specialized knowledge to understand.

Lay opinions are permitted under Rule 701 on matters such as the appearance of people or things, identity, the manner of conduct, competency of a person, degrees of light or darkness, sound, size, weight, distance, speed, mental state, whether another was healthy, and the value of one's property (*Asplundh Manufacturing Division v. Benton Harbor Engineering*, 57 F.3d 1190, 1196, 1997–98 (3d Cir. 1995)). The following statements are all permissible as lay opinions, so long as they are helpful to the jury and based on the witness' own perceptions:

- "He was going at least 60 miles an hour."
- "When I told him what his wife did, he got real mad, like he wanted to hit something."
- "I'd say I was about 15 feet from the truck when it passed by."
- "My mother wasn't feeling very well about that time."
- "I walked into the room, and it wasn't very well lit."
- "He was acting strange."
- "She looked terrible, like she'd gotten dressed in the dark that morning."

Objections to the competence of a lay witness to render an opinion can often be made before the opinion is actually stated, based on the question asked by the examining attorney. If the attorney asks, for instance, "Was the gun properly loaded?," opposing counsel could object that the question *calls* for an opinion that the witness is not competent to make. Attorneys must exercise tactical care in such situations, however, because it is possible that a lay witness can possess technical knowledge sufficient to qualify as an expert on the subject matter of the opinion. In that case, a brief expert *voir dire* of the witness (see below) might not only lay a foundation sufficient to allow the witness to offer his/her opinion, but it might also increase the witness' credibility by establishing his/her qualifications to give that opinion.

Expert Witnesses

Often, a criminal case requires a witness to render an opinion on matters that the average person would not be qualified to render. This is particular true of forensic evidence, such as the results of blood tests or DNA analysis. Where such issues arise, **expert witnesses** are permitted to give the jury opinions based on their specialized knowledge and experience in the relevant field of study.

Rule 702 lays out five requirements for expert testimony:

1. The witness is qualified to testify as an expert based on the witness' knowledge, skill, experience, training, or education.
2. The expert's specialized knowledge will help the trier of fact to understand the evidence or to determine a fact in issue.
3. The expert's testimony is based on sufficient facts or data.
4. The expert's testimony is the product of reliable principles and methods.
5. The expert has reliably applied the principles and methods to the facts of the case.

PRACTICE TIP

When deposing a witness who may be asked to render an improper lay opinion, it may be a good idea to explore the witness' credentials to see if that witness is in fact competent to testify on that issue.

expert witness
A witness who is qualified to render an expert opinion on an issue of fact in a case.

LEARNING OBJECTIVE 7
Illustrate the standards for admissibility of expert opinions.

specialized knowledge
Knowledge based on expertise, training, and/or experience in a given field, which lies beyond that of an average, reasonably intelligent person.

expert *voir dire*
A process of establishing the competence of a witness to testify as an expert.

LEARNING OBJECTIVE 8
Understand and apply the *Frye* and *Daubert* tests to the content of expert testimony.

Qualification.   An expert witness is qualified to give testimony in a particular case if that expert has a reasonable claim to **specialized knowledge** on the subject under investigation. Such "specialized knowledge" doesn't necessarily require formal training, although it certainly helps. The knowledge required to qualify as an expert can be gained through education, experience, or a combination of both. The qualifications of an expert witness must be established through an **expert *voir dire*** in which the credentials of the expert are proven by the party offering the testimony and challenged, as far as possible, by the opposing party.

SAMPLE TRIAL TRANSCRIPT 7-3

Voir Dire of an Expert Witness

Attorney:	Mr. Forester, what is your occupation?
Witness:	I am an electrical engineer.
Attorney:	Could you briefly describe your training in electrical engineering?
Witness:	I received a Bachelor's degree in Electrical Engineering from Hubert College, and a Master of Science in Engineering from Humphrey University. I've been certified as a Master Electrical Engineer by the Electrician's Society of America, and I've taught classes in electrical engineering at Local State University for the last three years.
Attorney:	How long have you been designing and installing residential electrical systems?
Witness:	For 25 years. [Once the expert's knowledge in a given field has been established, the attorney asks the court to qualify the witness as an expert.]
Attorney:	(To the judge) Your Honor, I ask that this witness be qualified as an expert in the field of residential electrical systems.
Judge:	(To opposing counsel) Any questions or objections? [At this point, the opposing counsel has the opportunity to cross-examine the witness on his qualifications. Often, there is no reasonable basis to challenge the qualifications of the witness.]
Opposing counsel:	No, Your Honor.
Judge:	The witness is qualified as an expert in residential electrical systems.

Evaluating whether Expert Testimony Will Assist the Trier of Fact.   The court's evaluation of whether expert testimony will assist the trier of fact actually encompasses the second through fifth factors set forth in Rule 702. It involves two questions: (1) is expert testimony needed in order for the jury to understand and analyze the evidence and draw conclusions from that evidence; and (2) is the expert testimony based on sound data, principles, and methods?

Even if an expert is qualified, his/her testimony will not be permitted if it is not needed for the jury to understand the evidence presented at trial. A jury does not need the testimony of an expert witness, for example, to help it understand that falling off of a collapsing ladder will cause the plaintiff to hit the ground and be injured. The average person understands enough about ladders, gravity, and the result of impact on the human body to make these decisions for himself/herself. But the jury might need help to understand *why* the ladder collapsed, or how the impact affected a particular part of the plaintiff's body.

With respect to the data underlying an expert's testimony, Rule 703 provides that these data can be, but do not have to be, based on the expert's own research and observations. An expert testifying about the cause of a medical condition can, for instance, base his/her opinion on his/her own examination of the patient, or make conclusions based on medical records and tests conducted by someone else. As long as the data are sufficient to support the expert's conclusion, they do not need to be created by the expert.

Rule 703 also provides that the underlying data supporting an expert's opinion do not have to be admissible so long as the data are the type reasonably relied on by experts in that field to make conclusions. Even if the data are not themselves admissible, Rule 703 allows the jury to see data only if their value in helping the jury understand the opinion does not outweigh any prejudicial effect data might have on the jury. If the data are otherwise admissible, then of course they can be used like any other admissible evidence.

Expert witnesses are often called at trial to render opinions about matters of scientific knowledge, such as engineering, physics, chemistry, medicine, or biology. The problem with scientific testimony is that not all scientific theories are valid, but a jury of nonscientists might have trouble distinguishing good science from so-called "junk" science. Judges might have just as much trouble making this distinction. So how does a court determine if the last two requirements of Rule 702 have been met?

One test of scientific validity was set forth in the case of *Frye* v. *United States*, 54 App.D.C. 46, 293 F. 1030 (1923), which held that a scientific theory or practice is sufficiently reliable if it has achieved general acceptance within the relevant scientific community (the "**Frye test**"). While some states still follow this test, it was rejected by the U.S. Supreme Court as a valid test in federal courts in the civil case of *Daubert* v. *Merrell Dow Pharmaceuticals*, 509 U.S. 579 (1993).

In *Daubert*, the plaintiffs had sued Merrell Dow because of birth defects allegedly caused by Bendectin, an anti-nausea drug. The defendant called an expert who testified that there was no indication in the prevailing scientific literature that Bendectin was capable of causing birth defects. To counter this testimony, the plaintiffs called eight highly qualified expert witnesses who testified, based on *in vitro* and live studies of the effect of Bendectin on animals along with chemical structure analyses, that the drug was capable of causing birth defects.

The trial court concluded that the studies the plaintiffs offered into evidence were not admissible because they were not based on principles that had been sufficiently established and accepted within the medical community. The Ninth Circuit Court of Appeals affirmed, applying the *Frye* test

Frye **test**
A standard for the competence of expert witnesses that requires an expert's methods and principles to be accepted within the scientific community to which the expert belongs.

discussed above. The U.S. Supreme Court agreed to hear the plaintiff's appeal in order to settle the debate over what standards should be used to interpret Rule 702 and admit expert testimony in federal courts.

Rejecting the *Frye* test, the *Daubert* court held that medical and other scientific experts should be assessed under Rule 702 based on a flexible standard of general reliability, not merely on whether it has been "generally accepted" in the scientific community. The court stated that it was the job of the federal judge, not the scientific community, to determine whether the basis of an expert's opinion was sufficient, and that the judge could make that decision based on factors such as testing, known or potential rates of error, and peer review and publication, as well as general acceptance.

The **Daubert test** has become the standard for admissibility of expert opinions in civil and criminal cases throughout the federal court system. It was further refined in the case of *Kumho Tire Co.* v. *Carmichael*, 526 U.S. 137, 119 S.Ct. 1167, 143 L.Ed.2d 238 (1999), which held that the standard applied to both scientific and nonscientific (technical) expert testimony, and that the *Daubert* criteria for admissibility were not meant to be a rigid, inflexible test, but to suggest factors that a judge might consider, along with others, in determining the reliability of expert testimony. The effect of *Daubert* and *Kumho Tire* has been to make Rule 702 a flexible standard for all expert testimony that allows judges to employ common sense in determining whether expert testimony should be allowed. As the *Daubert* court noted, even where expert testimony meets the *Daubert* test, the parties are still free to vigorously cross-examine each other's expert witnesses in order to shake out weak points in their conclusions and test the validity of their methods.

In the following case, the Third Circuit Court of Appeals used *Daubert* and *Kumho Tire* to assess the expert testimony of a police officer who was asked to offer a hypothetical opinion based on his years' experience with drug traffickers. The trial court allowed the officer to testify as an expert, and the defendant appealed.

Daubert test
A standard of competence for expert witnesses that is more flexible than the *Frye* test, and that focuses on the reliability of the methods and principles used by an expert rather than the general acceptance of those principles within the scientific community.

Expert witnesses are called upon testify and give opinions about subjects that are beyond the knowledge of the average juror, such as DNA evidence.

Source: http://www.gettyimages.com/detail/photo/witness-discusses-dna-evidence-with-lawer-and-judge-royalty-free-image/200393253-001.

PNC/Photodisc/Getty Images

COURT OPINION 7-3

UNITED STATES V. DAVIS, 397 F.3d 173 (3d Cir. 2005)

Two police officers traveling in South Philadelphia in an unmarked car saw six or seven shots fired from the passenger side of a black Honda automobile one block in front of them on 17th and Annin streets. The officers immediately activated their lights and siren, and pursued the Honda when the Honda did not stop. Within a few minutes, a marked police car also joined the chase led by the fleeing vehicle as it traveled at a high rate of speed, passed a number of red lights and stop signs, and on several occasions drove the wrong way on one-way streets. The police cars never lost sight of the Honda, and they eventually forced it to stop. All four doors immediately opened and the passengers attempted to exit.

Officer Brook, one of the officers in the marked car, testified that he observed Reginal Scott exit from the back passenger seat and Kevin Davis emerge from the front passenger seat. According to Officer Brook, Scott initially put up his hands and surrendered, but then began inching away from the car. At the same time, Davis attempted to flee on foot and Officer Brook pursued him. According to Officer Brook, Davis pointed his firearm at him and he then fired one shot and hit Davis. A pistol was recovered from the area where Davis fell. Davis was then taken to the hospital by Officers Haines and Thomas who recovered from Davis $169.00 in cash and one plastic baggie containing nineteen zip-lock packets of cocaine base.

Officer Bucceroni, who was with Officer Brook, observed Kevin Minnis exiting the vehicle with a semi-automatic firearm in his right hand. Officer Bucceroni instructed Minnis to drop the firearm. After he complied the officer retrieved the weapon, placed Minnis under arrest, and, in the search incident to the arrest, recovered twelve packets containing cocaine base. At approximately the same time, Officer Dawsonia, who arrived on the scene after responding to the radio call for assistance, was instructed to stop Scott who had been slowly attempting to inch away. Upon hearing this instruction, Scott threw a handgun onto the ground and was arrested by Officer Dawsonia, who searched Scott and recovered forty-four packets of cocaine base from his pocket. Ballistics tests later confirmed that the firearm recovered from Scott was the weapon fired at 17th and Annin Streets.

Defendants were convicted following a jury trial on the drug and weapons charges referred to above. . . . Defendants filed a timely appeal.

Defendants argue first that the District Court erred in admitting as expert testimony the responses of Officer Garner to the following hypothetical question: whether, assuming that "five persons were in a car, four of whom possessed handguns," and that "one person possessed a handgun with 12 packets, another person possessed a handgun with 19 packets, [and] one person . . . possessed a handgun with 44 packets," "would you say that would be consistent with drug trafficking or consistent with possession, simple possession." Jt.App. at 314a. Officer Garner responded, "It would be my opinion that would be possession with intent to deliver the narcotics." Id. He further explained that the bases for his opinion were "[t]he gun would be one factor, the narcotics would be the other," and "[t]he number of people in the vehicle and the circumstances of the arrest" would all play a factor." Id. at 314a-15a.

. . .

Defendants also argue that there is no objective basis for Officer Garner's testimony and that it fails the analysis required by *Daubert v. Merrell Dow Pharmaceuticals, Inc.*, 509 U.S. 579, 113 S.Ct. 2786, 125 L.Ed.2d 469 (1993), because "there was absolutely no pretense of scientific method, scientific testing, peer review in publication, a known or potential rate of error, and the extent to which [Officer Garner's] theory is generally accepted." Jt.App. at 41a. However, the factors enumerated in *Daubert* were intended to apply to the evaluation of scientific testimony, and they have little bearing in this case.

In *Kumho Tire Co. v. Carmichael*, 526 U.S. 137, 119 S.Ct. 1167, 143 L.Ed.2d 238 (1999), the Supreme Court recognized that "there are many different kinds of experts, and many different kinds of expertise," id. at 150, 119 S.Ct. 1167, and "*Daubert's* list of specific factors neither necessarily nor exclusively applies to all experts or in every case." Id. at 141, 119 S.Ct. 1167. The Court held that *Daubert's* list of specific factors would often be of little use in evaluating non-scientific expert

(continued)

(continued)

testimony and, as a result, the Court expanded *Daubert's* general holding to apply to expert testimony based on "technical or other specialized knowledge." *Id.* at 141, 113 S.Ct. 2786.

Federal Rule of Evidence 702 states that a court may permit expert testimony if it "will assist the trier of fact to understand the evidence or to determine a fact in issue." Under *Daubert*, a trial court must evaluate such testimony and make sure it "rests on a reliable foundation and is relevant to the task at hand." 509 U.S. at 597, 113 S.Ct. 2786. Officer Garner's testimony fully satisfied both these requirements. He was a fourteen-year veteran of the Philadelphia police force with twelve years of experience in narcotics. His testimony concerned the methods of operation for drug traffickers in the South Philadelphia area, a topic which we have held is a suitable topic for expert testimony because it is not within the common knowledge of the average juror. *United States v. Theodoropoulos*, 866 F.2d 587, 590-92 (3d Cir. 1989), *overruled on other grounds as recognized in United States v. Price*, 76 F.3d 526 (3d Cir. 1996). We are satisfied that Officer Garner's testimony concerned a proper subject matter for expert testimony, and he provided a reliable opinion based on years of experience. His testimony was thus admissible under both the Federal Rules of Evidence and *Daubert*.

Questions

1. On what grounds did the trial court determine that Officer Garner was qualified to testify as an expert witness?
2. What does this case tell us about the ability of police officers to offer expert testimony on their areas of specialty, such as narcotics?

Daubert, although it is a U.S. Supreme Court case, interprets Federal Rules of Evidence rather than the U.S. Constitution, and its holding is not, therefore, binding on the states. Indeed, each state has its own rules of evidence, which may or may not be similar to the federal rules. Since many states have fashioned their rules after the federal ones, however, the courts in those states will often look to federal courts' interpretation of federal rules to help understand and apply their own rules. For this reason, most states have adopted, either directly or through their own body of case law, the flexible standard for expert testimony embraced in *Daubert*.

EVIDENCE AND TECHNOLOGY

THE USE OF FORENSIC COMPUTER EXPERTS UNDER THE *DAUBERT* TEST

There are few areas of expertise more mysterious to the average person than the forensic analysis of digital resources. Jurors who are faced with such evidence will in virtually all cases need expert testimony to understand how such evidence was gathered, what it means, and how it is to be interpreted in light of the facts the jury is obligated to decide. At the same time, the level of general expertise needed by forensic digital experts may be decreasing due to advances in the development of hardware and software used to conduct such analyses. As Daniel Garrie and J. David Morrisy recently wrote,

"Over the last several years, commercial hardware and software vendors who specialize in digital forensic analysis tools and applications have made

(continued)

significant improvements in the methodologies necessary to analyze digital evidence. As a result, what was once an almost entirely ad hoc manual-analysis process is now structured to a point where years of experience and training are no longer necessary for the production of a digital forensic report. This trend increased the number of forensic examiners and lowered costs, but also reduced the depth of knowledge held by the average forensic examiner."[2]

Garrie and Morrisy also suggest that education and experience with the more generally accessible hardware and software used to conduct a forensic digital analysis would be greater factors under *Daubert* to qualify an expert than the more traditional route of certification in those specific computer resources. This is in keeping with *Daubert*'s more flexible approach to expert qualification, but also, as Garrie and Morrisy note, opens the door to less qualified experts who are more easily able to be impeached on cross-examination.

In *United States* v. *Gardner*, 2012 WL 6680395 (D.Utah 2012), the U.S. District Court for the District of Utah provided some indication of how a judge might approach an assessment of the conclusions of a computer forensic expert. In that case, the defendant's expert supplied 13 conclusions based on his analysis of the defendant's computer, using the same software as the prosecutor's computer forensics expert. Noting that the defendant's expert was generally qualified under Rule 702 and *Daubert*, *id.* at 3, the court nevertheless examined each of the defendant's expert's conclusions to determine whether, among other factors such as relevance and prejudice, the conclusions fell within the scope of his expertise. The court refused to allow the expert to testify about 9 of the 13 conclusions because the court found, despite his general qualifications, he did not have sufficient scientific, technical or other expertise to support *those* conclusions (*Id.* at 2–5).

Reasonable Certainty of Expert Testimony.   Even a well-qualified expert using generally accepted scientific principles will usually not be able to resolve an issue of scientific fact with absolute certainty. This is one of the reasons why, in many cases, a jury is required to choose between two equally credible expert opinions that reach the opposite conclusion about an issue of fact, each of whom testifies that the conclusions reached by the other are not correct. This so-called "battle of experts" happens because there is always some room for debate over the conclusions one draws when applying scientific principles to the facts of a particular case. For this reason, the law of evidence does not require absolute certainty in order to admit expert evidence. Instead, it requires a "reasonable degree of **professional certainty**."

professional certainty
A level of certainty that a professional would expect to achieve in the normal course of practicing his/her profession.

SAMPLE TRIAL TRANSCRIPT 7-4

Professional Certainty

After being qualified as a witness, a doctor testifies about his diagnosis of the victim's condition, and why the prosecutor's expert testimony was wrong. At the end of this testimony, the following dialogue takes place:

Defense counsel: Dr. Paul, have you reached your conclusion that you testified to today to a reasonable degree of medical certainty?

Witness: Yes, I have.

KEY TERMS

CHAPTER SUMMARY

- The competence of a witness is a foundational requirement to admit the witness' testimony into evidence.
- Under Rule 602, competence is generally established by producing evidence that the witness has personal knowledge of the substance of his/her testimony.
- Rule 603 requires a witness to take an oath or affirmation to testify truthfully. The oath needs to be sufficient to impress the duty to tell the truth on the witness' conscience.
- Where the competence of a witness is questioned based on age or mental condition, a *voir dire* may be conducted to examine the witness' ability to testify.
- A *voir dire* to establish general competence often takes place out of the jury's hearing.
- Where a witness does not speak English well enough to testify properly, Rule 604 requires that a qualified interpreter be provided.
- Judges are never competent to testify in cases over which they are presiding.
- Jurors are only competent to testify in matters affecting the validity of the jury's verdict, including extraneous information, improper influence, and mistakes on the jury verdict form.

- A nonexpert witness is permitted to state an opinion as long as it is rationally based on the witness' own perceptions, needed to help the jury understand the facts, and not based on any specialized knowledge.
- An expert witness must be qualified by demonstrating knowledge beyond the average person, based on experience, education, or training.
- An expert will only be permitted to state an opinion where it will help the jury understand and analyze the facts of the case.
- Expert testimony requires that the judge determine whether the expert's opinion is based on sound data, principles, and methods.
- Under the *Frye* test, used in some states, an expert opinion may only be offered if it is based on principles and methods generally accepted within the scientific or professional community to which the expert belongs.
- Under the *Daubert* test, used in federal and some state courts, an expert opinion may be offered so long as it is based on scientifically valid principles and methods.
- In all cases, an expert must testify that his/her opinion is held within a reasonable degree of professional certainty.

WEB EXCURSIONS

1. Locate your state's Rules of Evidence online, and review the rules your state follows regarding competence of witnesses. Does your state have any significant difference in how it addresses the competence of witnesses from Rules 601 et seq. in the federal rules? Which set of rules do you think would make it easier to prove the competence of a witness?
2. The National Association of Judiciary Interpreters and Translators (NAJIT) maintains an online national directory of translators for a wide variety of languages. Visit NAJIT's website at www.najit.org and locate the membership directory. Using that directory, determine whether there are any translators in your state for the following languages: Spanish, French, German, Portuguese, Arabic, Mandarin Chinese, Cantonese Chinese, Hebrew, Polish, Vietnamese, Russian, Japanese, Armenian, American sign language, Finnish, Haitian, Creole, Catalan, Korean, Mongolian, and Turkish.

PRACTICAL EXERCISE

1. Think of a fact about yourself—a hobby, where you attended school, etc.—that someone other than you would know something about. Now pretend that you are involved in a court case that requires you to prove that fact. Make a list of every person you can think of who would be competent to testify about that fact on your behalf at trial. What questions would you ask to lay a foundation for the competence of each person on your list? Would some people on your list make better witnesses than others? Why?

ENDNOTES

1. The words "swear or affirm" are often used in order to accommodate those who, for religious reasons, will not swear an oath.
2. Garrie, D.B., and Morrissy, J.D. (2014). Digital forensic evidence in the courtroom: Understanding content and quality. *Northwestern Journal of Technology and Intellectual Property*, 12(2), 121.

LEARNING OBJECTIVES

After reading this chapter, the student will be able to:

1. Explain the basic requirement of authentication of real evidence.

2. Illustrate how to authenticate real evidence using firsthand testimony.

3. Identify the requirements for authentication of handwriting by nonexpert testimony and comparison to a specimen.

4. Explain the use of distinctive characteristics to authenticate real evidence.

5. Describe the use of metadata to authenticate electronically stored information.

6. Illustrate the means of authentication of telephone conversations, voice recordings, public records, and ancient documents.

7. Explain how to authenticate real evidence by proof of a process or system.

8. Explain when a document is self-authenticating under Rule 902.

9. Explain the Best Evidence Rule and its exceptions.

10. Discuss how the loss or destruction of a document affects the presentation of evidence.

Authenticity and the Best Evidence Rule

CHAPTER 8

■ INTRODUCTION

Authenticity addresses a simple but critical question: how do we know that the piece of paper, videotape, drawing, gun, or other piece of real evidence that is being offered in court is, in fact, what the offering party says it is? **Authentication** means proving that a piece of real evidence is what it purports (appears or is claimed) to be. Whether real evidence is authentic is connected to the issue of its relevance, because if a piece of evidence is not authentic, then it is not capable of proving or disproving any fact at issue in the case.

■ THE GENERAL RULE OF AUTHENTICATION: RULE 901(a)

Authentication is addressed in Rule 901 of the Federal Rules of Evidence. The general rule is found in Rule 901(a): "To satisfy the requirement of authenticating or identifying an item of evidence, the proponent must produce evidence sufficient to support a finding that the item is what the proponent claims it is." This general rule opens the door to any evidence that bears on the identity of the evidence being offered.

LEARNING OBJECTIVE 1
Explain the basic requirement of authentication of real evidence.

authentication
Proof that a piece of real evidence is what its proponent claims it to be.

Of course, the burden of authenticating evidence is on the party offering it. But this burden is not great. To authenticate a piece of real evidence, "the proponent need only prove a rational basis for the claim that the [evidence] is what the proponent asserts it to be" (*United States* v. *Long*, 857 F.2d 436, 442 (8th Cir. 1988)). This proof does not need to prove that the evidence is reliable or accurate, which are questions for the jury to decide as a matter of weight (*Id.*). Authenticity can be proven by direct or circumstantial evidence.

There is no specific requirement for proof of authenticity; any evidence that meets the standard set forth in Rule 901(a) is sufficient.

■ THE RULE 901(b) EXAMPLES OF AUTHENTICATION

Rule 901(b) provides examples of methods that can be used to establish authenticity, but the rule is clear that those examples are not exhaustive, and the failure of a party to provide evidence that falls within one of the Rule 901(b) categories does not mean that the party has failed to authenticate the evidence. With that caveat in mind, we will now look at the examples set forth in Rule 901(b).

Firsthand Knowledge (Rule 901(b)(1))

The most effective way to authenticate real evidence is with the testimony of someone with **firsthand knowledge** of the evidence's identity. Such testimony would be direct evidence of authenticity. Before such testimony can be offered, the witness' competence must be established by proving that the witness does, in fact, have firsthand knowledge about the evidence. Once the witness' competence is proven, the evidence can be authenticated simply by asking the witness to identify the evidence, as illustrated in Sample Trial Transcript 8-1.

SAMPLE TRIAL TRANSCRIPT 8-1

Authentication of Real Evidence by Firsthand Knowledge

Attorney:	Mr. Smith, did your wife own a porcelain figurine of a swan?
Witness:	She owned quite a few of those. She collected them.
Attorney:	Were you familiar with her collection?
Witness:	Oh yes, very familiar. I had to dust them every week for 15 years.
Attorney:	I'm showing you a porcelain figurine that has been marked as Exhibit "B". Can you identify it?
Witness:	Yes, that's one from my wife's collection. It sat on the third shelf of her curio cabinet.
Attorney:	Your Honor, I'd like to introduce Exhibit "B" into evidence at this time.

Notice two things about this testimony. First, Mr. Smith's competence as an authenticating witness had to be established with regard to the specific piece of evidence he was authenticating. It would not have been enough for him to have firsthand knowledge of his wife's swan collection in general. He

LEARNING OBJECTIVE 2

Illustrate how to authenticate real evidence using firsthand testimony.

firsthand knowledge
Direct evidence of authenticity based on the testimony of a witness with direct knowledge of the item's identity and nature.

had to have firsthand knowledge of the specific piece of that collection being offered into evidence, which he established by testifying that he personally dusted each piece every week for 15 years. Second, his authenticating testimony had nothing to do with the relevance of the evidence, only its authenticity. This shows that an authenticating witness does not need to have any knowledge whatsoever about the connection between the evidence and the crime it is being offered to prove. It is the witness' knowledge about the object that matters.

Nonexpert Authentication of Handwriting (Rule 901(b)(2))

In order to authenticate a handwritten document (or the signature on a printed document) through a nonexpert witness, two conditions must be met: (1) the witness must be familiar with the handwriting, and (2) the familiarity must not have been acquired solely for purposes of the litigation. There is no requirement of a particular relationship between the witness and the person whose handwriting is being authenticated, so the witness could be a family member, friend, associate, employee, or even a complete stranger who, for some reason, has the requisite familiarity with the handwriting.

LEARNING OBJECTIVE 3
Identify the requirements for authentication of handwriting by nonexpert testimony and comparison to a specimen.

SAMPLE TRIAL TRANSCRIPT 8-2

Nonexpert Authentication of Handwriting

Attorney:	Miss Taylor, are you familiar with the handwriting of the defendant, Jim Carter?
Witness:	Yes, I am familiar with his handwriting.
Attorney:	How did you come to be familiar with his handwriting?
Witness:	I was his secretary for 15 years, and he often handwrote letters and other documents for me to type up.
Attorney:	Could you please take a look at the document we have marked as Exhibit "P6". There are some handwritten notes on the margins of page 2 of that document. Can you identify that handwriting?
Witness:	Yes, it's Jim Carter's.

Comparison by an Expert Witness or the Trier of Fact (Rule 901(b)(3))

Rule 901(b)(3) allows a comparison of the evidence in question with an authenticated specimen to determine whether the evidence is authentic. For example, if a birthday card signed by a person is authenticated by a witness, then the signature can be compared either by a handwriting expert or by the jury itself to the signature on the document offered as evidence. An authenticated specimen eliminates the need for personal familiarity with the handwriting. The specimen can be authenticated by any means complying with Rule 901.

SAMPLE TRIAL TRANSCRIPT 8-3

Comparison to a Specimen

Attorney:	Mr. Johnson, could you please tell me what this is?
Witness:	It's a thank-you note the defendant gave me two years ago.
Attorney:	How do you know it's from the defendant?
Witness:	I remember when he gave it to me. He was thanking me for attending his daughter's wedding.
Attorney:	Does that thank-you note contain his signature?
Witness:	Yes, right here at the bottom, "Joseph P. Kincaid." [The specimen has now been authenticated by a witness with firsthand knowledge, and can be compared by an expert witness or the jury to another document containing the defendant's signature in order to prove that the defendant signed that document.]

Rule 901(b)(3) permits either an expert witness or the "trier of fact" (a jury in most cases) to make the comparison between an offered piece of evidence and a specimen. The rule does not, however, provide specific guidelines about when expert testimony would be required for the comparison. This issue was addressed in the following opinion by the Ninth Circuit Court of Appeals, which provided the jury wide latitude in conducting its own comparison even where an expert was not able to determine for sure whether the specimen and evidence contained the same signature. The opinion also demonstrates how physical evidence, in this case stolen jet engine parts, can be authenticated in general under Rule 901.

COURT OPINION 8-1 _____

UNITED STATES V. WOODSON, 526 F.2d 550 (9th Cir. 1975)

Appellant (Woodson), an employee of the Alameda Naval Air Station (NAS), was convicted by a jury of all of the four counts of the indictment. Two charged theft of government property and two charged the sale of that property. 18 U.S.C. § 641. Woodson appeals from the resulting judgments of sentence, claiming error in two respects: (1) insufficiency of the evidence as to ownership and source of the property involved, and (2) error in the jury instructions as to handwriting. We affirm.

The property involved consisted of two separate batches of jet engine parts-one a group of stator vane blades, and the other a number of turbine blades.

The government's evidence showed that a scrap metal dealer bought, on November 3 and November 17, 1973, two separate batches of aircraft parts from a person identified by the dealer as Woodson. The dealer said the seller of the scrap signed the invoices as 'S. Bell' and 'Samuel Bell.' On one of the two occasions, the seller was driving a vehicle registered to Woodson. On a third occasion, the same person offered to sell other aircraft parts to the scrap dealer. When asked the sources, that person told the dealer the parts were 'hot' and that he had brought them from 'Alameda.'

Government employees identified some of the parts as bearing stamps they affixed as part of the inspection process. Other evidence showed the items sold, in all likelihood, could only have come from the NAS at Alameda, and were like the parts missing at about the time of the sales to the scrap dealer.

(continued)

(continued)

Under these circumstances, the evidence was clearly sufficient to permit the jury to conclude that the parts purchased by the scrap dealer were both (a) property belonging to the government, and (b) stolen.

Woodson's other assignment of error is based on the government's handwriting expert's inability to say that the 'Bell' signatures on the invoices and defendant's handwriting exemplars were of common or dissimilar authorship. Hence defendant claims it was error to instruct the jury that it was free, under the usual rule permitting it to either accept or reject part or all of the testimony of an expert, to find the questioned and admitted signatures were those of the same person. Woodson cites us no case authority for this novel proposition, nor does reason support it. In the absence of extreme or unusual circumstances not present here, we see no reason why handwriting comparisons cannot be made by jurors, and conclusions drawn from them, either in the presence or absence of expert opinion. 28 U.S.C. §1731; Federal Rules of Evidence, Rule 901(b)(3); *People v. Weiskopf*, 60 Cal.App.2d 214, 140 P.2d 201, 203 (1943). Indeed, the dealer here testified that Woodson was the one who signed the 'Bell' invoices. Under these circumstances, the instruction permitting the jury to find common authorship, and to base verdicts thereon was not only not erroneous, but was entirely proper. U.S. v. Ranta, 482 F.2d 1344 (8 Cir. 1973).

Questions

1. How did the government prosecutors authenticate the parts obtained from the scrap metal dealer?
2. What does this case tell us about the power of a jury to rely on its own judgment in determining whether evidence is authentic?

Distinctive Characteristics (Rule 901(b)(4))

LEARNING OBJECTIVE 4
Explain the use of distinctive characteristics to authenticate real evidence.

Rule 901(b)(4) relates to the authentication of real evidence by **distinctive characteristics**. Under that rule, a piece of real evidence can be authenticated based on "the appearance, contents, substance, internal patterns, or other distinctive characteristics of the item, taken together with all the circumstances."

Very often, documents are prepared or created with very distinctive features that serve to prove the authenticity of the document even in the absence of firsthand testimony. For instance, a document created by a particular office may have a peculiar letterhead, logo, or watermark that verifies that document's place of origin. Distinctive characteristics can include writing habits, such as dotting ones i's with little hearts or circles instead of dots, forming the number "8" by placing one circle over another rather than a stricken-through "S", or placing a small line through the center of the number "7". Nearly everyone has peculiarities in their writing style that would serve to identify their writing as distinct from anyone else's.

distinctive characteristics
Attributes of an item's appearance, contents, substance, internal patterns, or other characteristics that allow it to be authenticated without firsthand knowledge.

Another example of distinctive characteristics would be the addition of one's initials to a piece of real evidence. Suppose a gun is found at a crime scene that has the initials "DH" scratched into the handle, which happen to be the defendant's initials, with a small line above and below the initials. It would be very difficult to identify the initials by a handwriting comparison, but if it can be proven that the defendant scratches those initials in that same manner into *all* of his guns, then the initials could be considered a distinctive characteristic. Similarly, the inspection stamps affixed to the jet engine parts authenticated in *United States v. Woodson* (above) would also constitute distinctive characteristics under this rule.

Distinctive characteristics can also be helpful in proving that a piece of real evidence is not authentic. For instance, suppose an attorney is trying to authenticate a letter from Jane, and it is known that Jane always dots her i's with circles. The letter contains i's that are not dotted with circles. The testimony of someone familiar with Jane's writing habit would help to prove that the letter was not actually written by Jane. At the same time, the mere presence of circles above the i's may not be enough to prove conclusively that Jane did write the letter, because Jane is not the only person who has that habit. This is why Rule 901 requires that distinctive characteristics must be considered "together with all of the circumstances."

In the following case, a federal judge held that e-mails offered as evidence in a government fraud case could be identified by distinctive characteristics, and also that those e-mails could then be used to authenticate others by comparison under Rule 901(b)(3).

COURT OPINION 8-2

UNITED STATES V. SAFAVIAN, 435 F.Supp.2d 36 (D.C.D.C. 2006)

[The court considered and rejects an argument that the e-mails were self-authenticating under Rule 902.] Because it is not appropriate for these e-mails to be admitted as self-authenticating under Rule 902 of the Federal Rules of Evidence, the Court turns to the authentication requirements set forth in Rule 901. The question under Rule 901 is whether there is sufficient evidence "to support a finding that the matter in question is what its proponent claims," FED.R.EVID. 901(a)-in this case, e-mails between Mr. Safavian, Mr. Abramoff, and other individuals. . . . For the reasons that follow, the Court finds that there is ample evidence for the jury to find that these exhibits are, in fact, e-mail exchanges between Mr. Safavian, Mr. Abramoff, and other individuals.

One method of authentication identified under Rule 901 is to examine the evidence's "distinctive characteristics and the like," including "[a]ppearance, contents, substance, internal patterns, or other distinctive characteristics, taken in conjunction with circumstances." FED.R.EVID. 901(b)(4). Most of the proffered exhibits can be authenticated in this manner. The e-mails in question have many distinctive characteristics, including the actual e-mail addresses containing the "@" symbol, widely known to be part of an e-mail address, and certainly a distinctive mark that identifies the document in question as an e-mail. See *United States v. Siddiqui*, 235 F.3d 1318, 1322 (11th Cir. 2000). In addition, most of the e-mail addresses themselves contain the name of the person connected to the address, such as "abramoffj@gtlaw.com," "David.Safavian@ mail.house.gov," or "david.safavian @gsa.gov." *See, e.g.*, Exhibits 101, 105, 106. Frequently these e-mails contain the name of the sender or recipient in the bodies of the e-mail,

in the signature blocks at the end of the e-mail, in the "To:" and "From:" headings, and by signature of the sender. The contents of the e-mails also authenticate them as being from the purported sender and to the purported recipient, containing as they do discussions of various identifiable matters, such as Mr. Safavian's work at the General Services Administration ("GSA"), Mr. Abramoff's work as a lobbyist, Mr. Abramoff's restaurant, Signatures, and various other personal and professional matters.

Those e-mails that are not clearly identifiable on their own can be authenticated under Rule 901(b)(3), which states that such evidence may be authenticated by comparison by the trier of fact (the jury) with "specimens which have been [otherwise] authenticated"-in this case, those e-mails that already have been independently authenticated under Rule 901(b)(4). For instance, certain e-mails contain the address "MerrittDC@aol.com" with no further indication of what person uses that e-mail address either through the contents or in the e-mail heading itself. *See, e.g.*, Exhibit 134. This e-mail address on its own does not clearly demonstrate who was the sender or receiver using that address. When these e-mails are examined alongside Exhibit 100 (which the Court finds is authenticated under Rule 901(b)(4) by its distinctive characteristics), however, it becomes clear that MerrittDC@aol.com was an address used by the defendant. Exhibit 100 is also an e-mail sent from that address, but the signature within the e-mail gives the defendant's name and the name of his business, Janus-Merritt Strategies, L.L.C., located in Washington, D.C. (as well as other information, such as the business' address, telephone and fax numbers), thereby connecting the defendant to that e-mail

(continued)

(continued)

address and clarifying the meaning of both "Merritt" and "DC" in it. The comparison of those e-mails containing MerrittDC@aol.com with Exhibit 100 thereby can provide the jury with a sufficient basis to find that these two exhibits are what they purport to be—that is, e-mails to or from Mr. Safavian. The Court will not perform this exercise with respect to each exhibit. Suffice it to say that the Court has examined each of these e-mails and found that all those that the Court is admitting in whole or in part meet the requirements for authentication under Rule 901.

Questions

1. What "distinctive characteristics" did the court use to determine that there was sufficient evidence of authenticity to allow the e-mails to be offered into evidence?
2. What points of comparison did the court find between the e-mails authenticated by distinctive characteristics and those that could not be authenticated in that way?

EVIDENCE AND TECHNOLOGY

LEARNING OBJECTIVE 5
Describe the use of metadata to authenticate electronically stored information.

USING METADATA TO AUTHENTICATE AN ELECTRONIC DOCUMENT

In *Lorraine* v. *Markel American Insurance Company*, 241 F.R.D. 534 (D.Md. 2007), Chief U.S. Magistrate Judge Grimm looked carefully at the various ways **electronically stored information (ESI)** could be authenticated. In his opinion, he examined the use of **metadata** as a distinctive characteristic of ESI, in order to determine whether metadata could be used to authenticate ESI under Rule 901(b)(4). In that opinion, he wrote:

Metadata,

"commonly described as 'data about data,' is defined as 'information describing the history, tracking, or management of an electronic document.' Appendix F to *The Sedona Guidelines: Best Practice Guidelines & Commentary for Managing Information & Records in the Electronic Age* defines metadata as 'information about a particular data set which describes how, when and by whom it was collected, created, accessed, or modified and how it is formatted (including data demographics such as size, location, storage requirements and media information).' Technical Appendix E to *the Sedona Guidelines* provides an extended description of metadata. It further defines metadata to include 'all of the contextual, processing, and use information needed to identify and certify the scope, authenticity, and integrity of active or archival electronic information or records.' Some examples of metadata for electronic documents include: a file's name, a file's location (e.g., directory structure or path name), file format or file type, file size, file dates (e.g., creation date, date of last data modification, date of last data access, and date of last metadata modification), and file permissions (e.g., who can read the data, who can write to it, who can run it). Some metadata, such as file dates and sizes, can easily be seen by users; other metadata can be hidden or embedded and unavailable to computer users who are not technically adept."

Williams v. *Sprint/United Mgmt. Co.*, 230 F.R.D. at 646 (footnote omitted); Federal Judicial Center, Managing Discovery of Electronic Information: A Pocket Guide for Judges, Federal Judicial Center, 2007 at 24–25 (defining metadata as "[i]nformation about a particular data set or document which describes how, when, and by whom the data set or document was collected, created, accessed, or modified . . ."). Recently, revised Federal Rule of Civil Procedure 34 permits a party to discover electronically stored information and to identify the form or forms in which it is

electronically stored information (ESI)
Information that is stored in any electronic format, including information stored on a computer or any other electronic device.

metadata
Information describing the history, tracking, or management of an electronic document, often embedded in the document's electronic code.

(continued)

to be produced. A party therefore can request production of electronically stored information in its "native format", which includes the metadata for the electronic document. Because metadata shows the date, time and identity of the creator of an electronic record, as well as all changes made to it, metadata is a distinctive characteristic of all electronic evidence that can be used to authenticate it under Rule 901(b)(4). Although specific source code markers that constitute metadata can provide a useful method of authenticating electronically stored evidence, this method is not foolproof because "[a]n unauthorized person may be able to obtain access to an unattended computer. Moreover, a document or database located on a networked-computer system can be viewed by persons on the network who may modify it. In addition, many network computer systems usually provide for a selected network administrators to override an individual password identification number to gain access when necessary."

Weinstein at § 900.01[4][a]; *see also Fennell* v. *First Step Designs, Ltd.*, 83 F.3d 526, 530 (1st Cir. 1996) (discussing how metadata markers can reflect that a document was modified when in fact it simply was saved to a different location). Despite its lack of conclusiveness, however, "metadata certainly is a useful tool for authenticating electronic records by use of distinctive characteristics." (*Lorraine, supra*, at 547, 548).

"The *Lorraine* case also highlights the importance of requesting ESI in its native format, so that it captures key metadata such as date, time and identity of the creator of an electronic record, and any changes made to the record. Such information will make the record easier to authenticate and more likely to be admissible in court" (Isaza, J. (2010, November 1). Metadata in court: What RIM, legal, and IT need to know. ARMA International Educational Foundation, p. 6).

Authentication of a Voice Recording (Rule 901(b)(5))

The identification of someone's voice is often critical to the authentication of a recording. Rule 901(b)(5) allows such identification where the witness is personally familiar with the voice. In addition to familiarity, this method requires proof of circumstances that connect the voice with the speaker. If that familiarity can be established, then the witness can offer an opinion as to whether the voice belongs to a particular person.

Sample Trial Transcript 8-4 contains a short dialogue that illustrates this type of authentication.

SAMPLE TRIAL TRANSCRIPT 8-4

Authentication of Voice Recording

Attorney:	Mrs. Johnson, I am going to play a short recording of a voice, and I would ask you if you recognize that voice. (Recording played)
Witness:	Yes, I do.
Attorney:	How is it that you recognize that voice?
Witness:	It's a voice I've heard many, many times during my marriage. It's my husband's voice.

At this point, the recording has been authenticated as being a recording of the husband's voice. The entire recording would be authenticated, so long as the husband's voice is the only voice.

Authentication of Telephone Conversation (Rule 901(b)(6))

Rule 901(b)(6) provides for the authentication of a telephone conversation where a direct voice identification is not available. While not strictly documentary in nature, telephone conversations must be authenticated in the sense that there must be proof that the person the witness was speaking to was actually the person he/she thought it was. This can be accomplished by proving that (1) the call was made to the person's phone number, and (2) circumstances (such as the content of the conversation or familiarity with the person's voice) support the identification. If the call is placed to a business, it is sufficiently authenticated if the conversation "related to business reasonably transacted over the telephone."

SAMPLE TRIAL TRANSCRIPT 8-5

Authentication of Telephone Call

Attorney:	Mr. Dodge, you had a telephone conversation with the defendant on April 13, didn't you?
Witness:	Yes, I did.
Attorney:	Did you call him?
Witness:	Yes.
Attorney:	When you called him, what number did you dial?
Witness:	The number he gave me. It was on his business card.
Attorney:	Did he answer the phone?
Witness:	Yes, it was him.
Attorney:	How do you know?
Witness:	Well, I had never spoken to him before, but when he answered he said, "Hello, Jim Carson speaking."
Attorney:	And there is no doubt that you were speaking to Mr. Carson?
Witness:	Well, we started talking about the Edison contract that he signed, and he was speaking about it as if he was familiar with the contents, so no, there is no doubt in my mind that I was actually speaking to him.

At this point, the witness can go forward and relate the contents of the telephone conversation to the extent those contents are otherwise admissible.

Authentication of Public Record (Rule 901(b)(7))

Under Rule 901(b)(7), where a document is recorded or filed in a public office or is claimed to be a public record of some type, the document can be authenticated by showing that it was either recorded or filed in a public office as authorized by law, or that it came from the office authorized by law to keep that record.

The question of what constitutes a "**public record**" appears to be addressed by Rule 901(b)(7), in that the record's public nature depends on the nature of the office where it is filed, recorded, or kept. It does not matter whether the record was produced and filed by a public official or a private individual, so long as its filing and maintenance in a public office is authorized by law (*cf. Sternberg Dredging Co.* v. *Moran Towing & Transp. Co.,* 196 F.2d 1002 (2nd Cir. 1952)).

public record
A document the authenticity of which is established by the fact that it is filed or maintained in a public office.

 SAMPLE TRIAL TRANSCRIPT 8-6

Authentication of Public Record

Attorney:	Mr. Frank, I am showing you a copy of a real estate tax bill. Is that an official tax bill issued by the county for the property in question?
Witness:	Yes, it is.
Attorney:	And is this document maintained at the county tax office as part of its normal public records on real estate taxes?
Witness:	Yes.

Authentication of Ancient Documents and Data Compilations (Rule 901(b)(8))

ancient document
A document that is 20 or more years old.

Rule 901(b)(8) provides that an **ancient document** or data compilation is authentic if it is 20 or more years old, its condition does not create any suspicion about its authenticity, and it was in a place where it would normally be kept.

 SAMPLE TRIAL TRANSCRIPT 8-7

Authentication of Ancient Document

Attorney:	Mrs. Barnes, I am showing you a document. Can you identify it?
Witness:	It's my mother's will.
Attorney:	How long ago did she make this will?
Witness:	Almost 40 years ago.
Attorney:	Did you find this will in your mother's home?
Witness:	Yes, I did.
Attorney:	Where did you find it?
Witness:	In with her other financial papers.
Attorney:	Is that where she normally would keep her will?
Witness:	Oh yes, she keeps all of her important papers in the same drawer of her desk.

Authentication by Proof of Process or System (Rule 901(b)(9))

Under Rule 901(b)(9), a document can also be authenticated by evidence showing that a particular process or system was used to produce the document and that the process or system generally produces an accurate result.

SAMPLE TRIAL TRANSCRIPT 8-8

Authentication by Proof of Process

Attorney:	Mrs. Asher, I am showing you a document. Can you identify it?
Witness:	It appears to be a printout of our firm's ledger for 2006.
Attorney:	How is that ledger normally produced?
Witness:	There is a software program that we use, which I use and my predecessor used also, where you tell it to compile a ledger for a particular range of dates, and it prints out this ledger.
Attorney:	Is this the way the ledge appears when it prints out?
Witness:	Yes, with three columns and a small red logo here at the top.
Attorney:	To your knowledge, do the ledgers produced by this software accurately reflect your firm's financial transactions?
Witness:	Yes, I've never known it to make a mistake.

The 901(b)(9) method of authenticating documents is particularly useful when evidence consists of records taken from a defendant's computer, cell phone, or other electronic device. Obviously, government investigators will usually not have any firsthand knowledge of the identity of such records, and it is unlikely that the defendant will supply authenticating testimony. If, however, an investigator can prove that such records were recovered from the defendant's computer by a reliable process, this would be enough under Rule 901(b)(9) to authenticate the document, as illustrated in the following case.

COURT OPINION 8-3

UNITED STATES V. WHITAKER, 127 F.3d 595 (7th Cir. 1997)

Frank Whitaker was involved in a large-scale narcotics conspiracy, headed by co-defendant Ralph Solis, which was responsible for distributing large quantities of marijuana from early 1991 until March 22, 1994. After an investigation and statements by cooperating codefendants, a superseding indictment was returned on November 22, 1994 against Whitaker, Ralph Solis, Peter Krell, Jeffrey Freund, John Follman,

(continued)

(continued)

Anthony Gibbons, and Gary Frost, charging them with being members of this drug conspiracy. Testimony at trial established that the marijuana distribution organization operated in the Southern District of Illinois, the Eastern District of Missouri, Texas, Minnesota, and elsewhere.

. . .

In addition to testimonial evidence as to Whitaker's position and role in Solis' organization, the government also introduced . . . printouts of computer records into evidence. Frost used the computer records to keep track of drug transactions from approximately October 5, 1993 until February 24, 1994. Frost had shown the records and his computerized method for keeping track of drug transactions to Hartline, and other coconspirators knew that Frost kept computer records of the drug business. These computer records were seized from Frost's residence on February 25, 1994. . . .

1. *Admission of Computer Printouts*

Whitaker's first argument on appeal is that the district court erred in admitting the printouts of Frost's computer records against him because they were not properly authenticated and because the government did not lay a proper foundation.

. . .

Federal Rule of Evidence 901(a) provides the requirement for authentication of evidence:

> The requirement of authentication or identification as a condition precedent to admissibility is satisfied by evidence sufficient to support a finding that the matter in question is what its proponent claims.

Fed.R.Evid. 901(a). Whitaker argues that the prosecution failed to comply with the requirements of Rule 901(a) with respect to the computer printouts because it never supplied witnesses who had personal knowledge of the computer system's operation or who could confirm the accuracy of the input to and output from the computer.

The government laid the foundation for the computer records and provided their authentication through the testimony of FBI Special Agent Jay Keeven. Agent Keeven testified that the records were retrieved from Frost's computer, which was seized during the execution of a federal search warrant of Frost's home in February 1994. The records were retrieved from the computer using the Microsoft Money program. Agent Keeven was present when that program was installed on the computer and when the records were retrieved. Agent Keeven testified concerning his personal knowledge and his personal participation in obtaining the printouts. On cross-examination, the defense did not ask Agent Keeven any questions about how the disks were formatted, what type of computer was used, or any other questions of a technical nature. In sum, his testimony was sufficient to establish the authenticity of the computer records of the drug business, and the district court was correct in admitting the records . . ..

Questions

1. On what basis did Whitaker claim that the government had failed to properly authenticate Frost's computer records?
2. What evidence did the court find sufficient to authenticate the computer records despite the lack of firsthand testimony?

PRACTICE TIP

Whenever computer records are going to be used as evidence, the process by which those records are retrieved and analyzed should be carefully recorded and tracked to make sure they can be authenticated properly under Rule 901(b)(9).

Authentication by Statute or Rule of Court (Rule 901(b)(10))

Finally, Rule 901(b)(10) allows other methods of authentication provided for by statute or rule of court. For example, Section 1746 of the Federal Judiciary and Judicial Procedure Code provides that an unsworn statement can be treated as a sworn statement when properly endorsed with the date of execution and the words "I declare under penalty of perjury that the foregoing is true and correct" (or words to that effect). Compliance with this statute has been held sufficient to authenticate statements under Rule 901(b)(10) (*Trustees of Metal Polishers Local 8A–28A Funds* v. *Prestige Restoration and Maintenance, LLC*, 986 F.Supp.2d 159 (E.D.N.Y. 2013)).

■ SELF-AUTHENTICATING DOCUMENTS: RULE 902

LEARNING OBJECTIVE 8
Explain when a document is self-authenticating under Rule 902.

Rule 902 provides that "extrinsic evidence of authenticity as a condition precedent to admissibility is not required with respect to" certain types of documents. These documents are known as "**self-authenticating**," because extrinsic evidence, meaning evidence other than the document itself, is not required to authenticate such documents.

self-authentication
The authentication of a document based on its nature, without the need for further proof of authenticity.

The documents that are self-authenticating under Rule 902 including certain types of public documents, records, and publications; newspapers and periodicals; certain types of commercial documents; and certain records of regularly conducted activity. When a document is self-authenticating, the document can be introduced into evidence without laying any further foundation for authenticity. All a party has to do is prove that the document satisfies the requirements of self-authentication.

SAMPLE TRIAL TRANSCRIPT 8-9

Self-Authentication of Tax Record

Attorney:	Your Honor, I have here a record of taxes paid on Mr. Wise's property that is certified from the Township of Clinton, and bears the seal of the tax clerk of Clinton Township. I ask that it be entered in the record at this time.
Judge:	Very well.

■ THE BEST EVIDENCE RULE

Article X of the Federal Rules of Evidence limits the admissibility of real evidence to ensure that the evidence is as trustworthy as possible. It also provides for exceptions in situations where the most reliable version of evidence is not available or would cause confusion for the jury.

Types of Documents

Rule 1001 provides several definitions of types of documents relevant to the provisions of Article X. These definitions include:

- Writings
- Recordings

- Photographs
- Originals
- Duplicates

Writings and Recordings

"Writings" and "recordings" consist of letters, words, or numbers, or their equivalent, set down in any form or recorded in any manner. Under this definition, each of the following would be considered a "writing":

- A typewritten letter on a piece of paper
- The numbers and letters on a telephone key pad or a computer keyboard
- The engraving on a tombstone
- The washing instructions on a label inside the collar of a shirt
- Notations in the margin of your textbook
- The source code for the word processing program you use
- The numbers and letters on the license plate of your car
- Letters carved by young lovers on a tree in the middle of a forest
- The words "Let's Party" on a T-shirt
- The name and registration numbers painted on the side of a cruise ship

Rule 1001(a) defines more than "writing"; it also defines "recording." The word "recording" is used to denote an aural rendition of words, numbers, or letters. The scope of such renditions is more limited than writings, because recordings are much more dependent on the current state of technology. A hundred years ago, wax and tinfoil were used to record sound. Sixty years ago, vinyl was state of the art. As few as 30 years ago, magnetic tapes were the most sophisticated form of sound reproduction. Then came electronic recordings, the accuracy and durability of which has been improving with remarkable speed over time. Now, one can download hundreds of songs on an MP3 player small enough to carry in a shirt pocket.

As the sophistication of recording has increased over time, so have concerns about the accuracy of such recordings. Wax, tinfoil, and vinyl were impossible to meddle with; once they were made, the only way they could be eliminated as evidence was to destroy them. Magnetic tapes were more easily destroyed, but they were still very difficult to change in a way that could not be easily detected. Now, electronic recordings can be manipulated in a thousand different ways to change the pitch, tone, speed, and quality of the sound, and such recordings can be seamlessly dissected, spliced, and reorganized to create entirely new sounds.

Photographs

"Photographs" include all photographic images or the equivalent, stored in any form. Any form of visual recording would be included in this definition, including electronic recordings such as photos and videos taken with a cell phone camera and image files downloaded from the Internet. The same concerns exist with respect to photographs as sound recordings or written documents. Current technology is capable of editing and manipulating images as effectively as sounds, so this definition includes many forms of "photographs" that would raise serious credibility issues.

Original

An "**original**" of a writing or recording is the writing or recording itself, or any counterpart intended to have the same effect by a person executing or issuing it. An "original" of a photograph includes the negative or any print therefrom. If data are stored in a computer or similar device, any printout or other output readable by sight, shown to reflect the data accurately, is an "original."

The definition of an "original" must be carefully considered, because the rule that we will be discussing shortly depends heavily on this definition. First, the word "counterpart" should not be confused with "copy." A copy is not an original, but a "counterpart" is a duplicate original made at the same time as the first original, and intended to be an original by the party creating it.

An example would be the documents signed at a real estate closing, which is a conference between attorneys, seller, buyer, and bank representative where all of the documents relating to the sale of real estate are signed. "A blizzard of paper" is a common way of describing such a conference. Not only are a number of documents signed at such a conference, but enough counterparts of each document are signed that every person present (usually at least a half-dozen, often more) can receive an original of many of them. The real estate settlement sheet, for instance, will be signed at least six or seven times. Each one of those documents is a counterpart, and each one is considered an original for legal purposes. Not one of them is considered a copy. If someone receives a copy, that copy is made on a copy machine and does not contain an actual signature.

The same holds true for photographs that are made from the original negative. Each print made from the negative is an original; copies would be those photographs created by placing an original in a color copy machine, or by scanning the photograph into a computer and printing out the scanned file.

With respect to electronic documents (such as e-mails), an original is any printout of that document. Multiple "originals" can be produced this way, but copies made on a copy machine from the printout are not originals. The electronic file itself is also an original under this definition, and could be displayed on a screen in a courtroom equipped with the proper technology, and used as an original without the need for a printout.

Duplicate

A "**duplicate**" is a counterpart produced by any means that accurately reproduces the original. Consider, for example, a tombstone. The tombstone is the original writing. Tombstones are very difficult to bring into court, so a party wishing to introduce the writing takes a photograph of it. The photograph is a duplicate of the writing on the tombstone. It is the original photograph, however. The party then has more photographs made from the original negative. Each of those photographs is an original of the photograph that was taken first, but each one is a duplicate of the writing on the tombstone.

It is easier to think of a duplicate as any version of a writing, recording, or photograph that does not fit the definition of an original.

original
As applied to real evidence, the actual piece of real evidence or a counterpart intended to function as an original.

duplicate
A counterpart to an original that is not intended to function as the original.

The Best Evidence Rule (Rule 1002)

the Best Evidence Rule
A rule that requires that the original of a document be produced in order to prove its contents.

Now that we understand the difference between an original and a duplicate, it is time to look at Rule 1002, which embodies **the Best Evidence Rule**:

> An original writing, recording, or photograph is required in order to prove its content unless these rules or a federal statute provides otherwise. (F.R.E. 1002)

If the content of a writing, recording, or photograph is to be proven, the original must be produced unless the rules or a federal statute provides otherwise. Under this rule, the content of the writing must be the focus of the evidence that the party is offering. Consider, for example, the deed to a piece of real estate. If that deed is being offered to prove that the deed contained an accurate description of the property that was being transferred, then the content of the document itself is the evidence that is being offered. If, on the other hand, the deed is being offered to prove who the owner of the property is, the document itself is not what is being proved; it is merely evidence of something else. The owner of the property could be proven in other ways, such as testimony or a real estate tax bill. In such a case, the Best Evidence Rule would not apply to the admissibility of the deed, and a properly authenticated copy would serve just as well.

If the document is being offered to prove its contents, then Rule 1002 requires, as a general rule, that the original be produced. This allows the opposing party and the jury to examine the actual document to check for changes, erasures, or other problems that might affect the document's credibility.

LEARNING OBJECTIVE 9
Explain the Best Evidence Rule and its exceptions.

The Exception to the Best Evidence Rule (Rule 1003)

Rule 1003 contains a significant exception to the Best Evidence Rule. Under Rule 1003, a duplicate can be used to the same extent as the original unless (1) a genuine question is raised as to the authenticity of the original or (2) in the circumstances it would be unfair to admit the duplicate in lieu of the original.

An example of a situation where fairness requires the production of the original of a document would be where a photograph is being used that, when copied, is not as clear as the original, or where the party introducing the document had an expert look at the original to draw a conclusion, and the original has to be made available in order to properly evaluate the expert's opinion.

Unavailability of the Original (Rule 1004)

Even if the original would be required under Rule 1002, there are times when it is simply not available. Under such circumstances, Rule 1004 provides that evidence other than the original of the document may be admitted to prove the documents' contents. Such circumstances include the following.

Originals Lost or Destroyed

Originals of documents can be lost, or accidentally destroyed. In such a case, other evidence can be used, unless the person offering the document lost or destroyed it deliberately in order to deprive the other party of access or to avoid producing it at trial. This is what the rule means by "bad faith."

Note that the concept of "losing" and "destroying" electronic documents changes drastically depending on the forms the documents were in. Paper documents, if lost or destroyed, are usually unrecoverable, but a deleted e-mail can often be recovered. Even information stored on a computer hard drive that has been overwritten or deleted can sometimes be restored by methods available to computer technicians. Someone who is going to claim that an electronic document has been lost or destroyed is probably going to have to produce some kind of technical evidence regarding what efforts were made to recover the document. In any case, a party claiming loss or destruction will have to prove that a reasonable effort was made to find or recover the document before other evidence will be admitted under this rule.

Original Not Obtainable

This part of Rule 1004 covers situations where the document is known to exist, but it is in the possession of someone who cannot be summoned to court or ordered to produce the document by any legal means. Generally, this would apply where the document is in the hands of someone in a foreign country, where a judge's order or subpoena would not have any effect.

Original in Possession of Opponent

At a time when an original was under the control of the party against whom offered, that party was put on notice, by the pleadings or otherwise, that the contents would be a subject of proof at the hearing, and that party does not produce the original at the hearing.

One of the problems with obtaining an original of a document is, what if the other party has it and won't produce it? Normally this would not be permitted, since each party is required to cooperate with reasonable discovery requests of the other party. But a party might require the other party to produce a document at a hearing (by issuing a subpoena, for instance) and the other party simply does not bring it. In such a case, the party failing to produce the document can hardly complain if the court allows other evidence of the document's contents at trial.

LEARNING OBJECTIVE 10
Discuss how the loss or destruction of a document affects the presentation of evidence.

KEY TERMS

authentication   161
firsthand knowledge   162
distinctive characteristics   165
electronically stored
    information (ESI)   167

metadata   167
public record   170
ancient document   170
self-authentication   173
original   175

duplicate   175
the Best Evidence
    Rule   176

CHAPTER SUMMARY

- Under Rule 901(a), real evidence must be authenticated before it can be admitted, meaning that the party offering the evidence must prove that it is what the party claims it to be.
- Evidence can be authenticated by any evidence that meets the standard of Rule 901(a).
- The authenticity of real evidence can be directly proven by the testimony of someone who has firsthand knowledge of the evidence.
- Nonexperts are permitted to authenticate handwriting so long as their familiarity with the handwriting is established and not obtained solely for the purpose of litigation.
- An expert witness or trier of fact (i.e., jury) can compare evidence to an authenticated specimen to determine the authenticity of the evidence.
- The distinctive characteristics of an item's appearance, content, substance, or internal patterns can be used to authenticate the item.
- E-mails can be authenticated using distinctive characteristics such as the address of the sender and recipient, the content of the message, and other information typically supplied in an e-mail.
- Metadata embedded in electronically stored information can be used to authenticate that information.
- Voice recordings can be authenticated by anyone familiar with the voice contained in the recording.
- Telephone conversations can be authenticated by circumstantial evidence such as the number called and the content of the conversation.
- A public record can be authenticated by proof that it is filed, recorded, or maintained in a public office.
- Ancient documents and data compilations 20 years old or more can be authenticated by showing that they were stored in a place typical for that type of information, and there is no evidence to create suspicion about their authenticity.
- Any real evidence can be authenticated by proof of the process or system by which it was created and that such process or system generally creates an accurate result.
- In addition to the methods specified in Rule 901(b), real evidence can be authenticated by any means provided by statute or rule of court.
- Rule 902 allows some documents to be self-authenticating, meaning that no additional evidence needs to be presented to authenticate the document.
- The Best Evidence Rule states that the original of a document must be produced to prove its contents, unless otherwise provided in the rules.
- A duplicate can be used instead of an original when original is lost or destroyed, is unavailable, or will not be produced by the opposing party.

WEB EXCURSIONS

1. Search the Internet for any website of a business or organization. Find information on that website that might be offered as evidence in court. Using the website as a source, make a list of all of the information you could use to authenticate the website and the evidence you have selected, including the names of any person who might be called as an authenticating witness.

2. Using Google or a similar search engine, find your state's version of the Best Evidence Rule. Compare it to F.R.E. Article X. Are there any significant differences in how your state treats the introduction of originals and duplicates as evidence?

PRACTICAL EXERCISES

1. Think of a document or thing that relates to you personally—a mortgage, a will, a bicycle, and so on. Now pretend that you need to introduce that document or thing as real evidence in court. If you yourself were unable to testify, how would you authenticate the

evidence? Think about other witnesses who might have firsthand knowledge, or about other ways you might be able to authenticate the evidence under Rule 901(b).

2. Think about a document that you have signed or that has some impact on your life (e.g., a lease, a car loan, or a mortgage). Suppose that document and all duplicates were destroyed. What evidence could you produce to prove the contents of the document? Would that evidence be admissible under Article X of the Federal Rules?

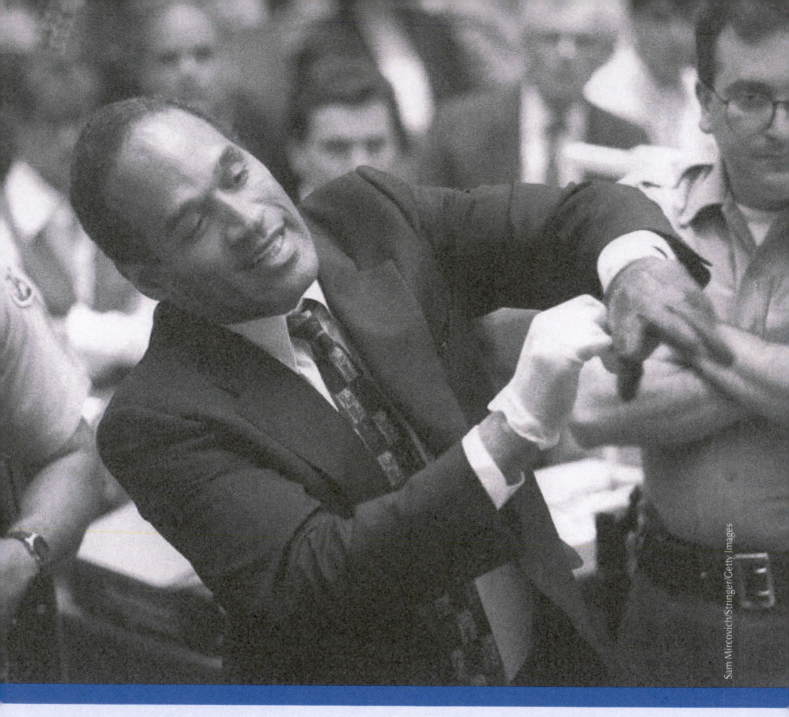

Sam Mircovich/Stringer/Getty Images

LEARNING OBJECTIVES

After reading this chapter, the student will be able to:

1. Explain what makes evidence relevant.

2. Distinguish between relevant and irrelevant evidence based on issues of fact.

3. Understand when character evidence is relevant and how it is introduced.

4. Illustrate when crimes, wrongful acts, and reputation can be introduced to show character.

5. Explain the introduction of habit or routine as relevant testimony.

Relevance

CHAPTER 9

■ INTRODUCTION

When a witness is competent, the witness can testify. When a piece of real evidence is authentic, the document can be brought into court. But testimony and real evidence must still pass one final test to be admissible and become part of the record: they must be relevant. In this chapter, you will explore the meaning of "relevance" as it applies to evidence offered in court. After looking at the general meaning of relevance, you will be introduced to special rules relating to the relevance of character evidence. You will also look at how a person's habit or routine can become relevant in a criminal case.

■ THE MEANING OF "RELEVANCE"

Under Rule 401, evidence is "relevant" if it has "any tendency to make the existence of any fact that is of consequence to the determination of the action more probable or less probable than it would be without the evidence." **Relevance** is the most critical test of admissibility, because it eliminates from a trial all testimony and real evidence that is not helpful to the factfinder in determining whether the elements of the case have been proven.

LEARNING OBJECTIVE 1
Explain what makes evidence relevant.

relevance
The tendency of evidence to prove or disprove a fact of consequence to the determination of an action.

Suppose a jury must determine whether Alvin Carson was driving at a dangerous speed at 5:30 P.M. on May 13. Four facts are being presented to help the jury make this decision:

1. The speed Alvin was driving at precisely 5:30 P.M. on May 13. This is relevant because the greater Alvin's speed, the most likely it is he was driving at a dangerous speed. The lower the Alvin's speed, the less likely it is his speed was dangerous.

2. The speed limit on the road where Alvin was traveling. This is relevant because the speed limit is an indication as to what is legally considered a safe speed on a given road. Driving over the speed limit makes it more likely that Alvin's speed was dangerous.

3. The road conditions on the road where Alvin was traveling. This is relevant because the road conditions will determine what a "safe speed" is on a given road. The worse the conditions, the more likely it is that Alvin was driving at an unsafe speed.

4. The speed Alvin was driving at 5:00 P.M. on May 13. This is irrelevant, because there is no logical connection between Alvin's speed at 5:00 P.M. and whether he was driving at a safe speed at 5:30 P.M.. He could easily have gone faster or slower or stopped any number of times between 5:00 P.M. and 5:30 P.M.. How fast he was going at 5:00 P.M. makes it neither more nor less likely that he was driving at a safe speed at 5:30 P.M..

As Rule 401 indicates, the relevance of evidence cannot be determined in a vacuum. Evidence can be relevant if it tends to prove or disprove *any fact of consequence* in the case. This includes not only the facts of the crime itself and whether the defendant committed it, but also any defenses the defendant may wish to raise, as well as the credibility (i.e., believability) of witnesses. For instance, suppose the eyewitness to a robbery is called to testify about what she saw. Certainly, her account of the events of the robbery would be relevant. But suppose the witness had herself been convicted of perjury in her testimony in a completely different criminal case. That fact has nothing to do with the robbery, or the defendant's guilt or innocence, but it is relevant because it tends to prove that the witness may be lying when she testified about the robbery.

SAMPLE TRIAL TRANSCRIPT 9-1

Objecting to Irrelevant Testimony

Prosecutor:	Mr. Carson, how fast were you driving at 5:30 P.M. on May 13?
Witness:	I was driving at 45 miles an hour, more or less.
Prosecutor:	Do you know the speed limit for this road where you were driving?
Witness:	Yes, it's 40 miles an hour.
Prosecutor:	What were the road conditions during this time?
Witness:	The road was dry, but it had just started to rain.
Prosecutor:	And how fast were you driving at 5:00 that same evening?
Defense:	Objection, your Honor, that's irrelevant.
Judge:	Sustained.

In the case of *United States* v. *Deruise*, the defendant was convicted of conspiring to possess marijuana with intent to distribute. The judge allowed the introduction of 103 pounds of marijuana into evidence, which was seized after the conspiracy allegedly ended and the indictment was issued by a grand jury. The defendant argued that the marijuana was irrelevant because it was not seized during the period the alleged conspiracy took place.

COURT OPINION 9-1

UNITED STATES V. DERUISE, 31 Fed.Appx. 151 (C.A.5, 2001)

Kenneth Deruise and Frederick Stemley were convicted of one count of conspiring to possess marijuana with intent to distribute, in violation of 21 U.S.C. §§ 841(a)(1) and 846. The district court denied their motions for judgment of acquittal and for a new trial. Deruise was sentenced to three years' probation and a $2000 fine. Stemley was sentenced to sixty-three months' imprisonment, five years' supervised release, and a $3000 fine. We affirm both convictions . . ..

On appeal, the defendants contend that . . . the district court erred in admitting into evidence 103 pounds of marijuana that FBI agents seized on September 8, 1998, after the conspiracy charged in the indictment had ended and after the indictment was returned.

. . .

Deruise and Stemley further contend that the district court abused its discretion in admitting into evidence the 103 pounds of marijuana seized on September 8, 1998. They argue this was not relevant evidence under Federal Rule of Evidence ("FRE") 401, and that it was unduly prejudicial evidence of other bad acts under Federal Rules of Evidence 403 and 404(b) and *United States v. Beechum*, 582 F.2d 898 (5th Cir. 1978) (en banc). The defendants objected to the admission of this evidence at trial, and we review the district court's evidentiary ruling on this matter for an abuse of discretion. *United States v. Navarro*, 169 F.3d 228, 232 (5th Cir. 1999), *cert. denied*, 528 U.S. 845 (1999).

"'Other act' evidence is 'intrinsic' when the evidence of the other act and evidence of the crime charged are 'inextricably intertwined' or both acts are part of a 'single criminal episode' or the other acts were 'necessary preliminaries' to the crime charged." *United States v. Williams*, 900 F.2d 823, 825 (5th Cir. 1990). Such evidence is admissible to complete the story of a crime by proving the immediate context of events in time and place. *United States v. Kloock*, 652 F.2d 492, 494–95 (5th Cir. 1981). Intrinsic evidence does not implicate Rule 404(b), and "consideration of its admissibility pursuant to Rule 404(b) is unnecessary." *United States v. Garcia*, 27 F.3d 1009, 1014 (5th Cir.), *cert. denied*, 513 U.S. 1009 (1994). We believe this evidence was intrinsic, in that it was part of the single conspiracy to possess and distribute marijuana charged by the government, i.e., part of a "single criminal episode." Although the indictment charged a conspiracy from May through July 1998, evidence seized after these dates can be probative of that conspiracy. Thus there is no need to consider FRE 404(b). Further, although the evidence here was seized after the return of the indictment, we have previously upheld the admission of evidence seized after the alleged conspiracy had ended and the indictment had been returned. *See United States v. Navarro*, 169 F.3d 228, 231–33 (5th Cir. 1999). Thus it was not an abuse of discretion to admit the marijuana simply because it was seized after the return of the indictment.

We must also consider whether the admission of the marijuana into evidence was unduly prejudicial under FRE 403. The parties point to *United States v. Torres*, 685 F.2d 921 (5th Cir. 1982) and to *Navarro*. In *Torres*, the district court admitted evidence of "sample transactions" that occurred prior to the dates alleged in the indictment, because the evidence of the sample transactions and the evidence of the charged conspiracy were "inextricably intertwined" and formed a "natural and integral" part of the surrounding circumstances. 685 F.2d at 924. In *Navarro*, the district court admitted evidence of drugs seized in January 1997, even though the alleged conspiracy ended in September 1996. The court concluded that the 1997 evidence

(continued)

(continued)

"demonstrated the structure of the drug organization, as well as the continuing contact between" the defendants. 169 F.3d at 233.

The evidence here was part of the single conspiracy alleged, and demonstrated its nature and scope. It was probative, and given its intrinsic nature was not unduly prejudicial. We hold that the district court did not abuse its discretion in admitting this evidence.

Questions

1. Why did the court permit introduction of the marijuana even though it wasn't part of what the defendants were accused of conspiring to distribute?
2. What facts were the marijuana introduced to prove?

LEARNING OBJECTIVE 2
Distinguish between relevant and irrelevant evidence based on issues of fact.

■ GENERAL LIMITATIONS ON RELEVANCE: RULE 403

Relevance is not the only test of admissibility. While irrelevant evidence is never admissible, relevant evidence can be excluded on a number of other grounds. In Chapter 6, for instance, you learned about a number of limitations on evidence imposed under the Fourth, Fifth, and Sixth Amendments to the U.S. Constitution. These limitations will be enforced through the exclusionary rule and exclude evidence that, in many cases, is extremely relevant to a defendant's guilt.

Beyond these constitutional concerns, the court is responsible to make sure that evidence is presented to the jury so that the jury can understand and apply to the law in order to reach a fair verdict. If the court believes that evidence, even though it is relevant, will confuse or mislead the jury, that evidence can be excluded under Rule 403. Of course, relevant evidence will not be excluded merely because it is complex. It is the responsibility of the prosecutor and defense to make sure complex evidence is presented in a way the jury can understand.

To illustrate this point, suppose a man is accused of participating in a riot by setting fire to cars parked along a street next to a courthouse where a jury has acquitted a police officer accused of shooting an unarmed youth. The details of the police officer's trial, while strictly relevant in showing the man's motive in committing his crime, may confuse the jury into thinking that the man was justified in doing what he did because the verdict was, in fact, unfair. The jury may not be able to distinguish between the justification of the man's anger and his motive for committing the crime.

Similarly, if a defendant is accused of raping and murdering a child, photos of the child's mangled body, while relevant, may incite such anger in the jury that it loses the ability to dispassionately assess the defendant's guilt. Again, such evidence will not be excluded merely because it is complex or graphic. The court must determine that it will somehow prevent the jury from carrying out its function, regardless of attempts by the court or the attorneys to clarify the proper role of the evidence in the jury's deliberations.

Undue delay and wasting time: Courts are not required to allow the introduction of evidence that will add little or nothing to the jury's understanding of the case, or that will cause needless delay in the proper administration of justice. If a prosecutor has a hundred witnesses to a crime, all of whose testimony will recount the same story, there is no need to allow the prosecutor to call all one hundred witnesses. If a defendant wishes to call his/her mother as a character witness, but she is on vacation and won't return until three weeks after the trial is scheduled to start, and there are other character witnesses available who can provide testimony just as effectively, then the court will not need to delay trial until the mother returns. Here again, though, the question is whether the evidence will *unduly* delay or waste the court's time. If a witness is essential to the presentation of the prosecutor or defendant's case, a delay in trial may not be unwarranted. If 20 witnesses can testify about different aspects of an event rather than simply repeat the same story 20 times, then calling all of those witnesses might be justified.

PRACTICE TIP

When evidence is being considered for use at trial that may create issues of prejudice, confusion, or undue delay, steps should be taken to carefully and clearly defend the probative value of that evidence as a counterweight to any negative factors under Rule 403.

■ RELEVANCE OF CHARACTER TESTIMONY: RULE 404

Character evidence relates to a person's traits or qualities rather than his/her actions or state of mind. In other words, this type of evidence shows whether a person is "good" or "bad," or has traits of "goodness" or "badness." The following statements are examples of character evidence:

- He is a bad-tempered man on his good days.
- She is the most generous person I've ever known.
- He's as honest as can be.
- She wouldn't tell the truth to her own mother.

Under Rule 404(a), character evidence "is not admissible to prove that on a particular occasion the person acted in accordance with the character or trait." The reason for this rule is to prevent a person's character from being used to prove his/her actions, instead of evidence that directly relates to those actions. For instance, just because a woman has a bad temper doesn't mean she assaulted her husband on a particular night. Just because a person is generally dishonest doesn't mean he/she took money from his/her employer. Human beings are not machines—their behavior can vary greatly from one occasion to another. So, in most instances, evidence of a person's character is irrelevant if it is being used to prove specific behavior at a particular time and place.

LEARNING OBJECTIVE 3
Understand when character evidence is relevant and how it is introduced.

character evidence
Evidence that relates to a person's traits or character, and that is generally inadmissible to show that the person's actions were in accordance with that trait or character.

SAMPLE TRIAL TRANSCRIPT 9-2

Objection to Improper Use of Character Evidence

Prosecutor: Mrs. Jones, how well do you know Mr. Smith?
Witness: Oh, I know him quite well.

Prosecutor:	Now, Mr. Smith is accused today of assaulting Mr. Martin. Mr. Martin claims that Mr. Smith hit him in anger. From what you know of Mr. Smith, do you think that would be in line with his character?
Witness:	Absolutely. Mr. Smith has a hair-trigger temper. It wouldn't surprise me at all if he punched Mr. Martin.
Defense:	Objection, Your Honor. Character testimony is not relevant to prove specific actions on a particular occasion.
Judge:	Sustained.

Here, the evidence about Mr. Smith's temper is being introduced in order to prove that, in the particular incident at issue in the case, Mr. Smith's actions were in line with his character. This is the type of evidence that Rule 404(a)(1) prohibits.

Exceptions to the Rule of Inadmissibility

Rule 404 contains several exceptions to the general rule of inadmissibility of lay opinions about actions taken in a particular instance. Of course, character evidence, like all evidence, is still subject to the general rule of relevance: it must tend to prove or disprove a fact of consequence to the case. The following exceptions wouldn't apply unless the character evidence met this general rule.

Evidence of Defendant's Character

While a prosecutor may not introduce evidence of a defendant's character, the defendant may. For instance, a defendant may offer evidence of his/her own honesty to help refute a charge that he/she embezzled money from his/her employer. This evidence is relevant in criminal cases because, while the defendant's character doesn't *prove* he/she behaved in a certain way at a particular time, it can create a *reasonable doubt* as to whether he/she did if such behavior is contrary to the defendant's character. Introducing character evidence is not without risk, however, because Rule 404(a)(1) also allows a prosecutor to introduce character evidence to rebut that offered by the defendant. In other words, by introducing evidence of his/her own character, the defendant opens the door to any evidence that might show that his/her character is not as benign as he/she wants the jury to believe.

SAMPLE TRIAL TRANSCRIPT 9-3

Evidence of Character to Disprove Guilt

| Defense: | Mrs. Jones, how well do you know Mr. Smith? |
| Witness: | Oh, I know him quite well. |

Defense:	Now, Mr. Smith is accused today of assaulting Mr. Martin. Mr. Martin claims that Mr. Smith hit him in anger. From what you know of Mr. Smith, do you think that would be in line with his character?
Witness:	Not at all. Mr. Smith is the gentlest man I know. He wouldn't hurt a fly. The idea of him punching Mr. Martin is ridiculous, no matter what Mr. Martin might have said to him.

If this testimony were offered by Mr. Smith to show that he wasn't guilty of assault, it would be admissible under Rule 404(a)(2). It would also open the door to any contrary evidence about Mr. Smith's character that the prosecutor might want to present.

Evidence of a Victim's Character

Rule 404(a)(2)(B) also provides an exception to the general prohibition against character testimony where the defendant offers evidence of the character of the victim. For instance, suppose a defendant is accused of assaulting a man in a bar, but the defendant claims that his assault was in self-defense because the man attacked him first. The defendant may support his defense under Rule 404(a)(2) by introducing evidence that the victim is a hot-tempered individual who often picks fights for no reason. In doing so, the defendant once again opens the door to rebuttal evidence by the prosecutor. The rule allows a prosecutor to present evidence that the victim's character is contrary to what the defendant claims. It also allows the prosecutor to show that the defendant has the same character trait as the victim (e.g., that the defendant is also a hothead who likes to pick fights with strangers). If the defendant is charged with homicide, the prosecutor may also introduce evidence that the witness is peaceful in order to rebut a defendant's claim that the victim was the first aggressor (Rule 404(a)(2)(C)).

SAMPLE TRIAL TRANSCRIPT 9-4

Evidence of Victim's Character to Refute Guilt

In this example, the defendant is presenting testimony in a case where he is accused of selling an elderly gentleman, Mr. Wampler, the rights to a nonexistent oil well in Texas.

Defense:	Mrs. Vale, are you familiar with Mr. Wampler?
Witness:	Yes, I've known him for years.
Defense:	How would you describe Mr. Wampler's character when it comes to spending his money?
Witness:	Oh, he's extremely careful with his money.
Defense:	Is he the kind of man who would write a check for $5,000 for the rights to an oil well he's never seen?
Witness:	Oh, heavens, no. Mr. Wampler is far too suspicious of swindlers to ever get involved with anything like that.

Again, the prosecutor may now present evidence to rebut this testimony and prove that Mr. Wampler wasn't the financially cautious man Mrs. Vale believed him to be.

The admissibility of evidence of a victim's character under Rule 404(a)(2)(B) is limited by the restriction on such evidence in sex offense cases set forth in Rule 412. Historically, if a woman was raped, evidence could be introduced to show that she was promiscuous, on the theory that a promiscuous woman was probably willing to engage in sexual activity. This assumption essentially placed the victim on trial, making her character rather than the defendant's actions the main focus of attention. The federal courts eventually realized that even a sexually active woman had the right to say no, and so they created Rule 412, which makes evidence of a sexual offense victim's other sexual behavior or sexual predisposition inadmissible.

Rule 412 has several important exceptions. One is that evidence can be introduced to show that the victim previously had sexual relations with the *defendant*, in order to support the defendant's defense of consent. The victim's other sexual activities can also be used to prove that someone other than the defendant was the source of semen, injury, or other physical evidence being used against the defendant. Essentially, these exceptions make it possible for the defendant to refute evidence specifically relating to the incident of sexual activity that resulted in the charges against him. An additional exception covers any evidence the exclusion of which would violate the defendant's constitutional rights.

Unlike other evidence of character, evidence cannot be offered under Rule 412 unless the court has granted leave at least two weeks prior to trial, with notice being given not only to the prosecutor, but also to the victim (Rule 412(c)).

The following case illustrates the application of Rule 412 in the context of a military court applying the identical Rule 412 of the Military Rules of Evidence. In this case, a private was accused of raping a woman, and he sought to introduce evidence of her prior sexual relations with him as proof that she consented to sexual intercourse. The court draws a clear and careful connection between Rule 412 and the question of relevance.

COURT OPINION 9-2

UNITED STATES V. BROWN, 17 M.J. 544 (U.S. Army Ct. of Mil. Rev., 1983)

At a pretrial Article 39(a), 10 U.S.C. § 839(a) session, the appellant's defense counsel advised the military judge that he intended to present evidence under Military Rule of Evidence (MRE) 412(b)(2) (A), of injury to Joanne Brown occurring on 20 May during her sexual activity with a person other than the appellant. He offered no evidence or information of specific instances. He did state,

(continued)

(continued)

however, that the source of his information regarding these injuries came from comments Joanne made to the physician who examined her after the alleged rape by the appellant. The defense counsel further advised the military judge that he had received this information at the Article 32(b)1 investigation that took place at least a month before the trial and that he had made no effort to follow up on it. The military judge disallowed the presentation of this evidence of Joanne's prior sexual conduct.

The defense counsel also advised the military judge that he intended to introduce certain evidence under MRE 412(b)(2)(B) "of prior consensual sexual intercourse between the accused and the victim." Again no specific instances were provided other than the defense counsel's statement that "consensual sex" had occurred between Joanne Brown and the appellant on two prior occasions. Likewise no prior notice of intention to introduce this evidence had been given to the military judge as required by MRE 412(c)(1), although on the evening before the trial the defense counsel had advised the trial counsel of his intention. When the military judge indicated his displeasure with the lack of notice the defense counsel acknowledged that he had no explanation other than simply having neglected to provide the required notice.

The military judge delayed ruling on the evidence of Joanne's sexual involvement with the appellant until the close of the government's case. At that time he disallowed its admission because of the lack of notice, the failure to provide specific information on time and place of prior sexual contact and because the evidence in question was "not constitutionally required." Nevertheless, in response to a question during cross-examination the appellant testified that he knew Joanne had been satisfied as a result of his performance during the alleged rape, because he "had sex with her before" and that she had been satisfied then.

Disallowing this evidence offered under MRE 412(b)(2)(B) by the defense was erroneous. In several recent cases the United States Court of Military Appeals has interpreted MRE 412. *United States v. Dorsey*, 16 M.J. 1 (C.M.A.1983); *United States v. Elvine*, 16 M.J. 14 (C.M.A.1983); *United States v. Colon-Angueira*, 16 M.J. 20 (C.M.A.1983);

United States v. Hollimon, 16 M.J. 164 (C.M.A.1983). From the holdings in these cases it is clear that relevance is the appropriate standard for determining the admissibility of evidence under MRE 412. "Whatever type of evidence may be offered as to past sexual behavior of an alleged victim, the underlying analysis is the same; and . . .. it centers on the relevance, materiality, and favorability to the defense of such evidence." *United States v. Hollimon*, *supra* at 165. Evidence of recent sexual intercourse between the appellant and the alleged victim in this case was relevant to the rape charge because of the inference of consent by the victim that could have been drawn by the fact-finders with respect to the incidents giving rise to the charge. Obviously, the purpose behind the defense offer of this evidence was to support its theory in defense of the rape charge that coitus between the appellant and Joanne Brown in the appellant's room on 27 May 1981 was with Joanne's consent. Thus the evidence also was material because whether or not Joanne did consent to coitus was the decisive issue in dispute at this trial. The evidence of prior sexual activity between the appellant and Joanne was favorable to the defense in that if an inference of consent had been drawn by the fact-finders it would have corroborated the testimony of the appellant that Joanne had consented to sexual intercourse with him on the fateful night. Thus the evidence was constitutionally required and within the right of the appellant to present. *See United States v. Dorsey*, *supra*. The appellant's response on cross-examination, wherein he referred to prior sexual relations with Joanne, did not satisfy the requirement for admissibility of the defense offered evidence under MRE 412(b)(2)(B) as it did not fully develop the evidence.

Questions

1. Why did the court find that evidence of prior sexual relations between the victim and the defendant was relevant to his defense of consent?

2. If this were a civilian jury trial, would a jury realistically be able to distinguish between prior acts offered to prove consent and prior acts offered to prove that the victim was promiscuous?

Evidence of Character of a Witness (Rule 404(a)(3))

Rule 404(a)(3) authorizes the use of character evidence relating to a witness to *impeach* (disprove the credibility of) the witness under Rule 607, to show that the witness is truthful or untruthful under Rule 608, or to impeach the witness based on criminal convictions under Rule 609. These rules will be covered in more detail later in the chapter discussing the credibility of witnesses.

Evidence of Crimes or Wrongful Acts to Show Character

Under Rule 404(b), evidence that a person committed a crime, wrong, or other act is not admissible to prove a person's character in order to show that the person acted in accordance with that character on a particular occasion. Such evidence can be used, however, to prove motive, opportunity, intent, preparation, plan, knowledge, identity, absence of mistake, or lack of accident.

To illustrate this rather complex rule, suppose that a man is accused of raping a woman in her home. The prosecutor can prove that the man had previously visited the home and made inappropriate sexual comments to the woman. This cannot be introduced to prove that the man's character was such that it is likely he committed the rape. But it can be introduced to show that (a) he knew where the woman lived, (b) he had access to the home, and (c) he had a sexual interest in the woman. His prior wrong acts (making inappropriate sexual comments) are not being used to show his character, but rather to show motive, opportunity, and intent.

In the following case, Rule 404(b) was applied to a rather unusual piece of evidence: rap lyrics written in a notebook by a suspected drug dealer: *Key for Key, Pound for pound I'm the biggest Dope Dealer and I serve all over town. Rock 4 Rock Self 4 Self. Give me a key let me go to work more Dollars than your average bussiness [sic] man.* The lyrics were discovered by federal agents when they searched a duffel bag and two suitcases being dragged across a train platform by the defendant, Foster. At Foster's trial for possession with intent to distribute, the prosecutor wanted the lyrics admitted to prove that the defendant was guilty of drug trafficking, but the District Court admitted them under the Rule 404(b) "other acts" exception solely for the purpose of proving that the defendant had knowledge about the drug trade and intended to engage in that trade. The defendant appealed the District Court's decision on the ground that the lyrics were irrelevant and highly prejudicial to the defendant.

COURT OPINION 9-3

UNITED STATES V. FOSTER, 939 F.2d 445 (7th Cir. 1991)

Foster's second evidentiary challenge to his conviction is that the district court erred in admitting the verse found in his notebook. Although the government argued that the verse was admissible without limitation because it was "'intricately related to the facts of the case,'" *United States v. Monzon*, 869 F.2d 338, 343 (7th Cir.), *cert. denied*, 490 U.S. 1075, 109 S.Ct. 2087, 104 L.Ed.2d 650 (1989), the district court concluded otherwise and admitted the verse under the government's fall-back argument—Rule 404(b). It then gave a contemporaneous instruction:

> The document is received for a limited purpose. It is not received to establish that the defendant is, in fact, the biggest dope dealer. It is not received that the defendant makes more dollars than the average

(continued)

(continued)

businessman. It is not received for that purpose. It is received for a limited purpose.

The admissibility of evidence of other acts or crimes is governed by Rule 404(b) of the Federal Rules of Evidence, which provides that such evidence may not be used to prove a person's bad character or his propensity to commit crimes in conformity with that character, but may be used for other purposes, such as proof of motive, opportunity, intent, preparation, plan, knowledge or absence of mistake or accident.

The limited purpose for which the document is received is only as to evidence of knowledge and intent. The defendant is accused in the indictment of having knowledge and intention; that he knowingly and intentionally did something.

This instruction illustrates the care with which the district court treated this issue, and in large part supports our conclusion that the decision to admit the verse did not constitute an abuse of discretion.

. . . As to relevance, [Foster] argues that the verse "certainly was nothing that could show knowledge of what was in the suitcases" because the verse "made no reference to the suitcases he carried, or to the trip he was making." . . . This view of relevance, however, is unduly restrictive. The verse, standing alone, need not have been enough to prove knowledge; it is sufficient that the verse made it more probable that Foster had knowledge (and, therefore, more probable that he was guilty of the crime charged). *United States v. York*, 933 F.2d 1343, 1351 (7th Cir. 1991) (citing FED.R.EVID. 401). In our view, the verse clearly meets that test; it indicated, at a minimum, that Foster was familiar with drug code words and, to a certain extent, narcotics trafficking, a familiarity that made it more probable that he knew that he was carrying illegal drugs.

Foster's knowledge, moreover, was relevant to the charges that he faced and was, in Foster's words, "the only issue in the case." . . . [T]he verse achieved heightened relevance by virtue of the fact that it also rebutted Foster's protestations of naiveté. . . .

Before moving on to prejudice, however, it is necessary to discuss one further point. Foster attempts to destroy, or at least diminish, the relevance of the verse by claiming that it was written for eventual incorporation into a rap song. These are rap lyrics, he claims. They have artistic value. They are fiction, just like Dashiel Hammett's description of violent acts in *The Maltese Falcon*. And as such, they cannot be relevant to his guilt.

This court has not faced such an argument in the past nor, does it appear, have many others. Indeed, the parties have cited no cases that are really on point, and this court has discovered only one case discussing the admission of a defendant's own literary or artistic work under a Rule 404(b) theory (*State v. Hanson*, 46 Wash.App. 656, 731 P.2d 1140 (1987)).

If nothing else, *Hanson* underscores the need to recall that the rap verse was not admitted to show that Foster was, in fact, "the biggest dope dealer"; it was not admitted to establish that Foster was the character portrayed in the lyrics. But in writing about this "fictional" character, Foster exhibited knowledge of an activity that is far from fictional. He exhibited some knowledge of narcotics trafficking, and in particular drug code words. It was for this limited purpose that the verse was admitted, and it is for this limited purpose that its relevance is clear. . . .

Much of Foster's argument on this point is therefore of limited usefulness because, to answer his concerns by the same type of analogy, admitting the rap verse was not the equivalent of admitting *The Godfather* as evidence that Mario Puzo was a mafia don or admitting "The Pit and the Pendulum" as evidence that Edgar Allen Poe had tortured someone. It was, instead, the equivalent of admitting *The Godfather* to illustrate Puzo's knowledge of the inner workings of an organized crime family and admitting "The Pit and the Pendulum" to illustrate Poe's knowledge of medieval torture devices. Rap music, under Foster's definition, "constitutes a popular musical style that describes urban life"; it describes the reality around its author. And it is Foster's knowledge of this reality, as evidenced by the verse that he has admittedly authored, that was relevant to the crimes for which he was charged.

[The court rejected Foster's claim that the rap lyrics were prejudicial, and upheld the District Court's decision to admit them under Rule 404(b).]

Questions

1. Assuming that the person referred to in defendant's verse was fictional and not Foster, what does the verse tell us about Foster himself that made the verse relevant?
2. How did Foster's claim that he lacked knowledge of the suitcase's contents make his rap lyrics even more relevant?

If the prosecutor wishes to introduce character evidence for a purpose permitted under Rule 404(b), then the prosecutor must give reasonable notice to the defendant prior to trial, unless there is good cause why such notice cannot be given. Also, care must be given to instruct the jury that it may only consider such evidence for the purposes permitted under Rule 404(b), as the District Court did in *Foster*. As noted above, if the evidence is so prejudicial that the jury would not reasonably be able to limit its consideration to the proper purposes, then the court could exclude the evidence despite its admissibility.

SAMPLE TRIAL TRANSCRIPT 9-5

Evidence of Character to Prove Motive

In the following dialogue, in which a prosecuting attorney is examining the sister of a murder victim, Mr. Kenna, who was shot by the defendant during an argument about a car the defendant had bought from Mr. Kenna that turned out to be a lemon.

Prosecutor:	Miss Kenna, did you ever see the defendant and your brother together before the night your brother died?
Witness:	Yeah, I saw them together a lot. They used to hang out together almost every night.
Prosecutor:	Did you ever see the defendant get into a fight with anyone?
Witness:	Yeah, a few times. The only serious one was a few months before.
Prosecutor:	What happened then?
Witness:	The defendant and my brother were up against these two guys over a bet and the defendant pulled a gun out of his pocket and stuck it in the one guy's face.
Prosecutor:	What else happened?
Witness:	He told the guy I'll kill anyone who tries to cheat me, no matter who, no matter what.

This evidence does not relate to the murder of Mr. Kenna itself, except to show that the defendant had a motive for shooting Mr. Kenna, and to prove that the shooting was not an accident. For this limited purpose, the prior incident of assault was admissible, unless the court felt (as it very well might) that the jury would not be able to distinguish the limited purpose of the admissibility (motive and deliberateness) from the conclusion that the defendant was guilty because he had previously committed a violent act.

Methods of Proving Character (Rule 405)

The methods of proving the character of a defendant, victim, or witness under Rule 404 are covered by Rule 405. Two methods are permitted under this rule: reputation or opinion evidence and evidence of specific instances of conduct.

Reputation or Opinion Evidence

The character of a person can be proven through testimony about the person's **reputation** or testimony in the form of an **opinion**. Sample Trial Transcripts 9-3 and 9-4 are examples of opinion testimony regarding character. For a witness to offer such an opinion, it is necessary to lay a foundation by showing that the witness is familiar enough with that person's character that there is some basis for the opinion. This is usually done by demonstration of firsthand familiarity with the person, preferably through long acquaintance. A short acquaintance or single experience with a person would not be sufficient to support an opinion about the person's character.

"Reputation" evidence is exactly what it sounds like—a person's reputation within the community. In this case, personal familiarity with the person is not necessary, so long as the witness is familiar with the person's reputation. Rule 405 also provides that the prosecutor may inquire into specific instances of conduct where a witness has offered an opinion or testified about reputation relating to character.

reputation
The sense of a person's character held throughout the community in which the person lives.

opinion
A witness' belief as to the character of a person based on firsthand experience with the person.

Nbah Peka/123RF

Computer use can provide evidence that may be relevant to a number of issues in a criminal case, including character and reputation.

Source: http://www.123rf.com/search.php?word=young+man+using+laptop+cafe&start=100&t_word=&t_lang=en&imgtype=0&oriSearch=young%20man%20using%20laptop&searchopts=&itemsperpage=100&sti=mqmaf9mjynait78yc|&mediapopup=50336856.

EVIDENCE AND TECHNOLOGY

USING SOCIAL NETWORKING SITES AS EVIDENCE OF CHARACTER

Social networking sites are more than just modes of communication. Statuses, comments, photos, and shared material provide an unprecedented look into the hearts and minds of users, reflecting thoughts and emotions that would not normally be put on public display. Like all statements, messages posted to a social media site can be used as evidence in a criminal trial, assuming they meet all of the standards of admissibility that are discussed in this text.

(continued)

Social media sites can be investigated in a number of ways, from obtaining information directly through a user's public page to subpoenaing information from the servers of the social media service itself. If there is good reason to believe that information relevant to a crime has been posted on social media, it becomes as much fair game for the target of an investigation as any other statements made by the defendant. As blogger and attorney Josh Gilliland wrote, "A lawyer recently expressed to me serious doubts about using evidence from social media websites. According to him, electronically stored information (ESI) can never be trusted without the proffering party proving each step of creation to guarantee its authenticity. But that would be the equivalent of requiring a team of experts to authenticate a hard-copy document. You'd start with a lumberjack to explain how a tree was cut down. An expert on how trees are made into paper would follow. Another expert would detail how ink works, and so on and so on.

The law simply does not require such a metaphysical discussion of existence for social media information to be admissible. It is treated no differently than any other evidence. For admission in court, a party must show that the ESI is relevant; authenticate it; address issues of unfair prejudice and probative value; address hearsay (show an exception or non-hearsay use of the ESI); and demonstrate that the ESI conforms to the original writing (the best evidence rule)."[1]

One danger in using social media statements as criminal evidence is that such statements are not necessarily reflective of what the user was actually thinking or feeling at the time the statements were made. The Internet is often used as a place for playing out fantasy, and the question arises whether a comment or status truly captures the nature and character of a user's thoughts, or whether the user was just pretending to have those thoughts in order to shock, amuse, or titillate his/her friends.

This issue is particularly important when social media evidence is used as evidence of a user's character. As we see in this chapter, the admissibility of character evidence is limited because of its potential for prejudice and the low relevance it bears to the question of the defendant's actual guilt. But where it is admissible, social media statements are as legitimate a means of proving character as any other, assuming that the statements do, in fact, reflect the character of the person writing them.

The few cases that have addressed this issue in a criminal context have consistently held that information from social media sites cannot be admitted if all it shows is that the defendant has a bad character and does not directly prove any fact relevant to the crime of which the defendant is accused. In *United States* v. *Drummond*, 2010 WL 1329059 (M.D.Pa. 2010), the court refused to admit photos of the defendant holding and throwing cash at a time when he had no job, even though the photos were somewhat relevant to the issue of whether defendant was dealing drugs, because the prejudicial effect of such photos outweighed any probative value they might have (*Id.* at 2). As the court stated, it would be unfair to admit the photos because the jury could conclude that "he is a drug dealer because he looks like a drug dealer" (*Id*).

A similar conclusion was reached in *United States* v. *Phaknikone*, 605 F.3d 1099 (11th Cir. 2010). There, photographs from the defendant's MySpace account depicting the defendant in a car with a child, holding a gun sideways, depicted only that the defendant had a "gangster-type personality," and could not be used to make the jury infer that "because Phaknikone is willing to publish these kinds of photographs online, under an incendiary alias, he is a gangster who is likely to rob banks" (*Id.* at 1109).

(continued)

These cases make it clear that evidence taken from social media sites cannot be used simply to show that the user is a bad person, or at least pretends to be a bad person when displaying himself/herself to his/her social media friends. If a status or photograph posted to social media site does not relate to the specific crime with which the defendant is charged, then it will likely not be admissible under the rules governing character evidence.

The opinion in *United States* v. *Reich* illustrates the use of opinion and reputation evidence where a defendant's character is at issue. In this case, the defendant, Perry Reich, was convicted of forgery and obstruction of justice in the creation and transmittal of a forged court order. At trial, Reich presented a character witness, James Pelzer, who testified about Reich's reputation for honesty. The Court allowed the prosecution to cross-examine Pelzer about an incident, unrelated to the forgery charge, where Reich, without authority, changed the beneficiary under his dying law partner's life insurance policy. This evidence of Reich's prior bad act was intended to impeach the character witness. Following his conviction, Reich moved for a new trial on a number of grounds, including the claim that the trial court improperly permitted the prosecution to present evidence of Reich's unauthorized change to his partner's life insurance policy.

COURT OPINION 9-4 _____

UNITED STATES V. REICH, 420 F.Supp.2d 75 (E.D.N.Y. 2006)

Defendant's Rule 29 motion based on improper impeachment of Reich's character argues that the Government improperly cross-examined James Pelzer, a character witness for Reich. Pelzer testified on direct examination that Reich is "a person of high honesty and integrity, a person that you can trust . . . and . . . others share that same opinion." (Tr. 813.) On cross-examination, the Government sought to attack Reich's character by asking about an unauthorized change in his law partner's life insurance policy in violation of the partnership agreement. (Tr. 817.) At a hearing, I examined a partnership agreement between the partner and Reich, in which each had life insurance paid by Reich, the proceeds of which went to their own families in the event of their death. (Tr. 822.) The agreement stated that if Reich sought to change the terms of the agreement, that he would have to notify his partner. (Tr. 823.) Lastly, I examined correspondence that established that Reich changed the terms of the agreement after the partner was diagnosed with cancer without consulting the partner. (Tr.

823–25.) Based on that proffer, I allowed the following question over defense counsel's objection:

> Mr. Pelzer, if I told you that Mr. Reich had changed the beneficiary of an insurance policy away from Mr. Schapiro's family members, designating the law firm the beneficiary in the event of Mr. Schapiro's death, without notice to Mr. Schapiro and in violation of the partnership agreement that the two of them had, would that change your opinion or the opinion of the community . . . with regard to the defendant's honesty or good character?

(Tr. 847.)

"Once a defendant offers character testimony, the prosecution is afforded substantial latitude to rebut such evidence." *United States v. Russo*, 110 F.3d 948, 952 (2d Cir. 1997). Federal Rule of Evidence 405 provides that if the defense puts forward a character witness to testify to the defendant's good reputation, that "[o]n cross-examination, inquiry is allowable into relevant instances of conduct." F.R.E. 405(a). The cross-examination is

(continued)

(continued)

permitted to evaluate the character witness's credibility and knowledge of the defendant. *United States v. Birney*, 686 F.2d 102, 108 (2d Cir. 1982). Before allowing the prosecution to attack a defendant's credibility by asking character witnesses on cross-examination about a specific instance of conduct, the trial court should ascertain that the prosecution has a good faith belief that the act occurred, and that the incident is relevant to the character trait at issue. *Michelson v. United States*, 335 U.S. 469, 481 n. 18, 69 S.Ct. 213, 93 L.Ed. 168 (1948). The Second Circuit reviews "a trial court's ruling on the admissibility of character evidence for an abuse of discretion." *United States v. Damblu*, 134 F.3d 490, 494 (2d Cir. 1998); *see also Michelson v. United States*, 335 U.S. 469, 480, 69 S.Ct. 213, 93 L.Ed. 168 (1948).

With these principles in mind, there is no substantial question presented as to whether this question was permissible under Federal Rule of Evidence 405. The defense counsel offered a character witness who testified to Reich's reputation for honesty and integrity in the New York legal community. On cross-examination, the prosecution is entitled to ask the witness about an act, based upon a good faith basis to believe that the act occurred, that tended to show Reich's character for dishonesty. Further, Reich's propensity for integrity and honesty was rel-

evant to the charges that he would seek to deceive an adversary's counsel and obstruct a judicial proceeding through the use of a forged Order.

. . .

Whether the Prosecution was entitled to question Pelzer about Reich's change to his law partner's life insurance policy under Federal Rule of Evidence 405, after this court determined that there was a good faith basis for the question and that it was relevant to the charged offenses, does not present a close question. Moreover, even if this ruling were incorrect, it would be harmless error, as there was strong evidence as to Reich's guilt. Accordingly, there is no substantial question raised for appeal purposes by this court's decision to permit the Prosecution to question Pelzer about Reich's violation of the partnership agreement.

Questions

1. How did the testimony of Pelzer relate to the charges brought against Reich?
2. Re-read Rule 405(a). Was the prosecutor's use of Reich's unauthorized change to his law partner's life insurance policy in compliance with that rule?

PRACTICE TIP

Whenever the character of a witness may be called into question, the witness should be thoroughly vetted to ensure that any evidence of bad character is known beforehand, and can be addressed adequately at trial.

Evidence of Specific Instances of Conduct

This type of evidence is demonstrated in the testimony of Miss Kenna in Sample Trial Transcript 9-5. Evidence of specific instances of conduct is admissible to prove character in only three instances:

1. Where such evidence is used to cross-examine a reputation witness (Rule 405(a)). In other words, once a witness has testified about a person's character, the other side can present specific instance of that person's conduct that demonstrates that the witness' assessment of that person's character was not accurate. This is the type of evidence that was used in *United States v. Reich*, above.
2. In a civil case where such evidence is used to prove a character trait that is an element of a claim or defense (Rule 405(b)(1)). For example, in a civil action for defamation of character, a key element of the plaintiff's case is to show that the plaintiff's reputation among his/her neighbors

and associates was harmed. In such a case, it would be proper for the defendant to present specific instances of the plaintiff's conduct to show that his/her reputation was such that the defendant's statement did not harm his/her reputation.

3. In a criminal case to prove a victim's character under Rule 404(a)(2) (Rule 405(b)(2)).

■ HABIT AND ROUTINE: RULE 406

Rule 406 allows evidence of **habit or routine** in order to show that a person or an organization acted in accordance with that habit or routine.

LEARNING OBJECTIVE 5
Explain the introduction of habit or routine as relevant testimony.

habit or routine
Evidence that is admissible to show that a person or an organization acted in accordance with established habits or routines.

SAMPLE TRIAL TRANSCRIPT 9-6

Evidence of Habit or Routine

Prosecutor:	Mr. Johns, were you familiar with the deceased's usual morning routine?
Witness:	Yes, I was. I knew him for many years, and he was a man of very regular habits.
Prosecutor:	What was his morning routine?
Witness:	He would get up at precisely 6:00 A.M., do some calisthenics, and then go for a brisk walk in the park two blocks from his home. He did this every morning, rain or shine, unless it was too cold.
Prosecutor:	So his presence in that park at 6:30 the morning of the murder was in line with his routine?
Witness:	Absolutely. You could've set your clock by it.

The reason for allowing this testimony is that, although the complexity of an individual's personality may not permit the inference that a person's action are dictated by his/her character, habits and routines are much more directly related to a person's choices, and are far more likely to influence his/her actions. This rule focuses on habits of action, so while a prosecutor may not be able to prove that a man beat his wife by showing he had a bad temper, he can prove it by showing that he routinely engaged in fistfights at a local bar every weekend, thereby demonstrating that physical violence was, for him, a habitual or routine occurrence.

■ OTHER LIMITATIONS ON RELEVANCY

F.R.E. Article IV places several other limitations on the general rule that relevant evidence is admissible. Those limitations include prejudicial evidence, cumulative evidence, evidence the admission of which would violate public policy, and evidence that is privileged. These limitations will all be discussed in detail in the following chapters.

KEY TERMS

relevance 181	reputation 193	habit or routine 197
character evidence 185	opinion 193	

CHAPTER SUMMARY

- In order to be admissible, evidence must be relevant, which means it must tend to prove or disprove a fact of consequence to the case.
- The relevance of evidence is determined based on all of the facts that may impact a case, not merely the guilt or innocence of the defendant.
- Even if relevant, evidence can be excluded if it violates constitutional limitations, if it would confuse, mislead, or prejudice the jury, or if it would cause undue delay or the waste of the court's time.
- Character evidence, or evidence of the person's qualities or traits, is not admissible to prove that the person acted in accordance with his/her character on a particular occasion.
- A defendant may introduce evidence of his/her own character to create a reasonable doubt as to whether he/she committed the crime of which he/she is accused.
- Where a defendant introduces evidence of character in his/her own defense, the prosecutor may introduce evidence to rebut that character evidence.
- Evidence of the character of a victim is admissible where the victim's character is an issue in the case, particularly where a defense (such as self-defense) is based on the victim's character.
- Evidence of past sexual conduct by the victim in a sex offense case is not admissible unless it relates specifically to sexual conduct between the victim and the defendant, or if it shows that someone other than the defendant was the source of physical evidence.
- Evidence of a witness' character can be used to show that the witness is untruthful or to otherwise impeach the testimony of a witness.
- Evidence of specific crimes or wrongful acts can be used to prove a defendant's motive, opportunity, intent, preparation, plan, knowledge, identity, absence of mistake, or lack of accident.
- Character can be proven by testimony showing the reputation of the person's character, or expressing the opinion of the witness as to the person's character.
- Evidence of specific instances of conduct cannot be used to prove character except where such evidence is being used to cross-examine a character witness.
- Evidence of a person's habit or routine is admissible to prove that a person's actions were in accordance with that habit or routine.

WEB EXCURSIONS

1. Using Google or a similar search engine, look up the Rules of Evidence for your state. Read the rules relating to relevance and character evidence. Can you identify any significant differences between your rules and the Federal Rules of Procedure?

2. Using the rules you found for your state, take another look at the *United States* v. *Deruise* case. Would that case have been decided the same in your state as it was under the federal rules?

PRACTICAL EXERCISES

1. Select a single fact about yourself (e.g., where you grew up, who your parents are, or your favorite hobby). Make a list of five pieces of evidence that would be relevant to prove that fact. List the evidence according to whether it proves the fact directly or circumstantially, and how well it proves the fact.
2. Suppose that you are the defendant in a criminal case, and your truthfulness is relevant to the charges. Make a list of five people you feel would be competent to testify about your reputation for honesty. For each witness, make a list of three questions that your attorney could ask the witness. Can you identify any specific instances of conduct that a prosecutor might be able to use to impeach your witness (as occurred in *United States* v. *Reich*)?

ENDNOTE

1. "The admissibility of social media evidence," Litigation News, ABA Section of Litigation. (n.d.). Retrieved from http://apps.americanbar. org/litigation/litigationnews/trial_skills/030413-tips-admissibility-ESI.html.

Robert Daly/Getty Images

LEARNING OBJECTIVES

After reading this chapter, the student will be able to:

1. Explain the meaning of unfairly prejudicial evidence, and when it can be excluded at trial.

2. Identify the methods available to courts to remedy the presentation of unfairly prejudicial evidence.

3. Determine when evidence is likely to mislead or confuse a jury, waste time, or cause undue delay in a manner that outweighs its probative value.

4. Identify the pleas and statements relating to plea proceedings and discussions that are excluded under Rule 410.

Relevance Exceptions: Prejudice, Cumulativeness, and Public Policy

CHAPTER 10

◼ INTRODUCTION

In Chapter 9, we examined what it means for evidence to be "relevant." As we noted at the end of that chapter, F.R.E. Article IV places several limitations on the general rule that relevant evidence is admissible. In this chapter, we will be examining the following limitations:

- Unfair prejudice and other concerns outweighing probative value (Rule 403)
- Cumulativeness (Rule 403)
- Exceptions based on public policy

    - Compromise offers and negotiations (Rule 408)
    - Pleas and plea discussions (Rule 410)

■ UNFAIR PREJUDICE AND OTHER CONCERNS OUTWEIGHING PROBATIVE VALUE

Rule 403 provides a balancing test for the exclusion of otherwise relevant evidence. Under that rule, relevant evidence can be excluded if its probative value is outweighed by any of the following concerns:

- Unfair prejudice
- Confusion of the issues
- Misleading the jury
- Undue delay
- Wasting time

We will now take a look at each of these concerns.

LEARNING OBJECTIVE 1
Explain the meaning of unfairly prejudicial evidence, and when it can be excluded at trial.

prejudicial effect
The effect of evidence on a juror, which may lead him/her to base a decision on emotional or other factors instead of the evidence.

Unfair Prejudice

As we learned in Chapter 3, any general or specific prejudice that might affect a juror's ability to fairly hear the evidence in a case is brought out during jury selection. But this does not take into account the possibility that specific evidence presented during the trial could itself have a **prejudicial effect** on the jury.

There is no question that evidence presented at a trial may have a serious emotional impact on the jury. Jurors are not computers, and they are not capable of a completely dispassionate evaluation of the evidence. When a rape victim testifies about the assault against her, or a parent testifies about seeing his/her child being murdered, or an elderly woman testifies about the despair she felt after realizing she'd lost her life's savings to a con artist, jurors will feel the emotions any human being would feel, and that is exactly what we expect of them. They are going to feel angry, upset, and sad, and those emotions are going to have a profound impact on how they view the evidence.

The question is not whether jurors will have an emotional response to evidence, but whether the value of the evidence in proving a fact at issue in the case is great enough to justify the risk that the emotional impact of the evidence will prejudice the jury's decision. In other words, does the prejudice that evidence may create in a juror's mind *outweigh* the value that evidence has in proving or disproving the facts at issue in the case?

This question was addressed and answered in the following case, where the Fifth Circuit Court of Appeals reviewed the trial court's decision to allow graphic photographs of a murder scene into evidence.

COURT OPINION 10-1 _____

UNITED STATES V. MCRAE, 593 F.2d 700 (5th Cir. 1979)

[The defendant, McRae, was convicted of first-degree murder in the shooting death of his wife. At trial, the prosecution introduced graphic color photographs of the death scene and the wife's body in order to establish cause and manner of death. The court allowed the photographs into evidence over the objections of defense counsel.]

. . .

[Defendant challenges] the admission of various photographs of the deceased and of the death

(continued)

(continued)

scene. It is said that these should have been excluded under Rule 403, Federal Rules of Evidence, as relevant matter the probative value of which is substantially outweighed by the danger of unfair prejudice. Two of these color prints are indeed as the trial court characterized them gross, distasteful and disturbing. Exhibit 29 is a view of Mrs. McRae's corpse, clothed in her bloody garments, bent forward so as to display an exit wound in the back of her skull produced by part of McRae's dum-dum bullet, which exploded in her brain. Exhibit 22 shows a front view of her body, seated in the chair where she died, her left eye disfigured by the bullet's entry and her head broken by its force. By comparison with these, the other photographs are mild; but these are not pretty even to the hardened eye. Neither, however, was the crime, and these exhibits are not flagrantly or deliberately gruesome depictions of it. See *United States v. Kaiser*, 545 F.2d 467, 496 (5th Cir. 1977). The trial court carefully reviewed the government's photographic exhibits, excluding some of little probative value. It found those admitted important to establishing elements of the offense such as Mrs. McRae's position and that of the rifle when it was fired, as bearing on McRae's defense of accident.

Relevant evidence is inherently prejudicial; but it is only unfair prejudice, substantially outweighing probative value, which permits exclusion of relevant matter under Rule 403. Unless trials are to be conducted on scenarios, on unreal facts tailored and sanitized for the occasion, the application of Rule 403 must be cautious and sparing. Its major function is limited to excluding matter of scant or cumulative probative force, dragged in by the heels for the sake of its prejudicial effect. As to such, Rule 403 is meant to relax the iron rule of relevance, to permit the trial judge to preserve the fairness of the proceedings by exclusion despite its relevance. It is not designed to permit the court to "even out" the weight of the evidence, to mitigate a crime, or to make a contest where there is little or none. Here was no parade of horrors. We refuse to interfere with the trial court's exercise of its discretion.

Questions

1. What does the *McRae* court's holding tell us about the difference between probative value and prejudicial effect?
2. What does the court mean by its comment that "relevant evidence is inherently prejudicial"?

Prejudice can also occur when evidence points to a fact that may lead the jury to draw an improper inference. For instance, suppose a man is accused of driving while intoxicated. A report showing his blood alcohol level would be highly probative evidence on the question of whether he was above the legal limit. But suppose the only evidence that he was intoxicated was eyewitness testimony that he was seen drinking at a bar an hour before being arrested. That evidence would not really prove, or even tend to prove, that he was intoxicated to the point required to be convicted of driving under the influence, but a jury could easily assume that if he was drinking, then he must have been intoxicated. The prejudicial effect of such evidence would outweigh its low probative value on the issue of the defendant's guilt.

In the case of *Turner* v. *White*, a police officer shot and killed a man while shooting at another man the officer believed was armed. In the civil rights case that followed, counsel for the officer offered evidence that both of the men had been drinking shortly before the incident. The plaintiff's counsel objected on the grounds that whether the men were drinking had no probative value on whether the officer properly used deadly force, and that the evidence was therefore unfairly prejudicial. The trial judge allowed the evidence, and the plaintiff filed an appeal.

COURT OPINION 10-2 _____

TURNER V. WHITE, 980 F.2d 1180 (8th Cir. 1992)

On the night of February 15, 1989, Keith Turner was driving Joseph Downing's white Cadillac with Tyrone Downing in the front passenger seat and Joseph Downing in the back seat on the passenger's side. At approximately 10:15 p.m., Officers Joseph Tuhill and Roy White of the St. Louis Police Department, Mobile Reserve Unit, observed the three men driving slowly south on Newstead Avenue and following a female pedestrian. The Cadillac turned around in a loading dock area and then proceeded north on Newstead Avenue. The officers, their suspicions aroused, followed the car up Newstead Avenue. Keith Turner saw the police car was following him, so he turned right on Labadie Avenue and pulled over to the side of the street.

The police officers pulled up behind the stopped car. Officer White, carrying a department-issued shotgun, and Officer Tuhill, his revolver drawn, got out of the patrol car. The officers testified that they twice commanded the occupants to get out of their car and that they did not respond; the Downings testified that they did not hear any such commands.

The officers observed the occupants moving in the car, and Officer White testified that the back-seat passenger, Joseph Downing, leaned down to the floor and his shoulders and arms dropped down and to the left. Officer White testified that Joseph Downing then quickly rose up, lifting his arms, turning back, and looking directly at Officer White. Officer White, believing that Joseph Downing had a firearm and was about to shoot him, fired one shot at Joseph Downing through the rear window of the Cadillac. The shotgun fire blasted a hole in the glass of the rear window, missed Joseph Downing, and hit and killed Keith Turner. Joseph Downing, it turned out, did not have a firearm.

. . .

Turner argues that it was reversible error for the trial judge to admit evidence concerning Keith Turner's and Joseph Downing's alcohol consumption.

We disagree. We review trial court rulings on the admissibility of evidence under the abuse of discretion standard. *United States v. Drew*, 894 F.2d 965, 969 (8th Cir.), *cert. denied*, 494 U.S. 1089, 110 S.Ct. 1830, 108 L.Ed.2d 959 (1990). Here, the court refused to exclude the evidence of alcohol consumption under Federal Rule of Evidence 403, ruling that this evidence was relevant to the question of Keith Turner's and Joseph Downing's actions and reactions when the officers shouted at them to get out of the car, and that the probative value of the evidence outweighed any unfair prejudice. We see no error in that ruling. In reaching its verdict, it was incumbent upon the jury to consider Officer White's actions in relation to all the circumstances of the situation that confronted him. We therefore believe the evidence of alcohol consumption was relevant to the jury's assessment of that situation, and we conclude that in balancing its probative value against the risk of undue prejudice, and in ruling it admissible, the trial court did not abuse its discretion. See *Saladino v. Winkler*, 609 F.2d 1211, 1214 (7th Cir. 1979) (in action against police officer for use of excessive force in disarming the plaintiff, evidence of the plaintiff's intoxication held admissible under Rule 403 as it "tends to make [it] more probable that the plaintiff acted as the defendant contended he did or that plaintiff otherwise conducted himself in such a manner as to place the defendant reasonably in fear of his life.").

Questions

1. For what purpose did the court find that evidence of Turner's and Downing's drinking was relevant to the actions of Officer White?
2. If this case were a criminal prosecution of Turner and Downing for resisting arrest, would the court's reason for admitting the evidence still be valid?

LEARNING OBJECTIVE 2
Identify the methods available to courts to remedy the presentation of unfairly prejudicial evidence.

Remedies for Prejudice

Where evidence is prejudicial, what happens if the jury hears evidence that the court has ruled as prejudicial and excluded under Rule 403?

This can happen in several ways. First, inadmissible information might come out by accident. A witness might say something in the course of testifying that contains prejudicial information, despite the attempts by the examining attorney to prevent it. Or, an attorney who feels that a piece of information is crucial even though it has been ruled inadmissible might attempt to make the jury aware of it by some other means. For instance, we have already seen in Chapter 9 that evidence of a rape victim's general promiscuity is not relevant to show that she consented to sexual intercourse with the accused. Suppose a defendant is accused of raping a prostitute. Obviously, the victim's profession would not be admissible under Rule 412. But suppose the defendant's attorney called a friend of the victim to testify to statements that the victim made about the rape, and in the course of that testimony it was revealed that the statements were made while the victim was standing on a street corner waiting for clients. That testimony would reveal the victim's profession to the jury, even though no direct question about that profession was ever asked or answered.

Where a jury has heard overly prejudicial evidence, a court has two options. The first is to instruct the jury that it should not take the information it just heard into account in its deliberations (a cautionary instruction). The second is to declare a **mistrial**, which essentially terminates the trial and reschedules the case for another trial in front of a different jury. Which of these options is appropriate depends on the severity of the prejudice that might result from the improper evidence. If the judge feels that the evidence will poison the jury's minds to such an extent that the jury cannot possibly render a fair verdict on the facts of the case, then a mistrial is in order. Otherwise, a cautionary instruction to the jury would suffice.

The problem with a mistrial is primarily that it wastes time and resources. The entire trial to that point is rendered meaningless, and a new trial must be scheduled, with both parties starting literally at square one. An instruction not to consider the evidence is preferable because the trial can continue from that point, but there is no guarantee that the jury will follow that instruction and ignore the prejudicial evidence when it deliberates. Since a jury's deliberations are secret, it is extremely difficult to prove that a single piece of prejudicial evidence resulted in an improper verdict.

The decision of how to respond to the disclosure of prejudicial evidence is within the discretion of the trial judge. One of the parties (usually the defendant in a criminal case) may demand a mistrial, but they are seldom granted. This is probably more a matter of economy than a matter of trust: the cost of a new trial is so great that judges will seldom want to incur that expense where there is a reasonable chance that the jury will be able to render a fair verdict despite the improper evidence.

mistrial
The termination of a trial prior to its conclusion due to a prejudicial event that cannot be remedied by a cautionary instruction.

Confusing or Misleading the Jury

The task of a jury is not an easy one. A jury may be called upon to coordinate, evaluate, and synthesize facts presented through dozens of witnesses and exhibits, and then deliberate on those facts, often guided by nothing but memory, to reach a clear verdict. In cases involving multiple counts or crimes with complex elements, the jury's job is even more difficult. The lawyers and judges do their best to help the jury understand the evidence and navigate the legal principles surrounding the case, but the ultimate responsibility still lies with the jurors.

In this environment, it is critical that the judge not allow the jury to be confused or misled by evidence that, while relevant, will cause the juror's minds to stray from the factual issues they are there to decide. Such confusion can occur in a number of ways. Evidence might distract the jury's attention from the central issues to be decided. In *United States* v. *Mohamed*, 418 F.Supp. 2d 913 (D.C.S.D., 2005), for instance, a defendant was not permitted to cross-examine a prosecution witness about his antiterrorism activities to prove that he was

LEARNING OBJECTIVE 3
Determine when evidence is likely to mislead or confuse a jury, waste time, or cause undue delay in a manner that outweighs its probative value.

biased against Moslems (of which the defendant was one), because there was no suggestion that the defendant was a terrorist and raising such an issue in light of the attention given to the September 11, 2001, terrorist attacks would simply confuse the jury and divert its attention from the real issue of the defendant's guilt (*Id.* at 916, 917). See *also United States* v. *Iron Hawk*, 612 F.3d 1031, 1039, 1040 (8th Cir. 2010) (evidence that victim's mother's apartment had steep stairs was not admissible to support alternate theory of how victim was injured, where there was no proof that the victim fell down stairs and such evidence could have led the jury to reach a verdict based on improper reasoning).

Wasting Time/Undue Delay

Judicial resources are a valuable commodity, and the testimony of a witness can take hours, even days, depending on the scope of that testimony and the objections and other issues that may arise. Understandably, judges have an interest in moving cases along, and not allowing proceedings to be bogged down with pointless testimony that adds nothing to the body of evidence a jury will need to resolve matters of guilt.

Rule 403 accommodates these concerns by giving judges the power to exclude evidence where probative value is outweighed by the likelihood that presenting the evidence will waste the court's time or cause undue delay. Again, this is a balancing test. The fact that evidence will take a long time to present, or might result in a delay of the trial, is not grounds for exclusion if the evidence will actually help the jury reach a decision on the merits of the case.

To evaluate the applicability of Rule 403 in such instances, it is necessary for a court to determine whether proffered evidence has any probative value. If not, then it is fairly easy to conclude that the evidence can be excluded under Rule 403. This is the analysis that took place in the case of *United States* v. *Cutolo*, where the court first addressed the defendant's reasons for wanting to present evidence relating to an FBI agent's actions, and then, finding such reasons lacking, ruled that the evidence could be excluded under Rule 403 as a waste of time.

COURT OPINION 10-3 _____

UNITED STATES V. CUTOLO, 868 F.Supp. 39 (E.D.N.Y. 1994)

Count Three of the indictment in this case charges that the seven defendants conspired to murder members of the Persico faction of the Colombo Organized Crime Family in order to maintain or enhance their positions in that Family.

The court has before it an application by the government to preclude defendants from obtaining discovery of or offering evidence as to whether an F.B.I. agent gave information to Gregory Scarpa, a member of the Persico faction in the "war" with the Orena faction of which defendants were members.

The defendants advance two main arguments as to why evidence should be admitted that an F.B.I. agent gave information to Scarpa.

The first is that the evidence would be relevant to a defense of entrapment by showing that "Scarpa, a government agent, was sent out by the F.B.I. in order to spread fear among the defendants and to incite them to react."

A defense of entrapment presupposes that the defendants illegally conspired to kill Persico faction members in order to maintain or enhance their positions in the family, but may not be found guilty because they would not have committed the crime without the government's inducement.

Leaving aside the fact that defendants have pointed to no facts from which it can be inferred that the F.B.I. purposely "incited" defendants to conspire to

(continued)

(continued)

kill members of the Persico faction, the court concludes that in any event there is no basis for an entrapment defense. Indeed, there is no contention that an F.B.I. agent sought to induce defendants to conspire to maintain or enhance their positions in the Colombo family by murder. Moreover, there is no claim that anyone in the F.B.I. (or Scarpa himself) communicated with defendants and persuaded them to conspire to kill members of the Persico faction. . . . This court holds that there is no basis for a defense of entrapment.

The defendants' second argument for allowing the discovery requested is that it is relevant to their defense that they did not intentionally conspire to kill members of the Persico faction to maintain or enhance their positions in the family, but merely agreed to get ready to defend themselves if they were attacked by that faction.

This argument assumes that the defendants will offer evidence permitting the jury to find that the defendants agreed to shoot at the Persico faction only to defend themselves against attack and then only when they could do so legally, that is, only when they could not avoid using deadly force by retreating or seeking the assistance of law enforcement officials.

Defendants say that evidence that Scarpa, who, they assert was for many years a mad, blood thirsty killer with an animus against the Orena faction, was receiving information from an F.B.I. agent is relevant to defendants' intent. The contention is that knowledge of Scarpa's receipt of such information would strengthen defendants' intent to agree to prepare to defend themselves against Scarpa.

The jury could infer from defendants' alleged knowledge of Scarpa's propensities as a "lethal" and unrestrained killer that defendants had a motive and intent to agree to defend themselves. But even if they had suspected that Scarpa was receiving information from an F.B.I. agent, that would hardly have added significantly to their putative determination, aroused by their knowledge of Scarpa's blood thirsty character, to defend themselves.

Under Rule 403 of the Federal Rules of Evidence the court rules out evidence that an F.B.I. agent gave information to Scarpa, because to admit it would require a diversionary trial of issues of no critical or substantial probative value in the case.

Questions

1. Why did the court decide that the FBI agent's alleged passing of information to Scarpa had no probative value on the issue of self-defense?
2. How did the court's ruling on the entrapment and self-defense issues affect its application of Rule 403?

It is important to make a distinction between evidence that will substantially hurt one party's case and evidence that will improperly prejudice the jury. Relevant evidence cannot be excluded simply because it is going to make the jury more likely to render a verdict against one party and in favor of the other; in fact, that is the whole purpose of presenting evidence in the first place. The only issue is whether the evidence will cause the jury's verdict to be something other than a fair and just verdict based on the facts of the case.

■ CUMULATIVE EVIDENCE

In addition to excluding overly prejudicial evidence, Rule 403 also excludes relevant evidence where it is merely cumulative. **Cumulative evidence** is evidence that has limited probative value because it proves facts that are adequately proven by other evidence already on the record. To give a simple example, suppose 15 people are standing at 15 windows in a house when it is raining. Since each window provides the same information about whether it is raining outside, there is no need to have all 15 testify about the rain. Any one of them would suffice, and the remaining 14 would merely be cumulative.

cumulative evidence
Evidence that has little or no probative value, because the fact it proves or disproves is adequately established by other evidence.

It is important to note that cumulativeness goes to the question of how probative the evidence is. Cumulative evidence is not necessary because it does not add anything to the body of evidence that is not already there. If evidence proves a fact that is not already established on the record, then it is not cumulative even if it also proves other facts that are adequately established.

It is important to draw a distinction between cumulative evidence and corroborative evidence. Corroborative evidence, as we have seen, adds weight to other evidence by supporting its credibility or probative value. A witness who can testify to hearing an assault victim's scream coming from an apartment upstairs will corroborate the testimony of another witness who saw the victim being assaulted from a building across the street. The testimony is not cumulative, because the testimony of both witnesses proves the assault to a greater degree than either one alone would. Cumulative evidence, by contrast, adds little or nothing to the probative value of the evidence, so that inclusion of that evidence does not make it any more or less likely that a fact is true.

In the following case, the defendant was charged with receipt, distribution, and possession of child pornography. In order to prove the character of the videos found on the defendant's computer and his knowledge that those videos contained child pornography, the prosecutor offered a series of clips from two videos seized from that computer. The trial court, over the defendant's objections, permitted the jury to view a number of clips, including some that depicted heinous and brutal sexual acts being performed on young children. The defendant appealed his conviction on the grounds that the more graphic of the clips were cumulative, and therefore of insufficient probative value to justify the serious prejudicial effect they had on the jury.

COURT OPINION 10-4

UNITED STATES V. CUNNINGHAM, 694 F.3d 372 (3rd Cir. 2012)

Cunningham also argues that the District Court abused its discretion under Rule 403 by not limiting or excluding the video excerpts. . . .

We begin our analysis by setting forth the elements of the charged crimes that the government had to prove. [The court noted that the counts required that the defendant *knowingly* receive and distribute and *knowingly* possess child pornography.] The parties stipulated that the videos recovered contained "visual depictions of real children under the age of 18 years of age engaging in sexually explicit conduct." (App. at 196–97.)

. . . . [W]e recognize that showing the video excerpts here had some probative value because they had a tendency to show that the offender knew the videos contain child pornography. . . .

[The court noted that the videos clips which were offered into evidence, had probative value because they were taken from the actual videos seized from the defendant's computers, and therefore constituted the actual instrument of the crime.]

Even though the two sets of videos were probative, however, the law of diminishing marginal returns still operates. The probative value of each clip was reduced by the existence of the clips before it. Once one video excerpt from each of the two videos was shown, the fact being proven—i.e., that the person distributing, receiving, and possessing that pornography would know that it contained images of real minors engaging in sexually explicit activity—may well have been established. As a result, after one excerpt from each video was displayed, the probative value of the remaining excerpts became diminished because knowledge of distribution, receipt, and possession had already been established in some degree by the prior video excerpts. Thus, any of the three excerpts from the first video would have diminished probative value if

(continued)

(continued)

one or two of the other video excerpts from the first video had already been shown. Likewise, any of the four excerpts from the second video would have diminished probative value if one or two of the other video excerpts from the second video had already been shown.

The question in the end, of course, is whether the probative value of the clips shown was substantially outweighed by the danger of unfair prejudice or the needless presentation of cumulative evidence. *See* Fed.R.Evid. 403. As Rule 403 clarifies, a party is not protected from all prejudice—only unfair prejudice. . . .

Here, the aggregate risk of unfair prejudice was tremendous. Although the videos in question were not presented to this Court, the detailed descriptions we have received show that at least two of them should clearly have been excluded under Rule 403. Those two video excerpts, part of the second set of video clips, portray bondage or actual violence. . . .

"While all depictions of an adult engaging in sexual acts with a young child are bound to be repulsive, the impact on the jury will depend upon the nature and severity of the acts depicted." . . .. Even in the cesspool of evidence presented here, Excerpts 1 and 3 in the second set of video clips stand out. . . . Without those two videos, the government still had the entire footage of the first set of videos and additional material from the second set. We disagree with the government's contention, made to the District Court, that all of those video excerpts needed to be shown to "fully appreciate the nature of child pornography crimes." (App. at 227.) Given the other available evidence, the government did not need to show videos of pre-pubescent children being bound, raped, and violently assaulted to prove that Cunningham knowingly possessed, received, and distributed child pornography. In addition, the more video excerpts were shown, the more it became a needless presentation of unfairly prejudicial and cumulative evidence. *See* Fed.R.Evid. 403.

We recognize that a district court "is not required to scrub the trial clean of all evidence that may have an emotional impact.'" *Ganoe*, 538 F.3d at 1124 (citation and internal quotation marks omitted). . . . However, in light of the content of the videos besides the bondage clips, the probative value of those two violent excerpts was extremely limited. Accordingly, this is a case where we can confidently say that the probative value of some of the video excerpts was "so minimal that it [was] obvious . . . that the potential prejudice to the defendant substantially outweigh[ed] any probative value that [they] might have." . . . Therefore, the Court abused its discretion in admitting the bondage videos.

Questions

1. On what grounds did the court determine that the two video clips in questions were cumulative and therefore of limited probative value?
2. What does this case tell us about the interaction between the prejudicial effect and cumulativeness of evidence?

■ PUBLIC POLICY EXCLUSIONS OF RELEVANT EVIDENCE

Evidence that is otherwise relevant can be excluded where its inclusion would violate a **public policy** recognized under the federal rules. For purposes of criminal actions, these exclusions are found in Rules 408 (maybe) and 410.

public policy (exceptions to relevance)
Evidence that is excluded from evidence despite its relevance, in order to advance a policy beneficial to the public.

Rule 408: Compromise Offers and Negotiations

Rule 408 provides that neither an offer or payment made or intended to compromise a disputed claim nor any conduct or statement made during negotiations regarding such a compromise is admissible to prove either liability for or the amount of the disputed claim. This rule clearly applies to the admissibility of settlements and negotiations to settle in civil lawsuits, but the question of whether this rule prevents such evidence from being used in criminal cases is far from clear. There is no reference to criminal cases or criminal proceedings in either the rule or any of the official comments to the rule.

Furthermore, courts have provided little consistent guidance on this issue. Some have ruled that Rule 408 does apply in criminal proceedings. See, for example, *United States* v. *Bailey*, 327 F.3d 1131 (10th Cir. 2003); *United States* v. *Davis*, 664 F.Supp.2d. 86 (D.D.C. 2009); *United States* v. *Skeddle*, 176 F.R.D. 254 (N.D.Ohio, 1997); and *United States* v. *Baker*, 926 F.2d 179 (2nd Cir. 1991). Other courts have held that Rule 408 does not prevent evidence of being offered in criminal cases (*United States* v. *Prewitt*, 34 F.3d 436 (7th Cir. 1994); *United States* v. *Mercado*, 2003 WL 21756084 (S.D.N.Y., 2003)). Anomalously, three months after flatly rejecting a criminal application of Rule 408 in *Prewitt*, the Seventh Circuit applied Rule 408 to determine the admissibility of evidence of a taxpayer's conduct during a tax audit in a criminal action for tax evasion (*United States* v. *Hauert*, 40 F.3d 197 (7th Cir. 1994)).

All that is clear from the case law on this issue is that Rule 408 can be used in some but not all federal circuits to exclude the use of civil settlements and settlement negotiations to prove guilt in a criminal action. What is clear, however, is that Rule 408 does not apply to the admissibility of negotiations and compromises *of* criminal cases. That subject is covered by Rule 410.

LEARNING OBJECTIVE 4
Identify the pleas and statements relating to plea proceedings and discussions that are excluded under Rule 410.

plea discussion
A discussion between defendant and prosecutor specifically aimed at reaching an agreement regarding the defendant's plea to a criminal charge.

Rule 410: Pleas, Plea Discussions, and Related Statements

Under Rule 410, evidence of any of the following cannot be used in either a civil or criminal case against the defendant who made the plea or participated in the plea discussions:

- a guilty plea that is later withdrawn,
- a plea of *nolo contendere* (no contest),
- any statements made in proceedings during a proceeding on either of those pleas, or
- any statement made in a **plea discussion** that did not result in a guilty plea, or resulted in a guilty plea that was later withdrawn.

The statements listed above may be used under certain circumstances in a criminal proceeding for perjury or false statement, or where fairness dictates the inclusion of such a statement in conjunction with other statements made during the same proceedings or discussions.

The purpose of this rule is clear. Pleas are beneficial to the criminal justice system, both from an economy standpoint (trials are expensive!) and from a justice standpoint. The vast majority of criminal cases end in some kind of plea, so it is in the best interests of society to encourage participation in discussions leading to pleas. If defendants knew that "anything they say can be used against them" when they participate in a plea discussion, they wouldn't be as willing to do it. So this rule encourages defendants to enter into those discussions.

Notice that guilty pleas are only covered by this rule if they are withdrawn. As we saw in Chapter 3, a guilty plea can be used as an admission of liability in a civil action arising from the criminal conduct. This rule does not change that doctrine. Nor does Rule 410 apply to every statement made by a defendant in discussions with prosecutors relating to a criminal case. A defendant's voluntary cooperation with law enforcement or prosecutors is not enough to bring statements within the protection of Rule 410, even if those discussions are motivated by a hope that a plea deal can be reached. See *United States* v. *Edelmann*, 458 F.3d 791 804–806 (8th Cir. 2006) (incriminating statements made by a defendant in pre-indictment discussions with prosecutors not covered by Rule 410, where no specific plea deal was sought by the defendant or offered by the prosecutor).

In the following case, the defendant Paden, charged with arson, participated in plea negotiations that broke off for eight months before resuming and finally ending in a guilty plea. At his sentencing hearing, statements made by Paden during these negotiations were used to prove that he was a leader of the group that committed the arson, resulting in an increased sentence. He appealed, claiming that these statements were not admissible under Rule 410, because they were made during the early stages of his plea negotiations, not the later stages that actually resulted in a guilty plea.

COURT OPINION 10-5 _____

UNITED STATES V. PADEN, 908 F.2d 1229 (5th Cir. 1990)

Paden argues that the district court erred in concluding that statements made by Paden during the course of plea bargaining were admissible in the sentencing phase of his trial. Paden cites Fed.R.Crim.P. 11(e)(6)(D), which is based upon (and virtually identical to) Fed.R.Evid. 410(4). Rule 11(e)(6)(D) provides that "any statement made in the course of plea discussions with an attorney for the government which do not result in a plea of guilty or which result in a plea of guilty later withdrawn" is not admissible against the criminal defendant who made the statement.

The incriminating statements in question were made during plea negotiations in August 1988. According to Paden, the Government unilaterally ended these negotiations, and consequently cut off the Government's opportunity to use any statements Paden made during the negotiations. Paden maintains that his subsequent plea agreement with the Government in April 1989 did not resurrect the Government's opportunity to use the incriminating statements.

This Court disagrees. We find nothing in either Fed.R.Crim.P. 11(e)(6)(D) or Fed.R.Evid. 410(4) requiring that a particular discussion or series of discussions must produce a plea agreement. Neither do we find anything in these rules that prevents either side from discontinuing negotiations for a time. Progress toward a plea is rarely smooth and unbroken. Both rules look only to the end result of the process. Here, the end result of Paden's discussions

with the Government was a guilty plea. By their express language, Fed.R.Crim.P. 11(e)(6)(D) and Fed.R.Evid. 410(4) do not prohibit statements made during plea negotiations that lead to a plea of guilty.

At sentencing, the district court may rely upon any evidence of the defendant's credibility and responsibility that is "sufficiently reliable." *United States v. Flores*, 875 F.2d 1110, 1112 (5th Cir. 1989). In this case, the statements are sufficiently reliable, because they came directly from Paden. Once it was shown that the statements were sufficiently reliable, Paden had "the burden of showing that this information upon which the district court relied in sentencing was materially untrue." *Flores*, 875 F.2d at 1113. Paden has not satisfied this burden. He insists that the statements he made during the plea negotiations were coerced by threats from the Government prosecutors, but he has not denied on appeal that the statements he made were accurate. Even if Paden may be said to have denied the truth of his incriminating statements, he has not alleged a colorable claim that his statements were involuntary. He claims that Government prosecutors pressured him to "tell the truth," and suggested that Paden might receive the death penalty or life imprisonment if he did not admit that he was the one who lit the match that sparked the Lakeland Stationers fire. Encouraging a defendant to tell the truth, however, does not render a statement involuntary. *United States v. Ballard*, 586 F.2d 1060, 1063 (5th Cir. 1978). Neither does a recitation of

(continued)

(continued)

the potential sentence a defendant might receive render a statement involuntary. *Id.* at 1062–63.

In this case, the district court, based on all the available evidence, reached a decision that Paden's prior incriminating statements during plea negotiations were relevant and helpful to a determination of the sentence Paden would receive. This Court cannot conclude that the district court's decision was in error.

Questions

1. On what basis did the Court conclude that Paden's August 1988 statements were part of the same plea negotiations that bore fruit in April 1989?
2. Would the outcome have been the same if the August 1988 negotiations had been terminated by Paden rather than the government?

KEY TERMS

prejudicial effect   202
mistrial   205
cumulative evidence   207

public policy (exceptions to
relevance)   209

plea discussion   210

CHAPTER SUMMARY

- Under Rule 403, evidence may be excluded that causes unfair prejudice, confuses or misleads the jury, or causes undue delay or wastes time in a manner that outweighs the probative value of the evidence.
- Evidence is unfairly prejudicial when the probative value of the evidence does not justify the risk that the jury will be improperly influenced by the evidence, or led to draw an improper inference not supported by the evidence.
- Where unfair prejudice has occurred, a court may remedy the prejudicial effect with a cautionary instruction to the jury, or, if such an instruction is insufficient, by declaring a mistrial.
- Evidence will confuse and mislead the jury when it draws the jury's attention away from the central issues of the case.

- Where evidence is of low probative value, the fact that it will take time away from the presentation of more probative evidence or cause delay in the trial is grounds for exclusion.
- Evidence that is cumulative has little or no probative value and can therefore be excluded under Rule 403.
- Cumulative evidence should not be confused with corroborative evidence that significantly adds to the probative value of other evidence.
- It is unclear whether Rule 408, excluding evidence of offers of compromise and the negotiation of such offers, applies in criminal proceedings.
- Under Rule 410, withdrawn guilty pleas, pleas of *nolo contendere*, and statements made during proceedings on such pleas or during plea discussions are excluded from evidence as a matter of public policy.

WEB EXCURSION

1. Using an Internet search engine, locate your state's rules of evidence relating to prejudicial and cumulative evidence. Does your state allow judges to exclude such evidence to the same, a lesser, or a greater extent than the federal rules? Does your state provide exclusions for evidence relating to compromise negotiations and plea discussions?

PRACTICAL EXERCISE

1. Imagine you're the defense counsel in a murder case. The prosecutor wants to introduce a series of high-definition full-color photographs of the crime scene, including extremely gruesome pictures of the victim's body. There are 30 photos, taken from a series of angles, many of which are very similar. You know the jury will be emotionally affected by the photos, and you are concerned that so many pictures will inflame their anger against your client. Using the principles and rules cited in this chapter, prepare an outline of arguments to include in a motion to suppress the photos on the grounds that they are too prejudicial, and that they are also cumulative.

Burlingham/Shutterstock

LEARNING OBJECTIVES

After reading this chapter, the student will be able to:

1. Define hearsay and apply that definition to specific statements in testimony.

2. Explain the meaning of an out-of-court statement.

3. Contrast statements offered to prove their truth and statements offered to prove they were made.

4. Apply the Rule 801 hearsay exclusions.

5. Explain and apply the various hearsay exceptions under Rules 803 and 804.

6. Explain the requirements for the "residual" exception under Rule 807.

Hearsay | CHAPTER 11

■ INTRODUCTION

One of the biggest concerns that the law of evidence addresses is how we can be sure that evidence presented in court is trustworthy. In this chapter, we'll be exploring the rules that govern a particular application of that concern: when a witness' testimony or real evidence contains statements that were made by someone who was not in court or under oath at the time. Such statements, known as hearsay, are dealt with in Chapter 8 of the Federal Rules of Evidence, which makes such statements generally inadmissible (the "Hearsay Rule"). Chapter 8 also provides exceptions to that general rule for instances where such statements are inherently trustworthy.

LEARNING OBJECTIVE 1
Define hearsay and apply that definition to specific statements in testimony.

hearsay
An out-of-court statement offered to prove the truth of the matter asserted in the statement.

■ THE HEARSAY RULE

Rule 801 defines "**hearsay**" as "a statement, other than one made by the declarant while testifying at the trial or hearing, offered in evidence to prove the truth of the matter asserted in the statement" (P.R.E. 801(c)). The "**declarant**" is the person who makes the statement being offered as evidence.

declarant
The person who makes an out-of-court statement being offered as evidence.

To clarify what we mean by hearsay, consider the following example. Suppose John looks out of his window and sees the defendant commit a murder. Later, he testifies in court that the defendant killed the victim. He is basing that testimony on his own observations, what we referred to in Chapter 7 as "personal knowledge." Now, suppose that John didn't see the murder, but he was told about it by Jim, who did see it. John goes into court. What can John testify to based on personal knowledge? He can testify that Jim *told* him that the defendant committed the murder, because he personally experienced Jim making that statement. But he cannot testify from personal knowledge that defendant actually committed the murder. If John states in court, "Jim told me that the defendant committed the murder," and if the purpose of that testimony is to prove that the defendant did, in fact, commit the murder, then the words "the defendant committed the murder" are hearsay, because they were spoken by Jim (the declarant) when he was not in court. And since Jim was not on the witness stand, under oath and subject to cross-examination, when he spoke those words, we have no way of testing the truthfulness of the statement he made to John.

Hearsay Rule
Hearsay is not admissible unless it falls within one of the exceptions set forth in F.R.E. 803, 804, or 807, or if it is otherwise made admissible by rule of court or statute.

Rule 802 sets forth the "**Hearsay Rule**," which is the general rule governing the admissibility of hearsay. Under Rule 802, hearsay is not admissible except as provided by the rules of evidence, other rules of court, or statute. Federal Rules of Evidence 803, 804, and 807, which are discussed in greater detail below, provide exceptions to the Hearsay Rule by identifying hearsay statements that are inherently trustworthy and therefore admissible.

An example of a case where a statute authorized the use of a hearsay document as evidence is *United States* v. *Clarke*, 628 F.Supp.2d 15 (D.C.D.C. 2009). In that case, the defendants were charged with conspiracy to commit hostage taking resulting in the death of a U.S. citizen abroad, and the government offered the victim's passport as evidence to prove his citizenship (*Id*. at 16–17). The court held that 22 U.S.C. §2705, which provides that passports will have the same effect as proof of U.S. citizenship as certificates of naturalization, provided a statutory exception to the Hearsay Rule (*Id*. at 22).

To determine whether the Hearsay Rule applies, four questions must be answered:

1. Does the offered testimony contain a "statement"?
2. If so, was the "statement" originally made out of court?
3. If so, is the statement being offered to prove the truth of the matter asserted in the statement (in other words, is it being offered to prove that the statement is true)?
4. If so, does the statement fall within one of the exceptions to the Hearsay Rule in Rule 803, 803.1, or 804? If it does, then the statement is admissible even though it is hearsay (assuming it meets the other requirements of admissibility, such as relevance). Otherwise, it not admissible.

Figure 11-1 illustrates the entire process of determining whether testimony is inadmissible under the Hearsay Rule. Each of the elements in this diagram is discussed in detail below.

Does the Testimony Contain a "Statement"?

statement
An oral or written assertion or nonverbal conduct intended as an assertion.

Rule 801 defines a **statement** to include "a person's oral assertion, written assertion, or nonverbal conduct, if the person intended it as an assertion" (Rule 801(a)). This means that spoken or written words can constitute hearsay, but so can a nod, shake of the head, or any other bodily movement intended to take the place of words.

Figure 11-1 The Hearsay Rule

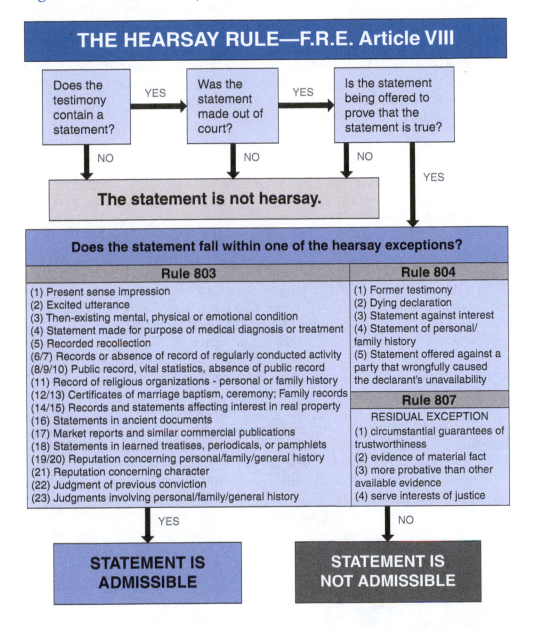

Examples:

- John asks Fred whether he saw the murder take place. Fred replies, "Yes, I saw the murder, and the defendant committed it." Fred has made a statement.
- John asks Fred whether the defendant killed the victim. Fred nods. Fred has made a statement.
- John asks a group of people whether any of them saw the defendant kill the victim. Fred raises his hand. Fred has made a statement.
- John asks Fred how many people were involved in the killing. Fred holds up two fingers. Fred has made a statement.
- John sees Fred and calls to him. In response, Fred waves his hand as a greeting. Fred has not made a statement, because waving a hand in greeting does not assert anything.

- John asks Fred whether he saw the defendant kill the victim. Fred doesn't respond, either verbally or by any bodily movement. Fred has not made a statement.

Statements can also be introduced through documents, so long as the information is being conveyed through words. A contract, will, or affidavit would be considered a statement under Rule 801, as would a videotape of someone speaking. A photograph or a video that does not include verbal content would not be considered a statement.

> **PRACTICE TIP**
>
> Documents should always be carefully reviewed to determine what statements they contain, and whether those statements might be subject to an objection to admissibility based on the Hearsay Rule.

Was the Statement Made Out of Court?

LEARNING OBJECTIVE 2
Explain the meaning of an out-of-court statement.

out-of-court statement
A statement made while the declarant was not testifying under oath at the proceeding in which the statement is offered as evidence.

Rule 801 specifically excludes from the definition of "hearsay" any statement made while the declarant is testifying under oath. Statements made while the declarant is not testifying under oath are subject to the Hearsay Rule. We refer to these as **"out-of-court" statements**, although that term is a little confusing, because a statement is considered "out-of-court" even if the declarant is sitting in the courtroom at the time he/she makes the statement, so long as he/she is not testifying under oath.

To properly apply this aspect of the Hearsay Rule, we need to carefully distinguish between the testimony being offered by the witness and the out-of-court statement that that testimony contains. Only the out-of-court statement is subject to the Hearsay Rule.

Suppose a witness gives the following testimony under oath: "John told me that he saw the shooting." This testimony can be represented as follows:

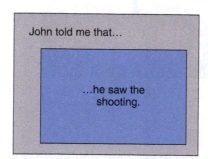

Everything inside the red box was testified to by the witness. But the statement in the blue box was made by the declarant, John, when he was not testifying under oath. The statement in the blue box is the only part of the testimony subject to the Hearsay Rule.

Hearsay within Hearsay

hearsay within hearsay
An out-of-court statement contained within another out-of-court statement, the admissibility of which is subject to Rule 805.

An out-of-court statement can also include other out-of-court statements. This is known as **hearsay within hearsay**. Under Rule 805, when hearsay contains hearsay in this manner, each part of the statement must be admissible in order for the entire statement to be admissible. Consider this testimony: "The officer told me that the coroner's report listed the time of death as 12:30 P.M." Here is a diagram of that testimony:

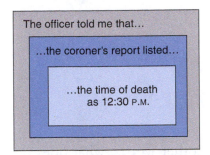

Again, the red box contains all of the testimony. The blue box contains the statement that the officer made out of court. The green box contains the statement from the coroner's report, which was also made out of court. Both of these statements are subject to the Hearsay Rule.

The Witness as Declarant

A statement can be subject to the Hearsay Rule even if it was made by the testifying witness, as long as the statement itself was made out of court. Suppose John testifies under oath as follows: "I told Mildred that I saw the defendant shoot the victim." Here is that testimony broken down into in-court and out-of-court components:

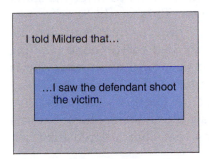

John is both the witness and the declarant, but the words he spoke to Mildred are considered an out-of-court statement, because he wasn't under oath when he spoke those words to her.

Is the Out-of-Court Statement Being Offered to Prove the Truth of the Matter Asserted in the Statement?

The third question relates to *why* the out-of-court statement is being offered. There are two possible answers to that question:

1. The statement is being offered into evidence to prove that the statement was *made*. In other words, the party offering the statement wants the jury to believe that the declarant spoke or wrote those words, whether or not the words are true.
2. The statement is being offered to prove that the statement is *true*. In other words, the party offering the statement wants the jury to believe the statement itself.

To illustrate the difference between these two reasons for offering an out-of-court statement, let's revisit the first example above:

LEARNING OBJECTIVE 3
Contrast statements offered to prove their truth and statements offered to prove they were made.

Why is this testimony being offered? In other words, what does the party offering this testimony want the jury to believe? If that party wants the jury to believe that John did, in fact, see the shooting, then John's statement is being offered to prove the truth of the matter asserted in the statement, and the Hearsay Rule would apply. If, on the other hand, the party wants the jury to believe that John *said* he saw the shooting (whether or not he actually did see it), then the testimony is not being offered to prove the truth of John's statement, and then the Hearsay Rule would not apply.

Why might a party offer a statement simply to prove that it was said? There are many reasons, but one of the most common is to impeach the credibility of the declarant. Suppose John had testified under oath that he hadn't seen the shooting, and the prosecutor wants to offer his statement to prove that he is not a truthful witness. This would be effective, because if John said out of court that he saw the shooting, and then he testified in court that he didn't, he obviously lied to someone. Calling John to the stand to accomplish this would be pointless, because he is unlikely to admit that he lied. So the prosecutor calls to the stand someone who heard John's out-of-court statement. The prosecutor doesn't want the jury to believe that John actually saw the shooting; he/she wants the jury to believe that John said something that contradicted his testimony in court.

■ HEARSAY EXCLUSIONS: RULE 801(D)

LEARNING OBJECTIVE 4
Apply the Rule 801 hearsay exclusions.

Two types of statements are explicitly excluded from the general definition of hearsay in Rule 801. These exclusions involve (1) statements by a declarant-witness (i.e., a trial witness who made the out-of-court statement), and (2) statements by an opposing party.

An out-of-court statement by a witness is not hearsay if it was made under penalty of perjury and it is inconsistent with the witness' testimony at the trial where it is being introduced. This allows a witness' statements in another, separate proceeding to be used to show that the witness is not testifying truthfully. A witness' own out-of-court statement can also be used to overcome a charge that the witness has recently fabricated his/her testimony, or has been improperly influenced to testify, by showing that he/she made consistent statements at an earlier time. Finally, a witness' out-of-court statement can be used if it identifies a person as someone the witness perceived before the statement was made.

Out-of-court statements by an opposing party can be used against that party for any reason. Rule 801(d) expands this rule to include statements made by the party himself/herself, or by the party's authorized agent, employee, or co-conspirator, and it also includes statements that the party adopted or expressly believed to be true. This latter application of the rule is often referred to as the "adoptive admission" exclusion.

In the following case, hearsay statements by the defendant Hamilton's co-conspirator, Hill, were held to have been adopted by him and therefore admissible under Rule 801(d), because the defendant had nodded while listening to his co-conspirator describe the details of two bank robberies he had committed. Note that the court addresses two different statements (Hill's statement bragging about the robberies, and Hamilton's affirmative head-shaking while listening to those statements), and find them both admissible under Rule 801(d).

COURT OPINION 11-1

UNITED STATES V. PRICE, 516 F.3D 597 (7TH CIR. 2008)

. . . Hamilton argues that the district court erred in admitting Troupe's testimony that a few days before the December 9, 2004, robbery, he attended a party during which he heard Hill bragging about previous robberies he had committed. As we previously noted, during Hill's commentary, Troupe observed Hamilton repeatedly nodding his head, suggesting to Troupe that Hamilton helped Hill commit these robberies. Because Hamilton failed to raise this issue before the district court, we review his argument only for plain error. *United States v. Reed*, 227 F.3d 763, 770 (7th Cir. 2000). And the argument has no merit.

First, Hill's statements about previous robberies he committed are admissible as coconspirator statements under Evidence Rule 801(d)(2)(E). Hamilton does not dispute that the government established by a preponderance of the evidence that a conspiracy to commit a new robbery existed, that the declarant (Hill) and the defendant (Hamilton) were members of that conspiracy, and that the statements—aimed at recruiting new members—were made in furtherance of the conspiracy. *See United States v. Skidmore*, 254 F.3d 635, 638 (7th Cir. 2001).

In addition, evidence of Hamilton's head-nodding during Hill's description of his previous criminal conquests was properly introduced as an adopted admission under Evidence Rule 801(d)(2)(E). Certainly, Hill's comment did not directly link Hamilton to the robbery and therefore doesn't fit into the category of statements that, if he were innocent, Hamilton would feel compelled to deny, *see United States v. Ward*, 377 F.3d 671, 676 (7th Cir. 2004). Likewise, Hamilton's head-nodding might suggest not that he was adopting Hill's statements, but that he was impressed by Hill's criminal exploits. Nevertheless, because Hill's statement was made in Hamilton's presence and because Hamilton appeared to adopt it as his own—signifying that he, too, participated in these crimes—the statement was admissible under Rule 801(d)(2)(E).

Questions

1. How did the court address the possibility that Hamilton's nodding could signify something other than an adoption of the truth of Hill's statements about the first two robberies?
2. What does this case tell us about the methods by which a defendant can adopt the statements of another under Rule 801(d)?

A key point to remember about the Rule 801(d) exclusions is that they involve out-of-court statements by individuals who are participating in the trial where the hearsay is being offered, either as a party or as a witness.

EVIDENCE AND TECHNOLOGY

CAN A "LIKE" BE AN ADOPTIVE ADMISSION?

We often think of the Internet as a global game-changer not only in terms of technology, but also in how we communicate with each other.[1] At the same time, the legal principles that apply to communications on the Internet are pretty much the same as those that apply to any other form of communication. In the legal sense, the Internet is not a game-changer, but simply a new player in the same old game. Whether a communication occurs by Facebook post, telephone, telegraph, or Pony Express, the legal principles governing its admission as evidence remain largely the same.

This is true of statements posted on social media sites such as Facebook. There is no question that written posts or messages on Facebook and other social media sites fall within the Hearsay Rule just like any other written statements. Courts have consistently analyzed such posts under traditional hearsay principles. Such posts have been admitted, for instance, as present sense impressions or admissions of party opponents (see the next section).

But social media sites provide users with the ability not just to write their own posts, but to "like" the posts of others. The question then arises whether a party's "liking" of another user's statements can make those statements admissible as adoptive admissions under Rule 801.[2]

Under Rule 801, statements are excluded from the Hearsay Rule, and therefore admissible, if they are offered against an opposing party who has "manifested" that the party "adopted" the statement or "believed [it] to be true." This can happen by an express agreement with the statement, or, as we saw in United States v. Price, above, by a simple nod of the head at the time the statement is made. As long as there is sufficient evidence that the defendant heard, understood, and unambiguously expressed some form of acquiescence in the statement, the statement can be admitted as an adoptive admission (see *United States* v. *Carter*, 760 F.2d 1568, 1579 (11th Cir. 1985); *United States* v. *Shulman*, 624 F.2d 384, 390 (2nd Cir. 1980)).

If "liking" a statement on Facebook constitutes an unambiguous manifestation of adoption or belief in the truth of the statement, then the statement would be excluded from the Hearsay Rule and could be used against the "liking" party as evidence. Given the wide propensity for use of social media sites among those who engage in criminal activity, and the widespread use of the "like" function to express approval of posts made by friends of users, the possibility that a "like" might turn a statement into an adoptive admission provides a very interesting addition to a prosecutor's evidentiary arsenal.

When a user clicks the "like" icon on Facebook, what exactly is he/she expressing? According to Facebook's online help page, "Clicking Like is a way to give positive feedback and connect with things you care about. Clicking Like below a post on Facebook is an easy way to let people know that you enjoy it without leaving a comment." It is unlikely that one would express "positive feedback" or "enjoy" a post with which one does not agree. It is commonly assumed that by "liking" a post, one is in fact *agreeing* with it.[3]

Based on this understanding of the meaning of a Facebook "like," it is reasonable to conclude that "liking" a statement on Facebook or any other social media would be tantamount to expressing agreement with the

(continued)

statement. There is certainly room for debate, however, as to whether such an expression is unambiguous enough to justify admitting the "liked" statement as an adoptive admission. Also, it is doubtful that any court would expand such a principle to include the adoption of entire pages as opposed to individual statements. Still, the likelihood that a suspect may "like" a statement that could implicate him/her in a crime or provide some other inculpatory evidence provides a great deal of incentive to explore this avenue of investigation where the circumstances justify it. We will have to wait and see, however, whether any court adopts such an interpretation of Rule 801 and makes such investigations worthwhile.

HEARSAY EXCEPTIONS

Once an out-of-court statement has been brought under the Hearsay Rule, it is inadmissible unless it falls within one of the **exceptions to the Hearsay Rule**. The rules divide these exceptions into three categories:

- Exceptions where it does not matter whether the declarant is available to testify (Rule 803).
- Exceptions where the declarant *must not* be available to testify (Rule 804).
- A "residual" exception to cover any statements not included in Rule 803 or 804.

These exceptions exist because the law recognizes that there are circumstances where a statement is inherently trustworthy, even though it was not made under oath. Keep in mind, though, that the admissibility of these hearsay statements does not mean that they *are* trustworthy, only that there is something about them that makes it reasonably *likely* that they can be trusted. Whether the statements are trustworthy or not is a matter of credibility for the jury to decide, and a party against whom a hearsay statement is admitted always has the option of proving that the statement is not trustworthy. These exceptions simply give the jury the opportunity to make that judgment.

Rule 803: Exceptions Where the Declarant's Availability Is Immaterial

Present Sense Impression (Rule 803(1))

A "**present sense impression**" is a statement describing something while the speaker is perceiving it. If an event is being perceived at the same moment it is being described, then we can assume that the description is accurate, because there is no time to make up a lie about it. This exception therefore *only* applies to descriptions of events or conditions that are made while the declarant is in the process of watching the event or observing the condition, or *immediately* thereafter. If there is any significant time lapse between the observation and the statement describing what the declarant saw or sensed, then this exception would not apply.

In Sample Trial Transcript 11-1, Mrs. Larimore's statement was made out of court, immediately after she saw a truck hit a little boy. Her statement would therefore be admissible as a present sense impression.

LEARNING OBJECTIVE 5
Explain and apply the various hearsay exceptions under Rules 803 and 804.

exception to the Hearsay Rule
One of the 30 circumstances specified in F.R.E. 803, 804, or 807, which allows a hearsay statement to be admitted into evidence.

present sense impression
A statement that describes an event or condition as it is being perceived by the declarant.

SAMPLE TRIAL TRANSCRIPT 11-1

Present Sense Impression

Prosecutor:	Mr. Larimore, you were indoors while your wife was outside, is that correct?
Witness:	That's right, but I ran outside right after the accident.
Prosecutor:	What caused you to go outside?
Witness:	I heard my wife screaming.
Prosecutor:	Was she saying anything?
Witness:	Yes. She screamed "Oh my God, that truck just hit that little boy!"

Excited Utterance (Rule 803(2))

excited utterance
A statement that describes a startling event or condition while the declarant is under the stress caused by the event or condition.

An "**excited utterance**" is a statement that relates to a startling event or condition, and that is made while the declarant was under the stress of excitement caused by the event or condition. An excited utterance is trustworthy because the declarant would presumably not be able to formulate a lie while under the mental stress caused by whatever he/she is talking about.

Sample Trial Transcript 11-1 illustrates an excited utterance as well as a present sense impression because Mrs. Larimore was clearly still under the stress of seeing the boy struck down at the time she made the statement. There are two important differences between an excited utterance and a present sense impression. First, a present sense impression does not have to be describing an event or condition that is startling or unusual, only one that is occurring as the statement is being made. Second, an excited utterance does not have to be made while the startling event is occurring, as long as the declarant is still under the mental stress it caused. Of course, the more time passes after an event, the less likely it is that the declarant will still be under the mental stress, but it is the stress, not the passage of time, that makes the excited utterance trustworthy.

Then-Existing Mental, Emotional, or Physical Condition (Rule 803(3))

then-existing mental, emotional, or physical condition
A statement describing the declarant's own physical, mental, or emotion condition as it is occurring.

A "**then-existing mental, emotional, or physical condition**" is a statement in which the declarant is describing his/her own emotional, mental, or physical condition as it is occurring. This can include a physical sensation (such as pain or pressure), an emotional condition (such as joy or fear), or a state of mind (such as an intention, motive, or plan). Think of this as a "present sense impression" turned inward. The basis for reliability of such a statement is the same for a present sense impression: if the statement is made as the physical, emotional, or mental condition is being perceived, there is no time to lie.

Each of the following statements would fall within this exception:

- "My leg is killing me." (Physical sensation)
- "I have a tickling feeling in my throat." (Physical sensation)
- "I feel feverish." (Physical sensation)
- "I've never been so angry." (Emotional condition)
- "I would love to go fishing next week." (State of mind)
- "This weather is really starting to annoy me." (Emotional condition)

- "I'm sick of my boss." (Emotional condition)
- "I am planning to take my vacation sometime in July." (State of mind)
- "I'm afraid I'm going to end up killing my wife." (State of mind)

However, the following statements would not fall within this exception, because they are not made at the time the physical, emotional, or mental condition is occurring:

- "Last night I couldn't sleep at all. My mind was racing and I couldn't relax."
- "I was really upset with my wife last week."
- "I usually get depressed around Christmastime."

In Sample Trial Transcript 11-2, two instances of this type of hearsay are seen. One was made by Prescott, expressing his then-existing frustration (emotional condition) with Walmer and his intention (mental condition) to fire him. The second was made by the witness herself, and expressed her immediate fear (emotional condition) concerning Ken's reaction to being fired.

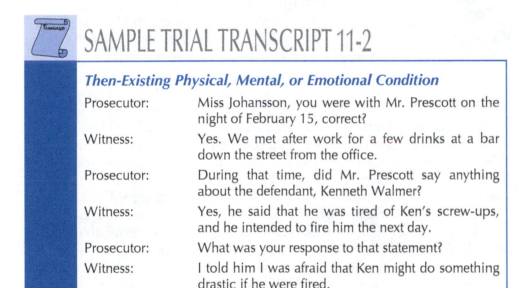

SAMPLE TRIAL TRANSCRIPT 11-2

Then-Existing Physical, Mental, or Emotional Condition

Prosecutor:	Miss Johansson, you were with Mr. Prescott on the night of February 15, correct?
Witness:	Yes. We met after work for a few drinks at a bar down the street from the office.
Prosecutor:	During that time, did Mr. Prescott say anything about the defendant, Kenneth Walmer?
Witness:	Yes, he said that he was tired of Ken's screw-ups, and he intended to fire him the next day.
Prosecutor:	What was your response to that statement?
Witness:	I told him I was afraid that Ken might do something drastic if he were fired.

Statement for Purpose of Medical Diagnosis or Treatment (Rule 803(4))

A statement that is made by the declarant in anticipation that the statement will be used by a medical professional to diagnose and treat a medical condition is inherently trustworthy, because presumably someone isn't going to give information that will result in the wrong diagnosis or treatment. While it is not inconceivable that someone might mislead his/her own doctor about his/her medical condition (perhaps to obtain prescription painkillers or to support a fraudulent lawsuit or worker's compensation claim), the rules of evidence consider these statements sufficiently trustworthy to admit them as hearsay.

Sample Trial Transcript 11-3 illustrates a statement made for the purpose of a medical diagnosis or treatment. Mrs. Petrie is testifying about statements she made to her doctor so that he could treat her condition. All of those statements are admissible under this exception. Note, however, that one of her statements, "it wasn't hurting that bad right then," would also be admissible as describing a then-existing physical condition, because she was telling her doctor how her arm was feeling at the moment she was speaking to him. This highlights that fact that a single statement can be admissible under more than one hearsay exception.

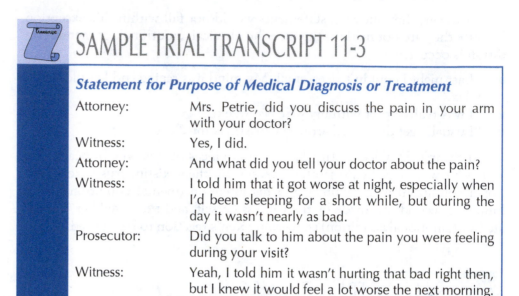

SAMPLE TRIAL TRANSCRIPT 11-3

Statement for Purpose of Medical Diagnosis or Treatment

Attorney:	Mrs. Petrie, did you discuss the pain in your arm with your doctor?
Witness:	Yes, I did.
Attorney:	And what did you tell your doctor about the pain?
Witness:	I told him that it got worse at night, especially when I'd been sleeping for a short while, but during the day it wasn't nearly as bad.
Prosecutor:	Did you talk to him about the pain you were feeling during your visit?
Witness:	Yeah, I told him it wasn't hurting that bad right then, but I knew it would feel a lot worse the next morning.

Recorded Recollection (Rule 803(5))

recorded recollection
A record made or adopted by the declarant while the subject matter of the record was still fresh in his/her mind.

A "**recorded recollection**" is a written record made or adopted by a witness while the subject matter of the record is still fresh in his/her mind. The record, although hearsay, can be used instead of the witness' testimony so long as the document can be authenticated and there is sufficient evidence that the record accurately reflects the witness' knowledge at the time the record was made.

This exception is extremely useful where a witness is called upon to testify about a matter that occurred years earlier, where no reasonable person could be expected to remember the details of the matter.

The key to this exception is the recording of the information at the time it was fresh in the witness' memory. The form of the record is not important; it can be a diary, a letter, a calendar entry, an e-mail, or any other kind of writing. The record could have been created long before the case arose.

> **PRACTICE TIP**
>
> Whenever you represent a client with a case where the facts are continuing to unfold (such as a divorce or custody case), instruct the client to keep a diary of everything that happens that could possibly relate to the case. Not only does such a diary provide important information in preparing for the case, but it also provides a record that can be used under this exception in the event that a particular detail escapes the client's memory at trial.

The question is whether, when the witness made the record, the matter was fresh in the witness' mind so that we can rely on the record's accuracy. For this reason, the record cannot be admitted unless the witness testifies to an inability to remember, and also attests to the authenticity of the record in open court.

In Sample Trial Transcript 11-4, Mr. Oscar's notations of his physical therapy appointments in his calendar are the statements being offered as recorded recollections. Note the questions the prosecutor must ask in order to authenticate the calendar entries and to establish that Mr. Oscar does not recall the specific dates of his appointments.

SAMPLE TRIAL TRANSCRIPT 11-4

Recorded Recollection

Prosecutor:	Mr. Oscar, do you recall on precisely what days you went to see the physical therapist following the assault?
Witness:	I don't recall all of them, no.
Prosecutor:	Did you keep any kind of a record of your appointments?
Witness:	Yes, I recorded them all on my calendar.
Prosecutor:	Is this the calendar you are referring to?
Witness:	Yes.
Prosecutor:	Are these calendar entries yours?
Witness:	Yes, they are.
Prosecutor:	And you made each of these entries as soon as the appointment was scheduled?
Witness:	Yes.
Prosecutor:	Mr. Oscar, does this calendar accurately reflect the dates on which you went to see the physical therapist?
Witness:	Yes, it does.
Prosecutor:	Your Honor, the people would ask to offer Mr. Oscar's record of his physical therapy appointments into evidence.
Judge:	The record is admitted.

Records of Regularly Conducted Activity or Absence Therefrom (Rules 803(6) and (7))

This exception includes records (i.e., documents, not oral statement) that are trustworthy because of their regularity. In other words, the records were made in the ordinary course of a regularly conducted activity, in accordance with regular practices of that activity. Here are some examples of such records:

- A business's balance sheet
- A golf player's scorecard
- A lawyer's time sheet
- A truck driver's mileage log
- A high school teacher's gradebook

Under Rule 803(7), an absence of information from a record can be used to establish that a fact is not true, if the fact, had it been true, would normally have been included in the record. For instance, suppose that a golf scorecard is used to prove that the three men listed on the card played golf together on a particular date. The same card could be used to prove that a fourth person did *not* play golf with them on that date, because had he played his name would have been included on the card.

Only the records custodian or another qualified individual may authenticate the regularity of the record, unless the record is certified by some lawful means. In addition, Rules 803(6) and (7) do not apply where there is evidence that the source of information contained in the record is not trustworthy. Sample Trial Transcript 11-5 illustrates how a foundation can be laid for the admission of a record of employee days off that will satisfy the requirements of Rules 803(6) and (7). Once that foundation is laid, any relevant information (or absence of information) contained in the record becomes admissible hearsay.

SAMPLE TRIAL TRANSCRIPT 11-5

Record of Regularly Conducted Activity

Prosecutor:	Mr. Barnes, you are the chief financial officer for ABC Company, is that correct?
Witness:	Yes.
Prosecutor:	And you regularly keep records of the days off taken by employees?
Witness:	That's right.
Prosecutor:	Is this document a record of those days off from July to August of 2006?
Witness:	Yes, it is.
Prosecutor:	And was this record maintained in the ordinary course of business according to your company's regular practices?
Witness:	Yes, it was.
Prosecutor:	Would you please tell the jury what this document says about the defendant's days off during those months?
Witness:	According to this, the defendant took off during the last week in July and the first four days in August.
Prosecutor:	Does the document give any indication that the defendant took off at any other time later in August?
Witness:	No. According to this, he didn't miss any days after August 4.

Public Records and Omissions Therefrom (Rules 803(8), (9), and (10))

Under these three exceptions, information contained in, or missing from, a record maintained by any public office is admissible so long as the information relates to the office's activities, vital statistics, or a matter that the office was under a legal duty to report. This exception works pretty much the same as the "record of regularly conducted activities" exception under Rules 803(6) and (7). The exception excludes the recorded observations of police officers in criminal cases, and also provides the same exclusion of records where the sources themselves are not trustworthy.

Statements Relating to Personal or Family History (Rules 803(11), (12), (13), and (19))

Records maintained by a religious organization that relate to personal or family history (such as statements recording births, deaths, marriages, and divorce) are admissible as long as they are regularly maintained by the religious organization. Similarly, certificates of marriage, baptism, sacraments, and other religious or public ceremonies are admissible so long as the certificates are made by a legally authorized person who performed the ceremony, and the certificate was made within a reasonable time after the ceremony was performed. Records of such events or facts maintained by families themselves are also admissible. These can include statements written in family Bibles and even engravings found on rings or burial markers. Finally, statements relating a reputation concerning such facts that is held among a person's family members are also admissible.

The following three sample trial transcripts illustrate various applications of the personal and family history exceptions.

SAMPLE TRIAL TRANSCRIPT 11-6

Record of Religious Organization/Record of Marriage or Other Religious Ceremony

Attorney:	Pastor Wilson, does your church regularly maintain records relating to individuals who are married at the church?
Witness:	Yes, we do.
Attorney:	Now, at my request, you reviewed and provided a copy of the records of your church relating to a wedding that took place on March 15, 1984. Is that correct?
Witness:	Yes.
Attorney:	Is this document I am showing you a copy of that record?
Witness:	Yes, that's what I gave you.
Attorney:	Does this record indicate who was married on that date?
Witness:	Yes, it says that the marriage was between James Corvair and Michelle Kreiser.
Attorney:	And what does this record indicate that the parties were, in fact, married on that date?
Witness:	Yes, it shows here that a marriage certificate was issued by the pastor at the time.

SAMPLE TRIAL TRANSCRIPT 11-7

Baptism Record

Attorney:	Mr. Smith, can you identify this document?
Witness:	Yes, this is my daughter's baptism certificate.
Attorney:	This certificate identifies the pastor who baptized your daughter on October 28, 2004?

(continued)

Witness:	That's right. Pastor Williams.
Attorney:	Does this certificate indicate your daughter's date of birth?
Witness:	Yes, it says it right here. September 1, 2004.

SAMPLE TRIAL TRANSCRIPT 11-8

Family Record

Attorney:	Mr. Franklin, I am going to show you an item and ask you to identify it.
Witness:	That's my mother's wedding ring.
Attorney:	Could you read the inscription on that ring?
Witness:	It says, "Joined in wedlock and love, 5/6/42."

Records of Documents Relating to Interests in Property (Rules 803(14) and (15))

Copies of documents relating to interests in property (such as deeds, mortgages, or easements) are often kept in public offices so that the public can, for instance, research the title to that property or determine its proper boundaries. Such records are not subject to the Hearsay Rule so long as they are maintained in a public office under statutory authority, and are used to prove the contents of the original document, or contain statements relating to the document's original purpose.

Statements in Ancient Documents (Rule 803(16))

A statement in an "ancient document," or a document that is proved to be at least 20 years old, is admissible, as long as the document is authenticated. Presumably, if a document that old contained a misrepresentation, someone would have discovered and corrected it at some point in time.

Objectively Prepared Documents (Rules 803(17) and (18))

Market reports and other commercial publications generally relied on by the public or in particular occupations, and statements contained in treatises, periodicals, or pamphlets used by expert witnesses as a basis for their opinions, are all admissible under these exceptions.

Reputation Concerning Boundaries or General History (Rule 803(20))

This exception allows the admission of statements relating to the reputation among members of a community regarding land boundaries and general historical events within that community, so long as the reputation arose before the events giving rise to the case where the statements are being introduced as evidence.

Reputation Concerning Character (Rule 803(21))

In keeping with the admissibility of reputation evidence of character that we discussed in Chapter 9, statements about the reputation of a person regarding his/her character are admissible as hearsay.

SAMPLE TRIAL TRANSCRIPT 11-9

> ### Reputation as to Character
>
> **Attorney:**   Mrs. Smith, you are a member of the community Mr. Trelaine belongs to, is that correct?
>
> **Witness:**   That's right. I've lived next to him for 17 years.
>
> **Attorney:**   Did you ever have the opportunity to discuss Mr. Trelaine with other members of community?
>
> **Witness:**   Well, yes, I've spoken about him a number of times with other neighbors.
>
> **Attorney:**   Do you know what Mr. Trelaine's reputation is in the community with respect to his character?
>
> **Witness:**   Yes, well, everyone in the community pretty much agrees that Mr. Trelaine is a bit of a shady character, and no one really trusts him.

Certain Judgments (Rules 803(22) and (23))

Where a court has entered a judgment in a previous case convicting a person of a crime after a guilty plea or a trial, that judgment can be admitted to prove any fact essential to the judgment (e.g., the person's guilt of that crime). In criminal cases, such a judgment of conviction can be used against someone other than the defendant only for purposes of challenging that person's credibility. For instance, a witness' prior conviction for perjury could be admitted under this exception to show that the witness cannot be trusted, but a prior conviction for arson could not be, because arson has nothing to do with the witness' honesty.

Judgments that decide matters of personal, family, or general history, or land boundaries, can also be admitted to prove facts essential to those judgments, in place of reputation evidence of those same facts.

Rule 804: Exceptions that Require the Declarant's Unavailability

Rule 804 contains a more modest list of five exceptions to the Hearsay Rule, but places an important limitation on those exceptions: in order to use them, the declarant must be **unavailable** to testify in person. Under Rule 804(a), a declarant can be "unavailable" in five ways:

unavailable
In the hearsay context, to be unable to testify in court for one of the reasons specified in F.R.E. 804(a).

- The declarant is exempt from testifying because of a privilege.
- The declarant refuses to testify despite a court order to do so.
- The declarant testifies that he/she doesn't remember the subject matter of the requested testimony.
- The declarant is dead or unable to testify due to physical or mental disability or illness.
- The party offering the statement has tried and failed to bring the declarant to court.

A declarant who falls within one of these categories will not be considered unavailable if the party seeking to offer the declarant's statement wrongfully procured or caused the declarant's unavailability.

Witnesses are not always easy to find, as evidenced by this plea for potential witnesses to a London murder.

Source: http://www.alamy.com/ stock-photo-police-murder-sign-appealing-for-witnesses-london-england-uk-7907009.html.

In *United States* v. *Lynch*, 499 F.2d 1011 (D.C.Cir. 1974), the trial judge allowed the prosecutor to admit a key witness' preliminary hearing testimony in lieu of her testimony at trial, finding that the witness was "unavailable" because she failed to appear when called at the close of the prosecutor's case-in-chief. The judge found that the prosecutor had attempted to contact the witness directly and through her family, and that she was therefore "unavailable" and her preliminary hearing testimony could be admitted under Rule 804 even though it was hearsay. The defendant appealed, arguing that the witness' hearsay testimony should not have been admitted because the witness was not "unavailable" as required under Rule 804.

The District of Columbia Court of Appeals reversed, finding that the prosecutor's efforts to locate the witness were not sufficient. The court stated:

> We conclude that the district court's determination that Miss Brown was 'unavailable' was erroneous. At least where the evidence indicates that a crucial government witness, who is physically and mentally capable of testifying, is within the jurisdiction of the court, the prosecution must demonstrate that it has been unable to obtain the witness' presence through a search exercised both in good faith and with reasonable diligence and care. In the ordinary case, this will require a search equally as vigorous as that which the government would undertake to find a critical witness if it has no preliminary hearing testimony to rely upon in the event of 'unavailability'.

The court found that the prosecutor's attempts to contact the witness were not sufficient because they did not include a search of "local hospitals, area police departments, the morgue, or of Miss Brown's employer." In addition, the court felt that insufficient manpower had been employed in attempting to locate the witness. For this reason, the court held that allowing the witness' preliminary hearing testimony under Rule 804 was improper because the witness had not been shown to be "unavailable."

A more recent decision applied the *Lynch* standards in a case involving a runaway minor witness. In the following case, *State v. Vinhaca*, the Supreme Court of Hawai'i ruled that efforts to locate the runaway were sufficient to justify the use of the minor's preliminary hearing testimony at trial. The prosecutor attempted to locate the minor by (1) assigning an investigator to search for her; (2) moving to delay the portion of the trial that relied on the minor's testimony to provide additional time to find her; and (3) subpoenaing the minor's guardian, who took further steps to attempt to locate her. Applying the standard for unavailability set forth in *Lynch*, the court examined whether these efforts were sufficient to conclude that the witness was unavailable, and to allow her preliminary hearing testimony under Rule 804. The decision and a strong dissenting opinion illustrate the room for disagreement that exists when prosecutors attempt to locate a missing witness.

COURT OPINION 11-2

STATE V. VINHACA, 124 HAWAI'I 128 (2010)

Preliminary hearing testimony from an unavailable witness is testimonial hearsay. *State v. Fields*, 115 Hawai'i 503, 513, 168 P.3d 955, 965 (2007) (quoting *Crawford v. Washington*, 541 U.S. 36, 64, 68, 124 S.Ct. 1354, 158 L.Ed.2d 177 (2004)). Testimonial hearsay "is admissible 'only where the declarant is unavailable, and only where the defendant has had a prior opportunity to cross-examine' [the declarant] about the statement." *Id.* (quoting *Crawford*, 541 U.S. at 59).

In determining whether the declarant is unavailable, the United States Supreme Court has held that the prosecution must prove that it made a "good faith" effort to secure the presence of the unavailable witness. *Ohio v. Roberts*, 448 U.S. 56, 74, 100 S.Ct. 2531, 65 L.Ed.2d 597 (1980) (quoting *Barber v. Page*, 390 U.S. 719, 724–25, 88 S.Ct. 1318, 20 L.Ed.2d 255 (1968)), *overruled on other grounds by Crawford*, 541 U.S. at 60–61, 68–69. The State's obligation to make a good faith effort is "context-specific. . . ." *Hamilton v. Morgan*, 474 F.3d 854, 858–59 (6th Cir. 2007); *see also* 30B Michael Graham, *Federal Practice & Procedure* § 7072 at 736–40 (2006) ("Whether the government has shown good faith in attempting to first locate and second procure the witness' attendance by process or voluntarily by reasonable means *must be determined on a case-by-case basis after careful review of the particular facts and circumstances*.") (emphasis added) (footnotes omitted). For instance, the Supreme Court explained that:

> The law does not require the doing of a futile act. Thus, if no possibility of procuring the witness exists (as, for example, the witness' intervening death), "good faith" demands nothing of the prosecution. But if there is a possibility, albeit remote, that affirmative measures might produce the declarant, the obligation of good faith *may* demand their effectuation.

Roberts, 448 U.S. at 74 (emphasis in original).

The Supreme Court also emphasized that the "lengths to which the prosecution must go to produce a witness . . . is a question of reasonableness." *Id.* (quoting *California v. Green*, 399 U.S. 149, 189 n. 22, 90 S.Ct. 1930, 26 L.Ed.2d 489 (1970) (Harlan, J., concurring)). To satisfy the unavailability requirement of the United States Constitution, the prosecution must show that "the witness is unavailable despite good-faith efforts undertaken prior to trial to locate and present that witness." *Id.* at 74–75.

This court has also explained that a good faith effort requires that the prosecution has made "vigorous and appropriate steps to procure the complaining witness' presence at trial. . . ." *State v. Lee*, 83 Hawai'i 267, 277, 925 P.2d 1091, 1101 (1996) (emphasis and block format omitted) (quoting *State v. Ortiz*, 74 Haw. 343, 363, 845 P.2d 547, 556–57 (1993)). In *Lee*, this court expressly adopted the unavailability standard announced in *United States v. Lynch*, "establishment of the prosecution's reasonable efforts to secure the presence of the declarant 'require[s] a search equally as vigorous as that which the government would undertake to find a critical witness if it has no prior testimony to rely upon in the event of 'unavailability [.]" *Id.* at 278, 925 P.2d 1091, 925 P.2d at 1102 (relying on *United States v. Lynch*, 499 F.2d 1011, 1.023 (D.C.Cir. 1974)). [T]he prosecution satisfied the tests announced in *Roberts* and *Lee* by moving to sever the trial when it became apparent Daughter 1 may not appear, having an investigator attempt to locate Daughter 1, subpoenaing Huerta to locate Daughter 1, and through Huerta's attempts to locate Daughter 1. . . .

(continued)

(continued)

Dissenting Opinion by ACOBA, J.

I respectfully dissent.

The solitary service of one subpoena on a social worker without physical custody of the subpoenaed witness only eleven days before trial, and three days *after* Respondent/Plaintiff-Appellee State of Hawai'i (Respondent or the prosecution) had already represented to the circuit court of the fifth circuit (the court) in a motion to sever that the subpoenaed witness's presence was "doubtful" for a trial involving an offense punishable by a prison term of twenty years, was a meaningless exercise not reasonably calculated to obtain the complaining witness's presence at trial and, thus, was violative of the defendant's Sixth Amendment right to confrontation under the United States Constitution. The federal constitution violation here is so fundamental and egregious, as to fall below the minimum standard that Respondent "ma[ke] a good-faith effort to obtain [the witness's] presence at trial" as set forth in *Barber v. Page*, 390 U.S. 719, 725, 88 S.Ct. 1318, 20 L. Ed.2d 255 (1968), and *Ohio v. Roberts*, 448 U.S. 56, 74, 100 S.Ct. 2531, 65 L.Ed.2d 597 (1980), *overruled on other grounds by Crawford v. Washington*, 541 U.S. 36, 60–61, 124 S.Ct. 1354, 158 L.Ed.2d 177 (2004). With all due respect, a request for further review by the United States Supreme Court may be warranted. Furthermore, under Article I, section 14, the parallel confrontation clause of the Hawai'i Constitution, Respondent has not established that the witness was unavailable under this jurisdiction's standard, which "requires a search equally as vigorous as that which the government would undertake to find a critical witness if it ha[d] no prior testimony to rely upon in the event of unavailability[.]" *State v. Lee*, 83 Hawai'i 267, 278, 925 P.2d 1091, 1102 (1996) (internal quotation marks, citation, and brackets omitted). . . .

Questions

1. Using the same standards, what were the differences between the prosecutor's efforts in *Lynch* and those in *Vinhaca* that would explain how the two courts reached opposite conclusions?
2. Do you agree with the dissenting judge in *Vinhaca* that the prosecutor should have taken further steps to find the witness before being allowed to use her preliminary hearing testimony?

If the declarant is unavailable, then one of the Rule 804 exceptions can be used to admit the declarant's statement.

PRACTICE TIP

Even if you expect a witness to be cooperative, subpoena him/her. If the witness for any reason is unable to appear at trial, the court will be much more likely to continue the trial or provide some other accommodation, such as permitting the use of prior testimony, if the witness was under subpoena.

Former Testimony (Rule 804(b)(1))

former testimony
Testimony given by a declarant as a witness under oath in a trial, hearing, or deposition, with an opportunity for cross-examination by the party against whom the testimony is now being offered.

"**Former testimony**" is testimony given by the declarant as a witness under oath in a trial, hearing, or deposition, where the party against whom the testimony is now being offered had the opportunity to cross-examine the declarant when the testimony was taken.

In order to use this exception, several factors must coalesce: (1) the prior testimony must be under oath, and (2) the party against whom the testimony is offered must have had a prior chance to develop the testimony through direct, cross-, or redirect examination. This means that the testimony does not need to come from the same hearing or even the same case, so long as the parties now were parties then. It also means that the testimony could be given at a hearing, a trial, a deposition, or in any other context where an oath is given and cross-examination is permitted.

Statement under Belief of Impending Death (Dying Declaration) (Rule 804(b)(2))

A statement is admissible if it was made when the declarant, who must be unavailable to testify, genuinely believed that his/her own death was imminent, so long as the statement concerned the cause or circumstances of that death. This exception, commonly referred to as a "**dying declaration**," is based on the notion that a person who believes he/she is about to die is not going to go to his/her eternal reward with a lie on his/her lips. It is a very limited exception, however, because it applies *only* to statements about the cause or circumstances of death. It does not apply to any other subject matter, nor does it apply unless the declarant actually believed that he/she was about to die.

dying declaration
A statement by a declarant who believes his/her death is imminent, concerning the cause or circumstances of his/her death.

In Sample Trial Transcript 11-10, take notice of how the prosecutor had to lay a foundation for the dying declaration exception by proving that the declarant actually believed he/she was dying.

SAMPLE TRIAL TRANSCRIPT 11-10

Dying Declaration

Prosecutor:	Officer Williams, did you speak to the victim at the hospital?
Witness:	Yes, I did.
Prosecutor:	Was he able to talk to you?
Witness:	He spoke clearly enough, and he seemed to be lucid, yes.
Prosecutor:	Did he say anything about his condition?
Witness:	Yes. He told me he knew he was going to die, and to tell his wife he loved her.
Prosecutor:	Did you ask him who shot him?
Witness:	Yes.
Prosecutor:	Did he identify the shooter?
Witness:	Yes. He told me the shooter was James Morgan.

Another limitation imposed on this exception is that it can only be used in a prosecution for homicide or in a civil case. The rule does not, however, state that the prosecution must be for the *declarant's* homicide. This creates the interesting if unlikely possibility that a declarant's statement could be used as a dying declaration even if the declarant survived. For instance, suppose two men are attacked and shot. One is killed instantly; the other believes himself to be mortally wounded. A police officer arrives and asks the surviving victim who shot him. The victim identifies the shooter as the cause of what he believes to be his own death. The victim is taken to the hospital and recovers. If the surviving victim is unavailable to testify at trial, nothing in Rule 804(b)(2) would prevent his "dying declaration" from being used in the homicide trial of the shooter for the other victim's killing. Since it is declarant's *belief* in his impending death that makes the statement trustworthy, there seems to be no reason why the declarant has to die to make a "dying declaration" admissible under this exception, although the declarant does need to be unavailable to testify.

Statement against Interest (Rule 804(b)(3))

statement against interest
A statement that is contrary to the declarant's own legal or financial interests, or operates against a claim or defense of the declarant.

A "**statement against interest**" is a statement that is so contrary to the declarant's own legal or financial interests that it is very unlikely the declarant would have made the statement if it weren't true. In other words, the law presumes that people will not tell a lie that will hurt them financially or subject them to legal liability. In a criminal case, a statement tending to expose the declarant to criminal liability is not admissible unless corroborating circumstances clearly indicate the trustworthiness of the statement.

The reliability of this type of statement is easy to see: no one would deliberately lie in a way that would hurt their own interests. So, if someone says something that gets him/her into serious trouble, or that hurts his/her chances of making a claim against someone else, or is otherwise harmful to his/her financial or personal interest, then we can assume that the statement is true.

This exception would apply to confessions in criminal cases only where other evidence is available to prove that the confession is trustworthy. Such a provision is needed to avoid situations where confessions are obtained through coercive means and then used as the sole evidence of guilt, or where a person confesses in order to protect someone else (such as a spouse or child) from criminal liability.

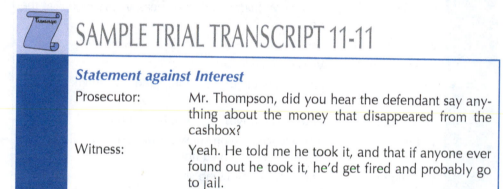

SAMPLE TRIAL TRANSCRIPT 11-11

Statement against Interest	
Prosecutor:	Mr. Thompson, did you hear the defendant say anything about the money that disappeared from the cashbox?
Witness:	Yeah. He told me he took it, and that if anyone ever found out he took it, he'd get fired and probably go to jail.

Statement of Personal or Family History (Rule 804(b)(4))

This exception admits statements by the declarant about his/her own personal or family history, even if (surprisingly) the declarant had *no way of acquiring personal knowledge* about those facts. This latter provision means there is no need to lay a foundation for hearsay statements about the declarant's own personal or family history. If the unavailable declarant said them, they're admissible.

This rule also allows statements about the personal or family history of someone else, if there is some basis (blood relationship or some other basis of intimate knowledge) to believe that the declarant's statements about that person are likely to be accurate.

Statement Offered against a Party that Wrongfully Caused the Declarant's Unavailability (Rule 804(b)(6))

A statement is admissible when it is offered against a party that has engaged or acquiesced in wrongdoing that was intended to, and did, procure the unavailability of the declarant as a witness.

Unlike all other hearsay exceptions, this one is not based on the inherent reliability of the declarant's statement, but upon considerations of fairness. A party who is wrongfully responsible for the unavailability of a declarant cannot be heard to complain if statements by the declarant are admitted in place of actual testimony. In such a case, that party has deprived himself/herself of the ability to cross-examine the declarant.

In order to use this exception, it would be necessary for the party offering the hearsay testimony to lay a foundation by proving that the other party was responsible for the declarant's unavailability.

SAMPLE TRIAL TRANSCRIPT 11-12

Laying a Foundation for Rule 804(b)(6)

Attorney:	Mrs. Philipps, were there any other witnesses to your husband's abusive behavior?
Witness:	Yes, my sister, Mary.
Attorney:	Is your sister Mary in court today?
Witness:	No, she isn't.
Attorney:	Why isn't she?
Witness:	She was afraid to come.
Attorney:	Do you know why?
Witness:	Because my husband told her that if she came and testified today he would treat her the same as he treated me. (NOTE: This would be admissible in order to lay a foundation for the sister's hearsay statements by showing the reason for the sister's absence, but not to prove that the husband actually intended to assault the sister if she testified.)
Attorney:	Did you hear him say this to her?
Witness:	Yes, I heard it myself.

PRACTICE TIP

Every piece of evidence you expect to use at trial, whether real or testimonial, should be carefully examined for hearsay statements, and any such statements should be analyzed to determine what exclusion or exception would apply.

Rule 807: The Residual Exception

Rule 807 sets forth the **"residual" exception to the Hearsay Rule**. This is a catch-all, discretionary exception that can be used to admit hearsay when it does not fall within one of the exceptions specified in Rules 803 and 804.

To use this exception, five requirements must be met:

- The statement must have circumstantial guarantees of trustworthiness equivalent to those described in the Rule 803 and 804 exceptions.
- The statement must be offered as evidence of a fact that is material to the case.
- The statement must prove the fact it is offered to prove better than any other evidence that the party can produce.
- Admitting the statement will serve the purpose of the Rules of Evidence and the interests of justice.
- The party offering the statement has given reasonable notice to the other party, including the declarant's name and address.

The following excerpt from the 2013 opinion of the U.S. District Court for the Western District of Kentucky in *United States* v. *Thurman* provides an excellent exposition on the meaning of the four substantive requirements of Rule 807.

LEARNING OBJECTIVE 6

Explain the requirements for the "residual" exception under Rule 807.

residual exception to the Hearsay Rule

A discretionary exception set forth in F.R.E. 807, which applies to hearsay statements that do not fall within one of the exceptions in F.R.E. 803 or 804.

COURT OPINION 11-3

UNITED STATES V. THURMAN, 915 F.SUPP.2D 836 (W.D.KY. 2013)

. . . .The Advisory Committee's Notes to prior Rule 803(24) explain that FRE 803(24) and 804(b)(5), now FRE 807, did not "contemplate an unfettered exercise of judicial discretion, but . . . do provide for treating new and presently unanticipated situations which demonstrate a trustworthiness within the spirit of the specifically stated exceptions." Advisory Committee's Note to former Rule 803(24). . . . Nevertheless, the federal courts have on several occasions cautioned that Rule 807 is in substance an exception of last resort to be applied in extraordinary circumstances lest it subsume the general prohibition against the admission of hearsay evidence under Rule 802. . . .

Perhaps the clearest warning that Rule 807 is to be cautiously applied comes from the report of the Senate Committee on the Judiciary, which cautions that "the residual hearsay exceptions will be used very rarely, and only in exceptional circumstances" . . . [as] the "committee does not intend to establish a broad license for trial judges to admit hearsay statements that do not fall within one or the other exceptions contained in Rules 803 and 804(b)." 7 Graham, *Handbook of Evidence at* § 807(1). . . .

While Rule 807 is not a panacea for the admission of hearsay statements that otherwise do not fall within the established hearsay exceptions of Rule 803 or 804, the rule nonetheless provides a means, albeit a limited one, for the admission of otherwise hearsay statements that meet five criteria, including the requirement of prior notice under subsection (b) of the rule. First, and perhaps foremost, is the requirement under the rule that the extrajudicial statement to be offered at trial has "equivalent circumstantial guarantees of trustworthiness." Fed.R.Evid. 807(a)(1). In other words, the circumstances that surround the making of the out-of-court statement must render the declarant particularly worthy of belief. . . .

Courts must look to the totality of the circumstances to determine the existence of independent indicia of reliability. . . . Included among the factors to be considered are: (1) the relationship of the declarant with the defendant(s) and the Government; (2) the motive of the declarant to make the extrajudicial statement; (3) the extent to which such statement reflects the personal knowledge of the declarant; (4) the past history of the declarant's statements, whether they are consistent or contradictory; (5) whether separate evidence beyond the declarant's extrajudicial statements corroborates the contents of such statements. *United States v. Darwich*, 337 F.3d 645, 658–60 (6th Cir. 2003).

Other factors that various courts and legal authority include in this analysis are the certainty of the declarant at the time the challenged statement was made, the passage of time between the out-of-court statement and the facts asserted therein, whether the statement was made in response to suggestive questions, and any partiality of the declarant. 7 Graham, *Handbook of Federal Evidence*, at § 807:1 nn. 13–16 (collecting cases). As one court has phrased the matter, the circumstantial guarantees of trustworthiness must be so evident that adversarial testing by cross-examination would add little to the reliability of the challenged statement. *United States v. Anderson*, 166 F.3d 1215 at *8 (6th Cir. 1998) (unpublished disposition). . . .

The second requirement for admission pursuant to FRE 807 is that the extrajudicial statement be offered as "evidence of a material fact." Fed.R.Evid. 807(a)(2). As this requirement has been explained, not only must the statement be offered as evidence of a fact that is relevant under Rule 401, but it must be offered on a fact that is "of substantial importance in determining the outcome of the litigation." . . . . Obviously, a statement offered to establish an element of the charged offense against a particular defendant would fall readily within the concept of a material fact under the rule.

The third requirement of FRE 807 is that the out-of-court statement be more probative on the point for which it is offered than any other evidence that could be obtained by the proponent through reasonable efforts. FRE 807(a)(3). To satisfy this requirement, the Government must explain what, if any, reasonable efforts were exerted to secure the equivalent testimony from other admissible sources. . . . What may or may not be a reasonable effort to obtain evidence is entirely dependent upon the nature of the fact(s) at issue in light of their relationship to the entire litigation. . . .

The fourth requirement of the rule, found at FRE 807(a)(4) is that the admission of the out-of-court statement will best serve the purposes of the rules of evidence and the interest of justice. Fed.R.Evid. 807(a)(4). This requirement is considered to be largely a restatement of Rule 102, "and as such is of little practical importance in

(continued)

(continued)

determining admissibility." . . . Rule 102, in turn, seeks to "promote the development of evidence law, to the end of ascertaining the truth and securing a just determination." Fed.R.Evid. 102. This language suggests to the Court that at the foundation of Rule 807, among the other factors, is a requirement for fundamental fairness when the admission of extrajudicial statements is considered pursuant to the residual hearsay exception of FRE 807. If the use of the rule to admit an otherwise inadmissible hearsay statement implicates the fairness of the trial, so as to potentially call into question the accuracy of the jury's verdict, then this requirement of FRE 807 weighs against admission.

Questions

1. How did the court envision the proper use of Rule 807 by trial judges?
2. Do you believe that Rule 807 became easier for judges to apply after this decision, or more difficult?

As the *Thurman* court notes, the application of Rule 807 was not intended to provide a way to admit all, most, or even many hearsay statements that fall outside of the Rule 803 and 804 exceptions. It is meant to be applied sparingly and in extraordinary circumstances.

Rule 807 was implicated in the notorious perjury case of Barry Bonds, the home-run king of the San Francisco Giants. As the following court opinion demonstrates, Rule 807 is not meant to provide a cure-all for hearsay, but is meant to be applied in a limited way to make sure that justice is done. In this case, the prosecution was required to prove that blood samples that tested positive for performance-enhancing drugs came from Bonds. After Greg Anderson, the only witness with firsthand knowledge of the identity of the blood samples, refused to testify, the government sought to introduce a lab assistant to whom Anderson had made statements identifying the samples as belonging to Bonds. The trial court rejected the government's argument that the lab assistant's testimony was admissible hearsay under Rule 807, and the government appealed.

COURT OPINION 11-4 _____

UNITED STATES V. BONDS, 608 F.3D 495 (9TH CIR. 2009)

. . . .The district court held that FRE 807, the residual exception, did not apply. The court observed that it was designed for "exceptional circumstances." *See Fong v. American Airlines*, 626 F.2d 759, 763 (9th Cir. 1980). FRE 807, previously FRE 803(24), provides:

> A statement specifically not covered by Rule 803 or 804 but having equivalent circumstantial guarantees of trustworthiness, is not excluded by the hearsay rule, if the court determines that (A) the statement is offered evidence of a material fact; (B) the statement is more probative on the point for which it is offered than any other evidence which the proponent can procure through reasonable efforts; and (C) the general purposes of these rules and the interests of justice will be served admission of the statement into evidence.

The court did not find Anderson's refusal to testify an exceptional circumstance because the effect was to make him an unavailable declarant, and FRE 804 already defines an "unavailable" declarant and

(continued)

(continued)

lists exceptions to inadmissibility that the government does not contend are applicable in this case.

FRE 807 involves discretion. It exists to provide judges a "fair degree of latitude" and "flexibility" to admit statements that would otherwise be hearsay. *See U.S. v. Valdez–Soto*, 31 F.3d 1467, 1471 (9th Cir. 1994).

Our sister circuits have also given district courts wide discretion in the application of FRE 807, whether it be to admit or exclude evidence. *See, e.g., U.S. v. Hughes*, 535 F.3d 880, 882–83 (8th Cir. 2008) (upholding district court decision not to admit evidence under FRE 807); *FTC v. Figgie Intern. Inc.*, 994 F.2d 595, 608–09 (9th Cir. 1993) (upholding admission under residual exception even where trial court failed adequately to explain reasoning). Our research has disclosed only one instance where a circuit court reversed a district court to require admission of a statement under FRE 807. *See U.S. v. Sanchez–Lima*, 161 F.3d 545, 547–48 (9th Cir. 1998). However, the hearsay statements in that case were videotaped and under oath, and thus had indicators of trustworthiness that Anderson's statements do not. *See id*. More important, the circumstances were "exceptional" because the government had deported the witnesses, so the statements remained the only way the defendants could present their defense. Therefore, the government is asking this Court to take an unprecedented step in using 807 to admit the statements of a declarant who has chosen not to testify and whose statements lack significant indicators of trustworthiness.

The government argues that the district court adopted an improperly narrow view of FRE 807 by not taking into account that Anderson's statements "almost" fell within several other hearsay exceptions. It also asserts the court did not give enough weight to Anderson's unavailability.

The government contends that Anderson's statements "almost" met several other hearsay exceptions, and for that reason the district court erred in not admitting them under FRE 807. Specifically the government points out that Anderson's statements came close to qualifying as statements against his penal interest and statements of a coconspirator. The government relies on *Valdez–Soto*. In upholding the admission of out of court statements under the 807

exception in *Valdez–Soto*, we said that where a statement "almost fit [s]" into other hearsay exceptions, the circumstance cuts in favor of admissibility under the residual exception. *See* 31 F.3d at 1471. We did not, however, hold the factor was determinative, only that it supported the district court's application of FRE 807 in that case to admit the evidence. In this case, even though this was a "near miss" it was nevertheless a "miss" that may have permitted, but did not alone compel the trial court to admit Anderson's statements under FRE 807.

The government next suggests that Anderson's unavailability is "exactly the type of scenario" FRE 807 was intended to remedy, but cites no authority supporting the proposition. It argues the district court misunderstood the rule and applied it too narrowly. The district court, however, correctly noted that courts use FRE 807 only in exceptional circumstances and found this situation unexceptional because it involves statements of an unavailable witness like those FRE 804 excludes, with limited exceptions here not applicable.

In addition, FRE 807 requires that the admissible statements have trustworthiness. The district court concluded Anderson's statements were untrustworthy, in major part because Valente admitted that he once mislabeled a sample when Anderson asked him to do so. To the extent the government contends that the district court improperly focused on Valente's trustworthiness instead of on the trustworthiness of Anderson's statements, the government misinterprets the district court's opinion. The district court finding properly focused on the record of untrustworthiness of the out of court declarant, Anderson, as required under the rule. There was support for its conclusion that Anderson's statements about the source of samples were not trustworthy. . . .

Questions

1. Why did the Ninth Circuit refuse to accept the "near-miss" argument in this case when it accepted it in the *Valdez–Soto* case?
2. Do you think that this case called for the application of Rule 807? How is your answer affected by the reason for Anderson's "unavailability" to testify?

KEY TERMS

CHAPTER SUMMARY

- Hearsay is any statement that was made outside of the court proceedings in which it is being offered, and intended to prove the truth of the matter asserted in the statement.
- A statement can be any written or oral assertion, or any nonverbal communication that is intended to be an assertion.
- Hearsay within hearsay is admissible if all of the hearsay included in the statement is admissible.
- Generally, hearsay is not admissible to prove the truth of the matter asserted in the statement.
- Hearsay statements by a witness that are introduced to impeach the witness are admissible.
- Hearsay statements made by and used against a party are admissible.
- If a hearsay statement falls within an exception set forth in Rule 803, 804, or 807, the statement is admissible.
- Rule 803 exceptions can be used whether or not the declarant is available to testify, and include the following:
    - Present sense impressions, which are statements describing an event or condition as it is being perceived by the declarant.
    - Excited utterances, which are statements describing a startling event or condition while the declarant is under the stress caused by the event or condition.
    - Statements describing the then-existing physical, emotional, or mental condition of the declarant.
    - Statements made for the purpose of obtaining a medical diagnosis or treatment.
    - Records created by the declarant when the subject matter is fresh in the declarant's mind.

- Certain records of regularly conducted activity, public records, vital statistics records, statements relating to personal or family history, records relating to interests in real property, and statement in documents 20 or more years old.
- Certain market reports and commercial publications used by the public or professionals, and treatises, periodicals, and pamphlets used by expert witnesses.
- Reputation evidence concerning character, general history, personal and family history, and boundaries of land.
- Certain judgments of conviction of a witness or defendant and judgments concerning general history or land boundaries.
- Rule 804 exceptions require that the declarant not be available to testify, and include the following:
    - Testimony given by the declarant under oath where the opposing part had the opportunity to cross-examine.
    - Statements made by the declarant under a belief of impending death, concerning the cause or circumstances of death.
    - Statement made by the declarant that operates against the declarant's legal or financial interests, or a legal claim or defense of the declarant.
    - Statement made by the declarant of the personal or family history of himself/herself or an intimate acquaintance.
    - Statement made by a declarant whose unavailability was wrongfully caused by the party against whom the statement is being used.
- A declarant is "unavailable" for purposes of Rule 804 if he/she is dead or physically or mentally incapable of testifying, refuses to testify

despite a court order, is privileged not to testify, doesn't remember the subject matter of the testimony, or unavailable despite the efforts of the party to bring him/her to court.

- Rule 807 provides a limited discretionary "residual" exception that can be used to admit hearsay that is not covered under Rule 803 or 804.

WEB EXCURSIONS

1. Locate your state's version of Article VIII of the Federal Rules of Evidence, and identify any differences between the hearsay exceptions in your state's rules of evidence and those in Rules 803, 804, and 807. Does your state have a "residual" exception? How is it defined?
2. Using Google or a similar search engine, find the transcript of a criminal trial or hearing. Can you locate any statements that would be considered hearsay? Are the statements objected to by opposing counsel? If not, what reason might there be for not raising an objection? Is the statement so clearly admissible that an objection would be unnecessary?

PRACTICAL EXERCISE

1. Listen to a conversation between two individuals on a news or talk show, and identify any statements that would be hearsay if said in court under oath. Try to identify any exceptions that would make those statement admissible.

ENDNOTES

1. The Internet's potential for meaningful communication has come a long way since 1999, when Federal District Judge Kent wrote: "While some look to the Internet as an innovative vehicle for communication, the Court continues to warily and wearily view it largely as one large catalyst for rumor, innuendo, and misinformation. . . . [T]his so-called Web provides no way of verifying the authenticity of the alleged contentions, [and t]here is no way Plaintiff can overcome the presumption that the information he discovered on the Internet is inherently untrustworthy. Anyone can put anything on the Internet. No website is monitored for accuracy and nothing contained therein is under oath or even subject to independent verification absent underlying documentation. Moreover, the Court holds no illusions that hackers can adulterate the content on any website from any location at any time. For these reasons, any evidence procured off the Internet is adequate for almost nothing, even under the most liberal interpretation of the hearsay exception rules found in FED.R.CIV.P. 807" (*St. Clair v. Johnny's Oyster & Shrimp, Inc.*, 76 F.Supp.2d 773, 774, 775 (S.D.Tex. 1999).

2. There is absolutely no answer to this question provided by the courts. The only court opinion that comes close is *People v. Johnson*, ___ N.Y.S.3d ___, 2015 N.Y.Slip.Op. 25431, 2015 WL 9595166, a New York County Court opinion. In *Johnson*, a defendant charged with sexually assaulting his minor stepdaughter sought to introduce evidence that the victim "liked" a Facebook page that contained mildly pornographic images (*Id.* at 1). The court briefly considered the question of whether the victim's "likes" themselves constituted hearsay, and concluded that they did and that they "fall within no existing hearsay exception" (*Id.* at 9). This case provides no help whatsoever in determining whether "likes" can constitute adoptive admissions of other hearsay statements.

3. In the case of *State v. Roach*, 457 S.W.3d 815 (Mo. 2014), for instance, a college professor posted a comment on Facebook that responded

to a colleague's post about how pointless it was to be asked how the semester was going when it was only the third day (*Id.* at 816 n.1). The defendant's response stated "But, yes. That's the beginning of the semester. I'm always optimistic. By October, I'll be wanting to get up to the top of the bell tower with a high powered rifle—with a good scope, and probably a gatling gun as well" (*Id.* at 816). The colleague responded with a flippant comment notifying the NSA that "I do not know this man," which the defendant gave a "thumbs-up," which on Facebook is a "like" (*Id.* at 816 n.1). Later, the defendant realized that his colleague's response to his comment had received seven "likes," while his comment had received none. He took this to mean that his friends disapproved of his comment, and eventually deleted it (*Id*).

LEARNING OBJECTIVES

After reading this chapter, the student will be able to:

1. Explain the role of privileges in determining what evidence is admissible at trial.

2. Apply the three elements of privileges to determine how each privilege works.

3. Identify evidence that is excluded by the spousal privileges, and how that privilege can be waived.

4. Identify evidence that is excluded by the attorney–client privilege and work-product doctrine, and how that privilege can be waived.

5. Identify evidence that is excluded by the physician–patient privilege.

6. Identify evidence that is excluded by the clergy–communicant privilege.

Privilege

■ INTRODUCTION

To this point, we have looked at several bases for excluding relevant evidence from the trial record. In this chapter, we will be exploring the final basis for excluding relevant evidence: privilege.

■ THE MEANING OF PRIVILEGE

A **privilege** is a rule that excludes evidence from trial, not because of its inherent lack of competence, relevance, or trustworthiness, but because disclosure would injure a relationship between the witness and another person (usually a party), and the law deems that relationship worthy of protection.

> Rules of privilege are substantive laws designed to influence the conduct of individuals. Unlike rules of exclusion which guard against unreliable, prejudicial, or misleading evidence, they do not aid in the discovery of truth. Instead, they serve to protect interests and relationships that society deems of sufficient importance to justify the suppression of facts necessary to the adjudicatory process.
>
> (Pachciarek, A. (2008). Federal Rules of Evidence–Testimonial privileges. *Journal of Criminal Law and Criminology*, 71(4), 594. Retrieved September 6, 2005, from http://scholarlycommons.law.northwestern.edu.)

LEARNING OBJECTIVE 1
Explain the role of privileges in determining what evidence is admissible at trial.

privilege
A rule that excludes evidence from trial where its disclosure would injure a relationship that the law deems worthy of protection.

245

While some privileges are prescribed by statute or rule of court, most have evolved over a long period of time through the development of the common law. Federal Rule of Evidence 501 provides:

> The common law—as interpreted by United States courts in the light of reason and experience—governs a claim of privilege unless any of the following provides otherwise:
>
> - the United States Constitution;
> - a federal statute; or
> - rules prescribed by the Supreme Court.
>
> But in a civil case, state law governs privilege regarding a claim or defense for which state law supplies the rule of decision. (F.R.E. 501)

Under this rule, if a federal court is applying state law (which it often does in civil cases), then it must apply the privileges that exist under that state's laws.

Privileges are intended to protect relationships, such as the relationships between attorneys and clients, husbands and wives, physicians and patients, and so on. Some privileges protect all communications between individuals in that relationship; others protect only specific kinds of information. Some privileges protect the fact that a communication took place; others only prevent disclosure of the information itself. Some privileges can be waived by the witness or the defendant, while others cannot.

Each privilege is defined by (a) the relationship it is intended to protect, (b) the communication or information it is intended to protect, and (c) whether it can be waived.

To determine whether evidence is privileged, several questions have to be answered:

1. Is the witness a party to a privileged relationship?
2. If a privileged relationship exists, is the information being offered into evidence subject to the privilege?
3. If the relationship and the information are both within the privilege, was the privilege waived?

If the relationship and the information are both within the privilege, and the privilege was not waived, then the evidence is inadmissible.

Privileges are often associated with the concept of **confidentiality**. While those terms are related in the sense that both are intended to prevent disclosure of information to protect important relationships, it is wrong to conclude that all confidential information is automatically privileged at trial, or that all privileged information is necessarily confidential. Confidentiality is a broad ethical concern that is rooted in the general duty imposed on certain professionals not to disclose information about their clients or patients. Privilege, by contrast, is a concept that applies only to the disclosure of information in court, and such disclosure might be required even though the information is considered confidential under the ethical rules governing the witness' profession. Conversely, information that is not necessarily considered confidential in an ethical sense (such as communications between a husband and wife) may be subject to a privilege that prevents its disclosure as evidence. So, while information is often covered by both confidentiality and privilege, these two concepts are not by any means interchangeable.

LEARNING OBJECTIVE 2
Apply the three elements of privileges to determine how each privilege works.

confidentiality
An ethical obligation, usually arising in a professional relationship, not to disclose information belonging to another person.

■ SPECIFIC PRIVILEGES

Privileges Arising from a Marriage

There are two basic privileges that apply in federal criminal courts to protect the spousal relationship: the confidential communications privilege and the testimonial privilege.

LEARNING OBJECTIVE 3
Identify evidence that is excluded by the spousal privileges, and how that privilege can be waived.

Confidential Communications Privilege

The marital relationship is one of the most sacred and protected under the law, and society demands that spouses be open and honest with each other and that their communications be accorded a high level of respect and privacy. The **confidential communications (marital) privilege** is designed to make sure that husbands and wives are able to communicate openly and honestly.

confidential communications (marital) privilege
A privilege that prevents the disclosure of confidential communications between spouses.

As a general rule, any confidential communication between spouses is considered privileged and not admissible in court. To determine if this privilege applies to a particular communication, we need to answer three questions:

1. Were the parties to the communication legally married when it was made?
2. Was there a "communication" between the married parties?
3. Did the married parties intend the communication to be confidential?

Marriage at the Time of Communication.   In order to invoke this privilege, the parties must be lawfully married at the time the communication takes place. While a legal marriage is usually fairly easy to prove, it is not always so.

Historically, there were two ways to get married: a ceremonial marriage and a common-law marriage. A **ceremonial marriage** requires a license issued by the county in which the parties intend to marry, and a ceremony conducted by a legally authorized official (such as a minister or a judge) in which the parties express their present intention to be married. After the ceremony is complete, the official signs a certificate of marriage, and the marriage is valid.

ceremonial marriage
A marriage that is conducted in a ceremony by an authorized official (usually a clergyman or judge) following the issuance of a marriage license.

A **common-law marriage** can be thought of as a "do-it-yourself" marriage, evolved during a time when courthouses and marrying officials were not always readily available. Many believe that a common-law marriage occurs automatically if parties live together for a certain number of years, but this is only a myth. Like a ceremonial marriage, a common-law marriage is a matter of intention. The parties must live together as spouses, and hold themselves out as spouses to the public. This can be done in a number of ways: by referring to each other as "my husband" or "my wife"; by the wife taking the husband's last name; by intermingling funds in a single bank account; or by purchasing property together as a married couple, to name a few. Once the parties have established themselves as having the intention of being married, they may then be considered "common-law" married even where there was no ceremony or license.

common-law marriage
A marriage that exists based on the intent of the parties to be married, evidence by behavior displaying that intent to the public.

Common-law marriage has been abolished by statute in most states, although common-law marriages that existed prior to the effective date of those statutes are still valid.

Even if a ceremonial or common-law marriage can be proven, that does not necessarily prove conclusively that the marriage is valid. There are many restrictions on who is allowed to marry in the United States. Most states have age restrictions on marriage that require parental or judicial consent for the marriage of an unemancipated minor. Close family members cannot be legally married. A person who is already legally married cannot marry another spouse. Most states also have restrictions on marriage of individuals who are mentally disabled, intoxicated, or under any kind of external coercion (*duress*) to get married.

For the most part, rules governing marriage are a matter of state law. The federal system never had a common-law marriage rule, but the federal courts have always been obligated to accept any marriage valid under state law, and each state is obligated to recognize a marriage valid in another state under the **"full faith and credit"** clause of the U.S. Constitution. The only notable exception to this general acceptance of state-sanctioned marriages was the Defense of Marriage Act, passed and signed in 1996, that explicitly denied federal recognition of same-sex marriages and permitted states to do the same in contravention of the "full faith and credit" clause. This law was struck down as unconstitutional by the U.S. Supreme Court in the cases of *United States* v. *Windsor*, 570 U.S. _____, 133 S.Ct. 2675, 186 L.Ed.2d 808 (2013) and *Obergefell* v. *Hodges*, 576 U.S. _____, 135 S.Ct. 2584, 192 L.Ed.2d 609 (2015), effectively legalizing same-sex marriage throughout the United States and requiring every state to recognize those marriages to the same extent as all others.

If the parties are legally married at the time of the communication, then it does not matter if they are still married at the time the witness is asked to disclose that communication in court. Conversely, if the parties are not married when the communication is made, then the privilege does not apply even if they are married when the spouse's testimony is solicited. For purposes of this rule, "not married" includes being permanently or legally separated.

Communication between Spouses. Once it has been determined that parties were legally married, it must then be proven that the subject matter of the evidence being offered involves an actual communication between those parties. Again, this seems like an easy question, since a "communication" simply means the transference of information. The means are unimportant; the spouses can communicate in person, by spoken word, in writing, by e-mail, by text, through a Facebook or other social networking account, through a gesture such as a nod or shake of the head, or in any other manner that is intended to convey information.

A question arises, however, where information that passes between spouses is not in the nature of a "communication" as it is generally thought of. For instance, suppose a wife sees her husband put a gun in his pocket in preparation for committing an armed robbery, or a husband watched his wife write out a check that they both know is not covered by funds in their joint back account. Are these observations of a spouse's behavior covered by the confidential communications privilege?

Generally, the answer is no. However, some courts look to the question of whether the observation itself took place within the boundaries of the marital relationship. Would the husband have allowed anyone other than his wife to see him pocket the weapon he planned to use in a robbery? Would the wife have openly signed a bad check if anyone but her husband had been present? If the answer to these questions is no, then it is arguable that the observation, even though it involved no transfer of information through

---

full faith and credit clause
A constitutional provision requiring states to recognize, among other things, valid marriages entered into in other states.

communication in the usual sense, was still a communication that took place between spouses and is therefore covered under the act.

Confidentiality of the Communication.   As discussed above, the concept of "confidentiality" is generally a matter of professional ethics, not privilege. However, when it comes to spouses, the law accords a level of privacy that is not found in any other nonprofessional relationship. In furtherance of its goal of protecting the marital relationship, the law presumes that any communication between husband and wife is confidential, so the party seeking to overcome the privilege has the burden of proving that the offered communications were not confidential.

    Spousal confidentiality is a matter of intent, but the intent that a communication be considered "confidential" can be determined by several factors. The first factor is the setting in which the communication takes place. If a communication is made in a setting where third parties might easily hear or see it (such as in a crowded room or one's Facebook wall), then it is not confidential no matter what the parties' intent. By contrast, a communication that is made in a setting that the parties *believe* is private can be confidential even if a third party, unbeknownst to them, happens to be eavesdropping or watching. If a husband sends an e-mail to his wife's private account from work, that e-mail can be considered confidential even though the system administrator can access it, unless the husband has reason to believe that it *will* be accessed.

    Another factor that can affect confidentiality is the content of the communication itself. If the communication would normally be considered the subject of privacy between spouses, then it would be confidential. Private discussions about a spouse's actions, experiences, thoughts, feelings or fears, family or medical history, political views, or other subjects of a personal or private nature would all probably fall within the meaning of "confidentiality."

spousal confidentiality
The confidentiality of communications that occur between spouses, within the context of the marital relationship.

> **PRACTICE TIP**
>
> Every client should be cautioned not to have potentially confidential discussions with his/her spouse when anyone else is present. While the spouse may not be able to testify, the third party would be able to testify about anything he/she heard.

Waiver.   States vary on whether a spouse can waive the confidential communications privilege alone, or whether the consent of both spouses is required for the privilege to be waived. The common rule is that the privilege can be waived if both spouses agree, either expressly or by failing to object to the disclosure of the information in court. The privilege is automatically waived if the confidential communication concerns a crime of which the testifying spouse or his/her child is the victim.

    United States v. *Brown* presents a rather unusual application of the confidential communications privilege. In this case, the defendant's co-conspirator, Heinritz, testified on behalf of the prosecution at Brown's trial. Brown wanted to call Heinritz's wife to testify about statements her husband had made to her indicating that he intended to commit perjury. The court refused to allow those statements based on the marital communications privilege, but only after allowing the wife to testify about the statements outside the jury's hearing.

COURT OPINION 12-1 _____

UNITED STATES V. BROWN, 634 F.2D 819 (5TH CIR. 1981)

Brown and Heinritz were charged together in a one-count indictment for transporting a fraudulently obtained check in interstate commerce. At the time of the offense charged in the indictment, Brown was the president and owner, and Heinritz was the executive vice-president and manager, of two insurance agencies. In brief, the indictment alleged that the two had devised a scheme to finance an existing indebtedness on expired insurance policies by submitting a false application to an agency in the business of financing insurance premiums; the financing agency approved the application, and Heinritz picked up the check for the proceeds of the loan and returned it (across state lines) to the office of Brown's insurance companies. Heinritz pled guilty and, prior to his testimony in this case, was sentenced to a term of probation.

Heinritz was the key witness in the government's case against Brown. Heinritz testified in some detail to the facts behind the formation and execution of the scheme alleged in the indictment, and to Brown's involvement in it. "The gist of Heinritz's testimony was that Brown had created the plan upon which Heinritz had acted, and that he had cooperated with Brown only out of a fear for his personal safety, an apprehension allegedly caused by threats made to him by Brown." United States v. Brown, supra, at 189.

In an attempt to impeach Mr. Heinritz, Brown called Mrs. Heinritz (Mr. Heinritz's former wife, who had been married to him during the events in question) to the stand. The prosecutor immediately requested a bench conference, and, along with defense counsel, held an off-the-record discussion with the court. Thereupon the jury was excused and the prosecutor and the defense counsel argued on the record whether Mr. Heinritz could validly claim a marital privilege in order to prevent his wife from testifying for the defense about private communications between them. Trial Transcript at 261–66. The court recessed for a time during this argument; on the basis of the discussion which took place after the recess, it appears that during the break the judge proposed, and the parties agreed, to allow the defense counsel to examine Mrs. Heinritz on the record but in the absence of the jury, after which the court was to inquire whether Mr. Heinritz wished to assert the privilege. In the event that the

court upheld the privilege, this examination was to serve as an offer of proof. Trial Transcript at 264–66. After the testimony of Mrs. Heinritz, the court explained to Mr. Heinritz that the conversations to which his wife had testified were confidential marital communications and were therefore privileged, and asked him whether he wished to assert his privilege. Mr. Heinritz replied that, upon the advice of his attorney, he would in fact claim the marital privilege. Trial Transcript at 281.

Mrs. Heinritz's testimony—as taken in Brown's offer of proof—contains two statements which Brown sought to use to impeach the truthfulness of Mr. Heinritz's testimony against him. First, Mrs. Heinritz stated that her husband had told her that he had lied to the grand jury about an important part of his story. Both before the grand jury and during Brown's trial, Mr. Heinritz testified that he had had a change of mind after picking up the check from the premium financing agency and had decided to return it. He failed to return it, so he testified, only because of his fear of Brown. As Mr. Heinritz stated at trial:

> (Brown) said to me, "where is that check from Agency Premium Services?" And I said, "It is in my desk," and he said, "Well, I want to see it." . . . I hesitated because this meant that I wouldn't have the opportunity to do what I planned, was to type a short letter of transmittal and then return it to Atlanta. . . . So, I hesitated and Mr. Brown stated, "Don't just stand there. I want to see that check, and if you don't get it," he said, "I won't have the boys kill you, I'll have them break your knee caps so you will never walk again."

Trial Transcript at 65–66. Mr. Heinritz was later asked whether he had in fact told his wife that his testimony before the grand jury as to Brown's physical threat against him was perjured. He admitted having discussed the matter with her but denied having made such a statement. Trial Transcript at 144–45. According to Mrs. Heinritz, however, Mr. Heinritz had told her that the statement about Brown's threat was untrue. As she stated during the offer of proof:

THE WITNESS (Mrs. Heinritz): He (Mr. Heinritz) had flown to Atlanta in the morning and when he came back that night, it was late, after supper, perhaps ten o'clock. But I'm guessing. And he had been

(continued)

(continued)

drinking, I presume that he had been drinking on the plane on the way back, and he came in and sat down and told me–I said, "Well, how did it go?" And he said he had lied before the Grand Jury.

Q. (By defense counsel): . . . Did he characterize the lie to the Grand Jury as relating to a statement that Mr. Brown had threatened him?

A. Yes. In that particular, he said that he had lied.

The second statement which Brown sought to use to impeach Mr. Heinritz involves the purpose for which Mr. Heinritz had entered the federal government's Witness Protection Program. On cross-examination, defense counsel sought to get Mr. Heinritz to admit that he had told his wife that he had entered the program not for protection against Brown, but instead to make his story more believable. Mr. Heinritz's answer was, however, limited to the following:

THE WITNESS (Mr. Heinritz): . . . I told my wife that a plea of guilty was required in order to enter the Witness Protection Program which would, in turn, strengthen the Government's case.

Q. (by defense counsel): Well, how did you think it would strengthen the Government's case? (Pause) Take your time, Mr. Heinritz.

A. By the mere fact that protection was afforded me.

Q. Because it would make Mr. Brown look like an evil man, right?

A. Mr. Brown is an evil man.

Trial Transcript at 222–23. Mrs. Heinritz's version of Mr. Heinritz's explanation to her of his reasons for entering the Witness Protection Program was somewhat closer to that suggested by defense counsel:

Q. (by defense counsel): Did there come a time, forward of that separation where you learned that Mr. Heinritz was going in to the program called the Witness Protection Program?

A. (Mrs. Heinritz): Yes.

Q. Did he discuss that with you?

A. Yes, he did.

Q. And what did he say about it and why he was going into it?

A. . . . he said he didn't want to leave New Orleans—he is a native and he likes the City—and that he didn't want to leave New Orleans, but that he had to do it to make it look good, to make his story believable.

Trial Transcript at 272–73. In both cases, Mrs. Heinritz's statements impeach the truthfulness of Mr. Heinritz's testimony: the first relays an admission of perjury before the grand jury on an important part of his story, and the second relays an admission of a general desire to make his story look more believable than he apparently felt it was. Moreover, both statements directly contradicted Mr. Heinritz's version of the confidential communications between them. . . .

Mr. Heinritz arguably waived his confidential marital communications privilege on two separate occasions. First, he allowed his wife to testify to the privileged communications as an offer of proof. It is true, as the government argues, that the court was informed that Mr. Heinritz wished to claim the privilege at the moment Mrs. Heinritz took the stand, and that Mr. Heinritz thereafter allowed his wife to testify as an offer of proof only because the judge explained that to be the proper procedure. Trial Transcript at 261–66. An important distinction can be made, however, between a privilege which protects against the introduction into evidence of certain testimony (such as the adverse spousal testimony privilege) and a privilege which protects only against the disclosure of certain communications (such as the confidential marital communications privilege at issue here). One can argue that the privileged party's consent to disclosure for any purpose waives the confidential communications privilege, for once the communication has been disclosed to any third party with the consent of the privileged party, the communication may no longer be "confidential" within the meaning of the privilege. See United States v. Lilley, 581 F.2d 182, 189 (8th Cir. 1978); Fraser v. United States, 145 F.2d 139, 144–45 (6th Cir. 1944), cert. denied, 324 U.S. 849, 65 S.Ct. 684, 89 L.Ed. 1409 (1945).

In the second place, Mr. Heinritz testified on cross-examination to the content of the confidential marital communications he later sought to prevent his wife from disclosing. As Wigmore states, the confidential marital communications privilege may be waived by "some act of testimony which in fairness places the person in a position not to object to further disclosure." 8 J. Wigmore, Evidence s 2340 at 671 (1961). Mr. Heinritz admitted on cross-examination that he had discussed with his wife both his testimony before the grand jury and his reasons for entering the Witness Protection Program; he specifically denied, however, both that he had told his wife he had lied to the grand jury and that

(continued)

(continued)

he had told his wife he had entered the Witness Protection Program in order to make his story more believable. Trial Transcript at 145, 221–22. Mr. Heinritz's answers on cross-examination at least arguably waived his privilege with respect to the particular communications he was willing to discuss on cross-examination, which included the two statements to which Mrs. Heinritz was willing to testify. The confidential marital communications privilege was not intended to allow one spouse to provide his or her own version of a particular communication while preventing the other version from being disclosed. See United States v. Burkhart, 501 F.2d 993, 995 (6th Cir. 1974) cert. denied, 420 U.S. 946, 95 S.Ct. 1326, 43 L.Ed.2d 424 (1975); United States v. Benford, 457 F.Supp. 589, 596–98 (E.D.Mich.1978); 81 Am.Jur.2d s 171 (1976).

We do not believe that the court's action can be characterized as plain error. In the first place, the sole waiver argument raised on appeal is hardly an "obvious" one; while a communications privilege may arguably be waived by any form of consented disclosure, a serious question is raised where, as here, the trial judge himself instructs the disclosure. In the second place, the allowance of the marital privilege cannot be said to have seriously affected the fairness of the proceeding. This follows from our decision in Fountain v. United States, supra. In Fountain, two separate lines of inquiry on cross-examination had been excluded by the judge because of the witness's privilege against self-incrimination. Fountain argued on appeal that both lines of inquiry would have led to admissions which would have impeached the truthfulness of the witness's direct testimony; in the second instance, however, Fountain's counsel had not explained the purpose of the questions to the trial judge and had

made no motion to strike the witness's direct testimony. We concluded that appeal on the basis of the second excluded line of inquiry was foreclosed by the plain error doctrine:

> Since the district court was neither apprised of the purpose of the inquiry nor asked to rule on the matter or to strike the direct testimony, the situation cannot require reversal unless it amounts to "plain error" within the meaning of Fed.R.Crim.P. 52(b). . . . In this case inability to inquire (into the excluded subject) did not deprive appellants of the right to test the truthfulness of (the witness's) testimony in any substantial way.

384 F.2d at 628–29 (citations omitted). The issue before us now is analogous to that decided in Fountain: Brown was precluded from introducing evidence that would have challenged the truthfulness of the testimony of the State's chief witness. But as we have already decided, in Part II, supra, the exclusion of Mrs. Heinritz's testimony did not substantially prejudice Brown by depriving him of the ability to test the truth of Mr. Heinritz's testimony. We conclude that whatever error may arguably have been committed by the trial court's allowance of Mr. Heinritz's claim of privilege was not plain error. Therefore we decline to address the merits of either waiver argument.

Questions

1. Why did the court believe that Heinritz's consent to his wife's courtroom testimony could have been a waiver of the confidential communications privilege?

2. Did the court's concern about including perjured testimony at trial outweigh its concern about upholding the marital privilege?

EVIDENCE AND TECHNOLOGY

MAINTAINING A PRIVILEGE IN ONLINE COMMUNICATIONS

With the increased predominance of electronically stored communications, all but replacing letters and phone calls, the very real danger arises that such communications will inadvertently compromise a privilege that would otherwise protect them. There is no question that an e-mail sent by an attorney to a client, or one spouse to another, would be subject to the same privilege as statements

(continued)

made in a private phone call of face-to-face meeting. But as we have seen, the root of privileged communications is confidentiality, and confidentiality is far more at risk in online communication than more traditional ones, simply because it is easy to share such communications with one, two, or a thousand third parties.

As attorneys Brenda Sharton and Gregory Lyons noted for the ABA when discussing waiver of the attorney–client privilege in business communications, "As a general rule, the disclosure of attorney–client communications (including sharing of an e-mail) to a third party waives the privilege. In the context of e-mail, the most common pitfall leading to inadvertent waivers stems from the ease with which e-mail containing legal advice can be sent to large groups of people via the Internet. Not only will a dissemination to a third party potentially waive the privilege (i.e., the "in confidence" element of the privilege is no longer met), but dissemination to too wide of an audience within the company also may cause a waiver. Business lawyers must be attentive because it is usually the business client who fails to keep a communication in confidence through mass distribution or forwarding of the e-mail 'from legal.'"[1]

If a communication occurs on Facebook or social media, it is even less likely to be subject to a privilege unless the method of communication (such as private message) justifies the conclusion that the communication was meant to be confidential. For instance, if a husband posts a status and his wife comments on it, that comment is not privileged (even if it was intended for the husband only) because all of the husband's friends can also read it. As Sharton and Lyons point out, the sharing of a communication with even one individual can waive the privilege; sharing it with several hundred friends would certainly do so.

This general rule would not apply, however, if the privilege is shared by everyone the communication is forwarded to. For instance, an attorney forwarding an e-mail from a client to another attorney in the same firm who is bound by the same obligation of confidentiality would probably not waive the privilege.

Because of the ease with which electronic communications can be shared, the prospect of inadvertent sharing of communications is a serious concern. Federal Rule of Civil Procedure 26(b)(5)(b) provides that privileged material inadvertently produced in response to a request for discovery must be returned, sequestered (i.e., set aside and not read or used), or destroyed upon notification by the disclosing party. But this rule would not apply to a privileged e-mail that is accidentally forwarded to a third party in any other context.

Clearly, caution in the handling of electronic privileged communications is called for. Many attorneys include in all potentially privileged e-mails notices of the privileged and confidential nature of the e-mails, and clear instructions on how to proceed should the e-mail be sent to the wrong person. Whether such notices by themselves are enough to prevent a waiver is questionable, however, especially where the transmission was deliberate and not inadvertent. Also, while lawyers are keenly aware of the need to preserve privileges in communications with their clients, other professionals such as clergymen and physicians, and especially nonprofessionals such as spouses, may not have the same awareness and therefore be more likely to compromise the privilege.

As was noted earlier, the rules of evidence do not change simply because technology is involved. The use of electronic communications does not change the rules governing privilege; such communications simply make those rules easier to break, and therefore demand a higher level of awareness and care.

The Spousal Testimonial Privilege

The **spousal testimonial privilege** is much broader than the one covering confidential communications between spouses. This privilege covers all testimony by one spouse against another, regardless of whether it involves communications, actions, or any other form of information.

To invoke this privilege, the parties must be lawfully married when the testimony is given. As with the confidential communications privilege, parties who are permanently separated are not considered married for purposes of the privilege. If the privilege applies, however, it bars *all* testimony by the spouse, even concerning events, communications, or actions that took place prior to the marriage. In this sense, then, the privilege has a much broader scope than the confidential communications privilege.

In criminal cases, the privilege can be waived by the spouse giving the testimony. This means that a husband or wife can testify against his or her spouse if he or she chooses to do so, but cannot be forced to do so, except in specific circumstances. These circumstances include where the criminal case is for desertion or maintenance (a criminal action designed to punish someone for failing to support his/her family), where the case involves a violent crime or injury against the defendant's spouse or a minor child of either party, where the testimony is needed to prove the parties' marriage in a case of bigamy (multiple marriage), or where the defendant is accused of a violent crime such as murder, involuntary deviate sexual intercourse, or rape.

Attorney–Client Privilege

Another privilege that protects an important relationship is the **attorney–client privilege**. An attorney learns a great deal of very personal and sometimes incriminating information in the course of representing a client. It is necessary that the client reveal this information so that the attorney can effectively advise and represent the client. Because of this, the attorney is usually privy to information about his/her client that would prove very useful to the opposing party at trial. Of course, if an attorney could testify against his/her own client, the client would never tell the attorney anything worth testifying about, and it would be impossible for the attorney to do his/her job.

Generally, an attorney is not permitted to testify to confidential communications made to him/her by his/her client, and a client cannot be forced to reveal such communications, unless the client waives the privilege. As with the marital privileges, the protected relationship must exist when the communication is made.

The Attorney–Client Relationship

What constitutes an **"attorney–client" relationship**? There are two ways this relationship can exist: (1) the attorney gives legal advice to the client, or (2) the attorney represents the client with respect to a legal case or transaction. Generally, this relationship exists whenever a person consults with a licensed attorney about a legal issue, no matter how simple or complex that issue may be. There does not need to be any formal arrangement between the attorney and client, nor does there need to be a written contract for the attorneys' services. The relationship is a matter of the client's intention: is the client intentionally seeking legal advice or legal representation from the attorney? If the answer is "yes," then regardless of the setting or circumstances, an attorney–client relationship has been formed.

The term "**legal advice**" is much broader than most people believe. It entails two aspects: (1) informing a client about his/her legal rights and obligations, or (2) advising a client about actions he/she should or shouldn't take based on the law. If an attorney engages in either of these activities, he/she is giving legal advice. If the legal advice is sought by the client with knowledge that it is being given by an attorney, then an attorney–client relationship has been established. In this way, even a casual conversation between an attorney and another person can create an attorney–client relationship.

Suppose a man and a woman are sitting at a bar. The man introduces himself with the purpose of initiating a conversation. The woman introduces herself and tells him that she is an attorney. This is not enough to create an attorney–client relationship, but it does set the stage for one. Now, the man tells the woman he is planning on leaving his wife soon and would like her phone number. Is this communication privileged? No, because he is not asking her for legal advice. Suppose he tells her he is planning on leaving his wife, and wants to know whether he can empty out their joint bank account. As long as she does not answer his question, she is still not his attorney, but if she gives him any kind of advice in response to his question, then an attorney–client relationship has been created, and anything he tells her about his marriage from that point on is privileged, even if they never see each other again.

Usually, an attorney–client relationship is not that casual. Attorneys will often refuse to give legal advice or provide any legal services unless it is clear that a formal professional relationship is being contemplated, because such a relationship has ethical implications far beyond the application of the attorney–client privilege. Still, there is no requirement of a formalization of the relationship for the privilege to apply. Of course, the attorney must be properly licensed to practice law at the time the information is communicated, or the attorney–client privilege would not apply under any circumstance.

Confidentiality of the Communication

The term "**confidential communication**" as it is used in the attorney–client privilege focuses on why the information passed between the attorney and his/her client. This is a two-way street; it does not matter whether the communication originates with the attorney or the client. What matters is whether the information passed because of or in furtherance of the attorney–client relationship. Suppose John hires his friend Amanda to be his attorney with respect to a contract case. Anything John tells Amanda, or Amanda tells John, regarding that case is privileged information. Now, suppose that one night John and Amanda are having drinks together at a local bar, after a particularly long negotiating session about John's contract. John tells Amanda that his wife is cheating on him. That information has nothing to do with the contract, so it is not a "confidential communication" protected by the attorney–client privilege *unless* John is telling it for the purpose of obtaining legal advice from Amanda about John's rights as the victim of adultery. Where someone reveals information with legal implications to someone he/she knows is an attorney, that information is generally going to be considered confidential. But the circumstances of the communication may prove otherwise, especially if the communication does not take place in a traditional professional setting.

legal advice
Information provided by an attorney to a client about the client's legal rights and obligations, or advice about actions the client should or shouldn't take under the law.

confidential communication (attorney–client)
Any communication between an attorney and his/her client relating to the attorney's legal representation of the client.

> **PRACTICE TIP**
>
> A meeting between an attorney and client that relates to the subject matter of the representation should *never* take place in the presence of anyone not working with the attorney on the case. Such a third-party presence in the room could destroy confidentiality even if the only ones talking are the attorney and client.

The attorney–client privilege does not necessarily cover everything a client tells an attorney, even where a formal attorney–client relationship is present. Sometimes, information disclosed to an attorney is so incidental to the subject of the representation that protecting it will not further the purpose of protecting the attorney–client relationship. This was the case in the following court opinion, in which a routine, relatively innocuous question on a client's intake form ended up being used as evidence of fraud and perjury against the client and her former attorney.

COURT OPINION 12-2 _____

UNITED STATES V. LEONARD–ALLEN, 739 F.3D 948 (7TH CIR. 2013)

Norma Leonard–Allen and Walter Stern became entangled in the financial arrangements that underlie this case during the aftermath of a lawsuit in which Stern served as Leonard–Allen's attorney. The government charged that Stern hid some of Leonard–Allen's assets so that she would not have to declare them in her bankruptcy proceeding. It maintained that Stern knew of Leonard–Allen's bankruptcy when he opened certificates of deposit (CDs) with Leonard–Allen's money, and thus that his action amounted to money laundering in violation of 18 U.S.C. § 1956(h). Leonard–Allen, it said, committed perjury in violation of 18 U.S.C. § 1623 when she testified that Stern had not referred her to her bankruptcy lawyer, contrary to her representation on a client-intake form on which she had listed "Walter Stern" as the person who referred her to the bankruptcy lawyer. Both were convicted after a jury trial.

On appeal, Leonard–Allen argues that the client-intake form was subject to attorney–client privilege and should not have been admitted against either defendant. Stern argues that even if the form were not subject to attorney–client privilege, the statement in the form is inadmissible hearsay. He also argues that the court erred when it excluded as hearsay his testimony about why he purchased the CDs and when it excluded as irrelevant testimony from Leonard–Allen's daughters. We affirm Leonard–Allen's conviction because the client-intake form was not a communication made in furtherance of the legal representation and therefore was not subject to the attorney–client privilege. Because the trial court wrongly prevented Stern from testifying about his own conduct—testimony central to Stern's defense

that he did not intend to conceal assets—we reverse Stern's conviction.

Stern met Leonard–Allen when he represented her in an employment discrimination suit. After the case settled, Stern and Leonard–Allen became romantically involved. They began living together in September 2006, months after Stern opened the first of two CD accounts underlying these charges. Leonard–Allen and her ex-husband had separated in June 2005 and had executed a Marital Settlement Agreement awarding Leonard–Allen $95,000, to be paid in four installments. In July 2005, Leonard–Allen visited a bankruptcy attorney, Mary Losey. In response to a question on Losey's client-intake form asking "How did you select this office?," she checked the box "Friend/Referral" and wrote in Walter Stern's name.

In September 2005, Leonard–Allen filed for bankruptcy, reporting $80,000 in liabilities and only $30,000 in assets. She did not disclose the $95,000 marital settlement. Between June 2005 and January 2006, while her bankruptcy was pending, Leonard–Allen received four personal checks, issued from the divorce attorney's trust account, for a total of $95,000. In January 2006, the bankruptcy court determined that Leonard–Allen had insufficient assets to pay her creditors and discharged her debt. A month later, Leonard–Allen used the proceeds of the first three divorce settlement checks to purchase a teller check; she promptly endorsed that check to Stern. In March 2006, Stern opened a CD account in his name with the proceeds of the check. In August 2006, Leonard–Allen used the proceeds of the fourth divorce settlement check to purchase another teller check, which

(continued)

(continued)

she also endorsed to Stern. In January 2007, Stern used the proceeds of the second teller check and the first CD to open another CD account in his name. In January 2007, Leonard–Allen's ex-husband's attorney informed the bankruptcy trustee that Leonard–Allen failed to disclose the $95,000 divorce settlement in the bankruptcy proceedings, and in October 2007, the bankruptcy judge revoked the discharge of Leonard–Allen's bankruptcy.

Criminal charges followed, and Leonard–Allen pleaded guilty to two counts of making a false declaration in a bankruptcy proceeding in violation of 18 U.S.C. § 152(3). After doing so, Leonard–Allen was subpoenaed to testify before a grand jury in the case against Stern. She told the grand jury that Stern had not referred her to Losey. The government subpoenaed records from Losey, including the client-intake form where Leonard–Allen had listed "Walter Stern" in the "Friend/Referral" box. Based on that evidence, the government charged Leonard–Allen with making a material false statement in a grand jury proceeding in violation of 18 U.S.C. § 1623. The court admitted the client-intake form as evidence of Leonard–Allen's perjury over Leonard–Allen's objection that it was subject to attorney–client privilege. She was convicted of the offense and sentenced to imprisonment for one year and a day.

. . . . Leonard–Allen argues that the intake form was protected by the attorney–client privilege and thus should not have been produced or introduced into evidence at the trial. The scope of attorney–client privilege is a question of law that we review *de novo*. *In re Subpoenaed Grand Jury Witness*, 171 F.3d 511, 512 (7th Cir. 1999). The privilege extends to confidential communications between client and attorney, made "in order to obtain legal assistance." *Fisher v. United States*, 425 U.S. 391, 403, 96 S.Ct. 1569, 48 L.Ed.2d 39 (1976). Its purpose is "to encourage clients to make full disclosure to their attorneys," and its scope is informed by this purpose. *Id*. Because the privilege may operate "in derogation of the search for truth," we "construe the privilege to apply only where necessary to achieve its purpose." *United States v. BDO Seidman, LLP*, 492 F.3d 806, 815 (7th Cir. 2007) (internal quotation marks and citations omitted). Accordingly, we have said that the privilege covers "only those communications which reflect the lawyer's thinking [or] are made for the purpose of eliciting the lawyer's professional advice or other legal assistance." *Id*. (internal quotation marks omitted).

Losey's form does not meet that description. Leonard–Allen's disclosure of who referred her does not reflect either the lawyer's or the client's thinking, and it

was not instrumental to the substance of the bankruptcy advice that Losey provided. The form is more akin to information about attorneys' fees. The latter information falls outside the scope of the privilege because fees are incidental to the substance of representation. *In re Subpoenaed Grand Jury Witness*, 171 F.3d at 513 (quoting *Matter of Witnesses Before Special March 1980 Grand Jury*, 729 F.2d 489, 491 (7th Cir. 1984)).

It is true that we have found that the privilege applies in the limited situation when a lawyer's disclosure of the identity of a third party who paid the defendant's fees would implicate another previously unknown client who was involved in the targeted criminal activity. *Id*. at 514. In that instance, the disclosure of the fee payor risks revealing another client's motive for seeking representation from the lawyer. This risk is not present in Leonard–Allen's acknowledgment that Stern referred her to Losey. That referral sheds no light on Leonard–Allen's motives for seeking legal assistance. On the other hand, her statement on the form was powerful evidence for the government's perjury case, since it contradicted her grand jury testimony.

While the form listed Leonard–Allen's reason for seeking representation as "financial," it was widely known that Losey represented Leonard–Allen for bankruptcy, and so that aspect of the intake form did not reveal otherwise confidential information about Leonard–Allen's motives. If Leonard–Allen had been concerned about the revelation that she had approached Losey for help in financial issues, she might have objected to that portion of the form. It could have been redacted, and the form would have been just as probative in the perjury proceeding. Because the referral statement is incidental to the representation and reveals nothing confidential about Leonard–Allen's motives, it falls outside the scope of the attorney–client privilege, and the district court did not err by admitting it as relevant evidence against both defendants. . . .

Questions

1. Why didn't Stern, Leonard–Allen's former attorney, also claim that the intake form was protected by the attorney–client privilege?

2. Considering that the purpose of an intake form is to provide basic information about a client and his/her case, what information on that form might be subject to the attorney–client privilege?

Waiver and Exceptions

Like the spousal privileges discussed earlier, the attorney–client privilege can be waived. Generally, the right to waive the privilege rests with the client, although waiver can be implied if the client allows the attorney to disclose information to a third party, unless that disclosure is part of the attorney's preparation of the client's case. For instance, a client may waive the attorney–client privilege in information that he/she authorizes his/her attorney to disclose to opposing counsel, but not information he/she allows the attorney to disclose to an investigator the attorney hires to help prepare the case for trial.

Federal Rule of Evidence 502 limits a criminal defendant's waiver of the attorney–client privilege or the work-product doctrine (see below) in certain cases. For instance, if a disclosure of information is inadvertent, and the disclosing party took reasonable steps to prevent the disclosure and to retrieve the information, then the privilege as to that information is not waived. An example would be if an e-mail between the attorney and his/her client was accidentally included in a group of nonprivileged e-mails provided to the prosecutor. Clearly, the disclosure was not meant to occur, so as long as reasonable steps were taken to make sure no such e-mails were included among the disclosure material, and the defense attorney promptly takes steps to retrieve the e-mail from the prosecutor, the privilege will remain intact. Otherwise, the privilege will be considered waived.

Rule 502 also limits waivers of certain other disclosures in federal and state proceedings, and where waiver of the attorney–client privilege is limited by court order or agreement between the parties.

There are some circumstances where the privilege does not apply even though there was never a formal waiver by the client. One of those circumstances exists where the client has attempted to use the attorney's services in furtherance of the commission of a crime. Not only is the attorney required ethically to refuse to provide such services, he/she is also free to disclose any communications his/her client made when attempting to secure them. Another exception occurs where the client has accused the attorney of professional malpractice or unethical conduct, or where the client has refused to pay the attorney for services rendered. In those cases, the attorney is free to disclose whatever confidential information is necessary to defend himself/herself against the accusation, or to prove his/her entitlement to his/her fee. An attorney is also ethically required to disclose a client's intention to harm anyone or to commit a crime in order to prevent that harm or crime from occurring.

The Work-Product Doctrine

work-product doctrine
A rule that prevents discovery or disclosure of an attorney's work product, including any records made by the defendant or his/her attorney during the case's investigation or defense.

In addition to the attorney–client privilege, the **work-product doctrine** prevents discovery or disclosure of any information in attorney's file that qualifies as "work product." This rule is embodied in Federal Rule of Criminal Procedure 16(b)(2):

Information Not Subject to Disclosure. Except for scientific or medical reports, Rule 16(b)(1) does not authorize discovery or inspection of:

(A) reports, memoranda, or other documents made by the defendant, or the defendant's attorney or agent, during the case's investigation or defense; or

(B) a statement made to the defendant, or the defendant's attorney or agent, by:
  (i) the defendant;
  (ii) a government or defense witness; or
  (iii) a prospective government or defense witness.

The work-product rule can be waived by a defendant to the same extent as the attorney–client privilege, and such waivers are subject to the same limitations under Rule 502.

Physician–Patient Privilege

Another common privilege is the physician–patient privilege that protects information obtained by doctors in the course of treating their patients. While federal courts do not recognize a **physician–patient privilege** in criminal cases (*United States* v. *Perryman*, 14 Fed.Appx. 328, 329 (6th Cir. 2001), citing *Hancock* v. *Dodson*, 958 F.2d 1367, 1373 (6th Cir. 1992)), the privilege exists in most state jurisdictions and should therefore be included in our discussion.

As with the attorney–client privilege, the relationship of doctor and patient must exist in order for the privilege to apply. Unlike the attorney–client privilege, this privilege protects not only confidential communications, but also *any* information obtained by a doctor in the course of diagnosing or treating a patient.

The physician–patient relationship generally begins when a patient first sees the physician for the purpose of diagnosing or treating a medical condition. This relationship is determined based on the patient's subjective understanding as to the purpose of a visit to the doctor. If the patient believes that he/she is being seen for diagnosis or treatment, then the relationship exists for purposes of the privilege. The relationship does not exist, however, if the patient is examined but refuses treatment.

Once the relationship exists, the privilege applies to all information that comes into possession of the doctor, regardless of source, relating to the diagnosis and treatment of that patient. In this sense, the privilege is much broader than either the spousal or attorney–client privilege discussed above, which only apply to confidential communications that take place between the spouses or between the attorney and his/her client. The physician privilege applies to *any* communications intended by the patient to be confidential, even if that information was provided to the doctor by a third person. It is not necessary for the patient to expressly request that information be kept confidential; any information relating to the diagnosis and treatment of the patient is considered to fall within the privilege.

In some jurisdictions, even information that is generated entirely by the doctor himself/herself can be subject to the privilege so long as that information is generated in the course of diagnosing and treating the patient. Therefore, the results of blood and urine tests, and other diagnostic measures, would fall within the privilege. In addition, a doctor's observations of a patient's behavior or condition while being examined or treated are also subject to the privilege. By contrast, some states limit the application of the privilege solely to information that would tend to blacken the reputation of the patient, thereby severely reducing the information to which the privilege applies.

Clergyman–Communicant Privilege

Many states protect the relationship between a clergyman and a communicant (i.e., member of the clergyman's faith or someone seeking his or her spiritual guidance) by imposing a **clergyman–communicant privilege** on confidential communications made to the clergyman in that capacity. Like all of the other privileges we have discussed, this privilege applies

LEARNING OBJECTIVE 5
Identify evidence that is excluded by the physician–patient privilege.

physician–patient privilege
A privilege protecting all information obtained by a doctor in the course of treating a patient.

LEARNING OBJECTIVE 6
Identify evidence that is excluded by the clergy–communicant privilege.

clergyman–communicant privilege
A privilege that protects confidential communications made to a clergyman.

only to communications that are intended by the communicant to be confidential.

This privilege presents a unique problem, because the definition of "clergyman" is a matter of religious as well as legal principle. Some states have interpreted the meaning broadly to encompass any minister of an organized church, whether or not that person is "ordained" in a formal sense. Others restrict the definition to ordained clergy. Generally, though, religious leaders and church officials who are not traditionally considered "clergy" (such as deacons and elders, and Sunday School teachers) and nonclergy leaders of religious organizations that cannot be properly characterized as "churches" (such as religious charities or associations) would not fall within the privilege. In some states, however, a person's reasonable belief that the individual they are speaking to is, in fact, a clergyman is sufficient to trigger the privilege.

In the following case from North Carolina, a defendant charged with murdering his wife unsuccessfully tried to invoke the clergy–communicant privilege to prevent incriminating testimony by his pastor.

COURT OPINION 12-3

STATE V. PULLEY, 180 N.C.APP. 54, 636 S.E.2D 231 (N.C.APP., 2006)

Defendant Eugene Ricky Pulley appeals from a judgment, sentencing him to life imprisonment without possibility of parole, entered upon his conviction by a jury for the first degree murder of his wife, Patty Jo Pulley. We find no error.

The State offered evidence at defendant's trial tending to show the following: In May of 1999, defendant and Patty Jo Pulley were married and living in Ringgold, Virginia. Defendant was employed as a youth pastor and music director with the River of Life Church in Ringgold. His wife cleaned homes and gave piano lessons.

On the morning of 14 May 1999, defendant drove his wife to a home she was to clean. He returned to pick her up sometime later that afternoon. A neighbor, Bethany Sudduth, called to ask for a ride to a school play and spoke with defendant, who told her Patty Jo was not feeling well. Later the same afternoon, defendant called and asked Bethany's mother, Judy Sudduth, if she had seen Patty Jo. Still later, defendant called and told Judy Sudduth that his dog had gotten loose and had chased a squirrel; he asked her to keep an eye out for the dog. Soon after, Judy Sudduth heard defendant calling the dog and went outside, where she saw defendant climbing an embankment. He had a red wound on the left side of his face.

In the late hours of 14 May 1999, defendant began informing people that Patty Jo had disappeared. He went with Rev. Sudduth, the pastor of the River of Life Church, to search for her. The following morning, several members of defendant's church joined the search and, at approximately 2:00 p.m., Richard Gardner found the Pulleys' red truck on River Bend Road, a short distance off of Highway 62.

. . .

There was evidence that prior to Patty Jo's disappearance, Rev. Sudduth had become concerned about defendant suffering from "burnout" and had offered him a sabbatical and a reduction in his involvement in the affairs of the church. Defendant reacted angrily and declined the opportunity. After Patty Jo's disappearance, during the summer of 1999 following defendant's return from a church-related trip to Texas, Rev. Sudduth and other ministers of nearby churches, as well as one of the elders of the River of Life Church, called a meeting with defendant to discuss some improper credit card charges which defendant had made on the church credit card. At that meeting, defendant disclosed that his relationship with Patty Jo had become strained because he had suffered from erectile dysfunction. In September 1999, defendant resigned from the church and moved to

(continued)

(continued)

Lebanon, Virginia. On 18 December 2002, skeletal remains identified as those of Patty Jo Pulley were found in Caswell County, North Carolina, near a bridge over Hyco Creek near the place where the Pulley's truck had been discovered roughly nineteen months earlier.

Defendant . . . assigns error to the admission of communications defendant contends were protected by the clergy–communicant privilege.

> No priest, rabbi, accredited Christian Science practitioner, or a clergyman or ordained minister of an established church shall be competent to testify in any action, suit or proceeding concerning any information which was communicated to him and entrusted to him in his professional capacity, and necessary to enable him to discharge the functions of his office according to the usual course of his practice or discipline, wherein such person so communicating such information about himself or another is seeking spiritual counsel and advice relative to and growing out of the information so imparted, provided, however, that this section shall not apply where communicant in open court waives the privilege conferred.

N.C. Gen.Stat. § 8–53.2 (2005).

To fall within the protection of the statute, the defendant must be seeking the counsel and advice of his minister and the information must be entrusted to the minister through a confidential communication. *State v. West*, 317 N.C. 219, 223, 345 S.E.2d 186, 189 (1986).

The clergy–communicant privilege is not applicable in this case. The trial court found, based on competent evidence offered at a *voir dire* hearing, that the purpose of the meeting [in the summer of 1999] was "to address issues involving the subject church and the status of the defendant in the administration of such churches' [sic] service." Further, a person to whom the privilege does not extend was present at the meeting between defendant, Rev. Sudduth, and others. This person was a church elder rather than an ordained minister or clergyman. . . . As a result, the clergy–communicant privilege does not apply in this case.

Questions

1. Why did the court conclude that the clergy–communicant privilege did not apply to the meeting between Pulley and Rev. Sudduth?

2. If Pulley had confessed that he murdered his wife to Rev. Sudduth, would that confession have fallen under the privilege?

KEY TERMS

CHAPTER SUMMARY

- A privilege is a rule that excludes competent, relevant testimony from evidence in order to protect an important relationship.
- Privilege is a rule governing the admission of evidence at trial, in contrast to the broader concept of confidentiality, which is an ethical concern usually arising in a professional relationship.
- The spousal relationship is protected by two privileges: the confidential communications privilege and the spousal testimonial privilege.

- The confidential communications privilege prevents disclosure of any confidential communications between spouses during their marriage.
- A "marriage" can be ceremonial, where the parties are married by an authorized official following issuance of a marriage license.
- A "marriage" can also be common-law, where the parties have indicated their intention to be married by behaving as husband and wife and holding themselves out as married to the community. Common-law marriages have been abolished by statute in most states.
- For the confidential communications privilege to apply, a communication must take place within the confines of the marriage relationship, and involve a subject that would normally be considered a private matter between a husband and wife.
- The confidential communications privilege can be waived by either spouse in most jurisdictions.
- The spousal testimonial privilege prevents a witness from testifying against his or her spouse during a valid marriage.
- In some jurisdictions, the spousal testimonial privilege cannot be waived; in others, it can only be waived with the consent of both spouses.
- The spousal privileges do not protect information in cases where the spouse or a minor child of the parties is the victim.
- The attorney–client privilege protects confidential communications by a client to an attorney made within the context of an attorney–client relationship.
- An attorney–client relationship exists when an attorney gives legal advice to a client, or represents the client in a case or transaction.
- An attorney gives legal advice when he/she informs a client about his/her legal rights and obligations, or advises the clients about actions he/she should or shouldn't take.
- An attorney's work product is also protected from disclosure or discovery.
- Work product includes any records or documents created by the attorney or defendant in the course of investigating a case or preparing a defense.
- The physician–patient privilege protects all information obtained by a physician in the course of diagnosing or treating a patient, although some states place limits on this privilege.
- Federal courts do not recognize a physician–patient privilege.
- The clergy–communicant privilege protects confidential communications by a communicant made to a clergyman in his capacity as such.
- A clergyman includes any religious leader who is considered as such by his church, but does not include deacons, elders, or other church leaders not generally considered clergy.

WEB EXCURSIONS

1. Privileges can vary widely from one jurisdiction to the next. Using Web resources, find the specific elements of the privileges discussed in this chapter in your own state. Do those privileges exist? If so, what are their specific elements? How can they be waived?
2. Using Web resources, find your state's code of professional ethics for attorneys. Compare your state's definition of "confidentiality" with the requirements for your state's attorney–client privilege. Are they similar? Is there any information that would be considered "confidential" for ethical purposes that would not fall under your state's attorney–client privilege?

PRACTICAL EXERCISE

1. John is a bank robber and Mary is his girlfriend. Every time John pulls off a caper, he comes home and tells Mary all about it. One day, John says, "Mary, you know a lot about my robberies, and if I'm ever caught, they're probably gonna try to make you testify against me. Let's get married so you won't have to testify." So, John and Mary get married. The next time John robs a bank, he's caught. While out on bail, John tells Mary about his latest bank robbery

and how he got caught. Mary then decides that she does not want to be married to a jailbird, and files for a divorce. The day before John's criminal trial, the divorce becomes final. At John's trial, the prosecutor calls Mary to the stand. Assume that neither Mary nor John will waive the confidential communications or spousal privileges. Answer the following questions in terms of whether the confidential communications privilege, the spousal privilege, or both would apply.

a. Can Mary be forced to testify about any of John's statements to her about his bank robberies before they were married?

b. Can Mary be forced to testify about John's statements to her concerning his last bank robbery?

ENDNOTE

1. The risks of e-mail communication: A guide to protecting privileged electronic communications. (n.d.). Retrieved from https://apps.americanbar.org/buslaw/blt/2007-09-10/lyons.shtml.

WavebreakMediaMicro/Fotolia

LEARNING OBJECTIVES

After reading this chapter, the student will be able to:

1. Identify the various types of witnesses.

2. Explain the various types of examination and the limitations imposed on each.

3. Illustrate leading questions and explain when they are permitted.

4. Know how to address unresponsive answers and questions that assume facts not in evidence.

5. Explain the sequestration of witnesses and when it is necessary.

6. Define credibility and explain how it is determined by a jury.

7. List and define the various methods of impeaching and rehabilitating witnesses.

Witnesses: Credibility and Impeachment

CHAPTER 13

■ INTRODUCTION

Witnesses are the most critical source of evidence in any criminal case. It is rare to find a case that can be decided on real evidence alone. The minds of human beings are required to recall and interpret events, statements, beliefs, intentions, and other matters relevant to the facts of the case. Because of this, the examination of witnesses is the key to the presentation of evidence to a jury. Much effort is usually spent in preparing one's own witnesses for trial, and in trying to "psych out" the witnesses of the other side to determine and take advantage of their weak spots and vulnerabilities.

PRACTICE TIP
Whenever a witness is going to be called at trial, he/she should be thoroughly prepared to testify, including being made familiar with likely cross-examination tactics and instructions on proper dress, deportment, and demeanor.

In order to understand the process of examining witnesses for trial, we need to look at the various purposes a witness might serve in a trial. There are four main types of witnesses:

LEARNING OBJECTIVE 1
Identify the various types of witnesses.

■ Eyewitnesses—those who can testify to events based on firsthand knowledge.

- Opinion witnesses—those who offer opinions helpful to the jury, either as experts or as lay witnesses.
- Character witnesses—those who testify about the character or reputation of another person.
- Authentication witnesses—those who provide testimony to authenticate a piece of real evidence.

Eyewitnesses are witnesses who are relating to the jury their own memories of events and conditions that occurred in their presence. The key concern for such witnesses is the clarity of their perception and the quality of their memory. Although they are called "eyewitnesses," their perceptions can also be based on senses other than sight. As long as the testimony is coming from the witness' memory of his/her own perceptions, he/she falls within this category.

Opinion witnesses, whom we discussed in Chapter 7, relate conclusions that they draw from events or conditions they themselves may not have perceived. The key concern here is the witness' qualification to render the opinion he/she is being asked to give under oath. If he/she is qualified, and if his/her opinion will help the jury understand a fact better than it would without his/her testimony, then his/her opinion is a valuable addition to the evidence.

Character witnesses, which were discussed in Chapter 9, are those who testify about the character of the defendant, the victim, or another witness. The key concern here is the witness' familiarity with the subject of his/her testimony. That familiarity can be based on personal experience, or on the subject's reputation within the community. So long as the witness' familiarity with the subject is established, his/her testimony is welcome where character is a relevant issue.

Finally, authentication witnesses testify about the authenticity of real evidence, which we discussed in Chapter 8. The key concern here is also familiarity, but with a document or thing rather than a person. An authentication witness' testimony, like that of an eyewitness, may be based on personal experience with the real evidence being authenticated, or it may provide a foundation for some other method of authenticity, such as an opinion regarding handwriting.

Keep in mind that more than one of these types can apply to a single person testifying at trial. For instance, a single witness might be called upon to (1) describe the events preceding and during an accident; (2) offer an opinion about the speed of one of the vehicles; (3) relate the character of another witness as truthful or untruthful; and (4) authenticate a picture of the accident scene that the witness drew for a police officer to illustrate his/her statement.

Table 13-1 summarizes the types of witnesses and their various characteristics.

Table 13-1   Types of Witnesses

	Substance of Testimony	Basis of Testimony	Use of Testimony
Eyewitness	Event or condition	Firsthand perception	Establish facts
Opinion witness	Conclusion about fact	Qualification to render opinion	Provide an opinion helpful to the jury
Character witness	Character of another person	Familiarity with subject or subject's reputation	Establish the character of a defendant, victim, or witness
Authentication witness	Authenticity of real evidence	Familiarity with real evidence	Authenticate real evidence

Defense attorney Perry Mason (center of picture) always managed to cross-examine witnesses on television and get them to confess to being the *real* killer. While cross-examinations in real courtrooms aren't always so dramatic, they are an effective way to test whether a witness is telling the truth.

Source: http://www.alamy.com/ stock-photo-william-talman-raymond-burr-perry-mason-1957-96977192.html.

■ EXAMINATION OF WITNESSES

Types of Examination

When a witness is called to testify by a party, that party's attorney asks the witness questions, which the witness answers as truthfully as possible. The initial questioning of a witness by the attorney for the party who called the witness is known as **direct examination**. After direct examination is over, the other party has the opportunity to ask questions of the witness. This is called **cross-examination**. Following cross-examination, the party calling the witness is given the chance to ask more questions. This is called **redirect examination**. Then, the other party can conduct recross-examination, after which, if there are still any facts to be obtained from the witness, there can occur re-redirect, re-recross, re-re-redirect, and so on. It is rare, however, that the questioning of a witness will go beyond recross.

The scope of cross-examination is limited by Rule 611(b). Cross-examination may not inquire into matters not raised in direct examination, unless those matters relate to the credibility of the witness. For instance, suppose a witness is called to testify as an eyewitness to a murder. The prosecutor asks him/her to relate the events as he/she saw them on the night of the murder, but does not ask him/her anything about his/her prior relationship with the victim. On cross-examination, the defense attorney would not be permitted to question him/her about his/her prior relationship with the victim, unless those questions were intended to attack his/her credibility as a witness by showing, for instance, that he/she was biased.

Similarly, the scope of redirect is limited to facts and issues explored on cross-examination, recross is limited to the scope of redirect, and so on. This prevents a witness from being endlessly examined about issues that properly belong elsewhere in the trial.

LEARNING OBJECTIVE 2
Explain the various types of examination and the limitations imposed on each.

direct examination
The questioning of a witness by the party who called the witness to testify.

cross-examination
The questioning of a witness by the opposing party or parties.

redirect examination
The questioning of a witness by the party who called the witness, following cross-examination.

The following case demonstrates what can happen when a witness is cross-examined too vigorously. The witness was a key prosecution witness, and during cross-examination by the defendant's attorney the witness revealed, unexpectedly, that he had been threatened. In affirming the trial judge's denial of a motion for mistrial, the Third Circuit expounded on the risk that a trial attorney takes when attempting to find holes in a witness' testimony during cross-examination.

COURT OPINION 13-1 _____

UNITED STATES V. BARBONE, 283 F.2D 628 (3RD CIR. 1960)

Appellants together with seven other persons were charged in a four count indictment with conspiracy to operate, etc., as well as the substantive crime of operating an illicit still.

. . . Error is alleged in the court's refusal to grant a mistrial, when on recross-examination, the government's main witness, Emidio Teti, answered that he had been threatened. A review of Teti's testimony and the circumstances surrounding his answer demonstrates that the trial judge's denial of the motion for mistrial was correct.

. . .

In their effort to discredit Teti counsel for the defendants extensively cross-examined him. . . . The cross-examination was persistent and minutely probing. It searched every aspect of the relationship between Teti and the [government] agents in the endeavor to establish that the witness had been coached and influenced by them. . . .

In his redirect examination Teti clarified certain portions of his testimony and re-affirmed the absence of any coaching or other undue influence.

On recross-examination the tactic utilized by defense counsel on cross-examination, was resumed. In response to defense counsel's questions Teti said that on the previous day when the court was not in session, an agent of the Alcohol Tax Unit had gone to Teti's home to pick him up and to give him certain witness fees. As the attorney insisted on further details of the association of the witness with the Alcohol Tax agents and the reasons therefore, the testimony continued:

Q. And where did you meet him? You must have met him sometimes time that day. Now, tell us where you first met him that day.
A. I met him in my home.

Q. He came down to your home on Friday, you mean, is that right?
A. Yes.

Q. What time did he come down to your home?
A. I don't recall the time, but I would say it was about 9:00 o'clock in the morning.

Q. Now, were you dressed when he came there or had you expected him there?
A. I had expected him there.

Q. Had you told him you wanted some more money?
A. No, sir.

Q. How did you expect him there? Did he tell you that he was coming down?
A. No. Sir.

Q. Well, how did you expect him there if he didn't tell you he would be down?
A. Well, I have been threatened in this case, sir.'

Following the last answer the defense attorneys immediately moved for a mistrial. In denying their motions, the trial judge correctly held that: [The answer was responsive to defense counsel's question and did not warrant a mistrial.]

Appellants urge that the answer and the inferences to be drawn therefrom were highly prejudicial and the motion for mistrial should have been granted. It seems to us that, in the context of the entire course of the cross and recross-examination, the answer was a natural and spontaneous response to the question. Teti had said that he expected the agent at his home that day. In seeking to uncover the precise reason why the agent had been looked for by Teti, defense counsel pinpointed his query. The answer was at least the beginning of the explanation. Defense counsel,

(continued)

(continued)

having persistently pursued that line of interrogation, cannot complain when the answer received is not tailored to fit their suggested theory. The well recognized rule that where an attorney puts this broad type of question, generally speaking, he cannot object to the response he receives is applicable. *United States v. Apuzzo*, 2 Cir. 1957, 245 F.2d 416. . . . In the Apuzzo trial, supra, defense counsel on cross-examination of a government agent propounded a question to him concerning the conversation between the agent and the defendant at the time of the latter's arrest. The witness answered that the defendant told him 'he had been arrested for policy 15 years ago.' Notwithstanding the inadmissibility of the statement, the Second Circuit held that defense counsel, having pursued this line of inquiry, could not object to the response elicited.

This appeal contains an even stronger factual basis for applying the rule, since the answer was responsive and admissible as relevant to the purpose of the cross and recross-examination, i.e., why was Teti in such close contact with the government agents. If the statement had effect at all, it was to clarify in some respects, the reasons why there was such close contact, and to neutralize the adverse inferences suggested, but never substantiated, by the defense attorneys.

. . .

In order that the full picture be developed and all necessary relevant evidence given the jury, considerable latitude in the examination of witnesses is allowed. As a corollary counsel must accept the hazard of uncovering evidence which although relevant, is unfavorable to his position. Chief Judge Clark puts this very well in *United States v. Apuzzo*, supra, 245 F.2d at page 422:

'It is inconceivable that defense counsel experienced in criminal cases would have indulged in all the extended cross-examination of the government agents without appreciation of the involved. His hope of finding some inconsistencies in the evidence must have been tempered by knowledge of the risk of turning up something he would not like. But in any event the sound general principle that a litigant cannot object to, or secure a mistrial for, evidence he himself produces cannot be controlled by the degree of naivete or sophistication of counsel. So far as the prosecution is concerned, there is nothing remotely to suggest impropriety on the part of the United States Attorney or indeed on the part of the witness unless answering responsively to a direct question can be so termed. But further, the implication that somehow the testimony should be geared to the defendant's objections is surely a dangerous one. It is hard to see how reversal here can be had without the implication that testimony should be manipulated, the last thing this court should even suggest.'

Questions

1. To what extent was the court's ruling affected by the fact that the challenged testimony was elicited on cross-examination by the defense attorney rather than on direct by the prosecutor?
2. What does this case tell us about the care that must be taken in eliciting information from an opposing witness through aggressive questioning?

Leading Questions

A **leading question** is a question that implies the answer the examining attorney wants the witness to give. Rule 611(c) does not allow leading questions during direct examination unless they are necessary to develop the witness' testimony.

Here are some examples of leading questions:

- Mrs. Henderson, isn't it true that your light didn't turn yellow until after you had already entered the intersection?

LEARNING OBJECTIVE 3
Illustrate leading questions and explain when they are permitted.

leading question
A question that implies the answer the examining party wishes the witness to give.

- Mr. Barnes, when you signed this agreement, you didn't expect the dollar amounts to be changed without your consent, did you?
- So, Miss Lane, when the defendant attacked you, you screamed and then you began to run, is that correct?

A question that requires a yes-or-no answer is not necessarily leading as long as it does not suggest what that answer should be. The question "You saw the defendant running from the parking lot, didn't you?" is leading, because it is clear that examining attorney wants the witness to answer "yes". The question "Did you see the defendant running from the parking lot?" is not leading, because the witness could answer "yes" or "no" depending on what he/she recalls, and there is nothing in the question's phrasing that would indicate which answer is desired.

The Hostile Witness

hostile witness
A witness whose sympathies lie with the party opposing the one who called the witness.

Rule 611(c) allows leading questions to be used on direct examination when examining a **hostile witness**. A hostile witness is one whose sympathies lie with the other side from the one examining him/her. The mother, father, or sibling of a defendant being called as a prosecution witness would be an example of a hostile witness. The examining party must lay a foundation by providing facts showing that the witness is hostile.

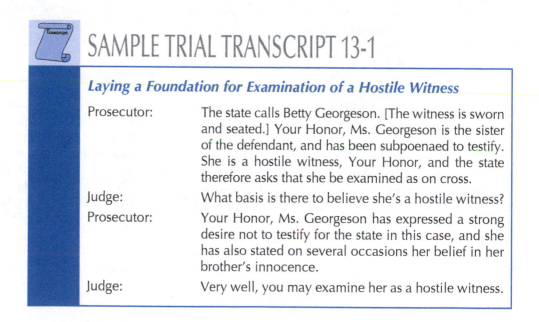

SAMPLE TRIAL TRANSCRIPT 13-1

Laying a Foundation for Examination of a Hostile Witness

Prosecutor:	The state calls Betty Georgeson. [The witness is sworn and seated.] Your Honor, Ms. Georgeson is the sister of the defendant, and has been subpoenaed to testify. She is a hostile witness, Your Honor, and the state therefore asks that she be examined as on cross.
Judge:	What basis is there to believe she's a hostile witness?
Prosecutor:	Your Honor, Ms. Georgeson has expressed a strong desire not to testify for the state in this case, and she has also stated on several occasions her belief in her brother's innocence.
Judge:	Very well, you may examine her as a hostile witness.

Once the decision is made that the witness is hostile, the party calling the witness may examine her with leading questions. The same rule applies if the witness is an opposing party or identified with an opposing party.

Assumption of Facts Not in Evidence

Many times, a question asked by an examiner must be based on facts that are implied in the question but not part of the question itself. An example would be, "Could you please tell the jury what you were doing at your house on the morning of September 5?" This question assumes that the witness was at his/her house on the morning of September 5. If a question assumes facts that are not already in evidence, opposing counsel can object, at which time the questioning attorney would be required to lay a foundation for the question by proving the facts that the question assumes. If the attorney cannot do so, then the question will not be permitted.

Unresponsive Answers

When a witness is examined, he/she must answer the questions put to him/her. When a witness fails to provide the answer a question calls for, or tries to provide information the question does not call for, the answer is **unresponsive**. If a witness gives an unresponsive answer, first the attorney and then the judge will instruct the witness to give an answer that is responsive.

LEARNING OBJECTIVE 4
Know how to address unresponsive answers and questions that assume facts not in evidence.

unresponsive answer
An answer to a question that does not address the substance of the question.

SAMPLE TRIAL TRANSCRIPT 13-2

Unresponsive Answer

Attorney:	Mr. Pickering, did you sign the lease?
Witness:	I talked to the landlord about it.
Attorney:	That wasn't my question, Mr. Pickering. I asked if you signed it.
Witness:	I told the landlord I wasn't going to sign until we discussed the rent.
Attorney:	Objection, Your Honor, the witness is being unresponsive.
Judge:	Mr. Pickering, please answer the question the attorney has asked you. Did you sign the lease?
Witness:	Yes, I did.

When a witness' unresponsive answer contains information that does not belong in front of a jury, the attorney asking the questions can also make a motion to strike the improper evidence from the record.

SAMPLE TRIAL TRANSCRIPT 13-3

Unresponsive Answer with Characterization

Attorney:	Mr. Pickering, did you sign the lease?
Witness:	I wanted to talk to that idiot of a landlord first.
Attorney:	Your Honor, objection, the witness is unresponsive, and I move to strike the characterization of my client as an idiot.
Judge:	Granted. The jury is instructed to disregard the characterization. Mr. Pickering, restrict your answers to the questions you are asked.
Witness:	Yes, I signed the lease.

A response to an open-ended question, one which calls for a narration from the witness, is only unresponsive if it ventures into areas not covered by the question.

SAMPLE TRIAL TRANSCRIPT 13-4

Unresponsive Answer with Incompetent Testimony

Attorney:	After you met with the defendant, what did you do?
Witness:	I went to the store to do some shopping, because I wanted to get my mind off the fight. I didn't know it, but the defendant had gone straight back to my house.
Opposing attorney:	Objection, not responsive and not competent.
Judge:	Sustained.
Attorney:	Please, I only asked you what you did, not what the defendant did.
Witness:	OK, I went to the store.
Attorney:	Now, when you returned home, was the defendant there?
Witness:	Yes.

Notice that the opposing counsel in this example raised two objections: unresponsiveness and incompetence. The witness admitted that the defendant's return to her house occurred when she wasn't there, so she wasn't competent to testify about that. She was competent to testify as to what she saw when she returned home. The jury could then infer that the defendant went to the witness' home while she was shopping, but the witness could not testify to that.

Sequestration

LEARNING OBJECTIVE 5
Explain the sequestration of witnesses and when it is necessary.

sequestration
The exclusion of a witness from the courtroom while another witness is testifying.

There are times when it is necessary to prevent one witness from hearing another witness' testimony. This often happens when the testimony of one witness might color or influence the testimony of another. Rule 615 authorizes the exclusion, or **sequestration**, of witnesses, which means that the witness who is not testifying at the moment is taken from the courtroom so that he/she cannot hear the testimony of another witness.

There are three exceptions to the court's power to sequester witnesses. First, a party who is a natural person (as opposed to a corporation or governmental body), and the parent or guardian of a minor who is a party, cannot be sequestered. Where a party is a corporation or similar entity, and a real person has been appointed as that entity's representative at trial, that person cannot be sequestered, either. Finally, a person whose presence in the courtroom is essential to the presentation of the party's case cannot be sequestered. An example would be an expert witness whose opinion testimony is going to be based on the testimony of another witness.

LEARNING OBJECTIVE 6
Define credibility and explain how it is determined by a jury.

■ CREDIBILITY

The *credibility* of a witness is one of the key elements in determining how much weight to give to a witness' testimony. If a witness is not credible, then his/her testimony, even if admissible, will have no influence on the jury's decision. "Credibility" is not simply a matter of whether a piece of evidence can be believed by the jury; it is a question of whether a piece of evidence will be believed by the jury. How do juries decide what to believe and what not to?

Every time a person is exposed to a statement of fact, he/she makes an assessment of whether or not he/she will believe it. People who believe everything they are told are called gullible; people who refuse to believe anything they are told are called cynical. Most of us lie somewhere in between. We don't necessarily take everyone's word for everything, but we don't believe everyone is lying, either. We decide whether to believe someone based on many factors, such as how well we know him/her, whether he/she has lied to us in the past, whether he/she can look us in the eye when he/she speaks, whether what he/she is saying makes sense to us, and whether what he/she is saying conforms to our own experiences.

A jury functions in pretty much the same way. The only factor that is usually not available to a jury is direct prior experience with the witness. After all, potential jurors who know the parties or key witnesses are not permitted to sit as jurors. Otherwise, jurors decide who and what to believe in a courtroom based on the same factors all of us use in our everyday lives. There is no magic formula to credibility; it is a matter of what the jury thinks is credible.

The factors that affect credibility can generally be reduced to three categories: reasonableness, consistency, and demeanor.

Reasonableness

In order for a jury to find evidence credible, the members have to find it sensible. If someone's testimony doesn't make sense, it won't be believed no matter how well it is presented.

Consider the testimony in Sample Trial Transcript 13-5, and ask yourself if it makes sense to you.

 SAMPLE TRIAL TRANSCRIPT 13-5

Unreasonable Testimony

Attorney:	Mr. Kent, what happened on the night of February 3?
Witness:	Well, I had just finished doing a few laps around the pool, and I got out and began toweling off. My girlfriend came outside and told me my mother was on the phone. So I picked it up and she started telling me that my dad was in the hospital and probably going to die that night. After that, I went out to dinner with my girlfriend, and then we stopped by the hospital, but dad was already in a coma by that point, so I went home and waited for Mom to call again. She never did. I found out later that Dad died that night, and I was really upset that she didn't call and tell me when it happened.

There are a few things about Mr. Kent's testimony that simply don't make sense. First, it doesn't seem reasonable that someone who just found out his father was dying would go to dinner with his girlfriend before he went to the hospital. It also doesn't make sense that the witness would leave the hospital while his dad was in a coma. These things do not conform to our own experience and certainly wouldn't seem reasonable to the average person.

But suppose the witness hated his father? Then his story would make sense, wouldn't it? But if that were true, why was he upset that his mother didn't call him when his father passed away? Why would he have gone to the hospital at all if that was his attitude? We can explain some aspects of the story, but taken together the story just doesn't make sense.

The testimony also contains a factual inconsistency. Supposedly, Mr. Kent took the call immediately after getting out of his swimming pool, outdoors, at night on February 3. Unless Mr. Kent lives in a climate where it is warm enough to swim in the dead of winter, this part of his story is clearly not credible.

It is entirely possible that Mr. Kent was being perfectly truthful when he told this story. But the average juror is going to have a hard time believing it, because so many elements of it run counter to common sense. An attorney who wishes the jury to believe this story is going to have to anticipate the problems and ask additional questions to explain away the contradictions if he wants the jury to accept the story as credible.

Consistency

Even when evidence seems perfectly reasonable, the jury may not believe it if it is inconsistent. There are two kinds of inconsistency: internal and external. Internal inconsistency means that a witness' testimony contradicts itself. External inconsistency means that it contradicts other evidence. In either case, a witness' credibility is going to be damaged unless the inconsistency is satisfactorily explained.

Internal inconsistency does more damage to a witness' testimony than external inconsistency because regardless of which of the inconsistent parts of the witness' testimony is true, we know who lied. Where two witnesses contradict one another, the jury has to make a decision as to which one is credible and which one is not.

Where a witness' testimony is internally inconsistent, it is often a mistake for opposing counsel to point out the inconsistency during the testimony, because it simply gives the witness the chance to explain it. And once explained, it is no longer an inconsistency.

SAMPLE TRIAL TRANSCRIPT 13-6

Explaining an Internal Inconsistency

Prosecutor (examining the defendant's mother):	Mrs. Herbert, you stated earlier that your son is a very conscientious young man who cared deeply about his family.
Witness:	That's exactly right. He is.

Prosecutor:	You also testified just now that your son failed to attend his own father's funeral, and in fact didn't call you for two weeks after his father's death.
Witness:	That's right.
Prosecutor:	So it is your testimony that a son who cares about his family would not only fail to attend his father's funeral, but also be completely out of touch for two weeks afterward?
Witness:	I didn't tell him his father died because I didn't think he could handle it emotionally so soon after his wife left him, so I kept it from him until two weeks after the funeral. He was furious with me for that, but I think I did the right thing.

As Sample Trial Transcript 13-6 makes clear, the credibility of a witness can easily be restored if an apparent inconsistency is explained to reconcile the inconsistency.

Demeanor

The aspect of credibility that captures the most attention of those who study law, and has perhaps the most profound if subtle effect on a juror, is the **demeanor** of the witness: his/her mannerisms, voice, gestures, expressions, eye contact, and so on. Some of the ways a person can nonverbally communicate a lack of credibility are nervousness, an inability to make eye contact, stammering, stuttering, repetition, defensiveness, anger, trembling, an uncharacteristic softness of voice, and an inability to sit still.

Of course, testifying in open court is a very nerve-wracking experience. It is difficult to tell whether a witness is nervous because he/she is lying, or just from the stress of testifying. Determining credibility from nonverbal signals is more art than science, and a perfectly truthful witness who happens to present poorly can end up not being believed over a pathological liar who is smooth in his/her demeanor and delivery. For this reason, attorneys devote much time and attention to preparing their witnesses for trial, which is discussed below.

demeanor
Nonverbal indicators of credibility.

Deference in Matters of Credibility

Trial transcripts contain nothing but the words spoken during the trial. This means that the nonverbal aspects of testimony used by the jury to assess credibility are not part of the record, and cannot, therefore, be evaluated after the trial is over. For this reason, a jury is given a wide degree of **deference** in matters of credibility. Deference means allowing a decision to rest within someone else's discretion, and not questioning it after it is made. While a jury is not permitted to make a decision that is not supported by the evidence, which evidence the jury chooses to believe or disbelieve will not be questioned by either the trial judge or any court on appeal.

When a trial judge or an appellate court reviews a jury's verdict to see if it is supported by the evidence, it assumes that all of the evidence that supports the verdict was found credible, and all of the evidence that

deference
In the context of credibility, the reluctance of a court to interfere with a jury's assessment of a witness' credibility.

would have dictated a different verdict was found not credible. If there is enough evidence in the record to support the verdict as a matter of law, then the jury's verdict will stand. The verdict will not be questioned simply because the trial judge believed a witness where the jury did not, or vice versa.

From a practical standpoint, this means that the focus of a witness' credibility must be on the jury. It makes no difference to the outcome of a trial if a judge finds a witness credible; all that matters is whether the jury does. Those who have attended trials know that the attention of a witness and a questioning attorney is always on the jury during questioning, and witnesses are often advised to speak directly to the jury when answering questions, so the jury can get a sense that the witness is being forthright.

■ IMPEACHMENT OF WITNESSES

LEARNING OBJECTIVE 7
List and define the various methods of impeaching and rehabilitating witnesses.

impeachment
The production of evidence demonstrating that a witness is not credible.

Although the jury is solely empowered to decide whether a witness is credible, the party opposing the witness can help the jury make that decision by presenting evidence that impeaches the witness. **Impeachment** means presenting evidence that tends to prove that the witness is not credible. Just because a witness is impeached does not mean that the jury will not believe the witness. It simply means that evidence has been presented attacking the witness' credibility.

Rule 607 provides that any party may attack the credibility of a witness, including the party who called the witness. Why would a party impeach its own witness? The usual reason is because the witness has given testimony that contradicts what the party expected or wanted the witness to say. This possibility is particularly problematic when the witness is hostile, as Sample Trial Transcript 13-7 shows.

Note that the prosecutor in this example is not trying to prove that *everything* Mrs. Herbert said during her direct testimony was untrue. In other words, he is not trying to impeach her credibility generally, but only with

To win a case, it is not enough to present the jury with testimony. A lawyer must also convince the jury that those witnesses can be believed.
Source: https://us.fotolia.com/id/77202442?by=serie.

SAMPLE TRIAL TRANSCRIPT 13-7

Impeachment of Own Witness

Prosecutor (direct examining the defendant's mother):	Mrs. Herbert, you told the police officer at the scene that your son was wearing a leather jacket when he left the house, is that correct?
Witness:	No, I didn't. He doesn't even own a leather jacket.
Prosecutor:	You didn't tell that to the police officer?
Witness:	No.

[Later, the prosecutor calls the arresting officer.]

Prosecutor:	Officer Bainbridge, did you interview the defendant's mother, Mrs. Herbert, on the night of the robbery?
Witness:	Yes.
Prosecutor:	And did Mrs. Herbert tell you at that time what the defendant was wearing?
Witness:	Yes. She told me he was wearing a black leather jacket, jeans, and white sneakers when he left her house that night.
Prosecutor:	Was that the source of the description of the suspect's clothing that appears in your report?
Witness:	Yes.
Prosecutor:	How do you know that's what the witness told you?
Witness:	I wrote it down as she told me, and then repeated it to her word for word, and she confirmed that it was an accurate description.

respect to the specific testimony regarding her statements about her son's clothing. Note also that the impeachment of Mrs. Herbert's testimony is conditioned upon the credibility of Officer Bainbridge. If the defense can impeach the officer's credibility, then the impeachment of Mrs. Herbert might be less effective.

Grounds for Impeachment

As a general rule, any evidence that tends to prove or disprove a witness' credibility is relevant. The Rules of Evidence discuss several specific methods of impeaching a witness' credibility.

Reputation or Opinion Evidence (Rule 608)

As you learned in Chapter 9, reputation and opinion evidence are relevant if they relate to a witness' credibility. This is one of the ways impeachment can occur: by having someone testify about the witness' reputation for dishonesty, or his or her own opinion about the witness' dishonesty based on personal experience.

SAMPLE TRIAL TRANSCRIPT 13-8

Reputation for Dishonesty

Defense:	Mr. Bain, you live in the same community as Mr. Harforth, the man who testified earlier, is that correct?
Witness:	Yes, I live right down the street from him.
Defense:	How long have you lived in that community?
Witness:	All my life.
Defense:	Can you tell the jury what Mr. Harforth's reputation is in your community? Is he generally considered to be an honest man?
Witness:	Well, no, not really. I mean, most of the people around there don't really trust him.
Defense:	Have you personally known Mr. Harforth?
Witness:	Yeah, I've known him for years.
Defense:	What is your opinion of his honesty?
Witness:	I guess I feel the same way everyone else does. He just isn't a very honest person.

Under Rule 608(a), once the testimony of Mr. Bain attacking Mr. Harforth's credibility has been placed on the record, this opens the door to any reputation or opinion evidence the prosecutor may want to produce showing that Mr. Harforth is honest.

Rule 608(b) also provides for evidence of specific instances of noncriminal conduct to prove the untruthfulness of a witness. (Criminal convictions are covered under Rule 609, discussed below.) Such evidence is not admissible except during cross-examination of the witness whose credibility is being impeached, or another witness whose direct testimony included opinion or reputation evidence about the witness' character.

As Court Opinion 13-2 shows, a defendant who takes the stand on his/her own behalf is subjected to the same methods of impeachment testimony as any other witness.

COURT OPINION 13-2

UNITED STATES V. LOLLAR, 606 F.2D 587 (5TH CIR. 1979)

Howard Lollar appeals from his conviction for interstate transportation of stolen property valued in excess of $5,000, 18 U.S.C.A. s 2314. The property was alleged to have been stolen by appellant and several of his employees from a warehouse in West Milford, New Jersey. We affirm.

After appellant testified at trial, the government recalled one of its witnesses and asked him whether he would believe appellant under oath. Defense counsel's objection was overruled, and the witness, a former employer, answered the question in the negative. Appellant now argues that it was error to allow the witness to offer his opinion on appellant's veracity.

Although a criminal defendant cannot be compelled to take the stand in his own defense, once he

(continued)

(continued)

chooses to testify "he places his credibility in issue as does any other witness." *United States v. Jackson*, 588 F.2d 1046, 1055 (5th Cir. 1979). . . . While the defendant's decision to testify does not open the door to attacks on his general character, it does free the government to offer evidence bearing on the defendant's believability as a witness. Historically, the most widely used method of impeaching a defendant's credibility was to call witnesses to testify that the defendant's reputation for truth and veracity was bad. The propriety of asking a more direct question, such as "would you believe this person under oath," caused a great deal of conflict among the courts and the commentators. Early cases in this Circuit adopted the position that such testimony could be used to impeach a witness' credibility. See Miller v. United States, 288 F. 816, 818 (5th Cir. 1923); Held v. United States, 260 F. 932, 933 (5th Cir. 1919). While this was the minority view among the courts, many commentators agreed that "the exclusion of opinion evidence was 'historically unsound'." 3 Weinstein's Evidence 608[04%], at 608–20 (1978); See McCormick, Evidence s 44, at 95 (1954); 7 Wigmore, Evidence ss 1981–1986 (3d ed. 1940); Ladd, Techniques of Character Testimony, 24 Iowa L. Rev. 498, 509–13 (1939). This conflict was resolved in 1976 with the enactment of Rule 608(a) of the Federal Rules of Evidence. Recognizing that "witnesses who testify to reputation seem in fact often to be giving their opinions, disguised somewhat misleadingly as reputation," Advisory Committee's Notes, Fed.R.Evid. 608(a), Rule 608(a)

provides that the credibility of a witness may be attacked "by evidence in the form of Opinion or reputation", Fed.R.Evid. 608(a) (emphasis added). While it may be more desirable to have counsel first ask the impeaching witness about his knowledge of the defendant's reputation for truth and veracity, and whether based on that knowledge he would believe the defendant under oath, Rule 608(a) imposes no such requirement:

> Witnesses may now be asked directly to state their opinion of the principal witness' character for truthfulness and they may answer for example, "I think X is a liar." The rule imposes no prerequisite conditioned upon long acquaintance or recent information about the witness; cross-examination can be expected to expose defects of lack of familiarity and to reveal reliance on isolated or irrelevant instances of misconduct or the existence of feelings of personal hostility towards the principal witness.

Weinstein's Evidence 608(04), at 608–20 (1978).

Accordingly, we hold that the district court was acting well within its discretion in overruling defense counsel's objection.

Questions

1. How would the prosecutor's ability to present a character witness against the defendant have been limited if the defendant had chosen not to testify?
2. Did the court approve or disapprove of the manner in which the prosecutor elicited character evidence to impeach the defendant?

Evidence of Criminal Conviction (Rule 609)

A criminal conviction of a witness can be used to impeach the witness' credibility in two instances under Rule 609. First, the conviction is admissible against any witness other than the defendant if it was punishable by death or imprisonment for more than one year. Second, a prior conviction for any crime can be admitted to impeach the defendant if proving the offense required showing a dishonest act or a false statement, so long as the probative value of the evidence in proving the defendant's dishonesty is not outweighed by the prejudicial effect of such evidence. With regard to this second provision, a conviction for murder or rape would not be admissible to impeach the defendant because those crimes do not involve falsity. A conviction for perjury, fraud, or embezzlement would be admissible. Rule 609 also limits such evidence if the conviction is more than 10 years old, if it has been nullified by pardon, annulment, or certification of rehabilitation, or if the conviction was obtained in juvenile proceedings, but not if the conviction is, at the time of trial, being appealed.

Religious Beliefs or Opinions (Rule 610)

Under Rule 610, religious beliefs or opinions cannot be used as a basis for impeachment or to support the credibility of a witness. Religious beliefs can, however, be introduced where they constitute substantive evidence of the defendant's guilt or relate to an issue other than credibility (see *United States v. Goxcon-Chagal*, 885 F.Supp.2d 1118 (D.N.M. 2012), *rev'd on other grounds*, *United States v. Medina-Copete*, 757 F.3d 1092 (10th Cir. 2014) (holding that Rule 610 did not prohibit the introduction of evidence that a drug dealer venerated and prayed to the alleged "narco-saint" Santa Muerte)).

Prior Inconsistent Statements (Rule 613)

prior inconsistent statements
Statements made by a witness prior to trial that contradict the witness' testimony.

Rule 613 permits the impeachment of a witness by using **prior statements inconsistent** with the witness' testimony on the stand. Recall that prior inconsistent statements are an exception to the Hearsay Rule that applies only when the witness testified at trial.

Prior inconsistent statements can be introduced in two ways. First, the witness himself/herself may be asked to acknowledge the prior inconsistent statement. In such a case, Rule 613 places no limitations on questioning, and does not require that the statement be in writing or that it be presented to the witness when he/she is being questioned. Upon request, the statement must be produced to opposing counsel, however.

Sample Trial Transcript 13-9 shows how evidence of a prior inconsistent statement might be introduced.

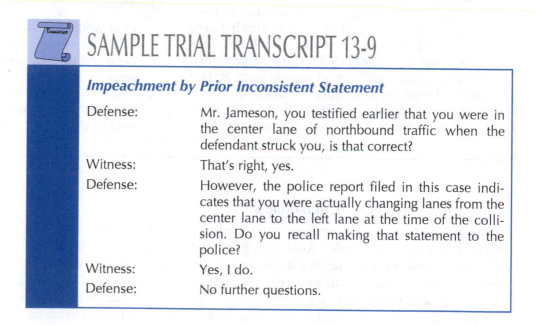

SAMPLE TRIAL TRANSCRIPT 13-9

Impeachment by Prior Inconsistent Statement

Defense:	Mr. Jameson, you testified earlier that you were in the center lane of northbound traffic when the defendant struck you, is that correct?
Witness:	That's right, yes.
Defense:	However, the police report filed in this case indicates that you were actually changing lanes from the center lane to the left lane at the time of the collision. Do you recall making that statement to the police?
Witness:	Yes, I do.
Defense:	No further questions.

Notice that the attorney here is not giving the witness the chance to explain the inconsistency. Had the witness tried to explain, then his testimony would have been objected to on the grounds that it was unresponsive. A "yes" or "no" question calls for nothing more than a "yes" or "no" answer. The prosecutor would, no doubt, elicit an explanation of the inconsistency on redirect examination.

The second way to introduce a prior inconsistent statement is through extrinsic evidence, which means the testimony of another witness or the introduction of a document containing the statement. Such evidence is admissible under Rule 613 only if the witness is given the opportunity to explain or deny the making of the statement.

In Sample Trial Transcript 13-9, suppose that Mr. Jameson denied making a contrary statement to the police. The defense attorney would then have to introduce the statement itself in order to impeach the witness, as shown in Sample Trial Transcript 13-10.

SAMPLE TRIAL TRANSCRIPT 13-10

Impeachment by Extrinsic Evidence of Prior Inconsistent Statement

Attorney:	Do you recall making that statement to the police?
Witness:	No, that's not what I told them.
Attorney:	Mr. Jameson, I am showing you a document that has been marked as Exhibit "C" and already introduced, which is the police report I am referring to. Would you please read the highlighted portion of that document?
Witness:	Certainly. It says, "W2 stated he was crossing from center to left lane when collision occurred."
Attorney:	And does the report indicate who W2 is?
Witness:	Yes, it's me.
Attorney:	Can you explain why you told the police that you were crossing from the center lane to the left lane when you were hit?
Witness:	I told them that because I had just started crossing over. I had my turn signal on and had just begun to make the change, but I was still in the center lane when I was hit.
Attorney:	No further questions.

Obviously, the impact of this testimony on the credibility of the witness is much less than if the witness simply admitted he made the inconsistent statement as in the first example.

Additional Grounds for Impeachment

In addition to the specific grounds set forth in Article VI of the Rules of Evidence, other grounds for impeachment are commonly used. These include establishing bias or prejudice on the part of a witness, or demonstrating that the witness was unable to observe the events about which he/she testified.

Bias or Prejudice. A person can be **biased** or **prejudiced** for or against a party for a number of reasons. These reasons can include demographic characteristics such as race, gender, and ethnicity. They can also include family connections, prior relationships, or any other factor that could color a witness' testimony or his/her perception or interpretation of events.

bias
The inclination of a witness to testify favorably toward one party.

prejudice
The inclination of a witness to testify unfavorably toward one party.

Bias or prejudice can be proven in a number of ways, but the most powerful is to have the witness admit the bias or prejudice on the witness stand. The witness' statements of bias or prejudice can also be used, but since they are being offered to prove that the witness is, in fact, biased or prejudiced, they must fall within one of the exceptions to the Hearsay Rule. Reputation evidence would not be admissible to prove bias or prejudice, because there is nothing inherently dishonest about holding a bias or prejudice.

Sample Trial Transcript 13-11 demonstrates how a witness might be impeached in this way. A mother is being cross-examined after testifying on behalf of the defense at her daughter's trial for assaulting her ex-husband.

SAMPLE TRIAL TRANSCRIPT 13-11

Bias and Prejudice

Attorney:	Mrs. Bouvier, you love your daughter, don't you?
Witness:	Absolutely.
Attorney:	And you wish to see your daughter found not guilty in this case?
Witness:	Of course.
Attorney:	You stated earlier in your testimony that you considered your son-in-law to be a, quote, "drunken slob", is that correct?
Witness:	That's right.
Attorney:	And you used that term in light of the fact that your son-in-law doesn't abstain from alcohol?
Witness:	Virtuous men don't drink alcohol. It's the devil's drink.
Attorney:	So you believe that anyone who does drink isn't virtuous?
Witness:	Yes.
Attorney:	You weren't happy when you learned your daughter was marrying a man who didn't abstain from alcohol?
Witness:	I think she could have done better, yes.
Attorney:	By marrying a teetotaler?
Witness:	Yes.
Attorney:	No further questions.

This questioning effectively challenged the witnesses' credibility in two ways: by showing that she was biased toward her daughter, and that she was prejudiced against her son-in-law because he drank alcohol. A jury may not discredit all of her testimony because of these two facts, but they do make it appear that the woman's perspective is colored by factors having nothing to do with the actual case.

Inability to Observe.   Despite the focus in impeachment testimony on truthfulness in general, impeachment often involves the question of whether the witness was merely mistaken rather than lying. A jury is not going to believe mistaken testimony any more than testimony that is deliberately fabricated.

A witness can be impeached by evidence of conditions that would have made it difficult or impossible for the witness to observe what he/she is describing in his/her testimony. If the witness is describing something he/she saw, the witness can be impeached by showing that he/she has poor eyesight or that there was an obstacle in the way. If the witness' testimony is aural in nature, proving the existence of other noises or poor hearing could show that the witness did not hear what he/she thought he/she heard, or at least did not hear it as well as he/she thinks.

Sample Trial Transcript 13-12 demonstrates this impeachment method where a witness is being questioned about a conversation he overheard between the defendant, charged with rape, and his friend.

 ## SAMPLE TRIAL TRANSCRIPT 13-12

Inability to Observe

Attorney:	Mr. Watson, you testified that you were sitting next to the defendant when you heard him say he raped Miss DeLane?
Witness:	Right next to him, yes.
Attorney:	How crowded was the bar that night?
Witness:	It was a pretty good crowd. It was Saturday night.
Attorney:	Was there a lot of noise from the crowd?
Witness:	It gets pretty loud, yes.
Attorney:	But you testified that the defendant was speaking softly to his friend, is that correct?
Witness:	Well, he wasn't shouting.
Attorney:	Your exact words were: "He was whispering so I could barely hear him." Isn't that correct?
Witness:	Yes, I said that. But. . . .
Attorney:	Just answer the question I ask, Mr. Watson. Now were you leaning toward the defendant at the time he said those words?
Witness:	Leaning? No, I was just sitting there. I don't normally listen in to other people's conversations.
Attorney:	You were with a date that night, weren't you?
Witness:	Yes, I was.
Attorney:	And she was sitting next to you?
Witness:	Yes.
Attorney:	Were the two of you engaged in conversation?
Witness:	Well, yeah. It was a little hard to talk with all the noise, but we were talking. Sometimes, we'd just sit there and watch the game on the TV above the bar.
Attorney:	So the TV was on, too. Was the sound turned up?
Witness:	Yeah, you could hear it a little. Not much.
Attorney:	Thank you, Mr. Watson. No further questions.

This attorney effectively demonstrated to the jury, each of whom had probably been in a crowded, noisy bar at some point, that the witness would have had a very difficult time hearing the defendant's confession to his friend in the environment he was in.

Rehabilitation.   Once a witness' credibility has been impeached, it is the job of the attorney who called the witness (assuming he/she isn't the one who impeached the witness) to **rehabilitate** the witness. In other words, the witness' credibility must be re-established. This can be done in one of the following ways:

rehabilitation
The production of evidence to re-establish the credibility of an impeached witness.

1. Having the witness explain any inconsistency in his/her testimony.
2. Introducing a prior consistent statement to counteract the effect of a prior inconsistent statement, which statement must have been made *after* the prior inconsistent statement used to impeach the witness.
3. Impeaching the impeachment witness by any method discussed above.
4. Presenting reputation or opinion evidence or instances of specific conduct showing that the witness is trustworthy.

As was noted above, impeachment is not a sure thing. There is no guarantee that the jury will fail to believe a witness whose credibility has been attacked. If the impeachment evidence is weak, and the attorney who is depending on the witness believes that the witness' credibility is still intact, rehabilitation may not be necessary. In the same way, there is no guarantee that rehabilitation will work, either. The bottom line is that credibility lies within the minds of the jurors. All the attorneys can do is give the jury reasons to either believe or not believe the witness.

■ PRESERVATION OF TESTIMONY

Because testimony is susceptible to loss through death or loss of memory, it is important to preserve testimony as soon as possible after a crime occurs. The most effective way, and from a constitutional standpoint the only way, to preserve oral testimony is through the taking of a witness' deposition.

Before explaining what a deposition is, it is necessary to point out why it is necessary. The Sixth Amendment of the U.S. Constitution, and most state constitutions, grants to the defendant in a criminal case the right to confront witnesses against him/her, and the right to cross-examine those witnesses. These rights are crucial to the underlying idea that the truth can only be determined through a thorough testing of a witness' memory and perceptions by the adversarial process.

A deposition is the questioning of a witness under oath by the prosecuting and defense attorneys, with a written, word-for-word transcript of that testimony being made for future use. Because both parties have the opportunity to participate in the examination of the witness, a deposition will generally be held to meet the Sixth Amendment requirement of confrontation and cross-examination. This is, therefore, the only constitutionally permissible means of preserving testimony.

Federal Rule of Criminal Procedure 15 permits depositions to be taken "in order to preserve testimony at trial," and only where such a deposition is justified "because of exceptional circumstances and in the interests of justice." This rule distinguishes depositions in criminal trials from the more common discovery depositions taken in civil trials, which are taken as a matter of course to determine what relevant information the witness possesses. In such depositions, it does not matter if the witness will be available to testify at trial; in fact, witnesses in civil cases are regularly deposed on the assumption that they *will* testify. Rule 15 is much more limiting, permitting depositions solely to *preserve* the testimony of witnesses who are unavailable to appear at trial.

The unavailability of a witness can occur for a number of reasons. A witness who has died or who is physically unable to come to court is an obvious example. Witnesses can also be unavailable if they refuse to testify and there is no legal means to force them to do so. In *United States* v. *Allie*, for example, three Mexican defendants who were in the United States illegally were required to be released from custody prior to the trial of the man charged with harboring them. In light of their imminent release from custody, the trial judge allowed the prosecutors to depose the three witnesses. The men were voluntarily deported to Mexico, but given permission to return to testify at the trial, and repeatedly assured the prosecutor that they would do so. They failed to show, and the court allowed their depositions to be used in lieu of their testimony at trial, a decision upheld by the Fifth Circuit Court of Appeals (*United States* v. *Allie*, 978 F.2d 1401 (5th Cir. 1992)).

Generally, courts will not permit the deposition of a witness in a criminal case in order to preserve that witness' testimony for trial unless there is good reason to believe that the witness will not be available to appear at trial in person. In the following case, the Supreme Court of Appeals of West Virginia had to decide whether a defendant would be permitted to take the deposition of a key witness who had been uncooperative in speaking with the defendant's attorney. The standards for depositions under West Virginia rules of court were very similar to those contained in F.R.Crim.P. 15.

COURT OPINION 13-3

STATE EX REL. SPAULDING V. WATT, 186 W.VA. 125, 411 S.E.2D 450 (1991)

[T]he . . . Prosecuting Attorney of Putnam County, seeks to prevent the respondent judge from requiring a potential witness for the State in a criminal prosecution to give a deposition to the defense. We find that the court exceeded its legitimate powers in ordering the deposition, and we grant the writ of prohibition prayed for.

The defendant below, Michael B. Pauley, was indicted in the Circuit Court of Putnam County on a charge of first-degree murder in connection with the August 29, 1990 death of James C. Lewis. The defendant had previously dated the decedent's granddaughter, Angela Lewis.

On January 17, 1991, the defendant filed a motion to compel Ms. Lewis to give a deposition to the defense. The motion stated that Ms. Lewis had refused to speak to defense counsel or his private investigator and had failed to appear at the preliminary hearing. The defense asserted that Ms. Lewis would be similarly "unavailable" for trial and sought a deposition for discovery purposes, apparently on the ground that the State had failed to obtain a detailed statement from her concerning her relationship with the defendant.

After a hearing, the circuit court, by order dated July 15, 1991, granted the motion. The prosecuting attorney subsequently instituted these proceedings to prevent enforcement of the circuit court's order.

Rule 15 of the West Virginia Rules of Criminal Procedure permits a deposition to be compelled in a criminal case only under very limited conditions, i.e., where, due to exceptional circumstances, the deposition is necessary, in the interest of justice, to preserve the deponent's testimony for use at trial. Our rule is patterned after Rule 15 of the Federal Rules of Criminal Procedure. There is virtual unanimity in federal cases that Rule 15 authorizes a court to order a deposition only when the witness is unavailable for trial and the deposition is needed to preserve the testimony for trial. [case citations omitted]

(continued)

(continued)

In *State v. Ferrell*, 174 W.Va. 697, 699, 329 S.E.2d 62, 64 (1985), we quoted from *United States v. Rich*, 580 F.2d 929, 934 (9th Cir.), *cert. denied*, 439 U.S. 935, 99 S.Ct. 330, 58 L.Ed.2d 331 (1978), where the court held that the exceptional circumstances which justify a court-ordered deposition were limited to criminal cases where the witness is unable to attend trial and stated that "'the rule contemplates a party taking the deposition of only his own witness, a requirement that comports with the purpose of preserving testimony.'" We have made similar statements about Rule 15 in other cases. [citations omitted]

In *Ferrell*, we also recognized that Rule 15 must be considered in the light of W.Va.Code, 62-3-1 (1981). The purpose of this provision, which lists some of the reasons for a court-ordered deposition, such as where a witness is aged or infirm or absent from the state, is to preserve testimony which the court has found to be "necessary and material" at trial.

In this case, the circuit court did not elaborate upon its reasons for ordering Ms. Lewis to submit to the defense deposition. There is, however, no showing that Ms. Lewis will be unavailable for trial. The fact that she was unwilling to talk to the defendant's attorney or investigator is not, alone, sufficient to authorize a court-ordered deposition under Rule 15 and W.Va.Code, 62-3-1. Moreover, it appears that the State had turned over to the defendant's attorney two written statements it had obtained from Ms. Lewis and that she had been interviewed by a private psychiatrist retained by the defendant. In light of these facts, we find no justification for the circuit court's order compelling Ms. Lewis to submit to the deposition.

Questions

1. For what reasons may a defendant take the deposition of his/her own witness?
2. Why did the court conclude that Ms. Lewis was not "unavailable" to testify despite the fact that she was not willing to talk to the defendant's attorney?

■ DISCLOSURE OF WITNESS STATEMENTS

Under Federal Rule of Criminal Procedure 26.2, the prosecutor and defense both have an obligation to disclose, when ordered, any written statement or contemporaneous recording of an oral statement of a witness other than the defendant who has testified on direct examination at trial, at a hearing on a motion to suppress, and, under certain circumstances, at a preliminary hearing and hearings relating to sentencing and detention. If a party fails to disclose such a statement after being ordered to do so by the court, the witness' testimony on direct can be stricken from the record.

Rule 26.2 includes statements made by witnesses to investigators that appear in the investigator's report, but not handwritten notes of investigators or counsel made during interviews with witnesses, or statements or report that the witness relies on during his/her testimony that were prepared by someone other than the witness. In addition, information contained in a statement that is not related to the substance of a witness' direct testimony can be redacted from the statement before it is disclosed.

KEY TERMS

direct examination 267
cross-examination 267
redirect examination 267
leading question 269
hostile witness 270

unresponsive answer 271
sequestration 272
demeanor 275
deference 275
impeachment 276

prior inconsistent statements 280
bias 281
prejudice 281
rehabilitation 284

CHAPTER SUMMARY

- There are four types of witnesses: eyewitnesses, character witnesses, opinion witnesses, and authentication witnesses.
- Direct examination of a witness is done by the party calling the witness, and does not allow the use of leading questions.
- Cross-examination is done by the opposing party and may include leading questions.
- Leading questions are questions that imply the answer that is desired.
- Hostile witnesses may be examined by the party calling them as if on cross.
- Question asked of a witness may not assume facts that are not part of the record.
- Witnesses are required to answer questions substantively, and unresponsive answers can be objected to.
- Rule 615 allows the exclusion or sequestration of witnesses except for parties or representatives of parties.

- Credibility is a determination by the jury regarding the truthfulness of a witness.
- Credibility is affected by the reasonableness and consistency of testimony and the demeanor of the witness.
- Courts will also defer to the jury in matters of credibility.
- The impeachment of a witness involves the production of evidence showing that the witness is not credible.
- A party can impeach any witness including its own.
- Impeachment can be done by reputation or opinion evidence, evidence of criminal convictions, prior inconsistent statements, establishing bias or prejudice, and proof that the witness was incapable of observing the matter testified to.
- An impeached witness can be rehabilitated by producing evidence of the witness' trustworthiness or by impeaching the impeachment witness.

WEB EXCURSION

1. One of the most disruptive and contentious trials in history was the trial of the so-called Chicago Seven that started in 1969 and lasted five months. The Chicago Seven were indicted for inciting riots at the 1968 Democratic National Convention in Chicago. Their trial was marked by the appearance of witnesses such as folk singer Judy Collins and civil rights activists Julian Bond and Jesse Jackson. It was also marred by battles between the defendants and the judge that led to contempt actions being filed against the defendant's attorney, William Kunstler. Read the excerpts of the trial transcript provided at http://law2.umkc.edu/faculty/projects/ftrials/Chicago7/Chi7_trial.html. Within the testimony, look for the application of various methods of impeachment that were discussed in this chapter.

PRACTICAL EXERCISE

1. Think about a memorable event that you personally experienced at least five years ago. If you were asked now to testify about that event in detail, how accurate would your testimony be? Write an account of the event in as much detail as you can, as if you were testifying in court. Think about questions the other side could ask on cross-examination that would impeach your testimony. Do you think they could successfully challenge your credibility? If so, what questions could be ask on redirect to rehabilitate your testimony? On the whole, do you believe you could convince a jury to believe your account?

THE FEDERAL RULES OF EVIDENCE

■ ARTICLE I. GENERAL PROVISIONS

Rule 101. Scope; Definitions

(a) **Scope.** These rules apply to proceedings in United States courts. The specific courts and proceedings to which the rules apply, along with exceptions, are set out in Rule 1101.

(b) **Definitions.** In these rules:
   (1) "civil case" means a civil action or proceeding;
   (2) "criminal case" includes a criminal proceeding;
   (3) "public office" includes a public agency;
   (4) "record" includes a memorandum, report, or data compilation;
   (5) a "rule prescribed by the Supreme Court" means a rule adopted by the Supreme Court under statutory authority; and
   (6) a reference to any kind of written material or any other medium includes electronically stored information.

Rule 102. Purpose

These rules should be construed so as to administer every proceeding fairly, eliminate unjustifiable expense and delay, and promote the development of evidence law, to the end of ascertaining the truth and securing a just determination.

Rule 103. Rulings on Evidence

(a) **Preserving a Claim of Error.** A party may claim error in a ruling to admit or exclude evidence only if the error affects a substantial right of the party and:
   (1) if the ruling admits evidence, a party, on the record:
      (A) timely objects or moves to strike; and
      (B) states the specific ground, unless it was apparent from the context; or
   (2) if the ruling excludes evidence, a party informs the court of its substance by an offer of proof, unless the substance was apparent from the context.

(b) **Not Needing to Renew an Objection or Offer of Proof.** Once the court rules definitively on the record—either before or at trial—a party need not renew an objection or offer of proof to preserve a claim of error for appeal.

(c) **Court's Statement About the Ruling; Directing an Offer of Proof.** The court may make any statement about the character or form of the evidence, the objection made, and the ruling. The court may direct that an offer of proof be made in question-and-answer form.

(d) **Preventing the Jury from Hearing Inadmissible Evidence**. To the extent practicable, the court must conduct a jury trial so that inadmissible evidence is not suggested to the jury by any means.

(e) **Taking Notice of Plain Error**. A court may take notice of a plain error affecting a substantial right, even if the claim of error was not properly preserved.

Rule 104. Preliminary Questions

(a) **In General**. The court must decide any preliminary question about whether a witness is qualified, a privilege exists, or evidence is admissible. In so deciding, the court is not bound by evidence rules, except those on privilege.

(b) **Relevance That Depends on a Fact**. When the relevance of evidence depends on whether a fact exists, proof must be introduced sufficient to support a finding that the fact does exist. The court may admit the proposed evidence on the condition that the proof be introduced later.

(c) **Conducting a Hearing So That the Jury Cannot Hear It**. The court must conduct any hearing on a preliminary question so that the jury cannot hear it if:
   (1) the hearing involves the admissibility of a confession;
   (2) a defendant in a criminal case is a witness and so requests; or
   (3) justice so requires.

(d) **Cross-Examining a Defendant in a Criminal Case**. By testifying on a preliminary question, a defendant in a criminal case does not become subject to cross-examination on other issues in the case.

(e) **Evidence Relevant to Weight and Credibility**. This rule does not limit a party's right to introduce before the jury evidence that is relevant to the weight or credibility of other evidence.

Rule 105. Limiting Evidence That is Not Admissible Against Other Parties or for Other Purposes

If the court admits evidence that is admissible against a party or for a purpose—but not against another party or for another purpose—the court, on timely request, must restrict the evidence to its proper scope and instruct the jury accordingly.

Rule 106. Remainder of or Related Writings or Recorded Statements

If a party introduces all or part of a writing or recorded statement, an adverse party may require the introduction, at that time, of any other part—or any other writing or recorded statement—that in fairness ought to be considered at the same time.

■ ARTICLE II. JUDICIAL NOTICE

Rule 201. Judicial Notice of Adjudicative Facts

(a) **Scope**. This rule governs judicial notice of an adjudicative fact only, not a legislative fact.

(b) **Kinds of Facts That May Be Judicially Noticed**. The court may judicially notice a fact that is not subject to reasonable dispute because it:

    (1) is generally known within the trial court's territorial jurisdiction; or

    (2) can be accurately and readily determined from sources whose accuracy cannot reasonably be questioned.

(c) **Taking Notice**. The court:

    (1) may take judicial notice on its own; or

    (2) must take judicial notice if a party requests it and the court is supplied with the necessary information.

(d) **Timing**. The court may take judicial notice at any stage of the proceeding.

(e) **Opportunity to Be Heard**. On timely request, a party is entitled to be heard on the propriety of taking judicial notice and the nature of the fact to be noticed. If the court takes judicial notice before notifying a party, the party, on request, is still entitled to be heard.

(f) **Instructing the Jury**. In a civil case, the court must instruct the jury to accept the noticed fact as conclusive. In a criminal case, the court must instruct the jury that it may or may not accept the noticed fact as conclusive.

■ ARTICLE III. PRESUMPTIONS IN CIVIL CASES

Rule 301. Presumptions in Civil Actions Generally

In a civil case, unless a federal statute or these rules provide otherwise, the party against whom a presumption is directed has the burden of producing evidence to rebut the presumption. But this rule does not shift the burden of persuasion, which remains on the party who had it originally.

Rule 302. Applying State Law to Presumptions in Civil Cases

In a civil case, state law governs the effect of a presumption regarding a claim or defense for which state law supplies the rule of decision.

■ ARTICLE IV. RELEVANCE AND ITS LIMITS

Rule 401. Test for Relevant Evidence

Evidence is relevant if:

(a) it has any tendency to make a fact more or less probable than it would be without the evidence; and

(b) the fact is of consequence in determining the action.

Rule 402. General Admissibility of Relevant Evidence

Relevant evidence is admissible unless any of the following provides otherwise:

- the United States Constitution;
- a federal statute;
- these rules; or
- other rules prescribed by the Supreme Court.

Irrelevant evidence is not admissible.

Rule 403. Excluding Relevant Evidence for Prejudice, Confusion, Waste of Time, or Other Reasons

The court may exclude relevant evidence if its probative value is substantially outweighed by a danger of one or more of the following: unfair prejudice, confusing the issues, misleading the jury, undue delay, wasting time, or needlessly presenting cumulative evidence.

Rule 404. Character Evidence; Crimes or Other Acts

(a) **Character Evidence.**
   (1) **Prohibited Uses.** Evidence of a person's character or character trait is not admissible to prove that on a particular occasion the person acted in accordance with the character or trait.
   (2) **Exceptions for a Defendant or Victim in a Criminal Case.** The following exceptions apply in a criminal case:
      (A) a defendant may offer evidence of the defendant's pertinent trait, and if the evidence is admitted, the prosecutor may offer evidence to rebut it;
      (B) subject to the limitations in Rule 412 [8], a defendant may offer evidence of an alleged victim's pertinent trait, and if the evidence is admitted, the prosecutor may:
         (i) offer evidence to rebut it; and
         (ii) offer evidence of the defendant's same trait; and
      (C) in a homicide case, the prosecutor may offer evidence of the alleged victim's trait of peacefulness to rebut evidence that the victim was the first aggressor.
   (3) **Exceptions for a Witness.** Evidence of a witness's character may be admitted under Rules 607 [9], 608 [10], and 609 [11].
(b) **Crimes, Wrongs, or Other Acts.**
   (1) **Prohibited Uses.** Evidence of a crime, wrong, or other act is not admissible to prove a person's character in order to show that on a particular occasion the person acted in accordance with the character.
   (2) **Permitted Uses; Notice in a Criminal Case.** This evidence may be admissible for another purpose, such as proving motive, opportunity, intent, preparation, plan, knowledge, identity, absence of mistake, or lack of accident. On request by a defendant in a criminal case, the prosecutor must:
      (A) provide reasonable notice of the general nature of any such evidence that the prosecutor intends to offer at trial; and
      (B) do so before trial—or during trial if the court, for good cause, excuses lack of pretrial notice.

Rule 405. Methods of Proving Character

(a) **By Reputation or Opinion.** When evidence of a person's character or character trait is admissible, it may be proved by testimony about the person's reputation or by testimony in the form of an opinion. On cross-examination of the character witness, the court may allow an inquiry into relevant specific instances of the person's conduct.
(b) **By Specific Instances of Conduct.** When a person's character or character trait is an essential element of a charge, claim, or defense, the

character or trait may also be proved by relevant specific instances of the person's conduct.

Rule 406. Habit; Routine Practice

Evidence of a person's habit or an organization's routine practice may be admitted to prove that on a particular occasion the person or organization acted in accordance with the habit or routine practice. The court may admit this evidence regardless of whether it is corroborated or whether there was an eyewitness.

Rule 407. Subsequent Remedial Measures

When measures are taken that would have made an earlier injury or harm less likely to occur, evidence of the subsequent measures is not admissible to prove:

- negligence;
- culpable conduct;
- a defect in a product or its design; or
- a need for a warning or instruction.

But the court may admit this evidence for another purpose, such as impeachment or—if disputed—proving ownership, control, or the feasibility of precautionary measures.

Rule 408. Compromise Offers and Negotiations

(a) **Prohibited uses**. Evidence of the following is not admissible—on behalf of any party—either to prove or disprove the validity or amount of a disputed claim or to impeach by a prior inconsistent statement or a contradiction:
   (1) furnishing, promising, or offering—or accepting, promising to accept, or offering to accept—a valuable consideration in compromising or attempting to compromise the claim; and
   (2) conduct or a statement made during compromise negotiations about the claim—except when offered in a criminal case and when the negotiations related to a claim by a public office in the exercise of its regulatory, investigative, or enforcement authority.
(b) **Exceptions**. The court may admit this evidence for another purpose, such as proving a witness's bias or prejudice, negating a contention of undue delay, or proving an effort to obstruct a criminal investigation or prosecution.

Rule 409. Offers to Pay Medical and Similar Expenses

Evidence of furnishing, promising to pay, or offering to pay medical, hospital, or similar expenses resulting from an injury is not admissible to prove liability for the injury.

Rule 410. Pleas, Plea Discussions, and Related Statements

(a) **Prohibited Uses**. In a civil or criminal case, evidence of the following is not admissible against the defendant who made the plea or participated in the plea discussions:
   (1) a guilty plea that was later withdrawn;
   (2) a nolo contendere plea;

(3) a statement made during a proceeding on either of those pleas under Federal Rule of Criminal Procedure 11 or a comparable state procedure; or

(4) a statement made during plea discussions with an attorney for the prosecuting authority if the discussions did not result in a guilty plea or they resulted in a later-withdrawn guilty plea.

(b) **Exceptions**. The court may admit a statement described in Rule 410(a) (3) or (4):

(1) in any proceeding in which another statement made during the same plea or plea discussions has been introduced, if in fairness the statements ought to be considered together; or

(2) in a criminal proceeding for perjury or false statement, if the defendant made the statement under oath, on the record, and with counsel present.

Rule 411. Liability Insurance

Evidence that a person was or was not insured against liability is not admissible to prove whether the person acted negligently or otherwise wrongfully. But the court may admit this evidence for another purpose, such as proving a witness's bias or prejudice or proving agency, ownership, or control.

Rule 412. Sex-Offense Cases: The Victim's Sexual Behavior or Predisposition

(a) **Prohibited Uses**. The following evidence is not admissible in a civil or criminal proceeding involving alleged sexual misconduct:

(1) evidence offered to prove that a victim engaged in other sexual behavior; or

(2) evidence offered to prove a victim's sexual predisposition.

(b) **Exceptions**.

(1) **Criminal Cases**. The court may admit the following evidence in a criminal case:

(A) evidence of specific instances of a victim's sexual behavior, if offered to prove that someone other than the defendant was the source of semen, injury, or other physical evidence;

(B) evidence of specific instances of a victim's sexual behavior with respect to the person accused of the sexual misconduct, if offered by the defendant to prove consent or if offered by the prosecutor; and

(C) evidence whose exclusion would violate the defendant's constitutional rights.

(2) **Civil Cases**. In a civil case, the court may admit evidence offered to prove a victim's sexual behavior or sexual predisposition if its probative value substantially outweighs the danger of harm to any victim and of unfair prejudice to any party. The court may admit evidence of a victim's reputation only if the victim has placed it in controversy.

(c) **Procedure To Determine Admissibility**.

(1) **Motion**. If a party intends to offer evidence under Rule 412(b), the party must:

(A) file a motion that specifically describes the evidence and states the purpose for which it is to be offered;

(B) do so at least 14 days before trial unless the court, for good cause, sets a different time;

(C) serve the motion on all parties; and

(D) notify the victim or, when appropriate, the victim's guardian or representative.

(2) **Hearing.** Before admitting evidence under this rule, the court must conduct an in camera hearing and give the victim and parties a right to attend and be heard. Unless the court orders otherwise, the motion, related materials, and the record of the hearing must be and remain sealed.

(d) **Definition of "Victim."** In this rule, "victim" includes an alleged victim.

Rule 413. Similar Crimes in Sexual-Assault Cases

(a) **Permitted Uses.** In a criminal case in which a defendant is accused of a sexual assault, the court may admit evidence that the defendant committed any other sexual assault. The evidence may be considered on any matter to which it is relevant.

(b) **Disclosure to the Defendant.** If the prosecutor intends to offer this evidence, the prosecutor must disclose it to the defendant, including witnesses' statements or a summary of the expected testimony. The prosecutor must do so at least 15 days before trial or at a later time that the court allows for good cause.

(c) **Effect on Other Rules.** This rule does not limit the admission or consideration of evidence under any other rule.

(d) **Definition of "Sexual Assault."** In this rule and Rule 415, "sexual assault" means a crime under federal law or under state law (as "state" is defined in 18 U.S.C. § 513) involving:

(1) any conduct prohibited by 18 U.S.C. chapter 109A;

(2) contact, without consent, between any part of the defendant's body—or an object—and another person's genitals or anus;

(3) contact, without consent, between the defendant's genitals or anus and any part of another person's body;

(4) deriving sexual pleasure or gratification from inflicting death, bodily injury, or physical pain on another person; or

(5) an attempt or conspiracy to engage in conduct described in subparagraphs (1)–(4).

Rule 414. Similar Crimes in Child-Molestation Cases

(a) **Permitted Uses.** In a criminal case in which a defendant is accused of child molestation, the court may admit evidence that the defendant committed any other child molestation. The evidence may be considered on any matter to which it is relevant.

(b) **Disclosure to the Defendant.** If the prosecutor intends to offer this evidence, the prosecutor must disclose it to the defendant, including witnesses' statements or a summary of the expected testimony. The prosecutor must do so at least 15 days before trial or at a later time that the court allows for good cause.

(c) **Effect on Other Rules.** This rule does not limit the admission or consideration of evidence under any other rule.

(d) **Definition of "Child" and "Child Molestation."** In this rule and Rule 415:

(1) "child" means a person below the age of 14; and

(2) "child molestation" means a crime under federal law or under state law (as "state" is defined in 18 U.S.C. § 513) involving:

(A) any conduct prohibited by 18 U.S.C. chapter 109A and committed with a child;

(B) any conduct prohibited by 18 U.S.C. chapter 110;

(C) contact between any part of the defendant's body—or an object—and a child's genitals or anus;

(D) contact between the defendant's genitals or anus and any part of a child's body;

(E) deriving sexual pleasure or gratification from inflicting death, bodily injury, or physical pain on a child; or

(F) an attempt or conspiracy to engage in conduct described in subparagraphs (A)–(E).

Rule 415. Similar Acts in Civil Cases Involving Sexual Assault or Child Molestation

(a) **Permitted Uses.** In a civil case involving a claim for relief based on a party's alleged sexual assault or child molestation, the court may admit evidence that the party committed any other sexual assault or child molestation. The evidence may be considered as provided in Rules 413 and 414.

(b) **Disclosure to the Opponent.** If a party intends to offer this evidence, the party must disclose it to the party against whom it will be offered, including witnesses' statements or a summary of the expected testimony. The party must do so at least 15 days before trial or at a later time that the court allows for good cause.

(c) **Effect on Other Rules.** This rule does not limit the admission or consideration of evidence under any other rule.

■ ARTICLE V. PRIVILEGES

Rule 501. Privileges in General

The common law—as interpreted by United States courts in the light of reason and experience—governs a claim of privilege unless any of the following provides otherwise:

- the United States Constitution;
- a federal statute; or
- rules prescribed by the Supreme Court.

But in a civil case, state law governs privilege regarding a claim or defense for which state law supplies the rule of decision.

Rule 502. Attorney–Client Privilege and Work Product; Limitations on Waiver

The following provisions apply, in the circumstances set out, to disclosure of a communication or information covered by the attorney-client privilege or work-product protection.

(a) **Disclosure Made in a Federal Proceeding or to a Federal Office or Agency; Scope of a Waiver.** When the disclosure is made in a federal proceeding or to a federal office or agency and waives the attorney–client privilege or work-product protection, the waiver extends to an undisclosed communication or information in a federal or state proceeding only if:

(1) the waiver is intentional;

(2) the disclosed and undisclosed communications or information concern the same subject matter; and

(3) they ought in fairness to be considered together.

(b) **Inadvertent Disclosure.** When made in a federal proceeding or to a federal office or agency, the disclosure does not operate as a waiver in a federal or state proceeding if:

(1) the disclosure is inadvertent;

(2) the holder of the privilege or protection took reasonable steps to prevent disclosure; and

(3) the holder promptly took reasonable steps to rectify the error, including (if applicable) following Federal Rule of Civil Procedure 26(b)(5)(B).

(c) **Disclosure Made in a State Proceeding.** When the disclosure is made in a state proceeding and is not the subject of a state-court order concerning waiver, the disclosure does not operate as a waiver in a federal proceeding if the disclosure:

(1) would not be a waiver under this rule if it had been made in a federal proceeding; or

(2) is not a waiver under the law of the State where the disclosure occurred.

(d) **Controlling Effect of a Court Order.** A federal court may order that the privilege or protection is not waived by disclosure connected with the litigation pending before the court—in which event the disclosure is also not a waiver in any other federal or state proceeding.

(e) **Controlling Effect of a Party Agreement.** An agreement on the effect of disclosure in a federal proceeding is binding only on the parties to the agreement, unless it is incorporated into a court order.

(f) **Controlling Effect of This Rule.** Notwithstanding Rules 101 [12] and 1101 [13], this rule applies to state proceedings and to federal court-annexed and federal court-mandated arbitration proceedings, in the circumstances set out in the rule. And notwithstanding Rule 501 [14], this rule applies even if State law provides the rule of decision.

(g) **Definitions.** In this rule:

(1) "attorney–client privilege" means the protection that applicable law provides for confidential attorney–client communications; and

(2) "work-product protection" means the protection that applicable law provides for tangible material (or its intangible equivalent) prepared in anticipation of litigation or for trial.

■ ARTICLE VI. WITNESSES

Rule 601. Competency to Testify in General

Every person is competent to be a witness unless these rules provide otherwise. But in a civil case, state law governs the witness's competency regarding a claim or defense for which state law supplies the rule of decision.

Rule 602. Need for Personal Knowledge

A witness may not testify to a matter unless evidence is introduced sufficient to support a finding that the witness has personal knowledge of the matter. Evidence to prove personal knowledge may, but need not, consist of the witness' own testimony. This rule is subject to the provisions of Rule 703, relating to opinion testimony by expert witnesses.

Rule 603. Oath or Affirmation to Testify Truthfully

Before testifying, a witness must give an oath or affirmation to testify truthfully. It must be in a form designed to impress that duty on the witness's conscience.

Rule 604. Interpreter

An interpreter must be qualified and must give an oath or affirmation to make a true translation.

Rule 605. Judge's Competency as a Witness

The presiding judge may not testify as a witness at the trial. A party need not object to preserve the issue.

Rule 606. Juror's Competency as a Witness

(a) **At the Trial.** A juror may not testify as a witness before the other jurors at the trial. If a juror is called to testify, the court must give a party an opportunity to object outside the jury's presence.

(b) **During an Inquiry into the Validity of a Verdict or Indictment.**
   (1) **Prohibited Testimony or Other Evidence.** During an inquiry into the validity of a verdict or indictment, a juror may not testify about any statement made or incident that occurred during the jury's deliberations; the effect of anything on that juror's or another juror's vote; or any juror's mental processes concerning the verdict or indictment. The court may not receive a juror's affidavit or evidence of a juror's statement on these matters.
   (2) **Exceptions.** A juror may testify about whether:
      (A) extraneous prejudicial information was improperly brought to the jury's attention;
      (B) an outside influence was improperly brought to bear on any juror; or
      (C) a mistake was made in entering the verdict on the verdict form.

Rule 607. Who May Impeach a Witness

Any party, including the party that called the witness, may attack the witness's credibility.

Rule 608. A Witness's Character for Truthfulness or Untruthfulness

(a) **Reputation or Opinion Evidence.** A witness's credibility may be attacked or supported by testimony about the witness's reputation for having a character for truthfulness or untruthfulness, or by testimony in the form of an opinion about that character. But evidence of truthful character is admissible only after the witness's character for truthfulness has been attacked.

(b) **Specific Instances of Conduct.**

Except for a criminal conviction under Rule 609, extrinsic evidence is not admissible to prove specific instances of a witness's conduct in order to attack or support the witness's character for truthfulness. But the court may, on cross-examination, allow them to be inquired into if they are probative of the character for truthfulness or untruthfulness of: (1) the witness; or (2)another witness whose character the witness being cross-examined has testified about. By testifying on another matter, a witness does not waive any privilege against self-incrimination for testimony that relates only to the witness's character for truthfulness.

Rule 609. Impeachment by Evidence of a Criminal Conviction

(a) **In General.** The following rules apply to attacking a witness's character for truthfulness by evidence of a criminal conviction:

(1) for a crime that, in the convicting jurisdiction, was punishable by death or by imprisonment for more than one year, the evidence:

(A) must be admitted, subject to Rule 403 [15], in a civil case or in a criminal case in which the witness is not a defendant; and

(B) must be admitted in a criminal case in which the witness is a defendant, if the probative value of the evidence outweighs its prejudicial effect to that defendant; and

(2) for any crime regardless of the punishment, the evidence must be admitted if the court can readily determine that establishing the elements of the crime required proving—or the witness's admitting—a dishonest act or false statement.

(b) **Limit on Using the Evidence After 10 Years.** This subdivision (b) applies if more than 10 years have passed since the witness's conviction or release from confinement for it, whichever is later. Evidence of the conviction is admissible only if:

(1) its probative value, supported by specific facts and circumstances, substantially outweighs its prejudicial effect; and

(2) the proponent gives an adverse party reasonable written notice of the intent to use it so that the party has a fair opportunity to contest its use.

(c) **Effect of a Pardon, Annulment, or Certificate of Rehabilitation.**

Evidence of a conviction is not admissible if:

(1) the conviction has been the subject of a pardon, annulment, certificate of rehabilitation, or other equivalent procedure based on a finding that the person has been rehabilitated, and the person has not been convicted of a later crime punishable by death or by imprisonment for more than one year; or

(2) the conviction has been the subject of a pardon, annulment, or other equivalent procedure based on a finding of innocence.

(d) **Juvenile Adjudications.**

Evidence of a juvenile adjudication is admissible under this rule only if:

(1) it is offered in a criminal case;

(2) the adjudication was of a witness other than the defendant;

(3) an adult's conviction for that offense would be admissible to attack the adult's credibility; and

(4) admitting the evidence is necessary to fairly determine guilt or innocence.

(e) **Pendency of an Appeal.** A conviction that satisfies this rule is admissible even if an appeal is pending. Evidence of the pendency is also admissible.

Rule 610. Religious Beliefs or Opinions

Evidence of a witness's religious beliefs or opinions is not admissible to attack or support the witness's credibility.

Rule 611. Mode and Order of Examining Witnesses and Presenting Evidence

(a) **Control by the Court; Purposes.** The court should exercise reasonable control over the mode and order of examining witnesses and presenting evidence so as to:

(1) make those procedures effective for determining the truth;

(2) avoid wasting time; and

(3) protect witnesses from harassment or undue embarrassment.

(b) **Scope of Cross-Examination.** Cross-examination should not go beyond the subject matter of the direct examination and matters affecting the witness's credibility. The court may allow inquiry into additional matters as if on direct examination.

(c) **Leading Questions.** Leading questions should not be used on direct examination except as necessary to develop the witness's testimony. Ordinarily, the court should allow leading questions:

(1) on cross-examination; and

(2) when a party calls a hostile witness, an adverse party, or a witness identified with an adverse party.

Rule 612. Writing Used to Refresh a Witness's Memory

(a) **Scope.** This rule gives an adverse party certain options when a witness uses a writing to refresh memory:

(1) while testifying; or

(2) before testifying, if the court decides that justice requires the party to have those options.

(b) **Adverse Party's Options; Deleting Unrelated Matter.** Unless 18 U.S.C. § 3500 provides otherwise in a criminal case, an adverse party is entitled to have the writing produced at the hearing, to inspect it, to cross-examine the witness about it, and to introduce in evidence any portion that relates to the witness's testimony. If the producing party claims that the writing includes unrelated matter, the court must examine the writing in camera, delete any unrelated portion, and order that the rest be delivered to the adverse party. Any portion deleted over objection must be preserved for the record.

(c) **Failure to Produce or Deliver the Writing.** If a writing is not produced or is not delivered as ordered, the court may issue any appropriate order. But if the prosecution does not comply in a criminal case, the court must strike the witness's testimony or—if justice so requires—declare a mistrial.

Rule 613. Witness's Prior Statement

(a) **Showing or Disclosing the Statement During Examination**. When examining a witness about the witness's prior statement, a party need not show it or disclose its contents to the witness. But the party must, on request, show it or disclose its contents to an adverse party's attorney.

(b) **Extrinsic Evidence of a Prior Inconsistent Statement**. Extrinsic evidence of a witness's prior inconsistent statement is admissible only if the witness is given an opportunity to explain or deny the statement and an adverse party is given an opportunity to examine the witness about it, or if justice so requires. This subdivision (b) does not apply to an opposing party's statement under Rule 801(d)(2) [16].

Rule 614. Court's Calling or Examining a Witness

(a) **Calling**. The court may call a witness on its own or at a party's request. Each party is entitled to cross-examine the witness.

(b) **Examining**. The court may examine a witness regardless of who calls the witness.

(c) **Objections**. A party may object to the court's calling or examining a witness either at that time or at the next opportunity when the jury is not present.

Rule 615. Excluding Witnesses

At a party's request, the court must order witnesses excluded so that they cannot hear other witnesses' testimony. Or the court may do so on its own. But this rule does not authorize excluding:

(a) a party who is a natural person;

(b) an officer or employee of a party that is not a natural person, after being designated as the party's representative by its attorney;

(c) a person whose presence a party shows to be essential to presenting the party's claim or defense; or

(d) a person authorized by statute to be present.

■ ARTICLE VII. OPINIONS AND EXPERT TESTIMONY

Rule 701. Opinion Testimony by Lay Witnesses

If a witness is not testifying as an expert, testimony in the form of an opinion is limited to one that is:

(a) rationally based on the witness's perception;

(b) helpful to clearly understanding the witness's testimony or to determining a fact in issue; and

(c) not based on scientific, technical, or other specialized knowledge within the scope of Rule 702 [17].

Rule 702. Testimony by Expert Witnesses

A witness who is qualified as an expert by knowledge, skill, experience, training, or education may testify in the form of an opinion or otherwise if:

(a) the expert's scientific, technical, or other specialized knowledge will help the trier of fact to understand the evidence or to determine a fact in issue;

(b) the testimony is based on sufficient facts or data;

(c) the testimony is the product of reliable principles and methods; and

(d) the expert has reliably applied the principles and methods to the facts of the case.

Rule 703. Bases of an Expert's Opinion Testimony

An expert may base an opinion on facts or data in the case that the expert has been made aware of or personally observed. If experts in the particular field would reasonably rely on those kinds of facts or data in forming an opinion on the subject, they need not be admissible for the opinion to be admitted. But if the facts or data would otherwise be inadmissible, the proponent of the opinion may disclose them to the jury only if their probative value in helping the jury evaluate the opinion substantially outweighs their prejudicial effect.

Rule 704. Opinion on an Ultimate Issue

(a) **In General**—Not Automatically Objectionable. An opinion is not objectionable just because it embraces an ultimate issue.

(b) **Exception**. In a criminal case, an expert witness must not state an opinion about whether the defendant did or did not have a mental state or condition that constitutes an element of the crime charged or of a defense. Those matters are for the trier of fact alone.

Rule 705. Disclosing the Facts or Data Underlying an Expert's Opinion

Unless the court orders otherwise, an expert may state an opinion—and give the reasons for it—without first testifying to the underlying facts or data. But the expert may be required to disclose those facts or data on cross-examination.

Rule 706. Court-Appointed Expert Witnesses

(a) **Appointment Process**. On a party's motion or on its own, the court may order the parties to show cause why expert witnesses should not be appointed and may ask the parties to submit nominations. The court may appoint any expert that the parties agree on and any of its own choosing. But the court may only appoint someone who consents to act.

(b) **Expert's Role**. The court must inform the expert of the expert's duties. The court may do so in writing and have a copy filed with the clerk or may do so orally at a conference in which the parties have an opportunity to participate. The expert:

   (1) must advise the parties of any findings the expert makes;

   (2) may be deposed by any party;

   (3) may be called to testify by the court or any party; and

   (4) may be cross-examined by any party, including the party that called the expert.

(c) **Compensation**. The expert is entitled to a reasonable compensation, as set by the court. The compensation is payable as follows:

   (1) in a criminal case or in a civil case involving just compensation under the Fifth Amendment, from any funds that are provided by law; and

(2) in any other civil case, by the parties in the proportion and at the time that the court directs—and the compensation is then charged like other costs.

(d) **Disclosing the Appointment to the Jury.** The court may authorize disclosure to the jury that the court appointed the expert.

(e) **Parties' Choice of Their Own Experts.** This rule does not limit a party in calling its own experts.

■ ARTICLE VIII. HEARSAY

Rule 801. Definitions That Apply to This Article; Exclusions from Hearsay

(a) **Statement.** "Statement" means a person's oral assertion, written assertion, or nonverbal conduct, if the person intended it as an assertion.

(b) **Declarant.** "Declarant" means the person who made the statement.

(c) **Hearsay.** "Hearsay" means a statement that:
  (1) the declarant does not make while testifying at the current trial or hearing; and
  (2) a party offers in evidence to prove the truth of the matter asserted in the statement.

(d) **Statements That Are Not Hearsay.** A statement that meets the following conditions is not hearsay:
  (1) **A Declarant-Witness's Prior Statement.** The declarant testifies and is subject to cross-examination about a prior statement, and the statement:
    (A) is inconsistent with the declarant's testimony and was given under penalty of perjury at a trial, hearing, or other proceeding or in a deposition;
    (B) is consistent with the declarant's testimony and is offered:
      (i) to rebut an express or implied charge that the declarant recently fabricated it or acted from a recent improper influence or motive in so testifying; or
      (ii) to rehabilitate the declarant's credibility as a witness when attacked on another ground; or
    (C) identifies a person as someone the declarant perceived earlier.
  (2) **An Opposing Party's Statement.** The statement is offered against an opposing party and:
    (A) was made by the party in an individual or representative capacity;
    (B) is one the party manifested that it adopted or believed to be true;
    (C) was made by a person whom the party authorized to make a statement on the subject;
    (D) was made by the party's agent or employee on a matter within the scope of that relationship and while it existed; or
    (E) was made by the party's coconspirator during and in furtherance of the conspiracy.

The statement must be considered but does not by itself establish the declarant's authority under (C); the existence or scope of the relationship under (D); or the existence of the conspiracy or participation in it under (E).

Rule 802. The Rule Against Hearsay

Hearsay is not admissible unless any of the following provides otherwise:

- a federal statute;
- these rules; or
- other rules prescribed by the Supreme Court.

Rule 803. Exceptions to the Rule Against Hearsay—Regardless of Whether the Declarant Is Available as a Witness

The following are not excluded by the rule against hearsay, regardless of whether the declarant is available as a witness:

(1) **Present Sense Impression.** A statement describing or explaining an event or condition, made while or immediately after the declarant perceived it.

(2) **Excited Utterance.** A statement relating to a startling event or condition, made while the declarant was under the stress of excitement that it caused.

(3) **Then-Existing Mental, Emotional, or Physical Condition.** A statement of the declarant's then-existing state of mind (such as motive, intent, or plan) or emotional, sensory, or physical condition (such as mental feeling, pain, or bodily health), but not including a statement of memory or belief to prove the fact remembered or believed unless it relates to the validity or terms of the declarant's will.

(4) **Statement Made for Medical Diagnosis or Treatment.** A statement that:

(A) is made for—and is reasonably pertinent to—medical diagnosis or treatment; and

(B) describes medical history; past or present symptoms or sensations; their inception; or their general cause.

(5) **Recorded Recollection.** A record that:

(A) is on a matter the witness once knew about but now cannot recall well enough to testify fully and accurately;

(B) was made or adopted by the witness when the matter was fresh in the witness's memory; and

(C) accurately reflects the witness's knowledge.

If admitted, the record may be read into evidence but may be received as an exhibit only if offered by an adverse party.

(6) **Records of a Regularly Conducted Activity.** A record of an act, event, condition, opinion, or diagnosis if:

(A) the record was made at or near the time by—or from information transmitted by—someone with knowledge;

(B) the record was kept in the course of a regularly conducted activity of a business, organization, occupation, or calling, whether or not for profit;

(C) making the record was a regular practice of that activity;

(D) all these conditions are shown by the testimony of the custodian or another qualified witness, or by a certification that complies with Rule 902(11) [18] or (12) [18] or with a statute permitting certification; and

(E) the opponent does not show that the source of information or the method or circumstances of preparation indicate a lack of trustworthiness.

(7) **Absence of a Record of a Regularly Conducted Activity.** Evidence that a matter is not included in a record described in paragraph (6) if:
  (A) the evidence is admitted to prove that the matter did not occur or exist;
  (B) a record was regularly kept for a matter of that kind; and
  (C) the opponent does not show that the possible source of the information or other circumstances indicate a lack of trustworthiness.

(8) **Public Records.** A record or statement of a public office if:
  (A) it sets out:
    (i)   the office's activities;
    (ii) a matter observed while under a legal duty to report, but not including, in a criminal case, a matter observed by law-enforcement personnel; or
    (iii) in a civil case or against the government in a criminal case, factual findings from a legally authorized investigation; and
  (B) the opponent does not show that the source of information or other circumstances indicate a lack of trustworthiness.

(9) **Public Records of Vital Statistics.** A record of a birth, death, or marriage, if reported to a public office in accordance with a legal duty.

(10) **Absence of a Public Record.** Testimony—or a certification under Rule 902 [18]—that a diligent search failed to disclose a public record or statement if:
  (A) the testimony or certification is admitted to prove that
    (i)   the record or statement does not exist;
          or
    (ii) a matter did not occur or exist, if a public office regularly kept a record or statement for a matter of that kind; and
  (B) in a criminal case, a prosecutor who intends to offer a certification provides written notice of that intent at least 14 days before trial, and the defendant does not object in writing within 7 days of receiving the notice—unless the court sets a different time for the notice or the objection.

(11) **Records of Religious Organizations Concerning Personal or Family History.** A statement of birth, legitimacy, ancestry, marriage, divorce, death, relationship by blood or marriage, or similar facts of personal or family history, contained in a regularly kept record of a religious organization.

(12) **Certificates of Marriage, Baptism, and Similar Ceremonies.** A statement of fact contained in a certificate:
  (A) made by a person who is authorized by a religious organization or by law to perform the act certified;
  (B) attesting that the person performed a marriage or similar ceremony or administered a sacrament; and
  (C) purporting to have been issued at the time of the act or within a reasonable time after it.

(13) **Family Records.** A statement of fact about personal or family history contained in a family record, such as a Bible, genealogy, chart, engraving on a ring, inscription on a portrait, or engraving on an urn or burial marker.

(14) **Records of Documents That Affect an Interest in Property.** The record of a document that purports to establish or affect an interest in property if:
  (A) the record is admitted to prove the content of the original recorded document, along with its signing and its delivery by each person who purports to have signed it;

(B) the record is kept in a public office; and

(C) a statute authorizes recording documents of that kind in that office.

(15) **Statements in Documents That Affect an Interest in Property.** A statement contained in a document that purports to establish or affect an interest in property if the matter stated was relevant to the document's purpose—unless later dealings with the property are inconsistent with the truth of the statement or the purport of the document.

(16) **Statements in Ancient Documents.** A statement in a document that is at least 20 years old and whose authenticity is established.

(17) **Market Reports and Similar Commercial Publications.** Market quotations, lists, directories, or other compilations that are generally relied on by the public or by persons in particular occupations.

(18) **Statements in Learned Treatises, Periodicals, or Pamphlets.** A statement contained in a treatise, periodical, or pamphlet if:

(A) the statement is called to the attention of an expert witness on cross-examination or relied on by the expert on direct examination; and

(B) the publication is established as a reliable authority by the expert's admission or testimony, by another expert's testimony, or by judicial notice.

If admitted, the statement may be read into evidence but not received as an exhibit.

(19) **Reputation Concerning Personal or Family History.** A reputation among a person's family by blood, adoption, or marriage—or among a person's associates or in the community—concerning the person's birth, adoption, legitimacy, ancestry, marriage, divorce, death, relationship by blood, adoption, or marriage, or similar facts of personal or family history.

(20) **Reputation Concerning Boundaries or General History.** A reputation in a community—arising before the controversy—concerning boundaries of land in the community or customs that affect the land, or concerning general historical events important to that community, state, or nation.

(21) **Reputation Concerning Character.** A reputation among a person's associates or in the community concerning the person's character.

(22) **Judgment of a Previous Conviction.** Evidence of a final judgment of conviction if:

(A) the judgment was entered after a trial or guilty plea, but not a nolo contendere plea;

(B) the conviction was for a crime punishable by death or by imprisonment for more than a year;

(C) the evidence is admitted to prove any fact essential to the judgment; and

(D) when offered by the prosecutor in a criminal case for a purpose other than impeachment, the judgment was against the defendant.

The pendency of an appeal may be shown but does not affect admissibility.

(23) **Judgments Involving Personal, Family, or General History, or a Boundary.** A judgment that is admitted to prove a matter of personal, family, or general history, or boundaries, if the matter:

(A) was essential to the judgment; and

(B) could be proved by evidence of reputation.

Rule 804. Hearsay Exceptions; Declarant Unavailable

(a) **Criteria for Being Unavailable**. A declarant is considered to be unavailable as a witness if the declarant:

    (1) is exempted from testifying about the subject matter of the declarant's statement because the court rules that a privilege applies;

    (2) refuses to testify about the subject matter despite a court order to do so;

    (3) testifies to not remembering the subject matter;

    (4) cannot be present or testify at the trial or hearing because of death or a then-existing infirmity, physical illness, or mental illness; or

    (5) is absent from the trial or hearing and the statement's proponent has not been able, by process or other reasonable means, to procure:

        (A) the declarant's attendance, in the case of a hearsay exception under Rule 804(b)(1) or (6) [20]; or

        (B) the declarant's attendance or testimony, in the case of a hearsay exception under Rule 804(b)(2), (3), or (4) [20].

But this subdivision (a) does not apply if the statement's proponent procured or wrongfully caused the declarant's unavailability as a witness in order to prevent the declarant from attending or testifying.

(b) **The Exceptions**. The following are not excluded by the rule against hearsay if the declarant is unavailable as a witness:

    (1) **Former Testimony**. Testimony that:

        (A) was given as a witness at a trial, hearing, or lawful deposition, whether given during the current proceeding or a different one; and

        (B) is now offered against a party who had—or, in a civil case, whose predecessor in interest had—an opportunity and similar motive to develop it by direct, cross-, or redirect examination.

    (2) **Statement Under the Belief of Imminent Death**. In a prosecution for homicide or in a civil case, a statement that the declarant, while believing the declarant's death to be imminent, made about its cause or circumstances.

    (3) **Statement Against Interest**. A statement that:

        (A) a reasonable person in the declarant's position would have made only if the person believed it to be true because, when made, it was so contrary to the declarant's proprietary or pecuniary interest or had so great a tendency to invalidate the declarant's claim against someone else or to expose the declarant to civil or criminal liability; and

        (B) is supported by corroborating circumstances that clearly indicate its trustworthiness, if it is offered in a criminal case as one that tends to expose the declarant to criminal liability.

    (4) **Statement of Personal or Family History**. A statement about:

        (A) the declarant's own birth, adoption, legitimacy, ancestry, marriage, divorce, relationship by blood, adoption, or marriage, or similar facts of personal or family history, even though the declarant had no way of acquiring personal knowledge about that fact; or

        (B) another person concerning any of these facts, as well as death, if the declarant was related to the person by blood, adoption, or marriage or was so intimately associated with the person's family that the declarant's information is likely to be accurate.

(5) [Other Exceptions.] [Transferred to Rule 807 [19].]

(6) **Statement Offered Against a Party That Wrongfully Caused the Declarant's Unavailability.** A statement offered against a party that wrongfully caused—or acquiesced in wrongfully causing—the declarant's unavailability as a witness, and did so intending that result.

Rule 805. Hearsay Within Hearsay

Hearsay within hearsay is not excluded by the rule against hearsay if each part of the combined statements conforms with an exception to the rule.

Rule 806. Attacking and Supporting the Declarant's Credibility

When a hearsay statement—or a statement described in Rule 801(d)(2)(C), (D), or (E) [16]—has been admitted in evidence, the declarant's credibility may be attacked, and then supported, by any evidence that would be admissible for those purposes if the declarant had testified as a witness. The court may admit evidence of the declarant's inconsistent statement or conduct, regardless of when it occurred or whether the declarant had an opportunity to explain or deny it. If the party against whom the statement was admitted calls the declarant as a witness, the party may examine the declarant on the statement as if on cross-examination.

Rule 807. Residual Exception

(a) **In General.** Under the following circumstances, a hearsay statement is not excluded by the rule against hearsay even if the statement is not specifically covered by a hearsay exception in Rule 803 [21] or 804 [20]:

    (1) the statement has equivalent circumstantial guarantees of trustworthiness;

    (2) it is offered as evidence of a material fact;

    (3) it is more probative on the point for which it is offered than any other evidence that the proponent can obtain through reasonable efforts; and

    (4) admitting it will best serve the purposes of these rules and the interests of justice.

(b) **Notice.** The statement is admissible only if, before the trial or hearing, the proponent gives an adverse party reasonable notice of the intent to offer the statement and its particulars, including the declarant's name and address, so that the party has a fair opportunity to meet it.

■ ARTICLE IX. AUTHENTICATION AND IDENTIFICATION

Rule 901. Authenticating or Identifying Evidence

(a) **In General.** To satisfy the requirement of authenticating or identifying an item of evidence, the proponent must produce evidence sufficient to support a finding that the item is what the proponent claims it is.

(b) **Examples.** The following are examples only—not a complete list—of evidence that satisfies the requirement:

(1) **Testimony of a Witness with Knowledge**. Testimony that an item is what it is claimed to be.

(2) **Nonexpert Opinion About Handwriting**. A nonexpert's opinion that handwriting is genuine, based on a familiarity with it that was not acquired for the current litigation.

(3) **Comparison by an Expert Witness or the Trier of Fact**. A comparison with an authenticated specimen by an expert witness or the trier of fact.

(4) **Distinctive Characteristics and the Like**. The appearance, contents, substance, internal patterns, or other distinctive characteristics of the item, taken together with all the circumstances.

(5) **Opinion About a Voice**. An opinion identifying a person's voice— whether heard firsthand or through mechanical or electronic transmission or recording—based on hearing the voice at any time under circumstances that connect it with the alleged speaker.

(6) **Evidence About a Telephone Conversation**. For a telephone conversation, evidence that a call was made to the number assigned at the time to:
   (A) a particular person, if circumstances, including self-identification, show that the person answering was the one called; or
   (B) a particular business, if the call was made to a business and the call related to business reasonably transacted over the telephone.

(7) **Evidence About Public Records**. Evidence that:
   (A) a document was recorded or filed in a public office as authorized by law; or
   (B) a purported public record or statement is from the office where items of this kind are kept.

(8) **Evidence About Ancient Documents or Data Compilations**. For a document or data compilation, evidence that it:
   (A) is in a condition that creates no suspicion about its authenticity;
   (B) was in a place where, if authentic, it would likely be; and
   (C) is at least 20 years old when offered.

(9) **Evidence About a Process or System**. Evidence describing a process or system and showing that it produces an accurate result.

(10) **Methods Provided by a Statute or Rule**. Any method of authentication or identification allowed by a federal statute or a rule prescribed by the Supreme Court.

Rule 902. Evidence That is Self-Authenticating

The following items of evidence are self-authenticating; they require no extrinsic evidence of authenticity in order to be admitted:

(1) **Domestic Public Documents That Are Sealed and Signed**. A document that bears:
   (A) a seal purporting to be that of the United States; any state, district, commonwealth, territory, or insular possession of the United States; the former Panama Canal Zone; the Trust Territory of the Pacific Islands; a political subdivision of any of these entities; or a department, agency, or officer of any entity named above; and
   (B) a signature purporting to be an execution or attestation.

(2) **Domestic Public Documents That Are Not Sealed But Are Signed and Certified**. A document that bears no seal if:

    (A) it bears the signature of an officer or employee of an entity named in Rule 902(1)(A); and

    (B) another public officer who has a seal and official duties within that same entity certifies under seal—or its equivalent—that the signer has the official capacity and that the signature is genuine.

(3) **Foreign Public Documents.** A document that purports to be signed or attested by a person who is authorized by a foreign country's law to do so. The document must be accompanied by a final certification that certifies the genuineness of the signature and official position of the signer or attester—or of any foreign official whose certificate of genuineness relates to the signature or attestation or is in a chain of certificates of genuineness relating to the signature or attestation. The certification may be made by a secretary of a United States embassy or legation; by a consul general, vice consul, or consular agent of the United States; or by a diplomatic or consular official of the foreign country assigned or accredited to the United States. If all parties have been given a reasonable opportunity to investigate the document's authenticity and accuracy, the court may, for good cause, either:

    (A) order that it be treated as presumptively authentic without final certification; or

    (B) allow it to be evidenced by an attested summary with or without final certification.

(4) **Certified Copies of Public Records.** A copy of an official record—or a copy of a document that was recorded or filed in a public office as authorized by law—if the copy is certified as correct by:

    (A) the custodian or another person authorized to make the certification; or

    (B) a certificate that complies with Rule 902(1), (2), or (3) [18], a federal statute, or a rule prescribed by the Supreme Court.

(5) **Official Publications.** A book, pamphlet, or other publication purporting to be issued by a public authority.

(6) **Newspapers and Periodicals.** Printed material purporting to be a newspaper or periodical.

(7) **Trade Inscriptions and the Like.** An inscription, sign, tag, or label purporting to have been affixed in the course of business and indicating origin, ownership, or control.

(8) **Acknowledged Documents.** A document accompanied by a certificate of acknowledgment that is lawfully executed by a notary public or another officer who is authorized to take acknowledgments.

(9) **Commercial Paper and Related Documents.** Commercial paper, a signature on it, and related documents, to the extent allowed by general commercial law.

(10) **Presumptions Under a Federal Statute.** A signature, document, or anything else that a federal statute declares to be presumptively or prima facie genuine or authentic.

(11) **Certified Domestic Records of a Regularly Conducted Activity.** The original or a copy of a domestic record that meets the requirements of Rule 803(6)(A)–(C) [21], as shown by a certification of the custodian or another qualified person that complies with a federal statute or a rule prescribed by the Supreme Court. Before the trial or hearing, the proponent must give an adverse party reasonable written notice of the intent to offer the record—and must make the record and certification

available for inspection—so that the party has a fair opportunity to challenge them.

(12) **Certified Foreign Records of a Regularly Conducted Activity**. In a civil case, the original or a copy of a foreign record that meets the requirements of Rule 902(11) [18], modified as follows: the certification, rather than complying with a federal statute or Supreme Court rule, must be signed in a manner that, if falsely made, would subject the maker to a criminal penalty in the country where the certification is signed. The proponent must also meet the notice requirements of Rule 902(11) [18].

Rule 903. Subscribing Witness's Testimony

A subscribing witness's testimony is necessary to authenticate a writing only if required by the law of the jurisdiction that governs its validity.

■ ARTICLE X. CONTENTS OF WRITINGS, RECORDINGS, AND PHOTOGRAPHS

Rule 1001. Definitions That Apply to This Article

In this article:

(a) A "writing" consists of letters, words, numbers, or their equivalent set down in any form.

(b) A "recording" consists of letters, words, numbers, or their equivalent recorded in any manner.

(c) A "photograph" means a photographic image or its equivalent stored in any form.

(d) An "original" of a writing or recording means the writing or recording itself or any counterpart intended to have the same effect by the person who executed or issued it. For electronically stored information, "original" means any printout—or other output readable by sight—if it accurately reflects the information. An "original" of a photograph includes the negative or a print from it.

(e) A "duplicate" means a counterpart produced by a mechanical, photographic, chemical, electronic, or other equivalent process or technique that accurately reproduces the original.

Rule 1002. Requirement of the Original

An original writing, recording, or photograph is required in order to prove its content unless these rules or a federal statute provides otherwise.

Rule 1003. Admissibility of Duplicates

A duplicate is admissible to the same extent as the original unless a genuine question is raised about the original's authenticity or the circumstances make it unfair to admit the duplicate.

Rule 1004. Admissibility of Other Evidence of Content

An original is not required and other evidence of the content of a writing, recording, or photograph is admissible if:

(a) all the originals are lost or destroyed, and not by the proponent acting in bad faith;
(b) an original cannot be obtained by any available judicial process;
(c) the party against whom the original would be offered had control of the original; was at that time put on notice, by pleadings or otherwise, that the original would be a subject of proof at the trial or hearing; and fails to produce it at the trial or hearing; or
(d) the writing, recording, or photograph is not closely related to a controlling issue.

Rule 1005. Copies of Public Records to Prove Content

The proponent may use a copy to prove the content of an official record—or of a document that was recorded or filed in a public office as authorized by law—if these conditions are met: the record or document is otherwise admissible; and the copy is certified as correct in accordance with Rule 902(4) [18] or is testified to be correct by a witness who has compared it with the original. If no such copy can be obtained by reasonable diligence, then the proponent may use other evidence to prove the content.

Rule 1006. Summaries to Prove Content

The proponent may use a summary, chart, or calculation to prove the content of voluminous writings, recordings, or photographs that cannot be conveniently examined in court. The proponent must make the originals or duplicates available for examination or copying, or both, by other parties at a reasonable time and place. And the court may order the proponent to produce them in court.

Rule 1007. Testimony or Statement of a Party to Prove Content

The proponent may prove the content of a writing, recording, or photograph by the testimony, deposition, or written statement of the party against whom the evidence is offered. The proponent need not account for the original.

Rule 1008. Functions of the Court and Jury

Ordinarily, the court determines whether the proponent has fulfilled the factual conditions for admitting other evidence of the content of a writing, recording, or photograph under Rule 1004 [22] or 1005 [23]. But in a jury trial, the jury determines—in accordance with Rule 104(b) [24] —any issue about whether:

(a) an asserted writing, recording, or photograph ever existed
(b) another one produced at the trial or hearing is the original; or
(c) other evidence of content accurately reflects the content.

■ ARTICLE XI. MISCELLANEOUS RULES

Rule 1101. Applicability of the Rules

(a) **To Courts and Judges**. These rules apply to proceedings before:
  - United States district courts;
  - United States bankruptcy and magistrate judges;

- United States courts of appeals;
- the United States Court of Federal Claims; and
- the district courts of Guam, the Virgin Islands, and the Northern Mariana Islands.

(b) **To Cases and Proceedings.** These rules apply in:
- civil cases and proceedings, including bankruptcy, admiralty, and maritime cases;
- criminal cases and proceedings; and
- contempt proceedings, except those in which the court may act summarily.

(c) **Rules on Privilege.** The rules on privilege apply to all stages of a case or proceeding.

(d) **Exceptions.** These rules—except for those on privilege—do not apply to the following:
    (1) the court's determination, under Rule 104(a) [24], on a preliminary question of fact governing admissibility;
    (2) grand-jury proceedings; and
    (3) miscellaneous proceedings such as:
        - extradition or rendition;
        - issuing an arrest warrant, criminal summons, or search warrant;
        - a preliminary examination in a criminal case;
        - sentencing;
        - granting or revoking probation or supervised release; and
        - considering whether to release on bail or otherwise.

(e) **Other Statutes and Rules.** A federal statute or a rule prescribed by the Supreme Court may provide for admitting or excluding evidence independently from these rules.

Rule 1102. Amendments

These rules may be amended as provided in 28 U.S.C. § 2072.

Rule 1103. Title

These rules may be cited as the Federal Rules of Evidence.

APPENDIX B

ANNOTATED TRIAL TRANSCRIPT

■ INTRODUCTION

The transcript contained in this appendix is the transcript of a real criminal trial. The names of the judge, witnesses, attorneys, and other persons have been changed, along with the names of streets and other locations, dates, and other various references. The words spoken by the judge, witnesses, and attorneys have not been altered. In modified form, here is the background of the case that led to this trial.

On March 15, 1996, Gregory Whitman drove the getaway car in a hold-up at Gerber's Food Market in Romersdale, Pennsylvania, perpetrated by Eddie Monroe. Later that same day, just before 7:00 P.M., Eddie Monroe held up another store, Northeast Drug Store. Both hold-ups were committed with the use of a gun. A security guard, Samuel Wilson, attempted to apprehend Monroe after he left the drug store following the second hold-up. As he was being led back to the store by Wilson, Monroe pulled his gun and shot Wilson, who died at the scene. Monroe escaped to Maryland, where he was apprehended on unrelated firearms charges and returned to Mallory County, Pennsylvania, to face murder and robbery charges stemming from the two March 15 hold-ups. He was eventually found guilty and sentenced to life in prison.

Gregory Whitman pled guilty as an accomplice to the Gerber's hold-up. With respect to the second hold-up at Northeast Drug Store, Whitman was charged with criminal homicide, robbery, and conspiracy to commit robbery, on the theory that he was involved as Monroe's getaway driver in the second hold-up in which Officer Wilson was murdered. At his trial, the prosecutor presented witnesses who placed Whitman at the scene of the crime in close proximity to Monroe's car, and who testified regarding Whitman's involvement in the first March 15 hold-up. Whitman's defense was that he was at home when the second hold-up took place, and his defense presents testimony to support that alibi.

Throughout the transcript, the author has added comments in brackets and boldface type to explain various aspects of the testimony, application of Rules of Evidence, and strategies used by the attorneys as they examine witnesses and introduce real evidence. Some of these comments are keyed to applicable portions of the textbook.

Commonwealth of Pennsylvania	Court of the Common Pleas
	Mallory County, Pennsylvania
V.	
Gregory Whitman	
	No. 453 CD 1996

TRANSCRIPT OF PROCEEDINGS JURY TRIAL

Before:	THE HONORABLE ALFRED A. ZEIGLER
Date:	Tuesday, August 6-9, 1996
PLACE:	Courtroom No. 4, Mallory County Courthouse, Romersdale, Penna.
APPEARANCES:	Clark B. Mendel, Esquire, Deputy District Attorney, for Commonwealth
	Kirby M. Wolfe, Esquire, for Defendant

MR. MENDEL: Your Honor, the next matter for trial is docketed to 453 CD 1996, The Commonwealth of Pennsylvania versus Gregory Whitman. The Defendant is present in the courtroom represented by his attorney, Mr. Kirby M. Wolfe.

He is presently charged with one count of criminal homicide, one count of robbery, one count of criminal conspiracy to commit robbery.

There is one outstanding motion that was a motion to compel discovery. Prior to this matter being called in court, we had an opportunity, Mr. Wolfe and myself, to discuss this matter in chambers with you. At that time I believe we resolved the outstanding motion to the satisfaction of both the Commonwealth and defense counsel. Would that be correct, Mr. Wolfe?

MR. WOLFE: That's correct, Your Honor. We have received copies of the requested statements that were requested in the motion to compel discovery.

[A motion to compel discovery was filed in this case and was not ruled upon by the court because the prosecutor provided the document requested by the defendant prior to trial. Ch. 3, "Disclosure of Evidence"]

THE COURT: Very well.

MR. MENDEL: And with that, Your Honor, I believe that we're prepared to begin with selection of the jury.

THE COURT: Fine.

(Whereupon, at 11:50 A.M., court was held in recess.)

AFTER RECESS

(Whereupon, at 2:00 P.M., the prospective jury panel entered the courtroom.)

THE COURT: Would you swear the prospective panel, please.

(Whereupon, all prospective jurors in the above-entitled matter were sworn or affirmed.)

[At this point, the jury is selected. The *voir dire* is not part of the record, however, so there is no need to include it here. Ch. 3, "Stage 1: Jury Selection"]

THE COURT: Ladies and gentlemen, now that you have been sworn and selected to be on this jury, you are to perform one of the most solemn duties of your citizenship. You are to sit in judgment upon a criminal charge made by the Commonwealth against one of your fellow citizens.

The services that you render as jurors in this case are as important to the administration of justice as those services rendered by the attorneys and by me as the Judge. You should pay close attention to what is said and to what occurs throughout the trial so that you can faithfully perform the duties that you now are going to undertake.

I want to describe briefly in a general way what's going to occur so that those of you who are not familiar or haven't been jurors before will have an idea of the procedure. The District Attorney will, if he wishes, make an opening statement to you. I presume that he will.

The purpose of opening statements whether made by the District Attorney or the defense is to outline generally the case as they will try to establish it for you ahead of time so that as you hear the witnesses you have some kind of framework and understanding of what those witnesses are going to talk about rather than not knowing anything about the case and just learn it as the witnesses tell you about it.

When the case in chief begins after the lawyers make their opening statements to you, the District Attorney will go first and present his witnesses, each of which will be examined by the District Attorney and then subject to cross examination. At the close of the Commonwealth's case, the Defendant's attorney may also and will present evidence for the Defendant.

Under Pennsylvania law, the Defendant has no obligation to offer evidence or to testify himself. Under the law, every Defendant is presumed innocent and has the right to remain silent. The burden is on the Commonwealth to prove the Defendant guilty beyond a reasonable doubt.

The District Attorney may cross examine any witnesses called by the defense. After all of the evidence is in, the lawyers will present closing arguments to you. They don't have to do that, but usually they do and I presume that they will do it in this case. The defense goes first and the District Attorney will finish.

It is my responsibility to decide the questions of law, and therefore you must accept any rulings that I make. And any instructions that I give you on the law, you must accept that as accurate. It is not for me or for the lawyers to determine the facts. That is your province and that is the job that you will perform when you undertake your deliberations.

You're the sole judges of the facts. It will be your responsibility to weigh the evidence, to determine the facts, and then apply the law that I give you to the facts that you have found.

You are not permitted in Pennsylvania to take any notes during a criminal proceeding. The reasons for that rule are basically two, I suppose: One is that the person who is taking notes, who has taken notes, may be given more consideration by the other jurors when you deliberate. You may tend to say well, Mrs. Smith took notes and she has them there, so that may be more accurate. Well, that's not necessarily the case, because the person who is taking the notes isn't listening.

The second reason is that the jury system works because it's the collective recollection of all of you that deliberate that determine the facts, not just one of you, but what you all remember as you deliberate about the case.

[Many jurisdictions are now changing this rule and allowing jurors to take notes in more complex proceedings. [Ch. 3, Stage 3: "Prosecutor's case-in-chief"]

We have a court reporter who sits right in front of me, Mrs. Shaffner, who is taking the testimony. If you fail to hear a question or to understand a response at any time during the trial, all you have to do is raise your hand and let us know that and we will read back the question and the answer as necessary.

At the end of the trial when you are deliberating, if you are unsure of any of the testimony, if you don't recall it, you can ask us to read back and go back over the testimony of that particular part. And if we're satisfied that that's crucial, we can do that. Generally and almost without exception that's not necessary because you will have remembered what the people say when you discuss it.

You are the judges of the credibility and weight of all evidence including the testimony of the witnesses. By credibility of testimony or other evidence, I mean its truthfulness and accuracy. In judging credibility and weight, you should use your understanding of human nature and common sense. Observe each witness as he or she testifies. Be alert for anything that in that person's words or manner or demeanor that would make you think that the person is accurate or not accurate.

In effect, bring into this jury box the common sense that has held you in good stead in your life outside of this courtroom. You should keep an open mind throughout the trial and you should not talk about the evidence or the case until you begin to deliberate.

Now, I want to tell you something very important about this case. As you indicated in your response from one of the lawyers, almost everybody has heard or you believe you've heard something about this case. I don't know whether or not the case is going to receive the attention of the media. But if it does, it will be in the newspapers or on the television and on the radio.

And what I'm telling you is that we don't want you to listen to any of that or watch it on television or read any of the newspaper accounts about it. The reason for that is this: If you do that, if there are any media presentations, that, after all, is just one person's impression of what is going on in this courtroom. That person probably will not have been here through the whole trial, whatever it is; they are taking what they hear and making an opinion out of it. And your performance of that function is the only one that counts. You are going to be here throughout the whole trial, and we don't want you to take anybody else's ideas about the case and consider them.

Now, sometime you may think it's hard to avoid any contact with the media presentation about this case if that occurs, but it's not. If you're in the living room and the 6:00 news comes on, get out of the living room. If it's in the paper, don't read the paper. It's not at all hard to do that.

And we found through the cases that the jurors do that. And after the first time their family respects them about that and the family aids in shielding you from anything about the case. But I want you to try very, very hard to exclude anything about this case outside of this courtroom from your knowledge.

Now, I want to tell you a few other things really just about our routine. We're going to start most days at 9:00 in the morning, which means that you should be in your jury deliberation room prepared to come down at 9:00. Sometimes we can't bring you right at 9:00 because there may be some other business that the court has, or the lawyers have a question which we may deal with in chambers. But you should prepare to come down at 9:00.

We will work about an hour and a half at a time before a recess, so that if we start at 9:00 you can expect a recess at 10:30. And we'll endeavor to have some refreshments in the jury room for you, and we will take a 15-minute recess.

We will then work to very close to 12:30. We'll come back a quarter of 2:00. We'll take a break at 3:00, and we'll work to 4:30. It will be very unusual for us to work later than 4:30. So that if you can contemplate that in your plans and so on, that that will be routine.

Again, most importantly, if any of you have any questions at all throughout the trial, either because you don't understand a part of the procedure or because you have a personal problem and it's making it difficult for you to function, if we're in the courtroom raise your hand and we'll deal with it. If you're in your jury deliberation room, all you have to do is tap on the door and tell one of the tip staffs and they'll inform the court and we'll deal with it.

Alright. The jury may now be excused for a 15-minute recess.

(Whereupon, at 3:00 P.M., the jury was excused.)

THE COURT: Recess the court until 3:15.

(Whereupon, at 3:00 P.M., court was held in recess.)

AFTER RECESS

(Whereupon, at 3:15 P.M., the following proceedings were had:)

MR. MENDEL: Thank you, Your Honor.

(Whereupon, at 3:17 P.M., Mr. Mendel began opening remarks to the jury.)

(Whereupon, at 3:23 P.M., Mr. Mendel concluded opening remarks to the jury.)

(Whereupon, at 3:23 P.M., Mr. Wolfe began opening remarks to the jury.)

(Whereupon, at 3:31 P.M., Mr. Wolfe concluded opening remarks to the jury.)

LINDA MARKS, called as a witness, being duly sworn, testified as follows:

MR. MENDEL: Your Honor, there was a request from counsel for the sequestration of certain witnesses. Some defense witnesses are here. I believe that most of the Commonwealth defense witnesses be sequestered as well.

[The sequestration of witnesses is a common practice to prevent their testimony from being affected by the testimony of other witnesses. Ch. 13, "Sequestration"]

THE COURT: Very well.

MR. WOLFE: I have no objections.

DIRECT EXAMINATION

BY MR. MENDEL:

Q Would you please state your full name, please.

A Linda Marks

Q And is that Mrs. Marks?

A Yes.

Q I'd like to direct your attention back to March 15, 1996, and ask you where you were employed on that date?

A Gerber's Food Market

Q And what was your position at Gerber's?

A Cashier.

Q And how long had you worked at Gerber's?

A Eight years.

Q And you just recently left the employ at Gerber's, is that correct?

A Saturday was my last.

Q Now, particularly I direct your attention to approximately a quarter to 4:00 in the afternoon of March 15. Would you tell the ladies and gentlemen of the jury what took place.

A I was working as a cashier, and about a quarter to 4:00 a black male entered the outdoor of the store. He went around the cashiers to the front. I got a customer which I was waiting on, and after I was done waiting on him I had another customer.

After I was finished packing her bag and giving her change, a black male came to the side of me with a small silver handgun and demanded—he said I want your money, and he looked at my customer which was still standing there and said don't open your mouth, just shut up.

So in panic I tried to open my register, and they're computered. I kept pushing the buttons. I couldn't open the register.

So I left the second register which I was on, went to the third checkout. No one was working at the time. And I came to my senses and I thought you have to push the no sale. I pushed the no sale button and started to get the money out. I took a brown paper bag off of the checkout, put the money in. I was letting the Food Stamps and checks in the one slot. He said I want all the money. I put those in, too.

[Technically, anything Monroe says to her during the robbery is hearsay, but it is not being offered here to prove the truth of what he is saying, but rather to provide a full picture of what is taking place. Hearsay is often not objected to when it is simply part of the overall story and does not specifically incriminate the defendant or support his defense.]

Put the brown paper bag on the checkout, left my checkout, started into my checkout thinking since he had gotten the money he was going to leave. Instead I felt he put the gun to my head and said lady, I'm not fooling, I want this money, too.

So I knew I couldn't open it before and I must have just went into shock. I started pushing buttons—all kind of buttons. The next thing, you know, he must have ran out of the store. I don't know if a customer came up that he ran out, and I started screaming, and that's all I can remember.

Q Mrs. Marks, how much money was taken from the store?

A $1,399.90.

Q And since that time have you had an opportunity to identify the individual who robbed you on March 15?

A Yes, I did.

Q And what is that individual's name?

A Eddie Monroe.

[This testimony may seem unrelated to the defendant's case, which involves a completely different hold-up, but as you'll see it is laying a factual foundation for evidence that the defendant himself was involved in this first hold-up, in order to prove that he was engaged in an overall course of criminal conduct with Monroe on this date. Ch. 9, "The Meaning of 'Relevance'"]

MR. MENDEL: Thank you, Mrs. Marks.

CROSS EXAMINATION

BY MR. WOLFE:

Q Ma'am, you said that you've identified a picture of Eddie Monroe as the person who robbed you that afternoon, is that correct?

A Not the picture. I seen him in person.

Q And you've identified him?

A Yes, I did.

Q The man that's seated to my left, Mr. Whitman, did you see him at all at Gerber's that afternoon?

A No, I did not.

Q You have no idea based on what you said as to how Mr. Monroe got away from the store, do you?

A No, I don't.

[Again, this testimony would seem to call the relevance of her previous testimony into question, but she is not being offered as an eyewitness to the defendant's activities, only laying a foundation for what follows. With these questions, Wolfe is simply pointing out to the jury that this testimony does not, in itself, incriminate his client.]

MR. WOLFE: Thank you. I have no further questions.

MR. MENDEL: Thank you, Mrs. Marks.

THE WITNESS: Thank you.

MR. MENDEL: With the court's permission, if Mrs. Marks could be permitted to be excused?

[The witness is being excused because there is no intention of calling her as a witness for the defense.]

MR. WOLFE: We have no objection.

THE COURT: Certainly.

MR. MENDEL: Thank you.

(Witness excused.)

MR. MENDEL: Chief Willis

ROBERT WILLIS, called as a witness, being duly sworn, testified as follows:

DIRECT EXAMINATION

BY MR. MENDEL:

Q Would you please state your name and spell your last name please.

A Robert Willis, W-i-l-l-i-s

Q Sir, how are you employed?

A Chief of Police, Severton Police Department

Q Sir, you're going to have to slow down and speak a little louder so everyone can hear you.

   Chief, I'd like to direct your attention to March 15, 1996, and the incident which Mrs. Marks just spoke about, that namely being the robbery at Gerber's. What time did your office receive the call concerning that incident?

A Approximately 4:00.

Q And through your investigation were you able to determine the time the offense took place?

A Just a minute. 15:45.

Q Which would be 3:45?

A 3:45 P.M.

Q Now, you weren't the initial officer on the scene, is that correct?

A I was not.

Q Did you subsequently take control of the investigation?

A I did the following day.

Q Well, basically your investigation, did it reveal who the robber of the store was, who the individual who went in the store was?

A Yes, sir.

Q And who was that individual?

A Eddie Monroe.

Q And has Mr. Monroe been charged?

A He has.

Q And has he been brought to trial yet on that?

A He has not.

Q And presently are you aware of the status of that case?

A Yes, sir.

Q And could you explain to the ladies and gentlemen of the jury where it is at the present time.

A At the present time it's pending court action here in Mallory County.

Q So he's awaiting trial?

A Yes, sir.

Q Now, as a result of your investigation, were you able to determine how he escaped from Gerber's or the perpetrator left the store?

A Yes, sir.

Q And how was that?

A A brown or copper-colored vehicle, the vehicle Pennsylvania registration GCK405. The vehicle was a 1983. It belonged to Eddie Monroe from 501 Meckler Street, Romersdale.

Q Now, what was the number of that vehicle?

A GCK405.

Q And who was identified as the operator of that vehicle?

A Gregory Whitman.

Q And for the record, who is Gregory Whitman?

A The Defendant sitting right there (indicating).

MR. MENDEL: Indicating the Defendant.

[Despite the clearly incriminating nature of this testimony and the fact that the testifying officer has no first-hand knowledge of the defendant's involvement in the robbery at Gerber's, he is testifying about the first hold-up, not the second, and the defendant already pleaded guilty to his involvement in the first hold-up, so there is no question that this evidence is admissible.]

MR. MENDEL:

Q Since that time has Mr. Whitman made any statements concerning whether or not he was in Severton on that date and at that time?

A Yes, sir, he has.

Q And basically what was the essence of that statement?

A During the afternoon hours, he was in Severton in that vehicle in the rear of Gerber's, and he has admitted being the operator of that vehicle during the Gerber's incident.

Q And has he made any statement concerning his knowledge of whether a robbery has taken place and whether or not he had agreed to commit a robbery?

A Yes, sir he has.

Q And basically could you explain that.

A Yes, sir. On that date and that time he was the lookout man and the operator of the vehicle during Gerber's robbery.

[Any confession like this made by the defendant in the course of an investigation of his own criminal conduct would be admissible both as an admission of a party opponent and as a statement against interest.]

Q Now, I believe you testified that the vehicle was parked or the statement the vehicle was parked to the rear of Gerber's?

A Yes, sir, it was.

Q Now, could you explain to the ladies and gentlemen where Gerber's is situated.

A It's located at Frank and Chivers Streets in the Borough of Severton. It's a fairly large store. The front of it would face the—yeah, the west or the river. The rear of the building would face St. Paul's Church on the east side. The vehicle was parked on the east side of the building, which would be the rear where there is not ample parking places for vehicles.

Q Now, Chief, were you able to determine through your investigation the route of travel that the vehicle used in leaving the scene?

A Yes, sir. The vehicle after the incident went out the back portion of Gerber's, up Second Street which is a one way street the wrong way, to St. Paul's Drive.

Q And at that time do you know where the vehicle went?

A No, sir, I do not.

Q And through your investigation were you able to determine where that vehicle went?

A I was told the vehicle went to 24G Hiller Court.

[Again, this is clearly hearsay, especially since he is not stating who told him this. Later, he indicates that the source of this information was the defendant himself. But even so, this is not the crime the defendant is being tried for, and he already pled guilty to being the getaway driver for the first hold-up.]

Q And that being the residence of the Defendant?

A Yes, sir.

Q Do you know if any money was recovered from either Mr. Monroe or from the Defendant?

A Sir, I believe from Mr. Monroe.

Q But as from the Defendant?

A No, sir.

[It is not necessary to show that the defendant profited from the robbery in order for him to be held liable as an accomplice.]

MR. MENDEL: Thank you Chief.

CROSS EXAMINATION

BY MR. WOLFE:

Q Chief Willis, heading up the investigation of the robbery in Severton, would you indicate to the jury the manner in which Mr. Whitman came into custody.

A Yes, sir.

Q How would that be?

A On March the 16th at approximately 10:45 A.M., Mr. Whitman came into the Severton Police Station. The secretary advised me of this and placed him under arrest, advised him of his constitutional rights. He voluntarily walked into the police station.

Q He voluntarily turned himself in the next day?

A Yes, sir, he did.

[The point being made here is that Mr. Whitman was willing to accept full responsibility for his involvement in the first hold-up, implying that he would have been equally willing to admit his guilt in the second hold-up, if he had in fact been involved. As it turns out, Mr. Whitman turned himself in because he heard the police were looking for him, and he did at first deny his involvement in the first hold-up, as Mr Mendel makes clear on redirect.]

Q Are you familiar under the circumstances under which Mr. Monroe was apprehended?

A A little, sir. He was arrested by the Romersdale Police and the Baltimore Police.

Q Where was he arrested?

A In Baltimore, Maryland.

Q You've indicated that based on your investigation the vehicle in question was registered to Eddie Monroe?

A Yes, sir, it was.

Q And you've indicated that through the source of your investigation that after the incident the vehicle proceeded to 24 G Hiller Court?

A Yes sir.

Q And your investigation further revealed that at that point Mr. Whitman was dropped off at his residence?

A From Mr. Whitman, okay. He explained this to me.

MR. WOLFE: Thank you. I have no further questions.

REDIRECT EXAMINATION

BY MR. MENDEL:

Q Chief, I have a couple questions. When Mr. Whitman turned himself in on the 16th of March, did you question him concerning his involvement in the robbery at Gerber's?

A I did, sir.

Q And what did he tell you at that time concerning his involvement?

A At first he denied any knowledge of the incident.

Q And knowledge whatsoever?

A Yes, sir.

Q What exactly did he tell you that he was doing at that time?

A I believe he told me—well, he did tell me he was with George Munns in Romersdale.

Q And did he tell you how he got in contact with Mr. Munns on that day in question.

A Initially he told me he called him.

[This testimony lays a foundation later to show that the defendant is not truthful, since the testimony shows that Munns does not have a phone.]

Q Did you later have an opportunity or some member of your force have an opportunity to interview Mr. Munns?

A We did, sir.

Q And were you able to determine if that story was indeed accurate?

A No, sir, it was not.

Q And how were you able to determine that?

A By speaking to Mr. Munns and also further speaking with Mr. Whitman.

Q If I can stop you for a second, speaking with Mr. Munns. After speaking with Mr. Munns, did you then question Mr. Whitman again?

A I did.

Q And what did Mr. Whitman tell you at this time?

A That originally he did not tell the truth.

Q And what did he say this time?

A If I may refer to my notes?

Q Yes, sir.

A Or my reports.

At 1:15 that afternoon Whitman agreed to be truthful about the knowledge of the incident involving Gerber's robbery. At that time, he indicated that he was a passenger in Monroe's vehicle.

Q Chief, if I could interrupt, if you could please speak up a little bit, a little slower. I believe some members of the jury may be having trouble understanding you.

A Okay. At that time he indicated he was a passenger in Monroe's vehicle and that Monroe did park in Gerber's lot yesterday and that Monroe went inside and came back to the car within 5 minutes. He stated Monroe drove out the wrong way from Gerber's and they drove to Hiller Court and that is where Whitman got out.

He stated he had no knowledge of Monroe robbing Gerber's before, during, or after the incident.

Q Did he indicate whether or not he got any money as a result of this?

A He told me he received no money.

Q And I believe you did say he indicated he had no knowledge of what took place?

A Yes, sir.

Q Now, you heard Mr. Whitman today, is that correct?

A Yes, sir, I did.

Q And today did he again deny any knowledge of that?

A No, sir, he didn't.

Q So is that the third time you've heard him speak about this?

A Yes.

Q And would this be the third different version?

A Yes, sir.

[This testimony essentially negates any benefit the defendant might have received from the jury knowing that he came to the police station voluntarily. He wasn't there to admit to his crimes, but rather to attempt, rather inartfully, to cover them up.]

MR. MENDEL: Thank you, Chief.

MR. WOLFE: I have no further questions.

THE COURT: Just a second, Chief. Would counsel approach the bench.

(Whereupon, the following discussion was held at side bar:)

THE COURT: What did he come in to say? I don't want to ask him, but he voluntarily came in.

MR. WOLFE: He turned himself in.

THE COURT: For what?

MR. MENDEL: It was his understanding there were warrants out for his arrest for the robbery charge down in Severton. Apparently one of the officers, I think it was Joseph Moreland of the Severton Police Department, phoned Mr. Whitman's mother and said they were looking for him and then he came down.

THE COURT: Do you think maybe a couple more questions because at least in my mind I didn't understand that. He came in, voluntarily turned himself in, and said he didn't know anything about it. And there's not going to—it's up to you, but I had that question.

MR. MENDEL: Maybe while we're here, in chambers before we started the trial we discussed bringing this evidence in and Mr. Wolfe indicated that basically he would not be objecting to it as to hearsay as to the Chief.

[The judge here is expressing a concern about the possibility of the jury's confusion over the question of why the defendant turned himself in. Obviously, the attorneys do not believe that any further explanation is necessary. Also, this is a good example of a stipulation that relates directly to the admissibility of evidence. Wolfe agreed beforehand that the Chief's hearsay testimony would not be challenged, although as we have seen any statements made by the defendant would be admissible anyway. Ch. 4, "Stipulations"]

MR. WOLFE: I didn't make any objection.

MR. MENDEL: I just want to put that on the record.

MR. WOLFE: We entered a plea to the charge.

MR. MENDEL: Okay.

(Whereupon, the discussion at side bar was concluded.)

MR. MENDEL: Thank you. Do you have any questions?

MR. WOLFE: No.

(Witness excused.)

MR. MENDEL: George Munns.

Your Honor, at this time we'd ask that a number of witnesses who are here be excused. I don't believe in light of the Chief's testimony they'll be needed. Basically, they're Lewis Thoman, Harvey Jones, Betty Fordham, and Georgia Ingris.

MR. WOLFE: I'm sorry. Would you repeat those witnesses again?

MR. MENDEL: Lewis Thoman, Harvey Jones, Betty Fordham, Jane Forbes, and Georgia Ingris.

[These witnesses were being held in reserve to provide the factual testimony necessary if the Chief's hearsay testimony had been excluded. This is an important point in preparing a case: if a witness' testimony is arguably inadmissible, backup testimony should be ready. In this case, Wolfe knew these witnesses were available and could testify about his client's involvement in the first hold-up, so to save time and prevent his client being essentially tried for that crime in this proceeding, he chose to waive any objections to the chief's testimony. This is good lawyering on the part of both attorneys.]

MR. WOLFE: We have no problems.

THE COURT: Very well. They may be excused.

MR. MENDEL: If I may have a brief second to explain it to them.

THE COURT: Ladies and gentlemen, several minutes ago, before we started, there were some questions about sequestering the witnesses. All that means is that those witnesses are just outside of the courtroom, and the idea is that they don't want to—both sides agree that it's not good to have the witnesses who are going to testify sit here and hear all the testimony because that might color them or persuade them.

So we keep them outside and then they come in and tell you without benefit of what they heard somebody else say, and we do it almost every proceeding.

MR. MENDEL: Mr. Munns.

GEORGE MUNNS, called as a witness, being duly sworn, testifies as follows:

DIRECT EXAMINATION

BY MR. MENDEL:

Q Would you please state your name for the record, sir.

A George Munns.

Q Now, Mr. Munns, where do you live?

A 214 Peiffer Street.

Q And on the date of March 15, 1996, where did you live?

A 76 Ivory Lane.

Q Now, on that occasion did you have a telephone at your home?

A No, I didn't.

Q Now, did you encounter or meet Gregory Whitman on that date?

A Yes, I did. On a Friday.

Q That was a Friday?

A Yes, sir.

Q And where did you meet him?

A At his home.

Q And where was that located?

A In Hiller Court.

Q And for the record, that address would be 24 G, correct?

A I guess.

Q Well, approximately what time did you meet with Mr. Whitman?

A About 4:00.

Q And any particular reason why you stopped by Mr. Whitman's home?

A Well, I had seen him earlier that week and I had that day went out to look for a job. And somebody told me that he was hiring at this place so I came—when I went past his house I was telling him I filled out an application and they were supposed to be hiring at this place.

Q If I could interrupt you, you have to speak a little louder and a little slower.

A When I went over to his house, right, I was telling him that I filled out this application for a job, you know. You know, he could fill out one, too, you know, that they was hiring.

So he didn't say anything at that time, you know, so I was just sitting there. So he was telling me about him and his brother went down to York.

Q And when did he say he went with his brother to York?

A He said to sell some stereo equipment.

Q And when did he say that took place?

A That day I guess, that morning.

Q And did Mr. Whitman indicate what he had received for that stereo equipment?

A Oh, I guess about $500.

Q Now, did he show you any money?

A Well, he loaned me $20.

Q But did he show you any money?

A Well, I seen money.

Q And could you describe the money you saw?

A Well, it was about that much (indicating)?

Q And did he indicate how much it was?

A About $500.

Q Is that what Mr. Whitman told you sir?

A Yes, sir.

Q And he loaned you $20, correct?

A Yeah.

Q What did you do after getting the $20 from Mr. Whitman?

[This testimony, relating to the hours between the first and second hold-ups on March 15, raises the question of whether Mr. Whitman did, in fact, profit from his participation in the earlier robbery.]

A Well, I have some medicine for my daughter that I was taking up for my daughter, so I asked him if he wanted to ride with me. So he rode with me uptown to take the medicine for my daughter.

Q Your daughter was staying with a baby sitter?

A Yeah, on Lorant Street.

Q And did Mr. Whitman go along with you.

A Yes, he did.

Q And you drive what kind of car?

A It was an '80 Grand Prix.

Q What color is it?

A Silver.

Q And did you and Mr. Whitman then go up to Lorant Street?

A Yes, we did.

Q What did you do after that?

A Well, from there we went up to Lou's Bar on North Sixth Street, Sixth and Munich.

Q And is that near Lorant Street?

A About six blocks.

Q And what did you do up at Lou's Bar?

A We hung around up there for a while.

Q Then what took place.

A Well, he had to—well, from there I asked him if he wanted to go see if his old lady, you know, got home yet. So from there we went back out to his house and I has let him out and from there I let him out. This was about a little after 6:00—after—a little after 5:00 when I let him out. It was after 5:00. And I left.

    I went around my brother's house. He live at 23 C Hiller Court. So from there when I went to his house, his girlfriend told me that he went to the store. That's Joe's Store.

Q His girlfriend told you that?

A Yeah, my brother's girlfriend.

Q Oh, your brother's girlfriend. What's her name?

A Nebbles.

Q Is that her first name?

A Well, that's all I call her, Nebbles. I don't know no more than that. She told me my brother went to the store, so I went around the store. I seen my brother and Gregory Whitman. He was standing on the corner. So he said that his old lady didn't get back home yet, you know, from work, something like that, right, that she had went shopping.

    So I said, well, come on, go with me then, you know, because he wasn't doing anything else. So he got back in the car, and after I finished talking to my brother, we went back uptown.

Q Okay. Where did you go particularly?

A Well, I went straight down through Seventeenth Street. I hit Main Street, went down Main Street. From there I went—I didn't make no stops. I went, hit Clipper Street and I went on uptown.

Q Okay.

A Okay. From there we went back up to Lou's Bar again.

Q Okay. What happened at Lou's then?

A Well, we stayed up there for a good while and I seen my wife's cousin up there. Her name is—well, her last name is Ferguson.

Q Okay. Would that be Allison?

A Yeah. She asked me to take her home. She'd give me $3 to run her home.

Q Okay. And where did she live?

A She lived right off of—well, she lived right off of Parson Street.

Q Okay.

A Okay. She asked me to take her to the chicken place while she was in the car. The chicken place is on Thirteenth and Main.

Q Okay. Did you take her there?

A Yeah, I did.

Q What did you do then?

A Well, I was sitting outside about 10, 15 minutes waiting on her. And I seen these two girls that I knew, they came up.

Q Well, let me take you back a little bit. Gregory's still in the car with you, right?

A Okay, okay.

Q Okay. And you're heading up toward the chicken place.

A Right.

Q Did Mr. Whitman ask you to stop anywhere or honk at anyone?

A Okay. Alright. When we come up Main Street from Lou's Bar out on the hill, we stopped at Thirteenth and Main at the red light.

Q Okay. What took place there?

A Well, there was this guy on the corner. I don't know the guy. So Greg asked me to blow my horn at him, you know. So I said I didn't know him, you know. So he hollered at the guy and asked the guy would he come over to his house, you know.

Q Who said that?

A Greg. He asked the guy would he come over to his house.

Q Okay. Now, where exactly was your car, were you on the street or parked off to the side?

A I was at the light.

Q Okay. When you say Greg, you mean the Defendant?

A Yeah.

Q Asked this man to come over to his house?

A Right.

Q Did you later have an opportunity to identify this individual?

A Yes, I did.

Q And who was that man?

A Eddie Monroe.

[At this point, timing becomes critical because of the defendant's defense of alibi. The defendant's whereabouts between 4:00 and 7:00, and whether he did, in fact, meet up with Monroe before the second hold-up, is the focal point of a great deal of testimony from this point forward. This is why the testimony relating to these hours, and in particular the hours between 6:00 and 7:00, is elicited in such detail by both attorneys when examining any witnesses to the defendant's activities during that time.]

Q Now, you're back at the chicken place then with the lady you dropped off?

A Yeah.

Q Okay. Did you wait for her to come out of the chicken place?

A No, I didn't.

Q Okay, What happened then?

A Well, I picked up this other girl, other two girls.

Q Okay.

A You know, they said they wanted to go get some pot. And I said alright, I'll take them to go get some pot. So all four of us was in the car—me, the two girls, and Gregory Whitman.

[It may seem strange to allow a witness to testify that he was engaged in the illegal purchase of drugs for his companions during the critical hours for this case. Again, however, this is part of the story which was unfolding during those hours, and has nothing directly to do with the defendant's criminal conduct or his defense. Having the witness admit to this on the stand not only explains each leg of the trip from the chicken shop to the defendant's home, but also establishes the witness' credibility by showing he is not trying to hide anything. It also gives the jury an unfavorable initial impression of the two women who were riding with Munns and Whitman, both of whom will eventually testify as witnesses for the defense and will admit that they were getting high during the critical hour, thereby making their testimony about specific times questionable. Ch. 13, "Impeachment"]

Okay. We were riding uptown on Presser Street, Sixth and Presser, and we go get some pot. So from there we rode back out on the hill. So he stopped at his sister's house to get some papers.

Q Do you know what time you stopped at his sister's home?

A Well, I believe it was after 6:00.

Q Okay. And that was to get some papers for marijuana?

A Right?

Q Who went in the house?

A Gregory.

Q I assume there's two girls right?

A Yeah.

Q And you and Mr. Whitman?

A Right.

Q And you're the only people in the car?

A Right.

Q What did the three of you do?

A Just sat outside and waited.

Q Okay. How long was Mr. Whitman in the home?

A About 5 minutes, 6 minutes.

Q Then what happened?

A Well, we rode around. He come out of the house and we had rode out on south side, you know, and I got a pack of cigarettes in the store, a couple packs of cigarettes. So this one girl, she was saying that she had to meet her sister at this bar at 7:00. And so I said well, alright.

It was going on something to 7:00 and I took—me and him took both of the girls out on Thirteenth and Main. I dropped them off on Thirteenth Street.

Q Then what did you do?

A Well, from there I took Mr. Whitman back out south side and I went home.

Q When you say south side, you mean Hiller Court?

A Hiller Court.

Q And after you dropped the girls off, you took the Defendant home?

A Right.

Q Did you see where he went after you dropped him off?

A No. When I dropped him off, like I stopped him off facing his house.

Q Okay.

A When he got out of the car, he walked toward his house and I just turned around and pulled off.

Q Now Mr. Munns, how soon or how long after Mr. Whitman said anything to Mr. Monroe did you drop him off.

A Well, when we seen the guy, Monroe, it must have been something after 6:00 when we seen him, and it was awhile after that when I dropped Greg off.

Q Do you think you can make an estimation about what time it was?

A Maybe about—it could have been about an hour and 10 minutes.

[This testimony would seem to support the defendant's defense of alibi, since the second robbery and murder took place around 7:00 that evening. Later witnesses will place the defendant at the scene of that robbery and murder, but at this point it appears that Whitman was actually with Munns when the murder was taking place. This may have been a tactical error on the part of the prosecutor, who now immediately changes the subject of the examination and brings it to a close.]

Q And that's the hour and 10 minutes from the time you saw Mr. Monroe to the time you dropped Mr. Whitman off at his home?

A Right.

MR. MENDEL: With the court's indulgence for one moment.

THE COURT: Certainly.

BY MR. MENDEL:

Q Do you recall how Mr. Whitman was dressed on that day?

A He had on beige, tan, brown, like tan, brown pair of pants, beige, like, you know, brownish, with a blue shirt with some little thing on the front.

Q On the shirt?

A Yes.

Q And what color was the shirt?

A It was like the same color of that shirt you got on, black there, bluish like that color shirt. It was a T-shirt like, though.

Q You mean the man in the first row?

A Yeah. It was a shirt like.

Q Did you ask Mr. Whitman—do you recall whether he had a jacket on?

A No, he didn't have no jacket on.

Q Did you ask him if he thought he should have a jacket?

A Well, it was kind of chilly out, you know, and I asked him, hey, ain't you going to get your jacket? He said no, he don't need it. So we just went on.

Q Was he wearing a hat at all?

A No, he wasn't.

MR. MENDEL: Thank you, Mr. Munns.

CROSS EXAMINATION

BY MR. WOLFE:

Q Mr. Munns, let's go back a little bit if we can to the first time that you saw Mr. Whitman that afternoon. At approximately what time would that have been?

A 4:00.

Q And he was at his house at that particular time?

A Yes, he was.

Q And from that particular point you indicated that you took yourself and Mr. Whitman uptown?

A Yes, sir.

Q And you stopped at Lou's Bar?

A Yes, we did.

Q And could you give me an approximation as to the time you stopped at Lou's Bar the first time?

A Well, we stayed up there maybe—it was after 5:00 when we left there.

Q And you had a couple drinks when you were up there?

A No, we didn't drink anything.

Q You were just up there talking?

A Well, I know a lot of friends up that way.

Q And it was sometimes after 5:00 when you left Lou's Bar?

A Yes.

Q And Mr. Whitman was with you at that time?

A Yes, he was.

Q And at that time you've indicated that he was wearing tan-colored pants and a T-shirt?

A Yes.

Q And I assume that's the outfit that he had on when you stopped him off at his house?

A Yes, he did.

Q For the evening, he never changed clothes or never added any clothes?

A No.

Q So after you went from Lou's Bar you went where, after you left the first time that's when you met—

A After we left the first time we went back out to Greg Whitman's house, because like his old lady, this woman, right, had went shopping they said, you know, the next door neighbors.

Q And at whose request did you go back to his house?

A Well, I asked him, you know. I said do you want to go back. And, you know, you know, so he said yeah, you know.

Q So he went back some time after 5:00?

A Right.

Q And then a short time later Mr. Whitman goes to his house and you try to find your brother?

A Right.

Q And then a short time later you see Mr. Whitman at the store or standing on the corner?

A Yes, I did.

Q And what time would that have been?

A Well it could have been about 20 after 5:00, or something like that, maybe 25 after 5:00.

Q So the two of you get together again?

A Right.

Q And at this point you drive back down to Lou's?

A Right, we go up to Lou's.

Q And you would have got to Lou's about 5:30, somewhere around there, when you came down the second time after coming out from the store?

A Yeah.

Q And you stayed at Lou's for a while, didn't you, the second time?

A Yeah.

Q And it was while you were at the bar the second time that you met your cousin, correct?

A My wife's cousin.

Q Your wife's cousin. And she requested that you drive her up on the hill.

A She said she would pay me if I take her out on the hill, if I take her home.

Q And she gave you some money?

A Yeah. She gave me $3.

Q And you, Mr. Whitman and your wife's cousin then drove up on the hill?

A Yes, we did.

Q And you dropped her off?

A At the chicken place.

Q Well, you said that you got back to Lou's the second time around 5:30 and you just stayed there for a while, correct?

A Right.

Q Alright. Can you give us any estimation as to what time you got to the chicken place on Thirteenth Street with Gregory Whitman and your wife's cousin?

A Well, it might have been a little—maybe five after 6:00 or something like that.

Q Was it getting dark at that particular time?

A Yes, it was.

Q Now, at that time she gets out of the car, correct?

A Right.

Q And you're waiting for her for a period of time, correct?

A About 10 or 15 minutes she was in there.

Q So you get to the chicken shack or this store around 6:00, five after, and you wait for her about 10, 15 minutes, right?

A Yes.

Q She doesn't show up?

A No.

Q Two other girls you see that you recognize, correct?

A Yes, I did.

Q You started talking with them, correct?

A Yes, sir.

Q So if we assume, Mr. Munns, that you got to the chicken store at say five after 6:00 and waited 10 or 15 minutes, that would have been in the area of around a quarter after, 20 after 6:00, correct?

A Yes.

Q When you get involved with these two other girls, correct?

A Right.

Q And Mr. Whitman's in the car at that time?

A Yes.

Q And they ask you if you know if there's some place where you can buy some marijuana?

A Yes, they did.

Q And you tell them that you can find a place for them, right?

A Yes.

Q And from that point on you go to Mr. Whitman's sister's house?

A Right.

Q To get some papers to roll the marijuana?

A Yes, we did.

Q And he stays in the house for about how long?

A For about 5 minutes. It wasn't very long.

Q And from that point you then drove downtown or the uptown area of Romersdale correct?

A No.

Q Where did you go after you left his house?

A We rode around toward Hiller Court. And the girl said she had to meet her sister at 7:00 and it was something to 7:00.

Q Let me back you up. At what point did you buy the marijuana, you went to buy the marijuana?

[In testimony like this, where timing is so critical, the lawyers will often need to control the witness to prevent any confusion about exactly when certain actions took place. This is easier to do on cross-examination with leading questions, as Wolfe is doing here, than it is on direct where the witness cannot be led to testify about specific events at specific times. Ch. 13, "Leading Questions"]

A Okay. When I see the two girls at the chicken place.

Q Right. And this would have been about 20 after 6:00?

A Right. So we go uptown, Sixth and Presser Street. This one boy named Keith, he goes down the street and gets a bag of reefers for us. And when he come back we come back out on the hill. That's when we stopped at his sister's house.

Q Oh, from the chicken store on Thirteenth Street you go to the uptown area to buy the marijuana?

A Yes, we did.

Q And how long would it have taken you to drive up there and to buy the marijuana?

A No more than 4 or 5 minutes at the most.

Q Did you wait at all while you bought the marijuana, did you have to wait?

A About 3, 4 minutes maybe.

Q And it took you some time to get up there, didn't it, to drive up there from Thirteenth Street, right?

A It don't take but 3 or 4 or 5 minutes to drive from that area uptown.

Q So it took you 3 or 4 minutes to drive there and you waited another couple of minutes before the guy came back with the marijuana, right?

A Yes, we did.

Q So that would have put it around the area of 6:30, correct, somewhere in that area?

A Yes, sir.

Q So you buy the marijuana, you, the two girls that are with you and Mr. Whitman then go back up to his sister's house, right?

A Yes.

Q And how long did it take you to get there?

A Four or 5 minutes.

Q It would be some time after 6:30, or somewhere in that area?

A Yeah, after we got the marijuana.

Q Mr. Whitman then goes in his sister's house to get the papers, correct?

A Yes.

Q And he sits there for he's inside the house for a couple minutes?

A Yes.

Q And he comes back out. Where did you go from that particular point then, Mr. Munns, where did you, Mr. Whitman and the two girls go?

A We rode around for a few minutes.

Q Were you using the marijuana, did you roll some?

A No, I didn't.

Q Well, did any of the girls in the car roll it?

A Yes, they did.

Q So you were driving around while they were smoking marijuana, right?

A Yes.

Q Do you recall where you went?

A Well, we went out to Joe's Store. I bought a couple packs of cigarettes. I bought a pack for me and one pack for the girl that was in the front seat. So from there the girl said she had to meet her sister at 7:00 because I was—I was like riding. I don't go no further than out on the hill uptown. I was living out on Creston Lane, so when I got the cigarettes, I got in the car and started back out toward the hill.

Q These girls indicated that they had—while girl indicated that they had to be somewhere at 7:00?

A Not Holly but the other one.

Q One of the other girls that was with you?

A Yeah.

Q And where did she have to be?

A She said she had to meet her sister at the bar over by Thirteenth and Main.

Q And did you take her back to the bar at Thirteenth and Main?

A Yes, I did.

Q When you took her back to the bar at Thirteenth and Main, was Mr. Whitman with you at the time?

A Yes, he was.

Q And could you give an estimate as to what time this was that when he was with you?

A Well, I put it to be about when we dropped the girls off, about ten of 7:00.

Q Ten to 7:00?

A Yes, maybe 7:00.

Q Maybe 7:00. Now, after that you then take Mr. Whitman back to his house, correct?

A Yes.

Q And you drop him off at that point?

A Yes, I did.

Q And that would have been some time after 7:00, correct?

A Yes.

Q Now, when you saw Mr. Monroe on the corner of Thirteenth Street, was he alone at that particular time?

A Yes, he was.

Q What response, if any, did he make to Mr. Whitman's wave or suggestion that he stop over?

A He said –

MR. MENDEL: Objection, Your Honor. That would be hearsay.

MR. WOLFE: I don't know. We're not really offering it for the truth of the matter asserted, Your Honor. We're offering it for whatever response the other individual made in reply to the greeting or solicitation by Mr. Whitman.

Mr. MENDEL: There's no other indication except that it would be offered for the truth of the matter as asserted.

THE COURT: Overruled. You can answer that.

[**This is a good example of the limitations of a hearsay objection when the objecting attorney does not know what the hearsay statement will actually be. Mendel is technically correct—there is no question that Monroe's response to Whitman's greeting is being offered to prove to the jury of Monroe's intentions in light of Whitman's offer for him to come to his house. Remember that Monroe and Whitman already pulled off a hold-up a few hours earlier. If Monroe agreed to come to Whitman's house, that would create a strong inference that Whitman was involved with the second hold-up as well. If not, it would make Whitman's case of alibi even stronger. Wolfe probably knows from speaking with his client what Monroe's response was. Mendel does not. But until the response is actually heard, there is no way of knowing for sure if it constitutes inadmissible hearsay. This is probably why the judge overrules the objection.**]

BY MR. WOLFE:

Q What did Mr. Monroe say to Mr. Whitman?

A Well, when Mr. Whitman asked him could he come out to his house, he said no, he was waiting on somebody. And like I looked over at him and like he was looking all around like he was looking for someone.

Q Who is he now?

A Eddie Monroe.

Q And at that particular point you and Mr. Whitman drove off?

A Yes, we did.

Q And you then went through the activities and the route that we have just gone over for the jury, correct?

A Yes, we did.

MR. WOLFE: Thank you. I have no further questions.

REDIRECT EXAMINATION

BY MR. MENDEL:

Q Mr. Munns, I have a number of questions for you. First of all, on that date you weren't watching the clock, were you?

[**This is an example of an attorney attempting to impeach his own witness, both by demonstrating lack of opportunity to perceive (not watching the clock), and by use of his statement to the police. Clearly, Mendel is attempting to undo the damage which occurred when Munns testified that Whitman was with him until after 7:00, but as the following testimony shows, his attempt is not particularly successful. Ch. 13, "Impeachment"**]

A No.

Q Throughout that. Do you remember giving a statement to the police on March 23, 1996?

A Yes.

Q And do you recall telling the police how long you were with Gregory Whitman on that day?

A Well, I told the police when he first asked me, I said we was together from about 4:00 until about 7:30.

Q On September 23 do you recall being asked how long do you think you were with him that day?

A I can't recall.

THE COURT: Mr. Mendel, you said September 23.

BY MR. MENDEL

Q I'm sorry. March 23.

A Well, excuse me, but like when I was down at City Hall where was this one short police, he kept saying to me, he said are you sure you wasn't together for like 2 hours and a half instead of 3 hours and a half. You know, he kept asking me the same question over and over.

[This unsolicited testimony is even more damaging to the prosecution's case, because it makes it appear that the police were attempting to get him to limit the time he was with Whitman to a period which would still allow Whitman to participate in the second hold-up. Mendel has, at this point, pretty much lost control of the witness, whose testimony is far more supportive of the defendant's alibi defense than it is of his criminal guilt.]

Q Well, do you remember answering the question then maybe an hour, close to 2, maybe 2 and a half, I don't remember?

A No. We was together longer than that.

Q Okay. Now, after you saw Eddie Monroe you testified it was what, about an hour later you dropped Gregory off, at the most an hour and 10 minutes?

A Well, I believe it was—well, I know we left Lou's it was after 6:00 and—

Q Well, Mr. Munns, my question is simply after you saw Eddie Monroe how much longer did you spend with the Defendant?

A Till the time I dropped him off.

Q Which would have been what, approximately an hour and 10 minutes as you said before?

A Yes, sir.

Q Now, how long were you guys driving around with the girls after you got the marijuana?

A About 20 minutes.

Mr. MENDEL: With the court's indulgence.

Thank you, Mr. Munns. No further questions.

RECROSS EXAMINATION

BY MR. WOLFE:

Q Just one or two questions on clarification, Mr. Munns. You said when you were with these two young ladies your purpose in dropping them off is that one of them indicated they had to be somewhere at 7:00, correct?

A Yes, they did.

Q And it was your indication that it was getting close to 7:00 when you dropped these two young ladies off, correct?

A It was close to 7:00.

[Wolfe here is driving the point home. If there is a good reason for Munns to remember the exact time he dropped off his female passengers, then the issue of time prior to that becomes moot. By focusing on the time just before 7:00, which is almost the exact time the second robbery and murder were taking place, he has cemented his client's alibi in the mind of the jurors.]

Mr. WOLFE: Alright. Thank you. I have no further questions.

MR. MENDEL: Thank you, Mr. Munns.

(Witness excused.)

MR. MENDEL: Tonya Franklin, please.

TONYA FRANKLIN, called as a witness, being duly sworn, testified as follows:

DIRECT EXAMINATION

BY MR. MENDEL:

Q Would you please state your name and spell your last name please.

A Tonya Franklin, F-r-a-n-k-l-i-n.

Q And Tonya, where do you live?

A 703 Boxton Street.

Q And that's in the City of Romersdale, correct?

A Um-hum.

Q Where do you go to school?

A Bishop McDevitt.

Q And what grade will you be in this coming year?

A Twelfth.

Q Do you have a part-time job?

A SaveRite Market.

Q And where's that located?

A Twenty-ninth and Emerald Street.

Q How long have you worked there?

A About a year and a half.

Q Excuse me?

A About a year and a half.

Q Okay. I'd like to direct your attention back to the 15th of March, 1996. It was a Friday evening. Were you working that day?

A Yes.

Q And what time did you start working?

A 5:00.

Q And do you recall the incident concerning the shooting of Samuel Wilson on that day?

A Yes.

Q Do you recall what register number you were working?

A I was on Register 4.

Q And as the store's set up, where is Register 4 in relation to the front door of the store?

A To the front door?

Q Yes.

A It's about four registers down from the door.

Q And in feet could you approximately guess how many?

A No.

Q On that date did you observe any individuals come through your counter that drew your attention to them?

A Yes.

Q And could you tell the ladies and gentlemen what you saw?

A There was a tall black male came through my line and asked me to put a small object in a large bag.

Q Do you recall what the object was?

A No.

Q Put it in a large bag. What did he mean?

A Well, usually we put little objects in real small bags. And he wanted the big bags that we put all the large objects in.

Q How big are the big bags, regular grocery-sized bags?

A Yeah.

Q Do you recall what the other individual was—how was he dressed?

A He had a black baseball hat with white letters.

Q Do you recall anything else?

A No.

Q Who were the other individuals working the checkout counters close to you?

A Penny was on 5.

Q Penny is Penny Green, correct?

A Yeah. Maggie was on 3.

Q And what's Maggie's name?

A Maggie Fleischman. She was training—she was training somebody on 3.

Q And approximately how soon after you saw this individual come through your line did you become aware of the shooting?

A About 15 minutes.

Q Thank you Tonya. Are you able to identify the individual who came through your checkout counter?

A Probably.

Q But have you had an opportunity to see him?

A Yeah.

Q And is the individual you observed present in the courtroom here today?

A No.

MR. MENDEL: Thank you.

[This testimony may seem pointless since the witness did not see Whitman at the store, but again Mendel is laying a factual foundation for later testimony. This is the beginning of the story of the events leading up to the second robbery and murder with which the defendant is charged.]

MR. WOLFE: I have a few questions for you.

CROSS EXAMINATION

BY MR. WOLFE:

Q You've indicated that—first of all, it's my understanding of around 6:30 when you say you saw this individual the store was fairly crowded, correct?

A Yes.

Q Were you waiting on a lot of people?

A Um-hum.

Q And you took it—was it somewhat of an unusual request in your opinion that this individual requested a large bag for something that was of small size?

A Sometimes people ask for them, but they always have something else they want to put in it. He didn't have anything.

Q How long did it take to wait on him?

A Not too long.

Q And you said that he was in the store or this individual was in the store around 15 minutes before the shooting, correct?

A Um-hum.

Q And so, Tonya, if we were to assume that the shooting occurred at say 6:45, it would be your testimony that it was around 6:30 that this individual came to your store, correct, to your register?

A Yes.

Q And you don't recall whether he was with anyone, do you?

A No.

Q The gentleman that's seated to my left, do you recall seeing him go through your checkout counter at that particular time?

A No.

Q You've indicated that you at least spent enough time with the person who went through your counter to be able to identify him, is that correct?

A Yes.

Q And there's nothing based on your memory of that particular evening that indicated that he was with anyone else?

A He could have been.

[Since she already testified that she didn't see the defendant when Monroe was in the store, asking her this question was a tactical error. Before, her denial of the defendant's presence was strong; now some doubt has been raised about whether he might have been there with Monroe.]

Q You don't remember seeing him with anyone else?

A I don't remember.

Q Now, at the time of the shooting did you have the occasion to look out the window and see anything that may have transpired outside after you heard the shots?

[At this point, the prosecuting attorney should object. This testimony is clearly beyond the scope of direct examination. From here on, this witness is testifying as a defense witness. While the prosecutor may have decided to let this testimony go forward to save the witness from having to be recalled, cross examination allows the use of leading questions which are not available on direct, so there is good reason to object. Ch. 13, "Examination of Witnesses"]

A Yeah.

Q And what did you see at that particular time?

A After the shooting?

Q Yes.

A The guy running back down our porch.

Q Were you able to describe that man?

A He was tall and black with a hat.

Q With a cap?

A Yeah.

Q Was he the only black male that you were able to see running down the sidewalk?

A Yes.

Q And where were you at this particular time?

A By the window.

Q Looking, and you saw him running down?

A Yeah.

Q How many times did you see him run by the window?

A Twice.

Q Now, when you saw him run down the first time, were there any black males with him at that particular time?

A No.

Q Did you see him being taken back up the sidewalk to the Northeast Drug Store?

A No.

Q But you then saw him the second time?

A Yeah.

Q Correct. And it was after you saw him the second time that you heard the shots, correct?

A Right—no, after the first time.

Q The first time?

A The first time I saw him. After the first time then I heard the shots. Then I seen him the second time.

Q And again the second time that you see him no one's running with him?

A No.

Q No black males of the size or weight of Mr. Whitman?

A No.

MR. WOLFE: Thank you. I have no further questions.

REDIRECT EXAMINATION

BY MR. MENDEL:

Q Did you see any other people around?

A Yeah.

Q After the shots?

A After the shots?

Q Yes.

A No. Before the shots.

Q Before the shots?

A Yeah.

Q Tonya, where were you when you first saw the individual run by?

A By the window.

Q And what were you doing there?

A I went to get a check okayed.

Q And is that a normal procedure.

A Yeah, if it's not from our store.

Q Do you recall the individual who gave you the check?

A No.

Q Well, do you recall about how soon after you waited on the man with the baseball cap that the person with the check came through?

A I don't know. She had a big order because it was a large check.

Q Do you recall where she was in relationship to the other individual?

A No. There was people between them.

Q Do you recall making a statement to the Romersdale Police Department?

A Yeah.

Q At that time were the incidents fairly clear in your mind?

A Yeah.

Q Okay. I'd like to ask you to—

MR. WOLFE: Excuse me. Can I have a copy of that? I don't believe I—

MR. MENDEL: I don't have a copy of it. With the court's indulgence.

MR. WOLFE: If I may, Your Honor, have a chance to look at the statement that Mr. Mendel has.

MR. MENDEL: Certainly. I have no objection.

BY MR. MENDEL:

Q I'd like you to just review Page 2 toward the bottom and the top of Page 3 of your statement.

A (Witness complies.)

Q After reviewing that do you recall where the individual who had the check came through your counter in relationship to the man with the hat?

A No.

Q That doesn't refresh your recollection, is that correct?

A No.

MR. MENDEL: Thank you, Tonya. I have no further questions.

MR. WOLFE: I have nothing else, Your Honor.

THE COURT: That's all.

(Witness excused.)

MR. MENDEL: We have a number of witnesses we could be prepared to offer, or if you would like to break for the day.

THE COURT: Yes. I think we'll stop now.

Ladies and gentlemen, it's almost 4:30, and we are going to terminate for today. You'll be excused in a moment. As I indicated before, we'll be looking for you at 9:00 tomorrow morning. Please heed and consider very carefully the things I said to you about staying away from any publicity about the case. This is the place where we want you to learn about it. The jury may now be excused.

(Whereupon, at 4:25 P.M., the jury was excused.)

THE COURT: Adjourn court until 9:00 tomorrow morning.

(Whereupon, at 4:26 P.M., court was held in recess.)

9:30 A.M.

Wednesday, August 7, 1996

Courtroom No. 4

(Whereupon, the following proceedings were had in the absence of the jury:)

MR. MENDEL: Good morning, Your Honor. At this time the Commonwealth would call the case docketed to 453 CD 1996, The Commonwealth versus Gregory Whitman for trial.

For the record, Mr. Whitman is present represented by his attorney, Mr. Wolfe.

THE COURT: Very well. Before we bring the jury down, would you like to get on the record your request about reading into the record the statement by Mr. Monroe that we talked about yesterday?

MR. WOLFE: Yes, Your Honor, if the Court would like at this particular time for me to do so.

As indicated by Your Honor, we had met in chambers prior to the beginning of trial yesterday and indicated that a co-defendant in this particular case, Eddie Monroe, has given several statements to members of the Romersdale Police Department, a statement to a relative and a statement to an investigator from the Public Defender's Office.

In those particular statements he implicates himself and Mr. Whitman in the robbery at Gerber's earlier that afternoon of March 15, 1996. He also in those statements indicates, that is to the second robbery in which the court is hearing now before a jury concerning the shooting at Northeast Drug Store later that evening, he exculpates Mr. Whitman from being involved in that particular criminal activity.

We understand that Mr. Monroe has a court-appointed counsel here in Mallory County, Mr. Simon Leroy. We would further note for the record that Mr. Monroe has been—a court order has been issued for his appearance to testify in this particular matter, and with the discussion with his attorney, Mr. Leroy, Mr. Leroy has indicated that he would advise Mr. Monroe to take the Fifth Amendment and not offer any testimony at the trial of Mr. Whitman.

[Monroe's trial for murder and robbery arising from second hold-up on March 15 had not yet taken place. Under these circumstances, it would have been foolish of Monroe's attorney to allow him to testify about Whitman's involvement in the second hold-up, because his testimony could have been used against him at his own trial.]

Based on that sequence of events, it would be the defense's position that we would be entitled then to read before the jury the statements that Mr. Monroe has given on several occasions exculpating Mr. Whitman in any activity in the Northeast Drug Store shooting.

In support of that position, the defense counsel has provided Your Honor with the case of Chambers v. Mississippi which we allege governs the admissibility of the statements under the circumstances given here. We certainly allege that under due process requirements the evidence being offered is certainly essential and important to the defense's case.

We think that the statements given by Mr. Monroe are reliable in that they were given against his interest and given to members of the Romersdale Police Department on two separate occasions after having been advised of his Miranda warnings.

And we also think that this evidence is corroborated by other testimony which the court has heard already and which the court will hear during the rest of the trial, specifically that only one individual was seen shooting the victim in this case and only one individual was seen fleeing from the scene of the crime.

Several witnesses who witnessed this will testify that they did not view Mr. Whitman present during the scene of the shooting. In addition to the alibi witnesses that are being offered by Mr. Whitman who will indicate, one of which who testified yesterday, that at the time of the shooting Mr. Whitman was in their company and not present at the time of the shooting.

So for all the reasons that I have just indicated, we would request the Court to rule that the statements made by Mr. Monroe should be admitted and allowed to be read to the jury.

THE COURT: Very well. The Court will note that the District Attorney has provided the Court with an opinion filed July 13, 1984, Commonwealth of Pennsylvania versus Kevin Brinkley which is very, very close to the request of defense counsel in this situation.

[This demonstrates the importance not only of preparing factual testimony for trial, but also of anticipating legal issues that might arise and thoroughly researching them. Mendel knew, because Wolfe was required to disclose to him, that Wolfe intended to introduce Monroe's exculpatory statements in light of his refusal to testify. The case which Mendel provided the court was directly on point, and clearly excluded such evidence from the reach of the statement-against-interests exception to the hearsay rule. By providing the court with this legal precedent, Mendel guaranteed that this very damaging evidence would not be heard by the jury.]

Because of the general legal principles involved and supported by the authority of the Pennsylvania Supreme Court, we're going to rule that those statements by Mr. Monroe are not presently admissible. I also read the Supreme Court case and I don't want to discuss it in depth with you, but it's markedly different than what you have presented to the Court so far as your desires about the portions of Mr. Monroe's statement.

But you put it on the record. You're protected so far as that's concerned. Anything you want to add, Mr. Mendel?

[By "protected," the judge means that the issue was raised and ruled upon at trial, leaving Wolfe the option of appealing on that issue should it become necessary to do so.]

MR. MENDEL: No, Your Honor.

THE COURT: Very well. Alright. I'll return the book to you, Mr. Wolfe.

MR. WOLFE: Okay. Thank you.

THE COURT: Any reason, gentlemen, why we should not bring the jury down at this time?

MR. MENDEL: No, Your Honor.

THE COURT: Very well. Would you get the jury please.

(Whereupon at 9:37 A.M., the jury entered the courtroom.)

THE COURT: Good morning ladies and gentlemen. Sorry we're late seeing you this morning. Mr. Mendel.

MR. MENDEL: Thank you, Your Honor. Penny Green.

PENNY GREEN, called as a witness, being duly sworn, testified as follows:

DIRECT EXAMINATION

BY MR. MENDEL:

Q Could you please state your name and spell your first name, please.

A Penny Green. P-e-n-n-y.

Q You're going to have to speak up real loud so everybody can hear you, okay?

A Um-hum.

Q How old are you?

A Seventeen.

[It may seem strange to have a minor testify without further establishing her competence, but competence is not directly related to age. A 17-year-old would be able to understand the duty to tell the truth without a long voir dire establishing that understanding. Ch. 7, "Voir Dire to Establish General Competence"]

Q And do you go to school?

A Yes.

Q And where do you go?

A Eastern High

Q And what grade will you be in this upcoming year?

A Twelfth.

Q Back in March of 1996 did you have a part-time job during the school year?

A Yes, I did.

Q And where was that at?

A SaveRite Market.

Q And what did you do at SaveRite Market?

A I was a cashier.

Q And particularly at which store did you work?

A Twenty-ninth Street.

Q Are you still employed there?

A Yes.

Q And how long have you been with the store?

A A year.

Q On March 15, 1996 in the evening hours were you working then?

A Yes.

Q And do you recall what shirt you were wearing or what hours you were working?

A 5:00 to 10:00.

Q 5:00 to 10:00?

A Um-hum.

Q Do you recall what checkout counter you were working, what register number?

A Register No. 5.

Q Now, as I understand it, the registers in the store are numbered one through approximately eight, is that correct?

A Yes.

Q And they run across the front of the store, would that be correct?

A Um-hum.

Q Now, do you recall who was working the checkouts next to you?

A To the left of me was Tonya Franklin, the right was Carly Dwyer.

Q And Tonya Franklin was the young lady who testified yesterday, correct?

A Yes.

THE COURT: Ma'am, do you want to talk a little closer to the microphone. Pull it closer if you want to or sit up a little bit.

Thank you.

BY MR. MENDEL:

Q Now, Penny, did you hear the commotion which occurred later that evening?

A Yes.

Q Namely the shots being fired?

A Um-hum.

MR. WOLFE: Your Honor, the questions are becoming somewhat leading in areas that are very crucial to the testimony here. I would ask that the questions be phrased and be made more objective.

THE COURT: I think that that's a reasonable request, Mr. Mendel.

MR. MENDEL: Certainly.

BY MR. MENDEL:

Q Did anything unusual happen that evening?

A Yes.

Q And could you tell the ladies and gentlemen what you observed?

A I was ringing up a lady's grocery order and she came through my line and she said excuse me—

Q Excuse me a second, Penny. Can you speak up a little louder and a little slower so everyone can hear you.

A A lady came through my checkout line. She said excuse me but I just saw a man running past the window with a drawer full of money. I looked out the window and it was dark and I didn't see anything. I went back to work.

A couple seconds later I heard a gunshot and looked out and saw a man running with a gun.

Q And where did this individual run past? You said you saw him run by. Where did he run?

A Past the window.

Q And which way was he headed?

A Up toward Northeast Drug.

Q Just go back. You heard a gunshot, okay. Then what did you see?

A A man running with a gun.

Q And which way did he run?

A He was like running backward.

Q And which way was he facing?

A He was facing up toward the store.

Q And then he would be running the opposite way?

A Yes.

Q Now what did you do after that took place?

A Called for the security guard.

Q And who was the security guard at that time?

A Curtis Smith.

THE COURT: The people in the far end of the jury box, ma'am, can't hear you. So if you want to lean forward a little bit or talk a little louder.

THE WITNESS: Okay.

BY MR. MENDEL:

Q Now, before this took place had you seen anyone in the store that stuck out in your mind?

A Yes, I did.

Q And could you tell the ladies and gentlemen what you observed.

A I observed two men in the line next to me.

Q And which line would that be?

A Register No. 4.

Q And is that the line Tonya was at?

A Yes.

Q And what drew your attention to these two men?

A By the way they were looking around strangely, observing everybody.

Q Were you able to get a good look at both individuals?

A Not both.

Q Was there one of them you were able to identify?

A Yes.

Q And what was that individual wearing?

A Jeans, a plain shirt.

Q Do you recall whether or not this individual had a jacket on?

A I can't remember.

Q Now, Penny, did you describe anything about the other individual?

A I just remember that he had a hat on.

Q Now, getting back to when you saw the man running down the street, were you able to identify the man with the gun?

A No.

Q Did you notice anything about him, how he was—if he was wearing anything?

A No, I didn't.

Q Now, did you later have an opportunity to tell the police about what you observed?

A Yes.

Q Were you able to give a description about what the individual looked like who you identified as the one in the jeans?

A Yes.

Q And are you able to identify that person today, is that person in the courtroom?

A Yes.

Q Could you point him out, please.

A There (indicating).

MR. MENDEL: For the record, indicating the Defendant, Gregory Whitman.

BY MR. MENDEL:

Q Penny, is there any doubt in your mind the individual you observed in the SaveRite Market at that time?

A No.

Q And that is the Defendant?

[As far as placing the defendant at the scene is concerned, this is the strongest witness so far. Remember, however, that the jury must conclude that the evidence supports guilt beyond a reasonable doubt. The evidence to this point was devoid of any proof that the defendant was at the scene of the crime. This witness' testimony, while strong, merely places the issue in doubt. The issue is now a matter of credibility. This witness has testified in a way that contradicts the testimony of several previous witnesses. Whom will the jury believe? Ch. 13, "Burden of Proof"]

THE COURT: You have to say out loud.

THE WITNESS: Yes.

BY MR. MENDEL:

Q Penny, how long after you saw Mr. Whitman and this other individual in the store did you hear the shots?

A About 12 minutes.

Q And do you know how many people you waited on after—well, strike that.

You didn't wait on these people, is that correct?

A No, I didn't.

Q The individual who you've identified as—well, strike that.

[Mendel is probably wise not to question her further. Doing so would give her the opportunity to contradict or qualify what she has already said. He doesn't want to make the same mistake with this critical witness that Wolfe made with Tonya Franklin.]

MR. MENDEL: I have no further questions. Thank you.

CROSS-EXAMINATION

BY MR. WOLFE

Q Penny, you came to work that evening at 5:00, correct?

A Yes.

Q And that was a Friday evening when this incident occurred, correct?

A Yes.

Q Friday evenings at the SaveRite Market are pretty busy evenings?

A Yes.

Q A lot of people do their shopping that evening, correct?

A Um-hum.

Q And you had waited on a fair number of individuals prior to 6:00, 6:30, isn't that correct?

A Yes.

Q Are you able to describe or point out any other individuals that stuck out in your mind during that period of time?

A No.

Q Are you able to estimate at this time how many people you waited on in say an hour and a half, from 5:00 to 6:30?

A No, I'm not.

Q The two people that you indicated that you thought behaved somewhat strangely, they did not go through your checkout counter, did they?

A No.

Q And you indicated that—did they look in your general direction, did they look at you?

A They were looking around.

Q Did they look toward you at all?

A No.

Q And how long did you have a chance to observe these individuals, how long did you look at them?

A About 10 seconds.

Q About 10 seconds?

A Yes.

Q And you were able to observe two individuals?

A Yes.

[He is impeaching her testimony by proving a lack of opportunity to observe. Her responses, however, indicate that she is not backing down from her position that the defendant is the man she saw in the store. Ch. 13, "Additional Grounds for Impeachment"]

Q Now, Miss Franklin was the clerk who actually waited on these two gentlemen, isn't that correct?

A Yes.

Q And she was the one that would have rang up any purchases that they made, correct?

A Um-hum.

Q And she supposedly would have had as good or even a better opportunity to observe these two people because they went through her line, isn't that correct?

MR. MENDEL: I'm going to have to object. That's speculative.

THE COURT: Sustained.

[Asking a witness what someone else might have done or seen is always objectionable. No lay witness is competent to testify about what might have happened.]

BY MR. WOLFE:

Q Let me rephrase the question. The two gentlemen that you're saying you observed in the store went through Miss Franklin's counter, correct?

A Yes.

Q And it was Miss Franklin that supposedly waited on them or rang up whatever purchase they made, correct?

A Yes.

Q Now, you indicated that these two individuals were in your store approximately 12 minutes before you heard the shots, is that correct?

A Yes.

Q Now, you've had a chance prior to the jury coming down to review the statement that you gave, isn't that correct?

A Yes.

Q And you looked at this statement I guess for the first time since you gave it back on the 20th of March, isn't that correct?

A Yes.

Q You hadn't seen it in the last three and a half months?

A Yes.

Q Now, can you describe this individual as wearing jeans and a shirt. Can you describe the shirt?

A No. There wasn't nothing special about the shirt.

Q But it was a shirt. There was the jeans. What kind of jeans were they?

A I didn't notice what kind.

Q You didn't notice the jeans. You indicated that he didn't have a jacket on, is that correct?

A I wasn't sure.

Q Well, you're not sure whether he had a jacket on, is that what you're saying?

A No, I'm not.

Q I show you a copy of the statement that Mr. Mendel just showed you this morning and ask if you can, first of all, can you identify that statement?

A Yes.

Q I refer you to the second page of the statement, the last line. The last question, could you read and answer that for me, please.

A You want the question too?

Q Yes.

A "Do you recall how this man was dressed?"

"Just a plain shirt and jeans. I don't think he had a jacket."

[This testimony is damaging to her credibility because of Munns' testimony that Whitman was wearing tan or beige pants when he picked him up earlier that afternoon. This doesn't mean that Munns was telling the truth, however, nor does it mean that the word "jeans" can't include tan or beige pants.]

Q So back at the time you were—it was your first impression you didn't believe he was wearing a jacket?

A I didn't think so.

Q Now, you indicated that the first time that someone came to you, they said that someone was walking past the window with a cash register tray or something, correct?

A Yes.

Q Did you go to the window and look outside?

A No, I didn't.

Q You looked from your position at the register?

A Yes.

Q And you were able to see outside?

A Yes.

Q And did you see the man with the cash register at that time?

A Yes.

Q You saw that?

A Yes.

Q Was that the only person that you saw at that particular time?

A Yes.

Q And in which direction was he heading?

A Toward the back of the store.

Q Heading toward Northeast?

A No. The other way.

Q The other way, heading toward the doors of the SaveRite Market?

A Yes.

Q Now, you indicated, too, that when you looked out it was dark outside at that particular time?

A Yes.

Q Now, a short time later you heard shots fired, correct?

A Um-hum.

Q And when you heard these shots what did you do at this particular time?

A Called for the security guard.

Q You go to the window first, don't you?

A No.

Q You don't go to the window and look out?

A No.

Q And see anyone?

A Oh, I looked out the window, yes, I did.

Q So you looked out the window?

A Um-hum.

Q Did you go to the window at this particular time?

A No.

Q You stayed at the register?

A Um-hum.

Q And you had a chance to observe a black male, correct?

A Yes.

Q And you saw him with a gun at that particular time?

A Yes.

Q And you're watching him from your position at the register? What's he doing at that particular time?

A Shooting.

Q You see him taking aim and shooting. At which direction is he shooting?

A Toward Northeast Drug.

Q Toward Northeast Drug. You didn't see who he's shooting at or anything along those lines?

A No.

Q It's your testimony then that when you looked out the window you saw this black male take aim, point his weapon in the direction of Northeast Drug Store and fire a shot?

A Yes.

Q And was anyone else around him at that particular time?

A No.

Q And after that individual took that shot, where did he go, in what direction did he go?

A He just went fleeing into the parking lot.

Q Well, did he run along the sidewalk out in the general direction?

A Just out, not on the sidewalk.

Q Not on the sidewalk?

A No.

Q Did he run away from the building then in other words?

A Yes.

Q Out into the parking lot?

A Yes.

Q And you were at your register this entire period of time and watching all this?

A Yes.

Q For the jury's information, because we haven't seen any photographs of the scene yet, there's a sidewalk that runs right along the front of SaveRite Market, isn't that correct?

A Yes.

Q And it runs all the way to the end of the building, correct?

A Yes.

Q And it's your testimony now that after you heard the shot being fired by this man, he did not run along the sidewalk, along the front of SaveRite Market, but in other words just ran away from the store into the general parking lot which is out in front of SaveRite, is that correct?

A Yes.

Q And you were watching all this at this particular time from your register?

A Um-hum.

Q Did you see where he went to?

A No, I didn't.

Q Did you see anyone else follow him?

A No.

Q Did you see the individual who you've indicated as Mr. Whitman with him at that particular time or outside of the store?

A No.

Q You didn't see him anywhere in sight, did you?

A No, I didn't.

[By leading her through what she saw, Wolfe is establishing that she was in a position to observe what was going on outside the store immediately following the shooting. In this light, her failure to see Whitman with Monroe is exculpatory, even assuming Whitman was with Monroe in the store before the shooting.]

Q And it was after he fled into the general area or the parking lot that you went back and got Officer Smith, correct?

A No. I got Officer Smith before that.

Q At what point did you get Officer Smith.

A As soon as I heard a gunshot I got Officer Smith.

Q But before you got him—at what point then were you able to observe this man fleeing into the parking lot after the gunshot?

A You mean how many minutes after that or—

Q Let me go back. You see a man take aim with a gun and shoot the gun?

A Yes.

Q And then you've testified that after he shot the gun he ran away from the building into the parking lot, correct, is that what you've testified to?

A Yes.

Q And then he disappeared and you didn't know where he went to?

A While he was shooting I called Mr. Smith and Mr. Smith—

Q How did you call Mr. Smith?

A How did I call him?

Q Yes. Did you go to him or did you just scream out?

A I screamed at him.

Q In other words, what you're saying is that as you're watching the shooting, you're calling for Mr. Smith to come and render assistance or do whatever he could, is that correct?

A Yes.

Q Meanwhile, you still have the entire view of the parking lot and whatever's happening outside of the store, correct? I mean, you're still looking outside while you're calling Mr. Smith, correct?

A Yes.

Q And you saw Mr. Smith exit the store and go out in the parking lot area?

A Yes.

Q Did you see which direction he went to?

A No, I didn't.

Q And this entire time, though, you remained at your cash register, correct?

A Yes.

Q And during this entire time while you're at your cash register looking outside, you don't see Mr. Whitman running by or anywhere in that area, do you?

A No.

MR. WOLFE: I have no further questions. Thank you.

REDIRECT EXAMINATION

BY MR. MENDEL:

Q Penny, when you were inside the store how far away from you was Mr. Whitman?

A He was in the next line.

Q And how far feet-wise would that be?

A About five feet.

Q And what's the lighting like in the store?

A The lighting?

Q Yes.

A Bright.

[This is rehabilitation from the impeachment which took place earlier, questioning her ability to observe Whitman in line at SaveRite. Ch. 13, "Rehabilitation"]

Q Do you know how many gunshots you heard?

A About two or three.

MR. MENDEL: Thank you, Penny.

RECROSS EXAMINATION

BY MR. WOLFE:

Q Penny, we've talked last week, I interviewed you about what you saw at that particular time, isn't that correct?

A Yes.

Q Did you ever indicate at that time that you weren't sure whether you could identify the person in the store?

A No.

[This was a calculated gamble that failed. Wolfe was the only other person involved in his interview with Penny. If she denies expressing uncertainty about the identity of Whitman in the store, the only person who could impeach her testimony would be Wolfe himself, and he is not able to testify.]

MR. WOLFE: Thank you. I have no more questions.

THE COURT: Penny, one question. The shot that you observed the man take when you were looking through the window, was that the first shot that you heard or had you heard a shot before that?

THE WITNESS: It was the first one.

THE COURT: That was the first shot that you heard?

THE WITNESS: Um-hum.

THE COURT: And then you heard one or two shots after that?

THE WITNESS: Um-hum.

THE COURT: Very well.

MR. WOLFE: May I follow up on that, Judge?

[Judges are permitted to examine witnesses at trial when they feel additional testimony is required for the benefit of the jury. Once they have done so, both attorney are then free to cross-examine based on the judge's questions.]

BY MR. WOLFE:

Q You said that the first shot that you saw or that you heard was when you saw the man point in the direction of Northeast Drug, correct?

A Yes.

Q And that you heard shots after that time. Where did those shots come from, were you able to tell?

A No.

Q You didn't see the man take those other shots?

A No.

MR. WOLFE: Alright. Thank you. I have no further questions.

MR. MENDEL: Thank you Penny.

(Witness excused.)

MR. MENDEL: Laverne Platts, please.

LAVERNE PLATTS, called as a witness, being duly sworn, testified as follows:

DIRECT EXAMINATION

BY MR. MENDEL:

Q Would you please state your name and spell your first and last, please.

A Laverne Platts. L-a-v-e-r-n-e P-l-a-t-t-s.

Q And Laverne, you're going to have to speak up pretty loud so everyone can hear you, okay?

A Okay.

Q How old are you?

A Nineteen.

Q And where do you live?

A 1833 Holly Street.

Q That's in the City of Romersdale, correct?

A Yes, it is.

Q And where are you presently employed?

A Presently?

Q Presently.

A Pennsylvania Blue Shield.

Q And directing your attention back to March 15, 1996, where were you employed then?

A Northeast Drugs on 29th Street.

Q And what did you do at Northeast Drugs?

A I was a cashier.

Q How long had you worked at Northeast Drug until then, before then?

A About 6 months.

Q Do you recall the incident of that day?

A Yes, I do.

Q What day did you—what time did you start to work?

A I believe it was 5:00.

Q And to what hour were you scheduled to work?

A 9:30.

Q And is that what time the store closes?

A Yes.

Q Now, Laverne, were you the only employee at the store at that time?

A No.

Q Who else was there?

A The pharmacist and two other cashiers.

Q Was there a security guard employed at the store?

A Yes.

Q And what was his name?

A We called him Bud. That was his nickname.

Q And his last name would be Wilson, is that correct?

A Yes.

Q And do you remember on that day what Mr. Wilson was wearing?

A No. I knew he was wearing a heavy coat, though.

Q Anything unusual happen that evening?

A Yes. A young black man came into the store and he started to walk up an aisle. He walked up one aisle; he came around and started to walk up another. And he picked up a pack of batteries and I thought that was unusual because he didn't even look at the batteries. He just picked them up and he threw them up on the top of the counter.

Q Now, what time was this approximately?

A About 6:30, somewhere between 6:30 and 7:00.

Q And what did he do when he came up to put the batteries down on the counter?

A He came up and he put the batteries on the counter, and he told me to give him all the money out of the register. And then he pulled the gun out and he told me to stick all the money in a bag.

   And that's when I reached for a bag underneath and it wouldn't fit in the bag. And he got mad at me and told me to stick all the money in a bag or he would shoot me.

Q Slow down a little, slow down. She has to take down every word you're saying. You're starting to get a little quick.

A I started to stick it—I stuck it in a larger bag and he took the bag and he left.

Q And what did you do then?

A I went down and I told Bud. I walked down and I told Bud. And Bud had a newspaper and he stopped the newspaper and he jumped over the railing. There was a railing right there, and he went out the entrance door.

Q He went out the entrance door?

A Out the entrance door.

Q Do you know which door the individual who robbed you went out?

A He went out the exit door.

Q Now, have you since that time been able to identify the individual who robbed you?

A Yes.

Q And are you aware of his name?

A No, I don't know his name.

Q Would it be Eddie Monroe?

A Yeah. I get them confused.

Q Do you recall what he was wearing on that date?

A He had on a two-piece suit and a light colored shirt and a cap.

Q Do you recall what type of cap it was?

A I believe it was a baseball cap.

Q Was there anything about his shirt that you remember?

A It didn't have no collar.

(Whereupon, Commonwealth's Exhibit No. 1 was marked for identification.)

BY MR. MENDEL:

Q Laverne, I'd like to show you what's been marked previously for identification as Commonwealth's Exhibit No. 1 and ask you to look at it and see if you can identify it.

A That's the parking lot of SaveRite and Northeast Drugs.

Q And for the record, it also shows both stores, would that be correct?

A Yes, it does.

[Laverne's ability to authenticate the photographs has nothing to do with whether she took them or has any knowledge about how they were created. All that is required is that she is familiar enough with the scene depicted in the photograph to be able to identify it. The fact that she worked at Northeast Drug was sufficient to establish her competence as an authentication witness. Ch. 8, "Firsthand knowledge"]

Q And where on the picture is the SaveRite Market located?

A Right here on the right (indicating).

Q And that is to the right side?

A Right.

Q And the Northeast store is then where?

A Located on the left.

Q If you would, please, with an E could you mark where the entrance door to the Northeast Drug Store is located.

A (Witness complies.)

Q And with an O, could you mark where the outdoor is located.

A (Witness complies.)

Q Perhaps you can make those a little bigger so possible the ladies and gentlemen of the jury can see those.

A Okay. (Witness complies.)

[At this point, the photograph becomes demonstrative evidence, introduced solely for the purpose of allowing the jury to visualize the testimony of the eyewitnesses and provide a frame of reference for their testimony. There is no suggestion that the photograph itself is either direct or circumstantial evidence of the crime, as it would be if the photograph had been taken during the crime and actually showed the crime in progress. Ch. 4, "Demonstrative evidence"]

MR. MENDEL: Perhaps if I raise this with the court's permission to display to the jury.

MR. WOLFE: No objection, Your Honor.

THE COURT: Very well.

(Whereupon, Mr. Mendel displayed Commonwealth's Exhibit No. 1 to the jury.)

BY MR. MENDEL:

Q How did you mark these? Which one did you indicate as being the entrance?

A The one right here (indicating).

Q And the exit?

A Right here (indicating).

Q With the O.

Now, Laverne, was the money that was taken, was that later returned?

A I don't know.

Q After Bud left over the turnstile, how long after that was it before you heard anything else?

A About 10 minutes.

Q And what did you hear at that time?

A I heard two shots.

Q And then what did you do?

A We looked out—you know, we waited about 2 or 3 minutes and we looked out the window, and that's when we saw Bud laying on the ground.

Q And if you could mark on the photograph where you saw Mr. Wilson with an X I would imagine.

A (Witness complies.)

MR. MENDEL: And again with the court's permission.

THE COURT: Do you have any objection to that, Mr. Wolfe?

MR. WOLFE: None, your Honor.

(Whereupon, Mr. Mendel displayed Commonwealth's Exhibit No. 1 to the jury.)

MR. MENDEL: Cross examine.

CROSS EXAMINATION

BY MR. WOLFE:

Q Miss Platts, your indication is that you saw this black male come into the store, correct?

A No. I didn't see him coming into the store.

Q You didn't?

A No.

Q When was the first time then that you saw him?

A I saw him when he was coming in. He was walking up—he walked up one aisle and came back down the aisle. That's when I had noticed him.

Q And he was alone at that particular time?

A Yes, he was.

Q You didn't see any other young black males with him?

A No, I didn't.

Q And you would have no idea as to how long he may have been in the store prior to coming to your register, would you?

A No.

Q And you indicated that there were two other cashiers and a pharmacist in the store. Where were they at that particular time?

A The cashier was over in the cosmetic—one was over in the cosmetic department and one was in the back with the pharmacist.

Q And you were the only one then in the front?

A Yes.

Q The individual that pointed the gun at you and took the money, did you have any observations as to what kind of condition he was in, how did he appear to you?

A He looked like he was high, like he had been smoking something.

Q What makes you say that?

A Because his eyes were red.

Q And you indicated that he was in a two-piece suit?

A Yeah.

Q Similar to the suit that I have on?

A No.

Q What do you mean by a two-piece suit?

A It was an older suit, suit from like the 70's. It was just a jacket and a pair of it looked like straight legged pants.

Q Now, when you say jacket you mean jacket like I have on?

A Right, but it wasn't made like that, no.

Q It was different?

A Yeah. It was an older style.

Q I see. And it was green in color?

A Yeah, I believe it was a dark green.

Q A dark color?

A Yeah.

Q And after he left the store you went to get Mr. Wilson?

A Right.

Q And you didn't observe anything further then, what happened outside or didn't see the shooting, is that correct?

A Right.

Q And I assume then that after the black male left the store that that was the last time that you saw him?

A Right.

[Like the testimony of Myers and Franklin, this testimony, while relaying the details of the second hold-up itself, does nothing to directly incriminate Whitman, even assuming the jury believes that Whitman was with Monroe minutes before in the SaveRite Market. Nevertheless, because the defendant's liability is that of an accomplice to Monroe and not a principal, it is absolutely necessary to prove the details of the robbery to show that a crime was, in fact, committed by Monroe. This testimony also provides factual context for the testimony that follows, particularly that of Barbara Lee.]

MR. WOLFE: Thank you. I have no further questions.

MR. MENDEL: Thank you, Laverne.

(Witness excused.)

MR. MENDEL: Benjamin Carver, please.

BENJAMIN CARVER, called as a witness, being duly sworn, testified as follows.

MR. MENDEL: Your Honor, before we begin may we approach side bar briefly for something?

THE COURT: Certainly.

(Whereupon, a discussion was held off the record at side bar.)

DIRECT EXAMINATION

BY MR. MENDEL:

Q Would you please state your name for the record, please, and spell your last.

A Benjamin Carver, C-a-r-v-e-r.

Q And Mr. Carver, where do you live?

A 2469 Arbor Street, Romersdale.

Q And how are you presently employed?

A I'm employed by the county, Mallory County.

Q Now, I'd like to direct your attention to March 15, 1996, and ask you if you were in the vicinity of the Northeast Drug Store and the SaveRite Market located at Twenty-ninth and Emerald Street?

[Like the testimony of Laverne Platts which proved Monroe guilty of robbery, the prosecutor is using Carver's testimony to prove that Monroe

committed murder. It is necessary to, in a sense, try Monroe for these crimes in order to establish the legal prerequisites of Whitman's liability as an accomplice. If Monroe is not guilty of murder and robbery, it would be impossible for Whitman to be guilty of being an accomplice to those crimes.]

A Yes, I was.

Q And who were you there with?

A I was with my wife and two children.

Q And about what time did you arrive there on that date?

A I'd say approximately 6:00 in the evening.

Q And particularly why did you go to that shopping complex on that day?

A My daughter was having a couple of girlfriends over and we went there to get some junk food for their party at SaveRite Market.

Q Did you notice anything unusual happen that day?

A Yes. As we were leaving that SaveRite Market, we were just coming out the doors, and there was two men running in our direction.

Q And were you able to describe these two men?

A Yes.

Q And could you describe them to the ladies and gentlemen of the jury.

A The man that was in front of me was a black and white man was chasing him.

Q Do you remember how the black man was dressed?

A Yes. He had dark trousers on and had a bluish-gray sports coat or suit coat.

Q And do you know if he was wearing anything on his head?

A No, I don't know if he was or not.

Q Can you describe the other individual who was chasing him?

A Yes. Stocky build man also wearing a jacket, and that's about all I can.

Q Okay. Where did you first see these two people?

A First?

Q Yes. Where is the first time you saw them?

A Just as I was coming out of the SaveRite Market.

Q I'm going to show you what's been marked as Commonwealth's Exhibit No. 1 and, for the record, ask you if you can identify what this is.

A That's a photo of the SaveRite Market and Northeast Drug.

Q Now, if you could, please indicate with an F where you were when you first observed these two individuals running.

A Over by the doors where the exit door is on the SaveRite Market.

THE COURT: Speak up a little bit, Mr. Carver.

WITNESS: Where the exit door is here coming out of the SaveRite Market. They were coming from the direction of the Northeast Drug toward the SaveRite Market.

BY MR. MENDEL:

Q Okay. Could you please mark with an M where you saw the black man, where he was.

A Okay.

Q You're going to have to make that pretty big so everyone can see it.

A (Witness complies.)

Q Try this yellow pen and see if that will show up a little better. I guess not.

MR. WOLFE: Do you have any other ones?

THE CLERK: Black.

MR. MENDEL: Thank you, Mr. Stare.

BY MR. MENDEL:

Q Why don't you try that one.

A (Witness complies.)

Q The M indicates where you saw the black man, correct?

A Right.

Q And where did you observe the other individual chasing him?

A He was approximately here (indicating).

Q Can you mark that with an S.

A (Witness complies.)

Q And how far were you from the black men?

A At the time they were running where it's indicated, S was chasing me, I was approximately just coming out of the door.

Q Now, what did you observe take place?

A Well, I heard the white man holler at the black man, "Stop, I'm a police-man," which just as he passed the doors, the entrance, he stopped.

Q The black man stopped?

A Yes. And by that time the white man had caught up to him and grasped him by the arm.

Q Was the black man carrying anything at this time?

A Yes, he was. He was carrying a—looking like to be a grocery bag in his right hand or arm.

Q And how was he holding it?

A He was holding it like this (indicating).

Q Indicating—

A It was laying.

Q —on this forearm?

A Right. The open end was sort of at this end (indicating).

Q And what did you observe take place then after he grabbed?

A Some change had fell out of the bag, and I thought to myself at that point apparently he must have robbed some place. Looking at being a grocery bag, I thought it was the SaveRite Market at the moment, but I couldn't grasp why they were outside running from the Northeast Drug toward the SaveRite Market if they robbed the SaveRite Market.

Q What happened then after the white man grabbed the other individual?

A Just moments after he had had him by the arm, he broke loose from him and run in the direction of Emerald Street.

Q Which would be away from the Northeast Drug past the SaveRite Market?

A Yes.

Q What did the white guy do at that time?

A He then continued to chance him in the same direction. And then I said to my wife, I said, "You take the shopping cart and the two children and go back in the store. I'm going to go down to see if he needs any help, to see what's going on."

　　So I then also ran down to the corner. By the time I got to the corner, the white man had had the black man by the arm again beside the car.

Q And where was that area located?

A That was facing Emerald Street, the side of the building.

Q Again, I'm going to show you the photograph and ask you to mark with a C the point at which you saw the black man be apprehended for the second time.

A With a B?

Q With a C. If you could make that pretty good size so everybody can see it.

A (Witness complies.)

MR. MENDEL: You have no objection, Mr. Wolfe, to displaying this to the jury?

MR. WOLFE: No.

(Whereupon, Mr. Mendel displayed Commonwealth's Exhibit No. 1 to the jury.)

BY MR. MENDEL:

Q What took place after you saw the individual caught off to the side of the store?

A Okay. I was standing in front of the car which they were beside, and they took a few steps. And the white man said to the black man, he says, "You have a knife in your pocket don't you?"

　　And no words were exchanged other than him asking if he had a knife in his pocket.

Q And that was the white man that asked that?

A Yes. He asked the black man.

Q Were you later able to identify the white man?

A Yes.

Q And did you know his name?

A I knew him as Bud. I didn't know his last name at the time, but by going into Northeast Drug. And I grasped that he was a security guard at the Northeast Drug being that he was there quite a lot.

Q So Bud then said to the black man, "I know you have a knife," or something like that?

A Yes.

Q What did the black man do?

A At that time he didn't do anything.

Q Then what took place?

A Well, they continued walking to the corner and turned right to go into the direction of the Northeast Drug and continued walking until they passed the doors of the SaveRite Market. Just as we were passing the doors of the SaveRite Market, Bud had said to the black man again, he said, "You have a knife in your pocket."

And the black man looked at him and said, "I have more than just a knife in my pocket."

Q Now, where did that take place at?

A Approximately just as you're passing the doors of the SaveRite Market, the exit and the entrance door of the SaveRite Market.

Q Okay. What took place at that time?

A Okay. Then after he said that, I had taken notice to his jacket pocket, the right-hand jacket pocket was bulging.

Q That was on the black man?

A Yes, on the black man. So then we just continued walking in the direction of the Northeast Drug.

Q Now, were you walking with them or—

A Yes, I was directly in back of them, like four feet approximately.

Q What took place then?

A Well, we walked up—there's large windows in the SaveRite Market, and then there's a section at the end of the SaveRite Market that has no windows. Well, just before we got to the end of the windows, the black man threw a fist full of 20's on the ground.

Q That was right in front of the windows?

A Yeah, just at the end of the windows before you're getting to the end of the building.

Q So that is on the far end of the windows going toward Northeast?

A Northeast, yes. So Bud had said to him, the black man that is, he said, "Are you trying to be funny?" And he had attempted, he looked like he was, Bud that is, was going to pick the money up. And I said to Bud, I said, "Don't worry about it. I'll pick the money up. You just watch him."

So I did. I picked it all up and just shoved it in my pants pocket.

So then when he took a few more steps and the man, the black man that is, threw the whole bag and everything right on the ground, just dropped it down, just sort of left go of it. And then at that time I said to Bud again, I said, "I'll pick the change and stuff that fell out of the drawer."

The drawer had slid out of the bag. "I'll pick everything up and you just watch him." So I did. And I also—I had carried the bag and the drawer and we continued walking then.

Well, there's a section between the Northeast Drug and the SaveRite Market and it has a fence dividing the two buildings. Just as we got in front of that, the black man had grabbed Bud and threw him back against the fence and pulled out the gun and pointed it toward him. And Bud had said don't do it or don't shoot.

Q Then what took place?

A At that moment the man just didn't hesitate at all, he just shot.

Q Did you observe that shot?

A Yes. I saw the flame even come out of the end of the barrel.

Q Were you able to identify the individual who was making the escape or who was running away and being followed by Bud? When you first saw him, were you able to identify the black man who was running from Bud?

A When I first saw at the time?

Q As you're coming out of the SaveRite Market?

A No. Everything was happening too fast at that moment.

Q But it was the same individual that you saw shoot Bud Wilson?

A The man that was being chased?

Q Yes.

A Yes.

Q And since that time have you been able to identify that individual?

A Yes, I have.

Q And are you aware of the man's name?

A Yes.

Q And what is that?

A Mr. Monroe.

Q That would be Eddie Monroe, correct?

A Eddie Monroe, correct.

Q Now, after you observed Mr. Monroe shoot Mr. Wilson what happened, what happened to Mr. Wilson?

A Well, seconds—I didn't think it was real. I mean, the gun didn't sound loud or anything. I thought he was—in my mind I guess I thought he was really trying to pull something and it wasn't really real. Then I saw Bud slide off the fence, because when he was shot he just sort of went back against the fence that's in between the two buildings and he slid down off the fence and I knew it was real.

  Just at that time as he was sliding off the fence Mr. Monroe turned to face me and pulled the trigger. Well, at that moment I didn't know if I was hit or what. Apparently I didn't think I was anyhow. I turned with the drawer and ran toward—on the sidewalk toward Emerald Street.

Q And that would be down toward—past the SaveRite Market?

A Right.

Q Okay. Then what happened?

A Okay. The man, Mr. Monroe it was, was hollering at me give me that bag or give me that drawer or something like that. And I continued holding onto it until he fired at me again, and I just had got approximately to where the overhand of the SaveRite Market is by the doors and I thought well, I'll just drop it, maybe it will scatter all over.

  So I dropped the drawer and I could hear the change going and I ran over into the parking lot. At that time he continued running on the side-walk which goes by the SaveRite Market doors and he was still sort of like pointing the gun at me.

  So then I looked over and I saw him stop and directly behind him was my wife and two children against the wall. They have a handicap parking area at the end of the SaveRite Market there. And my wife was standing between the two children and she was screaming, "Please don't shoot. Please don't shoot."

So the only thing that could come to my mind, that maybe he might turn and shoot her for screaming. So I come out in the open thinking if he wanted to shoot he would shoot at me some more.

Q Now, you were out in the parking lot at that time, is that correct?

A Yes, I'm in the parking lot.

Q So after you picked up the cash drawer and dropped it in front of the store, at that point you ran out to the—

A Yes. I ran in the direction which would have been of Twenty-ninth Street when I started to run, and then I turned in the parking lot and ran toward Emerald Street.

Q Now, for the record, looking at the photograph, the front of the store would be facing what's Twenty-ninth Street, correct?

A Correct.

Q And then as the photograph indicates, to the left-hand side is the Northeast Store as you're looking at it, to the right-hand side is the SaveRite Market and beyond that Emerald Street?

A Yes.

Q After you came out in the open what happened?

A Well, he just continued pointing the gun at me and for no reason he just turned the corner and ran back along the side of the building. Well, as soon as I saw him running back toward the side of the building or the end of the building, I don't know which you'd say, excuse me, I continued running in the same direction that he was headed because my wife and two children were still hanging there at the side, the front of the building which I could see him.

And he turned and opened a car door and got in the car. I said to my wife, "Quick," I said, "You and the children go back in the store and pick up the cash drawer I threw down." I ran back around the corner to the car, was going to get the make and the color and the license number if I could.

Well, he turned on the seat and pointed the gun toward me at the window. I hurried and ran back to the corner and ran around the corner. Well, I could hear he was having trouble getting the car in gear because he was grinding the gears in the car. And as soon as I heard the car go in gear, I ran back around and got the color and the license number off the car.

Q And do you remember what you did with the license number after you obtained it?

A Yes. There was a car parked right on the corner of the building and I ran over and I continued saying the license number over and over. And I tried to write it down on the shoot of a car that was sitting there which I didn't see was working out, so there was a young lady sitting in the car and another lady.

I said to her, "Would you please do me a favor, would you write this license number down." Well, she shuffled through her pocketbook and found something to write it down, and at that time there was one of the plain clothes officers, Mr. Smith, had came down to the corner. And I handed it to him and told him approximately what kind of car it was and the color and handed him the license number and pointed in the direction he was headed.

Q Which was which way?

A Well, he had went—there's two entrances to the SaveRite Market coming off of Emerald Street.

Q If I can show you what's been marked at Commonwealth's Exhibit No. 2 for identification and ask if you can identify that.

A It's the SaveRite Market and Emerald Street and Twenty-ninth Street.

Q Okay. Can you indicate with your finger the area which you observed the car leave.

A Okay. There's an entrance up here and there's one here (indicating). He was parked here and left through the parking lot out this exit here and headed toward—there's a red light up in this area, right in here (indicating).

Q For the record, he's taken, that would be, the northwest exit?

A I'm not that good with directions.

MR. MENDEL: Would you agree that it's northwest

MR. WOLFE: I don't know if it's northwest.

THE COURT: Did you try that grease pen?

MR. MENDEL: We tried that one previously and it wouldn't mark. Perhaps this blue pen.

THE WITNESS: It's not working.

THE COURT: Just one moment.

Mr. Mendel, this one will work.

BY MR. MENDEL:

Q Mr. Carver, could you please indicate with a line where you observed the car pull out from and where it went.

A (Witness complies.)

MR. MENDEL: You're right, Judge. It does work.

BY MR. MENDEL:

Q And that's where you observed the vehicle, correct?

A Yes.

MR. MENDEL: Perhaps if I just pass this along.

THE COURT: Mr. Wharton, did you get a look at that?

JUROR NO. 7:   Yes, I did.

BY MR. MENDEL:

Q Mr. Carver, after you got the license number what took place?

A Well, as soon as I turned the license number over to the officer, I ran directly back up to Bud and my wife was already up there and the ambulance was there, so I just sort or stood out of the way.

Q Did you then make a statement to the police?

A Yes, I did.

Q And how soon after this incident took place did you make the statement?

A Approximately maybe an hour, 2 hours later.

Q Do you recall what time this incident took place?

A Well, my wife and I were in the line getting ready to be checked out of the SaveRite Market approximately 6:30 because she had asked me what time it was because my daughter's girlfriends were coming at 7:00 and she wanted to make sure that we were home. And I would say it had to be—it didn't take long for me to get checked out, so I couldn't—you know, maybe 5 minutes or so.

Q Sometime after 6:30 then?

A Yes.

MR. MENDEL: Thank you. Cross-examine.

(Whereupon, Commonwealth's Exhibit No. 2 was marked for identification.)

CROSS-EXAMINATION

BY MR. WOLFE:

Q Mr. Carver, as you've indicated, you had to be somewhere at 7:00 and you had examined your watch?

A Yes.

Q And the last time you remember looking at your watch was around 6:30?

A Yes.

Q So the shooting took place a short period of time after it took you to check through the line and come out of the store which you said may have been 5 minutes?

A Yeah, approximately. I don't know.

Q You indicated that Mr. Monroe, the person that you saw during this entire period of time, you indicated that he had dark trousers on and bluish-gray coat, I believe that was your description?

A Yes.

Q Was it a suit coat similar to what I have on?

A It seemed to be, like it should be part of a suit.

Q But it was dark in color?

A No, it wasn't real dark. It was light in color.

Q It was a blue or a gray?

A Bluish-gray, yes.

Q Now, to go over some of these photographs, referring here to Commonwealth's Exhibit No. 2, which gives you a little more broad-based viewpoints. Now, when you came out of the—let's see Commonwealth's Exhibit 1 because you've already marked that one. When you came out of the SaveRite Market the first time—

A Yes.

Q —you've marked here on the exhibit where you saw Mr. Monroe as the person you've identified running down the sidewalk.

A Yes.

Q And Mr. Wilson running behind him?

A Right.

Q And you viewed these individuals coming down and running past you, correct?

A Yeah.

Q Now, at this particular time do you notice any other black males in this area?

A No, I don't.

Q Either before running in front of Mr. Monroe or behind Mr. Wilson?

A No.

Q Anywhere?

A No.

Q For the jury's information, too, Mr. Carver, you've been subpoenaed as a defense witness as well, haven't you? We have you under subpoena?

A Yes.

Q We're trying to get your testimony taken care of in one day if we can.

A Yes.

Q So you won't have to come back again. That's the reason we're going to go over everything here.

[At this point, since Wolfe made it clear that he is planning to examine Carver essentially as a defense witness, Mendel could have raised an objection and requested that Wolfe examine him as on direct, meaning that he be restricted to non-leading questions. In any event, it is critical that neither attorney impeach Carver, because the prosecution needs to jury to believe him regarding the details of the murder, and the defense needs the jury to believe him regarding his observations of the events immediately following the murder, including Monroe's getaway.]

Now, you've indicated that they ran past you or he initially apprehended him, Mr. Monroe?

A Yes.

Q And he broke loose and he continued around the side of the building?

A Right.

Q You've marked here on Commonwealth's Exhibit No. 1, I guess it's C, this point here (indicating). This is where Mr. Monroe was apprehended by Mr Wilson?

A The second time, yes.

Q The second time after he broke away and was caught?

A Right.

Q And at this particular point you said that there was a car there?

A Yes.

Q And did you have occasion to look at that car?

A No, I didn't pay attention to the car at that time.

Q But you've indicated and you've marked the approximate area in which he was apprehended?

A Yes.

Q   And it was near a car?

A   Yes, right beside the car.

Q   Now, on Commonwealth's Exhibit No. 2 you've marked the route in which Mr. Monroe took after he got in the car and left the SaveRite Market, correct?

A   Right.

Q   Now, I note that the point here in which you indicate that he got in the car and left and the point here on Commonwealth's Exhibit No. 1 is approximately the same area in which the car was located, is that correct?

A   Yes.

Q   Now, at this particular point where the car's parked alongside the building, do you notice any other black males present at that particular time?

A   No, I didn't.

Q   Do you notice any black male in the car the first time that you—

A   I didn't look in the car but—

Q   You didn't notice anyone?

A   No, I didn't.

Q   And it's safe to assume then, Mr. Carver, that from that point on, from the time Mr. Monroe was apprehended by Mr. Wilson the first time and walked back up in the direction of Northeast, you were in constant sight of Mr. Monroe and Mr. Wilson, correct?

A   Right.

Q   The entire time?

A   Yes.

[Wolfe's painstaking examination of Carver on the details of his own actions and those of Monroe which follows serves two purposes. First, it shows that Carver was in a position during the entire period from the shooting until Monroe left the parking lot and even thereafter to see everything that was happening, and to observe Whitman had he been present and in any way involved with Monroe. Second, it anticipates the testimony of Barbara Lee, who will testify that she actually saw Whitman at Monroe's car immediately before the shooting occurred. Carver's credibility, founded on both his direct involvement in the events and the graphic detail of his testimony, is not being challenged by either side, so any testimony which contradicts his own will be met with at least skepticism.]

Q   Now, as he walked back the sidewalk up in the general direction of Northeast Drug Store, you indicated that you were what, three, four feet away?

A   I would say approximately.

Q   And you continued at around that distance all the way up the sidewalk.

A   Just about yes, until—I would say until the shooting occurred. I was a little bit further away.

Q   I don't know if you have indicated for us, if you can just point out where the shooting actually occurred.

A   Right here (indicating). There's a fence dividing the two buildings, and that's where the shooting occurred.

Q Indicating, for the record, we're looking at Commonwealth's Exhibit No. 1 and the fences in area between the Northeast and SaveRite Market, correct?

A Right.

Q So that's where this first shot occurred?

A Yes.

Q Now, prior to that time as you're being—or as you're following Mr. Monroe and Mr. Wilson up the sidewalk, at this point do you notice any young black males in addition to Mr. Monroe in the area?

A No. My eyes were directly on him and Bud.

Q Now, you've indicated that the first shot that took place was the shooting of Mr. Wilson?

A Yes.

Q And that was in the fenced-in area?

A Yes.

Q And immediately thereafter a second shot took place in which Mr. Monroe pointed the gun at you?

A Yes.

Q Not in front of any of the windows in front of the SaveRite Market?

A No. The second shot he fired at me was—

Q Was still in the fenced in area?

THE COURT: He didn't answer.

BY MR. WOLFE:

Q I'm sorry. Continue.

A The first shot was at Mr. Wilson.

Q And that occurred?

A At the fence.

Q And the second shot?

A The second shot was at the same area. The third shot was in the direction of the SaveRite Market, down in front of the SaveRite Market.

Q Where were you at when the third shot was fired?

A Right where the overhang is.

Q At this point right here (indicating)?

A Approximately in that area, yeah.

Q Do you have any indication as to where Mr. Monroe was at when he fired the third shot?

A Do I have any—

Q Where was Mr. Monroe at when the third shot was fired?

A Whenever I left him he stood off the fence and was sliding on the ground.

Q No. Mr. Monroe.

A Mr. Monroe, he was directly in back of me because I turned and was looking at him.

Q So he was somewhere in that area, he was in front of the SaveRite Market at that time?

A Yes. He was on the walk in front of SaveRite Market.

Q If he had taken a shot at you at this particular time he would be aiming down the sidewalk toward the SaveRite Market, isn't that correct?

A Yes.

Q He would never, to the best of your knowledge, have ever aimed any shots in the general direction of Northeast Drug, would he?

A No.

Q Now, at what particular point along the sidewalk, Mr. Carver, do you leave the sidewalk?

A Just if I can show you.

Q Sure.

A Approximately before we get to the overhang, in this area (indicating).

Q Indicating for the record, again, reference to Commonwealth's Exhibit No. 1 which has been marked M I suppose where the area in which—

A This is the overhang of the building and I'm just before you get to the overhang because he was running—we were both running in this direction (indicating).

Q In this direction indicating heading toward SaveRite?

A Emerald Street, yes.

Q And it was at this particular point which is marked as M that you broke away and headed into the parking lot?

A Yeah. I can over into here and then turned and came down in this direction (indicating).

Q Let me stop you for a second. Indicating when you broke away you cane to the first row of parked cars?

A Yes.

Q Which is indicated on the photograph, correct?

A Correct.

Q Mr. Monroe at this particular time continued on the sidewalk?

A Yes.

Q And once you got past this first row of cars, Mr. Carver, you still saw Mr Monroe?

A Yes.

Q And he never left your sight at this time?

A No.

Q I mean, you would have seen him. And would you indicate what route Mr. Monroe took after you broke away from the sidewalk and headed into the parking lot. Which direction did he head into?

A The direction of Emerald Street right past the SaveRite Market.

Q Indicating, however, he remained on the sidewalk?

A At all times, yes.

Q He never left the sidewalk to the best of your knowledge?

A To the best of my knowledge he didn't, no.

Q You never saw Mr. Monroe break away or head into the parking lot at any time?

A No, he didn't.

Q At this point now, Mr. Carver, you've indicated that at the point where the overhang meets is where you exited or exited the sidewalk and headed into the parking lot?

A Correct.

Q You turned around and kept Mr. Monroe in close observation, I mean he was shooting at you, wasn't he?

A Right.

Q Did you at this particular point notice any black males running after Mr. Monroe?

A No, I didn't.

Q In the area at all?

A None.

Q Was there anyone else on the sidewalk at this particular time?

A I couldn't say. My eyes were directed mostly on him.

Q And as Mr. Monroe continued down the sidewalk, you ran in a parallel direction to SaveRite Market along the first row of parked cars?

A Right with the line of cars. I stayed behind the cars.

Q You're behind the cars?

A Yes.

Q And you indicated that at this point, which is like the extreme right hand of the building, is where there's a handicapped area?

A Yes.

Q And that's where your family was located?

A Right.

Q And again, you were watching Mr. Monroe this entire time?

A Yes.

Q And he appeared obviously to you to be alone?

A Yes, at that time.

Q Now, at some particular point in time he goes around the corner, is that correct?

A Correct.

Q And at that point what did you do?

A Well, I ran in the same direction that he was—if I could show you.

Q Sure.

A Whenever I saw that my wife and two children were standing in this area and he was directly in front of them, I was standing out here in the open (indicating). And this is whenever he ran and I ran directly toward him.

Q Toward Mr. Monroe?

A Right.

Q Indicating the corner of the building?

A Yes, because my wife and children were standing in this area (indicating).

Q They obviously observed the same things that you did in the terms of Mr. Monroe coming down the sidewalk?

A Yes.

Q Were you able to observe Mr. Monroe getting into the car?

A Yes, I saw him getting into the car and I was running in the direction of my wife and two children.

Q On Commonwealth's Exhibit No. 2, you've indicated the approximate point in which the car was located, is that correct? Could you just make maybe a small X and indicate where you were at when you saw the car.

    Did you see Mr. Monroe get into the car?

A Yes.

Q Would you indicate where you were at when you saw Mr. Monroe get into the car.

THE COURT: Are there any other Xs on there?

THE WITNESS: None, Your Honor.

               Where I was at?

MR. WOLFE: Yes.

THE WITNESS: (Witness complies)

BY MR. WOLFE:

Q And at that point you saw Mr. Monroe enter the car?

A Yes.

Q Which side of the car did he enter?

A It would have been the driver's side.

Q The driver's side?

A Yes.

Q At this particular point which you've marked as an X, were you able to observe the license plate of the car?

A No, I wasn't at that time.

Q So what did you do?

A Well, as soon as I ran to my wife, which I saw him get in the car, I ran to my wife quickly and just shouted to her, you know, "Youens get into the store and get the drawer that I threw down." Ran directly toward him, toward the car.

Q You headed toward the direction of the car?

A Right.

Q And you were able to see Mr. Monroe in the car?

A Yes.

Q Was he in the car alone?

A As far as I could see. I couldn't tell you if there was anyone else. I mean, he's the only one I saw in the car.

Q And at what distance were you at that point in feet, if you can approximate?

A Maybe eight feet.

Q Close enough to get a license plate obviously?

A Yes, which I tried and I couldn't at that time.

Q And you've indicated that Mr. Monroe was driving the car?

A Yes.

Q And made some motion to you with a handgun out the window of the driver's side of the car?

A Well, no. He had turned toward the passenger's side window.

Q So he was pointing out the passenger's side window?

A Because the car was facing Emerald Street, the front of the car was facing Emerald Street. It was backed in the space.

Q So the driver's side—

A Would have been to your—your left.

Q So the driver's side would have—

A Would have been to the—

Q —to the left of the car.

A Right.

Q And you would have seen the passenger's side, that would have been closer to you than the driver's side?

A Yes.

Q And you didn't see anyone in the driver's side?

A No.

THE COURT: Slow it down a little bit, Mr. Wolfe.

MR. WOLFE: I'm sorry, Your Honor.

BY MR. WOLFE:

Q Mr. Carver, do you see the individual seated to my left?

A Yes.

Q Based on the observations that you made during the—to what you've just testified to concerning the actions of Mr. Monroe from the time you came out of SaveRite Market until the time Mr. Monroe drove away, at any point during that period of time, Mr. Carver, did you observe Mr. Whitman anywhere in that area?

A I didn't see him, no.

[This is probably the strongest evidence in support of the defendant to this point. A thoroughly credible witness, in a position to see everything that is taking place and who has testified convincingly about every detail of the events surrounding the shooting, did not see Mr. Whitman anywhere around the crime scene.]

MR. WOLFE: Thank you. I have no further questions.

REDIRECT EXAMINATION

BY MR. MENDEL:

Q Mr. Carver, until the point you heard your wife scream—

A Yes.

Q —and the time you left her, did you see him at all during that period of time?

A Pardon?

Q From the time you left your wife coming out of the SaveRite Market until the time you heard her scream, did you see her at all?

A My wife?

Q Yes.

A No. I didn't see her until I spotted her. When he stopped directly in front of her, I heard her scream.

Q And that was Mr. Monroe, correct?

A Yes.

Q Now, the entire time Mr. Monroe was chasing you or making his escape, he was pointing a gun at you, is that correct?

A Yes.

Q And I assume at that time, of course, you were watching Mr. Monroe?

A Yes.

Q Would you say your attention was directed on Mr. Monroe exclusively?

A Yes, very much.

Q Do you know if there were any other individuals around?

A At that time I couldn't—the sidewalk could have been filled with people and I probably wouldn't have seen them.

[The tactic here is clear. Without impeaching Carver, Mendel is making it clear that his attention was focused entirely on Monroe the whole time the crime was taking place. Small wonder, since Monroe was not only a danger to Carver, but to his wife and children as well. Under these circumstances, it is quite conceivable that Whitman could have been at the scene, and Carver simply didn't notice him.]

MR. MENDEL: Thank you.

RECROSS EXAMINATION

BY MR. WOLFE:

Q Mr. Carver, concerning your wife, when she came out of the store she stayed, to the best of your knowledge, in front of the store, correct?

A At which time?

Q Well, when you came out of the store and then you began to assist Mr. Wilson—

A Yes.

Q —you told your wife to remain there, correct?

A No. I said to her, "Take the cart and the children and go back in the store." There's where I thought she went.

Q And as we've indicated before, you proceeded up first, initially, up to Northeast Drug Store following behind and picking up the money that was falling?

A Right.

Q And you came back down after the shooting, running down and entering and running into the parking lot?

A Correct.

Q And as you've indicated you had, when you were looking back at the store, you saw Mr. Monroe the entire time?

A Yes.

Q And while your attention was focused on him you did not see anyone else either running before him or running after him?

A No.

MR. WOLFE: Thank you.

MR. MENDEL: Thank you, Mr. Carver.

THE COURT: That's all. We're going to take a recess, Mr. Mendel. That's all, sir. Thank you.

(Witness excused)

THE COURT: We'll take a 15-minute recess at this point. The jury may be excused.

(Whereupon, at 10:51 A.M., the jury was excused.)

THE COURT: Recess for 15 minutes.

(Whereupon, at 10:52 A.M., court was held in recess.)

AFTER RECESS

(Whereupon, at 11:19 A.M., the following proceedings were had:)

MR. MENDEL: Dr. Soong.

KIM SOONG, called as a witness, being duly sworn, testifies as follows:

DIRECT EXAMINATION

BY MR. MENDEL:

Q Sir, could you please state your full name.

A My name is Kim Soong; Soong spelled S-o-o-n-g.

Q And, sir, what is your profession?

A I'm a pathologist.

Q And, sir you are also a medical doctor, is that correct?

A Yes, sir.

Q And could you briefly explain your background and training to the members of the jury.

A I graduated from medical school in Indonesia. I had 1 year of internship at Aultmen Hospital in Canton, Ohio. I had 2 years of pathologic training at the New Jersey School of Medicine in Newark, New Jersey, and 2 more years of pathologic training at the University of Maryland in Baltimore.

Q Sir, where are you presently working?

A Romersdale Hospital.

Q And what is your position at Romersdale Hospital?

A I'm a pathologist at Romersdale Hospital.

MR. WOLFE: Your Honor, as we've indicated, we're willing to stipulate to the doctor's qualifications as an expert.

THE COURT: Alright. But I think it's necessary that the doctor's functions and what a pathologist does and so on which I think we're doing.

[This shows the limitations of stipulating to the qualifications of an expert witness, which is not unusual. Although his competence to testify is not in doubt, the jury still needs to understand his specialty in order to grasp the import of his testimony.]

BY MR. MENDEL:

Q Dr. Soong, could you briefly explain the functions of a pathologist?

A A pathologist is a physician who specializes in making this diagnosis based on the examination of the whole body, like performing an autopsy or by examining parts of the body like examining tissues, blood, urine, and so forth.

Q Sir, in conducting autopsies, what is a pathologist looking for?

A During autopsy the pathologist will do an external examination of the body and notes the abnormalities found on the external surface of the body. And then he will open the body and look at all the organs. This is called internal examination. And we also take sections from almost all the organs and examine these under the microscope to look for diseases or injuries and so on.

Q And as a result of an autopsy, are you often able to determine a cause of death for a specific individual?

A Yes, we can.

Q And, sir, as a pathologist approximately how many autopsies have you performed?

A Around 700 autopsies.

Q And have you had opportunity to testify in the courts of Mallory County as an expert concerning the cause of death of certain individuals?

A Yes, I have.

Q And approximately how many times have you done that?

A Between 30 and 35.

MR. MENDEL: Now, as Mr. Wolfe had stipulated to his qualifications, I will however, offer him to you for any questions.

MR. WOLFE: I have no questions.

BY MR. MENDEL:

Q Now, Dr. Soong, I'd like to direct your attention to an autopsy you performed on March 16, 1996, at approximately 9:00. Do you have your records concerning that with you?

A Yes, I have.

Q And who was the individual upon whom you performed the autopsy?

A Mr. Samuel Wilson.

MR. WOLFE: Your Honor, if it could expedite matters, we're willing to stipulate the cause of death of Mr. Wilson with a single gunshot wound, if that would make it easier for Mr. Mendel to proceed with the testimony. We aren't going to challenge that. Don't even plan to offer any cross examination on that issue.

MR. MENDEL: We'll certainly take that into account.

BY MR. MENDEL:

Q As a result of your autopsy of Mr. Wilson, were you able to determine what the cause of death was?

A Yes.

Q And what was that cause of death, Doctor?

A The cause of death was loss of blood due to a single gunshot wound which entered the chest wall and penetrated the left lung and the aorta.

[Again, while this testimony seems superfluous, it is not enough to prove that Wilson died. In order to prove that Monroe killed him, it is necessary to show the causal connection between the gunshot and Wilson's death. Although this seems obvious, it is an absolutely essential part of proving the legal elements of homicide, and thereby a critical step in establishing Whitman's guilt as an accomplice to homicide.]

Q And, sir, could you indicate on your person where the entrance wound was located?

A It is in the front of the chest between the left first and left second ribs.

MR. MENDEL: Thank you. Do you have any questions?

MR. WOLFE: I have no questions, Doctor.

MR. MENDEL: Thank you, Dr Soong. I appreciate your coming.

THE COURT: Thank you.

THE WITNESS: Thank you.

(Witness excused.)

MR. MENDEL: Barbara Lee, please.

BARBARA LEE, called as a witness, being duly sworn, testified as follows:

DIRECT EXAMINATION

BY MR. MENDEL:

Q Could you please state your full name for the record.

A Barbara Lee.

Q And could you spell your last name.

A L-e-e.

Q And, Mrs. Lee, where do you live?

A 827 South Seventeenth Street in Romersdale.

Q I'd like to direct your attention back to March 15, 1996, and ask you if in the evening hours you were near or in the vicinity of the Northeast

Drug Store and the SaveRite Market located at Twenty-ninth and Emerald Street. Were you there?

A Yes, I was.

Q At about what time did you arrive at the store?

A Approximately a quarter of 7:00, between 6:30 and a quarter of 7:00.

Q Now, Mrs. Lee, which store were you going to?

A To the SaveRite Market.

Q And did you travel there alone?

A Yes.

Q And how did you get into the SaveRite Market?

A I drove in my car.

Q I'd like to show you what's been marked at Commonwealth's Exhibit No. 1 for identification and ask you if you can identify what this is.

A That's the SaveRite Market where I drove that evening and the Northeast Drug Store.

Q If you could take this pen, please, mark with an L where you parked your car on that occasion.

A It's approximately one or two of these. I'm not sure which space exactly, but it's right in this area (indicating).

Q Could you mark that with an L then.

A (Witness complies.)

Q A little bigger than that, please so everybody can see it.

A (Witness complies.)

Q Now, Mrs. Lee, what did you observe at that time?

A Well, as I was pulling into the parking lot I noticed a big white man had a black man against the wall and there was another man picking something off the ground.

Q Now, where did you see the black man up against the wall?

A Light right across as I was pulling in.

Q And would that be on the wall next to—

A The SaveRite Market.

Q Park of the SaveRite Market building.

A Right.

Q And were you able to determine—or what did it appear to you to be taking place?

A Okay. As I was pulling in, as I said, there were—the black man was against the wall. The white man had his back to me, had him against the wall. Another man was picking up something in a brown paper bag. And I looked over and saw another black man sitting in the right fender of a car and I thought to myself at that time that's strange that there's two white men against one black man and the other man's not doing anything about it.

Q Now, could you indicate perhaps with a black circle where you observed this individual sitting on the car.

A Okay. That was approximately—

Q Again, you're going to have to speak up a lot louder.

A That was approximately in this area (indicating).

Q Okay. Toward where an S has been indicated previously, is that correct?

A Right.

Q Now, on what part of the car was this individual sitting?

A He was sitting on the right front fender.

Q And which way was the car facing?

A It was headed toward the direction of the Northeast Drug Store.

Q So would the individual have then been sitting closer to the sidewalk or closer to the parking lot?

A To the sidewalk.

Q Now, where did you pass in relationship to this car, did you walk in front of the car or behind the car.

A Yes, I walked in front of the car.

Q And approximately how far away from this individual on the car were you?

A I'd say approximately ten feet or less.

Q Now, did you describe how that individual was clothed?

A I don't remember exactly what he was wearing. I just remember he had light-colored clothes on and he did not have a coat and he did not have a hat.

Q Now, were you able to identify the other, the black man who was up against the wall?

A He was in darker clothes and he had a hat on. That's what really stuck out in my mind, the hat. He had a black and white or dark blue and white hat, baseball cap on.

Q And did you see what took place?

A Yes, I did.

Q Could you tell the ladies and gentlemen of the jury what you saw?

A As I was crossing the street they started up the hill toward Northeast Drug Store.

Q Now, when you say they, who do you mean?

A Okay. The man continued to sit on the car, the one black man. The other black man with the two white men started up the hill going toward Northeast Drug Store and SaveRite Market and there was like a struggle. I heard a blast. I looked up at that time just as the struggle was going on.

I heard a shot. I saw a flash of light and I saw the one man fall down.

Q Now, which individual did you see fall down?

A The white man that is against the wall.

Q And he was slightly bigger than the other individual?

A Yes. He was a little bigger from the rear. And I just watched this briefly as this all happened, and then the black man stepped away and pointed the gun in my direction. I looked up, saw he had a gun, and then I just ran.

Q Did you see what happened to the individual who was on the car?

A He was just sitting there and I ran past him.

Q And what did he appear to be doing?

A Just watching.

Q Watching what?

A What was going on.

Q After the individual with the gun pointed the gun at you, what did you do?

A I went into the SaveRite Store.

Q And what did you do once you got inside the store?

A Well, I run into the SaveRite Store. I thought I heard another shot as soon as I got inside the door. I thought he was shooting at me and I was so frightened at that time that I was too afraid to turn around to see what was going on for fear that he would be pointing the gun at me.

Q Now, getting back to the individual on the car, were you able to give a description of this individual?

A Yes I was.

Q And were you able to identify the individual's face?

A I chose two pictures at the police station. One was him and one was the other man that was involved and chose them as being the two men that were involved.

Q Now, the individual who you observed in the SaveRite Market—was sitting outside, is he present in court today?

A Yes, he is.

Q Could you identify him, please?

A He's got the gray suit on.

Q Could you point to him, please.

A Yes (indicating).

MR. MENDEL: Indicating the Defendant, Gregory Whitman.

BY MR. MENDEL:

Q Is there any doubt in your mind, Mrs. Lee, that the individual that you saw sitting on the car at the SaveRite Market shortly before the shooting is the Defendant, Mr. Whitman?

A I'm pretty sure that that's the man. He really looks like the man that was sitting there.

MR. MENDEL: Thank you. Cross examine.

MR. WOLFE: Your Honor, may we approach side bar? There's something that I'd like to put on the record at this time before we go into cross examination.

THE COURT: Alright.

(Whereupon, the following discussion was had at side bar:)

MR. WOLFE: I'm concerned with the witness' reference, Your Honor, to photos that she indicated during her direct testimony. I would consider that that makes reference or gives the jury the inference that the Defendant has a criminal record because there hasn't been any evidence of that introduced.

There was an unsolicited remark which she made reference to the fact that she identified the photographs at the police department. I believe that was the testimony.

And on the basis of that, I think the jury, as I said, can infer that Mr. Whitman has a prior criminal record and I feel compelled to make a motion for mistrial because of the statement made by the witness.

[If a witness makes an unsolicited comment which exposes the jury to information that could prejudice them unfairly, a mistrial is one possible, albeit extreme, way to protect the defendant's right to a fair trial. Obviously, there was no actual attempt to elicit this testimony, but witnesses sometimes say things in ignorance of the niceties of trial procedure. In this case, Lee's revelation that she selected Whitman's picture from an array of mug shots clearly announces to the jury that this is not the first time Whitman has been in trouble with the law. Ch. 10, "Remedies for Prejudice"]

MR. MENDEL: Your Honor, it wasn't objected to at the time she made the statement. He could have objected to it at the time and possibly have taken care of it then. I think it's a little late at this point to make the objection.

[This illustrates the critical importance of raising timely objections to inadmissible evidence. The delay here could not have been more than a few minutes, but nevertheless provides Mendel with an effective argument against Wolfe's objection. Whether the judge felt that he had, in fact, waived the objection by not raising it in a timely manner, or felt instead that her mention of the mug shots was not sufficiently prejudicial to justify a mistrial, is not known. Either argument would be sufficient to deny Wolfe's motion.]

THE COURT: Well, I'm going to deny your request.

(Whereupon, the discussion at side bar was concluded)

CROSS EXAMINATION

BY MR. WOLFE:

Q You said that you made an identification of the two men that were involved, correct, that was your phrase that you used?

A Yes.

Q Now, isn't it true that the man that you're saying was sitting on the seat—or I'm sorry. On the fender of the car, he didn't do anything?

A From what I could see he was just sitting there watching.

Q And if we could use the exhibits here, let's use Commonwealth's Exhibit No. 1 which you've already marked. You've indicated that where you've marked I guess this is a O—

A Um-hum.

Q —that that is the point at which this individual was sitting on the car?

A Approximately.

Q Now, at this particular point could you indicate where the black man was that was being put against the wall by the other individual?

A Approximately where that truck is.

Q So he would have been like maybe ten feet away from the car up against the wall?

A Yes.

Q And at that point in time as this black male was up against the wall, the man that's sitting on the car doesn't say anything to these people, does he?

A No.

Q He makes no attempt to assist this other individual?

A No.

Q You thought, in fact you said that you thought that that was kind of strange, didn't you, that one black man is watching another black man being accosted by two white men and he's not jumping in and helping out?

A Yes.

Q That struck you as being unusual?

A Yes.

Q Is it your belief that blacks automatically jump in when other blacks are being accosted, is that what you are saying?

A I guess I was thinking that.

[It's hard to tell, but it is possible here that Wolfe is trying to establish some kind of bias or prejudice against blacks on the part of the witness, perhaps as a means of impeaching her testimony. Ch. 13, "Bias or Prejudice"]

Q I take it then that you don't have a fair amount of black friends or people that are—black social acquaintances?

A Yes, I do.

Q And you still have that belief, though, that they come in and help each other out?

A Well, I believe everybody should help each other. I just thought—I don't know. I guess I assumed that they were together.

Q You assumed that they were together?

A I don't know.

Q There's nothing that that man on the car did in any way that would indicate to you that they were together?

A No.

Q You've described this individual as having light clothes on?

A Yes, light clothes.

Q You're not able to describe in particular the color of the clothes?

A No.

Q And it's safe to assume that if we could use for demonstration purposes, if this was the car that the individual was sitting on in this type of manner, leaning against the car, you said you walked in front of him, correct?

A Yes.

Q About ten feet away?

A Approximately.

Q And this was sometime after 6:30 at night?

A Yes.

Q It was dark?

A Yes.

Q And your main focus of attention was what was happening up on the sidewalk, isn't that correct?

A Yes.

Q The black man being pushed up against the wall. So as you're walking between the car and the sidewalk, you're looking generally in the direction of the wall, aren't you?

A Well, the windows were there and the lights from the store being the store was open and the bright lights from the store made it possible to see.

Q But what you're looking at on the whole, Mrs. Lee, is in the direction of the wall and the sidewalk where this confrontation is taking place?

A Yes.

Q The man that you pass ten feet away, did he say anything to you?

A No.

Q Did he do anything out of the unusual?

A No.

Q Did he make any attempt to get out of the car or enter the car to flee the scene?

A No.

Q In fact, you indicated that when you ran after the shots were fired, the individual was still sitting on the fender?

A Yes.

Q In essence what you're saying is as far as the black man who is sitting on the fender, essentially what you did is take a quick glance at him, correct?

A I looked at him briefly.

Q Briefly?

A Yes.

Q And this whole entire incident from the time you crossed the street into the sidewalk took a very short period of time, correct?

A Yes.

Q Now, Mr. Mendel indicated or asked you are you positive that the man seated next to me, Mr. Whitman, was the man on the fender and you said that you were sure. You're not entirely sure, are you?

A He does look like the man that was sitting on that car.

Q He resembles the man?

A Yes, he does.

[Wolfe is very effective at getting Lee to qualify her identification of the defendant as the man she saw in the parking lot. Saying he resembles the man and saying he is the man are two very different levels of identification.]

Q Now, as you indicated that these people were walking up the sidewalk, what did you do at this particular time? You were heading toward the SaveRite?

A Yes, I was going toward the grocery store.

Q And you were on the sidewalk at this time?

A Yes.

Q Would you then have passed the car that this man was sitting on? I mean, you would have been heading down the sidewalk toward the—

A I didn't pass the car until I—after the shooting.

Q Until after the shooting?

A Yes.

Q And what did you do as you were walking down the sidewalk, were you looking back at what was happening or did you assume that everything was okay?

A I'm not clear what you're asking me.

Q Well, you come up to the sidewalk, you've crossed the street and you come to the sidewalk and these gentlemen are off to your left, the group of three people?

A Right.

Q And the other man's sitting on the fender?

A Um-hum.

Q Now, once you get to the sidewalk, what do you do, do you start walking down the sidewalk?

A Yes.

Q Looking down the sidewalk toward SaveRite?

A I started, then I heard the struggle. I could tell there was a struggle going on. And I looked up there and that's when I saw the man being shot.

Q Are you able to identify the individual who did the shooting?

A I picked his picture out.

Q Would you estimate the amount of time that this incident took place, as you said, was relatively short?

A Yes.

Q A matter of seconds?

A It happened so quickly, yes.

Q And based on all that, you were able to, nevertheless, observe and take into account the characteristics of the person that was on the fender?

A Yes.

Q Were you able to describe his facial features at all or what he looked like?

A I don't remember.

Q You don't remember if he had a mustache or anything of that nature?

A I don't remember.

Q You don't remember seeing them or you don't remember being able to give a description of that?

A I don't remember giving a description that, you know, mustache or no mustache. I really don't remember.

Q So you at that particular time were unable to really get a look at him to determine whether or not he had a mustache on?

A I described him that night at the police station and I picked his picture out from several that were shown to me as being the man.

Q The question that I'm asking, Mrs. Lee, is at the time of the incident do you recall the man who's sitting here having a mustache.

MR. WOLFE: If the court will bear with me for one second.

BY MR. WOLFE:

Q Do you recall testifying at the preliminary hearing on this matter?

A Yes.

Q Do you recall being asked questions concerning the description of the individual?

MR. WOLFE: Page 65, Mr. Mendel, of the transcript.

BY MR. WOLFE:

Q You were asked questions concerning the description and the—

A Yes.

Q —facial features of the individual. Do you recall being asked the question, Line 12 of the transcript, page 65?

"Okay. The men seated on the front of the car, did you get any look as far as the size or facial features?

Answer. "Well, not really, because I just sort of glanced at him. I just noticed he was there. And I noticed that he was sort of watching what was happening. I didn't know if he was involved or not."

That was your statement at the preliminary hearing?

A Yes.

Q So in essence your testimony concerning what you observed as to the man on the fender was a quick glance?

A Yes.

Q And he did nothing to attract your attention or in any way give any indication to you that he was involved with this altercation with these other people?

A No.

[At this point Lee's value as an identification witness has been thoroughly negated, not only based on her lack of opportunity to observe, but on her prior statements which clearly did not provide any level of certainly about her ability to identify the man. It does not, however, change the fact that she was able to select the defendant from an array at the police station.]

Q Mrs. Lee, you've indicated that this car was parked in the curb along the sidewalk, correct?

A Yes.

Q And it's not unusual for cars to be parked in that area, is it?

A No.

Q In fact, you shop at SaveRite quite a bit?

A Yes.

Q I think you park your car there at times?

A Yes.

Q To help unload groceries?

A Yes.

Q And if you would have parked your car, would you be parking it in the same direction that this individual had parked their car?

A No.

Q If I may point this out to you. Commonwealth's Exhibit No. 1, the street or the area in front of the SaveRite Market, Ma'am, is a two-way street?

A Well, there's one lane for—to pick up your groceries. I guess it is a two lane because cars go in both directions.

Q And the car that was parked here is parked in the same direction that this truck is, right?

A Yes.

Q Facing Northeast Drug?

A Yes.

Q And in fact, you've indicated that this car was actually parked in front of the SaveRite Market, correct?

A Yes.

Q What would you estimate the distance to Northeast Drug from that point?

A I really don't know. I'm not very good at estimating distance.

MR. WOLFE: Thank you, ma'am. I have no further questions.

REDIRECT EXAMINATION

BY MR. MENDEL:

Q Mrs. Lee, in addition to identifying the Defendant on two previous occasions you've testified to, were you present at the preliminary hearing on March 29?

A Yes.

Q And on that occasion did you have an opportunity to identify the individual you saw?

A Yes, I did.

Q Sitting in the car. And who did you identify at that time?

A The gentleman in the gray suit.

Q Mr. Whitman?

A Mr. Whitman.

MR. MENDEL: Thank you, Mrs. Lee. I have no further questions.

RECROSS EXAMINATION

BY MR. WOLFE:

Q Just one or two questions concerning that identification that you made, ma'am. On Page 67 of the transcript you were asked at that time, at the time of the preliminary hearing: "In the courtroom today are you identify anyone who resembles the man who was on the front of the car?"

　　Your answer was: "I'm not sure. It might be that gentleman there in the green."

　　Was that your answer at that particular time?

A Yes.

Q The second question that you were asked, ma'am, was: "Are you telling us that you're not sure?"

Your answer at that time: "I don't know that I want to swear that he was the gentleman. I mean that it was so fast. He looks like the man that was on the car."

That was your answer at the preliminary hearing?

A Yes.

[Given the extremely qualified nature of her identification at the preliminary hearing, it was probably a tactical error for Mendel to ask her about it on redirect, thereby opening the door to further impeachment based on her prior testimony.]

Q And that preliminary hearing occurred on March the 29th?

A Yes.

Q Approximately 2 weeks after the shooting, correct?

A Yes.

Q And at that time you were not sure that Mr. Whitman was the man that was seated on the car, correct?

A Yes.

MR. WOLFE: Thank you. I have no further questions.

REDIRECT EXAMINATION

BY MR. MENDEL:

Q Mrs. Lee, could you describe your physical condition at the time of that hearing?

A I was in extreme pain because I have a chronic back problem and I had to come from my bed to the hearing. And then I went home and went back to bed. I was in an awful lot of pain at the time.

Q And who took you back and forth to the hearing?

A My husband.

Q And did you make a statement to your husband concerning the identification at that time?

MR. WOLFE: I'm going to object to that, Your Honor.

THE COURT: For what reason?

MR. WOLFE: Your Honor, it's beyond the scope of any particular cross examination that I've offered. He certainly could have asked questions concerning the testimony at a prior preliminary hearing. She's given an indication at that particular time as to what her statements were. That was the extent of the recross examination. I think Mr. Mendel is going beyond the scope of anything that we've ever asked.

THE COURT: That's your objection.

MR. WOLFE: Yes, Your Honor.

THE COURT: Overruled.

[The court seems surprised that Wolfe is basing his objection on Mendel's questions being beyond the scope of cross. A stronger argument here would have been that her statements were hearsay. Although they would have been admitted as prior consistent statements for the limited purpose of rehabilitation, they could not have been admitted to support the substance of her identification. By not raising this objection, Wolfe permitted the statements to be entered, as it were, as an alternative identification of the defendant as the man she saw sitting in the parking lot.]

BY MR. MENDEL:

Q Did you make a statement to your husband?

A Yes, I did.

Q And what did you tell your husband?

A I said I'm very, very sure that that was the man at the time.

[Rehabilitation based on prior consistent statements is a method of rehabilitation that can be very effective. In this case, however, her statements to her husband are less effective because they contradict her own sworn testimony which she gave shortly before these statements were made. The jury will probably give more credibility to statements she made under oath in court than those she said privately to her husband on the way home. Ch. 13, "Rehabilitation"]

MR. MENDEL: Thank you.

RECROSS EXAMINATION

BY MR. WOLFE:

Q Ma'am, I'm not sure what you're trying to say. Were you stating the fact you were in a lot of back pain affecting the way in which you could answer those questions?

A I was very nervous and I was in an awful lot of pain at that time, yes. And when we left the courtroom I did tell my husband that I was very sure that that was the man sitting on that car.

Q Ma'am, the questions that you were asked at the preliminary hearing, the ones that we have just gone over, you were under oath at that particular time, weren't you?

A Yes.

Q And you didn't offer at the time of the hearing any explanation as to any back pain or anything like that, did you?

A No. No one asked me.

Q In fact, the questions that I've asked you now or that we've gone over, those were questions that were asked you by the district attorney, weren't they?

A Yes.

MR. WOLFE: Alright. Thank you.

MR. MENDEL: Thank you, Mrs. Lee. No further questions.

THE COURT: That's all, Mrs. Lee. Thank you.

(Witness excused.)

MR. MENDEL: Your Honor, if we may approach the bench.

(Whereupon, a discussion was held off the record at side bar.)

THE COURT: Ladies and gentlemen, we have a missing witness who is probably in the courthouse because there are trials going on in all the courtrooms. So that the District Attorney is going to try and find his witness and he believes that he can do that in a minute or so.

So if you'll bear with us, we want to go a little bit longer before lunch.

MR. MENDEL: Mr. Wolfe and I have discussed the extent of the examination of the next witness. Perhaps it might be wise to break for lunch and possibly use him as the first witness back and then Officer Zweiger.

THE COURT: In fact, if he is going to be here in a couple of moments I would prefer to do it now because of problems that we have with scheduling this afternoon.

MR. MENDEL: He's in the Public Safety Building which is at most a 2-minute walk.

THE COURT: What we would really have to do to get him here is have a recess and he would walk in the door as soon as the last juror filed out of the courtroom.

CURTIS SMITH, called as a witness, being duly sworn, testified as follows:

DIRECT EXAMINATION

BY MR MENDEL:

Q Sir, could you please state your full name.

A Patrolman Curtis Smith.

Q And Officer Smith, you're with the Romersdale Police Department, is that correct?

A That's correct.

Q How long have you been a police officer with the city?

A My sixth year.

Q Do you also work part time anywhere?

A Yes, I do.

Q Where were you working at that time?

A The SaveRite Market.

Q Now, sir, that was a Friday. Do you recall what hours you were working?

A 6:00 to closing.

Q On that evening was there anything unusual that you recall taking place?

A There was a shooting.

Q Could you tell us how you first heard of the shooting?

A I was near the front of the store, near the office, right between the office and the—or I should say at the corner of the office and the corner of the express lane at which time I heard what appeared to be a pop and I took for granted that it was a firecracker.

Q What did you hear after that?

A I heard a second noise. It was much louder. It was a much louder pop which at that point in time it sounded more like a gunshot.

Q And what did you do after hearing that?

A I walked toward the window to look out to see where it came from because a lot of patrons were looking out the window. I couldn't see and I walked along the window toward the exit doors still looking back somewhat to see if I could see.

Q Now, is this the office as you face the store, was that to the right or the left?

A If you face the store?

Q If you face the store.

A That would be toward the left.

Q So as you're walking, you're walking down toward Emerald Street, would that be correct?

A Correct.

Q Now, as you're walking along, what did you observe?

A I observed a person run past the store. I was still on the inside of the store.

Q Could you describe that individual?

A It was a black male. That's all I could really tell.

Q Did you notice any clothing or anything?

A I don't recall. I really don't.

Q And which way was that individual running?

A Running toward Emerald Street.

Q Did you notice anything in his hands?

A No, I didn't.

Q And this was after you heard the sound which appeared to be a gunshot, is that correct?

A That's correct.

Q What did you do then?

A Well, a lady came into the store to the entrance way or the store. She came in the outdoor should I say hollering, "He's been shot, he's been shot" and crying at which time I speeded up, exiting the store.

   And as I was exiting the second exit door, I walked out and I observed— or should I say I hurried out. I observed a cash drawer on the ground by the exit door.

Q Did you observe anything else as you stepped outside?

A Yes, I did. I observed a second black male running toward me. I observed a lady that was in front of me, an elderly lady, and a grocery cart in front of me. I also observed a car in which she must have been putting groceries into.

   The black male that ran past me turned somewhat of a three-quarter position toward me to get between me and the cart.

Q Could you describe that individual please?

A Black male, approximately five seven, five eight, medium build.

Q Do you recall what the individual was wearing at that time?

A If I remember correctly, it was blue jeans, I believe a blue top and some sort of jacket or something of that nature, dark-colored jacket possibly.

[This is the point at which the defendant's jacket becomes an issue. All of the witnesses who saw the defendant in March 15 testified that he did not have a jacket on. Testimony that the second man was wearing a jacket is fairly damning in that it raises a serious question about whether the defendant was the man who ran past Officer Smith. Shortly, Officer Smith will worsen that problem by failing to identify the defendant as the man he saw.]

Q Now, Officer, the individual who ran by you, were you able to identify him?

A Yes, I was.

Q Could you describe how he passed in front of you?

A If I was standing here, if I was standing here and the car was here, he turned this position to get through (indicating).

Q And when you indicated three-quarter turn—

A Yes.

Q —did you indicate you saw three-quarters of his face or three-quarters of his body?

A Both.

Q And were you able to then identify the individual?

A Yes.

Q The individual that you saw go past you, is he present in the courtroom today?

A No, I don't see him.

[Smith's failure to identify the defendant is a serious blow to the prosecutor's case for accomplice liability. In essence, Smith has made himself a defense witness. This is why Wolfe argues later that Mendel is trying to impeach his own witness on redirect by bringing in his preliminary hearing identification of the defendant as the second man.]

Q Now, Officer Smith, at the time that you came out of the store, what did you see after the individual ran by you?

A I looked toward the area of Northeast Drugs and observed a person on the ground, a body on the ground, a lady kneeling somewhat over him.

Q And what did you do then?

A I ran toward the body.

Q And after you got to the body, were you able to identify the individual who was lying down?

A Yes, I was.

Q And who was that individual?

A Bud, Bud Wilson.

Q And had you known Mr. Wilson previously?

A Yes.

Q And how was he employed at the time?

A He was employed by Northeast Drugs as a security officer.

Q   Now, Officer Smith, after you saw Mr. Wilson, what did you do?

A   I asked the lady that was kneeling over him who did it, who did it, and she hollered the guy that ran—the guy that ran past you, them two.

MR. WOLFE: I would object to that, Your Honor, the statement made by the witness.

THE COURT: Alright, just a moment, Mr. Mendel. Your reason?

MR. WOLFE: The conversation was a hearsay statement being referred to as to what this woman told Officer Smith as to what she observed. She's obviously not in the court at this particular time.

We would object to her relation as to the statements made to Officer Smith.

THE COURT: Mr. Mendel.

MR. MENDEL: Our reaction is the officer's explaining what took place and it's part of what took place and a presentation on his part, and it goes to why he did what he did which he'll testify to.

THE COURT: I'm going to sustain the objection. I want the jury to disregard the statement by the officer as to what this woman who was over the body said to him.

[Unlike much of the hearsay that was included in the various accounts of the murder, this hearsay is incriminating because the woman referred to "them two." The idea of two direct participants in the second hold-up is a new element in the evidence, not corroborated by any previous witness except, to a small extent, by Penny Green. This is the reason for the judge's cautionary instruction.]

BY MR. MENDEL:

Q   After you spoke to this lady, what did you do?

A   Ran back toward the SaveRite Market toward Emerald Street.

Q   And how did you—what path did you take?

A   Straight down the sidewalk.

Q   Were other individuals in your way as you went down?

A   There were numerous people.

Q   Now, when you got to the end of the road, what happened?

A   I met a gentleman. He had stated, "There they go" at which time I observed a vehicle, something to that nature, "There they go," or—

MR. WOLFE: I would object to that as well, Your Honor.

THE COURT: We'll sustain the objection, Mr. Mendel.

BY MR. MENDEL:

A   I observed a vehicle exiting the parking area onto Emerald Street.

Q   How was the vehicle traveling?

A   It was traveling west on Emerald Street.

Q   And were you able to approximate a rate of speed?

A   Initially it wasn't going real fast because there was a grinding sound in the vehicle, like greats grinding. But once it did get started past Twenty-fifth street, it did speed up.

Q Did you see it pass through the light at Twenty-fifth and Overly?

A Yes, I did.

Q And did it have the light at that time, did I have a green light?

A I don't recall.

Q And, Officer, were you able to obtain any license plate number?

A Just a partial plate.

Q And do you recall whether it was the first part of the plate or the second part?

A It was the first part.

Q And do you recall the letters?

A GCK.

Q Now, Officer Smith, after you obtained the license plate number, did you receive any other information from the people who were there?

A I did. I received information from a gentleman that stopped me and said, "I have the license plate number."

THE COURT: Alright now. Mr. Mendel, I wish that you would make an effort to control your witness so that we don't get any hearsay testimony.

MR. MENDEL: Certainly.

[When a witness continuously includes inadmissible evidence in his testimony, it is not uncommon for the judge to hold the attorney liable to make sure the witness understands the rules of testimony and to prevent him from possibly making a statement that would require a mistrial.]

BY MR. MENDEL:

Q Did you speak to an individual by the name of Benjamin Carver?

A Yes, I did.

Q And Mr. Carver has testified in court, were you aware of that?

A Yes.

Q And after you spoke with Mr. Carver, where did you go?

A I ran back into the SaveRite Market to go to the phone.

Q And who were you on the phone with?

A The dispatcher, Romersdale Police Dispatcher.

Q And after that conversation, what was the next step you took?

A I came back outside the building, outside of the SaveRite Market, and went back over to Bud's body.

Q Did you have any involvement with the money that was—well, the cash drawer that was in front of the SaveRite Store?

A Yes, I did.

Q And what was that basically?

A I handed the money over to Detective Zweiger, I believe, and some money was given to another patrol officer on the scene.

Q And did that end your involvement in this matter?

A Yes.

MR. MENDEL: Thank you. Cross examine.

CROSS-EXAMINATION

BY MR. WOLFE:

Q Officer Smith, you indicated that after the shooting you were coming out of the store and you saw a black male run past you?

A Right.

Q In a three-quarter position, three-quarter angle at which you were able to observe him?

A Right.

Q Wearing a blue coat, correct?

A It was a dark blue or dark colored jacket of some sort.

Q It was a jacket of some sort?

A Yes.

Q And your testimony is here today that you're unable to identify that particular person that ran past you, is that what you're testifying to?

A The photograph I was shown—well, yes to answer your question.

Q You can't make an identification?

A Beg pardon?

Q You cannot make an identification?

A No, I didn't say that I cannot make an identification.

Q Mr. Mendel asked you can you identify the person that ran past you outside of the Northeast. Do you remember him asking you that question?

A He asked me if I see the person in the courtroom today?

Q And you said no?

A That's correct.

[Smith's statement that he *can* identify the second man to run past him only strengthens the inculpatory nature of his failure to identify the defendant as that man.]

MR. WOLFE: Thank you. I have no further questions.

REDIRECT EXAMINATION

BY MR. MENDEL:

Q Officer Smith, you attended a preliminary hearing in this matter, is that correct?

A Correct.

Q And at that time did you identify the individual you observed at that hearing?

A Yes, I did.

MR. WOLFE: Objection. I think that's going beyond the scope of anything we've asked him on cross examination. We've just asked him if he could make an identification in court. He says he's not been able to.

The Commonwealth is going beyond the scope of that and trying to further expand the direct examination that they've already completed.

THE COURT: Mr. Mendel, the purpose of your question is what?

MR. MENDEL: Well, Your Honor, there's been—

THE COURT: Come to side bar.

(Whereupon, the following discussion was had at side bar:)

MR. MENDEL: Basically, Your Honor, my initial response is the objection is late. It came after the answer. The objection was to the question and he did not object prior to the question.

Additionally, I think there's been indication in this, too, that a witness testified as to identification and as to the photograph that he observed. I'm bringing in the fact that there was an additional identification, and I think if it doesn't come in on redirect I'll just call back the witness and ask him on direct. I'll recall the witness.

MR. WOLFE: What they're trying to do, they're trying to impeach their own witness. This is the Commonwealth's witness. He's been called to make an in-court identification. He has been unable to do that. They're impeaching him through use or prior testimony and prior identification. He's their witness.

What his testimony is governed by, what he's called here to do, is to make an identification in court, now as what he made at a prior time through the use of a photograph or through testimony at a preliminary hearing. They've asked that question on direct, if he can identify the person in the courtroom. He's answered no and they're trying to impeach him.

[There is nothing wrong with a party impeaching his own witness. If a witness changes his story from previous testimony, it is perfectly acceptance, though not desirable, to prove that the witness' current testimony is inconsistent with his prior testimony. The problem here is not that the witness is being impeached, but that Mendel is attempting to replace the in-court testimony, where Smith stated he could not identify the defendant as the second man who ran toward him, with his preliminary hearing testimony. As Mendel shows later in this argument, however, his intention was not to have Smith tell the jury what his previous testimony was, but merely to testify that he had made a previous identification.]

MR. MENDEL: I'm not trying to impeach him. Did he make a prior identification? Yes, he did. That was the last question that was asked. The next step comes up bringing up the next officer who is going to say at a certain time that he identified him. It's a place where the individual cannot identify him, but at one time they were identify him. I don't think it's impeachment.

THE COURT: It seems to me if you're going to interrogate him now about the identification, it would have been appropriate to do it when he said to you I don't see the person in the courtroom. Now we're faced with a problem and I think that you are beyond the scope. You raised the question of identification. It came up that he could not recognize him in court. That's the end of it. I mean, you have other things you can do.

MR. MENDEL: That's the last question I was asking that witness. I'm done with him now.

[Mendel raises a valid point. If he was not going to actually ask Smith what his preliminary hearing testimony was, then his question was not intended to impeach Smith, but rather to lay a foundation for later testimony about Smith's identification of the second man.]

THE COURT: Your last question was going to be what?

MR. MENDEL: The one I asked to which he answered and then an objection came. Did you make a prior identification? Yes.

THE COURT: Okay. I'm going to sustain that objection.

MR. WOLFE: We would ask the jury to disregard that. We would ask for a caution.

THE COURT: No.

(Whereupon, the discussion at side bar was concluded.)

THE COURT: Do you recall your last question, Mr. Mendel?

MR. MENDEL: I believe the question was do you recall making a prior identification.

THE COURT: At which point there was an objection. After side bar conference, the Court is going to sustain that objection and direct that that question be stricken.

MR. MENDEL: Thank you. No further questions.

MR. WOLFE: We have nothing further.

THE COURT: That's all sir.

MR. MENDEL: Thank you, Officer.

(Witness excused.)

MR. MENDEL: Your Honor, the next witness we have is Detective Zweiger. He's indicated he will not be available after the lunch hour for some period of time.

THE COURT: Alright. We're going to break for the noon recess now. It's 20 after 12:00. We would ask the jury to make every effort to be back and ready to come down at 1:30, and we'll try to arrange our witness so what we can proceed.

If it occurs that we will not be able to proceed with a witness because of conflicts in the courthouse, we'll notify you in the jury room so that you can relax up there as much as you may be able to relax up there. I don't know how relaxing it is.

So we will adjourn for the noon recess at this time. The jury is excused. If I could see counsel for just a moment. The jury may be excused.

(Whereupon, at 12:19 P.M., the jury was excused.)

(Whereupon, a discussion was held off the record at side bar.)

(Whereupon, at 12:20 P.M., court was held in recess.)

AFTER RECESS

(Whereupon, at 2:45 P.M., the following proceedings were had in the absence of the jury:)

MR. MENDEL: For the record, this is the case docketed to 453 Criminal Division 1996, Commonwealth of Pennsylvania versus

Gregory Whitman. For the record, Mr. Whitman is present represented by his attorney, Mr. Kirby Wolfe.

THE COURT: Very well. Mr. Wolfe.

MR. WOLFE: Your Honor, we would also note for the record these statements are taken outside the presence of the jury, Your Honor. We would note that Your Honor has made a motion prior to the commencement of testimony this morning refusing the defense counsel's request to bring in certain statements made by a co-defendant in this case, Eddie Monroe.

What the Defendants would like to do at this particular time would be to have those statements introduced and entered into part of the record concerning the exact nature of the statements given by Mr. Monroe.

[Although the court failed to allow Monroe's statements to be read to the jury, those statements are now being read into the record outside the jury's hearing so their substance can be evaluated by an appellate court should Wolfe file an appeal on this issue. What follows is not, however, part of the evidence in this case, and the jury will never be made aware of these statements.]

For the record, the first statement that the defense was prepared to offer in this case was a statement from Eddie Monroe taken on the 16th of March, 1996, at the Baltimore City Police Department by Sergeant Linden Gates and Sergeant Bill Keim of the Romersdale Police Department.

In that statement, in a police report filed by Detective Gates, he indicated that, "I read Mr. Monroe his rights at 17:44 hours at the Baltimore City Jail at which time Monroe stated that he robbed a store, meaning Northeast Drug Store and Twenty-ninth Street and that two men chased him, caught him and were walking him back to the store.

And the one man kept punching or pushing him and saying that's a knife in your pocket isn't it. That's when he shot him. He stopped talking at this point. At that time I asked him if he would give a written statement to which he replied not at this time. He also stated that he was alone at the time of the robbery and the shooting. At this time the interview was concluded."

THE COURT: Alright. How would you like to mark that?

MR. MENDEL: Well, I believe it's been read into the record. I don't think we'll have to formally introduce the statement.

THE COURT: The Court reiterates its ruling. We do not believe it would be appropriate.

Mr. WOLFE: There are other statements we were prepared to offer. We would like the record to reflect them as well.

The second statement is a statement that was taken on the 24th of May, 1996, by Mr. Monroe at the Baltimore City Jail in Baltimore by Detective Ronald Zweiger, who is the investigating officer in this incident.

On Page 3 of that statement, a portion of that statement concerns the involvement of Mr. Monroe at Northeast Drug and the presence or lack of presence of Mr. Whitman. The following questions and answers were given:

THE COURT: Please read them slow enough in consideration of the reporter, please.

MR. WOLFE:

Question: "After Gregory Whitman got out of your car at Seventeenth and Overly Street, did you see him again that day?"

Answer.   "No."

Question.   "Since the robbery at Gerber's Food Market, have you seen or spoke with Gregory Whitman?"

Answer.   "No."

"Was Gregory Whitman with you when you robbed Northeast Drug?"

Answer.   "No."

"Was anyone with you when you robbed Northeast Drug Store?"

Answer.   "No."

"Did you use the same gun to rob Northeast Drug Store that you used to rob Gerber's?"

Answer.   "Yes."

That was the extent of the statement involved in the defense petition exculpating Mr. Whitman from any involvement in the Northeast Drug Store.

There's two other statements that were given orally that we would like to present testimony as to the recipient of those statements given by Mr. Monroe.

THE COURT: Who would those be?

MR. WOLFE: One would be Miss Judith Monroe who is the sister-in-law of Eddie Monroe and who would state that she had spoken with Mr. Monroe on several occasions since his arrest by phone and during these phone conversations Mr. Monroe has repeatedly indicated that he was alone during the shooting at Northeast Drug Store and that Mr. Whitman was not present or involved in the planning or robbery at Northeast Drug.

I think that would be sufficient for the purposes of the record, Your Honor. I don't know if it's necessary to have her testimony from the stand.

THE COURT: Well, I think if you did call that witness to testify and the District Attorney knew what that testimony would be, he would object to it as hearsay. Mr. Mendel's already indicated that and it is in the Court's opinion hearsay, so we would not even permit that witness to make those statements.

Therefore, I don't think it's necessary to put that on and then preclude that. I think you've protected the record with what the witnesses would say.

MR. WOLFE: There would be one more statement, Your Honor, a statement taken by Mr. Dan Bishop, an investigator with the Mallory County Public Defender's office. And Mr. Bishop would testify on May the 11th, 1996, he was present during an interview of Eddie Monroe at the Baltimore City Jail at which time Mr. Monroe again reiterated to both myself and Mr. Bishop that he participated in the Northeast Drug robbery alone and that Gregory Whitman was not present at the time nor did he participate in the robbery at Northeast Drug.

THE COURT: Very well.

MR. WOLFE: Thank you, Your Honor.

THE COURT: We will not adjourn again and wait for your prosecuting officer.

MR. MENDEL: Very well. I'll go and try and track him down.

(Whereupon, at 2:52 P.M., Court was held in recess.)

(Whereupon, at 3:29 P.M., the jury entered the courtroom.)

THE COURT: I take it, Mr. Mendel, that there is no change in our status.

MR. MENDEL: That's correct, Your Honor. He's still on the stand.

THE COURT: Ladies and gentlemen, there was a Romersdale Police Officer that is the prosecuting officer in this case who has been seated beside Mr. Mendel. He's involved in another case in another courtroom and began to testify at 1:30.

He just now began his cross examination and it's probably going to be another hour. And the lawyers and the court like to have the cases come in in the way that the prosecution and the defense plan. That is, they organize their witnesses in what they perceive to be a proper fashion so that you folks get the right continuity of what happened.

So in a case as serious as this one, we do not want to disturb their order of preference. Because of that, it looks like we're not going to be able to proceed until late this afternoon, and we're not going to hold you anymore. You've been waiting without doing anything now for 2 hours now, so I'm going to discharge you now and you can go home without having to wait any longer. It might give you a jump on the traffic.

We will not be able to proceed tomorrow morning until 9:45, so that is you're in your jury room close to 9:30 that will be time for us tomorrow. I'm sorry for the inconvenience, but if you ever contemplated how difficult it is to get all of these cases when you only have five courtrooms and you're dealing with a lot of the same lawyers, very often it's difficult to have all of them scheduled and run as smoothly as possible.

We've hit that kind of impairment. Therefore, we're going to dismiss you at this point. The jury may now be excused.

(Whereupon, at 3:32 P.M., the jury was excused.)

THE COURT: And we will excuse Mr. Wolfe and Mr. Mendel unless Mr. Mendel has something else or you have something else. And we're in the process of calling the Deputy Court

> Administrator, but I'm not too optimistic that anything is going to come in.
>
> So we'll excuse you gentlemen and then we'll recess the court until further call by the court.

MR. WOLFE: Thank you, Your Honor.

(Whereupon, at 3:33 P.M., the court was held in recess.)

9:55 A.M.
Thursday, August 8, 1996
Courtroom No. 4

THE COURT: Good morning ladies and gentlemen.

MR. MENDEL: Your Honor, at this time the Commonwealth would call the case docketed to 453 Criminal Division 1996, the Commonwealth of Pennsylvania versus Gregory Whitman.

For the record, Mr. Whitman is present represented by his attorney, Mr. Kirby Wolfe. Also present is the jury.

THE COURT: Very well. You may proceed.

MR. MENDEL: At this time we'd like to call Officer Smith to the stand.

MR. WOLFE: May we approach side bar, Your Honor, before the next witness takes the stand?

THE COURT: Yes.

(Whereupon, the following discussion was had at side bar:)

MR. WOLFE: First of all, Your Honor, we would object to the recalling of Officer Smith. It's our understanding that he would be called by the Commonwealth to change the testimony that was given yesterday afternoon concerning the identification of Mr. Whitman as being present at the scene.

We think the Commonwealth has had the opportunity to call that witness and to elicit the testimony, and this would be repeating the testimony in a contradictory presentation of testimony that the Court and the jury has heard yesterday. And we don't think that there's been any sufficient basis to justify the recalling of the witness and to reiterate and withdraw testimony that they've previously given.

And, therefore, on that basis we would object.

THE COURT: Mr. Mendel.

MR. MENDEL: Based upon the Commonwealth versus Whitman—I don't have the Pennsylvania site. I have the Atlantic Reporter site. It's a 396 Atlantic 2nd 726.

THE COURT: Just a minute. And the page?

MR. MENDEL: 726. The court may permit the recall of witnesses or permit the reopening of a case at its discretion to correct mistakes or to effect a just result.

I think the officer's testimony would be that of a mistake. On two prior occasions he identified the individual, and after coming down off the stand and before I had left the courtroom he came up to me and informed me that indeed he had made a mistake.

THE COURT:	You'll have to lay whatever basis, you know, that you think.
MR. MENDEL:	Certainly.
THE COURT:	Is that a Superior Court or a Supreme Court?
MR. MENDEL:	Superior Court.
THE COURT:	I'm glad to hear that they upheld what I said in chambers. I note your objection and I'll overrule your objection.
MR. WOLFE:	Prior to your coming on the bench my client informed me that earlier this morning Officer Smith viewed my client down in the holding area where he was being kept as he was in custody during the course of this trial, and had the opportunity to view and observe my client.
	And it's my client's assertion it was done for the specific purpose of viewing in order to make an identification. There is no explanation that I can think of that would require earlier in this morning when he's going to take the stand and withdraw his testimony given yesterday.
	And presumable I had my client—
THE COURT:	Well, we don't know what he's going to say. And he's a Romersdale City Police Officer, isn't he?
MR. WOLFE:	Yes.
MR. MENDEL:	I believe he's working today as a Deputy Sheriff. It's a part-time job he has.
THE COURT:	I can't exclude him because of that. We'll note your objection. I would think that that would be fertile ground for cross examination as I'm sure you appreciate.

[This exchanged illustrates the difference between admissibility of evidence and credibility of evidence. The day before Officer Smith stated that he did not see the second man who passed him at the crime scene in the courtroom. This testimony contradicts two other previous statements when he did identify that man as the defendant. Now, Mendel is recalling him on the grounds that Smith told him he had made a mistake in his testimony. The judge is allowing this recall of the witness in the interests of justice and creating a complete and accurate record. His comment about "fertile ground for cross-examination," however, recognizes that although Smith will be permitted to correct his testimony, he will be subject to impeachment on the grounds that such correction was necessary in the first place, and on the fact that he apparently viewed the defendant the night before in order to confirm an identification he stated he couldn't make at trial.]

(Whereupon, the discussion at side bar was concluded.)

MR. MENDEL: Officer Smith.

CURTIS SMITH, recalled.

DIRECT EXAMINATION

BY MR. MENDEL:

Q Sir, for the record, you testified yesterday, is that correct?
A That is correct.

Q And at that time you were placed under oath, is that correct?

A That is correct.

Q And, sir, you are still under that oath, are you aware of that?

A Yes, I am.

Q Now, Officer Smith, you testified before the lunch recess yesterday, is that correct?

A Correct.

Q Where were you immediately before you were called to testify?

A In the Police Communications Center. I'm a police screening officer.

Q And that is in the Public Safely Building, is that correct?

A That is correct.

Q And at that time did you receive a message to come into the courtroom?

A Yes, I did, approximately 2, 3 minutes before I arrived.

Q And at that time you left the Public Safety Building and what did you do?

A Came directly over.

Q And then you were placed on the stand, is that correct?

A That is correct.

Q Now, Officer Smith, after you got off the stand and before I had left the courtroom, did you have an opportunity to come up and speak to me in this courtroom?

A When I left the stand prior to your leaving the courtroom, no, I didn't.

Q Did you come up to me at all while I was standing at counsel table here?

A Yes. It was during—it was after they had recessed for lunch.

Q But I had not left the courtroom, is that correct?

A That is correct.

Q Now, what did you inform me at that time?

A I informed you that at that time I did not see the Defendant and that it wasn't until after I testified that I recognized who the Defendant was.

Q And the individual who you observed, the second individual you observed run past the door of the SaveRite Market, were you able to identify that individual at the time of the incident?

A Yes.

Q Are you able to identify that individual today?

A Yes, I am.

Q And were you able to identify that individual yesterday after you had taken the stand?

A Yes.

Q And who is that individual?

A The Defendant sitting beside counsel (indicating).

MR. MENDEL: For the record, indicating Mr. Whitman.

BY MR. MENDEL:

Q At the time you testified did you notice any difference between the—

MR. WOLFE: Objection. I think it's one of a leading question, Your Honor.

THE COURT: Overruled.

BY MR. MENDEL:

Q Was there any difference between the Defendant's appearance yesterday and his appearance as you recall it on March 15, 1996?

A Yes.

Q And could you describe that appearance, please?

A He appears to be a little bit thinner than what he was during the time of the incident and/or the hearing.

Q Now, you did testify at a hearing in this matter previously, is that correct?

A That is correct.

Q And the date of that hearing was March 29, 1996, is that correct?

A That's correct.

Q And at that time did you identify the individual you observed at the SaveRite Market on March 15?

A Yes, sir.

MR. WOLFE: I would object to that, Your Honor. I think the Commonwealth is trying to impeach their own witness and establish his reliability by introducing prior consistent statements with what he's offering in the court right now. He hasn't even been subject to cross examination this morning on the basis of his identification.

[Wolfe misspoke here, his point being that the Commonwealth is trying to rehabilitate its own witness with his prior consistent preliminary hearing testimony, even before the defense has a chance to impeach him.]

THE COURT: Overruled.

BY MR. MENDEL:

Q And at that time, did you identify an individual that you saw run past you at the SaveRite Market?

A I did.

Q And who did you identify at that time, Officer?

A Mr. Gregory Whitman.

Q And is he the individual present in the courtroom today?

A That is correct.

MR. MENDEL: Thank you. Cross examine.

CROSS EXAMINATION

BY MR. WOLFE:

Q Now, Officer Smith, let me get this straight. You took the stand yesterday before lunch and sitting there as you're sitting now, you were asked questions by Mr. Mendel concerning what you saw at Northeast Drug on the evening on March 15, weren't you?

A Yes.

Q And you, at that particular time, described an individual that ran past you in which you got a three-quarter angle glimpse at, correct?

A Correct.

Q Mr. Mendel asked you yesterday if you could identify any individual in the courtroom as the person who ran past you on the evening of March 15, isn't that correct?

A That's correct.

Q You sat in that chair in an open courtroom with all the time in the world, fairly look lighting conditions, and you looked around, you looked all over this courtroom, didn't you?

A I did.

Q You looked at the table over there, didn't you?

A Yes, I did.

Q And what was your response to the jury at that time? You couldn't identify him, could you?

A That's correct.

Q And you had other things on your mind as well at that time, isn't that correct?

A That is correct.

Q I mean you had heard gunshots, you came out of the door, and you saw a cash register that was laying in that immediate area, correct?

A That's correct.

Q And you also noted a body that was laying up on the sidewalk?

A That's correct.

Q All these things are running through your mind back on March the 15th?

A Correct.

Q You're looking at the register, you're looking up here, and people are running by you, and you have a three-quarter glimpse of a man that runs by you and you're unable to identify that man based on that three-quarter glimpse as Gregory Whitman, is that what you're saying.

A Correct.

Q And then you're saying that in open court with no pressure on you, no distractions and all the time that you have that you can possibly take in order to make an identification, you can't identify this man, that's what you're telling the jury, isn't that correct?

A No, I stated that I did not see him in the courtroom at the time.

Q He was sitting here, wasn't he?

A He had his head down and it was as if he was writing. I could barely see his face.

Q Are you saying that the opportunity to look at him yesterday in the courtroom was less than the opportunity you had at Northeast Drug?

A Oh, yes.

Q How long did you testify yesterday?

A I don't know the time period.

Q Ten, 15, 20 minutes?

A I don't know.

Q The entire time you were sitting there Mr. Whitman was sitting here, correct?

A Correct.

Q So you had, the entire time that you were on the stand, the opportunity to observe this man, isn't that correct?

A Correct.

Q And the time that you had at Northeast Drug to observe him was fleeting so to speak?

A Correct.

Q Now, one of your possible explanations is that he had his head down, he was writing, that's why you didn't get a good chance to observe him, is that correct?

A Correct.

Q And are you testifying now in front of the jury that Mr. Whitman had his head down the entire time that you were on the stand?

A For some reason he was writing. I don't know why, but he had his head down.

Q He had his head down when the question was asked by Mr. Mendel as to whether you could identify him, and you're saying he had his head down when I asked you the question?

A That's correct.

Q You didn't bother to ask him to put his head up or to indicate that that looked like the man anyhow?

A That's correct, I did not.

Q Even with his head down, Officer, you still got a full-face view at him, didn't you?

A No, sir, not the full face.

Q Would you have gotten as much as a three-quarter view of him as you did at Northeast Drug on the evening of March 15?

A Not at the same angle, no. And with the possible loss of weight he appears thinner to me.

Q Thinner. Alright Officer, I want to—you're saying this man weighed 250 pounds back on March the 15th, are you?

A No, I'm not.

Q Are you saying that there's an appreciable loss of weight in his characteristics now from March the 15th?

A There is some weight—appears to be some weight loss.

Q Could you estimate in terms of weight how much loss?

A No, I couldn't.

Q Officer, you remember testifying at the preliminary hearing, don't you?

A That's correct.

Q Page 106 of the transcript. You remember being asked questions concerning the description of the individual, correct?

A Correct.

Q And you indicated that—your answer on Page 106 in terms of the description of the second individual was: "The second individual that I observed was a black male in his mid 20s: height approximately five seven, five eight, somewhere around there; not thin build but in between thin and medium build. I would say medium build, closer to a medium build.''

So at that particular time the description that you gave back on March the 15th was between a thin and a medium build, correct?

A Correct.

Q What would you describe Mr. Whitman's build as today; thin, medium?

A In between thin and medium.

Q So there isn't much difference between his build now and the build that you observed of the individual that ran past you on March the 15th, is there?

A Not in the build, no. If the face there is—seems to be somewhat of a loss in the face.

Q And it's based on that loss of the face that caused you—is one of your explanations as to why you can't identify this man?

A Correct.

Q Well, let me ask you this. Did you ever have the opportunity since yesterday, since you testified on the stand, have you ever had the opportunity to see Mr. Whitman again?

A When I came back into the courtroom.

Q Did you see him this morning?

A Not until I walked in.

Q That was the only time you saw him?

A This morning, yes.

Q When you took the stand?

A I walked back in and we started the proceedings.

Q Did those observations that you saw at that particular time assist you at all in making the identification of Mr. Whitman?

A Yes.

Q So the fact that you saw him walking around and had a greater opportunity to observe him helped you identify him?

A Yes.

Q You didn't have that ability to have any individual walk around at Northeast Drug on the 15th of March, did you?

A I'm sorry?

Q You didn't have the opportunity to have that individual walk in front of you and concentrate your attention fully on the 15th of March at Northeast Drug, did you?

A Are you indicating the Defendant?

Q No. Concerning the person that you saw at that time.

A No, I did not.

MR. WOLFE: Thank you. I have no further questions.

[This cross-examination was not as successful as it might have been, in part because Wolfe gave Smith plenty of opportunities to explain why he was unable to identify the defendant the day before. Another problem was that Smith denied viewing the defendant after trial the night before,

and the only witness who could contradict that testimony would be the defendant himself, who does not want to take the stand. By grilling Smith so assiduously on the change in his testimony, Wolfe actually made it possible for him to seem more credible to the jury than if he had simply allowed the contradiction to stand after direct examination.]

MR. MENDEL: Just to touch a couple of things.

REDIRECT EXAMINATION

BY MR. MENDEL:

Q The individual you observed at Northeast Drug, who you have identified as the Defendant, walked and ran past you, isn't that correct?

A That's correct.

Q Now, Officer Smith, after the lunch recess, were you present in court ready to testify at that time?

A Yes, I was.

Q And it was immediately after you got off the stand or shortly thereafter that you informed me—

MR. WOLFE: Objection. He's leading the witness.

THE COURT: Sustained.

BY MR. MENDEL:

Q Just recall at what time did you inform me?

A I left the courtroom during the recess. I went to Detective Zweiger and I stated that it looked like the individual but he appears to be thinner at which time I came back in to you and informed you of that fact.

Q And at a preliminary hearing—well, the evening of this incident took place, did you have an opportunity to look at a number of photographs?

A Yes, I did.

Q And at that time did you—

MR. WOLFE: I would object to that time of questioning.

MR. MENDEL: Your Honor, if we may approach side bar?

THE COURT: Alright.

(Whereupon, the following discussion was had at side bar:)

THE COURT: First of all, tell me about the pictures.

MR. MENDEL: There was a gallery of nine Romersdale Police Department which were shown to all the witnesses. There's been some testimony or evidence through cross examination showing recent photographs prepared by Sergeant Gates, I believe it was, of the fabrication or possible misidentification.

I think that case law is clear that opportunity for prior identification, even if they are photographs, permit—he is permitted to rehabilitate the witness which is what I'm attempting to do. There's been no reference to mug shots. There's been no reference to anything that would give rise to prior criminal activity.

Simply the fact he had an opportunity to review some photos.

MR. WOLFE: I object to Mr. Mendel's assertion that there is no indication that this jury can infer that he's making reference to mug shots, and, therefore, draw the conclusion that Mr. Whitman has a prior criminal record. He's been asked if he made an identification on the evening of the shooting at the police station. How else could they have pictures of Mr. Whitman at that particular time if, in fact, they weren't mug shots of Mr. Whitman?

This is a police officer. It's the Commonwealth's witness. I think the jury has heard evidence here that would clearly allow them to infer that Mr. Whitman has a prior record because of the circumstances under which he's making a photo identification at the police station on the night of the shooting. They've already heard that.

[The question of whether the jury knows about the defendant's criminal record is a serious one that could potentially result in a mistrial. There was already a suggestion of this issue during Barbara Lee's testimony, and now it becomes even more serious because this is an identification by a police officer based on what, as Wolfe notes, is obviously a series of mug shots. Because no actual testimony was elicited about the photographs from Mr. Smith, the prejudicial effect of the evidence is less severe than it might have been, but the court clearly agrees with Wolfe that allowing evidence which demonstrates Whitman's prior criminal record would be prejudicial to a point that would outweigh any probative value of that evidence as a method of rehabilitation. Ch. 10, "Unfair Prejudice"]

THE COURT: I think it's prejudicial. I think it's potentially prejudicial.

MR. MENDEL: I do have a case back there. I can give you a citation. They were permitted after a witness has been impeached and another witness could testify to the fact that photos were shown and that there was no prejudice to the Defendant by the fact the identification was made out of photos and that testimony not only is hearsay because someone else is saying it, but it also has the photo issue in it.

And that was permitted by the Superior Court in that instance. It's Commonwealth versus Berrios, B-e-r-r-i-o-s.

THE COURT: I don't want you to ask the question. I'm going to sustain the objection. I don't want you to ask the question about the photographs.

MR. MENDEL: The question then comes can I ask him the evening of the incident he did identify the individual, Mr. Whitman, as the person he observed without mentioning photographs?

THE COURT: He already said he did that a couple times.

MR. MENDEL: Not on the evening in question. I don't believe he said that. He said he identified him at the preliminary hearing.

THE COURT: What do you mean? What does that mean?

MR. MENDEL: Basically the fact that on the evening of the shooting he identified Gregory Whitman as the person.

THE COURT:	When you say identified, what do you mean?
MR. MENDEL:	He identified him through photographs but I'm not going to be asking him through photographs.
THE COURT:	No, because then you're going to come right back in. You're going to ask him how he made the identification. He made the identification from photographs and we're right back in and I think it's—
MR. MENDEL:	Okay.

(Whereupon, the discussion at side bar was concluded.)

MR. MENDEL: I have no further questions for the Officer.

RECROSS EXAMINATION

BY MR. WOLFE:

Q The clothing description of the individual.

MR. MENDEL: I'm going to have to object. It's outside the scope of redirect.

THE COURT: Sustained.

MR. WOLFE: Alright. Thank you. I have no further questions.

THE COURT: That's all.

MR. MENDEL: Thank you, Officer Smith.

(Witness excused.)

MR. MENDEL: Detective Zweiger

RONALD ZWEIGER, called as a witness, being duly sworn, testified as follows:

DIRECT EXAMINATION

BY MR. MENDEL:

Q For the record, would you please state your name and spell your last name please.

A Ronald E. Zweiger. Z-w-e-i-g-e-r.

Q Sir, how are you employed?

A Police Officer for the City of Romersdale assigned to the Detective Division.

Q And how long have you been a police officer with the City?

A I've been a police officer 13 years and assigned to the Detective Division six and a half years.

Q And, sir, you were assigned to the investigation into the shooting death of Samuel W. Wilson, Jr., is that correct?

A That's correct.

Q When did you first learn about a shooting at Northeast Drug?

A Very shortly after it occurred. I'd say probably within 2 minutes after it occurred.

Q What were the circumstances concerning how you were made aware of this?

A I was working off duty at the Old Market Food Store on Twenty-ninth Street which is across the road from the SaveRite Market/Northeast

Drug Store complex. The assistant store manager received a phone call from a City police officer advising him of a shooting at the SaveRite Store.

He immediately informed me. I informed him that we have police officers that work over there and I was going over.

So I left the Old Market Store and proceeded directly to the Northeast Drug Store/SaveRite Market complex.

Q And what time did you arrive there?

A Approximately 6:50 P.M., between 6:50 and 6:55 P.M.

Q And what did you observe at that time?

A Initially I observed a white male—well, initially I observed an ambulance coming across the lot as I was running across. There were people standing around, and I continued onto the sidewalk at the Northeast Drug Store, I observed a white male laying on the pavement at the north corner of the Northeast Drug Store.

Q Where would that be in relationship to the chain link fence between the two stores?

A Immediately beside it. There's the SaveRite Market, a chain link fence, and then the Northeast Drug Store. And Mr. Wilson was laying on the pavement right at the corner of the Northeast Drug Store beside the chain link fence.

Q Were you able to identify the individual as Samuel Wilson?

A Yes. I knew Mr. Wilson personally for probably 9 years now and I was able to identify him as Samuel Wilson.

Q And what was taking place in that area at that time?

A There were uniformed police officers there who were attempting to secure the scene. The ambulance attendants were attending to Mr. Wilson.

Q Were there a bunch of people around the area?

A Yes. There were a lot of people in the area.

Q Now, the ambulance people were taking care of Mr. Wilson, is that correct?

A That's correct.

Q How soon after your arrival was Mr. Wilson transported from the scene?

A I would estimate probably 5 to 7 minutes after I arrived he was removed.

Q And what did you do after reviewing the scene and seeing what was taking place?

A I started talking to the uniformed officers to secure certain areas and then started talking to the people that were there to try and obtain information to find out what had exactly occurred.

Q No, when you refer to securing the area, what do you mean by that?

A Well, the immediate area where Mr. Wilson was found, to get that secured, to stop anybody from walking through there, contaminating any possible evidence that may be there.

Q And how was the scene secured?

A Well, physically by police officers standing there and with the aid of what we call police tape. It's a yellow tape that's strung up and it has on it police lines, do not cross.

Q Now, after the scene was secured, what did you do?

A I then started to interview people at the scene.

Q And basically why were you speaking to these individuals?

A No. 1, to find out if we had any eye witnesses to the event who could identify the perpetrator.

Q And by perpetrator, you meant whom?

A The individual who shot Mr. Wilson.

Q Now, at any time that evening did you come into contact with the money?

A Yes. Shortly after arriving there Officer Smith, who was already off duty from the City but working part time in SaveRite Market, approached me. He had his hat, it was his personal hat which was a black apple-type hat in his hands, and inside that hat there was money. There were $20 bills. There was rolled change and there was loose change.

Q And what did you do with that money?

A I secured it in my—I had a field jacket on and I secured it in one of the pockets. I made sure there was nothing else in the pocket, and then I put the money in that pocket. And the jacket has a snap on the pocket.

After I put the money in the pocket, I snapped it.

Q I just want to take you back a second. When you observed Samuel Wilson, how was he dressed?

A He had a gray or bluish-gray heavy overcoat on, a winter-type coat. He had a pair of trousers that if I recall had a stripe down the side of them.

His normal job or primary job was manager of a—of the Brinks Armored Company here in Romersdale, and he apparently had that uniform on with a civilian jacket covering the shirt.

Q Now, Officer, after you came in contact with the money that you received from Officer Smith, what did you do with the money after you secured it?

A Later I turned all that money over to Sergeant Keim who is our evidence technician for the purpose of him examining it for latent fingerprints or anything that he could obtain from it.

Q After you received the money what did you do?

A I made arrangements for people that were there who advised me that they had seen something, heard something, whatever, who they may have told, a police officer or they told me when I was talking to them. I made arrangements to have those people transported to the criminal investigation section for the purpose of written statements.

Q Where is the criminal investigation section located?

A The Public Safety Building which houses the police department. It's on the third floor of that building at 26 Chester Street.

Q And that's in the city?

A Yes, sir.

Q Now, did you then leave the scene and if so approximately what time?

A I left the scene I'd say probably 19:15 to 19:20 hours or 7:15 to 20 after 7:00 in the evening. I left the scene and immediately traveled to the Criminal Investigation Section.

Q And what did you do upon arrival there?

A Ensured that all the witnesses were separated. I think there were five initially transported and a sixth one was allowed to make arrangements for her children before coming to City Hall.

 I ensured initially that each one was separated so that they wouldn't talk to each other about the events and that what we reported from them would be in their own words.

Q And approximately how many statements did you then take?

A Over the course of that evening I took six written statements.

Q And if you could, who are the people from whom you took the statements?

A The people I took them in the order that they were taken: Laverne Platts, Benjamin G. Carver, Scott Lawrence, Harold LaVey, L-a-v-e-y, Barbara Lee, and Officer Curtis Smith.

Q And all six of these statements were taken on the evening of March 15?

A That's right. We started taking the statements at 19:45 hours or 15 minutes of 8:00 P.M.

Q And approximately what time did you conclude the statements?

A Somewhere after 11:00 P.M. We called in extra officers to assist in the taking of statements. If I had taken six individual statements myself it would have went well past 11:00. But we had other officers called in to assist in the taking of statements.

Q Now, when you take the statements are the statements reduced to writing?

A They are.

Q And do the individuals have an opportunity to review their statements?

A They do.

Q And after the review of the statements what takes place?

A Okay, Initially when I take the statement—

MR. WOLFE: Judge, I would have to question the relevance of this type of line of questioning. I don't see were we're really going with the kind of questioning that's being asked by the officer here concerning how statements are adopted and taken.

THE COURT: Well, we'll wait and see, Mr. Wolfe.

BY MR. MENDEL:

Q How are the statements—after they have an opportunity to review, what takes place?

A Alright. When we're taking the statement, the individual, myself and a typist are seated together. We start with a narrative portion of the statement which the individual speaks and the typist types.

 Then there's a question and answer session where I ask the questions and the person responds. Those questions and answers are also typed. Each page is reviewed by the person giving the statement. They're instructed to ensure that what is typed there is what they said, that it's not the words of myself or the typist.

 The bottom of each statement is initialed by myself and the person giving the statement. Then the last page of the statement is signed by the individual giving the statement and signed as a witness by myself.

Q And prior to that you've taken oral statement from the individual, is that correct?

A Yes.

Q And now, I'd like to direct your attention then to the following day during the morning and ask you if you saw the Defendant, Gregory Whitman, on that date?

A I did.

Q And where did you first see him?

A I first saw Mr. Whitman at the Severton Police Headquarters in Severton, Pennsylvania.

Q And approximately what time was that?

A At approximately 11:15 A.M.

Q Who else was present at the time besides Mr. Whitman and yourself?

A Chief of Police for Severton Borough, Willis, Sergeant Gates from my department, and I believe Officer Joseph Moreland from the Severton Police Department.

Q Now, at that time did you have an opportunity to question Mr. Whitman?

A I did.

Q And prior to that had Mr. Whitman been advised of his constitutional rights?

A He had been.

Q And did you check with Mr. Whitman to verify that?

A I did. When I first entered the room I was introduced to Mr. Whitman. My first question to the police officers was has he been advised of his constitutional rights. They stated he was.

I then asked Mr. Whitman if he had been advised of his constitutional rights. He said he had been advised and he understood them.

Q Now, sir, is one of those rights the fact that any statements he may make will be used against him in a court of law?

A It is.

Q Now, specifically was Mr. Whitman being interviewed—well, strike that.

What incident was Mr. Whitman being interviewed about?

A Mr. Whitman was being interviewed about both incidents.

Q By both you mean what?

A The robbery at Gerber's Food Market in the afternoon hours of March 15 and the robbery/homicide at the Northeast Drug Store in the evening hours of March 15.

Q What was Mr. Whitman's initial statement concerning these incidents?

A He denied any involvement in either incident.

Q Shortly thereafter did you ask Mr. Whitman when he had last seen Eddie Monroe?

A I did. He stated that the last time he had seen Eddie Monroe—

MR. WOLFE: Your Honor, I would interpose at this time a note that the witness is reading off notes that he has in front of him. I would like the District Attorney to determine if the witness has an independent recollection of the statements given by Mr. Whitman or whether he's relying on the notes in order to testify.

[The interplay between recorded recollections and refreshed recollections is going to figure heavily in Zweiger's testimony. As the judge explains later to the jury, the use of notes to refresh one's recollection of events that one no longer remembers is acceptable so long as the witness can authenticate those notes and testify as to their accuracy when made. The notes are not being used as evidence; rather, they are being used as a means of bringing back to mind details that would otherwise be lost in the witness' testimony. The use of as notes as recorded recollections is a different matter. In that case, the notes are being used as evidence in place of testimony. Recorded recollections may be admitted where a witness testified that he no longer has any recollection of the subject of his testimony. In the case of Zweiger, he would not be able to convincingly argue that he could not remember events that occurred only a few months before, so the use of his notes must be restricted to the more limited purpose of refreshing his memory. Ch. 11, "Recorded Recollection"]

BY MR. MENDEL:

Q Well, Officer, do you have an independent recollection of the exact responses made by Mr. Whitman at the time?

A I do. The only thing I read from these notes were the names of the people I took the statements from. I'm glancing down to keep a chronological order, but I haven't read from it other than those names.

MR. WOLFE: So you have an independent—

THE WITNESS: If you want, I'll cover it up.

MR. WOLFE: So you have an independent recollection of these things?

THE WITNESS: Yes.

BY MR. MENDEL:

Q Now, Detective Zweiger, did you ask Mr. Whitman the last time he had seen Eddie Monroe?

A I did. He stated first that the last time he saw Eddie was between 5:00 and 5:30 P.M. on March 16—March 15 when he observed him standing at the corner of Thirteenth and Main Street talking with his brother.

Q And when you say his brother, who do you mean?

A Eddie's brother.

Q And did you obtain a name from Mr. Whitman concerning Eddie's brother?

A Yes. He said it was Brian Monroe.

Q Now, did Mr. Whitman indicate who he was with at that time?

A He stated at that time he was with George Munns.

Q And did he indicate—well, strike that.

He did indicate that he observed Mr. Monroe with Brian Monroe, is that correct?

A That's correct.

Q Did you question Mr. Whitman concerning his whereabouts that afternoon?

A I did.

Q And what did he indicate to you as to where he was?

A I'm going to have to ask to go back to my report for this one.

THE COURT: You certainly may review your notes.

BY MR. MENDEL:

A Mr. Whitman was asked what his activities were on Friday, March 15, '96. He replied around 13:30 to 14:00 hours or 1:30 P.M. to 2:00 P.M. that he was with Eddie Monroe, Josie Whitman and Frank Avard, A-v-a-r-d. They were in Eddie's car, a brown Cricket, and they were coming from 24G Hiller Court.

MR. WOLFE: I would have to object at this time because I think it's clear the witness does not remember the statement and is relying upon the note and the papers in front of him in order to give testimony.

And I don't think it satisfies on this particular point that it's been a past recollection recorded that would allow the statement itself to come in as opposed to his independent memory as to what the statements were.

THE COURT: We're going to direct that the officer may make reference to his notes to refresh his recollection about the events that he's testifying about.

MR. WOLFE: Well, the objection, Your Honor, is I don't think he's refreshing himself. I think he's using the notes solely to testify from. That's the objection by defense counsel.

MR. MENDEL: We'll take them step by step. If he says he can't recall, then we'll ask him if he would review his notes whether that would refresh his recollection. And we'll proceed that way.

THE COURT: Very well.

BY MR. MENDEL:

Q Now, Officer, concerning the initial question about Mr. Whitman's whereabouts in the afternoon, do you recall what he had stated at that time?

[A substantial part of Zweiger's testimony consists of relating Whitman's own statements during his interrogation after he turned himself in to police the night of the hold-ups. This information is admissible as statements of a party opponent and, in some cases, statements against interest. Since the defendant was advised of his constitutional rights and was answering questions upon the advice of counsel, the statements are also not a violation of his Fifth Amendment right against self-incrimination. In essence, Zweiger's testimony is going to be a substitute for the testimony of the defendant himself, although that testimony is limited to what the defendant said during his interrogation, much of which was admittedly false.]

A Yes.

Q And what did he indicate to you?

A He initially stated that he was with Eddie Monroe, that Eddie drove him from 24G Hiller Court to his mother's house in Severton.

Q Now, did Mr. Whitman indicate anyone was with him at that time?

A Frank Avard and Josie Whitman was with him, Josie Whitman being his brother.

Q And Josie is a nickname, is that correct?

A That's correct.

Q Now, 24G Hiller Court is the Defendant's address, is that correct?

A That's where he was residing at the time, yes.

Q And did Mr. Whitman indicate what happened—well, you say he took him to his mother's house. Is that what he said?

A Yes.

Q And do you recall where the Defendant's mother resides?

A At a subsequent requestioning, he gave her address as 20 Kennedy Lane, Severton.

Q And Mr. Whitman said he was dropped off there, is that correct?

A That's correct. The one time he stated that he was dropped off there. And Frank Avard went home from there. He went in the house and called George Munns.

Q He called George Munns?

A He called George Munns on the telephone.

Q And prior to Eddie Monroe leaving, did Mr. Whitman say anything as to what Eddie Monroe intended to do?

A I have to look.

Q Well, do you recall?

A No, I don't recall. I have to look at my notes.

Q If you looked at your notes would that refresh your recollection concerning the events Mr. Whitman related to you?

A Yes.

Q Please review those.

A Okay. On the one occasion he said that Eddie left alone saying that he was going to get his brother and do things.

Q Is the term do things a quote from Mr. Whitman?

A Yes.

THE COURT: I didn't hear you Mr. Mendel.

MR. MENDEL: Excuse me.

BY MR. MENDEL:

Q Is the phrase do things an exact quote from Mr. Whitman?

A It is.

Q And he was going to—Mr. Monroe was going to do things with his brother?

A That's what he said, yes.

Q Now, at what time did Mr. Whitman say he called George Munns to pick him up in Severton?

A I believe around 1:30 he said that he called George Munns on the telephone to come to his mother's residence and pick him up.

Q And did Mr. Whitman indicate what time Mr. Munns arrived to pick him up?

A At one point in the session he said it was exactly 2:00 P.M. that Hendy Munns arrived at his mother's residence.

Q And did he say where—did Mr. Whitman tell you where they went?

A He said that they returned to 24G Hiller Court and remained there. And then the second occasion he said that they returned to 24G Hiller Court and he did a load of wash while George Munns waited in the interior of the residence and then they went out and drove around.

Q How long did they stay at 24G Hiller Court according to Mr. Whitman?

A The first time he stated that he stayed at least 15:45 hours or 3:45 P.M., that George Munns was in his house and his next-door neighbor, John Siegel, he was inside his house.

   Then the second time—the second time he just said George—around 4:00 he took the key to 24G Hiller Court to 24H Hiller Court which is next door meaning the residence for 24G. He left it there with the neighbors and him and George went out.

Q From interviewing Mr. Whitman were you able to determine how many keys there were to the residence?

A From what I understood there was only one key to the residence.

Q And that was transported back and forth between the neighbor's home?

A Yes. If he would use the key to go out, he would leave it with a neighbor so that his girlfriend would be able to pick up the key and get inside the house when she returned home.

Q Did you question Mr. Whitman as to his acts after leaving the home with George Munns?

A Yes I did.

Q And what was his first response to that?

A His first response is that they were just riding around until approximately 17:30, or 5:30 P.M., that they had gone to his sister Judith's house on Wallace Street and that he returned to 24G Hiller Court.

Q Did he indicate during this time period whether or not he had seen Eddie Monroe and Brian Monroe?

A He did on the first interview. He stated that he observed Eddie and Brian standing at the corner or Thirteenth and Main Streets.

Q Now, did he indicate to you at what time he arrived home after driving around with George Munns?

A He did. On both occasions or both interviews he stated the time that he arrived home was around 5:30 P.M.

Q And the first occasion when you were going over this the first time, after he said he was home at 5:30 did he say he had left the home at all?

A No. He said from the time he arrived there at 17:30 or 5:30 P.M., he stayed there until the next morning which would have been March 16th until around 10:00 hours in the morning.

Q So Mr. Whitman indicated he stayed from 5:30 until 10:00 the next morning?

A That's what he stated.

Q Now, did you ask Mr. Whitman if he had spoken to Eddie Monroe since he was dropped off, since Mr. Whitman was dropped off at his mother's home in Severton?

A Yes.

Q And what did he respond or how did he respond?

A On the second interview he stated that after Eddie left his mother's house he only saw him again and that was at Thirteenth and Main Street when he was driving past. He acknowledged Eddie and Eddie responded by saying what's up.

Q Now, prior to that did you ask Mr. Whitman whether he had spoken to Eddie?

MR. WOLFE: Your Honor, I'm going to object to the constant reference by this witness to his notes here. I think it's clear that he doesn't have any independent recollection of the events that he's being asked to testify to. He's referring constantly to these notes, and I don't think that the prosecution has established the criteria that shows that these notes were conducted, at what period of time they were reduced to writing, and the memory of Detective Zweiger at the time he prepared the notes from which he's testifying.

THE COURT: Detective, when did you make those notes?

THE WITNESS: These notes were—the notes were made at the time I interviewed Mr. Whitman in the Borough of Severton Police Department. As he was writing—as he was speaking, I'd ask the questions and his responses. This report was typed, the final report was typed on March 27.

THE COURT: Are they notes that you made, they were yours?

THE WITNESS: They were my notes. They're available here.

THE COURT: And is the report that you're looking at accurate so far as you're concerned?

THE WITNESS: It is.

THE COURT: Alright. The Court's going to permit you to use that to refresh your recollection in response to the questions by the attorneys.

MR. WOLFE: We would ask our objection be noted for the record, sir.

THE COURT: Certainly, sir.

Now, your last question, Mr. Mendel, was what?

BY MR. MENDEL:

Q I believe the last question, Detective Zweiger, was the first tie you were speaking to Mr. Whitman did he say whether or not he had spoken to Eddie Monroe since Mr. Whitman was dropped off at his mother's home.

A No. He did not speak with Eddie after he was dropped off other than to acknowledge him at Thirteenth and Main Streets.

Q Now, did you ask Mr. Whitman where he was at a quarter to 4:00 or the time of the Severton Robbery?

A I did.

Q And what was his response to that question?

A That he was inside his residence at 24G Hiller Court with George Munns.

Q And did he indicate that there was anyone else who could verify that?

A He stated his next-door neighbor, John, could say that he was inside the house at that time.

Q Now, after receiving that information did you again ask Mr. Whitman to relate to you the events of that day?

A I did. I asked him to start over again with what occurred on that day.

Q And what did he say at this time concerning his whereabouts in the afternoon?

A He stated that between 13:30 and 14:00 hours or 1:30 and 2:00 P.M., that he was with Eddie, that Eddie had taken him to his mom's house at 20 Kennedy Lane in Severton.

Q Excuse me. And what did Mr. Whitman indicate that he did after arriving at the home in Severton?

A When they arrived at the house it was again Frank Avard and Josie Whitman, that Frank Avard went home, Josie went in and went to bed, and that he went in and called George Munns by telephone at George's residence to come down and pick him up.

Q And approximately what time did George Munns arrive there according to Mr. Whitman?

A Somewhere around 2:00 I believe.

Q And for how long and for what time period did Mr. Whitman indicate he was with George Munns in his home in Hiller Court?

A He stated that after George Munns picked him up in Severton they proceeded to 24G Hiller Court until around 16:00 or 4:00 P.M.

Q Were you able to verify whether or not George Munns had a telephone?

A I spoke with George Munns at the Borough of Severton Police Department, asked him if he had a phone. He said he did not. Further than that, I asked him if he had a beeper that somebody could call him to talk to him. He stated he did not. And I asked him if he know Gregory Whitman's phone number and he said that he didn't even know that Gregory had a phone. Any time he wanted to take to Gregory he'd go to the house to talk to him.

[It's difficult to imagine why Wolfe is not objecting to these statements on hearsay grounds. If they are being offered solely to impeach Mr. Whitman's statements, then they would be admissible, but at the very least it is surprising that Wolfe does not ask for a limiting instruction to the jury so it understands that Munns' statements are not to be considered evidence toward establishing Whitman's guilt.]

Q Now, after they left the home at 4:00 I believe you asked them Mr. Whitman where he went?

A I did.

Q And where did he indicate that he traveled?

A He just stated that he drove around with George Munns until between 17:00 and 17:30 or 5:00 and 5:30 P.M.

Q And again did he indicate what he did with the key at home?

A That he took the key to his next-door neighbor. The first time he said he left the key with Miss Liz. The second time he said he left the key with John at 24H Hiller Court.

Q And he indicated then he did what?

A That him and George Munns drove around for a while, that they went to his sister's—his sister's house. His sister is married to Eddie's brother.

Q And Eddie being Eddie Monroe?

A Eddie Monroe's brother, right. So it gets a little complicated at times. So he went to his sister, Rita Monroe's house on Wallace Street sometime after 5:00 P.M., and while he was there he informed her that he was on his way home.

Q And prior to that had he indicated if he saw anyone he know on the street?

A He stated that he saw Eddie and Brian Monroe standing on the corner of Thirteenth and Main Street.

Q And was anything said to these individuals at this time?

A Yes. He said Gregory said what's happening, what's up. Eddie just waved and said Greg.

Q And that was what Mr. Whitman told you?

A That's what Mr. Whitman said.

Q Now, after stopping at his sister's did Mr. Whitman tell you where he went?

A He stated that he went home and he arrived home between 17:00 and 17:30 hours.

Q Which is between what time?

A Between 5:00 and 5:30 P.M. that he arrived at 24G Hiller Court.

Q Did he indicate how he received the key?

A He got the key from John at 24H Hiller Court.

Q Then did he indicate what he did the rest of the evening?

A He did. He stated that he went inside 24G Hiller Court and that he watched TV. He stayed inside that residence until the next morning.

George Munns came over around 9:55 A.M., stayed a few minutes and then he went to the Severton Police Station.

Q Now, if I can just take you back one step. After Mr. Whitman indicated he got the key from John, did he mention seeing John or any involvement with John the rest of the interview or the rest of the night?

A Not at all. The only mention he made about John was that he got the key from John.

Q And that was before he walked in the home?

A Before he walked in the home. Both times, both interviews, he stated that he—once he arrived at 24G between 5:00and 5:30 he stayed inside there until the next morning.

Q Now, did Mr. Whitman indicate whether or not his girlfriend was home when he arrived home?

A No. She was out shopping.

Q And did he indicate at what time she did arrive home?

A Yes. He stated Robyn got back from the store between 17:30 and 18:00 or 5:30 and 6:00.

Q Did he indicate whether or not he had any conversation with Robyn when she arrived home between 5:30 and 6:00?

A He stated that she had informed him that there was a commotion going on –

MR. WOLFE: I'm going to object, Your Honor. He's starting to introduce statements or hearsay statements made by people other than the Defendant in this particular case.

MR. MENDEL: Your Honor, basically what we're introducing is a statement made by the Defendant, Mr. Whitman, indicating what he told the police officer. It certainly goes to his impressions and statement he made at the time and what was going through his mind.

THE COURT: Overruled.

[The reason why the hearsay statements of Whitman's girlfriend are of a different character than the previous statements of George Munns concerning his telephone is that Robyn's statements were made to the defendant and then related in his statement to police, whereas Munns' statements about his telephone were made directly to the testifying witness. Ironically, the statements of Robyn are hearsay within hearsay, which is why Mendel has to defend their admissibility by acknowledging that they are being admitted to show Whitman's state of mind, not as substantive evidence of his guilt. Again, it's surprising that Wolfe does not request a clarifying instruction to the jury, since it is unlikely the jurors could make such a subtle distinction on their own.]

BY MR. MENDEL:

Q Now, what did Mr. Whitman tell you that his girlfriend told him?

A Mr. Whitman said that when Robyn got home she told him that there had been a commotion doing on across the street at the SaveRite Store from where she was shopping.

Q And what time did he say she arrived home?

A Between 5:30 and 6:00 P.M.

Q And, Officer, what time was Samuel Wilson shot?

A 18:46 or 6:46 P.M.

Q A quarter to 7:00?

A A quarter of 7:00.

Q I believe you said the Defendant indicated he watched TV then, is that correct?

A Yes, he did.

Q Did he indicate to you what he watched and at what hours?

A Excuse me. I asked him what television programs he watched that evening. I'm going to have to read this now to get it exact.

    Okay. He was asked what television programs that he watched. He responded by saying Fresh Prince of Bel Air and Friends. He stated Fresh Prince comes on at 18:30 or 6:30.

Q And what hour is Friends on?

A They come on at 7:00, and he watched both shows on Channel 28 from 6:30 to 7:30 P.M.

Q Did he indicate what he had watched before that?

A He stated Fresh Prince is on before Friends.

Q Were you able to verify whether or not these shows were indeed on?

A I have reviewed the televisions listings for March 15, 1996, at the times, both in the TV Guide booklet and copies of the Evening News and Patriot News for March 15, and the shows are not listed at those times or on those stations that he said they were on.

Q Now, what did Defendant indicate he watched after Friends was over?

A After Friends they watched X-files on Channel 17, that there was a movie on Channel 22 which was on for 2 hours but he went to bed at 9:00 P.M. He stayed in bed until 6:00 A.M. the next morning and he got up and ironed clothes for the kids and Robyn and fixed breakfast.

Q If I could take you back a little bit. Were you able to determine what was on at 8:00 on Channel 22?

A Picket Fences.

Q And following that—was that a 2-hour special that evening?

A For Picket Fences?

Q Yes.

A I'm not sure. I don't believe it was. I believe it was the regular 1 hour.

Q So there was no movie on channel 22 that evening?

A No.

Q And you indicated that the Defendant then said he went to bed at 9:00?

A That's correct.

Q Now, is there any indication that the Defendant—did the Defendant say he read the newspaper that day?

THE COURT: You talk so fast Mr. Mendel, I didn't hear your question. I'm sorry.

Q Did the Defendant indicate whether he read a newspaper the following day?

A I believe that he did, that that was when he—that he read about the robbery/shooting in the paper, yes.

Q Now, what did Mr. Whitman tell you he did shortly before he turned himself in to the Severton Police?

A He stated that George Munns had come over to the house in the morning and that after Mr. Munns had left the house that he went to the Severton Police and turned himself in.

Q During the interview did you inform Mr. Whitman that he had been identified by an individual who know him as driving the car in Severton?

A I did. I told him that he had been observed by a witness who personally knew him at the time the robbery at Gerber's occurred, and at that time he said, oh, yes, I did wave to a guy as I drove across the parking lot.

Q Did he also indicate that, after being advised Frank Avard had said he was driving, did he make any statement?

A I told him that we had spoke to Frank Avard and that Frank advised us there were three people in the vehicle which was Frank, Gregory and Josie; and according to Frank Avard, Gregory was driving the car.
    Gregory replied that Frank's mistaken, I can even drive a stick shift.

Q And since that time you were present when Mr. Whitman indicated that indeed he was driving the car?

A Yes.

Q And that was at 3:45 on March 15th?

A That's correct.

Q Now, after speaking to Mr. Munns did you advise Mr. Whitman about the results of your conversation?

A I did. I told Mr. Whitman that I had spoke with George Munns about calling him on the phone, and Mr. Whitman replied okay, I lied about talking to George on the phone but I was not with Eddie at Northeast Drug.

Q And did he indicate at that time whether or not he was in Severton?

A No.

Q Did he indicate any involvement in the Severton incident?

A No.

Q And after that statement did you later obtain an arrest warrant for Mr. Whitman?

A I did.

Q Now, you are aware, Detective Zweiger, of the location of 24G Hiller Court, is that correct?

A Yes, sir, I am.

Q Of course, you're aware of the location of Northeast Drug Store?

A Yes.

Q Did you have occasion as part of your investigation to travel the distance between the two points on numerous occasions?

A I did. I made four different trips from 24G Hiller Court to the Northeast/SaveRite Market complex at Twenty-ninth and Emerald Street by vehicle.

Q And what was the longest amount of time that it took to travel between the two?

A Okay. The longest amount of time on the one route which would include the most stop signs, signal lights and turns, it took 7 minutes and 52 seconds.

Q And, sir, what speed were you traveling?

A On the first—on the first four runs I did not exceed a speed of 30 miles an hour. The maximum speed I traveled at any time was 30 miles an hour.

Q Now, those first four runs you made, what were the times and the distances between?

A Okay. On the first run I started at 12:09 and 5 seconds P.M. The mileage was 42,753.8 miles. Do you want the exact route I was traveling?

Q If you would, please.

A Okay. On the first tin the exact route was I stopped—started at the parking area of 24G Hill Manor, backed in that parking space, proceeded east on Overly Street to Nineteenth Street, turned left on Nineteenth Street and traveled north to Barnaby Street.

I caught the red light at Nineteenth and Barnaby Street. After the light changed, I turned right only Barnaby and traveled out Barnaby Street to Twenty-ninth Street. I turned left on Twenty-ninth Street and traveled north to Emerald Street, turning left and traveling west on Emerald Street and drove into the parking lot of SaveRite Market.

Q And that was the area indicated by some eye witnesses of where Mr. Monroe's vehicle was parked, is that correct?

A That is correct.

Q And what was the mileage on that trip?

A The mileage was 2.2 miles and it took 5 minutes and 40 seconds to travel that distance.

Q And that was not exceeding?

A That was not exceeding 30 miles an hour.

Q The second trip you took slightly different route, is that correct?

A I did.

Q But substantially the same?

A Substantially the same. Instead of going across Overly Street to Nineteenth, I turned left on Seventeenth Street and traveled up Seventeenth Street to Barnaby.

At Seventeenth and Willow there's a four-way stop sign which I stopped for. I then went to Seventeenth and Barnaby and turned right. This time the signal light at Seventeenth and Barnaby was green for my turn, so I continued to turn.

The rest of the trip was the same, out Barnaby to Twenty-ninth, out Twenty-ninth to Emerald. That was 2.3 miles and it took 7 minutes and 52 seconds.

Q That time?

A I'm sorry, 6 minutes and 52 seconds.

Q Now, the third trip you took how did the route differ there?

A The route would have been the same as coming from Hiller Court, but I ran it backward from the SaveRite Store to Hiller Court. And this route would have been, the initial part of it was the direction and route that the car traveled when it left the SaveRite Market Store the night of the incident.

Q And that would be what, do you know?

A It was west on Emerald to Hale Street and south on Hale Street. Then I continued to Berry and traveled from Berry to Parson, a small portion of Parson to Nineteenth, down Nineteenth Street to Overly, up Overly Street right to 24G Hiller Court.

Q And that was, time-wise, a long trip?

A This was the time of the longest trip. I think the first time I may have said the longest trip was 7 minutes and 52 seconds. That time was 6 minutes and 52 seconds. This is the longest trip because it involves the most turns, stop signs, and signal lights. It took 7 minutes and 35 seconds and covered a distance of 1.9 miles.

Q So this was the shortest distance in mileage but the longest in time?

A Yes.

Q Your fourth trip, what was the route you took on that?

A The fourth trip I left 24G Hiller Court, the parking lot right there at 24G. Again I backed from the space, traveled across Overly Street to Nineteenth, north on Nineteenth to Willow, down Willow to Barnaby, out Barnaby Street to Twenty-ninth and up Twenty-ninth to Emerald Street and onto the lot.

Q And what was the distance of that trip?

A 2.1 miles

Q And the time?

A Three minutes and 33 seconds because I didn't—I traveled—I did not limit it to 30 miles an hour.

Q And approximately how fast did you go?

A The maximum speed I reached was on Barnaby Street. I accelerated to 50 miles an hour.

Q And that trip took three and a half minutes, approximately?

A Three minutes and 33 seconds exactly.

THE COURT: Mr. Mendel, do you have much more on direct examination?

MR. MENDEL: No, Your Honor. As a matter of fact, I was going to offer the witness now for cross.

THE COURT: Alright. We'll take a recess at this point. The jury may now be excused. We'll be taking a 15 minutes recess until 11:15.

(Whereupon, at 11:02 A.M., the jury was excused.)

(Whereupon, at 11:02 A.M., court was held in recess)

AFTER RECESS

(Whereupon, at 11:20 A.M., the following in-chambers discussion was had:)

QUESTION OF THE JURY

[What follows is an illustration of how jurors can interact with the court during the course of a trial, and how requests for clarification are handled between the court and the attorneys.]

THE COURT: The question is two questions. Please explain why lawyers can talk directly from notes but a person on the stand is being questioned because he is talking from his notes.

     No. 2, if we need clarification on any point how do we get it?

     On the second question I'll tell them that they should reserve their questions until the case is over and they're deliberating, and then they should do this and we will deal with the questions. If they have any other physical problems, they should tell us or any other kind of a problem.

Now, on the other thing, what do you think about that, Mr. Wolfe?

MR. WOLFE: The only thing that has me a little concerned, Judge, it appears the jury to some extent is beginning to deliberate the case a little bit.

THE COURT: I'm sorry?

MR. WOLFE: Beginning to discuss the case among themselves while they're being in recess here. I think the question illustrates that there's some deliberation going on during the course of the trial.

THE COURT: I think they don't understand the question about why the man can, but I'll tell them. I'll tell them not to deliberate about the case.

MR. WOLFE: Do you intend to answer the question I guess?

THE COURT: Well, these two questions, yes, there's nothing the matter with that. It seems harmless to me. It seems you were asking questions about the officer, you know, whether from recollection or from his notes. And then you guys, like you always do, are sitting there and you're reading from your pads and going over things.

I don't perceive it's any big deal at all, but if you want to, if you want to say anything to me now about that?

MR. MENDEL: I can't think of any kind of response.

THE COURT: Tell me what you think the appropriate law is, a witness who is—

MR. WOLFE: Refreshing?

THE COURT: Yes. Give me the dichotomy between refreshing your recollection and putting the writing in the record or whatever.

MR. WOLFE: If he's refreshing his memory, the purpose is for him to examine it and to—and for the witness to indicate that based on his examination he is able to testify from memory and that as the notes say—as the exception says, directly based on his own recollection of the events.

A past recollection recorded, I think the requirements are stronger, that the witness would indicate that he has no present or individual memory as to the events that occurred and that these notes that he's testifying to or this writing is the actual belief that he had at the time that he subscribed those notes at that time.

THE COURT: And he doesn't recall if those events are true or not. Do you have anything to add, Mr. Mendel?

MR. MENDEL: Well, I think there's a little difference here, the type of evidence. We're not talking about a statement about general things, things he's observed. We're talking about, specifically about statements made by the Defendant to try to recall what he said as opposed to testifying as to what he took down as he is saying it, I think there's a very big difference.

[This portion of the colloquy between judge and lawyers relates back to the admissibility of Eddie Monroe's statement exculpating Whitman in the second hold-up. Monroe's attorney states on the record that he will advise his client, if called in this trial, to take the Fifth Amendment and refuse to testify, which Wolfe argues makes him unavailable, thereby opening the door to the introduction of his statement as evidence.]

THE COURT: I'll talk to them about that. What do you want to do here with Mr. Monroe's lawyer? How do we want to proceed with that?

MR. WOLFE: Just to have something on the record, I guess, to indicate that Mr. Monroe has been subpoenaed as a defense witness in this case under the belief that he would possibly, if he would agree to testify, exculpate Mr. Whitman from any involvement in the Northeast Drug Store incident.

Mr. Leroy, who is present in chambers, is the court-appointed attorney for Mr. Monroe. And I have, as I'm bound to do, informed him that it is our intent to call his client as a witness.

Mr. Leroy has represented to me that—

THE COURT: Well, suppose Mr. Leroy tells us what he—

MR. LEROY: For the record, I'm Simon T. Leroy. I'm the attorney of record for Eddie Monroe who is currently under arrest for what I believe to be the same charges here at trial.

He has had his preliminary hearing and is facing formal arraignment for criminal charges arising out of the death of Samuel Wilson and the robbery of Gerber's Market in Severton.

Mr. Wolfe has indicated to me that he obtained a writ of habeas corpus ad testificandum for Mr. Monroe, and based on that representation I have spoken with Mr. Monroe on two occasions, the last one being this morning. I have made him aware of the fact that he could be brought to this courtroom to testify as a defense witness.

Without making any representation whatsoever as to what his testimony would or would not be, I can say that Mr. Monroe, if called to this courtroom by either side, would take the Fifth Amendment to each and every subsequent question asked of him concerning the events here at trial.

THE COURT: Very well.

MR. WOLFE: That establishes his unavailability.

THE COURT: Anything further, gentlemen?

MR. MENDEL: Not from the Commonwealth.

MR. WOLFE: Not from the Defendant.

THE COURT: Very well. Thank you very much, Mr. Leroy.

(Whereupon, at 11:29 A.M., the in-camera discussion was concluded.)

(Whereupon, at 11:33 A.M., the following proceedings were had in Courtroom no. 4:)

THE COURT: Ladies and gentlemen, you directed an inquiry to the Court which we have made a part of the record. And the note was opened in the presence of counsel and we've read the questions and discussed them.

I'm going to answer your second question first. The second question is if we need clarification on any point how do we get it. And by writing a note to the Court, as you did in this instance, is the appropriate way.

Now, if you have—I don't mean to say if somebody does not feel good and you think you're going to be ill, don't write me a note, tell me. If you have any question about the procedure, though, this is the way that it should be done so that we can have everybody present when we go over it.

I would suggest to you, and I think that the question that you asked is a reasonable one and I will answer that. If you have any question on the law, however, or anything about the trial or any legal question that comes up, those should wait until we have instructed you on the law and you've begun your deliberations.

If during the course of your deliberations you are not sure about a point of law, then you can ask us about that and we'll consider, you know, how to deal with it. I don't want to say we'll do this or do that, it depends upon the question.

As I read the writer's pencilship, please explain why lawyers can talk, I think, directly from notes but the person on the stand is being questioned because he is talking from his notes.

Well, first of all, the lawyers of course have very carefully prepared for the case and they've written down beforehand the questions that they ask or things that they want to key them into questions and then as a witness is testifying question occur to them and they write them down. And it's perfectly all right for them to look and read those questions.

Some lawyers as they begin their practice write down everything and then after 20 years they can keep it all in their mind as the trial goes along. But anyway, it's perfectly all right for them to read, to prepare all the questions they want to ask and to read those questions.

The question about the witness is basically this. The law is interested in having the evidence come in at the highest possible quality. Now, you could have a witness who investigated something that happened some time ago and made a full report about that and that witness no longer remembers those events. In that case, the piece of paper, his report, if he says in 1980 when I made that report it was accurate, then the report is the piece of evidence because the witness no longer recalls those events with clarity.

But in this situation and in this particular situation, the officer and the other witnesses are testifying about events that occurred no further back than March 15, 1996. And so it's their memory, their recollection of what happened, that we want to hear.

But reasonably when you get into very detailed questions, it's beyond the scope of what a normally busy person can remember to recall with complete clarity exactly what happened. That is why the law permits a witness, if he has notes made at that time, as he testifies to read those notes, to go over them to refresh his recollection and then the testimony he gives you is his recollection refreshed.

Very well. Detective Zweiger.

(Whereupon, Detective Zweiger resumed the witness stand.)

CROSS EXAMINATION

BY MR. WOLFE:

Q Detective Zweiger, you went into a great deal of detail when you were questioned by Mr. Mendel about how you took statements from witnesses that were present at Northeast Drug Store on the evening of March the 15th, isn't that correct?

A The written statements?

Q Yes. You explained or Mr. Mendel asked you how you met with the witness, you have a typist there and you ask them questions and the typist takes everything down and they take the answers down and the witness or the person giving the statement has the opportunity to review that statement to make sure that it's accurate and signs it. Isn't that what you indicated you did with these witnesses?

A Yes, sir.

Q And you said that you took statements I think from a number of witnesses including a Scott Lawrence and a Harold LaVey, correct?

A That's correct.

Q Later on in the course of your investigation you've also taken notes—or a written statement from George Munns, correct?

A Yes.

Q And I believe you took statements from individual by the name of Holly Peterson?

A That's correct.

Q Valerie Helpern?

A Correct.

Q And they all had the opportunity to review the statements and sign them?

A Yes, they did.

Q And that's the standard procedure, what you do in most cases, isn't that correct?

A When we're reducing statements to writing, yes.

Q The statement that you indicated that you discussed, concerning the statements that were made by Mr. Whitman, that wasn't done in this case, was it?

A No. Mr. Whitman did not give a written statement. He gave a verbal statement.

Q So there wasn't any opportunity to have a typist present to take down the exact answers of Mr. Whitman and your questions?

MR. MENDEL: I'm going to have to object. May we come to side bar real briefly?

THE COURT: Alright.

(Whereupon, the following discussion was had at side bar:)

MR. MENDEL: Your Honor, my objection is basically he's getting into the point which I couldn't touch because it brings reference to the Defendant's invocation of his Fifth Amendment right. He asked for an attorney and that's why a written statement wasn't taken.

[Like his prior criminal record, the fact that the defendant refused to give a written statement based on his Fifth Amendment right against self-incrimination is something the jury is not permitted to know, because it raises an improper inference that the defendant has something to hide. Mendel, ironically, is raising this issue in order to prevent Wolfe from examining Zweiger as to the reasons why Whitman did not give a written statement. The court resolves the issue by suggesting that Wolfe ask Zweiger how he made the notes of Whitman's oral statements.]

Now he's cross examining concerning the fact that he didn't—I think where it's leading, that he didn't make a written statement. I can't get into that and I'm just wondering if he proceeds in this manner whether or not I would be permitted to then cross examine him on it. I don't think as a matter of law I can cross examine him on his invocation of his Fifth Amendment right.

THE COURT: Did he or did he not invoke?

MR. MENDEL: His statement was this time I'll tell you the truth but first let me talk to an attorney. And that ended his questioning right there. He talked to his attorney, and on the advice of counsel he didn't give a written statement.

MR. WOLFE: That has nothing to do—Your Honor, I'm sorry. Are you finished?

MR. MENDEL: Yes.

MR. WOLFE: That has nothing to do with the fact that the statements that the officer is testifying to now were not reduced to writing. I'm trying to get to the accuracy of his recollection of the event that—and statements were made by the Defendant.

Obviously his recollection as to what those statements were. I think it's certainly proper for limit the focus of the questioning to statements that the officer testified to let the jury know that those statements weren't reduced to writing.

MR. MENDEL: And I think I have the obligation on behalf of the Commonwealth to ask the officer to explain why they weren't reduced to writing, and the only way I can testify to that is to refer to the Defendant's invocation of his Fifth Amendment rights.

THE COURT: And you don't want him to do that?

MR. WOLFE: Certainly not. At some stage he indicated that he decided to make no further statements.

THE COURT: I think that there's merit to what both of you say. I think the District Attorney does have a point, but I think as well as that you're entitled to have the jury understand how the notes that he's made were taken, but don't beat it and beat it and beat it. He read from those statements. Ask him how they were made.

MR. WOLFE: Okay.

(Whereupon, the discussion at side bar was concluded.)

Q Again, Officer, just concerning the statements that you said that Mr. Whitman gave you, those statements were not reduced to writing, correct? The statement, to make sure you understand my question, the statement that you testified to on direct examination but with the questions from Mr. Mendel were oral statements of Mr. Whitman, correct?

A That's correct. As he was speaking I was writing. There was not a typist present at that point of the interview, that's correct.

Q And there wasn't any opportunity for Mr. Whitman to review your notes or to sign them concerning the accuracy, was there?

A No.

Q Now, you said you went to the Pennsylvania—I'm sorry. The Severton Police Station where Mr. Whitman was at, isn't that correct?

A That is correct.

Q And that present during that questioning—and you were there at what time?

A I arrived at approximately 11:00 in the morning, 11:00 A.M., on March 16.

Q And you were present then for all questioning that took place of Mr. Whitman?

A I don't know how much questioning preceded my arrival. Chief Willis, of course, was investigating the incident in Severton, and I don't know what questioning transpired before I arrived.

Q But afterward?

A After I arrived I would say I was there for all of the questioning with the exception of leaving the room on a brief occasion like when Frank Avard was brought in or George Munns was brought in. And at those time I would leave for 2 or 3 minutes maximum, go out and talk to each one of those individuals which is how I was able to confront Mr. Whitman with the discrepancies of him driving the vehicle, No. 1, which he said he couldn't do and that Frank Avard said he did, in fact, do and the fact that he couldn't have called George Munns because George doesn't have a—

Q So the answer to the question is that you were present then for the essential part of the questioning of Mr. Whitman from 11:00 A.M.?

A Yes.

Q Were you present during questioning offered by Chief Willis?

A I'm sorry?

Q Were you present when Chief Willis questioned Mr. Whitman concerning his involvement?

A Yes.

Q Are you aware of the existence of a written statement that was taken by Mr. Whitman from Chief Willis?

A No, I'm not. That may have occurred after I left.

Q Now, this is a question and answer from Chief Willis to Gregory Whitman. Do you recall, with your notes, the question that was asked to Mr. Whitman by Chief Willis?
  "About what time were you dropped off at home?"

Answer.   "About 4:00."

Question.   "What did you do next?"

               "I stayed home until George came home and I left the key next-door."

THE COURT: Let's find out, Mr. Wolfe, whether the officer was there and remembers that question. If he wasn't there—

MR. WOLFE: I'm asking him if that's the question.

BY MR. WOLFE:

Q Do you recall these questions being asked to Mr. Whitman?

A When I was there most of the questioning of Mr. Whitman was conducted by me okay. Chief Willis was there and he would make, you know, maybe a question or two relative to the Gerber's incident. These questions that you're reading from a statement, I was not present.

Q You weren't present when Mr. Whitman said that?

MR. MENDEL: Your Honor, I object. He's already indicate he wasn't there.

THE COURT: The reason my concern is that if this officer wasn't there, then he doesn't know anything about that. And I don't think it's proper for you to read in responses that he doesn't know about.

[Wolfe is taking a big chance here. By reading questions into the record directly from Whitman's statement to Chief Willis, he is opening the door for Mendel to have read into the record any other portion of that statement.]

BY MR. WOLFE:

Q You have no recollection of certain questions that were asked to Mr. Whitman by Chief Willis about what time he left the house and what he did after he left the house with Mr. Munns?

A After I arrived in Severton, the Severton Police Station, the majority of the questioning of Mr. Whitman was conducted by me. As I said Chief Willis may have inserted a question or two. I don't recall those exact questions, no. The notes that I made and the report that I made were my questions and Mr. Whitman's responses to me of my questions.

Q Well, do your notes indicate in terms of asking what—did you ever ask Mr. Whitman what he did or where he went with George Munns?

A Yes. He said that he went to his sister's house, Judith Monroe, on Wallace Street some time shortly after 5:00 and that he informed her that he was going home, on his way home, and then that was it.

Q Mr. Whitman never told you, according to your recollection, that he drove around with George until around 7:00 at night?

A No.

Q None of that indicates that on your report?

A He said on both times that he was home between 5:00 and 5:30.

Q And that's based on your notes and your recollection of the statements?

A That's what Mr. Whitman told me.

Q You indicated that you were the—well, you prepared the notes. What happened to the notes after that time?

A They're right there in that file.

Q But who transcribed the report and what you're testifying to now?

A I dictated it to our secretary, Ann Dreyer.

Q And that was done when?

A March 27.

Q And after that time—strike that question.

You indicated that you were responsible from the time of the shooting to conducting the investigation at Northeast, correct?

A That's correct.

Q And it's based on your investigation in the affidavit of probable cause that the shooting took place at 6:46 P.M., correct?

A That's correct.

Q And you've given indication here to the distances and the relative times that it would take depending on a route to travel from Mr. Whitman's house to Northeast Drug, correct?

A That's correct.

Q And they carried I think from three and a half—three minutes and 33 seconds going 55 miles an hour up to around—

A I don't believe I said 55 miles an hour. Fifty on Barnaby Street.

Q Fifty?

A Yes.

Q And the maximum period taking almost seven, 6.52?

A No. The maximum time was 7 minutes and 35 seconds and that was the shortest route in mileage, but it consisted of the most stop signs, signal lights, and turns.

Q In the course of your statements from Mr. Whitman, did he indicate to you that in any course of the statements that he had lied about calling George Munns from his mother's house?

A He did.

Q And he indicate that the reason that he lied was because he didn't want to become involved, he didn't want to become implicated in the Gerber's situation?

A No. He just said okay, I lied about talking to George on the phone, but I wasn't with Eddie at Northeast Drug.

Q But he then indicated initially during the course of your questioning, which took place I guess over several hours, that he initially denied being at Gerber's, is that correct?

A He has denied being involved in Gerber's as far as I know up until—

Q Sergeant Zweiger, the question I asked you was when you were asking him on that afternoon of March the 16th, he initially denied at that time having even been present with Eddie Monroe at Gerber's, correct, initially?

A That's correct.

Q And then later on during the course of that investigation he at least admitted that he was present in the parking lot at Gerber's, correct?

A All that he said to that was that he drove around the parking lot of Gerber's and he waved to a gentleman he knew as Billy.

Q You indicated that during the—you recited or detailed the statements that were made by Mr. Whitman to you, and in response to a question by Mr. Mendel about reading a newspaper you indicated that Mr. Whitman indicated to you that he had read a newspaper, is that correct?

A There was—in the case there was a mention of reading a newspaper article concerning this incident, okay, and I believe that Mr. Whitman indicated that he had obtained a newspaper and read about it or something like that.

Q Is that listed in your report that you indicate?

A Do you want me to look?

Q Yes.

A No.

Q So that that much of your report that you've made reference to in testifying concerning the statements of Mr. Whitman is incomplete, there's no mention in your report that Mr. Whitman indicated to you that he had read a newspaper, is there?

A No, there's not in my report, no.

Q And you were taking notes of the statements of Mr. Whitman as he was being questioned by the police and as you were questioning him?

A Yes.

Q And that issue of the newspaper evidently according to you came up somewhere during the questioning?

A I said that there was something said about a newspaper through the investigation and I thought possibly it was said by Mr. Whitman. I'm not positive who said anything about the newspaper. It could have been George Munns, when I interviewed George Munns.

Q But you indicated, if my memory is correct, that Mr. Mendel asked you the question on direct examination did Mr. Whitman say to you that he had read a newspaper and your response to that question was yes. Now you recall saying that on direct examination?

A I don't recall—I recall Mr. Mendel saying something about a newspaper, but I don't know what the question was, no. If you could read it back.

THE COURT: Well, we're not going to take the time now to sort that question back.

BY MR. WOLFE:

Q So your testimony is you're not sure if Mr. Whitman made a statement concerning reading a newspaper concerning the situation or the activity at Northeast Drug?

A No, I'm not.

Q And if he had made that statement, assuming for a second that he told you that I read about Northeast Drug in the newspaper, you didn't include that in your statement?

A I'd have to say that he didn't say anything about the newspaper because it's not in my report. He told me he heard about the incident when his girlfriend came home at 5:30, shortly after 5:30 and told him that there was a commotion going on across the street at SaveRite Store from where she was shopping.

Q But you don't have anything in your report about any statements made by Mr. Whitman concerning the reading of the newspaper?

A No.

MR. WOLFE: Thank you. I have no further questions.

REDIRECT EXAMINATION

BY MR. MENDEL:

Q Detective Zweiger, I'd like to refer you to Page 10 of your report, particularly the third paragraph, and ask you to review that and could you indicate whether or not that would refresh your recollection as to the existence of a newspaper.

A Yes.

Q And, Detective Zweiger –

MR. WOLFE: I don't have a copy of Page 10 of the report.

BY MR. MENDEL:

Q Sir, does that refresh your recollection concerning the testimony about a newspaper?

A Yes, it does.

Q And what was the information you learned about a newspaper?

A This is an interview with George Munns on March 22, '96. And the last sentence of this part of my report, Mr. Munns is relaying to me that Mr. Whitman told him that Eddie shot somebody and that the information was in the newspaper and that the police had been around his mother's house looking for him.

Q Now, sir, Mr. Wolfe asked you if you had taken statements from some individuals, and he named a number of them. I believe Harold LaVey?

A Correct.

Q Scott Lawrence?

A Correct.

Q Valerie Helpern?

A Yes.

Q Holly Peterson?

A Correct.

Q Your statement from Mr. Whitman, did he mention any of those individuals by name?

A Only—no, none of those individuals, no.

MR. MENDEL: Thank you. I have no further questions.

RECROSS EXAMINATION

BY MR. WOLFE:

Q So your testimony concerning the issue of the newspaper is that Mr. Whitman then made no statements to you during the course of your—during the course of the afternoon of March of 16th about reading—making statements to you now about reading about the incident in the newspaper?

A Would you repeat that one more time?

Q When you discussed the incident at Northeast Drug with Mr. Whitman on the afternoon of March the 16th, during that period of time it's your testimony now that Mr. Whitman did not make any statements to you that he read about the incident at Northeast Drug in the newspaper?

A That is correct.

MR. WOLFE: Thank you. Nothing further.

MR. MENDEL: Your Honor, at this time we'd move for the admission of Commonwealth Exhibits Nos. 1 and 2.

MR. WOLFE: We have no objection.

THE COURT: Very well. Let them be admitted.

MR. MENDEL: With that, Your Honor, the Commonwealth would rest.

THE COURT: Very well.

MR. WOLFE: We would like to approach side bar, Your Honor.

(Whereupon, the following discussion was had at side bar:)

[Now that the prosecution has rested its case, the defendant makes a motion for the judge to enter a directed verdict (a "demurrer") based on the failure of the prosecution to meet its burden of proving the charges. Wolfe's focus is on the absence of any evidence which shows any involvement by Whitman in the robbery of Northeast Drug Store or the murder of Sam Wilson. The court denies this motion. Judges are notoriously reluctant to take a case away from a jury where there is any possibility that it could interpret the evidence to find a verdict of guilty.]

MR. WOLFE: The defense, Your Honor, would demur to the prosecution's case at this particular time. We feel that in viewing the case in the light most favorable to the Commonwealth, that the jury, based on the evidence presented by the prosecution, cannot prove beyond a reasonable doubt that Gregory Whitman was present as an accomplice and participated in the robbery at Northeast Drug Store.

The Commonwealth has established, if you view their evidence most favorable, his presence at the scene through three separate witnesses, not participating in or aiding in any extent with the robbery at Northeast Drug. One witness places him at the scene. The second witness indicates that there is a flight, if believed, from the scene after the shooting.

We believe that they have that plus the earlier involvement in the prior robbery which goes to the issue of identity which they have already established through their other witness, and we would ask the court to dismiss the charges against Mr. Whitman.

MR. MENDEL: In response, Your Honor, we would say that viewing the light most favorable to the Commonwealth the following is shown: Earlier in the day, some 3 hours before, the robbery took place in the Borough of Severton close by. At the time the Defendant was the getaway driver, the car was parked to the rear of the store. The individual went in. Eddie Monroe came out, made his getaway in the car driven by the Defendant.

Now some 3 hours later Eddie Monroe's car is again off to the side of the food store in the Mallory County area—well, prior to that we have the statement by Gregory Whitman, come over to my house. And Eddie says not now, I'm busy.

But come over to my house. Sometime later the car is parked to the side of the SaveRite Market. Inside the SaveRite Market Gregory Whitman is identified by Penny Green as being there and looking around the store and acting suspicious. He's with another individual who is wearing the cap identified later as the robber, as a cap on.

And after he's apprehended Mr. Whitman is standing in position where he's observing what's taking place.

Our theory is this, and I think it's a reasonable inference to draw, that there was no flight along with Eddie Monroe because the security guard came right out and he's in a position to watch. There's no flight for that reason.

After the shooting takes place Eddie Monroe takes off, the shooter, and there's evidence of Gregory Whitman leaving the scene. We think there's more than sufficient evidence to show robbery and conspiracy to commit robbery and felony II murder.

THE COURT: I deny your motion, Mr. Wolfe.

(Whereupon, a discussion was held off the record.)

(Whereupon, the discussion at side bar was concluded.)

MR. WOLFE: Your Honor, the defense is ready to begin its case at this time and would call Valerie Helpern to the stand.

VALERIE HELPERN, called as a witness, being duly sworn, testified as follows:

DIRECT EXAMINATION

BY MR. WOLFE:

[Wolfe's examination of the defense witnesses Helpern, Siegel, Peterson, and LaVey, are directed at establishing the defendant's alibi defense, which the defendant has the burden of proving by a preponderance of the evidence. Most of this testimony is a moment-by-moment account of the activities of Whitman from shortly before 6:00 to shortly after 7:00 P.M. on the evening of March 15. This is very similar to the kind of testimony which was elicited from George Munns during the prosecutor's case-in-chief.]

Q   Ma'am, would you please state and spell your name for the record.

A   Valerie Helpern, V-a-l-e-r-i-e. H-e-l-p-e-r-n.

Q   And where do you live, ma'am?

A   11 South Seventeenth Street.

Q   I would like to refer your attention back to the afternoon or early evening of March the 15th, 1996, and ask if you recall that evening?

A   Me and Holly Peterson, we just left the bar at Thirteenth and Wallace.

Q   Could I back up a second. You and who, who was with you?

A   Holly Peterson.

Q   Where were you at the time?

A   Down at Thirteenth and Main, down at Flint's.

Q   And what time was this?

A   It was around about 5:30.

Q   Now, what happened after you left the bar?

A   Me and Holly, we was walking up Main Street and we stopped— we was coming across the light at KFC, and that's when Gregory and George was in the car and Holly walked over.

Q   Let me stop you for a second here. Now, who saw you at that time?

A   George and Gregory.

Q   And about what time would this have been?

A   It had to be around a quarter to 6:00 when we first walked up to KFC.

Q   Now, Mr. Whitman, was he present at that time?

A   Yes. He was sitting in the front seat of the car.

Q   And who was in the car with him?

A   Just George.

Q   And what transpired at that time?

A   Well, George Munns was waiting on somebody to come out of KFC, a female that he took there.

Q   Then what happened after that.

A   We was sitting outside. Well, me and Holly got in the car and we was just sitting there talking for a while, and then when we left there—

Q   Well, let me just stop you at that point. You said you were talking for a while. How long would you estimate that you are talking with Mr. Munns and Mr. Whitman?

A   About 10, 15 minutes before we, you know, rode around.

Q So could you estimate for us and the jury as to what time you left the parking lot at KFC?

A It would be about 6:00, 6:05.

Q At that particular point where did you go then?

A We rode around—well, we was going to get some reefer, right, and we rode around.

Q And let me stop you. Whose suggestion was it to get some reefers?

A Me and Holly was looking for a reefer.

Q And who indicated that they would be able to get some?

A George.

Q Was Mr. Whitman present at this time?

A Yes, he was.

Q Now, after you left the KFC lot, where did you go at that time?

A To Gregory's sister's house.

Q Which was located where?

A It was—I think it's Pine Street, Thirteenth and Pine, something like that.

Q And what did you do when you went to Gregory's sister's house?

A Me, George and Holly sat in the car, and that's when Greg went in.

Q And how long did Gregory remain in the house?

A Maybe—the longest was 5 minutes.

Q And what was the purpose of Gregory going to his sister's house?

A To get some papers.

Q What were they to be used for?

A For the reefer.

Q Did he come out?

A Um-hum.

Q And where did you go from that particular point?

A After he came out, that's when we rode uptown to Presser Street.

Q You rode from Thirteenth and Pine Street, is that what you said?

A Um-hum.

Q Up to?

A Presser.

Q Now, where is Presser Street at?

A Sixth and Presser.

Q In the uptown area of Romersdale?

A Um-hum.

Q Now, Thirteenth and Pine is up in the hill, correct?

A Um-hum.

Q So you drove from Thirteenth and Pine to Sixth and Presser. Who was present at this particular time while you were driving?

A Holly was sitting in the front seat, George was driving and Greg was in the back with me. We rode up there and we was—

Q   What happened when you got to Presser?

A   We didn't even have to get out of the car. This dude walked up to the car, and that's when we got the nickel.

[Phrases like "got the nickel," which is street slang for purchasing marijuana, are often confusing to a jury, and should in many cases be explained. Here, the context probably provides as much explanation as is required for defense purposes.]

Q   And how long would you estimate you stayed at Sixth and Presser Street?

A   We wasn't up there long, about—not even 10 minutes, in between 5 and 10 minutes.

Q   You were at Presser Street?

A   Um-hum.

Q   And this was after having left Thirteenth and Pine?

A   Right.

Q   Stopping at Gregory's sister's house and buying the marijuana at Sixth and Presser?

A   Right.

Q   Now, after you bought the marijuana, where did you go at that particular time?

A   We was riding around getting high.

Q   Who's we?

A   Me, Greg, George and Holly, and that's when after that we dropped Greg off down on south side.

Q   You were riding around. Do you recall where you went and what you were doing?

A   We was just riding around, you know, just getting high that's all.

Q   What are of town were you at when you were riding around?

A   On the hill.

Q   Now, after this happened you indicated that you dropped Greg off. Where did you drop him off?

A   At Seventeenth and Overly up at Hiller Court.

Q   And what's there at Seventeenth and Overly, is there anything there?

A   I didn't know where he was going. I just know we dropped him off.

Q   And what happened after you dropped him off?

A   We went to the store, Joe's Store, and George went in the store to get Holly some cigarettes. And that's when Gregory—well, I didn't see him go in the store but I seen him come out of the store.

Q   So you had dropped Gregory off?

A   Right.

Q   And then went to the store.

A   Right.

Q   Now, as you were at the store Gregory comes back to the store?

A   Um-hum.

Q Could you estimate for the jury about what time it was that he came back to the store?

A We had to be parked at the store 3 minutes, you know, just to run in and get some cigarettes and come out. And then that's when George— George came out and Greg got back in the car and then rode us over the Thirteenth and Main Street.

Q Let me stop you. Gregory got back in the car with you at this time?

A Um-hum.

Q And where did you proceed to at that point?

A To Thirteenth and Main.

Q And what happened at Thirteenth and Main?

A He dropped Holly off at her house and he dropped me off at Thirteenth, at the corner of Thirteenth and Main.

Q Do you have any estimation as to what time it was that you were dropped off?

A Well, I had an appointment to be at around about 7:00, so it was in between quarter to 7:00 and 7:00 when he dropped us off.

Q And that was where?

A Thirteenth and Main.

Q So sometime between quarter to 7:00 and 7:00 you were dropped off by George Munns and Gregory Whitman?

A Um-hum.

Q Let me ask you this. Now, when Gregory got back in the car at the grocery store was there any discussion of any activities that he wanted to do or suggested that you do later that evening together?

A Him and George Munns, they was talking about going out to a motel, going to a motel. And me and Holly said no.

Q So Mr. Whitman and Mr. Munns had suggested that perhaps that four of you should go to a motel that evening and that offer was rejected by you and Miss Peterson?

A Um-hum.

Q Had you, prior to March the 15th, 1996, ever seen Gregory Jonson, had you ever known him?

A No, I didn't. I didn't know Gregory or George Munns until Holly introduced them to me.

Q Have you since that time, since the 15th of March seen Gregory Whitman at all?

A Huh-uh.

MR. WOLFE: Thank you. I have no further questions.

[This testimony is remarkably consistent with that of George Munns and, as will be seen, with that of Holly Peterson, the other woman in Munns' car. While such consistency will often bolster the credibility of the witnesses, moment-by-moment consistency as exists here can often be a sign that the witnesses collaborated on their story. This can provide an effective means of arguing against credibility during closing arguments, especially where, as here, two of the witnesses testified that they were under the influence of drugs for at least part of the period of time covered by their testimony.]

CROSS EXAMINATION

BY MR. MENDEL:

Q Miss Helpern, I have a number of questions. First of all, you gave a statement to the Romersdale Police Department on March 20, 1996, is that correct?

A Yes.

Q And is that statement correct?

A Yes. I told them everything in the statement was correct except at that time we wasn't paying—we didn't have no concept of time because we was just riding around getting high, wasn't nobody paying attention to the time. And I told them when they dropped us off and everything. I told them everything.

Q But you had no concept of time at that time, that was just 4 day, 5 days afterward, correct?

A Well, yeah, yeah.

Q Now, today, August 8, nearly 5 months later, you know where you were at the specific time, correct?

A I didn't say I know where at the specific times. I said—everything he asked me I said around about.

Q Now, isn't it true you told the police that it was about a quarter to 6:00, just as you testified here today, that you the individuals?

A Right.

Q Is it also true that you said you were only with George and Gregory for half an hour?

A No, I did not. I said 45 minutes.

Q You did not say that?

A I said 45 minutes to an hour.

Q Okay. I'd like to show you a statement and ask you if you can identify those initials on the bottom of Page 3.

A Um-hum.

Q Are those your initials?

A Yes.

Q And to the last page, that is your signature?

A Yes.

Q Now, I'd like you to, the question I'm indicating, it's approximately the fourth question, ask you to read that question and the answer that is circled.

A It says, "How long were you and Holly and George Munns and Gregory Whitman together on Friday, 3/15/96?" And it says, "A half an hour."

Q And you're saying that is not the answer that you gave to the police?

A No, it is not.

[Mendel's use of the statements during cross-examination here highlights the possibility that this witness' testimony has been refined to conform to that of her friends who were allegedly with Whitman from 6:00 to 7:00 the evening of March 15.]

Q Now, if I can, does it indicate who the witness was to this statement, the signature right there?

A Ronald Zweiger.

Q Ronald Zweiger. Now, ma'am, you testified you went to Flint's Bar?

A Yes.

Q Correct?

A After they dropped us off.

Q And you came from Flint's Bar to begin with?

A Um-hum.

Q And you testified Flint's Bar is located at Thirteenth and Wallace?

A Um-hum.

Q Isn't it correct that Flint's is at Main and Pine Streets?

A Right. You're right. It is at Main and Pine.

Q Now, ma'am, the statement that you gave the police, you were driving around in George Munns's car?

A Right.

Q And isn't it true you told the police that George drives a burgundy Pontiac Grand Prix, the body being burgundy and the hood being burgundy?

A I said I didn't know exactly the make of the car but I said it was a wine burgundy.

Q And are you aware that George Munns testified his car is silver?

A It's not all silver. I knew that the car was burgundy or wine or something like that, yes.

Q Do you recall being asked the following question: "Do you recall what time it was when you got out of George Munns's car at Thirteenth and Main?" And your answer being: "No, I don't."

   The next question being: "Would it have been past 6:30?" Your answer being: "It would have been around 6:15. It wasn't that late."

A Um-hum. I told him we was together an hour to 45 minutes.

Q An hour to 45 minutes?

A Right. So that means if he picked up at 6:00, 45 minutes would be a quarter to 7:00 and an hour would be 7:00.

Q Okay, ma'am. If you would please read the answer that's circled.

MR. WOLFE: Mr. Mendel, could you indicate to me where on the statement you are?

MR. MENDEL: Certainly. We're on the next to last page, the third question and answer.

BY MR. MENDEL:

A "It would have been around 6:15. It wasn't that late."

Q Now, you're saying that you told the police or are you saying that was not a correct statement?"

A That's not correct.

Q That's not correct. Now, you just said you told the police you were with them 45 minutes to an hour?

A Right.

Q Now, would you please read the last question and answer on that page.

A "I was. I was. At least a half an hour to an hour to 45 minutes. That was the longest. I had to be somewhere at 7:00."

Q A half hour to 45 minutes. Now if I understand your testimony, you're saying what you told the police is it was 45 minutes to an hour?

A That's what I did. That's what I told the constable and everybody else that asked me.

Q So this statement half hour to 45 minutes is incorrect?

A Right.

Q The statement it would have been around 6:15 is not correct?

MR WOLFE: Your Honor, he's not giving the witness a response to the question.

MR. MENDEL: I asked her a yes or no and she said no.

THE COURT: You interrupted her the last time, Mr. Mendel. Slow down a little bit and give her an opportunity.

Q Miss Helpern, are you indicating then that your statement to the police that it was a half hour to 45 minutes is the longest is an inaccurate statement?

A Right.

Q And your statement –

THE COURT: Now, do you have anything else to say, ma'am, in response to that?

THE WITNESS: I was about to say when they asked me this I said a half an hour to 45 minutes—I mean an hour to 45 minutes.

BY MR. MENDEL:

Q So you meant an hour to 45 minutes?

A Right.

Q And the statement that it would have been around 6:15 that you got out of George Munns's car, it wasn't that late is an inaccurate statement as well?

A Right.

Q And the statement that you made that you were with Holly and George about half an hour would be another incorrect statement?

A Well, see, when he was asking me these questions I didn't pay that much attention to it because I didn't—you know, when he asked me the questions, right, I answered them the way that at that point in time thinking about the time that's how I answered them, because we wasn't keeping conception of no time at all.

[This witness has now been pretty thoroughly impeached. Not only was her testimony at odds with her previous statement made days after the event, she contradicts herself by first saying that the report of her statements is wrong, and then saying that the report wasn't wrong but that the statements she made weren't what she meant to say. Now, she admits that all of her statements regarding time—the most critical element of the alibi defense—are suspect because she wasn't paying attention to how much time was going by.]

Q You weren't keeping separate notes?

A We wasn't keeping a concept of time. When he asked me these questions I had to think back and try to remember because he kept asking me what time, what time, and I had to think back and remember.

Q And you had to think back 5 days?

A Yeah.

Q And today you have to think back 5 months?

A Yeah.

Q Holly Peterson's a good friend of yours, isn't that correct?

A Um-hum.

Q And she's a good friend of George Munns's?

A Um-hum.

Q Now, on March 15 isn't it true that the Defendant, Mr. Whitman, was wearing jeans?

A I don't know what kind of pants he had on, but he had on a blue shirt, I remember that.

Q A blue shirt. And your statement to the police, you testified that he did not have a jacket, is that correct?

A No, he didn't.

MR. MENDEL: No further questions.

REDIRECT EXAMINATION

BY MR. WOLFE:

Q One or two questions, ma'am. You did indicate to the police when you gave the statement back in March, you told them where Mr. Munns and Mr. Whitman picked you up, correct?

A Um-hum.

Q And you told them that you went to Gregory's sister's house?

A Yes.

Q And you told them you went uptown to buy some marijuana?

A Yes.

Q And you told them that you waited up at the KFC for about 15 to 20 minutes?

A Well, see, we didn't leave right away because he was waiting on the female that he took to KFC to come back out. And after he waited for a while he just said forget it, and that's when we left.

Q So you waited when you—could you estimate now?

A That's all I did. I just estimated. I said we was there around 15 minutes.

Q What time was it that you met them at KFC?

A It was a quarter of 6:00.

Q And you waited there for a period of time?

A Um-hum.

Q And then afterward, as you indicated before, you traveled to his sister's house, to the uptown area, back to the grocery store, Mr. Whitman according to you had got out of the car at that period of time and came back?

A Um-hum.

Q And then from that point you then drove down to Thirteenth Street, correct?

A Right.

Q And your estimate now as to how long that took from the time you first met Mr. Whitman until the time they dropped you off at Thirteenth Street is how long?

A Forty-five minutes to an hour.

MR. WOLFE: Alright. Thank you. I have no further questions.

MR. MENDEL: Thank you. Nothing further.

(Witness excused.)

THE COURT: Alright. We will take the noon recess at this point, Mr. Wolfe. Be prepared, ladies and gentlemen, to come back at 1:30. We'll call you when we're ready. The jury may now be excused.

(Whereupon, at 12:18 P.M., the jury was excused.)

THE COURT: Adjourn court until 1:30.

(Whereupon, at 12:18 P.M., court was held in recess.)

AFTER RECESS

MR. WOLFE: Good afternoon, Your Honor. The defense is prepared to call their next witness.

THE COURT: Very well, sir. Please proceed.

MR. WOLFE: Holly Peterson.

She was down in the cafeteria.

Call John Siegel.

MR. MENDEL: Your Honor, we request an offer of proof at this time.

THE COURT: You don't know about this witness, Mr. Mendel?

MR. MENDEL: Well, I assume he's going to testify to alibi.

MR. WOLFE: We did file notice of alibi listing him as an alibi witness.

MR. MENDEL: The alibi limits the time he testifies between 6:00 and 6:15, the Defendant was present, and to the extent that it goes beyond that we would object to the testimony being outside.

MR. WOLFE: We don't anticipate it going beyond that.

THE COURT: Very well.

MR. WOLFE: John, would you please take the stand.

JOHN SIEGEL, called as a witness, being duly sworn, testified as follows:

DIRECT EXAMINATION

BY MR. WOLFE:

Q Mr. Siegel, would you please state and spell your name for the record.

A John Siegel, J-o-h-n.

Q Last name?

A S-i-e-g-e-l

Q And where do you live, Mr. Siegel?

A 24H Hiller Court.

Q Were you living back in that area on the 15th of March, 1996?

A Yes.

Q Do you know the individual seated next to me, Mr. Whitman?

A Yes.

Q Where did he live at that time?

A Right next door, 24—what's that? H, G? H, I think.

[Impeachment of this witness shouldn't be difficult. He just testified that he lives at 24H, and now gets confused about whether the defendant lives at 24 G or H, and concludes the defendant's address is H, which is in fact his own address.]

Q He lived next door to you?

A Next door, yes.

Q And he was living next door to you on the 15th of March, 1996?

A Yes.

Q I refer your attention back to the evening hours of the 15th of March, and I would ask if you had occasion to see Mr. Whitman at your house that evening.

A Yes.

Q And could you give the jury an indication as to when you saw Mr. Whitman and under what circumstances?

A Well, Robyn West, she was at work. He left that day and asked me to give her a key.

Q What time did Mr. Whitman leave?

A 4:00.

Q And did you see who he left with or what he did?

A No.

Q But he left the key to your house?

A Yes.

Q And what was the purpose of him leaving the key at your apartment?

A I don't know.

Q Well, is that the only key to the apartment, if you know?

A Yes.

Q So after he left, dropped the key off at your apartment at 4:00, what then happened?

A Well, Robyn West came home from work. She gets off at 5:30, and her and my mother was going to the grocery store. And I gave her the key, I gave her the key and told her that he was here. So she took the key.

Q She meaning who?

A Robyn West, and they went to the grocery store.

Q Who's they?

A Robyn West and my mother.

[It is important for the examining lawyer to clear up confusion in a witness' testimony about who is being referred to, which is happening here in the use of pronouns by the witness without being clear about who the pronouns are referring to.]

Q And could you estimate for the jury what time the two of them went to the grocery store?

A 6:00.

Q And what occurred after Miss West and your mother went to the grocery store, did you see Mr. Whitman after that?

A No.

Q Did he come back to your apartment?

A He came back later on that evening.

Q Do you have any idea as to what time that would have been?

A No, I don't, but it was dusk.

Q It was dusk?

A Yeah.

Q Was it at a point after your mother and Robyn went shopping?

A Yes.

MR. WOLFE: Thank you. I have no further questions.

Well, just to clarify.

Q You said your mother and Robyn went shopping at 6:00?

A Yeah.

Q And he came there sometime after?

A Yes.

MR. WOLFE: Thank you.

THE COURT;   I can't understand, Mr. Siegel, the name of the other lady who went with your mother, what was her last name?

THE WITNESS: Robyn West.

THE COURT: Robyn is the first name?

THE WITNESS: Yes.

THE COURT: And what's her last name?

THE WITNESS: Weston.

[Here is another opportunity for impeachment. The witness has several times referred to Whitman's girlfriend as "West," and the attorney called her "Miss West," but now he not only gets her name confused, he even spells it "Weston."]

THE COURT: How do you spell that, W-e-s-t-o-n, something like that?

THE WITNESS: Yes.

MR. MENDEL: For the record, Your Honor, it would be Robyn West, W-e-s-t.

BY MR. MENDEL:

Q Mr. Siegel, I have a number of questions. Were you with Gregory Whitman at 3:45?

A No, I wasn't.

Q And you're positive about that?

A Yes.

Q Do you know where he was at 3;45?

A No, I don't.

Q So if Mr. Whitman would—

MR. WOLFE: Objection, Your Honor. It's going beyond the scope of the direct examination. We've offered this witness here as an alibi for his actions around 6:00, and that's the sole purpose of which this witness was offered by the defense.

[In fact, Wolfe asked Siegel questions about Whitman's activities as far back as 4:00, so even though the purpose of his testimony may have been limited to 6:00, the scope of his testimony was not.]

THE COURT: His credibility may be attacked by the prosecution. We'll overrule your objection.

Q But at 3:45 you were not with Gregory Whitman?

A No, I wasn't.

Q Now, it's your testimony that Robyn picked up the key at 6:00?

A Yes.

Q Correct?

A Yes.

Q Do you know what Gregory Whitman was doing between 4:00 and 6:00?

A No, I don't. At 4:00 he came by my house and give me the key.

Q After you got the key—

A Yes.

Q —did you know what he was doing?

A No, I didn't.

Q After that?

A No, sir.

Q And did you see him again?

A No, I did not until later on that evening when it was dusk when he came back.

Q And when he came back did he come to your house?

A Yes.

Q Or did he go right to his home?

A No. He came right to my home.

Q And that was sometime after Robyn and your mother went shopping, correct?

A Yes.

Q And you don't know how long afterward?

A No, I don't.

Q There's nothing that would cause you to remember that, is that correct?

A That's correct.

MR. MENDEL: Thank you.

MR. WOLFE: You may step down. Thank you.

(Witness excused.)

MR. WOLFE: Holly Peterson.

Your Honor, if I may have a second, please.

THE COURT: Certainly.

MR WOLFE: This is Miss Peterson, Your Honor.

HOLLY PETERSON, called as a witness, being duly sworn, testified as follows:

DIRECT EXAMINATION

BY MR. WOLFE:

[As before, this testimony is very consistent with that of Valerie Helpern and George Munns, once again raising questions about collusion between the witnesses. Mendel effectively establishes on the record that these three are close friends.]

Q Ma'am, would you please state and spell your name for the record.

A Holly Marie Peterson. Spell my last name?

Q Yes.

A P-e-t-e-r-s-o-n.

Q And, Holly, where do you live?

A 366 and a half Crescent.

Q Are you okay?

A I'm out of breath.

Q I would like to direct your attention back to the 15th of March 1996. Do you recall that day?

A Yes.

Q Did you have occasion during the evening hours of the 15th of March to see the individual seated next to me, Gregory Whitman?

A Yes.

Q Could you explain to the jury the circumstances under which you saw Mr. Whitman?

A We were—

Q Who's we? Let me stop you there.

A Well, me, Valerie, George Dobbs, we was—and Gregory, we was in the car. We wanted to go get some reefer.

Q Let me stop you. First of all, where did you meet Mr. Munns and Mr. Whitman?

A KFC.

Q And where is that located at?

A Fourteenth and Main.

Q And could you indicate for the jury approximately what time you saw or you first met Mr. Munns and Mr. Whitman?

A I can't give you an exact time, but I could tell you about 10 minutes to 6:00.

Q What did you do then when you met up with Mr. Whitman and Mr. Munns at KFC?

A Mr. and Valerie stood on—at the side of the car, the driver's side. And we talked to them for a while and I asked George did he know where to get some reefer from and he said yes. And so he said come on and get in the car, but he was waiting for somebody.

Q Who was waiting for somebody?

A George.

Q Okay. And where was Mr. Whitman at this time?

A On the passenger's side.

Q But he was there with Mr. Munns?

A Yes.

Q So could you give an estimate as to how long Mr. Munns waited for this person to come out of the KFC?

A When I came up to the car we waited about 5 minutes, and then he said the hell with it and left.

Q Who's we, who left?

A Me. Valerie, Gregory, and George.

Q And where did you go at that particular point?

A We drove down Main Street and stopped at Gregory's sister's house on Thirteenth and Wallace to get some papers because didn't nobody got no papers. And he went in his sister's house about 5 minutes.

Q Who's he?

A Gregory. And then we left and went upstairs to Sixth and Presser and copped some reefer.

Q Again, who is present at this time?

A Me, Gregory, Valerie, and George.

Q And you bought some marijuana at Sixth and Presser?

A Yes.

Q Could you give the jury an estimate as to approximately what time it was when you were at Sixth and Presser?

A It was about 25 minutes after 6:00, close to 6:30.

Q Now, after you brought the marijuana where did you do at that particular time, where did you go then?

A We rode around and smoked a couple of joints. Then we went on the south side to drop Gregory off.

Q Did you drop Gregory off?

A Yes.

Q And where did you go then?

A Excuse me?

Q Let's back up for a second. You said that around 25 after 6:00 or 6:30 you were at Sixth and Presser Streets?

A Yeah.

Q To buy the marijuana. And after you bought the Marijuana you drove around for a while, smoked a couple of joints. How long would you estimate that that took?

A We drove around for about 5 minutes.

Q And then you went back up on the hill?

A Yes, and we went straight out to the south side.

Q And you dropped Mr. Whitman off at that time?

A At Seventeenth and Overly.

Q What did you do then?

A George, me, and Valerie dropped Gregory off and we went to the store, Joe's Store, on Seventeenth Street. And George—

Q Can you estimate for us how long you were at the store?

A About 5 minutes.

Q And what happened at the store?

A George asked me did I need any cigarettes and I said yeah. He went to the store. He wasn't in there that long until Gregory came around the corner and went in the store. They must have been talking in the store or something, and they both came out of the store and got in the car together.

Q So Mr. Whitman then got in the car with you again?

A Yes.

Q After having been dropped off earlier?

A Yes.

Q How long of a period of time could you estimate it was from the time you dropped him off until the time you met up with him again at the store?

A It wasn't even 5 minutes.

Q Now, how long of a distance is it from where the store is to where you dropped Mr. Whitman off?

A It's about half a block.

Q Now, after Mr. Whitman gets back to the store with you, what do you do next?

A We drove off.

Q Who's we? Well, let me—was Mr. Whitman with you?

A Yes. We talked before we drove off.

Q What did you talk about?

A George asked us, asked me and Valerie, if we want to go to a hotel and we said no. Valerie said she had an appointment at 7:00 to meet her sister, so they took us on the hill and dropped me off at 20 Thirteenth Street at my sister's house, and from there they got to the light at Thirteenth and Main and made a right going toward Flint's Bar on Pine and Main.

Q And when you were dropped off, who was in the car at that time?

A Valerie, Gregory and George.

Q And could you estimate for the jury at what time of the evening it was when you were dropped off?

A It was about 6:45, 6:50, close to 7:00.

Q And is that the last time you saw Mr. Whitman that evening?

A Yes.

Q Prior to that time did you know Mr. Whitman?

A Yes, I knew him from the street.

Q Would you consider yourself a close friend of his?

A No.

MR. WOLFE: Thank you. I have no further questions.

CROSS EXAMINATION

BY MR. MENDEL:

Q Miss Peterson, you know Mr. Munns, though, don't you?

A Yes, I know him.

Q And would you consider yourself a very close friend of Mr. Munns's?

A Yes.

Q And how long have you known Mr. Munns?

A For years

Q Approximately how many years?

A I'd round it off about 2 years.

Q Now, as I understand your testimony, you met Mr. Munns and Mr. Whitman at approximately ten under 6:00?

A Not approximately—I can't give you an exact time.

Q You said I believe about 5:50?

A Yes.

Q Now, your testimony today was that you rode around with them and approximately 6:45 or 6:50, about an hour later, you dropped—you were dropped off by Mr. Whitman and Mr. Munns?

A Yes.

Q Do you remember giving a statement to the Romersdale Police on March 20, 1996?

A Yes.

Q And at that time you spoke with Detective Zweiger, would that be correct?

A Yes.

Q And at that time isn't it true that you told Detective Zweiger that the longest you were with George and Gregory was a half hour to 45 minutes?

A Uh-hum.

Q And not an hour as you've testified here today?

A I didn't say I was with him for an hour because it wasn't an hour.

Q It wasn't an hour?

A No. It had to be, like I said, a half an hour to about 45 or 50 minutes. It was close to an hour.

Q Half hour to 45 or 50 minutes?

A Um-hum.

[The impeachment here is effective as well, not only because she contradicted her statement to police, but because here she seems to confirm the truth of her statement and contradict her prior testimony of a few minutes before.]

MR. MENDEL: Thank you.

REDIRECT EXAMINATION

BY MR. WOLFE:

Q In the statement that you gave to the police you indicated to them essentially what you testified to today as to where you went and what you did, isn't that correct?

MR. MENDEL: Your Honor, I'm going to have to object. I don't think that would be proper examination to no impeachment as to that statement. I'm not questioning that. It's just improper to—

THE COURT: Overruled.

[This objection may have been overruled because the judge didn't understand what Mendel was saying. This illustrates the limitation of written transcripts. Mendel's objection may have made sense when spoken and interpreted based on tone, gestures, and body language, but the mere words themselves make no sense.]

BY MR. WOLFE:

Q Would you like me to repeat the question? Did you understand what I've asked you?

A Yes, I understand.

Q Did you tell the police essentially the same thing you've testified to today as to where you went and what you did?

A Yes.

Q And who you were with?

A Yes.

MR. WOLFE: Thank you. I have no further questions.

MR. MENDEL: Thank you, Miss Peterson.

(Witness excused.)

MR. WOLFE: The defense calls Harold LaVey.

HAROLD LAVEY, called as a witness, being duly sworn, testified as follows:

DIRECT EXAMINATION

BY MR. WOLFE:

[This witness is a rebuttal witness, testifying to challenge the testimony of other eyewitnesses to the robbery and shooting at Northeast Drug Store. The sole purpose of this testimony is to present an eyewitness who did not see Whitman anywhere near the scene of that crime. Like the other eyewitnesses, Mendel's cross-examination focuses on the fact that the failure

of this witness to see Mr. Whitman does not mean he wasn't there, since the witness is unable to testify with certainty that he was not.]

Q Mr. LaVey, would you please state and spell your last name for the record.

A LaVey, L-a-capital-V-e-y.

Q And how are you employed, sir?

A Workforce Temporary Services.

Q And where do you work?

A Jenkins-Harbor Equipment Company.

Q And where is that located?

A 2500 Barnaby Street.

Q How old are you, Mr. LaVey?

A Twenty-four.

Q Do you have any schooling or do you have any education?

A Three years of college.

Q Where at?

A Sutton University.

Q Mr. LaVey, I'll refer you back to March the 15th, 1996, and ask if you had occasion to be in the area of the SaveRite Market in Romersberg at that time?

A Yes, I did.

Q Could you indicate to the jury at approximately what time you were at the SaveRite Market?

A Of, it was in the evening hours. It just recently turned dark. I guess around 6:30, 7:00.

Q It was in your estimation dusk at that time?

A Yeah, it was already dark recently.

Q What were you doing there?

A I just received a check from PELL. It's a college load institution, and I had gone out to Weis to buy some food.

Q And did you, in fact, shop at SaveRite that evening?

A Yes, I did.

Q And what did you do after you were leaving SaveRite?

A I exited the store and walked toward my car.

Q If I may, if you could point out for the jury on what's been marked as Commonwealth's Exhibit 1, which is a photograph of the parking lot of SaveRite, could you please indicate for the jury just by pointing out— can everybody see—as to where your car was located at.

A Roughly right where this car with the dark top is, right here (indicating).

Q For the record, in the second row of cars in the parking lot facing SaveRite Market?

A Um-hum.

Q What did you happen to observe, Mr. LaVey, when you were in that position?

A At the car?

Q Yes.

A What I had seen actually took place while I was on the sidewalk?

Q Well, let's start it there when you were on the sidewalk.

A Okay.

Q What did you see when you were on the sidewalk?

A I heard change falling to my right at the read, so I looked over to my right and I saw a black male running with a paper bag in his hand.

Q Now, again just for the record and for the jury's information, where were you on the sidewalk when you saw this black male running with the change?

A Right out just a step off the curb in front of the doors here (indicating).

Q Indicating for the record the doors that are in the front of SaveRite Market, correct?

A Yes, the exit door.

Q And the black male was running in which direction, sir?

A Along from Northeast Drug past the front of SaveRite.

Q Indicating again for the record going from left to right on the photo?

A On the picture, right.

Q Did this individual have occasion to pass you?

A Yes, he did eventually pass me. I kept on walking. I didn't think anything of the incident. I thought he was dropping money and he was late for something carrying a grocery bag.

I got out to the first row of cars and then somebody did pass me.

Q What did you happen to observe after he passed you?

A Two males chasing him.

Q Could you describe these two males?

A Not very well, no.

Q What happened, what were they doing? They were chasing—

A They were chasing the black male who had the bag.

Q Were these two other males, were they white or black?

A They were both white, yes, sir.

Q Now, what occurred after you observed them chasing the black male?

A The fellow went around the corner and along with the two other men chasing him. I walked around the corner to see what was going on and they had already apprehended the man I would say about ten feet past the corner.

Q What actions did you take after the black male was apprehended?

A I didn't see any real need for myself to stay around there so I turned to go back to my car. I went back to my car, started it up and was ready to leave when I figured it would be interesting to see what had occurred.

So I turned around and went past in front of SaveRite, and that's from SaveRite to Northeast Drug Store along that lane there (indicating).

Q And where did you happen to observe at that time?

A Nothing right away. I got to the point right between SaveRite and Northeast Drug where you make a left-hand turn to head toward Twenty-Ninth

Street. Right prior to making the turn I heard a shot, looked up, and I saw a man fall and one of the white males running away again from Northeast to SaveRite from a black male with a gun in his hands.

Q Then what occurred?

A The black male with the gun rounded the same corner, the far corner from SaveRite.

Q Let me stop you for a second. Could you indicate again for the jury where you were located at when you saw the shooting?

A When I saw the shooting?

Q Yes. Where was your car at?

A Approximately here in the lane to make a left-hand turn (indicating)

Q And where according to your testimony did the shooting occur?

A Right just in front of the pay phone here (indicating).

Q The pay phone again for the record at the corner of the Northeast building?

A Right.

Q And what did you do after you heard the shot?

A I stopped my car and looked up, and the white male ran approximately here where he broke off and headed out into the cars (indicating). And the black male continued running across in front of the SaveRite Market and went out that way (indicating).

Q Did you have occasion to see him run all the way across the sidewalk and around the corner?

A Yes, I did.

Q Did you happen to see a second black male running along with this black male that did the shooting?

A No, I didn't.

Q Did you see a second black male thin to medium build in their mid 20s anywhere in the sidewalk at that particular time?

A Not that I can remember, no.

Q And you were able as you testified to observe the black male running all the way around the corner?

A Yes, I did.

Q Until he rounded the bend?

A He rounded the corner and that's the last I saw of him.

Q And according to your recollection no one, another black male similar to this individual, was nowhere around that you were able to observe?

A I don't recall seeing him, no.

Q Do you recall seeing any black males running behind the man that made—

A Running?

Q Yes.

A No.

Q Were you interviewed by the Romersdale Police concerning what you observed?

A Yes, I was.

Q And you gave a statement to them?

A Yes, I did.

MR. WOLFE: Thank you. I have no further questions.

CROSS EXAMINATION

BY MR. MENDEL:

Q Mr. LaVey, a number of questions. As you were observing the shooting and after you've seen that, your car was facing where, toward Northeast Drug?

A Toward Northeast, about 15, 20 feet from the ice machine.

Q Now, to look backward did you use your rear view mirror or did you turn around and look?

A I exited the car.

Q Okay. And as you're watching the individual who was running, that would be the individual who's doing the shooting, correct?

A Yes, yes, sir.

Q And did you watch him the whole time?

A Yes, I did.

Q And your attention was drawn to that man, is that correct?

A Yes.

Q Are you able to say that the Defendant, Gregory Whitman, was not there?

A No.

Q Is it possible he could have been there?

MR. WOLFE: Objection. The witness has no way to answer that question. It requires speculation on his part.

THE COURT: Overruled.

MR. MENDEL: I'll withdraw the question, Your Honor.

BY MR. MENDEL:

Q Is it possible to say that he was not there?

A Yes.

Q Is it possible to say he was there?

A Yes.

Q Do you know an individual by the name of Barbara Lee?

A No. The name doesn't mean anything to me.

Q Did you observe any blond woman on the sidewalk or walking along that way as you approached the scene?

A There could have been. I don't remember any.

Q But you didn't any in particular?

A No.

Q Can you estimate the number of people you saw standing on the porch?

A That would be the sidewalk in front of SaveRite?

Q Yes, sir.

A Approximately ten.

Q Do you know Officer Curtis Smith of the Romersdale Police Department?

A Only recently.

Q Did you observe Officer Smith on that occasion?

A No.

MR. MENDEL: Thank you.

REDIRECT EXAMINATION

MR. WOLFE:

Q Mr. LaVey, in response to the questions that you were asked by the Romersdale Police, you were asked a question, "Did you notice any other black males in the area who may have appeared to be an accomplice of the black male who did the shooting?"

　　And your answer to that statement was: "Neither the first nor the second time that I saw him running did I see anybody that looked like that that may be with him." Is that what your testimony is concerning what you observed at that time?

A Right.

MR. WOLFE: Thank you. I have no further questions.

RECROSS EXAMINATION

BY MR. MENDEL:

Q But again, you can't say whether or not the Defendant was there?

A Right.

MR. MENDEL: Thank you, Mr. LaVey.

THE COURT: That's all, sir. Thank you.

(Witness excused.)

MR. WOLFE: Mr. Bishop.

DANIEL BISHOP, called as a witness, being duly sworn, testified as follows:

DIRECT EXAMINATION

[This witness' testimony is to rebut the testimony of one of the prosecutor's strongest witnesses, Penny Green, who testified that she saw Mr. Whitman acting suspiciously in the company of Monroe just before the second hold-up. She is the only witness who testified about any direct interaction between Whitman and Monroe on that date. This witness interviewed Green and testifies about her uncertainty as to the identification of the Defendant.]

BY MR. WOLFE:

Q Mr. Bishop, will you please state and spell your name for the record.

A Daniel Bishop, B-i-s-h-o-p.

Q And how are you employed, Mr. Bishop?

A As an investigator for the Mallory County Public Defender's office.

Q Mr. Bishop, did you have occasion to be present when an interview was conducted of Penny Green?

A Yes.

Q Could you indicate as to when that interview was conducted?

A Last Friday.

Q Were you present when certain questions were put to Miss Green concerning her ability to identify the person that she said she saw in the checkout line at the SaveRite Market?

A Yes.

Q And what was Miss Green's response to her ability?

THE COURT: I'm not clear to what time the questions that you're referring to were asked. You mean in court or last Friday?

MR. WOLFE: I'm sorry. I'll clarify it, Your Honor.

BY MR. WOLFE:

Q The questions asked of Miss Green occurred during an interview, isn't that correct?

A Yes.

Q And it was conducted by myself, and Miss Green and you were present during that interview?

A Yes, sir.

Q And that occurred when?

A Last Friday afternoon.

Q And in response to those questions concerning Miss Green's ability to identify the person that she was at the register at the SaveRite Market, what was Miss Green's response at that time?

A She said I'm not sure I could pick it now.

THE COURT: I didn't hear you.

THE WITNESS: She said I'm not sure I could pick it now.

MR. WOLFE: Thank you.

CROSS EXAMINATION

BY MR. MENDEL:

Q I believe you said I'm not sure I could pick it now?

A Yes.

Q And particularly what were you referring to?

A The photo from the photo array, his picture.

Q Did you question whether or not she would be able to pick out the Defendant himself?

A No, sir.

Q So the questions were basically would she be able to pick out a photograph of an individual?

A Yes. We were discussing the photo array that she went over with the policeman during the initial investigation.

Q And do you know when that photo array was shown to her?

A It was during the initial investigation. I don't recall exactly what.

Q Did she indicate whether or not she had previously identified Mr. Whitman?

A She indicated she had, yes.

Q And did she indicate any doubt or reservations concerning that identification?

A She said I'm pretty sure is what she said.

MR. MENDEL: Thank you Mr. Bishop.

MR. WOLFE: I have no further questions.

(Witness excused.)

MR. WOLFE: Mr. Lawrence, Scott Lawrence.

SCOTT LAWRENCE, called as a witness, being duly sworn, testified as follows:

DIRECT EXAMINATION

[This last witness to testify provides testimony very similar to that of Harold LaVey. He was present at the scene of the second hold-up, saw the entire event take place, and did not recall seeing Whitman anywhere in the vicinity. On cross, the witness admits that he cannot say for certain that Whitman was not in the area, because his attention was focused on the shooting and its aftermath.]

BY MR. WOLFE:

Q Mr. Lawrence, would you please state and spell your name for the record.

A Scott Lawrence, L-a-w-r-e-n-c-e.

Q How old are you, Mr. Lawrence?

A Eighteen.

Q And where do you live?

A 2407 Varner Road, Romersdale.

Q Back on March the 15th, 1996, were you employed at that particular time?

A Yes.

Q And where were you working at?

A I was working at SaveRite.

Q Were you working on the evening of March the 15th, 1996?

A Yes.

Q I have occasion to refer you back to the evening of March the 15th and indicate to the jury if you can did you see—well, tell the jury, first of all, what you saw concerning the incident that occurred at the—both the Northeast Drug and the SaveRite Market that evening.

A I was working porch which means go out and collecting all the carts. And I see a man come running toward me with a bag with change falling out of it and with Sam Wilson following him.

And I looked at Bud and indicated to the man that was running if he wanted me to chase after him. And he said yes, so I chased after him. And he ran around the corner of our store to the road side and I was chasing him at the time.

And he had passed the cars that were there, and when I got pretty close to him he stopped, turned around and pulled a gun out of his pocket and pointed it toward me. And when he did, I veered to the right and at that time Bud had caught up with him and apprehended him.

Q What did you then observe happening after Mr. Wilson apprehended the black male?

A Well, the first thing he said was: "If you have a knife, give it to me." And then I don't believe the man said anything. And Bud repeated the question.

And at that time I walked up to him and asked him if he wanted me to go get our security man. And he looked at me and said, "Who's on, Curt Smith?" And I said, "Yes."

And so then I went into the store to find Curtis Smith.

Q Did you have the occasion to find Officer Smith?

A I couldn't locate him at the time.

Q What then happened after you went in the store, were in the store?

A I was walking around looking for Officer Smith, and then somebody come in the store saying somebody had been shot outside. And then I went back outside to see what, you know.

Q As you were going outside did you have occasion to see Officer Smith?

A Yes. He came running past me.

Q And where were you at when Officer Smith came running past you?

A Just outside the door.

Q You were outside the door?

A Um-hum.

Q When you were outside the door just as Officer Smith ran past you, did you see anyone, any black male, running past you at that particular point?

A No.

Q Concerning the individual that you saw running with the bag out of the store, did you have the occasion to see him earlier that evening?

A Yes. He came in the store.

Q At approximately what time?

A I'm not sure. I would estimate it at about 6:30 or close to that.

Q When he came in the store, you're saying that the person who you observed running down or being pursued by Sam Wilson was in the store earlier about 6:30?

A Um-hum.

Q Where did you see him at in the store, Mr. Lawrence?

A I never saw him in the store. I saw him walking inside into the in door.

Q Into the in door?

A Um-hum.

Q Where were you at that particular time?

A Just about two feet off to the left of the out—the going outdoor.

Q When he entered the store at about 6:30, did there appear to be anyone with him at that time?

A No.

Q He was alone?

A Um-hum.

Q Do you see the individual seated to my left?

A Yes.

Q Did you have the occasion to see this individual at the SaveRite Market any time that particular evening?

A No.

Q You gave a statement to the police concerning your observations, didn't you?

A Um-hum.

Q And you gave a statement the evening of the shooting, correct?

A Yes.

Q And you were asked in that statement, "Did you see anyone else in the area who would have appeared to have been connected with this black male," and your answer was "No, I saw another person chasing him"?

A Um-hum.

Q So you didn't see anyone during your observations on the evening of March the 15th that appeared to be associated with the black male that was apprehended by Samuel Wilson?

A I saw no one else.

MR. WOLFE: Thank you.

CROSS EXAMINATION

BY MR. MENDEL:

Q Mr. Lawrence, a number of questions. First of all, do you know say like ten people that went in before this individual you saw getting apprehended, can you identify the ten individuals who went in before?

A No.

Q How about the ten afterward?

A No.

Q Was your attention on that door the whole time?

A No.

Q Is it possible people could have come in minutes before or even seconds before and seconds after the individual you saw?

A Um-hum?

Q Now, when Officer Smith ran by you he was already outside the store, is that correct?

A Yes.

Q And he was running down the direction from Northeast Drug, correct?

A Um-hum.

Q Now, at the time of the shooting you were inside the store, correct?

A Um-hum.

Q Can you say the individual seated there was not in the vicinity of the SaveRite Market on that occasion?

A No.

MR. MENDEL: Thank you. I have no further questions.

REDIRECT EXAMINATION

BY MR. WOLFE:

Q Just one or two questions. You didn't see this individual there, did you, Mr. Lawrence?

A No.

Q And when you were outside the door and Officer Smith came running past you, were you already outside at that point?

A Yes.

Q When he came running by you?

A Yes.

Q When you were outside of the door did you see a black male running past you at any time?

A Only Officer Smith.

MR. WOLFE: Thank you. I have no further questions.

RECROSS EXAMINATION

BY MR. MENDEL:

Q When you came out of the store which way were you looking?

A To the right.

Q And that would be up toward where the body was?

A Um-hum.

Q And Officer Smith was already outside, correct?

A Yes.

MR. MENDEL: Thank you, Mr. Lawrence.

THE COURT: That's all, sir. Thank you.

(Witness excused.)

MR. WOLFE: The defense has no further testimony, Your Honor. We rest.

THE COURT: Very well.

MR. MENDEL: Your Honor, we have no rebuttal.

THE COURT: Alright. We'll take a recess now, ladies and gentlemen for 15 minutes. I'll give you 20 minutes. You should be prepared to come back down at a quarter of 3:00. The jury may now be excused.

(Whereupon, at 2:25 P.M., the jury was excused.)

THE COURT: Recess the court for 20 minutes. I'd like to see counsel in chambers.

(Whereupon, at 2:25 P.M., court was held in recess.)

■ EPILOGUE

On the afternoon of August 8, 1996, following the conclusion of testimony, the attorneys delivered their closing arguments to the jury, and the court instructed the jury on the law regarding burden of proof and the elements that need to be proven beyond a reasonable doubt in order to find the defendant guilty on the charges of criminal homicide, robbery, and conspiracy to commit robbery. The jury then retired to deliberate.

On August 9, 1996, the jury returned a verdict of not guilty on the counts of criminal homicide and robbery, and guilty on the count of conspiracy to commit robbery. In doing so, the jury apparently accepted the prosecutor's theory that Whitman was somehow involved with Monroe in his perpetration of the second hold-up, but not to the extent that Whitman could be held criminally liable for Monroe's crimes as an accomplice. While the jury's deliberations are not part of the transcript, it is likely that the jury accepted Whitman's defense of alibi, since his presence at the scene of the crime could easily have supported an inference that he was involved in the second hold-up as an accomplice, particularly given the testimony of his close proximity to Monroe's car in the Northeast Drug Store parking lot and his admitted role as getaway driver in the Gerber's hold-up earlier the same day.

GLOSSARY

Actus reus   The physical action that a criminal must take in order to commit a crime.

Admissibility   The ability to present evidence to a jury by satisfying legal requirements.

Affirm   A decision by an appellate court allowing a trial court's decision to stand where no prejudicial error has occurred.

Affirmative defense   A set of facts that relieves a defendant of liability for a crime. A defendant must present evidence to support an affirmative defense by a preponderance of the evidence.

Aggravating factors   Factors that may be considered by a judge in increasing a sentence above that prescribed by sentencing guidelines, or in imposing the death penalty.

Ancient document   A document that is 20 or more years old.

Appellate court   A court that reviews legal decisions made by a lower court to determine whether any legal errors occurred that affected the outcome of the case.

Arraignment   A proceeding at which a defendant is given the opportunity to enter a plea to criminal charges.

Arrest   Indefinite detention of a suspect upon probable cause that the suspect has committed a crime.

Arrest warrant   A warrant issued by a magistrate on probable cause to believe that the suspect named in the warrant has committed a crime.

Attorney–client privilege   A privilege that protects confidential communications between an attorney and his/her client.

Attorney–client relationship   A professional relationship that is formed when an attorney gives legal advice to a client or represents him/her in a legal case or transaction.

Authentication   Proof that a piece of real evidence is what its proponent claims it to be.

Beyond a reasonable doubt   The burden of proof applicable in criminal cases, in which evidence of guilt so outweighs evidence against guilt that no reasonable person could doubt the defendant's guilt.

Bias   The inclination of a witness to testify favorably toward one party based on factors other than the merits of that party's legal case.

Booking   The administrative process a criminal suspect is subjected to immediately following arrest.

Burden of proof   The level of proof required in order to prove a fact under the law.

Castle exception   A limitation to the retreat doctrine that holds that a defendant is not required to retreat from his/her own home before using deadly force to counter a threat of imminent harm.

Causation The connection between a defendant's actions and the harm that results from those actions. Causation must be proven in order to convict a defendant of a harm crime.

Cause-in-fact A step in proving causation that requires proof that the harm to the victim would not have occurred but for the defendant's actions.

Cautionary instruction An instruction by the court to the jury to disregard evidence in its deliberations.

Ceremonial marriage A marriage that is conducted in a ceremony by an authorized official (usually a clergyman or judge) following the issuance of a marriage license.

Character evidence Evidence that relates to a person's traits or character, and that is generally inadmissible to show that the person's actions were in accordance with that trait or character.

Circuit The main divisions of the federal court system. There are 11 regional circuits comprised of various states and territories, along with the federal circuit and the D.C. Circuit.

Circumstantial evidence Evidence that proves a fact by inference. A jury can accept circumstantial evidence as true without accepting the fact the evidence seeks to prove.

Clergyman–communicant privilege A privilege that protects confidential communications made to a clergyman.

Closing arguments Arguments by each side in a criminal case to persuade the jury that the presented evidence requires a verdict in that side's favor.

Collateral use rule Exception to the exclusionary rule that allows evidence obtained in violation of a defendant's rights to be used for purposes other than proving guilt at trial.

Common-law marriage A marriage that exists based on the intent of the parties to be married, evidenced by behavior displaying that intent to the public.

Competence The ability of a witness to testify truthfully.

Complaint A written statement of essential facts of the offenses with which a defendant is charged.

Conclusive presumption A presumption that requires a fact to be taken as true if other facts are proven or disproven, notwithstanding evidence that the presumed fact is not true.

Concurrence The connection between a defendant's mental state and his/her actions, by which the mental state triggers the actions.

Condition A fact other than the defendant's actions or mental state that must exist to make the defendant's actions criminal.

Confidential communication (attorney–client) Any communication between an attorney and his/her client relating to the attorney's legal representation of the client.

Confidential communications (marital) privilege A privilege that prevents the disclosure of confidential communications between spouses.

Confidentiality An ethical obligation, usually arising in a professional relationship, not to disclose information belonging to another person.

Consent (to search) Permission given by a suspect to conduct a search.

Consent (defense) A defense to criminal liability based on the willing acceptance of a crime by the victim.

Container search   The warrantless seizure of a container upon probable cause that the container contains evidence of a crime.

Contraband   Anything that is illegal to possess.

Corroboration   The degree to which the credibility of a piece of evidence is supported by other credible evidence.

Court of final appeal   An appellate court that hears appeals from an intermediate appellate court, or from a trial court where a state has no intermediate appellate court. Where an intermediate appellate court is available, appealing to a court of final appeal is a matter of permission, not of right.

Credibility   The degree to which a witness or piece of evidence is believed by the jury.

Crime scene investigation   The initial investigation of the location where a crime took place, usually conducted by specially trained law enforcement officers.

Crime of omission   A crime that is committed by failing to perform a legally required action.

Crime of possession   A crime in which the *actus reus* is the knowing possession of contraband rather than a physical action.

Criminal code   A set of statutes that contain the criminal law in a particular jurisdiction.

Criminal law   The branch of law that defines the parameters of criminal liability.

Criminal trial   A proceeding at which evidence is presented for the purpose of determining whether a defendant is guilty of the crimes charged.

Cross-examination   The questioning of a witness by the opposing party or parties.

Cumulative evidence   Evidence that has little or no probative value, because the fact it proves or disproves is adequately established by other evidence.

***Daubert* test**   A standard of competence for expert witnesses that is more flexible than the *Frye* test, and that focuses on the reliability of the methods and principles used by an expert rather than the general acceptance of those principles within the scientific community.

Declarant   The person who makes an out-of-court statement being offered as evidence.

Defendant's case-in-chief   The presentation of evidence by the defendant for the purpose of rebutting evidence of guilt and establishing facts supporting the defendant's innocence or proving affirmative defenses.

Defense   see "Affirmative Defense."

Deference   The acceptance by a court of a jury's judgment about the credibility of evidence and conclusions about the facts of a case.

Demeanor   Nonverbal indicators of credibility.

Demonstrative evidence   Evidence that demonstrates a fact to a jury (e.g., a model, illustration, chart, photograph, etc.).

Direct evidence   Evidence that proves a fact without the need for an inference by the trier of fact. If a jury accepts direct evidence as true, then it must conclude that the fact the evidence is offered to prove is also true.

Direct examination   The questioning of a witness by the party who called the witness to testify.

Discovery   The disclosure of evidence by one side in a criminal case to the other.

Distinctive characteristics   Attributes of an item's appearance, contents, substance, internal patterns, or other characteristics that allow it to be authenticated without firsthand knowledge.

District   Subdivisions of federal circuits along state or territorial lines. Each state and territory has between one and four districts, depending on population.

Documentary evidence (document)   Evidence that proves a fact based upon information that the evidence contains or states.

Double jeopardy   The trying of a defendant for a crime of which the defendant has already been convicted or acquitted.

Duplicate   A counterpart to an original that is not intended to function as the original.

Duress   An excuse for criminal liability based on the fact that the defendant was forced or pressured to commit a crime.

Dying declaration   A hearsay statement made by an unavailable declarant who believes his/her death is imminent, concerning the cause or circumstances of his/her death.

Electronically stored information (ESI)   Information that is stored in any electronic format, including information stored on a computer or any other electronic device.

Elements of crimes   Facts that must be proven in order to find a defendant guilty of a crime.

Error   A legal mistake committed by a trial judge.

Exception to the Hearsay Rule   One of the circumstances specified in F.R.E. 803, 804, or 807, which allows a hearsay statement to be admitted into evidence.

Excited utterance   An admissible hearsay statement that describes a startling event or condition while the declarant is under the stress caused by the event or condition.

Exclusionary rule   The rule that evidence obtained in violation of a defendant's constitutional rights cannot be used to prove his/her guilt at trial.

Excuse   A defense that claims that, under the circumstances, the defendant should not be punished for committing a crime despite its wrongness.

Expert *voir dire*   A process of establishing the competence of a witness to testify as an expert.

Expert witness   A witness who is qualified to render an expert opinion on an issue of fact in a case.

Extradition   The constitutionally mandated process by which a fugitive from justice is arrested and held in the state where he is located, for delivery into the custody of agents of the prosecuting state.

Factors of admissibility   The factors that determine whether evidence is admissible. They are competence, authenticity, relevance, hearsay, prejudice, privilege, cumulativeness, and public policy.

Federal Reporter   The reporter that contains opinions handed down by judges of the U.S. circuit courts of appeals, now in its third series.

Federal Rules Decisions   The reporter that compiles decisions handed down by U.S. district courts and circuits courts of appeal that relate directly to the interpretation and application of federal rules.

Federal Rules of Evidence   Rules that govern the use and admissibility of evidence in federal trial courts. These rules have been used by many states as a model for their own rules of evidence.

Federal Supplement   The reporter that contains opinions written by U.S. district judges, now in its second series.

Firsthand knowledge   Direct evidence of authenticity based on the testimony of a witness with direct knowledge of the item's identity and nature.

First appearance   A brief hearing in which a defendant appears before a magistrate and is informed of the charges against him/her and given the opportunity to request appointment of counsel.

Foreseeability   The ability of a defendant to reasonably predict that his/her actions will constitute a crime or result in prohibited harm.

Former testimony   Testimony given by a declarant as a witness under oath in a trial, hearing, or deposition, with an opportunity for cross-examination by the party against whom the testimony is now being offered as admissible hearsay.

Fourteenth Amendment   Constitutional amendment that has been used to apply specific federal constitutional rights to states.

Frisk   A pat-down of a suspect's clothing during a *Terry* stop for the purpose of determining whether the suspect is armed.

The fruit of the poisonous tree doctrine   The application of the exclusionary rule to all evidence resulting from a constitutional violation.

Frye test   A standard for the competence of expert witnesses that requires an expert's methods and principles to be accepted within the scientific community to which the expert belongs.

Full faith and credit clause   A constitutional provision requiring states to recognize, among other things, valid marriages entered into in other states.

General intent   The intent to commit the *actus reus* of a crime.

Grand jury   A panel of 16 to 23 citizens empowered to bring indictments against criminal defendants.

Guilt   The ultimate fact that must be proven in a criminal case in order to punish the defendant.

Guilty plea   A plea by a criminal defendant that has the same effect as a conviction at trial.

Habit or routine   A common practice of a person or an organization that is admitted to prove that the person or organization acted in accordance with that practice.

Harm crime   A crime that requires the proof of a particular harm in order to find the defendant guilty.

Harmless error   A legal mistake by a trial judge that does not meaningfully affect the outcome of the trial or a party's ability to fairly present his/her case.

Hearsay within hearsay   An out-of-court statement contained within another out-of-court statement, the admissibility of which is subject to Rule 805.

Hearsay   An out-of-court statement offered as evidence to prove the truth of the matter asserted in the statement.

Hostile witness   A witness whose sympathies lie with the party opposing the one who called the witness.

Hung jury   A jury that, after deliberating, is unable to agree on a unanimous verdict of either guilty or not guilty.

Impeachment   The production of evidence demonstrating that a witness is not credible.

Inadmissible   Evidence that does not meet the legal requirements for admissibility and cannot be presented to a jury.

Independent source rule Exception to the fruit of the poisonous tree doctrine that admits evidence that could have been obtained from a constitutionally valid source.

Indictment A decision made by a grand jury to bring charges against a defendant, following presentation of evidence by a prosecutor sufficient to find probable cause that such charges are justified.

Inevitable discovery rule Exception to the fruit of the poisonous tree doctrine that admits evidence that would inevitably have been discovered even without the constitutionally improper evidence.

Information A formal written accusation against the defendant filed by a government attorney.

Insanity An excuse that relieves the defendant of criminal liability because of a mental disease or defect that prevents the defendant from recognizing the wrongness of his/her actions or from being able to conform his/her actions to the requirements of the law.

Intention A mental state that requires proof that the defendant acted with a conscious purpose of committing the prohibited act or causing the prohibited harm.

Intermediate appellate court A court that hears appeals directly from a trial court. Appealing to this level of court is a matter of right, but not all states have intermediate appellate courts.

Interpreter One skilled in the ability to translate from one language and dialect into another.

Interrogation The questioning of a suspect, or any other deliberate attempt to obtain information from a suspect's mind.

Judicial notice A declaration by a court that a fact is true without supporting evidence, usually used for facts that are common knowledge.

Jurisdiction The power of a court to hear a particular case.

Jury deliberations The conference of jurors following the conclusion of the presentation of evidence in which the jury considers the evidence and attempts to form a verdict.

Jury instructions Also known as the "charge to the jury," the instructions on the law relevant to a case given by a judge to a jury before it deliberates.

Jury poll The questioning of each individual juror as to his or her agreement with the verdict announced by the foreman.

Jury selection The process by which a jury is chosen for a particular criminal trial.

Justification A defense that avoids criminal liability by claiming that a defendant's criminal actions were the right thing to do under the circumstances.

Knowledge A mental state that requires proof that the defendant acted with knowledge or substantial certainty that a condition exists, or harm will result, which makes his actions criminal.

Lay witness An opinion witness who is not offering an opinion as an expert.

Laying a foundation for competence The production of evidence necessary to establish the competence of a witness.

Leading question A question that implies the answer the examining party wishes the witness to give.

Legal advice Information provided by an attorney to a client about the client's legal rights and obligations, or advice about actions the client should or shouldn't take under the law.

Limitations period   A period of time, prescribed by statute, within which the prosecution of a defendant must be started after the crime is committed.

Local rules   Rules that govern proceedings in individual courts, as opposed to the entire court system as a whole.

Long-arm statute   A state statute that allows punishment of a defendant for acts committed outside the state, where those acts violate that state's criminal law.

Mens rea   The mental state that the defendant must have in order to make his/her actions criminal.

Metadata   Information describing the history, tracking, or management of an electronic document, often embedded in the document's electronic code.

Minor courts   Courts of limited jurisdiction that hear small civil claims, issue arrest and search warrants, and conduct preliminary criminal proceedings.

Miranda **rights**   Three rights, prescribed by the U.S. Supreme Court in *Miranda* v. *Arizona*, that a suspect must be made aware of before he/she can be interrogated following arrest. These rights include: the right to remain silent, the right to counsel, and the right to have counsel provided if the suspect is unable to afford his/her own. The suspect must also be notified that anything said by him/her can be used against him/her in court.

Mistrial   The termination of a trial, usually because of the exposure of the jury to inadmissible evidence that cannot be adequately remedied through a cautionary instruction.

Mitigating factors   Factors that may be considered by a judge in decreasing a sentence below that prescribed by sentencing guidelines, or in determining whether to impose the death penalty.

Model jury instructions   Instructions prescribed by a court as a guide for lawyers and judges in formulating a charge to the jury.

Motion for a judgment of acquittal   A motion made by the defendant asking the court to rule as a matter of law that the prosecutor's evidence is insufficient to support a conviction. Granting this motion has the same effect as a verdict of not guilty.

Motion to suppress   A motion filed by a defendant seeking a pretrial ruling that evidence is not admissible.

Necessity   A justification in which a defendant commits a crime to avoid a greater harm than the crime itself would cause.

Negligence   A mental state in which the defendant unreasonably fails to perceive a substantial risk that a condition exists, or harm will result, which makes his/her actions criminal.

Nolo contendere   A plea of "no contest" that has the same effect as a guilty plea, but that cannot be used as an admission of wrongdoing in subsequent civil or criminal actions filed against the same defendant.

Objections   Challenges to the admissibility of evidence raised during the course of a trial.

Offer   To seek to bring evidence before a jury.

Offer of proof   A presentation of information about evidence that helps the judge determine its admissibility.

Open fields search   The search of open land that is not fenced in or otherwise protected from public access.

Opening statements   Statements to the jury by each side in a criminal case, providing the jury with a summary or "roadmap" of the evidence to be presented at trial.

Opinion (testimony) A statement of a witness' conclusion about a fact.

Opinion (character evidence) A witness' belief as to the character of a person based on firsthand experience with the person.

Opinion (legal resource) A judge's or justice's formal written explanation of the factual and legal reasoning behind a decision on an issue of law.

Original As applied to real evidence, the actual piece of real evidence or a counterpart intended to function as an original.

Out-of-court statement A statement made while the declarant was not testifying under oath at the proceeding in which the statement is offered as evidence.

Overrule A ruling by a trial judge that an objection to the admissibility of evidence is not correct, and that the evidence should be admitted.

Peremptory objections Objections, limited in number, that either side can raise to the inclusion of a juror in the jury for a particular criminal trial, and that do not need to be based on any specific cause for excluding the juror.

Personal knowledge Knowledge that originates in the mind of a witness through his/her own perception or mental processes.

Physical evidence (thing) Non-testimonial evidence that proves a fact based upon the physical properties of the evidence.

Physician–patient privilege A privilege protecting information obtained by a doctor in the course of treating a patient.

Plea discussion A discussion between defendant and prosecutor specifically aimed at reaching an agreement regarding the defendant's plea to a criminal charge.

Plain error A prejudicial error that seriously affects the fairness, integrity, or public reputation of judicial proceedings, and that does not need to be preserved for appeal.

Plain-view search A "non-search" in which a police officer comes upon evidence of a crime in a location where the officer has a right to be.

Prejudice (witness) The inclination of a witness to testify unfavorably toward one party.

Prejudicial effect The effect of evidence on a juror, which may lead him/her to base a decision on emotional or other factors instead of the evidence.

Prejudicial error An error that affects a substantial right of a party by denying him/her the ability to present his/her case fully and fairly.

Preliminary hearing A hearing at which the prosecutor's case is tested by a magistrate to determine whether there is sufficient evidence to proceed to trial.

Preponderance of the evidence The burden of proof applicable to criminal defenses, in which evidence supporting the defense must slightly outweigh evidence against the defense.

Present sense impression An admissible hearsay statement that describes an event or condition as it is being perceived by the declarant.

Presentencing report A report prepared by a probation officer, providing a judge with facts that will affect the judge's decision regarding a defendant's sentence.

Presumption of legitimacy A rebuttable presumption that the man who is married to a woman who gives birth to a child is the father of the child.

Presumption A fact that is taken as true when another fact is proven or disproven.

Prior inconsistent statements Statements made by a witness prior to trial that contradict the witness' testimony.

Privilege (defense)   A justification in which the defendant has the legal right to commit the crime.

Privilege (basis for exclusion)   A rule that excludes evidence from trial where its disclosure would injure a relationship that the law deems worthy of protection.

Probable cause   Articulable facts that support a reasonable belief that a crime is being or has been committed.

Probable cause affidavit   A sworn statement by a police officer containing facts to support the issuance of a search or arrest warrant.

Probable cause hearing   A hearing that determines whether there was probable cause for a warrantless arrest.

Probative value   The degree to which a piece of evidence proves the fact it is offered to prove.

Professional certainty   A level of certainty that a professional would expect to achieve in the normal course of practicing his/her profession.

Proffer session   An informal meeting between the prosecutor and defense counsel where evidence of guilt is presented to open the door to plea negotiations.

Prosecutor's case-in-chief   The trial stage at which the prosecutor must present sufficient evidence to prove the defendant's guilt beyond a reasonable doubt.

Public record   A document the authenticity of which is established by the fact that it is filed or maintained in a public office.

Public policy exception to relevance   Evidence that is inadmissible despite its relevance, in order to advance a policy beneficial to the public.

Purposeful   see "intentional."

Real evidence   Evidence that exists apart from the mind of a witness. Real evidence can be categorized as documentary evidence (or documents) and physical evidence (or things).

Rebuttable presumption   A presumption that can be overcome by presenting evidence that the presumed fact is not true.

Recklessness   A mental state in which the defendant consciously disregards a substantial risk that a condition exists, or harm will result, that makes his/her actions criminal.

Record   The body of evidence admitted at trial, consisting of the transcript of oral testimony, exhibits, and other evidence, along with arguments, rulings, and other matters placed on the record by the court or the parties during trial.

Recorded recollection   A record made or adopted by the declarant while the subject matter of the record was still fresh in his/her mind.

Redirect examination   The questioning of a witness by the party who called the witness, following cross-examination.

Rehabilitation   The production of evidence to re-establish the credibility of an impeached witness.

Relevance   The tendency of evidence to prove or disprove a fact of consequence to the determination of an action.

Remand   The return of a case to a trial court for further proceedings in compliance with an appellate court's interpretation of the law.

Reputation   The sense of a person's character held throughout the community in which the person lives.

Residual exception to the Hearsay Rule   A discretionary exception set forth in F.R.E. 807, which applies to hearsay statements that do not fall within one of the exceptions in F.R.E. 803 or 804.

Retreat doctrine   A doctrine limiting the use of deadly force in self-defense to situations where the defendant has no safe means of retreating from the danger.

Reverse   An appellate court's decision overturning of the decision of a trial court where prejudicial error has occurred.

Rule of court   Specific procedural instructions that apply to all courts within a certain jurisdiction. Rules of court are generally created, modified, and rescinded by the highest court within that jurisdiction.

Rule of Four   The rule that four U.S. Supreme Court justices must agree to hear an appeal before a *writ of certiorari* is granted.

Rules of Evidence   Rules of court that govern the admissibility and use of evidence before a trial court.

Search incident to an arrest   A search of a suspect's body, clothing, and immediate vicinity, conducted during the course of a valid arrest.

Search warrant   A warrant issued by a magistrate on probable cause to believe that the location identified in the warrant contains evidence of a crime.

Self-authentication   The authentication of a document based on its nature, without the need for further proof of authenticity.

Self-defense   A justification relieving a defendant of criminal liability where the crime was committed to avoid an imminent threat of bodily harm.

Sequestration (jurors)   The isolation of jurors during trial to prevent them from being exposed to any external information related to the case.

Sequestration (witnesses)   The exclusion of a witness from the courtroom while another witness is testifying.

Sidebar   A discussion between a judge and attorneys during trial on a question of admissibility, taking place out of the jury's hearing.

Specialized knowledge   Knowledge based on expertise, training, and/or experience in a given field, which lies beyond that of an average, reasonably intelligent person.

Specific intent   The intent to perform a prohibited action other than the *actus reus* of the crime itself.

Specific intent crime   A crime that requires proof of both a general intent to commit the *actus reus* of the crime, and a specific intent to commit another prohibited action.

Speedy trial   Trial without undue delay, the right to which is guaranteed under the Sixth Amendment of the U.S. Constitution.

Spoliation   The loss or destruction of real evidence.

Spousal confidentiality   The confidentiality of communications that occur between spouses, within the context of the marital relationship.

Spousal testimonial privilege   A privilege that prevents one spouse from testifying against another.

Stand-your-ground rule   A rule that permits a person to use deadly force to defend himself/herself against imminent danger even where he/she can safely retreat and avoid harm.

Statement against interest   A statement that is contrary to the declarant's own legal or financial interests, or operates against a claim or defense of the declarant.

Statement   An oral or written assertion or nonverbal conduct intended as an assertion.

Status crime   A crime that prohibits a state of being (such as intoxication) rather than a physical act.

Stipulation   An agreement between a prosecutor and defense attorney that a fact is true without evidence.

Strict liability crime   A crime that does not require proof of the defendant's mental state.

Suppression of evidence   A determination by a judge prior to trial that evidence is not admissible.

Sustain   A ruling by a trial judge that an objection to the admissibility of evidence is correct, and that the evidence should not be admitted.

Terry **stop**   A brief investigative stop of a suspect for the purpose of determining whether there is probable cause to arrest.

Testimonial evidence   Evidence that comes from the mind of a witness, usually through an oral statement by the witness.

The Best Evidence Rule   A rule that requires that the original of a document be produced in order to prove its contents.

Hearsay Rule   A rule embodied in F.R.E. 802 which states that hearsay is not admissible unless it falls within one of the exceptions set forth in F.R.E. 803, 804, or 807, or if it is otherwise made admissible by rule of court or statute.

The United States Reports   The official reporter of opinions issued by the U.S. Supreme Court.

The weight formula   A formula that loosely demonstrates the association between probative value, credibility, and corroboration in determining the weight of evidence.

Then-existing mental, emotional, or physical condition   An admissible hearsay statement describing the declarant's own physical, mental, or emotional condition as it is occurring.

Trial court   Courts that conduct criminal trials and sentencing proceedings, and rule upon legal issues that arise in the pretrial process, including the admissibility of evidence.

Trial judge   A judge who presides over a trial court.

True bill   A decision of a grand jury that leads to an indictment.

Unavailable   In the hearsay context, to be unable to testify in court for one of the reasons specified in F.R.E. 804(a).

U.S. circuit court of appeals   A federal court that hears appeals from U.S. district courts within a particular circuit.

U.S. district court   A federal court that hears cases involving federal crimes that arise within a particular district. These are the trial courts of the federal court system.

U.S. district judge   A federal judge who presides over a U.S. district court. These judges are appointed by the President of the United States with the approval of the Senate.

U.S. Supreme Court   The court of final appeal in the federal system, consisting of nine justices appointed by the President of the United States and confirmed by the Senate. This court has the final authority to declare the meaning of federal law, including the U.S. Constitution.

Unresponsive answer   An answer to a question that does not address the substance of the question.

Vehicle search   A warrantless search of a vehicle on probable cause that the vehicle contains evidence of a crime.

Verdict   The decision of a jury regarding the defendant's guilt.

Void for vagueness   A violation of due process by a statute that fails to clearly identify the behavior that is being criminalized.

Voir dire **(jury)**   The process of examining jurors to determine their fitness to sit on the jury of a particular criminal trial.

Voir dire **(witness)**   A proceeding at which the competence of a witness is established.

Voluntary encounter   An encounter between a police officer and another person where the person is free to walk away.

Warrant   see "arrest warrant" and "search warrant."

Weight   The degree to which evidence influences a jury's decision.

Work-product doctrine   A rule that prevents discovery or disclosure of an attorney's work product, including any records made by the defendant or his/her attorney during the case's investigation or defense.

Writ of certiorari   Permission given by the U.S. Supreme Court to file an appeal before that court.

INDEX